Expert Performance Indexing in SQL Server 2019

Toward Faster Results and Lower Maintenance

Third Edition

Jason Strate

Apress®

Expert Performance Indexing in SQL Server 2019: Toward Faster Results and Lower Maintenance

Jason Strate
Hugo, MN, USA

ISBN-13 (pbk): 978-1-4842-5463-9 ISBN-13 (electronic): 978-1-4842-5464-6
https://doi.org/10.1007/978-1-4842-5464-6

Copyright © 2019 by Jason Strate

This work is subject to copyright. All rights are reserved by the Publisher, whether the whole or part of the material is concerned, specifically the rights of translation, reprinting, reuse of illustrations, recitation, broadcasting, reproduction on microfilms or in any other physical way, and transmission or information storage and retrieval, electronic adaptation, computer software, or by similar or dissimilar methodology now known or hereafter developed.

Trademarked names, logos, and images may appear in this book. Rather than use a trademark symbol with every occurrence of a trademarked name, logo, or image we use the names, logos, and images only in an editorial fashion and to the benefit of the trademark owner, with no intention of infringement of the trademark.

The use in this publication of trade names, trademarks, service marks, and similar terms, even if they are not identified as such, is not to be taken as an expression of opinion as to whether or not they are subject to proprietary rights.

While the advice and information in this book are believed to be true and accurate at the date of publication, neither the authors nor the editors nor the publisher can accept any legal responsibility for any errors or omissions that may be made. The publisher makes no warranty, express or implied, with respect to the material contained herein.

> Managing Director, Apress Media LLC: Welmoed Spahr
> Acquisitions Editor: Jonathan Gennick
> Development Editor: Laura Berendson
> Coordinating Editor: Jill Balzano

Cover image designed by Freepik (www.freepik.com)

Distributed to the book trade worldwide by Springer Science+Business Media New York, 233 Spring Street, 6th Floor, New York, NY 10013. Phone 1-800-SPRINGER, fax (201) 348-4505, e-mail orders-ny@springer-sbm.com, or visit www.springeronline.com. Apress Media, LLC is a California LLC and the sole member (owner) is Springer Science + Business Media Finance Inc (SSBM Finance Inc). SSBM Finance Inc is a **Delaware** corporation.

For information on translations, please e-mail rights@apress.com, or visit http://www.apress.com/rights-permissions.

Apress titles may be purchased in bulk for academic, corporate, or promotional use. eBook versions and licenses are also available for most titles. For more information, reference our Print and eBook Bulk Sales web page at http://www.apress.com/bulk-sales.

Any source code or other supplementary material referenced by the author in this book is available to readers on GitHub via the book's product page, located at www.apress.com/9781484254639. For more detailed information, please visit http://www.apress.com/source-code.

Printed on acid-free paper

Thanks to my family and friends for their support while I had to duck out early at times to try to avoid missing deadlines on this edition.

—*Jason Strate*

Table of Contents

About the Author ....**xv**

About the Technical Reviewer ....**xvii**

Introduction ....**xix**

Chapter 1: Index Fundamentals 1
   Why Build Indexes? 1
   Major Index Types 3
      Heap Tables 3
      Clustered Indexes 4
      Nonclustered Indexes 4
      Columnstore Indexes 5
   Other Index Types 6
      JSON and XML Indexes 6
      Spatial Indexes 7
      Hash and Range Indexes 8
      Full-Text Search 9
   Index Variations 9
      Primary Key 10
      Unique Index 10
      Included Columns 11
      Partitioned Indexes 11
      Filtered Indexes 12

TABLE OF CONTENTS

Compression and Indexing	13
Index Data Definition Language	14
Creating an Index	14
Altering an Index	18
Dropping an Index	21
Index Metadata	23
sys.indexes	23
sys.index_columns	24
sys.index_resumable_operations	24
sys.xml_indexes	24
sys.selective_xml_index_paths	24
sys.selective_xml_index_namespaces	24
sys.spatial_indexes	25
sys.spatial_index_tessellations	25
sys.column_store_dictionaries	25
sys.column_store_segments	25
sys.column_store_row_groups	25
sys.hash_indexes	26
sys.fulltext_catalogs	26
sys.fulltext_indexes	26
sys.fulltext_index_columns	26
Summary	26
Chapter 2: Index Storage Fundamentals	**29**
Storage Basics	30
Pages	30
Extents	31
Page Types	33
File Header Page	34
Boot Page	34
Page Free Space Page	35

Global Allocation Map Page	36
Shared Global Allocation Map Page	36
Differential Changed Map Page	37
Minimally Logged Page	37
Index Allocation Map Page	38
Data Page	38
Index Page	39
Large Object Page	39
Organizing Pages	40
Heap Structure	40
B-Tree Structure	42
Columnstore Structure	44
Examining Pages	47
Dynamic Management Functions	47
DBCC Commands	59
Page Fragmentation	80
Forwarded Records	81
Page Splits	83
Index Characteristics	87
Heap	87
Clustered Index	87
Nonclustered Index	88
Columnstore Index	89
Summary	90
Chapter 3: Index Metadata and Statistics	**91**
Column-Level Statistics	92
DBCC SHOW_STATISTICS	92
Catalog Views	99
STATS_DATE	101
sys.dm_db_stats_properties	102

- sys.dm_db_stats_histogram 107
- sys.dm_db_incremental_stats_properties 109
- Statistics DDL 109
- Colum-Level Statistics Summary 109
- Index Usage Statistics 110
  - Header Columns 110
  - User Columns 112
  - System Columns 119
  - Index Usage Stats Summary 122
- Index Operational Statistics 122
  - Header Columns 124
  - DML Activity 125
  - SELECT Activity 128
  - Locking Contention 132
  - Latch Contention 139
  - Page Allocation Cycle 144
  - Compression 147
  - LOB Access 149
  - Row Version 152
  - Index Operational Stats Summary 153
- Index Physical Statistics 153
  - Header Columns 154
  - Row Statistics 155
  - Fragmentation Statistics 156
  - Index Physical Stats Summary 158
- Columnstore Statistics 158
  - Columnstore Physical Stats 158
  - Columnstore Operational Stats 161
- Summary 162

Chapter 4: XML Indexes 163

XML Data 163
Benefits 164
Cautions 164

XML Indexes 165
Primary/Secondary XML Indexes 165
Selective XML Indexes 171

Summary 176

Chapter 5: Spatial Indexing 177

How Spatial Data Is Indexed 178
Creating Spatial Indexes 181
Supporting Methods with Indexes 188
Understanding Statistics, Properties, and Information 190
The Views 190
The Procedures 192

Tuning Spatial Indexes 194
Restrictions on Spatial Indexes 195
Summary 196

Chapter 6: Indexing Memory-Optimized Tables 197

Memory-Optimized Tables Overview 197
Hash Indexes 202
Range Indexes 208
Summary 211

Chapter 7: Full-Text Indexing 213

Full-Text Indexing 213
Creating a Full-Text Example 214
Creating a Full-Text Catalog 215
Creating a Full-Text Index 217
Full-Text Search Index Catalog Views and Properties 223

Summary 228

TABLE OF CONTENTS

Chapter 8: Indexing Myths and Best Practices 229

Index Myths 230

Myth 1: Databases Don't Need Indexes 230

Myth 2: Primary Keys Are Always Clustered 233

Myth 3: Online Index Operations Don't Block 235

Myth 4: Any Column Can Be Filtered in Multicolumn Indexes 239

Myth 5: Clustered Indexes Store Records in Physical Order 242

Myth 6: Indexes Always Output in the Same Order 244

Myth 7: Fill Factor Is Applied to Indexes During Inserts 249

Myth 8: Deleting from Heaps Results in Unrecoverable Space 251

Myth 9: Every Table Should Have a Heap/Clustered Index 253

Index Best Practices 255

Index to Your Current Workload 255

Use Clustered Indexes on Primary Keys by Default 256

Specify Fill Factors 256

Index Foreign Key Columns 257

Balance Index Count 258

Summary 259

Chapter 9: Index Maintenance 261

Index Fragmentation 261

Fragmentation Operations 262

Fragmentation Variants 276

Fragmentation Issues 288

Defragmentation Options 291

Defragmentation Strategies 296

Preventing Fragmentation 307

Index Statistics Maintenance 309

Automatically Maintaining Statistics 310

Manually Maintaining Statistics 312

Summary 318

Chapter 10: Indexing Tools 319

Missing Indexes 319
Explaining the DMOs 321
Using the DMOs 325

Database Engine Tuning Advisor 330
Explaining the DTA 331
Using the DTA GUI 333
Using the DTA Utility 339

Summary 351

Chapter 11: Indexing Strategies 353

Heaps 353
Temporary Objects 354
Other Heap Scenarios 358

Clustered Indexes 359
Identity Sequence 361
Natural Key 363
Foreign Key 366
Multiple Column 373
Globally Unique Identifier 380

Nonclustered Indexes 383
Search Columns 385
Index Intersection 388
Multiple Column 392
Covering Index 394
Included Columns 397
Filtered Indexes 403
Foreign Keys 408

Columnstore Index 413

JSON Indexing 420

xi

TABLE OF CONTENTS

Index Storage Strategies 425
    Row Compression 425
    Page Compression 429

Indexed Views 433

Summary 438

Chapter 12: Query Strategies 439

LIKE Comparison 439

Concatenation 444

Computed Columns 447

Scalar Functions 451

Data Conversion 455

Summary 460

Chapter 13: Monitoring Indexes 461

Performance Counters 462

Dynamic Management Objects 471
    Index Usage Stats 471
    Index Operational Stats 477
    Index Physical Stats 491
    Wait Statistics 497
    Data Cleanup 501

Event Tracing 502
    SQL Trace 503
    Extended Events 509

Query Store 513

Summary 514

Chapter 14: Index Analysis 515

Review of Server State 517
    Performance Counters 517
    Wait Statistics 553
    Buffer Allocation 569

Schema Discovery 572
    Identify Heaps 572
    Duplicate Indexes 574
    Overlapping Indexes 577
    Unindexed Foreign Keys 581
    Uncompressed Indexes 584
Database Engine Tuning Advisor 586
Unused Indexes 589
Index Plan Usage 591
Summary 594

Chapter 15: Indexing Methodology 595

The Indexing Method 595
Implement 597
    Communication 598
    Deployment Scripts 600
    Execution 602
Repeat 603
Summary 603

Index 605

About the Author

Jason Strate is senior database architect and developer working in the financial services industry. He has been making data cool again for nearly 20 years, which includes more than a decade of consulting with companies across the United States. A previous recipient of Microsoft Most Valuable Professional award for Data Platform (formerly SQL Server) from 2009 to 2016, Jason's done fun stuff like getting certifications, blogging, authoring books, and presenting on technologies. These days, he's most often splitting his time between reading, karaoke, and the PASS Cloud Virtual Group.

About the Technical Reviewer

Rodney Landrum went to school to be a poet and a writer. And then he graduated, so that dream was crushed. He followed another path, which was to become a professional in the fun-filled world of information technology. He has worked as a systems engineer, UNIX and network admin, data analyst, client services director, and finally database administrator (DBA). The old hankering to put words on paper, while paper still existed, got the best of him and in 2000 he began writing technical articles, some creative and humorous, some quite the opposite. In 2010, he wrote *SQL Server Tacklebox*, a title his editor disdained, but a book closest to the true creative potential he sought; he still yearned to do a full book without a single screenshot, which he accomplished in 2019 with his first novel, *Chronicles of Shameus*. He currently works from his castle office in Pensacola, FL, as a senior DBA consultant for Ntirety, a division of Hostway/Hosting.

Introduction

Today's world is all about the data. From the applications to manage our lives to the analytics we use to guide our decisions, data is everywhere. Behind data, databases provide the engine to get to our data, but without the right indexes we lack the fuel to access our data efficiently.

When it comes to indexes, no single structure aids in retrieving data from a database more than an index. New features in SQL Server provide new and unique ways to leverage and access your data, but without going back to the basics and ensuring that the data is properly indexed, you'll find that even the new features fail to live up to expectations.

Indexes represent both how data is stored and the access paths by which data can be retrieved from your database. Without indexes, a database is an unordered mess minus the roadmap to find the information you want.

Throughout my experience working on data platforms, one of the most common resolutions that I provide for performance tuning and application outages is to provide the right indexes for the underlying databases. Often, the effort of adding an index or two to the most accessed tables within a database provides significant performance improvements—much more so than tuning the database at a per SQL statement level. This is because an index affects many SQL statements that are being run against the database lifting performance across the workload.

Managing indexes may seem like an easy task. Unfortunately, their seeming simplicity is often the key to why they are overlooked. Often, there is an assumption from developers that the database administrators will take care of indexing. Or there is an assumption by the database administrators that the developers are building the necessary indexes as they develop features in their applications. While these are primarily cases of miscommunication, people need to know how to determine what indexes are necessary and the value of those indexes. This book provides that information.

Outside of the aforementioned scenarios is the fact that applications and the data they use change over time. Features created and used to tune the database may not be as useful as expected, or a small feature change may lead to a big change in how the

INTRODUCTION

application and underlying databases are used. All of this change affects the database and what needs to be accessed. As time goes on, databases and their indexes need to be reviewed to determine if the current indexing is accurate for the new load. This book also provides information in this regard.

What's in This Book?

From beginning to end, this book provides information that helps build your skills from a novice at indexing to an expert. The chapters are laid out such that you can start at any place to fill in the gaps in your knowledge and build out from there. Whether you can barely spell index, need to understand the fundamentals, or need to build an indexing methodology, the information is available here.

Chapter 1 covers index fundamentals. It lays the groundwork for all of the following chapters. This chapter provides information regarding the types of indexes available in SQL Server. It covers some of the Primary index types and defines what these are and how to build them. The chapter also explores the options available that can change the structure of indexes. From fill factor to included columns, the available attributes are defined and explained.

Chapter 2 picks up where the previous chapter left off. Going beyond defining the indexes available, the chapter looks at the physical and logical structure of indexes and the components that make up indexes. This internal understanding of indexes provides the basis for grasping why indexes behave in certain ways in certain situations. As you examine the structures of indexes, you'll become familiar with the tools you can use to begin digging into these structures on your own.

Armed with an understanding of the indexes available and how they are built, Chapter 3 explores the statistics that are stored on the indexes and how to use this information; these statistics provide insight into how SQL Server is utilizing indexes. The chapter also provides information necessary to decipher why an index may not be selected and why it is behaving in a certain way. You will gain a deeper understanding of how this information is collected by SQL Server through dynamic management views and what data is worthwhile to review.

Not every index type is fully discussed in the first chapter; the types not discussed are covered in Chapters 4, 5, and 6. Beyond the rowstore and columnstore index structures, there are a few other index types which are Extensible Markup Language (XML), spatial, full-text, and semantic search. These indexes are applicable to specific situations.

INTRODUCTION

In these chapters, you'll look into these other index types to understand what they have to offer. You'll also look at situations where they should be implemented.

In a similar fashion to the previous three chapters, Chapter 7 takes a dive into memory-optimized tables. Memory-optimized tables were new to SQL Server 2014 and provided a unique capability to provide improved performance with tables that reside in memory when online. This chapter will look at how indexes function on these types of tables and what restrictions still remain.

Chapter 8 identifies and debunks some commonly held myths about indexes. Also, it outlines some best practices in regard to indexing a table. As you move into using tools and strategies to build indexes in the chapters that follow, this information will be important to remember.

With a firm grasp of the options for indexing, the next thing that needs to be addressed is maintenance. In Chapter 9, you'll look at what needs to be considered when maintaining indexes in your environment. We'll look at both the fragmentation of the indexes and the underlying statistics that supports how SQL Server determines how the index can be used.

SQL Server is not without tools to automate your ability to build indexes. Chapter 10 explores these tools and looks at ways that you can begin building indexes in your environment today with minimal effort. The four tools discussed are the missing index dynamic management views (DMVs), Database Engine Tuning Advisor (DTA), Query Store, and Automatic Database Tuning. You'll look at the benefits and issues regarding these tools and get some guidance on how to use them effectively in your environment.

The tools alone won't give you everything you need to index your databases. In Chapter 11, you'll begin to look at how to determine the indexes that are needed for a database and a table. There are a number of strategies for selecting what indexes to build within a database. They can be built according to recommendations by the query optimizer. They also should be built to support metadata structures such as foreign keys. For each strategy of indexing, there are a number of considerations to take into account when deciding whether or not to build the index.

Part of effective indexing is writing queries that can utilize an index on a query. Chapter 12 discusses a number of strategies for indexing. Sometimes when querying data, the indexes that you assume will be used are not used after all. These situations are usually tied into how a query is structured or the data that is being retrieved. Indexes can be skipped due to SARGability issues (where the query isn't being properly selective on the index). They can also be skipped over due to tipping point issues, such as when

INTRODUCTION

the number of reads to retrieve data from an index potentially exceeds the reads to scan that or another index. These issues affect index selection as well as the effectiveness and justification for some indexes.

Today's DBA isn't in a position where they have only a single table to index. A database can have tens, hundreds, or thousands of tables, and all of them need to have the proper indexes. Beginning in Chapter 13, you'll learn some methods to approach indexing for a single database but also for all of the databases on a server and servers within your environment.

What's New in This Edition?

With three new versions of SQL Server released since the last edition of this book, there have been a significant number of changes to how indexes can be applied to your databases and data. Some of the key changes to SQL Server that involve indexing are as follows:

- Changes in indexing restrictions to memory-optimized tables and columnstore indexes

- Improvements to maintenance processes for indexes including improved processing and ability to pause and restart index rebuilds

- New tools to review query execution to identify and automate index selection

- Improvements to partitioning and statistics

- Changes in dynamic management objects (DMOs) available that improve capabilities to inspect indexes and data pages

All of these changes and more are spread throughout the book in all of the chapters. Even though there have been a number of releases of SQL Server since the last edition, the primary focus will be on SQL Server 2019 as the current state of SQL Server. Where applicable, information will be included to indicate features made available since the last edition, namely, calling out changes from SQL Server 2016 and 2017.

Summary

As previously mentioned, data is important, and indexes provide the way for you to get to that data. Through the chapters in this book, you will become armed with what you need to know about the indexes in your environment. You will also learn how to find the information you need to improve the performance of your environment.

CHAPTER 1

Index Fundamentals

The goal of this book is to help you improve the performance of your databases through the use of indexes. In order to accomplish this, you must first understand what indexes are and why you need them. You need to understand the differences between how data in a clustered index, columnstore index, and heap table is stored. You also will look at how nonclustered and other index types are built and how indexes interact with other indexes. This chapter will provide the building blocks for understanding the logical design of indexes.

Why Build Indexes?

The most important asset any business owns is its data. Databases exist to store that data. A key piece in providing the data is delivering it efficiently. Being able to efficiently access data improves the value that the business gains from the data. The way to do that is through indexes.

Indexes are the means to providing an efficient access path between the user and the data. By providing this access path, the user can ask for data from the database, and the database will know where to go to retrieve the data and how to do so with minimal effort.

Why not just have all the data in a table and return it when it is needed? Why go through the exercise of creating indexes? Returning data when needed is actually the point of indexes; they provide the path that is necessary to get to the data in the quickest manner possible. Without indexes to provide a map to where data is located, database systems have to search through all of the available data to know that the required data has been accessed. In today's world where terabytes of data is common, it's important to be able to quickly and efficiently get to the data needed.

To illustrate, let's consider an analogy that is often used to describe indexes—a library. When you go to the library, there are shelves upon shelves of books. In this library, a common task repeated over and over is finding a book. Most often you are particular on the book that you need, and you have a few options for finding that book.

CHAPTER 1   INDEX FUNDAMENTALS

In the library, books are stored on the shelves using the Dewey Decimal Classification system. This system assigns a number to a book based on its subject. Once the value is assigned, the book is stored in numerical order within the library. For instance, books on science are in the range of 500–599. From there, if you wanted a book on mathematics, you would look for books with a classification of 510–519. Then to find a book on geometry, you'd look for books numbered 516. With this classification system, finding a book on any subject is easy and efficient. Once you know the number of the book you are looking for, you can go directly to the stack in the library where the books with 516 are located, instead of wandering through the library until you happen upon the geometry books. This is exactly how indexes work; they provide an ordered manner to store information that allows users to easily find the data.

What happens, though, if you want to find all the books in a library written by Jason Strate? You could make an educated guess that they are all categorized under databases, but you would have to know that for certain. The only way to do that would be to walk through the library and check every stack. The library has a solution for this problem—the card catalog.

Most card catalogs are available through computer terminals these days, but back when I was a kid, they consisted of individual cards that were ordered by author, title, subject, and category. Using the card catalog, you would be able to find the Dewey Decimal number for any book. For instance, searching by author, you could find all books written by Jason Strate. Thus, instead of wandering through the stacks and checking each book to see whether I wrote it, you could instead go to the specific books in the library written by me. In essence, this is also how indexes work. The index provides a location of data so that queries can go directly to the data.

Without these mechanisms, finding books in a library, or information in a database, would be difficult. Instead of going straight to the information, you'd wander through the library aisle to aisle trying to find what you need. In smaller libraries, such as Little Free Libraries, this isn't much of a problem, since there are so few books. But as the library gets larger and settles into a building, it just isn't efficient to browse all the stacks. And when there is research that needs to be done and books need to be found, there isn't time to browse through everything.

This analogy has hopefully provided you with the basis to understand the purpose and the need for indexes. In the following sections, I'll dissect this analogy a bit more and pair it with the different indexing options that are available in SQL Server databases.

Major Index Types

You can categorize indexes in different ways. However, it's essential to understand the four major categories described in this particular section: heaps, clustered, columnstore, and nonclustered indexes. Heaps, clustered indexes, and clustered columnstore indexes directly affect how data in the underlying tables are stored. Nonclustered indexes are independent of data storage. The first step toward understanding indexing is to grasp this categorization scheme.

Heap Tables

As mentioned in the library analogy, in a Little Free Library, the books available change often; usually there are only one or two short shelves of books. In these cases, the owner doesn't spend time organizing the books under the Dewey Decimal system. Instead, the books are placed on the shelves as they are acquired. In this case, there is no order to how the books are stored in the library. When SQL Server stores data in a table in a similar fashion, when the data lacks an ordered structure, it is referred to as a *heap*.

In a heap, the first row added to the index is the first record in the table, the second row is the second record in the table, the third row is the third record in the table, and so on. There is nothing in the data that is used to specify the order in which the data has been added. The data and records are in the table without any particular order.

When a table is first created, the initial storage structure is called a *heap*. This is probably the simplest storage structure. Rows are inserted into the table in the order in which they are added. A table uses a heap until a clustered index or clustered columnstore index is created on the table or the table is created as memory-optimized, discussed in Chapter 7. A table can be a heap only if there are no other index types that define how the base data is stored on the table. Only a single heap structure is allowed per table.

Note Most people don't consider heaps to be indexes. That's fine. In the context of this discussion, we will treat them as indexes as they assist in determining where data will be located and how it will be accessed by queries.

Clustered Indexes

In the library analogy, you reviewed how the Dewey Decimal system defines how books are sorted and stored in the library. Regardless of when the book is added to the library, with the Dewey Decimal system, it is assigned a number based on its subject and placed on the shelf between other books of the same subject. The subject of the book, not when it is added, determines the location of the book. This structure is the most direct method to find a book within the library. In the context of a table, the index that provides this functionality in a database is called a *clustered index*.

With a clustered index, one or more columns are selected as the *key columns* for the index. Key columns are used to sort and determine where to locate data in the table. Where a library places books on the shelves based on their Dewey Decimal number, a clustered index determines the location of records in the table based on the logical order of the key columns of the index.

The columns used as the key columns for a clustered index are selected based on the most frequently used method for accessing the records in the table. For instance, in a table with states and provinces, the most common method of finding a record in the table would probably be through its abbreviation. In that situation, using the abbreviation for the clustering key column would be best. With most tables, the primary key or business key will serve as the clustered index key columns.

As with heaps, clustered indexes determine where data is located in a table. In a clustered index, the data outside the key columns is stored alongside the key columns. This equates to the clustered index determining the physical table itself, just as a heap defines the table. Due to this, a table cannot have more than one clustered index.

Nonclustered Indexes

As was noted in my analogy, the Dewey Decimal system doesn't account for every way in which a person may need to search for a book. If the author or title is known but not the subject, then the classification doesn't really provide any value. Libraries solve this problem with card catalogs, which provide a place to cross-reference the classification number of a book with the name of the author or the book title. Databases are also able to solve this problem with nonclustered indexes.

In a nonclustered index, columns are selected and sorted based on their values. These columns contain a reference to the heap or clustered index location of the data they are related to. This is nearly identical to how a card catalog works in a library. The order of the books, or the records in the tables, doesn't change, but a shortcut to the data is created based on the other search criteria.

Nonclustered indexes do not have the same restrictions as heaps and clustered indexes. There can be many nonclustered indexes on a table, in fact up to 999 nonclustered indexes. This allows alternative routes to be created for users to get to the data they need without having to traverse all records in a table. Just because a table can have many indexes doesn't mean that it should, as I'll discuss later in this book.

Columnstore Indexes

One of the problems with card catalogs in large libraries is that there could be dozens or hundreds of index cards that match a title of a book. Each of these index cards contains information such as the author, subject, title, International Standard Book Number (ISBN), page count, and publishing date, along with the Dewey Decimal number. In nearly all cases, this additional information is not needed, but it's there to help filter out index cards when necessary.

Imagine if instead of dozens or hundreds of index cards to look at, you had a few cards that had only the title and Dewey Decimal number or only the subject and Dewey Decimal number. Basically, instead of storing all attributes together, you stored them separately with an identifier, like a Dewey Decimal number, included to link them back together again. For each attribute, where you previously would have had to look through dozens or hundreds of index cards, you instead are left with a few consolidated index cards. This type of index would be called a *columnstore index*.

Columnstore indexes were new to SQL Server 2012 and greatly expanded in following SQL Server releases. Traditionally, indexes are stored in row-based organization, also known as *rowstore*. This form of storage is extremely efficient when one row or a small range is requested. When a large range or all rows are returned, rowstores can become inefficient, especially when there are aggregations or few columns are required. The columnstore index favors the return of large ranges of rows by storing data in column-wise organization.

When you create a columnstore index, you include all the columns in a table. This ensures that all columns are included in the enhanced performance benefits of the columnstore organization. In a columnstore index, instead of storing all the columns for a record together, each column is stored separately with all the other rows in an index. The benefit of this type of index is that only the columns and rows required for a query need to be read. In data warehousing scenarios, often less than 15 percent of the columns in an index are needed for the results of a query.[1]

Because of their structure, columnstore indexes provide significant value for data warehousing. Consider first that the index accesses only the columns required to execute the query. Additionally, compression is greatly improved since data within a single column has a higher likelihood for similarity. Between these two aspects, columnstore indexes provide significant performance improvements. I'll discuss these in more depth in later chapters.

Other Index Types

Besides the index types just discussed, a number of other index types are available. These other types cover specialized search, data, and table types that don't fit under traditional indexing structures. These types, which are XML, spatial, hash and range, and full-text search (FTS) indexes, each have dedicated chapters to focus on their specialized indexing structures. While these don't necessarily fit into the card catalog scenario that has been outlined so far, they are important options when working with their related data and table types. To help illustrate, I'll show how to add some new functionality to the library. Later chapters will further expand on the information presented here.

JSON and XML Indexes

Suppose you needed a method to be able to search the table of contents for all the books in the library. A table of contents provides a hierarchical view of a book. There are chapters that outline the main sections for the book, which are followed by subchapter heads that provide more details of the contents of the chapter. This relationship model is similar to how XML documents are designed; there are nodes and a relation between them that define the structure of the information.

---

[1] www.red-gate.com/simple-talk/wp-content/uploads/2013/07/Columnstore-Indexes-for-Fast-DW-QP-SQL-Server-11.pdf

As discussed with the card catalog, it would not be efficient to look through every book in the library to find those that were written by Jason Strate. It would be even less efficient to look through all the books in the library to find out whether any of the chapters in any of the books were written by Ted Krueger. Each book probably has more than one chapter, resulting in multiple values that would need to be checked for each book and no certainty as to how many chapters would need to be looked at before checking.

One method of solving this problem would be to make a list of every book in the library and list all the chapters for each book. Each book would have one or more chapter entries in the list. This provides the same benefit that a card catalog provides, but for some less than standard information. In a database, this is what *XML indexes* and indexing JavaScript Object Notation (JSON) can accomplish.

For every node in an XML document, an entry is made in the XML index. This information is persisted in internal tables that SQL Server can use to determine whether the XML document contains the data that is being queried. Similarly with JSON, the values to index are materialized with an index on a calculated column.

Creating and maintaining XML indexes can be quite costly. Every time the index is updated, it needs to shred all the nodes of the XML document into the XML index. The larger the XML document, the more costly this process will be. However, if data in an XML column will be queried often, the cost of creating and maintaining an XML index can be offset quickly by removing the need to shred all the XML documents at runtime.

Spatial Indexes

Every library has maps. Some maps cover the oceans; others are for continents, countries, states, or cities. Various maps can be found in a library, each providing a different view and information of perhaps the same areas. There are two basic challenges that exist with all these maps. First, you may want to know which maps overlap or include the same information. For instance, you may be interested in all the maps that include Minnesota. The second challenge is when you want to find all the books in the library that were written or published at a specific place. Again, in this case, how many books were written within 25 miles of Minneapolis?

Both of these present a problem because, traditionally, data in a database is fairly one-dimensional, meaning that data represents discrete facts. In the physical world, data often exists in more than one dimension. Maps are two-dimensional, and buildings and floor plans are three-dimensional. To solve this problem, SQL Server provides the capabilities for *spatial indexes*.

Spatial indexes dissect the spatial information that is provided into a four-level representation of the data. This representation allows SQL Server to plot out the spatial information, both geometry and geography, in the record to determine where rows overlap and the proximity of one point to another point.

There are a few restrictions that exist with spatial indexes. The main restriction is that spatial indexes must be created on tables that have primary keys. Without a primary key, the spatial index creation will not succeed. Additionally when creating spatial indexes, they are restricted from utilizing parallel processing; and only a single spatial index can be built on a table at a time, which impacts the speed in which they can be created. Also, spatial indexes cannot be used on indexed views. These and other restrictions are covered in Chapter 5.

Similar to XML indexes, spatial indexes have up-front and maintenance costs associated with their sizes. The benefit is that when spatial data needs to be queried using specific methods for querying spatial data, the value of the spatial index can be quickly realized. Spatial indexes will be discussed in more depth in Chapter 5.

Hash and Range Indexes

As books come into the library, sometimes the frequency in which they are returned exceeds the rate in which they are placed back into the stacks. It takes time to sort the books and put them where they go. At these times, a librarian is often there keeping track of what is returned. For these books, the librarian can often remember which books are where in the queue of returned books and get the book you want without the use of the card catalog. This is in essence what memory-optimized tables do with hash and range indexes. The only difference is that with hash and range indexes, millions of rows, or books, can be kept in memory without needing to rely on disk-based structures to support them.

A hash index allows a memory-optimized table to provide point lookups of data within the table. In other words, the index, or the librarian, can remember exactly where the book is in the table and index each time it is needed.

Alternatively, a range index provides memory-optimized tables with the capability to efficiently identify ranges of items. For instance, if the index, or librarian, needed all the books returned between 8 a.m. and 12 p.m., the index would be able to scan across the rows vs. accessing rows in row-by-row operations.

For both range and hash indexes, there are a few things to consider. First, hash and range indexes are allowed only on memory-optimized tables. The reference to remembering where the books are is really what is different about hash and range indexes over other index types. Between disk and memory, the structure of a clustered index is relatively unchanged. With hash and range indexes, the structure is designed specifically for fast memory access and leverages disk solely to support transaction consistency and the ability to rebuild the index in memory when the database comes online.

Full-Text Search

The last scenario to consider is the idea of finding specific terms within books. Card catalogs do a good job of providing information on finding books by author, title, or subject. The subject of a book isn't the only keyword you may want to use to search for books. At the back of many books are keyword indexes to help you find other subjects within a book. When this book is completed, there will be an index, and it will have the entry full-text search in it with a reference to this page and other pages where this is discussed in this book.

Consider for a moment if every book in the library had a keyword index. Furthermore, let's take all those keywords and place them in their own card catalog. With this card catalog, you'd be able to find every book in the library with references to every page that discusses full-text searches. Generally speaking, this is what an implementation of a full-text search provides except it covers nearly all words in the books.

Index Variations

Up to this point, you've looked at the different types of indexes available within SQL Server. These aren't the only ways in which indexes can be defined. There are a few index properties that can be used to create variations on the types of indexes discussed previously. Implementing these variations can assist in implementing business rules associated with the data and can help improve the performance of the index.

CHAPTER 1 ■ INDEX FUNDAMENTALS

Primary Key

In the library analogy, I discussed how all the books have a Dewey Decimal number. This unique number identifies each book and where it is in the library. In a similar fashion, one index on a table can be defined to uniquely identify records within a table. To do this, an index is created as the primary key. There are some differences between the Dewey Decimal number and a primary key, but conceptually they are the same.

A primary key is used to identify a record within a table. For this reason, none of the records in a table can have the same primary key value. Typically, a primary key will be created on a single column, though it can be composed of multiple columns.

There are a few other things that need to be remembered when using a primary key. First, a primary key is a unique value that identifies each record in a table. Because of this, all values within a primary key must be populated. No null values are allowed in a primary key. Also, there can be only one primary key on a table. There may be other identifying information in a table, but only a single column or set of columns can be identified as the primary key. Lastly, although it is not required, a primary key will typically be built on a clustered index. The primary key will be clustered by default, but this behavior can be overridden and will be ignored if a clustered index already exists. More information on why this is done will be included in Chapter 8.

Unique Index

As mentioned previously, there can be more than a single column or set of columns that can be used to uniquely identify a record in a table. This is similar to the fact that there is more than one way to uniquely identify a book in a library. Besides the Dewey Decimal number, a book can also be identified through its ISBN. Within a database, this type of information can be represented with a *unique index*.

Similar to the primary key, an index is constrained so that only a single value appears within the index. A unique index is similar in that it provides a mechanism to uniquely identify records in a table and can also be created across a single column or multiple columns.

One chief difference between a primary key and a unique index is the behavior when the possibility of null values is introduced. A unique index will allow null values within the columns being indexed. A null value is considered a discrete value, and only one combination of null values is allowed across the key column in a unique index.

Included Columns

Suppose you want to find all the books written by Douglas Adams and find out how many pages are in each book. You may at first be inclined to look up the books in the card catalog and then find each book and write down the number of pages. Doing this would be fairly time-consuming. It would be a better use of your time if instead of looking up each book, you had that information on hand. With a card catalog, you wouldn't actually need to find each book for a page count, though, since most card catalogs include the page count on the index card. When it comes to indexing, including information outside the indexed columns is done through *included columns*.

When a nonclustered index is built, there is an option to add included columns into the index. These columns are stored as nonsorted data within the sorted data in the index. Included columns cannot include any columns that have been used in the initial sorted column list of the index.

In terms of querying, included columns allow users to look up information outside the sorted columns. If everything they need for the query is in the included columns, the query does not need to access the heap or clustered index for the table to complete the results. Similar to the card catalog example, included columns can significantly improve the performance of a query.

Partitioned Indexes

Books that cover a lot of data can get fairly large. If you look at a dictionary or the complete works of William Shakespeare, these are often quite thick. Books can get large enough that the idea of containing them in a single volume just isn't practical. The best example of this is an encyclopedia.

It is rare that an encyclopedia is contained in a single book. The reason is quite simple—the size of the book and the width of the binding would be beyond the ability of nearly anyone to manage. Also, the time it takes to find all the subjects in the encyclopedia that start with the letter *S* is greatly improved because you can go directly to the S volume instead of paging through an enormous book to find where they start.

This problem isn't limited to books. A problem similar to this exists with tables. Tables and their indexes can get to a point where their size makes it difficult to continue to maintain the indexes in a reasonable time period. Along with that, if the table has millions or billions of rows, being able to scan across limited portions of the table vs. the whole table can provide significant performance improvements. To solve this problem on a table, indexes have the ability to be partitioned.

Partitioning can occur on both clustered and nonclustered indexes. It allows an index to be split along the values supplied by a function. By doing this, the data in the index is physically separated into multiple partitions, while the index itself is still a single logical object.

Filtered Indexes

By default, nonclustered indexes contain one record in them for every row in the table for which the index is associated. In most cases, this is ideal and provides the index an opportunity to assist in selectivity for any value in the column.

There are atypical situations where including all the records in a table in an index is less than ideal. For instance, the set of values most often queried may represent a small number of rows in a table. In this case, limiting the rows in the index will reduce the amount of work a query needs to perform, resulting in an improvement in the performance of the query. Another could be where the selectivity of a value is low compared to the number of rows in the table. This could be an active status or shipped Boolean values; indexing on these values wouldn't drastically improve performance, but filtering to just those records would provide a significant opportunity for query improvement.

To assist in these scenarios, nonclustered indexes can be filtered to reduce the number of records they contain. When the index is built, it can be defined to include or exclude records based on a simple comparison that reduces the size of the index.

Besides the performance improvements outlined, there are other benefits to using filtered indexes. The first improvement is reduced storage costs. Since filtered indexes have fewer records in them, because of the filtering, there will be less data in the index, which requires less storage space. Another benefit is reduced maintenance costs. Similar to the reduced storage costs, since there is less data to maintain, less time is required to maintain the index.

Compression and Indexing

Today's libraries have a lot of books in them. As the number of books increases, there comes a point where it becomes more and more difficult to manage the library with the existing staff and resources. Because of this, there are a number of ways that libraries find to store books, or the information within them, to allow better management without increasing the resources required to maintain the library. As an example, books can be stored on microfiche or made available only through electronic means. This provides the benefits of reducing the amount of space needed to store the materials and allows library patrons a means to look at more books more quickly.

Similarly, indexes can reach the point of becoming difficult to manage when they get too large. Also, the time required to access the records can increase beyond acceptable levels. There are two types of compression available in SQL Server: row-level and page-level compression.

With *row-level compression*, an index compresses each record at the row level. When row-level compression is enabled, a number of changes are made to each record. To begin with, the metadata for the row is stored in an alternative format that decreases the amount of information stored on each column, but because of another change, it may actually increase the size of the overhead. The main changes to the records are numerical data changes from fixed to variable length and blank spaces at the end of fixed-length string data types that are not stored. Another change is that null or zero values do not require any space to be stored.

Page-level compression is similar to row-level compression, but it also includes compression across a group of rows. When page-level compression is enabled, similarities between string values in columns are identified and compressed. This will be discussed in detail in Chapter 2.

With both row-level and page-level compression, there are some things to be taken into consideration. To begin with, compressing a record takes additional central processing unit (CPU) time. Although the row will take up less space, the CPU is the primary resource used to handle the compression task before it can be stored. Along with that, depending on the type of data in your tables and indexes, the effectiveness of the compression will vary.

CHAPTER 1 INDEX FUNDAMENTALS

Index Data Definition Language

Similar to the richness in types and variations of indexes available in SQL Server, there is also a rich data definition language (DDL) that surrounds building indexes. In this section, you will examine the DDL for building indexes. First, you'll look at the CREATE statement and its options and pair them with the concepts discussed previously in this chapter.

For the sake of brevity, I won't discuss the backward-compatible features of the index DDL; you can find information on those features in SQL Docs for SQL Server 2012. I'll discuss XML and spatial indexes and full-text search further in later chapters.

Creating an Index

Before an index can exist within your database, it must first be created. This is accomplished with the CREATE INDEX syntax shown in Listing 1-1. As the syntax illustrates, most of the index types and variations previously discussed are available through the basic syntax.

Listing 1-1. CREATE INDEX Syntax

```
CREATE [ UNIQUE ] [ CLUSTERED | NONCLUSTERED ] INDEX index_name
    ON <object> ( column [ ASC | DESC ] [ ,...n ] )
    [ INCLUDE ( column_name [ ,...n ] ) ]
    [ WHERE <filter_predicate> ]
    [ WITH ( <relational_index_option> [ ,...n ] ) ]
    [ ON { partition_scheme_name ( column_name )
         | filegroup_name
         | default
         }
    ]
    [ FILESTREAM_ON { filestream_filegroup_name | partition_scheme_name |
    "NULL" } ]
[ ; ]
```

The choice between CLUSTERED and NONCLUSTERED indexing determines whether an index will be built as one of those two basic types. Excluding either of these types will default the index to nonclustered.

CHAPTER 1 INDEX FUNDAMENTALS

The uniqueness of the index is determined by the UNIQUE keyword; including it within the CREATE INDEX syntax will make the index unique. The syntax for creating an index as a primary key will be included later in this chapter.

The <object> option determines the base object over which the index will be built. The syntax allows for indexes to be created on either tables or views. The specification of the object can include the database name and schema name, if needed.

After specifying the object for the index, the sorted columns of an index are listed. These columns are usually referred to as the *key columns*. Each column can appear in the index only a single time. By default, the columns will be sorted in the index in ascending order, but descending order can be specified instead. An index can include up to 32 columns as part of the index key with a total size not to excess 1,700 bytes. Prior to SQL Server 2016, it was 16 columns and 900 bytes.

As an option, included columns can be specified on any nonclustered index, which are added after the key columns for the index. There is no option for either ascending or descending since included columns are not sorted. Between the key and nonkey columns, there can be up to 1,023 columns in an index. The size restriction on the key columns does not affect included columns.

If an index will be filtered, this information is specified next. The filtering criteria are added to an index through a WHERE clause. The WHERE clause can use any of the following comparisons: IS, IS NOT, =, <>, !=, >, >=, !>, <, <=, and !<. Also, a filtered index cannot use comparisons against a computed column, a user-defined type (UDT) column, a spatial data type column, or a HierarchyID data type column.

You can use a number of options when creating an index. In Listing 1-1, there is a segment for adding index options, noted by the tag <relational_index_option>. These index options control both how indexes are created and how they will function in some scenarios. Listing 1-2 provides the DDL for the available options available for CREATE INDEX.

Listing 1-2. CREATE INDEX Options

```
PAD_INDEX = { ON | OFF }
 | FILLFACTOR = fillfactor
 | SORT_IN_TEMPDB = { ON | OFF }
 | IGNORE_DUP_KEY = { ON | OFF }
 | STATISTICS_NORECOMPUTE = { ON | OFF }
 | STATISTICS_INCREMENTAL = { ON | OFF }
```

15

```
| DROP_EXISTING = { ON | OFF }
| ONLINE = { ON | OFF }
| RESUMABLE = {ON | OF }
| MAX_DURATION = <time> [MINUTES]
| ALLOW_ROW_LOCKS = { ON | OFF }
| ALLOW_PAGE_LOCKS = { ON | OFF }
| MAXDOP = max_degree_of_parallelism
| DATA_COMPRESSION = { NONE | ROW | PAGE}
  [ ON PARTITIONS ( { <partition_number_expression> | <range> }
  [ , ...n ] ) ]
```

Each of the options allows for different levels of control on the index creation process. Table 1-1 lists all the options available for CREATE INDEX. In later chapters, I'll discuss examples and strategies for applying them. You can find more information on the CREATE INDEX syntax and examples of its use in SQL Docs for SQL Server.

Table 1-1. CREATE INDEX Syntax Options

Option Name	Description
FILLFACTOR	Defines the amount of empty space to leave in each data page of an index when it is created. This is applied only at the time an index is created or rebuilt.
PAD_INDEX	Specifies whether the FILLFACTOR for the index should be applied to the nonleaf data pages for the index. The PAD_INDEX option is used when data manipulation language (DML) operations that lead to excessive nonleaf-level page splitting need to be mitigated.
SORT_IN_TEMPDB	Determines whether to store temporary results from building the index in the tempdb database. This option will increase the amount of space required.
IGNORE_DUP_KEY	Changes the behavior when duplicate keys are encountered when performing inserts into a table. When enabled, rows violating the key constraint will fail. When the default behavior is disabled, the entire insert will fail.

(*continued*)

Table 1-1. (*continued*)

Option Name	Description
STATISTICS_NORECOMPUTE	Specifies whether any statistics related to the index should be re-created when the index is created.
STATISTICS_INCREMENTAL	Specifies whether statistics collected for the index should be created on the index as a whole or per partition.
DROP_EXISTING	Determines the behavior when an index of the same name on the table already exists. By default, when OFF, the index creation will fail. When set to ON, the index creation will overwrite the existing index.
ONLINE	Determines whether a table and its indexes are available for queries and data modification during index operations. When enabled, locking is minimized, and an intent shared is the primary lock held during index creation. When disabled, the locking will prevent data modifications to the index and underlying table for the duration of the operation. ONLINE is an Enterprise Edition–only feature.
RESUMABLE	Identifies whether an indexing operation will be resumable. New for SQL Server 2019.
MAX_DURATION	Determines the max number of minutes for a resumable indexing operation to execute for until pausing. New for SQL Server 2019.
ALLOW_ROW_LOCKS	Determines whether row locks are allowed on an index. By default, they are allowed.
ALLOW_PAGE_LOCKS	Determines whether page locks are allowed on an index. By default, they are allowed.
MAXDOP	Overrides the server-level maximum degree of parallelism during the index operation. The setting determines the maximum number of processors that an index can utilize during an index operation.
DATA_COMPRESSION	Determines the type of data compression to use on the index. By default, no compression is enabled. With this, both page- and row-level compression types can be specified.

To demonstrate the CREATE INDEX syntax, let's build an index on the table Sales. SalesOrderDetail in AdventureWorks2017. The key column for the index is ProductId with the columns OrderQty and UnitPrice included as nonkey columns. Additionally, the index will be PAGE compressed. The code in Listing 1-3 builds this index.

Listing 1-3. CREATE INDEX Example

```
USE AdventureWorks2017;
GO

CREATE INDEX IX_Sales_SalesOrderDetail_ProductId
ON Sales.SalesOrderDetail (ProductID)
INCLUDE (OrderQty, UnitPrice)
WITH (DATA_COMPRESSION = PAGE);
```

Altering an Index

After an index has been created, there will be a need, from time to time, to modify the index. There are a few reasons to alter an existing index. First, the index may need to be rebuilt or reorganized as part of ongoing index maintenance. Also, some of the index options, such as the type of compression, may need to change. In these cases, the index can be altered, and the options for the indexes are modified.

To modify an index, you use the ALTER INDEX syntax. Listing 1-4 shows the basic syntax for altering indexes.

Listing 1-4. ALTER INDEX Syntax

```
ALTER INDEX { index_name | ALL }
 ON <object>
 { REBUILD
   [ [PARTITION = ALL] [ WITH ( <rebuild_index_option> [ ,...n ] ) ]
   | [ PARTITION = partition_number [ WITH ( <single_partition_rebuild_
   index_option> [ ,...n ] ) ] ] ]
 | DISABLE
 | REORGANIZE
       [ PARTITION = partition_number ]
       [ WITH ( LOB_COMPACTION = { ON | OFF } ) ]
```

```
| SET ( <set_index_option> [ ,...n ] )
| RESUME [WITH (<resumable_index_options>,[...n])]
| PAUSE
| ABORT
  } [ ; ]
```

When using the ALTER INDEX syntax for index maintenance, there are two options in the syntax that can be used. These options are REBUILD and REORGANIZE. The REBUILD option re-creates the index using the existing index structure and options. It can also be used to enable a disabled index. The REORGANIZE option re-sorts the leaf-level pages of an index. This is similar to reshuffling the cards in a deck to get them back in sequential order. Both of these options will be discussed more thoroughly in Chapter 6.

Additionally, the ALTER INDEX syntax can be used to disable an index. This is accomplished through the DISABLE option under the ALTER INDEX syntax. A disabled index will not be used or made available by the database engine. After an index is disabled, it can be reenabled only by altering the index again with the REBUILD option.

Beyond those functions, many of the index options available through the CREATE INDEX syntax are also available with the ALTER INDEX syntax. The ALTER INDEX syntax can be used to modify the compression of an index. It can also be used to change the fill factor or the pad index settings. Depending on the changing needs for the index, this syntax can be used to change any of the available options, though there are some limitations with how the options are used. When you REBUILD ALL partitions on an index, you can modify all of the same options that were available with the CREATE INDEX syntax, as shown in Listing 1-5. However, when you REBUILD a single partition, the list of options available is greatly reduced, as shown in Listing 1-6. This is because the overall index isn't changing, just the partition and the unavailable options apply to the entire index.

Listing 1-5. ALTER INDEX Rebuild Options

```
PAD_INDEX = { ON | OFF }
 | FILLFACTOR = fillfactor
 | SORT_IN_TEMPDB = { ON | OFF }
 | IGNORE_DUP_KEY = { ON | OFF }
 | STATISTICS_NORECOMPUTE = { ON | OFF }
 | STATISTICS_INCREMENTAL = { ON | OFF }
 | ONLINE = { ON [ ( <low_priority_lock_wait> ) ] | OFF }
```

```
  | RESUMABLE = { ON | OFF }
  | MAX_DURATION = <time> [MINUTES}
  | ALLOW_ROW_LOCKS = { ON | OFF }
  | ALLOW_PAGE_LOCKS = { ON | OFF }
  | MAXDOP = max_degree_of_parallelism
| DATA_COMPRESSION = { NONE | ROW | PAGE }
    [ ON PARTITIONS ( {<partition_number> [ TO <partition_number>] } [ , ...n ] ) ]
```

Listing 1-6. ALTER INDEX Single Partition Rebuild Options

```
SORT_IN_TEMPDB = { ON | OFF }
  | MAXDOP = max_degree_of_parallelism
  | RESUMABLE = { ON | OFF }
  | MAX_DURATION = <time> [MINUTES}
  | DATA_COMPRESSION = { NONE | ROW | PAGE } }
  | ONLINE = { ON [ ( <low_priority_lock_wait> ) ] | OFF }
```

For REORGANIZE, the options for ALTER INDEX are limited to LOB_COMPACTION, shown in Listing 1-7. With LOB_COMPACTION, when set to ON, the reorganization will attempt to compact large object (LOB) pages, allowing space within the index associated with these pages to be reduced and released. Without activating this, the reorganization will not release these pages.

Listing 1-7. ALTER INDEX Reorganize Options

```
LOB_COMPACTION = { ON | OFF }
```

Similar to the CREATE INDEX syntax, starting with SQL Server 2019, it is possible to resume ALTER INDEX statements. Listing 1-8 shows that for the ALTER INDEX syntax, the options available are similar to CREATE INDEX with the exception of the inclusion of the low priority lock wait, which is discussed in the next paragraph.

Listing 1-8. ALTER INDEX Resumable Options

```
MAXDOP = max_degree_of_parallelism
  | MAX_DURATION =<time> [MINUTES]
  | <low_priority_lock_wait>
```

The low priority lock wait provides the ALTER INDEX syntax the ability to predefine how it will behave when blocked by a SCH-M lock, shown in Listing 1-9. This is supported on REBUILD, REORGANIZE, and resumable options. This option allows the ALTER INDEX to terminate its own or other transactions that are blocking the ALTER INDEX operation after a set amount of time. This can be useful when you have a queue of ALTER INDEX statements waiting to execute and one of them gets held up by another transaction.

Listing 1-9. ALTER INDEX Low Priority Lock Wait Options

```
WAIT_AT_LOW_PRIORITY ( MAX_DURATION = <time> [ MINUTES ] ,
 ABORT_AFTER_WAIT = { NONE | SELF | BLOCKERS } )
```

It is worth mentioning that there is one type of index modification that is not possible with the `ALTER INDEX` syntax. When altering an index, the key and included columns cannot be changed. To accomplish this, the `CREATE INDEX` syntax is used with the `DROP_EXISTING` option.

As an example of the ALTER INDEX syntax, we'll disable the index built in the last section. Using the script in Listing 1-10, the index is disabled, and as previously mentioned the index still exists as metadata without the underlying data structure. For more information on the `ALTER INDEX` syntax and examples of its use, you can search for it in SQL Docs.

Listing 1-10. ALTER INDEX Example

```
USE AdventureWorks2017;
GO

ALTER INDEX IX_Sales_SalesOrderDetail_ProductId
ON Sales.SalesOrderDetail
DISABLE;
```

Dropping an Index

There will be times when you no longer need an index. The index may no longer be necessary because of changing usage patterns of the database, or the index may be similar enough to another index that it isn't useful enough to warrant its existence.

To *drop*, or remove, an index, you use the DROP INDEX syntax. This syntax includes the name of the index and the table, or object, that the index is built against. Listing 1-11 shows the syntax for dropping an index. Starting with SQL Server 2016, DROP INDEX syntax supports the IF EXISTS clause, allowing you to drop indexes without first checking to verify that the indexes exist.

Listing 1-11. DROP INDEX Syntax

```
DROP INDEX [ IF EXISTS ]
        index_name ON <object>
   [ WITH ( <drop_clustered_index_option> [ ,...n ] ) ]
```

Besides just dropping an index, you can include a few additional options. These options primarily apply to dropping clustered indexes. Listing 1-12 details the options available to use for a DROP INDEX operation.

Listing 1-12. DROP INDEX Options

```
  MAXDOP = max_degree_of_parallelism
  | ONLINE = { ON | OFF }
| MOVE TO { partition_scheme_name ( column_name )
          | filegroup_name
          | "default"
          }
[ FILESTREAM_ON { partition_scheme_name
          | filestream_filegroup_name
          | "default" } ]
```

When a clustered index is dropped, the base structure of the table will change from clustered to heap. When built, a clustered index defines where the base data for a table is stored. When making a change from the clustered to the heap structure, SQL Server needs to know where to place the heap structure. If the location is anywhere other than the default filegroup, it will need to be specified. The location for the heap can be a single filegroup or defined by a partitioning scheme. This information is set through the MOVE TO option. Along with the data location, the FILESTREAM location may also need to be set through these options.

The performance impact of the drop index operation may be something that you need to consider. Because of this, there are options in the DROP INDEX syntax to specify the maximum number of processors to utilize along with whether the operation should be completed online. Both of these options function similar to the options of the same name in the CREATE INDEX syntax.

To remove the index used in the last two sections, we can use the code in Listing 1-13 to drop the index. For more information on the DROP INDEX syntax and examples of its use, you can search in SQL Docs.

Listing 1-13. ALTER INDEX Example

```
USE AdventureWorks2017;
GO

DROP INDEX IX_Sales_SalesOrderDetail_ProductId ON Sales.SalesOrderDetail;
```

Index Metadata

Before going too deep into indexing strategies, it is important to understand the information available in SQL Server on the indexes. When there is a need to understand or know how an index is built, there are catalog views that can be queried to provide this information. Four catalog views are available for indexes. User and system databases have these catalog views in them, and only specific indexes that are unique to each database in which they are queried will be returned. Each of these catalog views provides important details for each index.

sys.indexes

The sys.indexes catalog view provides information on each index in a database. For every table, index, or table-valued function, there is one row within the catalog view. This provides a full accounting of all indexes in a database.

The information in sys.indexes is useful in a few ways. First, the catalog view includes the name of the index. Along with that is the type of the index, identifying whether the index is clustered, nonclustered, and so forth. Along with that information are the properties on the definition of the index. This includes the fill factor, the filter definition, the uniqueness flag, and the other items that were used to define the index.

sys.index_columns

The `sys.index_columns` catalog view lists all the columns included in an index. For each key and included column that is a part of an index, there is one row in this catalog view. For each of the columns in the index, the order of columns is included along with the order in which the column is sorted in the index.

sys.index_resumable_operations

The sys.index_resumable_operations catalog view lists the execution status for resumable index rebuilds. For each index rebuild that is paused or currently executing, there is a record in this catalog view. The view describes the DDL for the resumable index rebuild operation and provides a state to identify if it is running or paused.

sys.xml_indexes

The catalog view `sys.xml_indexes` is similar to `sys.indexes`. This catalog view returns one row per XML index in a database. The chief difference with this catalog view is that it also provides some additional information. The view includes information on whether the XML index is a Primary or Secondary XML index. If the XML index is a Secondary XML index, the catalog view includes a type for the Secondary index.

sys.selective_xml_index_paths

The `sys.selective_xml_index_paths` catalog view is a subset of the indexes in `sys.indexes`, which contains only Selective XML indexes. For each Selective XML created for an XPath, there is one entry in this catalog view.

sys.selective_xml_index_namespaces

The sys.selective_xml_index_namespaces catalog view identifies the namespace associated with Selective XML indexes. For each namespace associated with an XML index, there is an entry in this catalog view identifying the namespace and indicating if it is the default.

sys.spatial_indexes

The `sys.spatial_indexes` catalog view is also similar to `sys.indexes`. This catalog view returns one row for every spatial index in a database. The main difference with this catalog view is that it provides additional information on spatial indexes. The view includes information on whether the spatial index is a geometric or geographic index.

sys.spatial_index_tessellations

The `sys.spatial_index_tessellations` catalog view augments the sys.spatial_indexes catalog view. This catalog view details the bounding boxes and grids associated with a spatial index.

sys.column_store_dictionaries

The `sys.column_store_dictionaries` catalog view supports columnstore indexes. This catalog view returns one row for each column in a columnstore index. The data describes the structure and type of dictionary built for the column.

sys.column_store_segments

The `sys.column_store_segments` catalog view supports columnstore indexes by returning at least one row for every column in a columnstore index. Columns can have multiple segments of approximately 1 million rows each. The rows in the catalog view describe base information on the segment (e.g., whether the segment has null values and what the minimum and maximum data IDs are for the segment).

sys.column_store_row_groups

The sys.column_store_row_groups catalog view supports maintenance of columnstore segments by return per-segment rowgroup details. This catalog view returns information on the number of rows in the rowgroup along with the current state of the rowgroup and its physical location in the database.

sys.hash_indexes

The `sys.hash_indexes` catalog view is similar to `sys.indexes` but contains an additional column that pertains specifically to hash indexes on memory-optimized tables. The additional column is `bucket_count`, for the count of the number of buckets created for the index. In the context of a hash index, *buckets* refer to the number of locations that are created to store values in the index. The relationship between buckets and indexed values is detailed in Chapters 2 and 7.

sys.fulltext_catalogs

The `sys.fulltext_catalogs` catalog view contains one row for every full-text catalog in a database.

sys.fulltext_indexes

The `sys.fulltext_indexes` catalog view contains one row for every full-text index in a database. The view describes the full-text catalog that the index is a part of and provides details on the state of the index and how it is being updated.

sys.fulltext_index_columns

The `sys.fulltext_index_columns` catalog view supports `sys.fulltext_indexes`. It contains one row for every column associated with a full-text index.

Summary

This chapter presented a number of fundamentals related to indexes. You looked at the type of indexes available within SQL Server. From heaps to nonclustered to spatial indexes, you looked at the type of the index and related it to the library Dewey Decimal system as a real-world analogy to indexing. This example helped illustrate how each of the index types interacted with the others and the scenarios where one type can provide value over another.

Next, you looked at the data definition language for indexes. Indexes can be created, modified, and dropped through the DDL. DDL has a lot of options that can be used to finely tune how an index is structured to help improve its usefulness within a database.

This chapter also included information on the metadata, or catalog views, available on indexes within SQL Server. Each of the catalog views provides information on the structure and makeup of the index. This information can assist in researching and understanding the view that is available.

The details in this chapter provide the framework for what will be discussed in later chapters. By leveraging this information, you'll be able to look deeper into your indexes and start applying the appropriate strategies to index your databases.

CHAPTER 2

Index Storage Fundamentals

Where the previous chapter discussed the logical design and syntax of indexes, this chapter will focus on the physical implementation of indexes. An understanding of the way in which indexes are laid out and interact with each other at the implementation and storage level will help you become better acquainted with the benefits that indexes provide and why they behave in certain ways.

To get to this understanding, the chapter will start with some of the basics about data storage. First, you'll look at data pages and how they are laid out. This examination will detail what comprises a data page and what can be found within it. Also, you'll examine the dynamic management functions (DMFs) and DBCC commands that can be used to inspect pages in the index.

From there, you'll look at the three ways in which pages are organized for storage within SQL Server. These storage methods relate back to heap, clustered, nonclustered, and columnstore indexes. For each type of structure, you'll examine how the pages are organized within the index. You'll also examine the requirements and restrictions associated with each index type.

You will finish this chapter with a deeper understanding of the fundamentals of index storage. With this information, you'll be better able to deal with, understand, and expect behaviors from the indexes in your databases.

CHAPTER 2 ■ INDEX STORAGE FUNDAMENTALS

Storage Basics

SQL Server uses a number of structures to store and organize data within databases. In the context of this book and chapter, you'll look at the storage structures that relate directly to tables and indexes. You'll start by focusing on pages and extents and how they relate to one another. Then you'll look at the different types of pages available in SQL Server and relate each of them back to indexes.

Pages

The most basic storage area is a page. Pages are used by SQL Server to store everything in the database. Everything from the rows in tables to the structures used to map out indexes at the lowest levels is stored on a page.

When space is allocated to database data files, all the space is divided into pages. During allocation, each page is created to use 8 KB (8,192 bytes) of space, and pages are numbered starting at 0, incrementing 1 for every page allocated. When SQL Server interacts with the database files, the smallest unit in which an input/output (I/O) operation can occur is at the page level.

There are three primary components to a page: the page header, records, and the offset array, as shown in Figure 2-1. All pages begin with the page header. The header is 96 bytes and contains meta-information about the page, such as the page number, the owning object, and the type of page. If rows will be stored on the pages, such as with data and index pages, the end of the page will contain an offset array. The offset array is 36 bytes and provides pointers to the byte location of the start of rows on the page. Between these two areas are 8,060 bytes where records and other page data are stored.

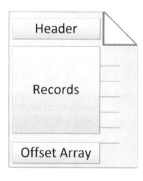

Figure 2-1. *Page structure*

30

If the page includes an offset array, it begins at the end of the page. As rows are added to a page, the row is added to the first open position in the records area of the page. After this, the starting location of the page is stored in the last available position in the offset array. For every row added, the data for the row is stored further away from the start of the page, and the offset is stored further away from the end of the page, as shown in Figure 2-2. Reading from the end of the page backward, the offset can be used to identify the starting position of every row, sometimes referred to as a *slot*, on the page.

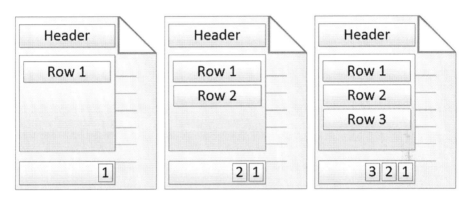

Figure 2-2. *Row placement and offset array*

While the basics of pages are the same, there are a number of ways in which pages are used. These uses include storing data pages, index structures, and large objects. These uses and how they interact with a SQL Server database will be discussed later in this chapter.

Extents

Moving up from pages, the next basic structure of the database are *extents*. These are groups of eight pages. An extent is simply eight physically contiguous data pages in a data file. All pages belong to an extent, and extents can't have fewer or more than eight pages. There are two types of extents used by SQL Server databases: *mixed* and *uniform* extents.

In mixed extents, the pages can be allocated to multiple objects. For example, when a table is first created and there are fewer than eight pages allocated to the table, it will be built as a mixed extent. The table will use mixed extents as long as the total size of the table is less than eight pages, as shown in Figure 2-3. By using mixed extents, databases can reduce the amount of space allocated to small tables.

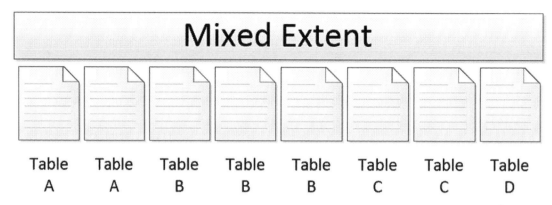

Figure 2-3. Mixed extent

Once the number of pages in a table exceeds eight pages, it will begin using uniform extents. In a uniform extent, all pages in the extent are allocated to a single object in the database (see Figure 2-4). Because of this, pages for an object will be contiguous, which increases the number of pages of an object that can be read in a single read. For more information on the benefits of contiguous reads, see Chapter 6.

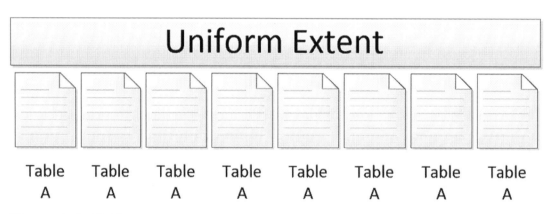

Figure 2-4. Uniform extent

Since SQL Server 2016, the use of uniform extents has become default behavior for all extent allocations for all databases. The behavior can be modified using the MIXED_PAGE_ALLOCATION database option, which will default the allocations to use mixed extents. With SQL Server 2014 and earlier versions, the behavior was opposite and defaulted to allocating mixed extents. And this behavior could be modified in those versions using trace flag 1118, which would modify SQL Server to using uniform extents, as is the current default behavior. While this may be a bit confusing, the important thing to remember is that SQL Server defaults to using uniform extents which mitigates a significant amount of page allocation contention issues.

Page Types

There are many ways in which a page can be used in a database. For each of these uses, there is a type associated with the page that defines how the page is being used. The page types available in a SQL Server database are

- File header page
- Boot page
- Page Free Space (PFS) page
- Global Allocation Map (GAM) page
- Shared Global Allocation Map (SGAM) page
- Differential Changed Map (DIFF) page
- Minimally Logged (ML) page
- Index Allocation Map (IAM) page
- Data page
- Index page
- Large object (Text and Image) page

The next few sections will expand on the types of pages and explain how they are used. While not all of page types deal directly with indexing, each will be defined and explained to help provide an understanding of the total picture. With every database, there are similarities in which the pages are laid out. For instance, in the first file of every database, the pages are laid out as shown in Figure 2-5. There are more page types available than the figure indicates, but as the examinations of each page type will show, only those in the first few pages are fixed. Many of the others appear in patterns that are dictated by the data in the database.

CHAPTER 2   INDEX STORAGE FUNDAMENTALS

Figure 2-5. *Data file pages*

Note   Database log files don't use the page architecture. Page structures apply only to database data files. A discussion of log file architecture is outside the scope of this book.

File Header Page

The first page in any database data file is the file header page, shown in Figure 2-5. Since this is the first page, it is always numbered 0. The file header page contains metadata information about the database file. The information on this page includes

- File ID
- Filegroup ID
- Current size of the file
- Max file size
- Sector size
- LSN information

There are a number of other details about the file on the file header page, but basically the information is immaterial to indexing internals.

Boot Page

The boot page is similar to the file header page in that it provides metadata information. This page, though, provides metadata information for the database itself instead of for the data file. There is one boot page per database, and it is located on page 9

34

in the first data file for a database (see Figure 2-5). Some of the information on the boot page includes the current version of the database, the create date and version for the database, the database name, the database ID, and the compatibility level.

One important attribute on the boot page is the attribute `dbi_dbccLastKnownGood`. This attribute provides the date that the last known DBCC CHECKDB completed successfully. While database maintenance isn't within the scope of this book, regular consistency checks of a database are critical to verifying that data remains available.

Page Free Space Page

To track whether pages have space available for inserting rows, each data file contains Page Free Space (PFS) pages. These pages, which are the second page of the data file (see Figure 2-5) and located every 8,088 pages after that, track the amount of free space in the database. Each byte on the PFS page represents one subsequent page in the data file and provides some simple allocation information regarding the page; namely, it determines the approximate amount of free space on the page.

When the database engine needs to store LOB data or data for heaps, it needs to know where the next available page is and how full the currently allocated pages are. This functionality is provided by PFS pages. Within each byte are flags that identify the current amount of space that is being used. Bits 0–2 determine whether the page is in one of the following free space states:

- Page is empty.
- 1–50 percent full.
- 51–80 percent full.
- 81–95 percent full.
- 96–100 percent full.

Along with free space, PFS pages also contain bits to identify a few other types of information for a page. For instance, bit 3 determines whether there are ghost records on a page. Bit 4 identifies whether the page is part of the Index Allocation Map, described later in this chapter. Bit 5 states whether the page is in a mixed extent. And finally, bit 6 identifies whether a page has been allocated.

Through the additional flags, or bits, SQL Server can determine what and how a page is being used from a high level. It can determine whether it is currently allocated. If not, is it available for LOB or heap data? If it is currently allocated, the PFS page then provides the first purpose described earlier in this section.

Finally, when the ghost cleanup process runs, the process doesn't need to check every page in a database for records to clean up. Instead, the PFS page can be checked, and only those pages with ghost records need to be accessed.

> **Note** The indexes themselves handle free space and page allocation for non-LOB data and indexes. The allocation of pages for these structures is determined by the definition of the structure.

Global Allocation Map Page

Similar to the PFS page is the Global Allocation Map (GAM) page. This page determines whether an extent has been designated for use as a uniform extent. A secondary purpose of the GAM page is helping determine whether the extent is free and available for allocation.

Each GAM page provides a map of all subsequent extents in each GAM interval. A GAM interval consists of the 64,000 extents, or 4 GB, that follow the GAM page. Each bit on the GAM page represents one extent following the GAM page. The first GAM page is located on page 2 of the database file (see Figure 2-5).

To determine whether an extent has been allocated to a uniform extent, SQL Server checks the bit in the GAM page that represents the extent. If the extent is allocated, then the bit is set to 0. When it is set to 1, the extent is free and available for other purposes.

Shared Global Allocation Map Page

Nearly identically to the GAM page is the Shared Global Allocation Map (SGAM) page. The primary difference between the pages is that the SGAM page determines whether an extent is allocated as a mixed extent. Like the GAM page, the SGAM page is also used to determine whether pages are available for allocation.

Each SGAM page provides a map of all subsequent extents in each SGAM interval. An SGAM interval consists of the 64,000 extents, or 4 GB, that follow the SGAM page.

Each bit on the SGAM page represents one extent following the SGAM page. The first SGAM page is located on page 3, after the GAM page of the database file (see Figure 2-5).

The SGAM pages determine when an extent has been allocated for use as a mixed extent. If the extent is allocated for this purpose and has a free page, the bit is set to 1. When it is set to 0, either the extent is not used as a mixed extent or it is a mixed extent with all pages in use.

Differential Changed Map Page

The next page to discuss is the Differential Changed Map (DCM) page. This page is used to determine whether an extent in a GAM interval has changed. When an extent changes, a bit value is changed from 0 to 1. These bits are stored in a bitmap row on the DCM page with each bit representing an extent.

DCM pages are used to track which extents have changed between full database backups. Whenever a full database backup occurs, all the bits on the DCM page are reset to 0. The bit then changes back to 1 when a change occurs within the associated extent.

The primary use for DCM pages is to provide a list of extents that have been modified for differential backups. Instead of checking every page or extent in the database to see whether it has changed, the DCM pages provide the list of extents to back up.

The first DCM page is located at page 6 of the data file. Subsequent DCM pages occur for each GAM interval in the data file.

Minimally Logged Page

After the DCM page is the Minimally Logged (ML) page, formerly known as the Bulk Changed Map page. The ML page is used to indicate when an extent in a GAM interval has been modified by a minimally logged operation. Any extent that is affected by a minimally logged operation will have its bit value set to 1, and those that have not will be set to 0. The bits are stored in a bitmap row on the ML page with each bit representing an extent in the GAM interval.

As the former name of ML pages implied (Bulk Changed Map), these pages are used in conjunction with the BULK_LOGGED recovery model. When the database uses this recovery model, the ML page is used to identify extents that were modified with a minimally logged operation since the last transaction log backup. When the transaction log backup completes, the bits on the ML page are reset to 0.

The first ML page is located at page 7 of the data file. Subsequent ML pages occur for each GAM interval in the data file.

Index Allocation Map Page

Most of the pages discussed so far provide information about whether there is data on the pages they cover. More important than whether a page is open and available, SQL Server needs to know whether the information on a page is associated to a specific table or index. The pages that provide this information are the Index Allocation Map (IAM) pages.

Every table or index first starts with an IAM page. This page indicates which extents within a GAM interval, discussed previously, are associated with the table or index. If a table or index crosses more than one GAM interval, there will be more than one IAM page for the table or index.

There are four types of pages that an IAM page associates with a table or index. These are data, index, large object, and small-large object pages. The IAM page accomplishes the association of the pages to the table or index through a bitmap row on the IAM page.

Besides the bitmap row, there is also an IAM header row on the IAM page. The IAM header provides the sequence number of IAM pages for a table or index. It also contains the starting page for the GAM interval that the IAM page is associated with. Finally, the row contains a single-page allocation array. This is used when less than an extent has been allocated to a table or index.

The value in understanding the IAM page is that it provides a map and root through which all the pages of a table or indexes come together. This page is used when all of the extents for a table or index need to be determined.

Data Page

Data pages are the most prevalent type of pages in any database. Data pages are used to store the data from rows in the database's tables. Except for a few data types, all data for a record is located on data pages. The exception to this rule is columns that store data in LOB data types. That information is stored on large object pages, discussed later in this section.

An understanding of data pages is important in relation to indexing internals. The understanding is important because data pages are the most common pages that will be looked at when looking at the internals of an index. When you get to the lowest levels of the index, data pages will always be found.

Index Page

Similar to data pages are index pages. These pages provide information on the structure of indexes and where data pages are located. For clustered indexes, the index pages are used to build the hierarchy of pages that are used to navigate the clustered index. With nonclustered indexes, index pages perform the same function but are also used to store the key values that comprise the index.

As mentioned, index pages are used to build the hierarchy of pages within an index. To accomplish this, the data contained in an index page provides a mapping of key values and page addresses. The key value is the key value from the index that the first sorted row on the child table contains, and the page address identifies where to locate this.

Index pages are constructed similarly to other page types. The page has a page header that contains all the standard information, such as page type, allocation unit, partition ID, and allocation status. The row offset array contains pointers to where the index data rows are located on the page. The index data rows contain two pieces of information: the key value and a page address (these were described earlier).

Understanding index pages is important since they provide a map of how all the data pages in an index are hooked together.

Large Object Page

As previously discussed, the limit for data on a single page is 8 KB. The maximum size, though, for some data types can be as high as 2 GB. For these data types, another storage mechanism is required to store the data. For this, there is a large object page type.

The data types that can utilize LOB pages include text, ntext, image, nvarchar(max), varchar(max), varbinary(max), and xml. When the data for one of these data types is stored on a data page, the LOB page will be used if the size of the row will exceed 8 KB. In these cases, the column will contain references to the LOB pages required for the data, and it will be stored on LOB pages instead (see Figure 2-6).

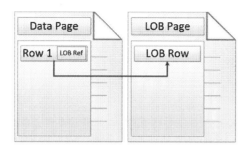

Figure 2-6. *Data page link to the LOB page*

Organizing Pages

So far you've looked at the low-level components that make up the internals for indexing. While these pieces are important to indexing, the structures in which these components are organized are where the value of indexing is realized. SQL Server utilizes a number of different organizational structures for storing data in the database.

The organizational structures in SQL Server are

- Heap
- Balanced-tree (B-tree)
- Columnar

These structures all map to specific index types that will be discussed later in this chapter. In this section, you'll examine each of the ways to organize pages to build that understanding.

Note In the structures for organizing indexes, the levels of the index that contain index pages are considered *nonleaf* levels. When referencing levels that contain data pages, the levels are called *leaf levels*.

Heap Structure

The default structure for organizing pages is called a *heap*. Heaps occur when a B-tree structure, discussed in the next section, is not used to organize the data pages in a table. Conceptually, a heap can be envisioned to be a pile of data pages in no particular order,

CHAPTER 2 INDEX STORAGE FUNDAMENTALS

as shown in Figure 2-7. In the example, the only way to retrieve all of the "Madison" records is to check each page to see whether "Madison" is on the page.

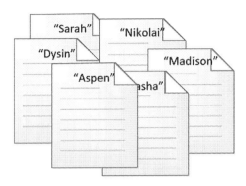

Figure 2-7. *Heap pile example*

From an internals perspective, though, heaps are more than a pile of pages. While unsorted, heaps have a few key components that organize the pages for easy access. All heaps start with an IAM page, shown in Figure 2-8. IAM pages, as discussed, map out which extents and single-page allocations within a GAM interval are associated with an index. For a heap, the IAM page is the only mechanism for associating data pages and extents to a heap. As mentioned, the heap structure does not enforce any sort of ordering on the pages that are associated with the heap. The first page available in a heap is the first page found in the database file for the heap.

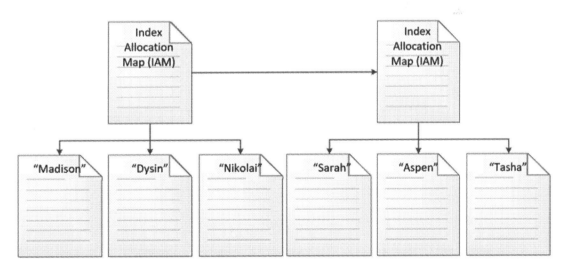

Figure 2-8. *Heap structure*

41

The IAM page lists all the data pages associated with the heap. The data pages for the heap store the rows for the table, with the use of LOB pages as needed. When the IAM page has no more pages available to allocate in the GAM interval, a new IAM page is allocated to the heap, and the next set of pages and their corresponding rows are added to the heap, as detailed in Figure 2-1. As the image shows, a heap structure is flat. From top to bottom, there is only ever one level from the IAM pages to the data pages of the structure.

While a heap provides a mechanism for organizing pages, it does not relate to an index type. A heap structure is used when a table does not have a clustered index. When a heap stores rows in a table, the rows are inserted without an enforced order. This happens because, as opposed to a clustered index, a sort order based on specific columns does not exist on a heap.

B-Tree Structure

The second available structure that can be used for indexing is the Balanced-tree, or *B-tree*, structure. It is the most commonly used structure for organizing indexes in SQL Server and is used by both clustered and nonclustered indexes.

In a B-tree, pages are organized in a hierarchical tree structure, as shown in Figure 2-9. Within the structure, pages are sorted to optimize searches for information within the structure. Along with the sorting, relationships between pages are maintained to allow sequential access to pages across the levels of the index.

Similar to heaps, B-trees start with an IAM page that identifies where the first page of the B-tree is located within the GAM interval. The first page of the B-tree is an index page and is often referred to as the *root level* of the index. As an index page, the root level contains key values and page addresses for the next pages in the index. Depending on the size of the index, the next level of the index may be data pages or additional index pages.

If the number of index rows required to sort all the rows on the data pages exceeds the space available, then the root page will be followed by another level of index pages. Additional levels of index pages in a B-tree are referred to as *intermediate levels*. In many cases, indexes built with a B-tree structure will not require more than one or two intermediate levels. Even with a wide indexing key, millions to billions of rows can be sorted with just a few levels.

CHAPTER 2 INDEX STORAGE FUNDAMENTALS

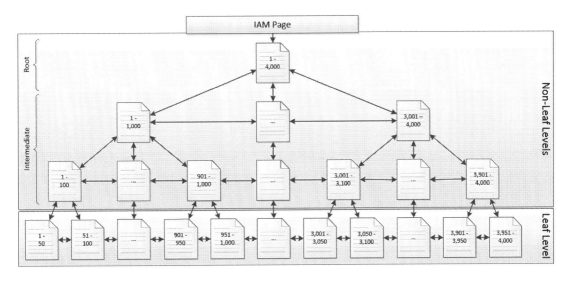

Figure 2-9. *B-tree structure*

The next level of pages below the root and intermediate levels of the indexes, referred to as the *nonleaf levels*, is the *leaf level* (see Figure 2-9). The leaf level contains all the data pages for the index. The data pages are where all the key values and the nonkey values for the row are stored. Nonkey values are never stored on the index pages.

Another differentiator between heaps and B-trees is the ability within the index levels to perform sequential page reads. Pages contain previous page and next page properties in the page headers. With index and data pages, these properties are populated and can be used to traverse the B-tree to find the next requested row from the B-tree without returning to the root level of the index. To illustrate this, consider a situation where you request the rows with key values between 925 and 3,025 from the index shown in Figure 2-9. Through a B-tree, this operation can be done by traversing the B-tree down to key value 925, shown in Figure 2-10. After that, the rows through key value 3,025 can be retrieved by accessing all pages after the first page in order, finishing the operation when the last key value is encountered.

CHAPTER 2   INDEX STORAGE FUNDAMENTALS

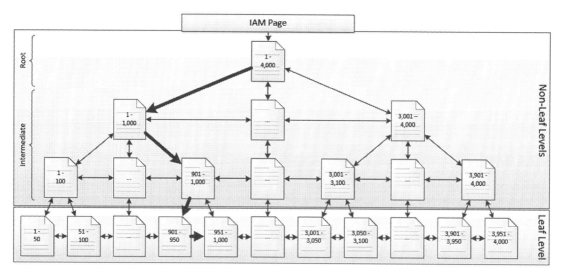

Figure 2-10. *B-tree sequential read*

One option available for tables and indexes is the ability to partition these structures. Partitioning changes the physical implementation of the index and how the index and data pages are organized. From the perspective of the B-tree structure, each partition in an index has its own B-tree. If a table is partitioned into three different partitions, there will then be three B-tree structures for the index.

Columnstore Structure

Columnstore, first introduced with SQL Server 2012, introduces a new organizational structure, which is based on Microsoft's Vertipaq technology. The columnstore structure is used by the clustered and nonclustered columnstore index types. The columnstore structure diverges from the traditional method of storing and indexing data from a row-wise to a column-wise format. This means that instead of storing all the values for a row with all the other values in the row, the values are stored with the values of the same column grouped together. For instance, in the example in Figure 2-11, instead of four row "groups" stored on the page, three column "groups" are stored.

CHAPTER 2 ■ INDEX STORAGE FUNDAMENTALS

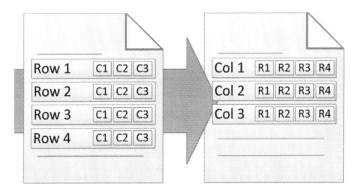

Figure 2-11. *Row-wise vs. column-wise storage*

The physical implementation of the columnstore structure does not introduce any new page types; it instead utilizes existing page types. Like other structures, a columnstore begins with an IAM page, shown in Figure 2-12. From the IAM page are LOB pages that contain the columnstore information. For each column stored in the columnstore, there are one or more segments. Segments contain up to about 1 million rows worth of data for the columns that they represent. An LOB page can contain one or more segments, and the segments can span multiple LOB pages.

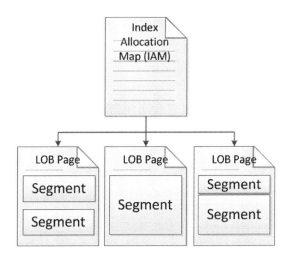

Figure 2-12. *Columnstore structure*

Within each segment is a hash dictionary that is used to map the data that comprises the segment of the columnstore. The hash dictionary also contains the minimum and maximum values for the data in the segment. This information is used by SQL Server during query execution to eliminate segments during query execution.

45

One of the advantages of the columnstore structure is its ability to leverage compression. Since each segment of the columnstore structure contains the same type of data, both from a data type and from a value perspective, SQL Server has a greater likelihood of being able to utilize compression on the data. The compression used by the columnstore is similar to page-level compression. It utilizes dictionary compression to remove similar values throughout the segment. There are two main differences between page and columnstore compressions. First, while page compression is optional, columnstore compression is mandatory and cannot be disabled. Second, page compression is limited to compressing the values on a single page. Alternately, columnstore compression is for the entire segment, which may span multiple pages or could have multiple segments on the same page. Regardless of the number of pages or segments on a page, columnstore compression is contained to the segment.

Another advantage of the columnstore is that only the columns requested from the columnstore are returned. It is often recommended not to use SELECT * when writing queries; instead, the best practice is to only SELECT the columns that are required. Unfortunately, even when this practice is followed, indexes based on heaps and B-trees read all the columns for the row from disk into memory. The practice reduces some network traffic and streamlines execution, but it doesn't assist with the bottleneck of reading data from disk. Columnstore indexes address this issue by reading from disk only the columns that are requested and moving that data into memory. Along these same lines, according to Microsoft, queries often access only 10–15 percent of the available columns in a table.[1] The reduction in the columns retrieved from a columnstore structure will have a significant impact on performance and I/O.

While the columnar structure is unchanged between clustered and nonclustered columnstore indexes, there are a few points of distinction between the two that are important to be aware of. A clustered columnstore index has an additional structure, called the *deltastore*, which allows write operations on the index. While segments of both types of columnstore are read-only, the deltastore allows insert, update, and delete actions against the index. Also, a clustered columnstore is the base copy of the data; it doesn't have a clustered index or heap that it relies on for a full copy of the data.

---

[1] "Columnstore Indexes: A New Feature in SQL Server known as Project 'Apollo,'" Microsoft SQL Server Team Blog, http://blogs.technet.com/b/dataplatforminsider/archive/2011/08/04/columnstore-indexes-a-new-feature-in-sql-server-known-as-project-apollo.aspx

All data is stored in a clustered columnstore index. Alternatively, the nonclustered columnstore index requires a traditional clustered index on the data it is using and generally represents a duplication of the data in the database.

> **Warning** The tools used in the next section are undocumented and unsupported. They do not appear in Books Online, and their functionality can change without notice. That being said, these tools have been around for quite some time, and there are many blog posts that describe their behavior. You can find additional resources for using these tools at `www.sqlskills.com`. When using older versions of SQL Server, it will be important to understand these tools, since the previously described DMFs may not be available.

Examining Pages

The first part of this chapter outlined the types of pages found in SQL Server databases. On top of that, you've looked at the structures available for organizing and managing the relationship between pages within your databases. In this next section, you will look at how to use dynamic management functions and DBCC commands to examine pages in your database. For current versions of SQL Server, you'll be able to use the DMFs, but on older releases you'll need to use the DBCC commands.

By using these tools, you'll gain the foundation from which you'll be able to look at the behaviors of indexes in this chapter and throughout the rest of the book. Also, this will provide you with the knowledge to do your own exploration of indexes and data in your databases.

Dynamic Management Functions

There are two dynamic management functions you'll be using to examine the pages within your SQL Server databases. These are

- sys.dm_db_database_page_allocations
- sys.dm_db_page_info

sys.dm_db_database_page_allocations

The DMF sys.dm_db_database_page_allocations provides information on page allocations within a database. The function can be used to investigate indexes and their associated pages. It can also be used to identify how extents have been allocated and whether the extents being used are mixed or uniform.

The DMF provides data similar to that which is provided from DBCC EXTENTINFO and DBCC IND, which are described later. An advantage of using the DMF is that the results can be filtered and merged with other DMFs. Additionally, it provides details on all pages allocated to an index even those without data on them. One restriction of the output is that it only returns pages associated with data allocation, such as the data, index, and IAM pages.

Listing 2-1 shows the syntax for using sys.dm_db_database_page_allocations. The execution requires five parameters, which are defined in Table 2-1.

Listing 2-1. sys.dm_db_database_page_allocations Syntax

```
SELECT * FROM sys.dm_db_database_page_allocations ({database_id},
{TableId | NULL}, {IndexId | NULL}, { PartitionId | NULL },
{DETAILED | LIMITED})
```

Table 2-1. *Parameters for sys.dm_db_database_page_allocations*

Parameter	Description
@DatabaseId	Database from which to return the page listing for tables and indexes. The parameter is required and accepts the use of the DB_ID() function.
@TableId	Object_id for the table from which to return the page listing. The parameter is required and accepts the use of the OBJECT_ID() function. NULL can also be used to return all tables.
@IndexId	Index_id from the table that the page list is from. The parameter is required and accepts the use of NULL to return information for all indexes.
@PartionId	ID of the partition that the page list is returning. The parameter is required and accepts the use of NULL to return information for all indexes.
@Mode	Defines the mode for returning data. The options are DETAILED and LIMITED. With LIMITED, the information is limited to page metadata, such as page allocation and relationship information. Under the DETAILED mode, additional information is provided, such as page type and interpage relationship chains.

CHAPTER 2 INDEX STORAGE FUNDAMENTALS

When executing sys.dm_db_database_page_allocations, results include the columns defined in Table 2-2. For every page allocation, there will be one row in the results.

Table 2-2. *Columns for sys.dm_db_database_page_allocations*

DMF Column	Description
database_id	ID of the database.
object_id	Object ID for the table or view.
index_id	ID for the index.
partition_id	Partition number for the index.
rowset_id	Partition ID for the index.
allocation_unit_id	ID of the allocation unit.
allocation_unit_type	Type of allocation unit.
allocation_unit_type_desc	Description of the allocation unit.
data_clone_id	Unknown.
clone_state	Unknown.
clone_state_desc	Unknown.
extent_file_id	File ID of the extent.
extent_page_id	Page ID for the extent.
allocated_page_iam_file_id	File ID for the index allocation map page associated with the page.
allocated_page_iam_page_id	Page ID for the index allocation map page associated with the page.
allocated_page_file_id	File ID of the allocated page.
allocated_page_page_id	Page ID for the allocated page.
is_allocated	Indicates whether a page is allocated.
is_iam_page	Indicates whether a page is the index allocation page.
is_mixed_page_allocation	Indicates whether a page is allocated.

(*continued*)

Table 2-2. (*continued*)

DMF Column	Description
page_free_space_percent	Percentage of space free on the page.
page_type	Page type ID for the allocated page.
page_type_desc	Description of the page type.
page_level	Level of the page in the B-tree index.
next_page_file_id	File ID for the next page.
next_page_page_id	Page ID for the next page.
previous_page_file_id	File ID for the previous page.
previous_page_page_id	Page ID for the previous page.
is_page_compressed	Indicates whether the page is compressed.
has_ghost_records	Indicates whether the page has ghost records.

With this DMF, there are a couple of use cases we can investigate that can help to demonstrate leveraging sys.dm_db_database_page_allocations. To begin, you want to create a database for this chapter and a table that has twelve rows in it using Listing 2-2.

Listing 2-2. Script for Creating dbo.IndexInternalsOne with 12 Rows

```
USE master;
GO
CREATE DATABASE Chapter2Internals;
GO
USE Chapter2Internals;
GO
CREATE TABLE dbo.IndexInternalsOne
(
    RowID INT IDENTITY(1, 1),
    FillerData CHAR(8000)
);
```

CHAPTER 2 INDEX STORAGE FUNDAMENTALS

```
GO
INSERT INTO dbo.IndexInternalsOne
DEFAULT VALUES;
GO 12
```

After creating the table, you'll use the script in Listing 2-3 to show how SQL Server stored the records in the table and how you can examine them with sys.dm_db_database_page_allocations. As Figure 2-13 shows, there is one Index Allocation Map page allocated to the table, which is within a mixed page allocation. This means the multiple indexes can use that extent to allocate these pages. And then there are eight pages allocated to the first data page extent of the index starting at page 312 and another four pages allocated from an extent starting at page 320. Additionally, you see that there are four pages allocated but not assigned a page type on the extent at page 320. This demonstrates and confirms what was discussed in the previous section on heap structures. There's an index allocation map and extents with data pages allocated to that map.

Listing 2-3. Extent Allocation with sys.dm_db_database_page_allocations

```
SELECT DPA.extent_file_id,
       DPA.extent_page_id,
       DPA.page_type_desc,
       DPA.allocation_unit_type_desc,
       DPA.is_iam_page,
       DPA.is_mixed_page_allocation,
       COUNT(*) AS page_count
FROM sys.dm_db_database_page_allocations(DB_ID(), OBJECT_ID('dbo.
IndexInternalsOne'), NULL, NULL, 'DETAILED') DPA
GROUP BY DPA.extent_file_id,
         DPA.extent_page_id,
         DPA.page_type_desc,
         DPA.allocation_unit_type_desc,
         DPA.is_iam_page,
         DPA.is_mixed_page_allocation
ORDER BY DPA.extent_page_id,
         DPA.page_type_desc;
```

CHAPTER 2 INDEX STORAGE FUNDAMENTALS

	extent_file_id	extent_page_id	page_type_desc	allocation_unit_type_desc	is_iam_page	is_mixed_page_allocation	page_count
1	1	232	IAM_PAGE	IN_ROW_DATA	1	1	1
2	1	312	DATA_PAGE	IN_ROW_DATA	0	0	8
3	1	320	NULL	IN_ROW_DATA	0	0	4
4	1	320	DATA_PAGE	IN_ROW_DATA	0	0	4

Figure 2-13. *Extent allocation results for dbo.IndexInternalsOne*

Index allocation map pages are always part of a mixed extent, since the allocation determines the index mapping for multiple tables. To demonstrate, you can run the script in Listing 2-4 which creates a second table that includes a clustered index via a primary key. Reviewing the results in Figure 2-14, the six rows were added to an extent that starts at page 328, bypassing the four pages that were allocated, but not used in the previous table. The index allocation map page though belongs to the same extent as that of dbo.IndexInternalsOne, which starts at page 232, showing that this extent is indeed mixed. Additionally, you'll see that an index page is allocated to the table to support the B-tree structure of the clustered index.

Listing 2-4. Script for Creating dbo.IndexInternalsTwo with 12 Rows

```
USE Chapter2Internals;
GO

CREATE TABLE dbo.IndexInternalsTwo
(
    RowID INT IDENTITY(1, 1) PRIMARY KEY,
    FillerData CHAR(8000)
);
GO
INSERT INTO dbo.IndexInternalsTwo
DEFAULT VALUES;
GO 6
SELECT DPA.extent_file_id,
       DPA.extent_page_id,
       DPA.page_type_desc,
       DPA.allocation_unit_type_desc,
       DPA.is_iam_page,
       DPA.is_mixed_page_allocation,
       COUNT(*) AS page_count
```

```
FROM sys.dm_db_database_page_allocations(DB_ID(), OBJECT_ID('dbo.
IndexInternalsTwo'), NULL, NULL, 'DETAILED') DPA
GROUP BY DPA.extent_file_id,
         DPA.extent_page_id,
         DPA.page_type_desc,
         DPA.allocation_unit_type_desc,
         DPA.is_iam_page,
         DPA.is_mixed_page_allocation
ORDER BY DPA.extent_page_id,
         DPA.page_type_desc;
```

	extent_file_id	extent_page_id	page_type_desc	allocation_unit_type_desc	is_iam_page	is_mixed_page_allocation	page_count
1	1	232	IAM_PAGE	IN_ROW_DATA	1	1	1
2	1	328	NULL	IN_ROW_DATA	0	0	1
3	1	328	DATA_PAGE	IN_ROW_DATA	0	0	6
4	1	328	INDEX_PAGE	IN_ROW_DATA	0	0	1

Figure 2-14. *Extent allocation results for dbo.IndexInternalsTwo*

Beyond extent-level details, you can use this DMF to investigate indexes down to the page level to understand all pages allocated to the table and the order in which they relate to other pages in an index. Using the script in Listing 2-5, you can once again see, in Figure 2-15, that the extent starting on page 232 includes the allocated pages 235 and 236 for the index allocation maps. And the page allocated to the extent starting at page 312 includes pages 312, 313, and so on which is similar to the extent starting at page 328 which includes pages 328, 329, and so on. Add to this the ability to see per page the page level within the B-tree and the connections between pages, verifying the ability to move up and down the index and from page to page at the data pages.

Listing 2-5. Script for Reviewing All Allocated Pages

```
SELECT DPA.page_type_desc,
       DPA.allocation_unit_type_desc,
       DPA.object_id,
       DPA.index_id,
       DPA.extent_page_id,
       DPA.allocated_page_iam_page_id,
       DPA.allocated_page_page_id,
```

```
    DPA.page_level,
    DPA.next_page_page_id,
    DPA.previous_page_page_id
FROM sys.dm_db_database_page_allocations(DB_ID(), OBJECT_ID('dbo.
IndexInternalsTwo'), NULL, NULL, 'DETAILED') DPA
```

	page_type_desc	allocation_unit_type_desc	object_id	index_id	extent_page_id	allocated_page_iam_page_id	allocated_page_page_id	page_level	next_page_page_id	previous_page_page_id
1	IAM_PAGE	IN_ROW_DATA	597577167	1	232	NULL	236	0	NULL	NULL
2	DATA_PAGE	IN_ROW_DATA	597577167	1	328	236	328	0	330	NULL
3	INDEX_PAGE	IN_ROW_DATA	597577167	1	328	236	329	1	NULL	NULL
4	DATA_PAGE	IN_ROW_DATA	597577167	1	328	236	330	0	331	328
5	DATA_PAGE	IN_ROW_DATA	597577167	1	328	236	331	0	332	330
6	DATA_PAGE	IN_ROW_DATA	597577167	1	328	236	332	0	333	331
7	DATA_PAGE	IN_ROW_DATA	597577167	1	328	236	333	0	334	332
8	DATA_PAGE	IN_ROW_DATA	597577167	1	328	236	334	0	NULL	333
9	NULL	IN_ROW_DATA	597577167	1	328	236	335	NULL	NULL	NULL

Figure 2-15. *Extent allocation results for reviewing all allocated pages*

sys.dm_db_page_info

Another dynamic management function that helps us understand how indexes operate is sys.dm_db_page_info. This DMF provides page header row information for database pages. This information includes number of slots, free bytes, minimally logged status, ghost records, and page linking details.

Listing 2-6 shows the syntax for using sys.dm_db_page_info. The execution requires four parameters, which are defined in Table 2-3. While Microsoft states that these parameters can be NULL, that is not the case, and the function errors when NULL values are provided.

Listing 2-6. sys.dm_db_page_info Syntax

```
SELECT * FROM sys.dm_db_database_page_allocations ({database_id},
{FileId}, {PageId}, {DETAILED | LIMITED})
```

CHAPTER 2 INDEX STORAGE FUNDAMENTALS

Table 2-3. Parameters for sys.dm_db_database_page_allocations

Parameter	Description
@DatabaseId	Database from which to return the page header information.
@FileID	FileId for the page that will be returned.
@PageId	Page_id for the page that will be returned.
@Mode	Defines the mode for returning data. The options are DETAILED and LIMITED. With LIMITED, the information is limited to page metadata. Under the DETAILED mode, page descriptive columns will be populated.

When executing sys.dm_db_page_info, results include the columns defined in Table 2-4. For every page requested, there will be one row of header information in the results.

Table 2-4. Columns for sys.dm_db_page_info

Column Name	Description
database_id	ID of the database.
file_id	ID of the data file.
page_id	ID of the page.
page_header_version	Version of the page header.
page_type	ID for the page type.
page_type_desc	Text description of the page type.
page_type_flag_bits	Type flag bits in the page header.
page_type_flag_bits_desc	Type flag bits description in the page header.
page_flag_bits	Flag bits in the page header.
page_flag_bits_desc	Flag bits text description in the page header.
page_lsn	Log sequence number associated with last page modification.
page_level	Level of the page in the index.
object_id	ID of the object associated with the page.

(continued)

Table 2-4. (*continued*)

Column Name	Description
index_id	ID of the index.
partition_id	ID of the partition.
alloc_unit_id	ID of the allocation unit.
is_encrypted	Indicates whether a page is encrypted.
has_checksum	Indicates whether a page has a checksum value.
checksum	Checksum value for a page.
is_iam_page	Indicates whether a page is the index allocation page.
is_mixed_extent	Indicates whether a page is part of a mixed extent.
has_ghost_records	Indicates whether the page has ghost records.
has_version_records	Indicates whether the page has version records.
has_persisted_version_records	Indicates whether the page has persisted version records.
pfs_page_id	Page ID of the PFS page associated with this page.
pfs_is_allocated	Indicates whether the PFS page has allocated this page.
pfs_alloc_percent	Allocation percentage as indicated by the PFS page.
pfs_status	Bit value for the PFS status.
pfs_status_desc	Text description of the PFS status.
gam_page_id	Page ID of the GAM page associated with this page.
gam_status	ID value indicating the GAM status of this page.
gam_status_desc	Text description of the GAM status of this page.
sgam_page_id	Page ID of the SGAM page associated with this page.
sgam_status	ID value indicating the SGAM status of this page.
sgam_status_desc	Text description of the SGAM status of this page.
diff_map_page_id	Page ID of the differential map page associated with this page.
diff_status	ID value indicating the differential map status of this page.
diff_status_desc	Text description of the differential map status of this page.

(*continued*)

CHAPTER 2　INDEX STORAGE FUNDAMENTALS

Table 2-4. (*continued*)

Column Name	Description
ml_map_page_id	Page ID of the minimally logged page associated with this page.
ml_status	ID value indicating the minimally logged page status of this page.
ml_status_desc	Text description of the minimally logged page status of this page.
prev_page_file_id	File ID for the next page.
prev_page_page_id	Page ID for the next page.
next_page_file_id	File ID for the previous page.
next_page_page_id	Page ID for the previous page.
fixed_length	Unknown.
slot_count	Total number of used and unused slots.
ghost_rec_count	Number of records marked as ghost on the page.
free_bytes	Number of free bytes on the page.
free_bytes_offset	Offset of free space at the end of data area.
reserved_bytes	Number of reserved bytes on the page.
reserved_bytes_by_xdes_id	Space contributed by m_xdesID to m_reservedCnt.
xdes_id	Latest transaction contributed by m_reserved.

You can use this header information to identify how pages are interrelated between different structures, such as PFS pages, or use it to inspect pages to verify checksum or number of slots and free space. To demonstrate, run the code in Listing 2-7, which retrieves all page allocations for the two previously created tables and retrieves page header information for all of the assigned pages.

Listing 2-7. Query Using sys.dm_db_page_info

```
SELECT T.name,
       DPA.page_type_desc,
       DPI.page_id,
       DPI.pfs_page_id,
       DPI.gam_page_id,
```

CHAPTER 2 INDEX STORAGE FUNDAMENTALS

```
    DPI.sgam_page_id,
    DPI.diff_map_page_id,
    DPI.ml_map_page_id,
    DPI.prev_page_page_id,
    DPI.next_page_page_id,
    DPI.fixed_length,
    DPI.slot_count,
    DPI.free_bytes
FROM sys.dm_db_database_page_allocations(DB_ID(), NULL, NULL, NULL,
'DETAILED') DPA
    INNER JOIN sys.tables T ON T.object_id = DPA.object_id
    CROSS APPLY sys.dm_db_page_info(DPA.database_id, DPA.allocated_page_
    file_id, DPA.allocated_page_page_id, DEFAULT) DPI;
```

Once executed, you'll have results similar to those in Figure 2-16. In these results, we see the same previous and next page connections for dbo.IndexInternalsTwo, but no page IDs listed for dbo.IndexInternalsone. Additionally, the PFS, GAM, SGAM, DIFF, and ML pages are identified for both tables, which are the same since the database is smaller than the threshold required for having multiples of these page types. Lastly, you'll see the number of slots, length, and free bytes per page. Of note, page 329, which is the index page for dbo.IndexInternalsTwo, has six slots, one for each page that the index page manages in the clustered index.

	name	page_type_desc	page_id	pfs_page_id	gam_page_id	sgam_page_id	diff_map_page_id	ml_map_page_id	prev_page_page_id	next_page_page_id	fixed_length	slot_count	free_bytes
1	IndexInternalsOne	IAM_PAGE	235	1	2	3	6	7	0	0	90	2	6
2	IndexInternalsOne	DATA_PAGE	312	1	2	3	6	7	0	0	8008	1	83
3	IndexInternalsOne	DATA_PAGE	313	1	2	3	6	7	0	0	8008	1	83
4	IndexInternalsOne	DATA_PAGE	314	1	2	3	6	7	0	0	8008	1	83
5	IndexInternalsOne	DATA_PAGE	315	1	2	3	6	7	0	0	8008	1	83
6	IndexInternalsOne	DATA_PAGE	316	1	2	3	6	7	0	0	8008	1	83
7	IndexInternalsOne	DATA_PAGE	317	1	2	3	6	7	0	0	8008	1	83
8	IndexInternalsOne	DATA_PAGE	318	1	2	3	6	7	0	0	8008	1	83
9	IndexInternalsOne	DATA_PAGE	319	1	2	3	6	7	0	0	8008	1	83
10	IndexInternalsOne	DATA_PAGE	320	1	2	3	6	7	0	0	8008	1	83
11	IndexInternalsOne	DATA_PAGE	321	1	2	3	6	7	0	0	8008	1	83
12	IndexInternalsOne	DATA_PAGE	322	1	2	3	6	7	0	0	8008	1	83
13	IndexInternalsOne	DATA_PAGE	323	1	2	3	6	7	0	0	8008	1	83
14	IndexInternalsOne	NULL	324	NULL	NULL	NULL	NULL	NULL	NULL	NULL	NULL	NULL	NULL
15	IndexInternalsOne	NULL	325	NULL	NULL	NULL	NULL	NULL	NULL	NULL	NULL	NULL	NULL
16	IndexInternalsOne	NULL	326	NULL	NULL	NULL	NULL	NULL	NULL	NULL	NULL	NULL	NULL
17	IndexInternalsOne	NULL	327	NULL	NULL	NULL	NULL	NULL	NULL	NULL	NULL	NULL	NULL
18	IndexInternalsTwo	IAM_PAGE	236	1	2	3	6	7	0	0	90	2	6
19	IndexInternalsTwo	DATA_PAGE	328	1	2	3	6	7	0	330	8008	1	83
20	IndexInternalsTwo	INDEX_PAGE	329	1	2	3	6	7	0	0	11	6	8018
21	IndexInternalsTwo	DATA_PAGE	330	1	2	3	6	7	328	331	8008	1	83
22	IndexInternalsTwo	DATA_PAGE	331	1	2	3	6	7	330	332	8008	1	83
23	IndexInternalsTwo	DATA_PAGE	332	1	2	3	6	7	331	333	8008	1	83
24	IndexInternalsTwo	DATA_PAGE	333	1	2	3	6	7	332	334	8008	1	83
25	IndexInternalsTwo	DATA_PAGE	334	1	2	3	6	7	333	0	8008	1	83
26	IndexInternalsTwo	NULL	335	NULL	NULL	NULL	NULL	NULL	NULL	NULL	NULL	NULL	NULL

Figure 2-16. Page header results from sys.dm_db_page_info

DBCC Commands

While you can do a lot of exploration of data structures with the dynamic management functions previously described in this chapter, there will be some occasions where you will want to dig deeper. To accomplish this in SQL Server, you can use the following DBCC commands:

- DBCC EXTENTINFO
- DBCC IND
- DBCC PAGE

In the next few sections, we'll explore these commands and review some examples of leveraging them in databases.

DBCC EXTENTINFO

The first DBCC command to explore is DBCC EXTENTINFO. Similar to sys.dm_db_database_page_allocations, this command provides information about extent allocations that occur within a database. This identifies how extents have been allocated and whether the extents being used are mixed or uniform. Listing 2-8 shows the syntax for using DBCC EXTENTINFO. When using the command, there are four parameters that can be populated; these are defined in Table 2-5.

Listing 2-8. DBCC EXTENTINFO Syntax

```
DBCC EXTENTINFO ( {database_name | database_id | 0}
    , {table_name | table_object_id}, { index_name | index_id | -1}
    , { partition_id | 0}
```

Table 2-5. *DBCC EXTENTINFO Parameters*

Parameter	Description
database_name | database_id	Specifies either the database name or the database ID where the page will be retrieved. If the value 0 is provided for this parameter or the parameter is not set, then the current database will be used.
table_name | table_object_id	Specifies which table to return in the output by providing either the table name or the `object_ID` for the table. If no value is provided, the output will include results for all tables.
index_name | index_id	Specifies which index to return in the output by providing either the index name or the `index_ID`. If -1 or no value is provided, then the output will include results for all indexes on the table.
partition_id	Specifies which partition of the index to return in the output by providing the partition number. If 0 or no value is provided, then the output will include results for all partitions on the index.

When executing `DBCC EXTENTINFO`, a dataset is returned. The results include the columns defined in Table 2-6. For every extent allocation, there will be one row in the results. Since extents are comprised of eight pages, there can be as many as eight allocations for an extent when there are single-page allocations, such as when mixed extents are used. When uniform extents are used, there will be only one extent allocation and one row returned for the extent.

Table 2-6. *DBCC EXTENTINFO Output Columns*

Parameter	Description
file_id	File number where the page is located.
page_id	Page number for the page.
pg_alloc	Number of pages allocated from the extent to the object.
ext_size	Size of the extent.
object_id	Object ID for the table.
index_id	Index ID associated with the heap or index.

(*continued*)

Table 2-6. (*continued*)

Parameter	Description
partition_number	Partition number for the heap or index.
partition_id	Partition ID for the heap or index.
iam_chain_type	The type of IAM chain the extent is used for. Values can be in-row data, LOB data, and overflow data.
pfs_bytes	Bytes array that identifies the amount of free space, whether there are ghost records, whether the page is an IAM page, whether it is allocated, and whether it is part of a mixed extent.

To demonstrate how the command works, let's walk through a couple examples to observe how extents are allocated. In the first example, shown in Listing 2-9, we'll reuse the dbo.IndexInternalsOne from the last section and run the DBCC EXTENTINFO command against that.

Listing 2-9. DBCC EXTENTINFO dbo.IndexInternalsOne

```
USE Chapter2Internals
GO
DBCC EXTENTINFO(0, IndexInternalsOne, -1)
```

In the results from the DBCC command, shown in Figure 2-17, you can see that there are 13 total pages allocated to the table. The items of interest in these results are the pg_alloc and ext_size columns. In the first row, the pages allocated are nine, accounting for the index allocation map page and eight pages of the extent. In the second row, there are 4 pages allocated, which is the balance of the 12 records inserted into the table. Both rows should have 8 for the extent size, since uniform extents are allocated.

	file_id	page_id	pg_alloc	ext_size	object_id	index_id	partition_number	partition_id	iam_chain_type	pfs_bytes
1	1	312	9	8	581577110	0	1	72057594043170816	In-row data	0x4444444444444444
2	1	320	4	8	581577110	0	1	72057594043170816	In-row data	0x4444444400000000

Figure 2-17. DBCC EXTENTINFO for pages in dbo.IndexInternalsOne

In SQL Server versions prior to SQL Server 2016, the behavior will be quite different since it will leverage single-page allocations for each transaction until the first extent is filled. This behavior change is due to the behavior of trace flag 1118 becoming default behavior for SQL Server.

Though DBCC EXTENTINFO doesn't provide as much detail as sys.dm_db_database_page_allocations, it can be useful for identifying extents assigned to a table, especially when using SQL Server versions prior to SQL Server 2012.

DBCC IND

The next command that can be used to investigate indexes and their associated pages is DBCC IND. This command returns a list of all the pages associated with the requested object, which can be scoped to the database, table, or index level, also similar to sys.dm_db_database_page_allocations. Listing 2-10 shows the syntax for using DBCC IND. When using the command, there are three parameters that can be populated; these are defined in Table 2-7.

Listing 2-10. DBCC IND Syntax

```
DBCC IND ( {'dbname' | dbid}, {'table_name' | table_object_id},
         {'index_name' | index_id | -1})
```

Table 2-7. DBCC IND Parameters

Parameter	Description
database_name | database_id	Specifies either the database name or the database ID where the page list will be retrieved. If the value 0 is provided for this parameter or the parameter is not set, then the current database will be used.
table_name | table_object_id	Specifies which table to return in the output by providing either the table name or the object_ID for the table. If no value is provided, the output will include results for all tables.
index_name | index_id	Specifies which index to return in the output by providing either the index name or the index_ID. If -1 or no value is provided, the output will include results for all indexes on the table.

DBCC IND returns a dataset when executed. For every page that is allocated to the requested objects, one row is returned in the dataset; the columns are defined in Table 2-8. Unlike the previous DBCC EXTENTINFO, DBCC IND does explicitly return the IAM page in the results.

Table 2-8. *DBCC IND Output Columns*

Column	Description
PageFID	File number where the page is located.
PagePID	Page number for the page.
IAMFID	File ID where the IAM page is located.
IAMPID	Page ID for the page in the data file.
ObjectID	Object ID for the associated table.
IndexID	Index ID associated with the heap or index.
PartitionNumber	Partition number for the heap or index.
PartitionID	Partition ID for the heap or index.
iam_chain_type	The type of IAM chain the extent is used for. Values can be in-row data, LOB data, and overflow data.
PageType	Number identifying the page type. These are listed in Table 2-9.
IndexLevel	Level at which the page exists in the page organizational structure. The levels are organized from 0 to N, where 0 is the lowest level of the index and N is the index root.
NextPageFID	File number where the next page at the index level is located.
NextPagePID	Page number for the next page at the index level.
PrevPageFID	File number where the previous page at the index level is located.
PrevPagePID	Page number for the previous page at the index level.

Within the results from DBCC EXTENTINFO is a PageType column. This column identifies what type of page is returned through the DBCC command. The page types can include data, index, GAM, or any other of the page types discussed earlier in the chapter. Table 2-9 shows a full list of the page types and the value identifying the page type.

Table 2-9. Page Type Mappings

Page Type	Description
1	Data page.
2	Index page.
3	Large object page.
4	Large object page.
8	Global Allocation Map page.
9	Share Global Allocation Map page.
10	Index Allocation Map page.
11	Page Free Space page.
13	Boot page.
15	File header page.
16	Differential Changed Map page.
17	Minimally Logged page.

The primary benefit of using DBCC IND is that it provides a list of all pages for a table or index with their locations in the database. You can use this to help investigate how indexes are behaving and where pages are ending up. To put this information into action, we'll walk through a couple of scenarios.

For the first example, you'll revisit the tables created in the last section and examine the output for each of these in comparison to the DBCC EXTENTINFO output. The code example includes DBCC IND commands for IndexInternalsOne and IndexInternalsTwo, shown in Listing 2-11. The database ID passed in is 0 for the current database, and the index ID is set to -1 to return pages for all indexes.

Listing 2-11. DBCC IND Example

```
USE Chapter2Internals;
GO

DBCC IND (0, 'IndexInternalsOne',-1);
```

CHAPTER 2 INDEX STORAGE FUNDAMENTALS

In the `DBCC EXTENTINFO` example, there were two extent allocations for the table IndexInternalsOne, shown in Figure 2-17. These results show that there were 13 pages allocated to the table. The `DBCC IND` results, shown in Figure 2-18, detail all the pages that were part of two extent allocations.

In these results, there was a single IAM page and twelve data pages allocated to the table. Where DBCC EXTENTINFO provided page 312 as the start of the extent allocations, containing nine pages, it was not possible to identify where the IAM page was based on that. It was instead in another extent that the results did not list, and the results for DBCC IND identify it as being on page 235. The benefit of using DBCC IND for listing the pages for an index is that you get the exact page numbers without having to make any guesses. Also, note that the index level in the results returns as level 0 with no intermediate levels. As stated earlier, heap structures are flat, and the pages are in no particular order.

	PageFID	PagePID	IAMFID	IAMPID	ObjectID	IndexID	PartitionNumber	PartitionID	iam_chain_type	PageType	IndexLevel	NextPageFID	NextPagePID	PrevPageFID	PrevPagePID
1	1	235	NULL	NULL	581577110	0	1	72057594043170816	In-row data	10	NULL	0	0	0	0
2	1	312	1	235	581577110	0	1	72057594043170816	In-row data	1	0	0	0	0	0
3	1	313	1	235	581577110	0	1	72057594043170816	In-row data	1	0	0	0	0	0
4	1	314	1	235	581577110	0	1	72057594043170816	In-row data	1	0	0	0	0	0
5	1	315	1	235	581577110	0	1	72057594043170816	In-row data	1	0	0	0	0	0
6	1	316	1	235	581577110	0	1	72057594043170816	In-row data	1	0	0	0	0	0
7	1	317	1	235	581577110	0	1	72057594043170816	In-row data	1	0	0	0	0	0
8	1	318	1	235	581577110	0	1	72057594043170816	In-row data	1	0	0	0	0	0
9	1	319	1	235	581577110	0	1	72057594043170816	In-row data	1	0	0	0	0	0
10	1	320	1	235	581577110	0	1	72057594043170816	In-row data	1	0	0	0	0	0
11	1	321	1	235	581577110	0	1	72057594043170816	In-row data	1	0	0	0	0	0
12	1	322	1	235	581577110	0	1	72057594043170816	In-row data	1	0	0	0	0	0
13	1	323	1	235	581577110	0	1	72057594043170816	In-row data	1	0	0	0	0	0

***Figure 2-18.** DBCC IND for dbo.IndexInternalsOne*

As mentioned, the tables in the previous example were organized in a heap structure. For the next example, you'll observe what the output from `DBCC IND` is when examining a table with a clustered index. In Listing 2-12, first the table `dbo.IndexInternalsThree` is created with a clustered index on the `RowID` column. Then, you'll insert four rows. Finally, the example executes `DBCC IND` on the table.

***Listing 2-12.** DBCC IND Clustered Index Example*

```
USE Chapter2Internals
GO

CREATE TABLE dbo.IndexInternalsThree
    (
    RowID INT IDENTITY(1,1)
    ,FillerData CHAR(8000)
```

CHAPTER 2 INDEX STORAGE FUNDAMENTALS

```
        ,CONSTRAINT PK_IndexInternalsThree  PRIMARY KEY CLUSTERED (RowID)
        )
GO
INSERT INTO dbo.IndexInternalsThree DEFAULT VALUES
GO 4
DBCC IND (0, 'IndexInternalsThree',-1)
```

Figure 2-19 shows the results from this example involving dbo.IndexInternalsThree. Notice the change in how IndexLevel is being returned as compared to the previous example (Figure 2-18).

	PageFID	PagePID	IAMFID	IAMPID	ObjectID	IndexID	PartitionNumber	PartitionID	iam_chain_type	PageType	IndexLevel	NextPageFID	NextPagePID	PrevPageFID	PrevPagePID
1	1	237	NULL	NULL	629577281	1	1	72057594043301888	In-row data	10	NULL	0	0	0	0
2	1	360	1	237	629577281	1	1	72057594043301888	In-row data	1	0	1	362	0	0
3	1	361	1	237	629577281	1	1	72057594043301888	In-row data	2	1	0	0	0	0
4	1	362	1	237	629577281	1	1	72057594043301888	In-row data	1	0	1	363	1	360
5	1	363	1	237	629577281	1	1	72057594043301888	In-row data	1	0	1	364	1	362
6	1	364	1	237	629577281	1	1	72057594043301888	In-row data	1	0	0	0	1	363

Figure 2-19. *DBCC IND for dbo.IndexInternalsThree*

In this example, the index level for the third row in the results has an IndexLevel of 1 and also a PageType of 2, which is an index page. With these results, there is enough information to rebuild the B-tree structure for the index, as shown in Figure 2-20. The B-tree starts with the IAM page, which is page number 1:237. This page is linked to page 1:361, which is an index page at index level 1. Following that, pages 1:360, 1:362, 1:363, and 1:364 are at index level 0 and doubly linked to each other.

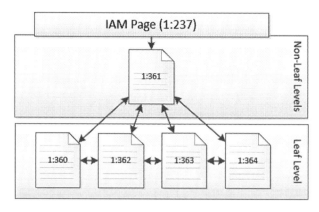

Figure 2-20. *DBCC IND for dbo.IndexInternalsThree*

CHAPTER 2 ■ INDEX STORAGE FUNDAMENTALS

Through both of these examples, you examined how to use DBCC IND to investigate the pages associated with a table or an index. As the examples showed, the command provides the information on all the pages of the table or index, including the IAM page. These pages include the page numbers to identify where they are in the database. The relationships between the pages are also included, even the next and previous page numbers that are used to navigate the index for B-tree indexes.

As previously noted, sys.dm_db_database_page_allocations can provide this same information and much more. To demonstrate this, Listing 2-13 shows how to get DBCC IND information from the sys.dm_db_database_page_allocations. If you compare the outputs, you'll note that they are nearly identical; there are a few instances where NULL and 0 are returned differently. With this ability, you should use the DMF in favor of using the DBCC command.

Listing 2-13. DBCC IND Output from sys.dm_db_database_page_allocations

```
USE Chapter2Internals;
GO

SELECT
allocated_page_file_id AS PageFID
,allocated_page_page_id AS PagePID
,allocated_page_iam_file_id AS IAMFID
,allocated_page_iam_page_id AS IAMPID
,object_id AS ObjectID
,index_id AS IndexID
,partition_id AS PartitionNumber
,rowset_id AS PartitionID
,allocation_unit_type_desc AS iam_chain_type
,page_type AS PageType
,page_level AS IndexLevel
,next_page_file_id AS NextPageFID
,next_page_page_id AS NextPagePID
,previous_page_file_id AS PrevPageFID
,previous_page_page_id AS PrevPagePID
```

```
FROM sys.dm_db_database_page_allocations(DB_ID(), OBJECT_ID('dbo.
IndexInternalsTwo'), 1, NULL, 'DETAILED')
WHERE is_allocated = 1;
GO

DBCC IND (0,'dbo.IndexInternalsTwo',1)
```

DBCC PAGE

The last command available for examining pages is DBCC PAGE. While the other two commands provide information on the pages associated with tables and indexes, the output from DBCC PAGE provides a look at the contents of a page. Also, even with the dynamic management functions, you'll still need to use DBCC PAGE since much of its capabilities are not yet available through DMFs. Listing 2-14 shows the syntax for using DBCC PAGE.

Listing 2-14. DBCC PAGE Syntax

```
DBCC PAGE ( { database_name | database_id | 0}, file_number, page_number
          [,print_option ={0|1|2|3} ])
```

The DBCC PAGE command accepts a number of parameters. Through the parameters, the command is able to determine the database and specific page requested, which is then returned in the requested format. Table 2-10 details the parameters for DBCC PAGE.

Table 2-10. *DBCC PAGE Parameters*

Parameter	Description
database_name | database_id	Specifies either the database name or the database ID where the page will be retrieved. If the value 0 is provided for this parameter or the parameter is not set, the current database will be used.
file_number	Specifies the file number for the data file in the database from where the page will be retrieved.
page_number	Specifies the page number in the database file that will be retrieved.

(continued)

Table 2-10. (*continued*)

Parameter	Description
print_option	Specifies how the output should be returned. There are four print options available: *0—page header only*: Returns only the page header information. *1—hex rows*: Returns the page header information, all the rows on the page, and the offset array. In this output, each row is returned individually. *2—hex data*: Returns the page header information, all the rows on the page, and the offset array. Unlike option 1, the output shows all the rows as a single block of data. *3—data rows*: Returns the page header information, all the rows on the page, and the offset array. This option differs from the other options in that the data in the columns for the row is translated as listed with their column names. This parameter is optional, and 0 is used as the default when no option is selected.

Note By default, the DBCC PAGE command outputs its messages to the SQL Server event log. In most situations, this is not the ideal output mechanism. Trace flag 3604 allows you to modify this behavior. By utilizing this trace flag, the output from the DBCC statements returns to the Messages tab in SQL Server Management Studio (SSMS).

Through DBCC PAGE and its print options, everything that is on a page can be retrieved. There are a few reasons why you might want to look at the contents of a page. To start with, looking at an index or data page can help you understand why an index is behaving in one manner or another. You gain insight into how the data within the row is structured, which may cause rows to be larger than expected. The sizes of rows do have an important impact on how indexes behave since as a row gets larger, the number of pages required to store the index increases. An increase in the number of pages for an index increases the resources required to use the index, which results in longer query

CHAPTER 2　INDEX STORAGE FUNDAMENTALS

times and, in some cases, a change in how or which indexes will be utilized. Another reason to use DBCC PAGE is to observe what happens to a data page when certain operations occur. As the examples later in this chapter will illustrate, DBCC PAGE can be used to uncover what happens during page splits and forwarded record operations.

To help demonstrate how to use DBCC PAGE, you'll run through a few demonstrations with each of the print options. These demos will be based on the code in Listing 2-15, which uses sys.dm_db_database_page_allocations to identify page numbers for the examples. For each example, you'll look at some of the ways the results can differ between page types. While the page numbers in your database may differ slightly, the demos are based on an IAM page of 238, index page of 377, and data pages of 376 and 378, as shown in Figure 2-21.

Listing 2-15. DBCC IND Query for DBCC PAGE Examples

```
USE [Chapter2Internals];
GO

CREATE TABLE dbo.IndexInternalsFour (
    RowID INT IDENTITY(1, 1) NOT NULL,
    FillerData VARCHAR(2000) NULL,
    CONSTRAINT PK_IndexInternalsFour
        PRIMARY KEY CLUSTERED ([RowID] ASC));

INSERT INTO dbo.IndexInternalsFour (FillerData)
VALUES (REPLICATE(1, 2000)),
(REPLICATE(2, 2000)), (REPLICATE(3, 2000)),
(REPLICATE(4, 2000)), (REPLICATE(5, 25));

SELECT allocated_page_file_id AS PageFID,
       allocated_page_page_id AS PagePID,
       allocated_page_iam_file_id AS IAMFID,
       allocated_page_iam_page_id AS IAMPID,
       index_id AS IndexID,
       allocation_unit_type_desc AS iam_chain_type,
       page_type_desc,
       page_level AS IndexLevel,
       next_page_file_id AS NextPageFID,
```

```
        next_page_page_id AS NextPagePID,
        previous_page_file_id AS PrevPageFID,
        previous_page_page_id AS PrevPagePID
FROM sys.dm_db_database_page_allocations(DB_ID(), OBJECT_ID('dbo.
IndexInternalsFour'), 1, NULL, 'DETAILED')
WHERE is_allocated = 1;
```

	PageFID	PagePID	IAMFID	IAMPID	IndexID	iam_chain_type	page_type_desc	IndexLevel	NextPageFID	NextPagePID	PrevPageFID	PrevPagePID
1	1	238	NULL	NULL	1	IN_ROW_DATA	IAM_PAGE	0	NULL	NULL	NULL	NULL
2	1	376	1	238	1	IN_ROW_DATA	DATA_PAGE	0	1	378	NULL	NULL
3	1	377	1	238	1	IN_ROW_DATA	INDEX_PAGE	1	NULL	NULL	NULL	NULL
4	1	378	1	238	1	IN_ROW_DATA	DATA_PAGE	0	NULL	NULL	1	376

Figure 2-21. Page allocations for dbo.IndexInternalsFour

Page Header–Only Print Option

The first print option available for DBCC PAGE is the page header only where print_option equals 0. With this option, only the page header is returned in the output from the DBCC command. The page header is returned with all DBCC PAGE requests; using this option just limits the results to only the page header. Two sections are returned as part of the page header.

The first section returned is the buffer information. The buffer provides information on where the page is currently located in memory in SQL Server. To read a page, the page must first be retrieved from disk and placed in memory. This section provides the address that could be used to find the memory location of the page.

The second section is the actual page header. The page header contains a number of attributes that describe the page and the contents of the page. Not all the attributes are currently in use by SQL Server, but there are a number of attributes that are worth understanding. These key attributes are listed and defined in Table 2-11.

Table 2-11. *Page Header Key Attribute Definitions*

Attribute	Definition
m_pageId	File ID and page number for the page.
m_type	The type of page returned; see the page type list in Table 2-5.
Metadata: AllocUnitId	Allocation unit ID that maps from the catalog view sys.allocation_units.
Metadata: PartitionId	Partition ID for the table or index. This maps to partition_ID in the catalog view sys.partitions.
Metadata: ObjectId	Object ID for the table. This maps to the object_ID in the catalog view sys.tables.
Metadata: IndexId	Index ID for the table or index. This maps to the index_ID in the catalog view sys.indexes.
m_prevPage	Previous page in the index structure. This is used in B-tree indexes to allow reading sequential pages along index levels.
m_nextPage	Next page in the index structure. This is used in B-tree indexes to allow reading sequential pages along index levels.
m_slotCnt	Number of slots, or rows, on the page.
Allocation Status	Lists the locations of the GAM, SGAM, PFS, DIFF (or DCM), and ML (or BCM) pages for the page requested. It also includes the status for each from those metadata pages.

To demonstrate the use of DBCC PAGE for the page header–only option, the code in Listing 2-16 can be used. Your results should be similar to those in Figure 2-22. In these results, you can see the page number at the top of the page indicating that it is page 1:377. The m_type is 2, which translates to being an index page. The m_slotCnt shows that there are two rows on the page. Referring to Figure 2-22, the row count would correlate to the two index records needed to map data pages 1:376 and 1:378 to the index. Finally, the allocation statuses show that the page is allocated on the GAM page, it is 0 percent full (per PFS page), and the page has been changed since the last full backup (per the DCM page).

CHAPTER 2 INDEX STORAGE FUNDAMENTALS

Listing 2-16. *DBCC PAGE with Page Header–Only Print Option*

```
DBCC TRACEON(3604)
DBCC PAGE(0,1,377,0)
```

```
PAGE: (1:377)

BUFFER:

BUF @0x00000153FC7BF900

bpage = 0x00000153D8700000          bPmmpage = 0x0000000000000000      bsort_r_nextbP = 0x00000153FC7BF6D0
bsort_r_prevbP = 0x0000000000000000 bhash = 0x0000000000000000          bpageno = (1:377)
bpart = 1                           ckptGen = 0x0000000000000000        bDirtyRefCount = 0
bstat = 0x9                         breferences = 1                     berrcode = 0
bUse1 = 10097                       bstat2 = 0x0                        blog = 0x15ab215a
bsampleCount = 0                    bIoCount = 0                        resPoolId = 0
bcputicks = 0                       bReadMicroSec = 126                 bDirtyContext = 0x0000000000000000
bDbPageBroker = 0x0000000000000000  bdbid = 9                           bpru = 0x00000153F4070040

PAGE HEADER:

Page @0x00000153D8700000

m_pageId = (1:377)                      m_headerVersion = 1              m_type = 2
m_typeFlagBits = 0x0                    m_level = 1                      m_flagBits = 0x8200
m_objId (AllocUnitId.idObj) = 182       m_indexId (AllocUnitId.idInd) = 256
Metadata: AllocUnitId = 72057594049855488
Metadata: PartitionId = 72057594043367424                                 Metadata: IndexId = 1
Metadata: ObjectId = 661577395          m_prevPage = (0:0)               m_nextPage = (0:0)
pminlen = 11                            m_slotCnt = 2                    m_freeCnt = 8070
m_freeData = 118                        m_reservedCnt = 0                m_lsn = (35:944:55)
m_xactReserved = 0                      m_xdesId = (0:0)                 m_ghostRecCnt = 0
m_tornBits = -191478502                 DB Frag ID = 1

Allocation Status

GAM (1:2) = ALLOCATED                   SGAM (1:3) = NOT ALLOCATED       PFS (1:1) = 0x40 ALLOCATED  0_PCT_FULL
DIFF (1:6) = CHANGED                    ML (1:7) = NOT MIN_LOGGED
```

Figure 2-22. *DBCC PAGE output for page header-only print option*

As the page header–only option shows, there is a lot of useful information in the page header. In fact, you are provided with enough information to envision how this page relates to the other pages in the index and the extent it occupies. This information is similar to sys.dm_db_page_info, but from this point forward, DBCC PAGE provides more information than the DMF.

Hex Rows Print Option

The next print option available for DBCC PAGE is the hex rows print option, where print_option equals 1. This print option expands on the previous option adding into the output an entry for every slot on the page and the offset array that describes the location of each slot on the page.

73

The data section of the page repeats for every row that is on the page and contains all the metadata and the data associated with that row. For the metadata, the row includes the slot number, page offset, record type, and record attributes. This information helps define the row and what contributes besides the size of the data to the row size. At the end of the slot is a memory dump of the row. The memory dump displays the row in a hex format that, while not easily read by humans, contains all the data for the row. For more on the attributes and their definitions, see Table 2-12.

The offset array is the last section of information included in the hex rows option results. The offset array contains two pieces of information for each row on the table. The first piece of information is the slot number with its hex representation. The second piece is the byte location for the slot on the page. With these two pieces of information, any row on the page can be located and returned.

Table 2-12. Hex Rows Key Attribute Definitions

Attribute	Definition
Slot	The position of the row on the page. The count is 0 based and starts immediately after the page header.
Offset	Physical byte location of the row on the page.
Length	The length of the row on the page.
Record Type	The type of row. Some possible values are INDEX_RECORD and PRIMARY_RECORD.
Record Attributes	List of attributes on the row that contribute to the size of the row. These can include the NULL_BITMAP and VARIABLE_COLUMNS array.
Record Size	The length of the row on the page.
Memory Dump	The memory location for the data on the page. For the hex rows option, it is limited to the information in that slot. The memory address is provided, and afterward a hex dump of the data is stored in the slot.

For the hex rows example, you'll continue to investigate the index page (1:279) that you looked at in the previous section. This time, you'll use the hex rows print option, which is when a print_option of 1 is used in DBCC PAGE, as shown in Listing 2-17.

The results for the DBCC PAGE command will be longer than the previous execution since this time it includes the row data with the page header. To focus on the new information,

CHAPTER 2 INDEX STORAGE FUNDAMENTALS

the buffer and page header results have been excluded in the sample output in Figure 2-23. In the data section, there are two slots shown, slot 0 and slot 1. These slots map to the two index rows on the page, which can be verified through the record type of INDEX_RECORD for each of the rows. The hex data for the rows contains the page and range information for the index record, but that isn't translated with this print option. The last section has the offset table containing the slot information for both of the rows on the table. Note that the offset ends with 0 and counts up from the bottom. This matches to how the offset array was described earlier in the chapter. The rows start after the header incrementing up, while the offset array starts at the end of the page incrementing backward. In this manner, new rows can be added to the table without reorganizing the page.

Listing 2-17. DBCC PAGE with Hex Rows Print Option

```
DBCC TRACEON(3604)
DBCC PAGE(0,1,377,1)
```

```
PAGE: (1:377)

BUFFER:
...

PAGE HEADER:
...

DATA:

Slot 0, Offset 0x60, Length 11, DumpStyle BYTE
Record Type = INDEX_RECORD        Record Attributes =              Record Size = 11
Memory Dump @0x0000003BCD3F8060
0000000000000000:   064edfce 3b780100 000100                 .NßÎ;x.....

Slot 1, Offset 0x6b, Length 11, DumpStyle BYTE
Record Type = INDEX_RECORD        Record Attributes =              Record Size = 11
Memory Dump @0x0000003BCD3F806B
0000000000000000:   06050000 007a0100 000100                 .....z.....

OFFSET TABLE:
Row - Offset
1 (0x1) - 107 (0x6b)
0 (0x0) - 96 (0x60)
```

Figure 2-23. *DBCC PAGE output for hex rows print option*

The hex rows print option is a bit more useful than the first print option. It includes the page header information but expands on it to provide insight into the actual rows on the page. This information can prove valuable when you want to look at a row to determine its size on the page and why it may be larger than expected.

Hex Data Print Option

The third print option available for DBCC PAGE is the hex data print option, where print_option equals 2. This print option, like the previous option, starts with the output from the page header–only print option and adds to it. The information added through this option includes the hex output of the data section of the page and the offset array. With the data section, the page is output complete and unformatted as it appears on the actual page. The output in this format can be useful when you want to see the page in its raw form.

To demonstrate the hex data print option, you'll use the script in Listing 2-18. In it the DBCC PAGE command is used to retrieve the page from dbo.IndexInternalsFour that contains the last row. This row contains 25 fives in the FillerData column.

Listing 2-18. DBCC PAGE with Hex Data Print Option

```
USE Chapter2Internals
GO

DBCC TRACEON(3604)
DBCC PAGE(0,1,377,2)
```

In the results, shown in Figure 2-24, the output contains a large block of characters in the data section. The block contains three components. On the far left is page address information, such as 0x0000003BCEBF8000. The page address identifies where on the page the information is located. The middle section contains the hex data that is contained in that section of the page. The right side of the character block contains the character representation of the hex data. For the most part, this data is not legible, except when it comes to character data being stored from character data types, such as char and nchar.

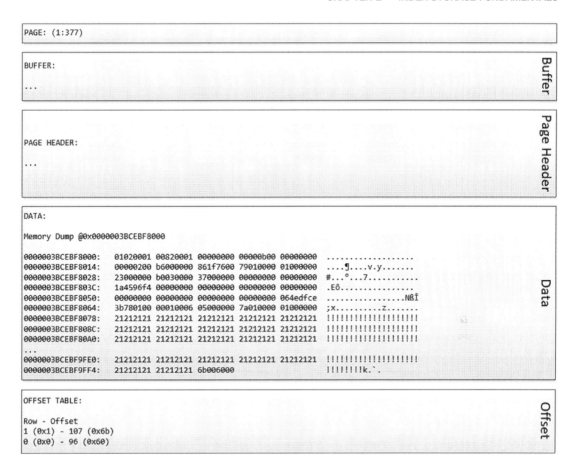

Figure 2-24. *DBCC PAGE output for hex data print option*

Initially, the hex data print option may seem less useful than the other print options. In many situations, this will be the case. The true value in this print option is that DBCC PAGE doesn't try to interpret the page for you. It displays the page as is. With the other print options, the output will sometimes be reordered to conform to expected slot orders; an example of this is demonstrated in Chapter 8.

Row Data Print Option

The last print option available for DBCC PAGE is the row data print option, where print_option equals 3. The output from this print option can change depending on the type of page that is being requested. The basic information returned for most pages is identical to that returned from the hex rows print option: the data split per row in the hex format. The output varies, though, when it comes to data pages and index pages. For these page types, this print option provides some extremely useful information about the page.

Note You can use the WITH TABLERESULTS option with DBCC PAGE to output the results from the command to a resultset instead of messages. This option is useful when you want to insert the results returned from the DBCC command into a table.

To show the differences between the data and index page outputs, let's walk through another example. This example will use the table dbo.IndexInternalsFour that was created in Listing 2-10. In the demo for this print option, shown in Listing 2-19, you'll execute DBCC PAGE against one of the data pages and the index page for the table.

Listing 2-19. DBCC PAGE with Row Data Print Option

```
USE Chapter2Internals
GO

DBCC TRACEON(3604)
DBCC PAGE(0,1,378,3) -- Data page
DBCC PAGE(0,1,377,3) -- Index page
```

Comparing the results from the data page, shown in Figure 2-25, to the output from the hex data print option, shown in Figure 2-24, there is one major difference. Underneath the hex memory dump for the slot, all the column details from the row are decoded and presented in a legible format. It starts with slot 0 column 1, which contains the RowID column, which it shows to have a value of 5. The next column, column 2, is the FillerData column, which contains 25 fives. For each of these columns, the physical length is noted along with the offset of the value within the row. The last value provided on the data section of the page is the KeyHashValue. This value isn't actually stored on the page. Instead, it is a hash value that was created when the page was placed in memory based on the keys on the page. This value is shown in tools that are used by SQL Server to report information about pages back to the end user; you may have seen this value before while investigating deadlocks.

CHAPTER 2 INDEX STORAGE FUNDAMENTALS

```
PAGE: (1:378)

BUFFER:
...

PAGE HEADER:
...

Slot 0 Offset 0x60 Length 40
Record Type = PRIMARY_RECORD        Record Attributes =  NULL_BITMAP VARIABLE_COLUMNS
Record Size = 40
Memory Dump @0x0000003BCC7F8060

0000000000000000:   30000800 05000000 02000001 00280035 35353535  0............(.55555
0000000000000014:   35353535 35353535 35353535 35353535 35353535  55555555555555555555

Slot 0 Column 1 Offset 0x4 Length 4 Length (physical) 4
RowID = 5

Slot 0 Column 2 Offset 0xf Length 25 Length (physical) 25
FillerData = 5555555555555555555555555

Slot 0 Offset 0x0 Length 0 Length (physical) 0
KeyHashValue = (59855d342c69)
```

Figure 2-25. DBCC PAGE output for row data print option for data page

With the index page, there isn't a change in the message output from other page types. Instead, the difference with this page is the resultset. Instead of just a message output, a table is also returned. The table returns one row for every index row on the page. Reviewing the output for the index page, shown in Figure 2-26, there are two rows returned. The first row indicates that page 1:376 is the child page to the index page. It also shows that the key value for the index is RowID, which is NULL for the first index row. This means that this is the start of the index and no values are limiting the first values on the child page. The second row maps to page 1:378 with a key value of 5. In this case, the key value indicates that the first row on the child page has a RowID of 5. Since the key value can change from index to index, the results from the DBCC PAGE command with these options will change as well. For every index variation, the output will return the relevant values for the index.

	FileId	PageId	Row	Level	ChildFileId	ChildPageId	RowID (key)	KeyHashValue	Row Size
1	1	377	0	1	1	376	NULL	NULL	11
2	1	377	1	1	1	378	5	NULL	11

Figure 2-26. *DBCC PAGE output for row data print option for index page*

The row data print option is one of the most useful options for the DBCC PAGE command. For data pages, it provides total insight into the data stored on the page, how much space it takes up, and its position. This allows you a direct line into understanding why only certain rows may be fitting on the page and why, for instance, a page split may have occurred. The resultset from the index page output is equally as useful. The ability to map the index rows to pages and return the key values can provide much insight into how the index is organized and how the pages are laid out.

Page Fragmentation

As discussed throughout this chapter, SQL Server stores information in the database on 8 KB pages. In general, records in tables are limited to that size; if they are smaller than 8 KB, SQL Server stores more than one record per page. One of the problems with storing more than a single record per page is handling situations where the total size of all the records on a page exceeds 8 KB of space. In these situations, SQL Server must change how the records on a page are stored. Depending on how the pages are organized, there are two ways in which SQL Server will handle the situations: forwarded records and page splits.

> **Note** This discussion does not consider two situations where single records can be larger than a page. These other situations are row-overflow and large objects. With row overflow, SQL Server will allow a single record on a page to exceed the 8 KB in certain situations. Also, when large object values exceed the 8 KB size, they utilize LOB pages instead of data pages. These do not have a direct impact on the page fragmentation discussed in this section.

CHAPTER 2 INDEX STORAGE FUNDAMENTALS

Forwarded Records

The first method for managing records when they exceed the size of a data page is through forwarded records. This method applies only when the heap structure is used. With forwarded records, when a row is updated and no longer fits on the data page, SQL Server will move that record to a new data page in the heap and add pointers between the two locations. The first pointer identifies the page on which the record now exists, often called the *forwarded record pointer*. The second is on the new page, pointing back to the original page on which the forwarded record existed; it's called the *back pointer*.

As an example of how this works, let's walk through a logical example of how forwarding operates. Consider a page, numbered 100, that exists on a table using a heap (see Figure 2-27). This page has four rows on it, and each row is approximately 2 KB in size, totaling 8 KB in space used. If the second row is updated to 2.5 KB in size, it will no longer be able to fit on the page. SQL Server selects another page in the heap or allocates a new page to the heap, the page numbered 101 in this case. The second row is then written to that page, and the pointer to the new page replaces the row on page 100.

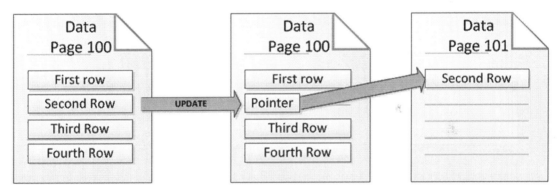

Figure 2-27. Forwarded record process diagram

Taking this logical example further, the next thing to do is examine how records are forwarded on a table. For example, create a table named dbo.HeapForwardedRecords, shown in Listing 2-20. To represent the rows from the logical example, you'll use the sys.objects table to add 24 rows to dbo.HeapForwardedRecords. Each of these rows has a RowID to identify the row and 2,000 characters, resulting in four rows per page in the table. Using sys.dm_db_index_physical_stats, you can verify (see Figure 2-28) that there are six pages in the table with a total of 24 records.

Listing 2-20. Forwarded Record Scenario

```
USE AdventureWorks2017
GO

CREATE TABLE dbo.HeapForwardedRecords
(
  RowId INT IDENTITY(1,1)
  ,FillerData VARCHAR(2500)
);

INSERT INTO dbo.HeapForwardedRecords (FillerData)
SELECT TOP 24 REPLICATE('X',2000)
FROM sys.objects;

DECLARE @ObjectID INT = OBJECT_ID('dbo.HeapForwardedRecords');

SELECT object_id, index_type_desc, page_count, record_count, forwarded_record_count
FROM sys.dm_db_index_physical_stats (DB_ID(), @ObjectID, NULL, NULL, 'DETAILED');
```

	object_id	index_type_desc	page_count	record_count	forwarded_record_count
1	660197402	HEAP	6	24	0

Figure 2-28. *Physical state of dbo.HeapForwardedRecords before forwarding records*

The next step in the demonstration is to cause forwarded records in the table. To do this, you'll update every other row in the table to expand the values of FillerData from 2,000 to 2,500 characters, shown in Listing 2-21. As a result, two of the rows will be too large to fit in the space remaining on the pages where these rows are located. Instead of 8 KB of data, there will be about 9 KB being written to the 8 KB page.

As a result, SQL Server will need to move records off the page to complete the updates. Since moving one of the records off the page will leave enough room on the page for the second row, only one record will be forwarded. The output from sys.dm_db_index_physical_stats (see Figure 2-29) verifies that this is the case. The page count increases to nine, and six records are logged as being forwarded. One item of particular interest is the record count. While the number of rows in the table did not increase, there

CHAPTER 2 INDEX STORAGE FUNDAMENTALS

are now six additional records in the table. This is because the original record for the row is still in the original position with a pointer to another record elsewhere that contains the data for the row.

Listing 2-21. Script to Cause Forwarded Records

```
USE AdventureWorks2017
GO

UPDATE dbo.HeapForwardedRecords
SET FillerData = REPLICATE('X',2500)
WHERE RowId % 2 = 0;

DECLARE @ObjectID INT = OBJECT_ID('dbo.HeapForwardedRecords');

SELECT object_id, index_type_desc, page_count, record_count, forwarded_record_count
FROM sys.dm_db_index_physical_stats (DB_ID(), @ObjectID, NULL, NULL, 'DETAILED');
```

	object_id	index_type_desc	page_count	record_count	forwarded_record_count
1	660197402	HEAP	9	30	6

Figure 2-29. Physical state of dbo.HeapForwardedRecords after forwarding records

The problem with forwarded records is that they cause rows in the table to have records in two locations, resulting in an increase in the amount of I/O activity required when retrieving data from and writing data to the table. The larger the table and the higher the number of forwarded records, the more likely that forwarded records can have a negative impact on performance.

Page Splits

The second approach for handling pages where the size of the rows on the page exceeds the size of the page is performing the page split. A page split is used on any index that is implemented under the B-tree index structure, which includes clustered and nonclustered indexes. With page splits, if a row is updated to a size that will no longer fit on the data page on which it currently exists, SQL Server will take half the records on the page and place them on a new page. Then SQL Server will attempt to write the data for the row to the page again. If the data will then fit on the page, the page will be written. If not, then the process will be repeated until it fits on the page.

To explain how page splits operate, let's walk through an update that results in a page split. Similar to the previous section, consider a table with a page numbered 100 (see Figure 2-30). There are four rows stored on page 100, and each is approximately 2 KB in size. Suppose that one of the rows, such as the second row, is updated to 2.5 KB in size. The data for the page will be 8.5 KB, which exceeds the available space, which causes a page split to occur. To split the page, a new page is allocated, numbered 101, and half the rows on the page (the third and fourth row) are written to the new page. At this point, the second row can be written to the page since there is now 4 KB of open space on the page.

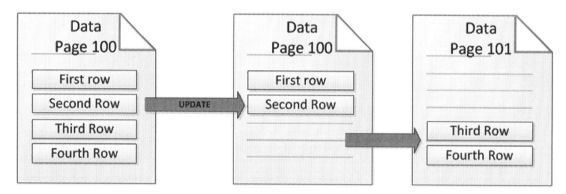

Figure 2-30. *Page split process diagram*

To demonstrate how page splits occur on a table, let's walk through an example similar to the one already described, which causes page splits to occur on the table. To start the example, create the table dbo.ClusteredPageSplits, provided in Listing 2-22. Into this table you'll insert 24 records that are about 2 KB in length. This should result in four rows per page and six data pages allocated to the table. Look at the information on index level 0, which is the leaf level. Since the table is using a B-tree, through the clustered index there will be an additional page that is used for the index tree structure. On index level 1, there are six records, which reference the six pages in the index. You can confirm this information with Figure 2-31.

CHAPTER 2 INDEX STORAGE FUNDAMENTALS

Listing 2-22. Page Split Scenario

```
USE AdventureWorks2017
GO

CREATE TABLE dbo.ClusteredPageSplits
(
  RowId INT IDENTITY(1,1)
  ,FillerData VARCHAR(2500)
  ,CONSTRAINT PK_ClusteredPageSplits PRIMARY KEY CLUSTERED (RowId)
);

INSERT INTO dbo.ClusteredPageSplits (FillerData)
SELECT TOP 24 REPLICATE('X',2000)
FROM sys.objects;

DECLARE @ObjectID INT = OBJECT_ID('dbo.ClusteredPageSplits');

SELECT object_id, index_type_desc, index_level, page_count, record_count
FROM sys.dm_db_index_physical_stats (DB_ID(), @ObjectID, NULL, NULL,
'DETAILED');
```

	object_id	index_type_desc	index_level	page_count	record_count
1	676197459	CLUSTERED INDEX	0	6	24
2	676197459	CLUSTERED INDEX	1	1	6

Figure 2-31. *Physical state of dbo.ClusteredPageSplits before page splits*

Causing the page splits on the table can be done by updating some of the records to exceed the size of the page. You'll do this by issuing an UPDATE statement that increases the FillerData column in every other row from 2,000 to 2,500 characters in length, using the script in Listing 2-23. The resulting rows on each page will be 9 KB in size, which, like the previous example, exceeds the available page size, thus causing SQL Server to use page spits to free up space on the page.

Investigating the results (Figure 2-32) after the page splits have occurred shows the effect of the page splits on the table. For starters, instead of 6 pages at the leaf level of the index, at index level 0 there are 12 pages. As mentioned, when a page split occurs, the page is split in half, and a new page is added. Since all the data pages were updated

85

in the table, all the pages were split, resulting in a doubling of the pages at the leaf level. The only change at index level 0 was the addition of six pages to reference the new pages in the index.

Listing 2-23. Script to Cause Page Splits

```
USE AdventureWorks2017
GO

UPDATE dbo.ClusteredPageSplits
SET FillerData = REPLICATE('X',2500)
WHERE RowId % 2 = 0;

DECLARE @ObjectID INT = OBJECT_ID('dbo.ClusteredPageSplits');

SELECT object_id, index_type_desc, index_level, page_count, record_count
FROM sys.dm_db_index_physical_stats (DB_ID(), @ObjectID, NULL, NULL,
'DETAILED');
```

	object_id	index_type_desc	index_level	page_count	record_count
1	676197459	CLUSTERED INDEX	0	12	24
2	676197459	CLUSTERED INDEX	1	1	12

Figure 2-32. Physical state of dbo.ClusteredPageSplits after page splits

There are two distinctions between page splits and forwarded records that are worth mentioning. First, when the page splits occurred, the number of records on the data pages did not increase. A page split moves the location of records to make room for the records within the logical index ordering. The second is that page splits do not increase the record count. Since page splits have made room for the records, there is no need for additional records to point to where data is stored.

Page splits can lead to performance issues similar to forwarded records. These performance issues occur both when the page split is occurring and afterward. During the page splits, the page that is being split needs to be locked exclusively while the records are split between two pages. This means that there can be contention when someone needs to access a row other than the one being updated when the page split happens. After the page is split, the physical order of the data pages in the index is almost always not in their logical order within the index. This interrupts SQL Server's ability to perform contiguous reads, decreasing the amount of data that can be read in single operations. Also, the more pages that need to be read into memory for a query to execute, the slower the query will perform compared to the same results on fewer pages.

Index Characteristics

The first part of this chapter discussed the physical structures that are used to store indexes. In those sections, a clear line between the types of indexes available and these structures was not defined. In this section, the main index types for SQL Server will be discussed, along with the indexing structure that they use. For each, you'll learn about the requirements and restrictions associated with the indexes.

Heap

The first index type to discuss is the heap. As pointed out earlier in the book, a heap is not actually a type of index. It is instead the result of the lack of a clustered index on a table. A heap index will, as the name implies, use the heap structure for organizing pages in a table.

There is only a single requirement for creating a table with a heap. The requirement is that a clustered index can't already be created on the table. If there is a clustered index, then a heap will not be used. Heaps and clustered indexes are mutually exclusive. Also, provided there is not a clustered index, there can be only a single heap on a table. The heap is used to store the data pages for the index, and this is done only once.

The primary concern when using heaps is that the data in the heaps is not ordered. There is no column that determines the sort for the data on the pages. The result of this is that, without other supporting nonclustered indexes, queries will always be forced to scan the information in the table.

Clustered Index

The second index type is the clustered index. Clustered indexes utilize a B-tree for storing data. For all practical purposes, a clustered index is the opposite of a heap. When a clustered index is built on a table, the heap is replaced with the B-tree structure, organizing the pages according to the key columns of the clustered index. The B-tree for a clustered index includes data pages with all the data for the rows in the table.

Clustered indexes have a few restrictions when considering the columns for the index. The first restriction is that the total length for the key columns cannot exceed 900 bytes. Second, the clustering key in a clustered index must be unique. If columns in a clustering key are not unique, SQL Server will add a hidden uniquifier column to the row when it is stored. The uniquifier is a 4-byte numeric value that is added to nonunique clustering keys to enforce uniqueness. The uniquifier size is not considered part of the 900-byte limit.

When building clustered indexes, there are a few things to consider. First, there can be only a single clustered index per table. Since the clustered index is stored in the order of the clustering key and the data in the row is stored with the key, there can't be an alternative sort on top of the table sorting it in a second manner. Also, when building a clustered index on an existing table with a heap, be sure to have enough space available for a second copy of the data. Until the build of the index is completed, both copies of the data will exist.

As will be discussed in later chapters, it is often preferable to create clustered indexes on all tables. This preference is not an absolute, and there are situations where clustered indexes are not appropriate. You will need to investigate in your own databases to determine which structure is best. Simply use this preference as a starting point.

Nonclustered Index

The next index type to discuss is the nonclustered index. Nonclustered indexes are similar to clustered indexes in a couple ways. For starters, nonclustered indexes use the B-tree structure for storing data. They are also limited to 900 bytes for their key columns.

Beyond the similarities to clustered indexes, there are some differences. First, there can be more than one nonclustered index on a table. In fact, there can be up to 999 nonclustered indexes on a table, each with no more than 16 columns. This upper limit isn't an invitation to create that many indexes; it is just an indication to the total number of nonclustered indexes that can be created. However, with filtered indexes, it may sometimes be worthwhile to create more indexes on a table than was traditionally considered appropriate. Also, instead of having a leaf level where data is stored in the B-tree, nonclustered indexes have page references to the locations in either the heap or clustered index on the table where the data is located.

Columnstore Index

The last index type discussed in this section is the columnstore index. Columnstore indexes use the columnstore structure, as the name implies. Columnstore indexes can be of both clustered and nonclustered types.

A number of restrictions need to be considered with both types of columnstore indexes. The first is that not all data types are available to be used in columnstore indexes. The data types that cannot be used are binary, varbinary, ntext, text, image, nvarchar(max), varchar(max), uniqueidentifier, rowversion, sql_variant, decimal (with greater than 18 digits), datetimeoffset, xml, and CLR-based types. While all columns in a table should be added to a clustered index, there is a limit of 1,024 columns in a columnstore index. Also, because of the nature of columnstore indexes, the index cannot be unique, be clustered, contain included columns, or have an ascending or descending order designated. Also, there can be only a single columnstore index on a table. This restriction is not a problem since it is advisable to include every column in a table in the columnstore index.

Additionally, with nonclustered columnstore indexes, there are a couple of additional restrictions. To begin with, a columnstore index is read-only. Once it has been created, there can be no data modifications to the data in the table. For this reason, it is often worthwhile to partition the underlying table to reduce the amount of data that needs to be contained in a columnstore index and to allow rebuilding of the index when new data is added to the table.

Clustered columnstore indexes, on the other hand, have some additional capabilities beyond nonclustered columnstore indexes. Clustered columnstores are writeable, which is allowed through a deltastore that is a hidden heap table that stores new rows as they are received and compresses them into columnstore rowgroups over time. The distinction of clustered in the case of clustered columnstore indexes indicates that it is the structure that all the data in a table is stored in. This means there are no other structures, such as a heap, that contain data in addition to the columnstore index.

When using columnstore indexes, there are some features within SQL Server that they cannot be combined with. Since columnstore uses its own compression technology, it can't be combined with row or page compression. It can't be used with replication, change tracking, or change data capture. These technologies would not make sense with columnstore since they assist in read-write scenarios, while columnstore indexes are read-only. The last feature restrictions are filestream and filetable, which can't be used with columnstore.

Summary

In this chapter, you looked at the components that are used as the building blocks for indexes. Now you have the fundamental foundation necessary to create indexes that will behave in the ways that you expect and anticipate. To review, you looked at the different types of pages that SQL Server uses to store data in the database and how these pages are arranged together in extents. Then you looked at the available structures for organizing pages, not for physical storage but in a logical fashion in order to access the data on those pages. Then you looked at the tools available for investigating the pages and structures of indexes through DBCC commands. The chapter concluded with a review of how the structures for indexes are associated with the available index types.

CHAPTER 3

Index Metadata and Statistics

Now that you understand the logical and physical fundamentals of indexes, you should look at the way in which statistics are stored for indexes. These statistics provide insight into how SQL Server can utilize and is utilizing indexes. It also provides the information needed to decipher why an index may not be selected and how it is behaving. This chapter will provide you with a deeper understanding about where and how this information is collected. You'll investigate some additional DBCC commands and dynamic management objects (DMOs) that are available and see how that information comes to be.

There are four domains of information that the statistics in this chapter will cover. The first domain is column-level statistics. This provides the query optimizer with information on the population of data within a column and, thus, an index. The next domain is index usage statistics. Information here provides insight into whether and how an index is being used. The third domain is operational statistics. This information is similar to usage statistics but provides deeper insight. The last domain of information is physical statistics, and it provides insight into the physical characteristics of the index and how the index is distributed within the database.

Additionally, in this chapter, you'll review the metadata and statistics that are available for columnstore indexes and explore the information that is collected. This information provides an understanding of what is being stored by the columnstore index and how it might impact the performance of queries against columnstore indexes.

Column-Level Statistics

Let's begin by looking at the first domain of statistics information, column-level statistics. This area is one of the most important within SQL Server when it comes to indexes. Column-level statistics provide information on how data and its values are distributed across the key column(s) of an index. SQL Server uses this information to determine the anticipated frequency and distribution of values within an index; this is referred to as *cardinality*.

Through cardinality, the query optimizer develops cost-based execution plans to find the best execution plan for executing the submitted request. If the statistics for an index are incorrect or no longer represent the data in the index, then the plan that is created will, likely, be inefficient. It is important to understand and be able to interact with statistics to be certain that indexes in your environment not only exist but also provide their expected benefits.

> **Note** Often when indexes are rebuilt to "fix" performance issues, the fragmentation is usually not the cause or direct solution to the issue. When rebuilt, indexes receive new statistics, and execution plans related to those indexes need to be recompiled, either of which is the likely cause of the performance issue vs. any index fragmentation.

There are many ways to interact with statistics within SQL Server. You'll review some of the most common mechanisms in the sections to follow. With each of these methods, you'll look what they are, what they provide, and the value in using each method.

DBCC SHOW_STATISTICS

The first, and likely most familiar, way to interact with statistics is through the DBCC command SHOW_STATISTICS. This command will return the statistics for the requested database object, either a table or an indexed view. The information returned is a statistics object that includes three different components: the header, the histogram, and the density vector. Each of these components provides SQL Server with an understanding of the data available in the index.

Returning the statistics object can be done with the DBCC syntax in Listing 3-1. This syntax accepts the name of the table or indexed view for the statistics, and then the target is returned. The target is either the name of the index or the column-level statistics that were created.

Listing 3-1. DBCC SHOW_STATISTICS Syntax

```
DBCC SHOW_STATISTICS ( table_or_indexed_view_name , target )
[ WITH [ < options > ]
```

There are four options that can be included with the DBCC command: NO_INFOMSGS, STAT_HEADER, DENSITY_VECTOR, and HISTOGRAM. Any or all of these options can be included in a comma-separated list.

The option NO_INFOMSGS suppresses all informational messages when the DBCC command is executed. These are error messages generated with severity from 0 to 10, with 10 being the highest severity error. In most cases, since these error messages are informational, they are not of value when using this DBCC statement.

The options STAT_HEADER, DENSITY_VECTOR, and HISTOGRAM limit the output from the DBCC command. If one or more of the options are included, then only the statistics components for the items included will be returned. If none of these is selected, then all the components are included. There is STATS_STREAM option that won't be discussed because it is not supported and may not be included in future releases.

With the DBCC command defined, let's walk through each of the statistics components. Each will be defined, and then an example of their contents from the AdventureWorks2017 database will be explored. The results that you'll be reviewing can be created with Listing 3-2.

Listing 3-2. DBCC SHOW_STATISTICS for Index on Sales.SalesOrderDetail Table

```
USE AdventureWorks2017
GO

DBCC SHOW_STATISTICS ( 'Sales.SalesOrderDetail'
, PK_SalesOrderDetail_SalesOrderID_SalesOrderDetailID )
```

Stats Header

The stats header is the metadata portion of the statistics object. These columns, listed in Table 3-1, are primarily informational. They inform on the number of rows that were considered when building the statistics and how those rows were selected through filtering. Table 3-1 also includes information on when the statistics were last updated, which can be useful when investigating potential issues with the quality of statistics.

Table 3-1. *Stats Header Columns from DBCC SHOW_STATISTICS*

Column Name	Description
Name	Name of the statistics object. For index statistics, this is the same name as the index.
Updated	Date and time that the statistics were last updated.
Rows	Total number of rows in the table or indexed view when the statistics were last updated. For filtered statistics or indexes, the count pertains to the number of rows that matched the filter criteria.
Rows Sampled	Total number of rows sampled for statistics calculations. Histogram and density values are estimates when the Rows Sampled value is less than the value in Rows.
Steps	Number of steps in the histogram. Each step spans a range of column values followed by an upper-bound column value. The histogram steps are defined on the first key column in the statistics. The maximum number of steps is 200.
Density	Calculated as 1/*distinct values* for all values in the first key column of the statistics object, excluding the histogram boundary values. As of SQL Server 2008, this value is no longer used by SQL Server.
Average Key Length	Average number of bytes per value for all the key columns in the statistics object.
String Index	Indicates whether the statistics object contains string summary statistics to improve the cardinality estimates for query predicates that use the LIKE operator.
Filter Expression	When populated, this is the predicate for the subset of table rows included in the statistics object.
Unfiltered Rows	Total number of rows in the table before applying the filter expression. If Filter Expression is NULL, Unfiltered Rows is equal to Rows.
Persisted Sample Percent	Added in SQL Server 2016, shows the sample percentage to use for updates to the statistics. If zero, then there is no sample percentage set for the statistics.

CHAPTER 3 INDEX METADATA AND STATISTICS

Reviewing the stats header information for PK_SalesOrderDetail_SalesOrderID_SalesOrderDetailID on Sales.SalesOrderDetail, shown in Figure 3-1, you'll see a number of items of interest. First, since the Rows and Rows Sampled values are the same, you know that the statistics are not based on estimates. Next, the statistics were last updated on October 27, 2017 (though this value may differ in your database). Another item is that there are 163 steps, of a possible max 200 steps, in the statistics histogram. The number of steps is equal to ranges. In this case, 163 steps mean there are 163 ranges, each with an upper-bound value in the statistics. The upper-bound value defines the max value within the range. If step 1 had an upper-bound value of 42, then step 1 would cover values 0–42. The next step would then start with 43 and include values up through its upper-bound. Note the lack of a filtered expression and unfiltered rows; neither the index nor statistics are filtering out rows. Lastly, the Persisted Sample Percent is set to 0, which means all rows were sampled for the statistics, which can be confirmed by comparing Rows with Rows Sampled.

	Name	Updated	Rows	Rows Sampled	Steps	Density	Average key length	String Index	Filter Expression	Unfiltered Rows	Persisted Sample Percent
1	PK_SalesOrderDetail_SalesOrderID_SalesOrderDeta...	Oct 27 2017 2:33PM	121317	121317	163	0.2703436	8	NO	NULL	121317	0

Figure 3-1. Stats header for index on Sales.SalesOrderDetail table

Density Vector

The next portion of the statistics components is the density vector. The density vector describes the columns within a statistics object. There is a row for each key value in the statistics or index object. For instance, if there are two columns in an index named SaleOrderID and SalesOrderDetailID, there will be two rows in the density vector. The density vector will have a row for SaleOrderID and a row for SaleOrderID and SalesOrderDetailID, shown in Figure 3-2. There are three pieces of information available for density vector: the density, average length, and columns included in the vector (column names detailed in Table 3-2).

	All density	Average Length	Columns
1	3.178134E-05	4	SalesOrderID
2	8.242868E-06	8	SalesOrderID, SalesOrderDetailID

Figure 3-2. Sample of the density vector for index on Sales.SalesOrderDetail table

95

The value of the density vector is that it helps the query optimizer adjust cardinality for multiple column statistics objects. As we'll discuss in the next section, the ranges within the histogram are based solely on the first column of the statistics object, and the density provides an adjustment between when single or multicolumn queries are executed. While the focus for updating statistics is often on changes in the histogram, the density vector provides a valuable means to adjust ranges in the histogram to adjust for differences in the distribution of data in beyond the first column of the index.

Table 3-2. *Density Vector Columns from DBCC SHOW_STATISTICS*

Column Name	Description
All Density	Returns the density for each prefix of columns in the statistics object, one row per density. The density is calculated as 1/*distinct column values*. The closer the density is to 1, the more uniform the values in the columns.
Average Length	Average length, in bytes, to store the column values for each level of the density vector.
Columns	Names of columns in each density vector level.

Histogram

The last piece from the DBCC SHOW_STATISTICS output is the histogram. The histogram provides the details of the statistics object that the query optimizer uses to determine cardinality. When building the histogram, SQL Server calculates a number of aggregates that are based on either a statistics sample or all the rows in the table or view. The aggregates measure the frequency in which values occur and group the values into no more than 200 segments, or *steps*. For each of these steps, a distribution of the statistics columns is computed that includes the number of rows in the step, the upper bound of the step, the number of rows matching the upper bound, the distinct rows in the step, and the average number of duplicate values in the step. Table 3-3 lists the columns that match these aggregates. With this information, the query optimizer is able to estimate the number of rows returned for ranges of values in an index, thus allowing it to calculate a cost associated with retrieving the row.

Table 3-3. *Histogram Columns from DBCC SHOW_STATISTICS*

Column Name	Description
RANGE_HI_KEY	Upper-bound column value for a histogram step. The column value is also called a *key value*.
RANGE_ROWS	Estimated number of rows whose column value falls within a histogram step, excluding the upper bound.
EQ_ROWS	Estimated number of rows whose column value equals the upper bound of the histogram step.
DISTINCT_RANGE_ROWS	Estimated number of rows with a distinct column value within a histogram step, excluding the upper bound.
AVG_RANGE_ROWS	Average number of rows with duplicate column values within a histogram step, excluding the upper bound (RANGE_ROWS/ DISTINCT_RANGE_ROWS for DISTINCT_RANGE_ROWS > 0).

As mentioned in the first section, there are 163 steps in the histogram. In Figure 3-2, which includes a number of rows from the histogram, you can see how a few of the steps in Sales.SalesOrderDetail are aggregated. If you look at the second item in Figure 3-3, it shows the RANGE_HI_KEY value of 43692; this means that all SalesOrderID values between 43660 and 43692 are included in these estimates. There are 282 rows in this series, based on the RANGE_ROWS value, with 32 distinct rows in the series. Translating these numbers to the SalesOrderDetail table, there are 32 distinct SalesOrderID values with 282 SalesOrderDetailID items between them. Lastly, there are 28 SalesOrderDetailID items for SalesOrderID 43692.

CHAPTER 3   INDEX METADATA AND STATISTICS

	RANGE_HI_KEY	RANGE_ROWS	EQ_ROWS	DISTINCT_RANGE_ROWS	AVG_RANGE_ROWS
1	43659	0	12	0	1
2	43692	282	28	32	8.8125
3	43898	716	28	205	3.492683
4	44079	403	27	180	2.238889
5	44288	766	34	208	3.682692
6	44488	570	27	199	2.864322
7	44538	614	35	49	12.53061
8	44570	370	32	31	11.93548
9	44758	409	27	187	2.187166
10	44801	504	26	42	12

Figure 3-3. *Sample of the histogram for index on Sales.SalesOrderDetail table*

This leaves one last column to look at: AVG_RANGE_ROWS. The value in this column is quite important and can result in a lot of pain when statistics are out-of-date. It states how many rows can be expected when any one value or range of values from the statistics are retrieved. To check the accuracy of the range average, execute Listing 3-3, which will aggregate some of the values in the second step. After it is complete, the results (shown in Figure 3-4) will show that the averages closely match the average range rows value of 8.8125.

Listing 3-3. Query to Check AVG_RANGE_ROWS Estimate

```
USE AdventureWorks2017
GO

SELECT (COUNT(*)*1.)/COUNT(DISTINCT SalesOrderID) AS AverageRows
FROM Sales.SalesOrderDetail
WHERE SalesOrderID BETWEEN 43672 AND 43677;

SELECT (COUNT(*)*1.)/COUNT(DISTINCT SalesOrderID) AS AverageRows
FROM Sales.SalesOrderDetail
WHERE SalesOrderID BETWEEN 43675 AND 43677;

SELECT (COUNT(*)*1.)/COUNT(DISTINCT SalesOrderID) AS AverageRows
FROM Sales.SalesOrderDetail
WHERE SalesOrderID BETWEEN 43675 AND 43680;
```

CHAPTER 3　INDEX METADATA AND STATISTICS

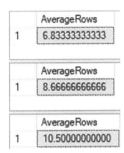

Figure 3-4. *Results of AVG_RANGE_ROWS estimate validation*

This histogram is a valuable tool to use when the statistics of an index are in question. If there is a need to determine why a query is behaving in a specific manner or you need to check why a query plan is estimating rows as it is, the histogram can be used to validate these behaviors and results.

Catalog Views

Using `DBCC SHOW_STATISTICS` provides the most detailed information on query optimization statistics. It does, however, rely on the user knowing that the statistics exist. With index statistics, it is easy to know about the statistics since all indexes have statistics. Column-level statistics require an alternative method for discovering the statistics. This is accomplished through two catalog views: `sys.stats` and `sys.stats_columns`.

sys.stats

The catalog view `sys.stats` returns one row for every query optimization statistics object that exists within the database. Whether the statistic was created based on an index or column, the statistics object is listed in the view. Table 3-4 lists the columns in `sys.stats`.

Table 3-4. Columns for sys.stats

Column Name	Data Type	Description
object_id	int	ID of the object to which these statistics belong.
name	sysname	Name of the statistics. This value must be unique for every object_id.
stats_id	int	ID of the statistics (unique within the object).
auto_created	bit	Statistics were autocreated by the query processor.
user_created	bit	Statistics were explicitly created by the user.
no_recompute	bit	Statistics were created with the NORECOMPUTE option.
has_filter	bit	Indicates whether the statistics are aggregated based on a filter or subset of rows.
filter_definition	nvarchar(max)	Expression for the subset of rows included in filtered statistics.
is_temporary	bit	Indicates whether the statistics are temporary. Added in SQL Server 2012.
is_is_incremental	bit	Indicates whether the statistics are temporary. Added in SQL Server 2014.
has_persisted_sample	bit	Indicates whether the statistics have a persisted sample rate. Added in SQL Server 2019.
stats_generation_method	int	Flag identifying the generation method for the statistics. Added in SQL Server 2019.
stats_generattion_method_desc	varchar(80)	Text description identifying the generation method for the statistics. Added in SQL Server 2019.

sys.stats_columns

As a companion to sys.stats, the catalog view `sys.stats_columns` provides one row for every column within a statistics object. Table 3-5 lists the columns in `sys.stats_columns`.

Table 3-5. Columns for sys.stats

Column Name	Data Type	Description
object_id	int	ID of the object of which this column is part.
stats_id	int	ID of the statistics of which this column is part.
stats_column_id	int	1-based ordinal within a set of stats columns.
column_id	int	ID of the column from `sys.columns`.

STATS_DATE

When it comes to statistics, one of the most important questions that is asked is whether the statistics are out-of-date. A frequent method for determining whether statistics are out-of-date is through the STATS_DATE function. The STATS_DATE function provides the date of the most recent update to statistics. The syntax for the function, shown in Listing 3-4, accepts an object_id and stats_id. In the case of indexes, the stats_id is the same value as the index_id.

Listing 3-4. STATS_DATE Syntax

```
STATS_DATE ( object_id , stats_id )
```

While the STATS_DATE function is routinely used to identify out-of-date statistics, that approach isn't effective for this task. The date that statistics were last updated does not necessarily reflect anything about the rate at which data has changed. A table that hasn't had an update in years with stats that are months old won't have out-of-date statistics, while a table with constant inserts, updates, and deletes with stats that were updated the previous day could have statistics that no longer represent the values in the index. While the function can be useful as a catchall for indexes whose statistics change slowly, it should be used with caution due to the example just given.

sys.dm_db_stats_properties

A better method for identifying the rate of change in statistics, which provides a qualifier that is reflective of the data, is the sys.dm_db_stats_properties DMO. The DMO, introduced in SQL Server 2008, provides the details on the number of rows that have changed since the statistics were last updated. The syntax for sys.dm_db_stats_properties, shown in Listing 3-5, accepts an object_id and stats_id. As with STATS_DATE, stats_id is the same value as the index_id. Table 3-6 lists the columns in sys.dm_db_stats_properties.

Listing 3-5. Syntax for sys.dm_db_stats_properties

sys.dm_db_stats_properties (object_id, stats_id)

Table 3-6. Columns for sys.dm_db_stats_properties

Column Name	Data Type	Description
object_id	int	ID of the object in question.
stats_id	int	ID of the statistics. For indexes, the ID matches the index ID.
last_updated	datetime2(7)	Date and time that the statistics were last updated.
rows	bigint	Total number of rows in the table or indexed view when the statistics were last updated. For filtered statistics or indexes, the count pertains to the number of rows that matched the filter criteria.
rows_sampled	bigint	Total number of rows sampled for statistics calculations. Histogram and density values are estimates when the rows_sampled value is less than the value in rows.
steps	int	Number of steps in the histogram. Each step spans a range of column values followed by an upper-bound column value. The histogram steps are defined on the first key column in the statistics. The maximum number of steps is 200.

(continued)

Table 3-6. (*continued*)

Column Name	Data Type	Description
unfiltered_rows	bigint	Total number of rows in the table before applying the filter expression. If Filter Expression is NULL, unfiltered_rows is equal to rows.
modification_counter	bigint	Count of the total number of inserted, deleted, or updated rows since the last time statistics were updated for the table.
persisted_sample_percent	Float	Added in SQL Server 2016.

Since sys.dm_db_stats_properties provides the opportunity for a better quality of understanding whether statistics are out-of-date, let's take a look at the output to see how changes to values in a table affect the modification_counter column. To do this, you'll start by creating the table dbo.SalesOrderHeaderStats, with Listing 3-6, and a number of indexes. To investigate modification_counter, you'll use the query in Listing 3-7 to see the changes in the column. From Figure 3-5, you see there are 20,000 rows in the table with a current modification_counter value of 0 for every index and statistic listed.

Listing 3-6. Prepare Tables for sys.dm_db_stats_properties Review

```
USE AdventureWorks2017
GO

DROP TABLE IF EXISTS dbo.SalesOrderHeaderStats;

SELECT SalesOrderID
,OrderDate
,SalesOrderNumber
INTO dbo.SalesOrderHeaderStats
FROM Sales.SalesOrderHeader
WHERE SalesOrderID <= 63658

CREATE CLUSTERED INDEX CIX_SalesOrderHeaderStats
    ON dbo.SalesOrderHeaderStats(SalesOrderID)
```

CHAPTER 3 INDEX METADATA AND STATISTICS

```
CREATE INDEX CIX_SalesOrderHeaderStats_OrderDate
    ON dbo.SalesOrderHeaderStats(OrderDate)
CREATE INDEX CIX_SalesOrderHeaderStats_SalesOrderNumber
    ON dbo.SalesOrderHeaderStats(SalesOrderNumber)
```

Listing 3-7. sys.dm_db_stats_properties Query for dbo.SalesOrderHeaderStats

```
USE AdventureWorks2017
GO

SELECT
    OBJECT_SCHEMA_NAME(s.object_id)
    +'.'+OBJECT_NAME(s.object_id) AS object_name
    ,s.name as statistics_name
    ,x.last_updated
    ,x.rows
    ,x.rows_sampled
    ,x.steps
    ,x.unfiltered_rows
    ,x.modification_counter
FROM sys.stats s
    CROSS APPLY sys.dm_db_stats_properties(s.object_id, s.stats_id) x
WHERE s.object_id = OBJECT_ID('dbo.SalesOrderHeaderStats')
```

	object_name	statistics_name	last_updated	rows	rows_sampled	steps	unfiltered_rows	modification_counter
1	dbo.SalesOrderHeaderStats	CIX_SalesOrderHeaderStats	2019-06-09 15:07:49.1800000	20000	20000	3	20000	0
2	dbo.SalesOrderHeaderStats	CIX_SalesOrderHeaderStats_OrderDate	2019-06-09 15:07:49.2866667	20000	20000	199	20000	0
3	dbo.SalesOrderHeaderStats	CIX_SalesOrderHeaderStats_SalesOrderNumber	2019-06-09 15:07:49.3166667	20000	20000	157	20000	0

Figure 3-5. *Query results for sys.dm_db_stats_properties on dbo.SalesOrderHeaderStats*

Now that you have a table to work with, let's look at what happens when changes occur to the data in the table. For the examples, you'll look at five different queries, provided in Listing 3-8. The first updates the OrderDate column resulting in 40 rows changed. The second query updates 50 rows where the SalesOrderNumber is updated to the same value it currently contains. The third query updates the SalesOrderNumber column again but reverses the value for the same 50 rows. The fourth query inserts

CHAPTER 3　INDEX METADATA AND STATISTICS

11,465 records into the table. The final query deletes the first 20,000 records from the table. Between each of the queries, execute the code in Listing 3-7; doing so will result in the output in Figure 3-6.

Listing 3-8. Sample DML Queries on dbo.SalesOrderHeaderStats

```
USE AdventureWorks2017
GO

UPDATE dbo.SalesOrderHeaderStats
set OrderDate = GETDATE()
WHERE SalesOrderID % 500 = 1

--execute code in Listing 3-7

UPDATE dbo.SalesOrderHeaderStats
SET SalesOrderNumber = SalesOrderNumber
WHERE SalesOrderID % 400 = 1

--execute code in Listing 3-7

UPDATE dbo.SalesOrderHeaderStats
SET SalesOrderNumber = REVERSE(SalesOrderNumber)
WHERE SalesOrderID % 400 = 1

--execute code in Listing 3-7

SET IDENTITY_INSERT dbo.SalesOrderHeaderStats ON
INSERT INTO dbo.SalesOrderHeaderStats (SalesOrderID
,OrderDate
,SalesOrderNumber)
SELECT SalesOrderID
,OrderDate
,SalesOrderNumber
FROM Sales.SalesOrderHeader
WHERE SalesOrderID > 63658
SET IDENTITY_INSERT dbo.SalesOrderHeaderStats OFF
```

CHAPTER 3   INDEX METADATA AND STATISTICS

```
--execute code in Listing 3-7

DELETE FROM dbo.SalesOrderHeaderStats
WHERE SalesOrderID <= 63658

--execute code in Listing 3-7
```

object_name	statistics_name	last_updated	rows	rows_sampled	steps	unfiltered_rows	modification_counter	
1 dbo.SalesOrderHeaderStats	CIX_SalesOrderHeaderStats	2019-06-09 15:07:49.1800000	20000	20000	3	20000	0	
2 dbo.SalesOrderHeaderStats	CIX_SalesOrderHeaderStats_OrderDate	2019-06-09 15:07:49.2866667	20000	20000	199	20000	40	1
3 dbo.SalesOrderHeaderStats	CIX_SalesOrderHeaderStats_SalesOrderNumber	2019-06-09 15:07:49.3166667	20000	20000	157	20000	0	
1 dbo.SalesOrderHeaderStats	CIX_SalesOrderHeaderStats	2019-06-09 15:07:49.1800000	20000	20000	3	20000	0	
2 dbo.SalesOrderHeaderStats	CIX_SalesOrderHeaderStats_OrderDate	2019-06-09 15:07:49.2866667	20000	20000	199	20000	40	2
3 dbo.SalesOrderHeaderStats	CIX_SalesOrderHeaderStats_SalesOrderNumber	2019-06-09 15:07:49.3166667	20000	20000	157	20000	50	
1 dbo.SalesOrderHeaderStats	CIX_SalesOrderHeaderStats	2019-06-09 15:07:49.1800000	20000	20000	3	20000	0	
2 dbo.SalesOrderHeaderStats	CIX_SalesOrderHeaderStats_OrderDate	2019-06-09 15:07:49.2866667	20000	20000	199	20000	40	3
3 dbo.SalesOrderHeaderStats	CIX_SalesOrderHeaderStats_SalesOrderNumber	2019-06-09 15:07:49.3166667	20000	20000	157	20000	100	
1 dbo.SalesOrderHeaderStats	CIX_SalesOrderHeaderStats	2019-06-09 15:07:49.1800000	20000	20000	3	20000	11465	
2 dbo.SalesOrderHeaderStats	CIX_SalesOrderHeaderStats_OrderDate	2019-06-09 15:07:49.2866667	20000	20000	199	20000	11505	4
3 dbo.SalesOrderHeaderStats	CIX_SalesOrderHeaderStats_SalesOrderNumber	2019-06-09 15:07:49.3166667	20000	20000	157	20000	11565	
1 dbo.SalesOrderHeaderStats	CIX_SalesOrderHeaderStats	2019-06-09 15:09:59.6800000	31465	31465	3	31465	20000	
2 dbo.SalesOrderHeaderStats	CIX_SalesOrderHeaderStats_OrderDate	2019-06-09 15:07:49.2866667	20000	20000	199	20000	31505	5
3 dbo.SalesOrderHeaderStats	CIX_SalesOrderHeaderStats_SalesOrderNumber	2019-06-09 15:07:49.3166667	20000	20000	157	20000	31565	

Figure 3-6. *Query results for sys.dm_db_stats_properties for sample queries on dbo.SalesOrderHeaderStats*

Reviewing the results in Figure 3-6 provides some interesting insight into how the `modification_counter` column is populated. To summarize, any insert, update, or delete is considered a single change for the index and statistics. Looking at the results for query 1, the 40 rows changed the result in `modification_counter` for `CIX_SalesOrderHeaderStats_OrderDate` to increase to 40. Similarly, when `SalesOrderNumber` is changed in queries 2 and 3, each query results in an increase of 50 to `modification_counter`, whether the value changed or not. Increasing the number of records causes all three indexes to increase the `modification_counter` value by 11,465, which coincides with the number of records inserted. Finally, in the query 5 results, you see the 20,000 records were deleted. Interestingly enough, in the results for the last query, the statistics from `CIX_SalesOrderHeaderStats` were updated to better reflect the changes in values in the index.

While `sys.dm_db_stats_properties` doesn't provide a list of all distinct records in a table and the impact that might have on statistics, it does provide details that identify the volume of change on an index and the statistics that support it. When trying to determine whether an index has statistics that may be out-of-date, this DMO is extremely useful.

sys.dm_db_stats_histogram

While getting the histogram for statistics can be done with DBCC SHOW_STATISTICS, SQL Server 2016 introduced the DMO function sys.dm_db_stats_histogram. This function returns output similar to the DBCC command with the added benefit that it can be joined with other DMOs to increase the usability of this data. The syntax for the function, shown in Listing 3-9, accepts an object_id and stats_id with the columns listed in Table 3-7 returned in the output.

Listing 3-9. Syntax for sys.dm_db_stats_histogram

```
sys.dm_db_stats_histogram (object_id, stats_id)
```

Table 3-7. Columns for sys.dm_db_stats_histogram

Column Name	Data Type	Description
object_id	int	ID of the object in question.
stats_id	int	ID of the statistics. For indexes, the ID matches the index ID.
step_number	int	Number of steps in the histogram. Max value 200.
range_high_key	sql_variant	Upper-bound column value for a histogram step. The column value is also called a *key value*.
range_rows	real	Estimated number of rows whose column value falls within a histogram step, excluding the upper bound.
equal_rows	real	Estimated number of rows whose column value equals the upper bound of the histogram step.
distinct_range_rows	bigint	Estimated number of rows with a distinct column value within a histogram step, excluding the upper bound.
average_range_rows	real	Average number of rows with duplicate column values in the histogram step, excluding the upper bound (range_rows/distinct_range_rows for distinct_range_rows > 0).

CHAPTER 3 INDEX METADATA AND STATISTICS

If you combine sys.stats with sys.dm_db_stats_histogram, as is done with Listing 3-10, you can get the histogram for all statistics on Sales.SalesOrderDetail. This provides information on all of the steps and their range values. Scroll through the results, shown in Figure 3-7, to rows 163 and 164; and you'll see where the range_high_key value changes from numeric to character data with the change between the statistics and steps.

Listing 3-10. sys.dm_db_stats_histogram Query for Sales.SalesOrderDetail

```
USE AdventureWorks2017;
GO

SELECT h.object_id,
       h.stats_id,
       h.step_number,
       h.range_high_key,
       h.range_rows,
       h.equal_rows,
       h.distinct_range_rows,
       h.average_range_rows
FROM sys.stats s
    CROSS APPLY sys.dm_db_stats_histogram(s.object_id, s.stats_id) h
WHERE s.object_id = OBJECT_ID('Sales.SalesOrderDetail');
```

	object_id	stats_id	step_number	range_high_key	range_rows	equal_rows	distinct_range_rows	average_range_rows
161	1810105489	1	161	74648	640	5	298	2.147651
162	1810105489	1	162	74869	511	7	220	2.322727
163	1810105489	1	163	75123	591	3	253	2.335968
164	1810105489	2	1	27520246-6C...	0	1	0	1
165	1810105489	2	2	B0AB9011-08...	966	1	966	1
166	1810105489	2	3	8E575E65-59...	2559	1	2559	1

Figure 3-7. *Query results for sys.dm_db_stats_histogram on Sales.SalesOrderDetail*

This new function is a great addition to your abilities to view and inspect histograms. For example, if you had multiple indexes and statistics on a column, you could write a query that includes just those statistics and then filter the range_high_key to only include the steps that match the records that you are concerned about. At that point, you can see the average_range_rows and get an understanding on why SQL Server may have chosen one index over another.

sys.dm_db_incremental_stats_properties

With incremental index maintenance, which is discussed in Chapter 9, statistics also require the ability for incremental updates to support that feature. As a companion to sys.dm_db_stats_properties, the function sys.dm_db_incremental_stats_properties provides visibility to stats properties of incremental statistics and indexes. The syntax for sys.dm_db_incremental_stats_properties, shown in Listing 3-11, includes the same two parameters as the other functions, object_id and stats_id. The columns returned are identical to those in Table 3-6 except this function includes a partition_number column indicating the partition for the incremental statistics.

Listing 3-11. Syntax for sys.dm_db_incremental_stats_properties

```
sys.dm_db_incremental_stats_properties (object_id, stats_id)
```

Statistics DDL

This section has primarily focused on discussing index-level statistics. Index statistics are automatically created when an index is created and automatically dropped when the index is dropped. Statistics can also be created and provide significant value on nonindexed columns. When manually creating or dropping statistics on nonindexed columns, there are two DDL statements that can be used to accomplish this: `CREATE` and `DROP STATISTICS`. Since they are outside the scope of this book, they will not be discussed. The third DDL statement, `UPDATE STATISTICS`, applies to all statistics including the index-level statistics. Since `UPDATE STATISTICS` is primarily tied to index maintenance, it is discussed in Chapter 7.

Colum-Level Statistics Summary

Query optimization statistics are a vital piece of indexing. They provide the information that the query optimizer requires in order to build cost-based query plans. Through this process, SQL Server can identify high-quality plans through their calculated costs. In this section, you looked at how statistics are stored and the tools you can use in order to investigate and begin to understand the statistics that are stored for an index.

CHAPTER 3 INDEX METADATA AND STATISTICS

Index Usage Statistics

The next domain of information to take a look at is index usage stats. Index usage statistics are accumulated through the DMO sys.dm_db_index_usage_stats. This DMO returns counts of different types of index operations and when the operation was last performed. Through this information, you can discern how frequently an index is being used and how current that usage is.

The DMO sys.dm_db_index_usage_stats is a dynamic management view (DMV). Because of this, it does not require any parameters. It can be joined to other tables or views through any of the JOIN operators. Indexes appear within the DMV after the indexes have been used for the first time or since the reset of the statistics.

Note Along with restarting the SQL Server service, closing or detaching a database will reset all the statistics for an index that have been accumulated in sys.dm_db_index_usage_stats.

Within the DMV sys.dm_db_index_usage_stats, three types of data are provided: header columns, user statistics, and system statistics. In the next few sections, you will explore each to gain an understanding of what information they hold and how you can use it.

Header Columns

The header columns for the DMV provide referential information that can be used to determine for which index the statistics were accumulated. Table 3-8 lists the columns that are part of this. These columns are primarily used to join the DMV to system catalog views and other DMOs.

Table 3-8. *Header Columns in sys.dm_db_index_usage_stats*

Column Name	Data Type	Description
database_id	smallint	ID of the database in which the table or view is defined.
object_id	int	ID of the table or view in which the index is defined.
index_id	int	ID of the index.

CHAPTER 3 INDEX METADATA AND STATISTICS

One of the first things that can be done with sys.dm_db_index_usage_stats is to check to see whether an index has been used since the last time the statistics in the DMV were reset. Using the header columns, similar to the T-SQL statement in Listing 3-12, can provide a list of the indexes that have not been used. If you are using the AdventureWorks2017 database, your results will look similar to those in Figure 3-8. In these results, indexes that have not been used are returned.

Listing 3-12. Query for Header Columns in sys.dm_db_index_usage_stats

```
USE AdventureWorks2017
GO

SELECT TOP 10 OBJECT_NAME(i.object_id) AS table_name
        ,i.name AS index_name
        ,ius.database_id
        ,ius.object_id
        ,ius.index_id
FROM sys.indexes i
        LEFT JOIN sys.dm_db_index_usage_stats ius
                ON i.object_id = ius.object_id
                AND i.index_id = ius.index_id
                AND ius.database_id = DB_ID()
WHERE ius.index_id IS NULL
AND OBJECTPROPERTY(i.object_id, 'IsUserTable') = 1
ORDER BY table_name, index_name
```

	table_name	index_name	database_id	object_id	index_id
1	Address	AK_Address_rowguid	NULL	NULL	NULL
2	Address	IX_Address_AddressLine1_AddressLine2_City_StatePr...	NULL	NULL	NULL
3	Address	IX_Address_StateProvinceID	NULL	NULL	NULL
4	Address	PK_Address_AddressID	NULL	NULL	NULL
5	AddressType	AK_AddressType_Name	NULL	NULL	NULL
6	AddressType	AK_AddressType_rowguid	NULL	NULL	NULL
7	AddressType	PK_AddressType_AddressTypeID	NULL	NULL	NULL
8	AWBuildVersion	PK_AWBuildVersion_SystemInformationID	NULL	NULL	NULL
9	BillOfMaterials	AK_BillOfMaterials_ProductAssemblyID_ComponentID...	NULL	NULL	NULL
10	BillOfMaterials	IX_BillOfMaterials_UnitMeasureCode	NULL	NULL	NULL

Figure 3-8. sys.dm_db_index_usage_stats header columns query results

This type of information can be useful for managing the indexes in your databases. It is an excellent resource for identifying the indexes that have not been used in a while. This strategy of index management is discussed further in later chapters.

User Columns

The next set of columns in the DMV `sys.dm_db_index_usage_stats` is the user columns. The user columns provide insight into how indexes are being specifically used within query plans. The columns are listed in Table 3-9; they include statistics on how many times each operation occurred and the time at which the last one occurred.

Table 3-9. *User Columns in sys.dm_db_index_usage_stats*

Column Name	Data Type	Description
user_seeks	bigint	Aggregate count of seeks by user queries.
user_scans	bigint	Aggregate count of scans by user queries.
user_lookups	bigint	Aggregate count of bookmark/key lookups by user queries.
user_updates	bigint	Aggregate count of updates by user queries.
last_user_seek	datetime	Date and time of last user seek.
last_user_scan	datetime	Date and time of last user scan.
last_user_lookup	datetime	Date and time of last user lookup.
last_user_update	datetime	Date and time of last user update.

`sys.dm_db_index_usage_stats` monitors four types of index operations. These are represented through the columns user_seeks, user_scans, user_lookups, and user_updates.

The first of the index usage columns is user_seeks. The operations for this column occur whenever a query executes and returns a single row or range of rows for which it has a direct access path. For instance, if a query executes and retrieves all the sales details for a single order or a small range of orders, similar to the queries in Listing 3-13, the query plan for these would use a seek operation (see Figure 3-9).

CHAPTER 3 INDEX METADATA AND STATISTICS

Listing 3-13. Index Seek Queries

```
USE AdventureWorks2017
GO

SELECT * FROM Sales.SalesOrderDetail
WHERE SalesOrderID = 43659;

SELECT * FROM Sales.SalesOrderDetail
WHERE SalesOrderID BETWEEN 43659 AND 44659;
```

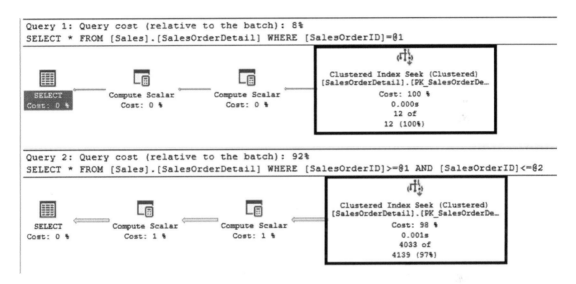

Figure 3-9. *Query plans for seek queries*

After running the queries from Listing 3-13, the DMV sys.dm_db_index_usage_stats will be counted into the user_seeks column. Listing 3-14 provides a query to investigate this. If you are following along, you should see the results in Figure 3-10. As the results show, the value in the user_seeks column is 5, which matches the count of operations from Listing 3-13. Based on this, you know that two queries were executed using the index and both were able to utilize the index to go directly to rows that were requested.

Listing 3-14. Query for index_seeks from sys.dm_db_index_usage_stats

```
USE AdventureWorks2017
GO

SELECT TOP 10
    OBJECT_NAME(i.object_id) AS table_name
    ,i.name AS index_name
    ,ius.user_seeks
    ,ius.last_user_seek
FROM sys.indexes i
    INNER JOIN sys.dm_db_index_usage_stats ius
            ON i.object_id = ius.object_id
            AND i.index_id = ius.index_id
            AND ius.database_id = DB_ID()
WHERE ius.object_id = OBJECT_ID('Sales.SalesOrderDetail');
```

	table_name	index_name	user_seeks	last_user_seek
1	SalesOrderDetail	PK_SalesOrderDetail_SalesOrderID_SalesOrderDet...	5	2019-08-26 18:10:00.700

Figure 3-10. *Query results for index_seeks*

The next usage column is user_scans. The value of this column is increased whenever a query executes, and it must scan through every row of an index. For instance, consider a query on sales details that is unfiltered and must return all records or a query that is filtered on a column that is unindexed. Both of these queries, shown in Listing 3-15, are asking SQL Server for either everything it has in a table or a few rows that it doesn't have a location on. The only way to accommodate this request would be through a scan of the SalesOrderDetail table. Figure 3-11 shows the execution plans for these two queries.

Listing 3-15. Index Scan Queries

```
USE AdventureWorks2017
GO

SELECT * FROM  Sales.SalesOrderDetail;

SELECT * FROM  Sales.SalesOrderDetail
WHERE CarrierTrackingNumber = '4911-403C-98';
```

CHAPTER 3 INDEX METADATA AND STATISTICS

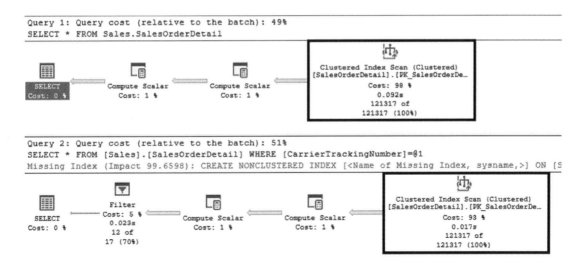

Figure 3-11. Query plans for seek queries

When index scans occur, they can be seen in sys.dm_db_index_usage_stats. The query in Listing 3-16 provides a view in the DMV to see the accumulation of the scans. Since there were two scans, one for each of the two queries, the results in Figure 3-12 show that there have been two operations under user_scans. This information can be useful when trying to troubleshoot situations where there are large numbers of scans on a table. By looking at this information, you are able to find the indexes with high scans and then begin to look at why queries using those indexes are using scans over more optimal operations such as index seeks.

Listing 3-16. Query for index_scans from sys.dm_db_index_usage_stats

```
USE AdventureWorks2017
GO

SELECT TOP 10
    OBJECT_NAME(i.object_id) AS table_name
    ,i.name AS index_name
    ,ius.user_scans
    ,ius.last_user_scan
```

115

```
FROM sys.indexes i
    INNER JOIN sys.dm_db_index_usage_stats ius
                ON i.object_id = ius.object_id
                AND i.index_id = ius.index_id
                AND ius.database_id = DB_ID()
WHERE ius.object_id = OBJECT_ID('Sales.SalesOrderDetail');
```

	table_name	index_name	user_scans	last_user_scan
1	SalesOrderDetail	PK_SalesOrderDetail_SalesOrderID_SalesOrderDet...	2	2019-06-09 19:38:49.773

Figure 3-12. *Query results for index_scans*

The third column in the DMV is user_lookups. User lookups occur when a seek on a nonclustered index occurs but the index does not have all of the required columns in it to satisfy the query. When this happens, the query must look up the columns from the clustered index. An example would be a query against the SalesOrderDetail table that is returning the ProductID and CarrierTrackingNumber columns, which is filtered on ProductID; Listing 3-17 shows this query. Figure 3-13 shows the query plan from this query. The query plan shows a seek on the nonclustered index and a key lookup on the clustered index.

Listing 3-17. Index Lookup Query

```
USE AdventureWorks2017
GO

SELECT ProductID, CarrierTrackingNumber
FROM Sales.SalesOrderDetail
WHERE ProductID = 778
GO
```

CHAPTER 3 INDEX METADATA AND STATISTICS

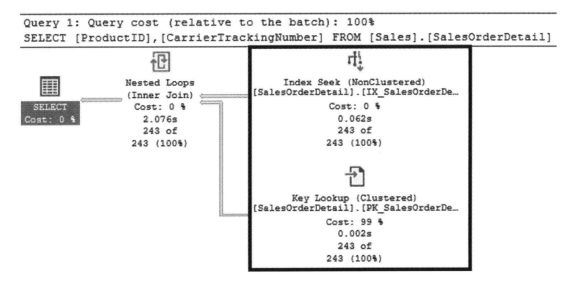

Figure 3-13. *Query plans for seek and key lookup*

In sys.dm_db_index_usage_stats, there will be a tally of one for both user_seeks and user_lookups. To access these values, use Listing 3-18, which will return the results in Figure 3-14. Patterns between these columns can help with determining proper clustering keys or identifying when to modify indexes to avoid the key lookups. Key lookups aren't necessarily bad but can be a performance bottleneck if overused and left unchecked. I'll discuss more on what to look for in regard to user_lookups in later chapters.

Listing 3-18. Query for index_lookups from sys.dm_db_index_usage_stats

```
SELECT TOP 10
    OBJECT_NAME(i.object_id) AS table_name
    ,i.name AS index_name
    ,ius.user_seeks
    ,ius.user_lookups
    ,ius.last_user_lookup
FROM sys.indexes i
    INNER JOIN sys.dm_db_index_usage_stats ius
            ON i.object_id = ius.object_id
            AND i.index_id = ius.index_id
            AND ius.database_id = DB_ID()
WHERE ius.object_id = OBJECT_ID('Sales.SalesOrderDetail');
```

117

	table_name	index_name	user_seeks	user_lookups	last_user_lookup
1	SalesOrderDetail	PK_SalesOrderDetail_SalesOrderID_SalesOrderDet...	5	1	2019-08-26 19:45:26.037
2	SalesOrderDetail	IX_SalesOrderDetail_ProductID	1	0	NULL

Figure 3-14. *Query results for index_lookups*

The last of the index operations is user_updates. The user_updates column is not limited to update operations on a table. In actuality, it covers all INSERT, UPDATE, and DELETE operations that occur on a table. To demonstrate this, you can execute the code in Listing 3-19. This code will insert a record into the SalesOrderDetail table, then update the record, and finally delete the record from the table. Since the execution plans for these are complex because of foreign key relationships, they have not been included in this example.

Listing 3-19. Index Update Queries

```
USE AdventureWorks2017
GO

INSERT INTO Sales.SalesOrderDetail
(SalesOrderID, CarrierTrackingNumber, OrderQty, ProductID, SpecialOfferID,
UnitPrice, UnitPriceDiscount, ModifiedDate)
SELECT SalesOrderID, CarrierTrackingNumber, OrderQty, ProductID,
SpecialOfferID, UnitPrice, UnitPriceDiscount, GETDATE() AS ModifiedDate
FROM Sales.SalesOrderDetail
WHERE SalesOrderDetailID = 1;

UPDATE Sales.SalesOrderDetail
SET CarrierTrackingNumber = '999-99-9999'
WHERE ModifiedDate > DATEADD(d, -1, GETDATE());

DELETE FROM Sales.SalesOrderDetail
WHERE ModifiedDate > DATEADD(d, -1, GETDATE());
```

At the completion of the execution of the code listing, there were three operations that occurred on the table. For each of these operations, sys.dm_db_index_usage_stats accumulated one tick in the user_updates column. Execute the code in Listing 3-20 to see the activity that occurred on the index. The results will be similar to those in Figure 3-15. Besides the changes made to the clustered index for SalesOrderDetail, the updates made

CHAPTER 3 INDEX METADATA AND STATISTICS

to the nonclustered indexes are also included. Being able to see the effects of an insert, update, or delete on a table can help provide an understanding of the impact of users and the volatility of your data.

Listing 3-20. Query for index_updates from sys.dm_db_index_usage_stats

```
USE AdventureWorks2017
GO
SELECT TOP 10
    OBJECT_NAME(i.object_id) AS table_name
    ,i.name AS index_name
    ,ius.user_updates
    ,ius.last_user_update
FROM sys.indexes i
    INNER JOIN sys.dm_db_index_usage_stats ius
                ON i.object_id = ius.object_id
                AND i.index_id = ius.index_id
                AND ius.database_id = DB_ID()
WHERE ius.object_id = OBJECT_ID('Sales.SalesOrderDetail');
```

	table_name	index_name	user_updates	last_user_update
1	SalesOrderDetail	AK_SalesOrderDetail_rowguid	2	2019-08-26 19:45:26.770
2	SalesOrderDetail	PK_SalesOrderDetail_SalesOrderID_SalesOrderDet...	3	2019-08-26 19:45:26.770
3	SalesOrderDetail	IX_SalesOrderDetail_ProductID	2	2019-08-26 19:45:26.770

Figure 3-15. Query results for index_updates

System Columns

The last set of columns in sys.dm_db_index_usage_stats is the system columns. The system columns return the same general information as the user columns, except these values are from the perspective of background processes. Whenever something triggers within SQL Server, such as a triggered statistics update, that activity will be tracked through these columns. Table 3-10 lists the system columns.

CHAPTER 3   INDEX METADATA AND STATISTICS

Table 3-10. *System Columns in sys.dm_db_index_usage_stats*

Column Name	Data Type	Description
system_seeks	bigint	Number of seeks by system queries.
system_scans	bigint	Number of scans by system queries.
system_lookups	bigint	Number of lookups by system queries.
system_updates	bigint	Number of updates by system queries.
last_system_seek	datetime	Time of last system seek.
last_system_scan	datetime	Time of last system scan.
last_system_lookup	datetime	Time of last system lookup.
last_system_update	datetime	Time of last system update.

For the most part, these columns can be ignored. It is good, though, to understand how they are aggregated. To see an example, execute the code in Listing 3-21, which may run up to a minute. This will change a majority of the rows in the SalesOrderDetail table. Since more than 20 percent of the rows have changed, an automatic statistics update will be triggered. The statistics update is not directly related to user activity and is instead a background, or system, process.

Listing 3-21. Update for Sales.SalesOrderDetail

```
USE AdventureWorks2017
GO

UPDATE Sales.SalesOrderDetail
SET UnitPriceDiscount = 0.01
WHERE UnitPriceDiscount = 0.00;
```

After the update has completed, run the T-SQL statements in Listing 3-22. This code will return results from sys.stats and the system columns from sys.dm_db_index_usage_stats, shown in Figure 3-16. Within these is the system_scans column which shows three system scans have occurred on Sales.SalesOrderDetail. These related to statistics updates, one of which occurred on the UnitPriceDiscount column. Looking at the times when the statistics were created, you can see that they were on CarrierTrackingNumber, then SalesOrderDetailId, ModifiedDate, and finally UnitPriceDiscount.

Listing 3-22. Query for System Columns in sys.dm_db_index_usage_stats

```
USE AdventureWorks2017
GO

SELECT S.object_id,
       S.name,
       S.auto_created,
       STATS_DATE(S.object_id, S.stats_id),
       X.stats_column_names
FROM sys.stats S
    CROSS APPLY
(
    SELECT STRING_AGG(C.name, ',') AS stats_column_names
    FROM sys.stats_columns SC
        INNER JOIN sys.columns C
            ON C.object_id = SC.object_id
                AND C.column_id = SC.column_id
    WHERE S.object_id = SC.object_id
          AND S.stats_id = SC.stats_id
) X
WHERE S.object_id = OBJECT_ID('Sales.SalesOrderDetail');

SELECT OBJECT_NAME(i.object_id) AS table_name
    ,i.name AS index_name
    ,ius.system_seeks
    ,ius.system_scans
    ,ius.system_lookups
    ,ius.system_updates
    ,ius.last_system_seek
    ,ius.last_system_scan
    ,ius.last_system_lookup
    ,ius.last_system_update
FROM sys.indexes i
```

CHAPTER 3 INDEX METADATA AND STATISTICS

```
        INNER JOIN sys.dm_db_index_usage_stats ius
                ON i.object_id = ius.object_id
                AND i.index_id = ius.index_id
                AND ius.database_id = DB_ID()
WHERE ius.object_id = OBJECT_ID('Sales.SalesOrderDetail');
```

Figure 3-16. sys.stats and sys.dm_db_index_usage_stats system columns query results

From a usefulness perspective, there isn't much of anything that can be gleaned from these columns. They are just the result of background processes and are more there to inform what is happening with indexes in the background.

Index Usage Stats Summary

In this section, I discussed the statistics found in DMV `sys.dm_db_index_usage_stats`. This DMV provides some extremely useful statistics about how and if indexes are being used in the database. By monitoring these statistics over the long run, you will be able to understand which indexes are providing some of the most value. Strategies for using all these columns to index for performance will be discussed in Chapter 8.

Index Operational Statistics

The third area of statistics to consider is index operational stats. These statistics are presented to users through the DMO `sys.dm_db_index_operational_stats`. From a high level, this DMO provides low-level information on I/O, locking, latching, and access methods that occur on indexes. Through this low-level information, you can identify indexes that may be encountering performance issues and start to understand what is leading to those performance issues. At the end of this section, you will understand the statistics provided in the DMO and know how to investigate indexes through these statistics.

Unlike the DMO in the previous section, sys.dm_db_index_operational_stats is a dynamic management function (DMF). Because of this, the DMF requires a number of parameters to be supplied when it is used. Table 3-11 details the parameters for the DMF.

Table 3-11. *Parameters for sys.dm_db_index_operational_stats*

Parameter Name	Data Type	Description
database_id	smallint	ID of the database where the indexes reside. Providing the value 0, NULL, or DEFAULT will return index information for all databases. The function DB_ID can be used in this parameter.
object_id	int	Object ID of the table or view for which statistics should be returned. Providing the value 0, NULL, or DEFAULT will return index information for all tables or views in the database.
index_id	int	Index ID of the index for which statistics should be returned. Providing the value -1, NULL, or DEFAULT will return statistics for all indexes on the table or view.
partition_number	int	Partition number on an index in which statistics should be returned. Providing the value 0, NULL, or DEFAULT will return statistics information for all partitions on an index.

Through the parameters, statistics on indexes can be as widely or narrowly focused as necessary. This flexibility is useful since sys.dm_db_index_operational_stats does not allow the use of the CROSS APPLY or OUTER APPLY operator. When passing the parameters into the DMF, the syntax for doing so is defined in Listing 3-23.

Listing 3-23. Index Operational Stats Syntax

```
sys.dm_db_index_operational_stats (
    { database_id | NULL | 0 | DEFAULT }
    , { object_id | NULL | 0 | DEFAULT }
    , { index_id | 0 | NULL | -1 | DEFAULT }
    , { partition_number | NULL | 0 | DEFAULT }
)
```

> **Note** The DMF sys.dm_db_index_operational_stats can accept the use of the Transact SQL functions DB_ID() and OBJECT_ID(). These functions can be used for the parameters database_id and object_id, respectively.

Header Columns

To start looking at the statistics, you need to identify the header columns that will be used with all the resulting queries. For every row that is returned through the DMF, there will be a database_id, object_id, index_id, and partition_number. These columns are defined further in Table 3-12. As is implied through the partition_number, the granularity of the results for this DMF is at the partition level. For nonpartitioned indexes, the partition number will be 1.

Table 3-12. Header Columns in sys.dm_db_index_operational_stats

Column Name	Data Type	Description
database_id	smallint	ID of the database on which the table or view is defined.
object_id	int	ID of the table or view on which the index is defined.
index_id	int	ID of the index.
partition_number	int	1-based partition number within the index or heap.
hobt_id	bigint	ID used to identify the heap or B-tree (hobt) associated with an index partition. New since SQL Server 2016.

The header columns provide the basis for understanding to which indexes the statistics apply. This will help provide perspective regarding the statistics returned. Also, they can be used to join to catalog views, such as sys.indexes, to provide the names of the indexes.

The useful information in this DMF comes in the rest of the columns returned by the function. The information that can be returned provides insight into DML activity, the page allocation cycle, data access patterns, index contention, and disk activity. In the following sections, you'll look into the columns of the DMF that provide statistics for this information.

DML Activity

The place to begin when investigating the operation stats on an index is with the DML activity on the index. Table 3-13 lists the columns that represent this activity. These columns provide a count of the number of rows that are affected by DML operations. The statistics that follow are similar to those in sys.dm_db_index_usage but with a few differences in perspective that will be discussed next.

Table 3-13. DML Activity Columns in sys.dm_db_index_operational_stats

Column Name	Data Type	Description
leaf_insert_count	bigint	Cumulative count of leaf-level rows inserted.
leaf_delete_count	bigint	Cumulative count of leaf-level rows deleted.
leaf_update_count	bigint	Cumulative count of leaf-level rows updated.
leaf_ghost_count	bigint	Cumulative count of leaf-level rows that are marked to be deleted but not yet removed.
nonleaf_insert_count	bigint	Cumulative count of inserts above the leaf level. For heaps, this value will always be 0.
nonleaf_delete_count	bigint	Cumulative count of deletes above the leaf level. For heaps, this value will always be 0.
nonleaf_update_count	bigint	Cumulative count of updates above the leaf level. For heaps, this value will always be 0.

Within sys.dm_db_index_operational_stats, there are two areas where DML activity can be tracked. These are at the leaf and nonleaf levels. These areas of DML activity were discussed in Chapter 2; for more information on leaf and nonleaf pages, refer to that chapter.

The difference between these two types of data changes is important to help identify whether there are changes as a result of DML operations. This means that leaf-level DML activity is a direct result of INSERT, UPDATE, and DELETE statements. The nonleaf-level DML activity happens when leaf-level activity results in a change in how the index is structured and isn't something that can be directly impacted with an INSERT, UPDATE, or DELETE statement.

Both leaf-level and nonleaf-level DML activities are broken apart into statistics based on the type of DML operation that has occurred. As previously indicated, DML activity monitors INSERT, UPDATE, and DELETE activities. For each of these operations, there is a column in `sys.dm_db_index_operational_stats`. Additionally, there is a column that counts records that have been ghosted off the leaf-level DML activity.

During DELETE operations, rows affected by the statement are deleted in a two-phase operation. Initially, the records are marked for deletion. When this occurs, the records are referred to as being *ghosted*; the rows in this state are counted in `leaf_ghost_count`. At regular intervals, a cleanup thread within SQL Server will go through and perform an actual delete operation on rows marked as ghosted. At that point, the records will be counted in the `leaf_delete_count`. This process helps in the performance of delete operations since the actual delete of a row happens after the transaction is committed. Also, in the event of transaction rollback, the ghost flag on a row is all that needs to change rather than an attempt to re-create the row in the table. This activity occurs only at the leaf level; nonleaf pages are deleted whenever all the rows associated with the pages have been deleted or otherwise removed.

As mentioned, this DML activity on this DMF is similar to that found in `sys.dm_db_index_usage_stats`. While it is similar, there are some stark differences. The first difference is that the information in `sys.dm_db_index_operational_stats` is much more granular than that in `sys.dm_db_index_usage_stats`. Operational stats report down to the leaf and nonleaf levels; usage stats do not. Along with the granularity is the difference in how the counts are tabulated. Usage stats count one for every plan that performs the operation on the index; whether 0 or 100 rows, the stats are collected. Operational stats differ in that the count increments for every row that has the DML operation performed. To summarize the difference, usage stats aggregate when the index is used, and operational stats aggregate based on how much of the index is used.

The code in Listing 3-24 illustrates how operational stats are tabulated. In the listing, 79 rows are added to the table `dbo.Karaoke`. Then 44 rows are deleted from the table. This is followed by 35 rows being updated in the table. The last query returns operational stats based on the DML activity. Figure 3-17 shows the results of the final query.

Listing 3-24. DML Activity Script

```
USE AdventureWorks2017
GO

IF OBJECT_ID('dbo.Karaoke') IS NOT NULL
  DROP TABLE dbo.Karaoke;
```

CHAPTER 3 ■ INDEX METADATA AND STATISTICS

```sql
CREATE TABLE dbo.Karaoke
(
 KaraokeID INT
,Duet BIT
,CONSTRAINT PK_Karaoke_KaraokeID PRIMARY KEY CLUSTERED (KaraokeID)
);

INSERT INTO dbo.Karaoke
    SELECT ROW_NUMBER() OVER (ORDER BY t.object_id)
        ,t.object_id % 2
    FROM sys.tables t;

DELETE FROM dbo.Karaoke
WHERE  Duet = 0;

UPDATE dbo.Karaoke
SET    Duet = 0
WHERE  Duet = 1;

SELECT OBJECT_SCHEMA_NAME(ios.object_id) + '.' + OBJECT_NAME(ios.object_id)
AS table_name
    ,i.name AS index_name
    ,ios.leaf_insert_count
    ,ios.leaf_update_count
    ,ios.leaf_delete_count
    ,ios.leaf_ghost_count
FROM sys.dm_db_index_operational_stats(DB_ID(),NULL,NULL,NULL) ios
    INNER JOIN sys.indexes i
      ON i.object_id = ios.object_id
        AND i.index_id = ios.index_id
WHERE ios.object_id = OBJECT_ID('dbo.Karaoke')
ORDER BY ios.range_scan_count DESC;
```

	table_name	index_name	leaf_insert_count	leaf_update_count	leaf_delete_count	leaf_ghost_count
1	dbo.Karaoke	PK_Karaoke_KaraokeID	79	35	0	44

Figure 3-17. DML activity query results (result may vary on your system)

The value in looking at the DML activity in an index is to help you understand what is happening to the data in an index. For example, if a nonclustered index is being updated often, it may be beneficial to look at the columns in the index to determine whether the volatility of the columns matches the benefit of the index. It is good to look at the indexes with high amounts of DML activity and consider whether the activity matches your own understanding of the database platform.

SELECT Activity

After DML activity, the next area of information that can be looked at is the information on SELECT activity. The SELECT activity columns, shown in Table 3-14, identify the type of physical operation that was used when queries were executed. There are three types of access that SQL Server collects information on: range scans, singleton lookups, and forwarded records.

Table 3-14. Access Pattern Columns in sys.dm_db_index_operational_stats

Column Name	Data Type	Description
range_scan_count	bigint	Cumulative count of range and table scans started on the index or heap.
singleton_lookup_count	bigint	Cumulative count of single row retrievals from the index or heap.
forwarded_fetch_count	bigint	Count of rows that were fetched through a forwarding record.

Range Scan

Range scans occur whenever a range of rows or a table scan is used to access data. When considering a range of rows, it can be anywhere from 1 to 1,000 or more rows. The number of rows in the range is not material in how SQL Server accesses the data. With table scans, the number of rows is also not important, but you already, likely, assume that it includes all records in the table. In sys.dm_db_index_operational_stats, these values are stored in the column range_scan_count.

To see this information collected in range_scan_count, execute the code in Listing 3-13 and Listing 3-15 from the previous section. Before doing this, take the AdventureWorks2017 database offline and then bring it back online which will reset the statistics returned from the DMOs. In these two code samples, four queries will be executed. The first two will result in index seeks in the query plan, shown in Figure 3-9. And the second two queries result in index scans, as shown in the execution plans in Figure 3-11. Running the code in Listing 3-25 will show, as displayed in Figure 3-18, that all four queries used a range scan to retrieve the data from the table.

Listing 3-25. Query for range_scan_count from sys.dm_db_index_operational_stats

```
USE AdventureWorks2017
GO

SELECT OBJECT_NAME(ios.object_id) AS table_name
    ,i.name AS index_name
    ,ios.range_scan_count
FROM sys.dm_db_index_operational_stats(DB_ID(),OBJECT_ID('Sales.SalesOrderDetail'),NULL,NULL) ios
    INNER JOIN sys.indexes i
        ON i.object_id = ios.object_id
        AND i.index_id = ios.index_id
ORDER BY ios.range_scan_count DESC;
```

	table_name	index_name	range_scan_count
1	SalesOrderDetail	PK_SalesOrderDetail_SalesOrderID_SalesOrderDet...	4

Figure 3-18. Query results for range_scan_count

Singleton Lookup

The next statistics column collected on SELECT activity is singleton_lookup_count. Values in this column are increased whenever the key lookup, formerly bookmark lookup, is used. In general terms, this is the same type of information as collected in the column user_lookups in sys.dm_db_index_usage_stats. There is a significant difference, though, between user_lookups and singleton_lookup_count. When a key lookup is used, user_lookups will increment by one to indicate that the index operation

CHAPTER 3   INDEX METADATA AND STATISTICS

had been used. With `singleton_lookup_count`, for every row that uses the key lookup operation, the value in this column will increase by one.

For instance, running the code in Listing 3-17 will result in a key lookup. This can be validated by examining the execution plan, shown in Figure 3-13. The statistics from this were discussed previously and shown in Figure 3-19. The new information to look at can be investigated by running the T-SQL statement in Listing 3-26. In the results, you can see that instead of there being a value of 1 in `singleton_lookup_count`, the value is 243. This is an important distinction for this column. Rather than knowing that key lookups have occurred, this statistic provides information on the scope of the lookups. You could consider that if the ratio of singleton lookups to range scans was high, there may be other indexing alternatives to consider.

Listing 3-26. Query for singleton_lookup_count from sys.dm_db_index_operational_stats

```
USE AdventureWorks2017
GO

SELECT OBJECT_NAME(ios.object_id) AS table_name
    ,i.name AS index_name
    ,ios.singleton_lookup_count
FROM sys.dm_db_index_operational_stats(DB_ID(),OBJECT_ID('Sales.
SalesOrderDetail'),NULL,NULL) ios
    INNER JOIN sys.indexes i
      ON i.object_id = ios.object_id
        AND i.index_id = ios.index_id
ORDER BY ios. singleton_lookup_count DESC;
```

	table_name	index_name	singleton_lookup_count
1	SalesOrderDetail	PK_SalesOrderDetail_SalesOrderID_SalesOrderDet...	243
2	SalesOrderDetail	AK_SalesOrderDetail_rowguid	0
3	SalesOrderDetail	IX_SalesOrderDetail_ProductID	0

Figure 3-19. Query results for singleton_lookup_count

CHAPTER 3 INDEX METADATA AND STATISTICS

Forwarded Fetch

The last column of statistics collected on SELECT activity is forwarded_fetch_count. As discussed in Chapter 2, forwarded records occur in heaps when a record increases in size and can no longer fit on the page that it is currently on. The column forwarded_fetch_count increases by one every time a record forward operation occurs.

To demonstrate, the code in Listing 3-27 builds a table with a heap and populates it with some values. Then an UPDATE statement increases the size of every third row. The size of the new row will exceed the available space on the page, resulting in a forwarded record.

Listing 3-27. T-SQL Script for Forwarded Records

```
USE AdventureWorks2017
GO

CREATE TABLE dbo.ForwardedRecords
    (
    ID INT IDENTITY(1,1)
    ,VALUE VARCHAR(8000)
    );
INSERT INTO dbo.ForwardedRecords (VALUE)
SELECT REPLICATE(type, 500)
FROM sys.objects;

UPDATE dbo.ForwardedRecords
SET VALUE = REPLICATE(VALUE, 16)
WHERE ID%3 = 1;
```

Once the script is completed, the sys.dm_db_index_operational_stats script in Listing 3-28 can be used to view the number of times that forwarded records have been fetched. In this case, the 222 records that were forwarded resulted in a forwarded_fetch_count of 222, shown in Figure 3-20. This column is useful when looking into the performance counter Forwarded Records/sec. Reviewing this column will help identify which heap is leading to the counter activity, providing a focus on the exact table to investigate.

Listing 3-28. Query for forwarded_fetch_count from sys.dm_db_index_operational_stats

```
SELECT OBJECT_NAME(ios.object_id) AS table_name
      ,i.name AS index_name
      ,ios.forwarded_fetch_count
FROM sys.dm_db_index_operational_stats(DB_ID(),OBJECT_ID('dbo.ForwardedRecords'),NULL,NULL) ios
      INNER JOIN sys.indexes i
        ON i.object_id = ios.object_id
          AND i.index_id = ios.index_id
ORDER BY ios.forwarded_fetch_count DESC
```

	table_name	index_name	forwarded_fetch_count
1	ForwardedRecords	NULL	222

Figure 3-20. *Query result for forwarded_fetch_count*

Locking Contention

As data is used within SQL Server databases, it is locked to provide consistency in the data that users are requesting and to prevent others from receiving incorrect results. At times, locking for one user can interfere with another user. To best monitor locking, `sys.dm_db_index_operational_stats` provides columns that detail the counts on locks and time spent waiting for locks to occur. Table 3-15 lists three groups of columns. There are three types of locks that are tracked in `sys.dm_db_index_operational_stats` to provide insight into locking contention: row locks, page locks, and index lock promotion.

CHAPTER 3 INDEX METADATA AND STATISTICS

Table 3-15. *Index Contention Columns in sys.dm_db_index_operational_stats*

Column Name	Data Type	Description
row_lock_count	bigint	Cumulative number of row locks requested.
row_lock_wait_count	bigint	Cumulative number of times the database engine waited on a row lock.
row_lock_wait_in_ms	bigint	Total number of milliseconds the database engine waited on a row lock.
page_lock_count	bigint	Cumulative number of page locks requested.
page_lock_wait_count	bigint	Cumulative number of times the database engine waited on a page lock.
page_lock_wait_in_ms	bigint	Total number of milliseconds the database engine waited on a page lock.
index_lock_promotion_attempt_count	bigint	Cumulative number of times the database engine tried to escalate locks.
index_lock_promotion_count	bigint	Cumulative number of times the database engine escalated locks.

Row Lock

The first set of columns consists of the row lock columns. These columns include row_lock_count, row_lock_wait_count, and row_lock_wait_in_ms. Through these columns, you are able to measure the number of locks that occur on a row and then whether there was any contention when acquiring the row lock. Row lock contention can often be observed by its effect on transaction performance through blocking and deadlocking.

To demonstrate how this information is collected, execute the code in Listing 3-29. In this script, rows from the Sales.SalesOrderDetail table are retrieved based on ProductID. In the AdventureWorks2017 database, the query retrieves 44 rows.

CHAPTER 3   INDEX METADATA AND STATISTICS

Listing 3-29. T-SQL Script to Generate Row Locks

```
USE AdventureWorks2017
GO

ALTER INDEX ALL ON Sales.SalesOrderDetail REBUILD;

SELECT SalesOrderID
    ,SalesOrderDetailID
    ,CarrierTrackingNumber
    ,OrderQty
FROM Sales.SalesOrderDetail
WHERE ProductID = 710;
```

To observe the row locks that were acquired by the query, use the row lock columns in the query provided in Listing 3-30. In these results, you see that for each row that was returned by the query against Sales.SalesOrderDetail, there is one lock included in the results of sys.dm_db_index_operational_stats, shown in Figure 3-21. As a result, there were 44 row locks placed on the index IX_SalesOrderDetail_ProductID.

Note that there is no information returned for the row_lock_wait_count and row_lock_wait_in_ms columns. This is because the script was not blocked by any other query. Had the query in Listing 3-29 been blocked by another transaction, then the values in these columns would have incremented.

Listing 3-30. Query for Row Locks in sys.dm_db_index_operational_stats

```
USE AdventureWorks2017
GO

SELECT OBJECT_NAME(ios.object_id) AS table_name
      ,i.name AS index_name
      ,ios.row_lock_count
      ,ios.row_lock_wait_count
      ,ios.row_lock_wait_in_ms
FROM sys.dm_db_index_operational_stats(DB_ID(),OBJECT_ID('Sales.
SalesOrderDetail'),NULL,NULL) ios
      INNER JOIN sys.indexes i
```

CHAPTER 3 INDEX METADATA AND STATISTICS

```
        ON i.object_id = ios.object_id
        AND i.index_id = ios.index_id
ORDER BY ios.range_scan_count DESC;
```

	table_name	index_name	row_lock_count	row_lock_wait_count	row_lock_wait_in_ms
1	SalesOrderDetail	IX_SalesOrderDetail_ProductID	44	0	0
2	SalesOrderDetail	PK_SalesOrderDetail_SalesOrderID_SalesOrderDet...	0	0	0
3	SalesOrderDetail	AK_SalesOrderDetail_rowguid	0	0	0

Figure 3-21. *Query results for row locks*

Page Lock

The next set of columns are the page lock columns. The columns in this group have similar characteristics to the row lock columns, with the exception that they are scoped at the page level instead of the row level. For every page that relates to an accessed row, a page lock is acquired. These columns are page_lock_count, page_lock_wait_count, and page_lock_wait_in_ms. When monitoring for locking contention on an index, it is important to look at both the page and row levels to identify whether the contention is on the individual rows being accessed or possibly different rows accessed on the same pages.

To review the differences, let's continue with the query from Listing 3-29 but retrieve the page lock statistics that were collected in sys.dm_db_index_operational_stats for the query. This information is available using the script in Listing 3-31. The results this time are a bit different than those for the row locks. For the page locks, see Figure 3-22; there are only two page locks on the index IX_SalesOrderDetail_ProductID. Along with that, there are 44 page locks on PK_SalesOrderDetail_SalesOrderID_SalesOrderDetailID, which did not encounter any row locks.

Listing 3-31. Query for Page Locks in sys.dm_db_index_operational_stats

```
USE AdventureWorks2017
GO

SELECT OBJECT_NAME(ios.object_id) AS table_name
      ,i.name AS index_name
      ,ios.page_lock_count
      ,ios.page_lock_wait_count
      ,ios.page_lock_wait_in_ms
```

CHAPTER 3 INDEX METADATA AND STATISTICS

```
FROM sys.dm_db_index_operational_stats(DB_ID(),OBJECT_ID('Sales.
SalesOrderDetail'),NULL,NULL) ios
        INNER JOIN sys.indexes i
            ON i.object_id = ios.object_id
            AND i.index_id = ios.index_id
ORDER BY ios.range_scan_count DESC;
```

	table_name	index_name	page_lock_count	page_lock_wait_count	page_lock_wait_in_ms
1	SalesOrderDetail	IX_SalesOrderDetail_ProductID	2	0	0
2	SalesOrderDetail	PK_SalesOrderDetail_SalesOrderID_SalesOrderDet...	44	0	0
3	SalesOrderDetail	AK_SalesOrderDetail_rowguid	0	0	0

Figure 3-22. Query results for page locks

The statistics for the locking behavior may not make sense initially, until you consider the activity that occurred when the query (from Listing 3-29) executed. When the query executed, it utilized an index seek and a key lookup (see the execution plan in Figure 3-23). The index seek on IX_SalesOrderDetail_ProductID accounts for the 2 page locks and the 44 row locks. There were 44 rows that matched the predicate for the query, and they spanned 2 pages. The 44 page locks on PK_SalesOrderDetail_SalesOrderID_SalesOrderDetailID are the result of the key lookup operations that occurred for all the rows from IX_SalesOrderDetail_ProductID. Together, the row and page lock columns help describe the activity that occurred.

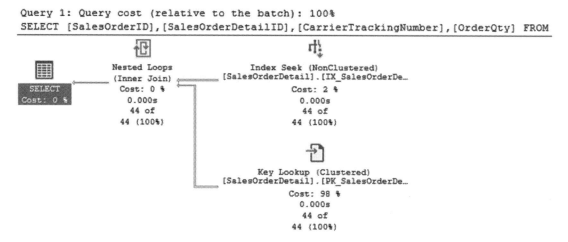

Figure 3-23. Execution plan for SELECT query

While row locking and page locking are useful for identifying when contention exists, there is one piece about locking that it does not provide. There is no information collected in the DMO about the types of locks that are being placed. All the locks could be shared locks, or they could also be exclusive locks. The lock wait count provides scope around the frequency of incompatible locks on the tables and the duration of those locks, but the locks themselves are not identified.

Lock Escalation

The last piece with locking contention to pay attention to is the amount of lock escalation that is occurring in the database. When the number of locks acquired for a transaction exceeds the locking threshold on an SQL Server instance, the locks will escalate to the next higher level of locking. This escalation can happen at the page, partition, and table levels. There are a number of reasons for escalating locks on a database. One reason is that locks require memory, so the more locks there are, the more memory is required and the more resources are needed to manage locks. Another reason is that many individual low-level locks open the opportunity for blocking to escalate into deadlocking. For these reasons, it is important to pay attention to lock escalations.

To help provide an understanding of lock escalation, let's use a modification of the demo query that was used previously in this section. Instead of selecting 44 rows, though, you'll update all the rows where `ProductID` is less than or equal to 712 (see Listing 3-32). The update will just change `ProductID` to its current value so as not to permanently change the data in AdventureWorks2017.

Listing 3-32. T-SQL Script to Generate Lock Promotion

```
USE AdventureWorks2017
GO

UPDATE Sales.SalesOrderDetail
SET ProductID = ProductID
WHERE ProductID <= 712
```

Now with the example script execution, you'll need to review the statistics in `sys.dm_db_index_operational_stats` to see whether there were any lock escalations by using the script in Listing 3-33. As the output from the script shows (Figure 3-24), the column `index_lock_promotion_attempt_count` recorded four events for PK_SalesOrderDetail_SalesOrderID_SalesOrderDetailID and IX_SalesOrderDetail_ProductID. This means that there were four opportunities for lock escalation that were triggered. Looking at the column index_lock_promotion_count, there was one lock escalation on IX_SalesOrderDetail_ProductID. Translating the results into less technical terms, for the two indexes there were four times when SQL Server considered whether a lock escalation was appropriate for the query. At the fourth check on IX_SalesOrderDetail_ProductID, SQL Server determined that a lock escalation was needed, and the lock was escalated.

Listing 3-33. Query for Lock Escalation in sys.dm_db_index_operational_stats

```
USE AdventureWorks2017
GO

SELECT OBJECT_NAME(ios.object_id) AS table_name
      ,i.name AS index_name
      ,ios.index_lock_promotion_attempt_count
      ,ios.index_lock_promotion_count
FROM sys.dm_db_index_operational_stats(DB_ID(),OBJECT_ID('Sales.SalesOrderDetail'),NULL,NULL) ios
      INNER JOIN sys.indexes i
          ON i.object_id = ios.object_id
              AND i.index_id = ios.index_id
ORDER BY ios.range_scan_count DESC;
```

	table_name	index_name	index_lock_promotion_attempt_count	index_lock_promotion_count
1	SalesOrderDetail	PK_SalesOrderDetail_SalesOrderID_SalesOrderDet...	5	0
2	SalesOrderDetail	IX_SalesOrderDetail_ProductID	4	1
3	SalesOrderDetail	AK_SalesOrderDetail_rowguid	0	0

Figure 3-24. *Query results for lock escalation*

Monitoring lock escalation goes hand in hand with monitoring row and page locks. When row and page lock contention increases, either through increased frequency or through duration of lock waits, evaluating lock escalation can help identify the number of times SQL Server considers escalating locks and when those locks have been escalated. In some cases where tables are improperly indexed, locks can escalate more frequently and lead to increased blocking and potentially deadlocking.

Latch Contention

Locking isn't the only type of contention that indexes can encounter. In addition to locking, there is latch contention. Latches are short, lightweight data synchronization objects. From a high level, latches provide controls on memory objects while activities are executing. One example of a latch is when data is transferred from disk to memory. If there are disk bottlenecks while this occurs, latch waits will accumulate while the disk transfer completes. The value in this information is that when latch waits are occurring, the columns (shown in Table 3-16) provide a mechanism to track the waits down to specific indexes, thus allowing you to focus on where indexes are stored as part of index management.

Table 3-16. Latch Activity Columns in sys.dm_db_index_operational_stats

Column Name	Data Type	Description
page_latch_wait_count	bigint	Cumulative number of times the database engine waited because of latch contention.
page_latch_wait_in_ms	bigint	Cumulative number of milliseconds the database engine waited because of latch contention.
page_io_latch_wait_count	bigint	Cumulative number of times the database engine waited on an I/O page latch.
page_io_latch_wait_in_ms	bigint	Cumulative number of milliseconds the database engine waited on a page I/O latch.
tree_page_latch_wait_count	bigint	Subset of page_latch_wait_count that includes only the upper-level B-tree pages. This is always 0 for a heap.
tree_page_latch_wait_in_ms	bigint	Subset of page_latch_wait_in_ms that includes only the upper-level B-tree pages. This is always 0 for a heap.
tree_page_io_latch_wait_count	bigint	Subset of page_io_latch_wait_count that includes only the upper-level B-tree pages. This is always 0 for a heap.
tree_page_io_latch_wait_in_ms	bigint	Subset of page_io_latch_wait_in_ms that includes only the upper-level B-tree pages. This is always 0 for a heap.

Page I/O Latch

When it comes to page I/O latches, two sets of data are collected: page-level latching and tree page latching. Page-level latching occurs when data pages at the leaf levels of an index, the data pages, need to be retrieved (as opposed to tree page latching, which happens at all the other levels of the index). Both of these statistics are measures of the number of latches created while moving data into the buffer and any time related to delays. Whenever time is accumulated in page_io_latch_wait_in_ms or tree_page_io_latch_wait_in_ms, it correlates to increases in wait times for the PAGEIOLATCH_* wait types.

To better understand how page I/O latches occur and the statistics you can collect, you'll review an example that will cause these waits to occur. In this demonstration, you'll return all the data from Sales.SalesOrderDetail, Sales.SalesOrderHeader, and Production.Product via the script in Listing 3-34. Before executing the script, the buffer cache will be purged to force SQL Server to have to retrieve the data for the pages from disk. Be sure to use this script only on a nonproduction server where clearing the buffer cache will not impact other processes.

Listing 3-34. T-SQL Script to Generate Page I/O Latch

```
USE AdventureWorks2017
GO

DBCC DROPCLEANBUFFERS
GO

SELECT *
FROM Sales.SalesOrderDetail sod
INNER JOIN Sales.SalesOrderHeader soh ON sod.SalesOrderID = soh.SalesOrderID
INNER JOIN Production.Product p ON sod.ProductID = p.ProductID;
```

When the query completes, a number of page I/O latches will have occurred while populating the pages for the tables and indexes into the buffer cache. To review the page I/O latches, query against sys.dm_db_index_operational_stats on the page I/O latch columns using the script in Listing 3-35. The results, shown in Figure 3-25, indicate that there were page I/O latch waits on all three of the tables in the example query, including a whole 1 millisecond incurred on Sales.SalesOrderHeader. The results here are highly dependent on the underlying storage, so if your numbers are radically different, that's a difference in hardware performance vs. an issue with the query. If they are excessively high, you may want to consider some analysis of the disk system.

Listing 3-35. Query for Page I/O Latch Statistics in sys.dm_db_index_ operational_stats

```
USE AdventureWorks2017
GO

SELECT OBJECT_SCHEMA_NAME(ios.object_id) + '.' + OBJECT_NAME(ios.object_id)
as table_name
    ,i.name as index_name
    ,page_io_latch_wait_count
    ,page_io_latch_wait_in_ms
    ,CAST(1. * page_io_latch_wait_in_ms
      / NULLIF(page_io_latch_wait_count ,0) AS decimal(12,2)) AS page_io_
      avg_lock_wait_ms
FROM sys.dm_db_index_operational_stats (DB_ID(), NULL, NULL, NULL) ios
INNER JOIN sys.indexes i ON i.object_id = ios.object_id AND i.index_id =
ios.index_id
WHERE i.object_id = OBJECT_ID('Sales.SalesOrderHeader')
OR i.object_id = OBJECT_ID('Sales.SalesOrderDetail')
OR i.object_id = OBJECT_ID('Production.Product')
ORDER BY 5 DESC;
```

	table_name	index_name	page_io_latch_wait_count	page_io_latch_wait_in_ms	page_io_avg_lock_wait_ms
1	Sales.SalesOrderHeader	IX_SalesOrderHeader_SalesPersonID	1	1	1.00
2	Sales.SalesOrderHeader	PK_SalesOrderHeader_SalesOrderID	77	60	0.78
3	Sales.SalesOrderDetail	PK_SalesOrderDetail_SalesOrderID_SalesOrderDet...	1	0	0.00
4	Production.Product	PK_Product_ProductID	4	0	0.00
5	Sales.SalesOrderHeader	IX_SalesOrderHeader_CustomerID	1	0	0.00
6	Sales.SalesOrderDetail	AK_SalesOrderDetail_rowguid	0	0	NULL
7	Sales.SalesOrderDetail	IX_SalesOrderDetail_ProductID	0	0	NULL
8	Production.Product	AK_Product_ProductNumber	0	0	NULL
9	Production.Product	AK_Product_Name	0	0	NULL
10	Production.Product	AK_Product_rowguid	0	0	NULL
11	Sales.SalesOrderHeader	AK_SalesOrderHeader_rowguid	0	0	NULL
12	Sales.SalesOrderHeader	AK_SalesOrderHeader_SalesOrderNumber	0	0	NULL

Figure 3-25. *Query results for page I/O latch*

Page Latch

The other kind of latching related to indexes that can occur in databases is page latching. Page latching covers any latching that occurs on nondata pages. Page latches include allocation of GAM and SGAM pages and DBCC and backup activities. As pages are allocated by different resources, contention can occur, and monitoring page latches can uncover this activity.

When it comes to an index, one common scenario in which page latches can occur is when a "hotspot" develops on an index because of frequent inserts or page allocations. To demonstrate this scenario, you'll create the table dbo.PageLatchDemo in Listing 3-36. Next, using your preferred load generator tool, execute five sessions of the code in Listing 3-37. To generate the load for this example, five query windows in SQL Server Management Studio run a copy of the load query. Through this example, hundreds of rows will be inserted quickly into the same series of pages, and numerous page allocations will be made. Since these inserts will be so close, a "hotspot" will be created, which will lead to page latch contention.

Listing 3-36. T-SQL Script to Generate Page Latch Scenario

```
USE AdventureWorks2017
GO

IF OBJECT_ID('dbo.PageLatchDemo') IS NOT NULL
        DROP TABLE dbo.PageLatchDemo;

CREATE TABLE dbo.PageLatchDemo
(
PageLatchDemoID INT IDENTITY (1,1)
,FillerData  bit
,CONSTRAINT PK_PageLatchDemo_PageLatchDemoID PRIMARY KEY
CLUSTERED  (PageLatchDemoID)
);
```

CHAPTER 3 INDEX METADATA AND STATISTICS

Listing 3-37. T-SQL Script to Generate Page Latch Load

```
USE AdventureWorks2017
GO

INSERT INTO dbo.PageLatchDemo
 (FillerData)
SELECT  t.object_id % 2
FROM sys.tables t;
GO 5000
```

To verify that the page latch contention did occur, use the script provided in Listing 3-38. The results, provided in Figure 3-26, show that there were numerous page latches and delays associated with them. In this example, the delay per page latch was over 20 milliseconds. In more critical situations, these values will be much higher and will help you identify when an index is interfering with accessing or writing data to an index.

Listing 3-38. Query for Page Latch Statistics in sys.dm_db_index_operational_stats

```
SELECT OBJECT_SCHEMA_NAME(ios.object_id) + '.' + OBJECT_NAME(ios.object_id)
as table_name
,i.name as index_name
,page_latch_wait_count
,page_latch_wait_in_ms
,CAST(100. * page_latch_wait_in_ms
      / NULLIF(page_latch_wait_count ,0) AS decimal(12,2)) AS page_avg_
      lock_wait_ms
FROM sys.dm_db_index_operational_stats (DB_ID(), NULL, NULL, NULL) ios
INNER JOIN sys.indexes i ON i.object_id = ios.object_id AND i.index_id =
ios.index_id
WHERE i.object_id = OBJECT_ID('dbo.PageLatchDemo');
```

	table_name	index_name	page_latch_wait_count	page_latch_wait_in_ms	page_avg_lock_wait_ms
1	dbo.PageLatchDemo	PK_PageLatchDemo_PageLatchDemoID	489858	105096	21.45

Figure 3-26. *Query results for page latch*

> **Note** Page I/O and page latch contentions are highly dependent on hardware. Your results for the demonstration queries in this section will not identically match the results shown.

Page Allocation Cycle

As a result of the DML activity, leaf and nonleaf pages are allocated or deallocated from indexes from time to time. Monitoring page allocations is an important part of monitoring an index (see Table 3-17 for options). Through this monitoring, it is possible to get a handle on how an index is "breathing" between maintenance windows. This breathing activity is the relationship between pages allocated to indexes through inserts and page splits and then the removal, or merging, of pages through deletes. By monitoring this activity, you can better maintain your indexes and get an idea of when it would be useful to increase the index FILLFACTOR value.

Table 3-17. Page Allocation Cycle Columns in sys.dm_db_index_operational_stats

Column Name	Data Type	Description
leaf_allocation_count	bigint	Cumulative count of leaf-level page allocations in the index or heap.
nonleaf_allocation_count	bigint	Cumulative count of page allocations caused by page splits above the leaf level.
leaf_page_merge_count	bigint	Cumulative count of page merges at the leaf level.
nonleaf_page_merge_count	bigint	Cumulative count of page merges above the leaf level.

As an example of how page allocation occurs on a table, execute the script in Listing 3-39. In this script, the table dbo.AllocationCycle is created. Afterward, 100,000 rows are inserted into the table. Since this is a new table, there is no contention on page allocations, and data is added in an orderly fashion. At this point, pages have been allocated to the table, and the allocations relate specifically to these inserts. This script will run for a minute or more. Be sure that Include Actual Execution Plan is not enabled when this is executed.

Listing 3-39. T-SQL Script to Generate Page Allocations

```
USE AdventureWorks2017;
GO

SET NOCOUNT ON

DROP TABLE IF EXISTS dbo.AllocationCycle;

CREATE TABLE dbo.AllocationCycle (
    ID INT IDENTITY,
    FillerData VARCHAR(1000),
    CreateDate DATETIME,
    CONSTRAINT PK_AllocationCycle PRIMARY KEY CLUSTERED (ID)
);
GO

INSERT INTO dbo.AllocationCycle (FillerData, CreateDate)
VALUES (NEWID(), GETDATE());
GO 100000
```

To verify the allocations, you can check the leaf and nonleaf allocation columns leaf_allocation_count and nonleaf_allocation_count from sys.dm_db_index_operational_stats. Using the script in Listing 3-40, you see that there are 758 allocations at the leaf level and 3 at the nonleaf level (see Figure 3-27). This is an important point to remember whenever using these columns: a portion of the pages allocated can be insert-related.

Listing 3-40. Query for Page Latch Statistics in sys.dm_db_index_operational_stats

```
USE AdventureWorks2017
GO

SELECT OBJECT_SCHEMA_NAME(ios.object_id) + '.' + OBJECT_NAME(ios.object_id)
as table_name
  ,i.name as index_name
  ,ios.leaf_allocation_count
  ,ios.nonleaf_allocation_count
  ,ios.leaf_page_merge_count
```

```
        ,ios.nonleaf_page_merge_count
FROM sys.dm_db_index_operational_stats(DB_ID(), OBJECT_ID('dbo.
AllocationCycle'), NULL,NULL) ios
    INNER JOIN sys.indexes i ON i.object_id = ios.object_id AND i.index_id =
    ios.index_id;
```

	table_name	index_name	leaf_allocation_count	nonleaf_allocation_count	leaf_page_merge_count	nonleaf_page_merge_count
1	dbo.AllocationCycle	PK_AllocationCycle	758	3	0	0

Figure 3-27. Query results for insert page allocations

Note After SQL Server 2014, the behavior for these columns changed. On bulk inserts, only a single page is recorded for the leaf_allocation_count.

At the start of this section, there was a reference to using page allocations to monitor for page splits and to identify where modifications to the fill factor can be useful. To understand this, you first need to generate page splits on the dbo.AllocationCycle table. You can do so using the script in Listing 3-41. This script increases the length of the FillerData column on every third row to 1,000 characters.

Listing 3-41. T-SQL Script to Increase Page Allocations

```
USE AdventureWorks2017;
GO

UPDATE  dbo.AllocationCycle
SET     FillerData = REPLICATE('x',1000)
WHERE   ID % 3 = 1;
```

Once the data is modified, the results from executing the sys.dm_db_index_operational_stats query in Listing 3-40 change drastically. With the size of the rows expanding, the number of pages allocated jumps up to 9,849 with a total of 35 nonleaf pages (Figure 3-28). Since the order of the rows hasn't changed, this activity is related to page splits from expanding the sizes of the rows. By monitoring these statistics, indexes affected by this pattern of activity can be identified.

	table_name	index_name	leaf_allocation_count	nonleaf_allocation_count	leaf_page_merge_count	nonleaf_page_merge_count
1	dbo.AllocationCycle	PK_AllocationCycle	9849	35	0	0

***Figure 3-28.** Query results for update page allocations*

Compression

While not the most exciting set of columns, there are two columns in `sys.dm_db_index_operational_stats` that are used for monitoring compression. These columns, listed in Table 3-18, count the number of attempts that have been made at compressing a page and then the number of successful attempts in doing so. The primary value in these columns is providing feedback on PAGE-level compression. Failures can lead to decisions to remove compression because it is usually not practical to have compression enabled when there is a high rate of failure with compression.

***Table 3-18.** Compression Columns in sys.dm_db_index_operational_stats*

Column Name	Data Type	Description
page_compression_attempt_count	bigint	Number of pages that were evaluated for PAGE-level compression for specific partitions of a table, index, or indexed view. Includes pages that were not compressed because significant savings could not be achieved.
page_compression_success_count	bigint	Number of data pages that were compressed by using PAGE-level compression for specific partitions of a table, index, or indexed view.

Page compression can fail when the cost to compress the data exceeds the value in uncompressing that data later. This is typically found in data that has low patterns of repeating data, such as images. When image data is compressed, it often does not receive sufficient benefit from the compression, and SQL Server will not store the page as a compressed page. To demonstrate this, execute the code in Listing 3-42, which creates a table with page compression enabled and inserts a number of images into it.

CHAPTER 3 INDEX METADATA AND STATISTICS

Listing 3-42. T-SQL Script to create table with page compression

```
USE AdventureWorks2017
GO

IF OBJECT_ID('dbo.PageCompression') IS NOT NULL
        DROP TABLE dbo.PageCompression;

CREATE TABLE dbo.PageCompression(
        ProductPhotoID int NOT NULL,
        ThumbNailPhoto varbinary(max) NULL,
        LargePhoto varbinary(max) NULL,
    CONSTRAINT PK_PageCompression PRIMARY KEY CLUSTERED (ProductPhotoID))
    WITH (DATA_COMPRESSION = PAGE);

INSERT INTO dbo.PageCompression
SELECT ProductPhotoID
    ,ThumbNailPhoto
    ,LargePhoto
FROM Production.ProductPhoto;
```

The insert into the table doesn't fail, but are all the pages compressed? To find out, execute the script in Listing 3-43; it returns the page_compression_attempt_count and page_compression_success_count columns. As the results show (Figure 3-29), 7 pages were successfully compressed, but another 46 pages failed to compress. With this ratio of success to failures for page compression, it is easy to see that the value of page compression on the clustered index on dbo.PageCompression is not very high.

Listing 3-43. Query for page compression attempts in sys.dm_db_index_operational_stats

```
USE AdventureWorks2017
GO

SELECT OBJECT_SCHEMA_NAME(ios.object_id) + '.' + OBJECT_NAME(ios.object_id)
as table_name
,i.name as index_name
,page_compression_attempt_count
,page_compression_success_count
```

```
FROM sys.dm_db_index_operational_stats (DB_ID(), OBJECT_ID('dbo.
PageCompression'), NULL, NULL) ios
    INNER JOIN sys.indexes i ON i.object_id = ios.object_id AND i.index_id
    = ios.index_id;
```

	table_name	index_name	page_compression_attempt_count	page_compression_success_count
1	dbo.PageCompression	PK_PageCompression	46	7

Figure 3-29. Query results for compression

LOB Access

The next group of columns in `sys.dm_db_index_operational_stats` pertains to large objects (LOBs). They provide information on the number of pages fetched and the size of those pages. Also, there are columns that measure the amount of LOB data that is pushed off and pulled into rows. Table 3-19 lists all these columns and others in this group.

Table 3-19. LOB Access Columns in sys.dm_db_index_operational_stats

Column Name	Data Type	Description
lob_fetch_in_pages	bigint	Cumulative count of LOB pages retrieved from the LOB_DATA allocation unit. These pages contain data that is stored in columns of type text, ntext, image, varchar(max), nvarchar(max), varbinary(max), and xml.
lob_fetch_in_bytes	bigint	Cumulative count of LOB data bytes retrieved.
lob_orphan_create_count	bigint	Cumulative count of orphan LOB values created for bulk operations.
lob_orphan_insert_count	bigint	Cumulative count of orphan LOB values inserted during bulk operations.
row_overflow_fetch_in_pages	bigint	Cumulative count of row-overflow data pages retrieved from the ROW_OVERFLOW_DATA allocation unit.
row_overflow_fetch_in_bytes	bigint	Cumulative count of row-overflow data bytes retrieved.

(continued)

Table 3-19. (*continued*)

Column Name	Data Type	Description
column_value_push_off_row_count	bigint	Cumulative count of column values for LOB data and row-overflow data that is pushed off-row to make an inserted or updated row fit within a page.
column_value_pull_in_row_count	bigint	Cumulative count of column values for LOB data and row-overflow data that is pulled in-row. This occurs when an update operation frees up space in a record and provides an opportunity to pull in one or more off-row values from the LOB_DATA or ROW_OVERFLOW_DATA allocation unit to the IN_ROW_DATA allocation unit.

The LOB access columns can be useful in determining the volume of large object activity and when data may be moving from large object to in-row-overflow storage. This is important when you are seeing performance issues related to retrieving or updating LOB data. For instance, the column lob_fetch_in_bytes measures the bytes from LOB columns retrieved by SQL Server for the index.

To demonstrate some LOB activity, run the script in Listing 3-44. This script doesn't represent all the possible activity, but it does cover the basics. At the start of the script, the table dbo.LOBAccess is created with the column LOBValue, which uses a large object data type. The first operation against the table inserts ten rows that are narrow enough that the LOBValue values can be stored on the data page with the rows. The second operation increases the size of the LOBValue column forcing it to expand outside the 8 KB max for a data row. The final operation retrieves all the rows from the table.

Listing 3-44. T-SQL Script to create table with LOB data

```
USE AdventureWorks2017
GO

IF OBJECT_ID('dbo.LOBAccess') IS NOT NULL
    DROP TABLE dbo.LOBAccess;

CREATE TABLE dbo.LOBAccess
  (
  ID INT IDENTITY(1,1) PRIMARY KEY CLUSTERED
  ,LOBValue VARCHAR(MAX)
```

CHAPTER 3 INDEX METADATA AND STATISTICS

```
,FillerData CHAR(2000) DEFAULT(REPLICATE('X',2000))
,FillerDate DATETIME DEFAULT(GETDATE())
);

INSERT INTO dbo.LOBAccess (LOBValue)
SELECT TOP 10 'Short Value'
FROM Production.ProductPhoto;

UPDATE dbo.LOBAccess
SET LOBValue = REPLICATE('Long Value',8000);

SELECT * FROM dbo.LOBAccess;
```

Using the LOB access columns listed in Table 3-20, you can observe what happens under the covers with the script in Listing 3-45. As the output in Figure 3-30 shows, the column column_value_push_off_row_count tracked ten row operations on the index where the row moved in-row data off into large object storage. The operation coincided with the update that increased the length of the rows. The other two statistics that were accumulated, lob_fetch_in_pages and lob_fetch_in_bytes, detail the number of pages and the size of the data retrieved during the SELECT statement. As these statistics show, the LOB access statistics provide granular tracking of LOB activity.

Listing 3-45. Query for LOB access in sys.dm_db_index_operational_stats

```
USE AdventureWorks2017
GO

SELECT OBJECT_SCHEMA_NAME(ios.object_id) + '.' + OBJECT_NAME(ios.object_id)
as table_name
    ,i.name as index_name
    ,lob_fetch_in_pages
    ,lob_fetch_in_bytes
    ,lob_orphan_create_count
    ,lob_orphan_insert_count
    ,row_overflow_fetch_in_pages
    ,row_overflow_fetch_in_bytes
    ,column_value_push_off_row_count
    ,column_value_pull_in_row_count
```

```
FROM sys.dm_db_index_operational_stats (DB_ID(), OBJECT_ID('dbo.
LOBAccess'), NULL, NULL) ios
INNER JOIN sys.indexes i ON i.object_id = ios.object_id AND i.index_id =
ios.index_id;
```

table_name	index_name	lob_fetch_in_pages	lob_fetch_in_bytes	lob_orphan_create_...	lob_orphan_insert_...	row_overflow_fetch_...	row_overflow_fetch_...	column_value_push_...	column_value_pull_...
dbo.LOBAccess	PK__LOBAcces__3214EC27485BDA59	30	80000	0	0	0	0	10	0

Figure 3-30. Query results for LOB access

Row Version

The last group of columns in sys.dm_db_index_operational_stats report on version counts within indexes due to snapshot isolation columns. These columns are new to SQL Server 2019. While this book won't demonstrate their use within snapshot isolation levels, they are included in the chapter for completeness.

Table 3-20. Row Version Columns in sys.dm_db_index_operational_stats

Column Name	Data Type	Description
version_generated_inrow	bigint	Number of in-row version records retained by snapshot isolation transaction.
version_generated_offrow	bigint	Number of off-row version records retained by snapshot isolation transaction.
ghost_version_inrow	bigint	Number of in-row ghost version records retained by snapshot isolation transaction.
ghost_version_offrow	bigint	Number of off-row ghost version records retained by snapshot isolation transaction.
insert_over_ghost_version_inrow	bigint	Number of in-row inserts over ghost version records retained by snapshot isolation transaction.
insert_over_ghost_version_offrow	bigint	Number of off-row inserts over ghost version records retained by snapshot isolation transaction.

Index Operational Stats Summary

This section discussed the statistics available in the DMO sys.dm_db_index_operational_stats. While it isn't a DMO that is widely used, it does provide a lot of low-level detail regarding indexes that can be leveraged to dig deep into how indexes are behaving. From the columns on DML and SELECT activity to locking contention to compression, the columns in this DMO provide a wealth of information.

Index Physical Statistics

The last area of statistics that SQL Server collects is the index physical stats. These statistics report information about the current structure of the index along with the physical effect of insert, update, and delete operations on indexes. These statistics are collected in the DMO sys.dm_db_index_physical_stats.

Just like sys.dm_db_index_operational_stats, sys.dm_db_index_physical_stats is a dynamic management function. To use the DMF, a number of parameters need to be supplied when it is used. Listing 3-46 details the parameters for the DMF.

Listing 3-46. Parameters for sys.dm_db_index_physical_stats

```
sys.dm_db_index_physical_stats (
    { database_id | NULL | 0 | DEFAULT }
  , { object_id | NULL | 0 | DEFAULT }
  , { index_id | NULL | 0 | -1 | DEFAULT }
  , { partition_number | NULL | 0 | DEFAULT }
  , { mode | NULL | DEFAULT }
)
```

The mode parameter for sys.dm_db_index_physical_stats accepts one of five values: DEFAULT, NULL, LIMITED, SAMPLED, or DETAILED. DEFAULT, NULL, and LIMITED are in effect the same value and will be described together. Table 3-21 lists the parameters.

> **Note** The DMF sys.dm_db_index_physical_stats can accept the use of the Transact SQL functions DB_ID() and OBJECT_ID(). These functions can be used for the parameters database_id and object_id, respectively.

Table 3-21. Parameters for sys.dm_db_index_physical_stats

Parameter Name	Description
LIMITED	The fastest mode that scans the smallest number of pages. For an index, only the parent-level pages of the B-tree are scanned. In a heap, only the associated PFS and IAM pages are examined.
SAMPLED	This mode returns statistics based on a 1 percent sample of all the pages in the index or heap. If the index or heap has fewer than 10,000 pages, DETAILED mode is used instead of SAMPLED.
DETAILED	This mode scans all pages, both leaf and nonleaf, of an index and returns all statistics.

When executed, there are three areas of information that are reported from the DMF: header columns, row statistics, and fragmentation statistics. One word of caution: This DMF gathers the information that it reports as it is executed. If your system is heavily used, this DMF can interfere with production workloads.

Header Columns

The first set of columns returned from sys.dm_db_index_physical_stats are the header columns. These columns provide metadata and descriptive information around the types of information that are included in that row of the results. The header columns for this are listed in Table 3-22. The most important information to pay attention to when looking at the header columns are the alloc_unit_type_desc and index_level. These two columns provide information on what type of data is being reported on and where in the index the statistics are originating from.

CHAPTER 3 INDEX METADATA AND STATISTICS

Table 3-22. Header Columns for sys.dm_db_index_physical_stats

Column Name	Data Type	Description
database_id	smallint	Database ID of the table or view.
object_id	int	Object ID of the table or view that the index is on.
index_id	int	Index ID of an index.
partition_number	int	1-based partition number within the owning object: a table, view, or index.
index_type_desc	nvarchar(60)	Description of the index type.
hobt_id	bigint	Heap or B-tree ID of the index or partition.
alloc_unit_type_desc	nvarchar(60)	Description of the allocation unit type.
index_depth	tinyint	Number of index levels.
index_level	tinyint	Current level of the index.

Row Statistics

The second group of columns in sys.dm_db_index_physical_stats are the row statistics columns. These columns provide statistics on the rows contained in the index, shown in Table 3-23. From the number of pages in the index to the record count, these columns provide some general statistics along these lines. There are a few items of interest in these columns that can be quite useful.

Table 3-23. Row Statistics Columns for sys.dm_db_index_physical_stats

Column Name	Data Type	Description
page_count	bigint	Total number of index or data pages.
record_count	bigint	Total number of records.
ghost_record_count	bigint	Number of ghost records ready for removal by the ghost cleanup task in the allocation unit.
version_ghost_record_count	bigint	Number of ghost records retained by an outstanding snapshot isolation transaction in an allocation unit.
min_record_size_in_bytes	int	Minimum record size in bytes.

(*continued*)

Table 3-23. (*continued*)

Column Name	Data Type	Description
max_record_size_in_bytes	int	Maximum record size in bytes.
avg_record_size_in_bytes	float	Average record size in bytes.
forwarded_record_count	bigint	Number of records in a heap that have forward pointers to another data location.
compressed_page_count	bigint	The number of compressed pages.

The first items of interest are the columns ghost_record_count and version_ghost_record_count. These columns provide a breakdown of the ghost_record_count found in sys.dm_db_index_operational_stats.

The next column to check is forwarded_record_count. This column provides an accounting to the number of forwarded records in a heap. This was discussed some in sys.dm_db_index_operational_stats with the forwarded_fetch_count column. In that DMF, the count was because of the number of times that forwarded records were accessed. In sys.dm_db_index_operational_stats, the count refers to the number of forwarded records that exist within the table.

The last column to look at is compressed_page_count. The compressed page count provides a count of all the pages in an index that have been compressed. This helps provide a measure of value in having pages compressed by PAGE-level compression.

Fragmentation Statistics

The last group of statistics in the DMF are the fragmentation statistics. For the most part, fragmentation is what most frequently turns people to looking at sys.dm_db_index_physical_stats. Fragmentation occurs in indexes when rows are inserted or modified in an index where the row no longer fits on the page where the index should be placed. When this happens, the page is split to move half of the page to another page. Since there usually isn't a contiguous page available after the page that has been split, the page gets moved to an available free page. This results in gaps in an index where pages are expected to be continuous, preventing SQL Server from completing sequential reads while reading an index on disk.

CHAPTER 3 ■ INDEX METADATA AND STATISTICS

There are four columns, shown in Table 3-24, that provide the information needed to analyze the state of fragmentation within an index. Each of these helps provide a view on the extent of the fragmentation and assists in determining how to resolve or mitigate the fragmentation.

Table 3-24. *Fragmentation Statistics Columns for sys.dm_db_index_physical_stats*

Column Name	Data Type	Description
avg_fragmentation_in_percent	float	Logical fragmentation for indexes or extent fragmentation for heaps in the IN_ROW_DATA allocation unit.
fragment_count	bigint	Number of fragments in the leaf level of an IN_ROW_DATA allocation unit.
avg_fragment_size_in_pages	float	Average number of pages in one fragment in the leaf level of an IN_ROW_DATA allocation unit.
avg_page_space_used_in_percent	float	Average percentage of available data storage space used in all pages.

The first fragment column is the avg_fragmentation_in_percent. This column provides a percent count of the amount of fragmentation in an index. As fragmentation increases, SQL Server will likely see an increase in the amount of physical I/Os required to retrieve data from the database. Using this column, you can build a maintenance plan to mitigate fragmentation by either rebuilding or reorganizing the index. The general guideline is to reorganize indexes with less than 30 percent fragmentation and to rebuild indexes with more than 30 percent fragmentation.

The next column, fragment_count, provides a count of all the fragments in an index. For each fragment created in an index, this column will summarize a count of those pages.

The third column is avg_fragment_size_in_pages. This column represents the average number of pages that are in each fragment. The higher this value is and the closer it is to page_count, the less I/O that SQL Server requires to read the data.

The last column is avg_page_space_used_in_percent. This column provides information on the amount of space available on pages. An index with little DML activity should be as close to 100 percent as possible. If there are no updates expected on an index, the goal should be to have the index as compacted as possible.

Index Physical Stats Summary

The primary purpose in looking at sys.dm_db_index_physical_stats is to help guide index maintenance. Through this DMF, statistics at every level of an index can be analyzed. Through this, the appropriate amount of maintenance for each level of an index can be identified. Whether the need is to defragment the index, modify the fill factor, or pad the index, the information in sys.dm_db_index_physical_stats can help guide this activity.

Columnstore Statistics

As discussed in the last chapter, columnstore indexes use a structure quite different from the typical B-tree or heap, sometimes considered rowstores. Due to these differences, there are some differences in the statistics collected for these indexes that relate to the underlying architecture and how it is accessed. To provide visibility to these different aspects, there are two DMOs that focus on the physical and operational statistics for columnstore statistics.

Columnstore Physical Stats

The first piece to look at is the physical statistics being collected on columnstore indexes. This information can be accessed through the DMO sys.dm_db_column_store_row_group_physical_stats. This DMO has a row-per-rowgroup within a columnstore index. Recalling in the last chapter, there will be a rowgroup per column and up to one per million records in the table.

Header Columns

As you've started with the previous sections, we'll start with the header columns for the DMO. Since there is a row-per-rowgroup, each row will include object_id, index_id, partition_number, row_group_id, and delta_store_hobt_id. These columns are defined further in Table 3-25. Like other indexes, the partition_number validates that columnstore indexes can be partitioned. For nonpartitioned columnstore indexes, the partition number will be 1.

Table 3-25. *Header Columns in sys.dm_db_column_store_row_group_physical_stats*

Column Name	Data Type	Description
object_id	int	ID of the table or view on which the index is defined.
index_id	int	ID of the index.
partition_number	int	1-based partition number within the index or heap.
row_group_id	bigint	ID of the rowgroup.
delta_store_hobt_id	bigint	ID of hobt_id of the rowgroup deltastore. If NULL, there is not an associated deltastore for the rowgroup.

Statistics Columns

The statistics columns for sys.dm_db_column_store_row_group_physical_stats provide a lot of metadata for columnstore indexes that can assist in understanding how the columnstore is constructed. The statistics, defined in Table 3-26, provide insight necessary for managing your columnstore indexes. For example, you can leverage total_rows and deleted_rows to determine the portion of a rowgroup that is still active. In some cases, aggressive modifications on a rowgroup could leave empty rowgroups on your tables. Also, when the rowgroups are smaller than the million rows, the state, trim reason, and transition to compressed information can help identify how rowgroups are being compressed. For instance, if you have a large number of small rowgroups that are being closed due to BULKLOAD, it may be worthwhile to rebuild those rowgroups or make modification to the load process to try to aim for rowgroups with more rows.

Table 3-26. *Stats Columns in sys.dm_db_column_store_row_group_physical_stats*

Column Name	Data Type	Description
state	tinyint	ID number associated with state_description.
state_desc	nvarchar(60)	Description of the rowgroup state, which can be INVISIBLE, OPEN, CLOSED, COMPRESSED, or TOMBSTONE.
total_rows	bigint	Full count of rows in the rowgroup including any row that has been marked deleted.
deleted_rows	bigint	Number of rows in the rowgroup marked for deletion.
size_in_bytes	bigint	Size of the rowgroup in bytes.
trim_reason	tinyint	ID number associated with the trim_reason_desc.
trim_reason_desc	nvarchar(60)	Description of why a COMPRESSED rowgroup has less than the million-row maximum of rows, which can be NO_TRIM, BULKLOAD, ROERG, DICTIONARY SIZE, MEMORY LIMITATION, RESIDUAL ROW GROUP, STATS MISMATCH, or SPILLOVER.
transition_to_compressed_state	tinyint	ID number associated with the transition_to_compressed_state_desc.
transition_to_compressed_state_desc	nvarchar(60)	Description of how the rowgroup transitions from a deltastore to a rowgroup, which includes NOT APPLICABLE, INDEX BUILD, TUPLE MOVER, REORG NORMAL, REORG FORCED, BULKLOAD, or MERGE.
has_vertipaq_optimization	bit	Boolean identifying whether Vertipaq optimization was used during compression. When not used, compression will not be as efficient as when it is used.
generation	bigint	Rowgroup generation associated with this rowgroup.
created_time	datetime2	Clock time for when this rowgroup was created.
closed_time	datetime2	Clock time for when this rowgroup was closed.

CHAPTER 3 INDEX METADATA AND STATISTICS

Columnstore Operational Stats

The other piece for columnstore indexes is to look at their operational statistics through the DMO sys.dm_db_column_store_row_group_operational_stats. This DMO also returns one row per rowgroup within a columnstore index. Recalling in the last chapter, there will be a rowgroup per column and up to one per million records in the table.

Header Columns

The header columns for sys.dm_db_column_store_row_group_operational_stats are similar to those of the columnstore physical stats DMO. The exception is that there isn't a deltastore reference, meaning this DMO returns the columns object_id, index_id, partition_number, and row_group_id. These columns are defined in Table 3-27.

Table 3-27. Header Columns in sys.dm_db_column_store_row_group_operational_stats

Column Name	Data Type	Description
object_id	int	ID of the table or view on which the index is defined.
index_id	int	ID of the index.
partition_number	int	1-based partition number within the index or heap.
row_group_id	bigint	ID of the rowgroup.

Statistics Columns

The interesting information for sys.dm_db_column_store_row_group_operational_stats comes from the stats columns. In these columns, defined in Table 3-28, there are details about the number of scans for the rowgroup, the number of times the delete rows were scanned, and the number of times the partition for the columnstore was scanned. This can help you identify how useful the rowgroup and its min and max values are for the queries that access the table and determine when the number of deleted rows might be becoming a hindrance to the usefulness of the rowgroup when they are being excessively accessed. Additionally, you can see if there are locks and blocking transactions negatively impacting the accessibility of the rowgroup, helping you know when there are potential IO or transactional bottlenecks that need to be addressed.

Table 3-28. *Stats Columns in sys.dm_db_column_store_row_group_operational_stats*

Column Name	Data Type	Description
scan_count	int	Number of scans through the rowgroup since the last SQL restart.
delete_buffer_scan_count	int	Number of times the delete buffer was used to determine deleted rows in this rowgroup. This includes accessing the in-memory hashtable and the underlying B-tree.
index_scan_count	int	Number of times the columnstore index partition was scanned. This is the same for all rowgroups in the partition.
rowgroup_lock_count	bigint	Cumulative count of lock requests for this rowgroup since the last SQL restart.
rowgroup_lock_wait_count	bigint	Cumulative number of times the database engine waited on this rowgroup lock since the last SQL restart.
rowgroup_lock_wait_in_ms	bigint	Cumulative number of milliseconds the database engine waited on this rowgroup lock since the last SQL restart.

Summary

In this chapter, you looked at the statistical information available in SQL Server on indexes. From statistics on cardinality to the physical layout of an index, you learned what information is available and how to retrieve it. For the most part, this information is the tip of the iceberg. In upcoming chapters, you'll leverage this information by looking at the statistics that have been captured and leveraging them to improve your ability to index your database.

CHAPTER 4

XML Indexes

The past couple chapters focused on indexing what is commonly referred to as *structured data*, where there is a common schema and organization around the data and its storage. In this chapter and the next few chapters, the indexing focus shifts to unstructured and semistructured data. With both structured and unstructured data, the task of indexing is to gain optimal efficiency for retrieving and manipulating data, but the data types that represent these types of data have differences in how they are stored in the database. These differences dictate how and why indexing is implemented as well as how the indexes are used by the query optimizer.

SQL Server has a specialized data type for storing the most common type of unstructured and semistructured data, XML. This chapter explores the types of indexes offered by SQL Server for dealing with XML data. The chapter will also show the impact of those indexes on the types of queries that can be written against XML data using XQuery and the impact on the choices made by the optimizer.

XML Data

Extensible Markup Language (XML) was developed through the 1990s and introduced as a standard by the World Wide Web Consortium in February 1998. XML data has been stored in databases for years but until SQL Server 2005 did not have a dedicated data type or access methods. When introduced, the XML data type extended the capabilities of SQL Server to appropriately manage this different data structure. With the acceptance of XML, the use and size of the total XML content within SQL Server databases grew. The growth was spurred by the advantages that XML offered application developers.

Benefits

The introduction of the XML data type allowed for the full capability of XML storage inside an SQL Server database. This included the ability to retrieve XML contents based on queries written against the XML itself. The strongest support that XML offers developers is that it is both text-based and, nominally, self-documenting. Being text-based means that XML is easily passed from one application to another, regardless of underlying operating system or programming language. The self-documenting nature of XML means that you don't need to actually have a structure defined in the same way as columns and tables are defined within a database. Instead, the elements and properties of the XML will tell you what they are. XML is referred to as *semistructured* because there is generally a template defining an expected structure in order to help validate that any given set of XML is considered to be well-formed.

Indexing XML can be a huge benefit if you are doing a lot XML processing on your system. The largest benefit for XML indexes will be in situations where you have large amounts of XML stored but you're retrieving only small subsets of that XML. XML indexes benefit this situation greatly. If you have a lot of queries on your XML, you may also see improvements here when XML indexes are implemented.

Cautions

Although the XML data type sounds like a perfect fit for every instance of XML, some considerations should be contemplated when designing a column in SQL Server that will be storing XML. One of the most critical is that the XML content should be well-formed. This ensures that the XML data type and features provided to utilize the data most efficiently are used to their full advantage. XML columns are stored as binary large objects, more commonly known as BLOBs. This storage means that runtime querying of the content is resource-intensive and slow in most cases. With any task that involves data retrieval, efficiency of that retrieval is of concern. In SQL Server, indexing is paramount to how efficient or nonefficient this can be. A complete lack of indexing or too many indexes will affect any data manipulation task. The XML data type also falls into this requirement. XML indexing is unique compared to the other indexing methods in SQL Server.

XML Indexes

XML indexes fall into two main categories: Primary/Secondary and Selective XML indexes. The main difference between these index types is how much of the XML data is included within the index. For Primary/Secondary indexes, all paths, nodes, and values are included in the index. This works well when it is unknown what portions of the XML will be most accessed. Alternatively, if only a limited portion of the XML will be accessed, then a Selective XML index can provide better performance since the volume of data indexed is reduced. The next two sections will explore and fully explain these categories of XML indexes.

Primary/Secondary XML Indexes

As the name implies, there are two types of indexes that fall under Primary/Secondary XML indexes, which are Primary and Secondary indexes. These two index types provide an indexing relationship within the XML documents similar to the relationship between clustered and nonclustered indexes. When implementing XML indexes, some basic rules apply to each:

- Only one Primary XML index can exist on a column, though multiple Primary XML indexes can exist on a table.

- Primary XML indexes cannot exist without a clustered index on the primary key of the table that the XML column is in. This clustered index is required for partitioning the table, and the XML index can use the same partitioning scheme and functioning.

- Primary XML indexes include all paths, tags, and values of the XML content.

- A Secondary XML index cannot exist without a Primary XML index.

- A Secondary XML index extends the Primary index including paths, values, and properties.

To demonstrate the Primary/Secondary XML indexes, we'll use the AdventureWorks2017 database and the table [Sales].[Store]. This table has an existing Primary XML index on [Demographics] that will need to be dropped using the code in Listing 4-1.

CHAPTER 4 XML INDEXES

Listing 4-1. Drop the Existing Primary XML Index on [Sales].[Store]

```
DROP INDEX IF EXISTS [PXML_Store_Demographics] ON [Sales].[Store]
```

Using this table, let's first get a benchmark of the cost to execute an example query. In the query, in Listing 4-2, we'll query [Sales].[Store] for the stores with annual sales equal to $1,500,000. For a query returning less than 200 records, the cost is 12.751, shown in Figure 4-1, which is quite expensive. This is due to the XML Reader with XPath filter, which had to shred the entire XML document for all rows to find the requested records, which is an extremely slow and resource-intensive process.

Listing 4-2. Query on [Sales].[Store] for AnnualSales

```
WITH XMLNAMESPACES
(DEFAULT 'http://schemas.microsoft.com/sqlserver/2004/07/adventure-works/
StoreSurvey')
SELECT BusinessEntityID, Name, Demographics
FROM [Sales].[Store]
WHERE Demographics.exist('/StoreSurvey/AnnualSales[.=1500000]') = 1;
```

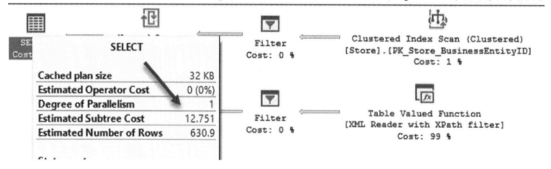

Figure 4-1. *XML query cost with no XML indexes*

> **Note** This chapter will use comparisons of estimated subtree cost vs. logical reads to demonstrate the value of XML indexes. While most analysis in this book focuses on reducing IO through the use of indexes, parsing XML is generally a computationally expensive operation which is why we will focus on query cost. You could alternatively look at statistics time to compare the CPU time changes.

CHAPTER 4 XML INDEXES

This query approach is costly, yet efficient with a small amount of data in the table. However, in real life, tables can become quite large, surpassing the point in which scanning through multiple XML documents is efficient. For instance, imagine if a point-of-sale system stored receipt information in XML documents for each sale. With this kind of data volume, performance would begin to suffer quickly.

Primary XML Index

Now that we know the cost of our example query without any XML indexes, let's look at what happens when we add a Primary XML index. Using the CREATE INDEX code in Listing 4-3, create the Primary XML index. More information on this syntax is in Chapter 1. This will create a Primary XML index on the Demographic column.

Listing 4-3. Primary XML Index on [Sales].[Store]

```
CREATE PRIMARY XML INDEX [PXML_Store_Demographics] ON [Sales].[Store]
([Demographics])
```

As previously stated, when the Primary XML index is created, all of the paths, tags, and nodes are indexed. For each of these items, a record is created in the XML index that contains that item along with information on how that item appears in the XML document and which row in the table is associated with the item. It's important to understand this because XML indexes will often dramatically increase the storage footprint of the underlying table. To demonstrate, run the code in Listing 4-4 to see the number of records and pages for each index. As the results in Figure 4-2 demonstrate, the number of records in the Primary XML index greatly exceeds the number of records in the table by a factor of 13.

Listing 4-4. Primary XML Index on [Sales].[Store]

```
SELECT [i].[name]
      ,[i].[index_id]
      ,[IPS].[index_level]
      ,[IPS].[index_type_desc]
      ,[IPS].[fragment_count]
      ,[IPS].[avg_page_space_used_in_percent]
      ,[IPS].[record_count]
      ,[IPS].[page_count]
```

CHAPTER 4 XML INDEXES

```
FROM [sys].[dm_db_index_physical_stats](DB_ID(N'AdventureWorks2017'),
OBJECT_ID(N'Sales.Store'), NULL, NULL, 'DETAILED') AS [IPS]
    INNER JOIN [sys].[indexes] AS [i]
        ON [i].[object_id] = [IPS].[object_id]
            AND [i].[index_id] = [IPS].[index_id]
WHERE [IPS].[index_type_desc] <> 'NONCLUSTERED INDEX'
ORDER BY [i].[index_id]
        ,[IPS].[index_level];
```

	name	index_id	index_level	index_type_desc	fragment_count	avg_page_space_used_in_percent	record_count	page_count
1	PK_Store_BusinessEntityID	1	0	CLUSTERED INDEX	4	91.902458611317	701	101
2	PK_Store_BusinessEntityID	1	1	CLUSTERED INDEX	1	16.1971830985915	101	1
3	PXML_Store_Demographics	256000	0	PRIMARY XML INDEX	6	98.4627996046454	9113	64
4	PXML_Store_Demographics	256000	1	PRIMARY XML INDEX	1	15.0976031628367	64	1

Figure 4-2. *Physical stats after creating Primary XML index*

With the Primary XML index in place, let's execute the code from Listing 4-2. Reviewing the execution plan, you can see that the execution plan takes on an extremely different pattern, as shown in Figure 4-3. Instead of an estimated subtree cost of over 12, this has been reduced to 0.1535; and the XML Reader with XPath filter is replaced by a clustered index scan of the Primary XML index. Under the covers, the query is still scanning the table, but it is doing so with much less effort. With larger tables, this indexing change will dramatically decrease the total duration of the query itself.

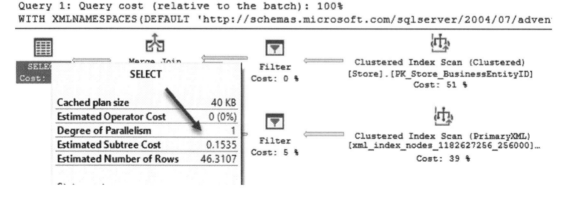

Figure 4-3. *XML query cost with Primary XML index*

You can now see that the optimizer is able to make choices that are more evenly balanced. The `clustered index scan` of the `PointOfSale` table is actually as high an estimated cost as the `clustered index seek` against the XML index you created. This shift in where the work is occurring within the query engine will result in improved performance.

> **Caution** If you create and then drop a primary XML index, any Secondary XML indexes will also be dropped because they are dependent on the primary. No warning will be shown for this action.

Secondary XML Index

Secondary XML indexes provide the ability to further improve querying XML data. With Secondary XML indexes, you'll choose between the PATH, VALUE, and PROPERTY types when building the index. What these options do is determine which elements from the Primary XML index will be included in the Secondary XML index. These options provide performance improvements based on the types of queries that are often run against the XML documents. For instance, if more queries are accessing property elements, then the PROPERTY type for the Secondary XML index would be appropriate.

Going back to our example query in Listing 4-2, the existing function call we are using is using both a path and value. Since we are first searching for a path to check a value and other paths are not being accessed, we'll create a Secondary XML index using PATH. The syntax for the CREATE INDEX statement is provided in Listing 4-5. Note that the CREATE INDEX syntax now includes a USING statement that references the Primary XML index and has the FOR PATH clause.

Listing 4-5. Creating a Secondary Index

```
CREATE XML INDEX [SXML_Store_Demographics] ON [Sales].[Store]
(Demographics)
USING XML INDEX [PXML_Store_Demographics]
FOR PATH;
```

Once you have created the Secondary XML index, we'll run our example query from Listing 4-2 again to see how the execution plan is changed. As shown in Figure 4-4, the execution plan is again dramatically improved. The estimated subtree cost has been reduced by about half from 0.1535 to 0.0888, and the clustered index scan on the Primary XML index is replaced with an index seek on the Secondary XML index. Now the highest-cost item on the query is the clustered index scan on the table's clustered index. In essence, through the use of the Secondary XML index, we've nearly removed the expense associated with accessing the XML data.

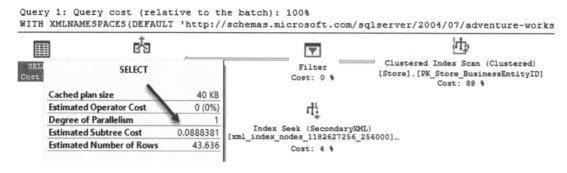

Figure 4-4. XML query cost with Secondary XML index

With the Secondary XML index, you'll find that it will in some cases be nearly as large as the Primary XML index. This is demonstrated by running the code in Listing 4-4, which shows in Figure 4-5 that the same number of records is in the Primary and Secondary XML indexes. In this case, this is to be expected since all of the data in the XML documents is values at XML paths. The advantage of the Secondary XML index in this case is an ordering based on those paths that allow the XML indexes to be more selective, as previously discussed.

	name	index_id	index_level	index_type_desc	fragment_count	avg_page_space_used_in_percent	record_count	page_count
1	PK_Store_BusinessEntityID	1	0	CLUSTERED INDEX	4	91.902458611317	701	101
2	PK_Store_BusinessEntityID	1	1	CLUSTERED INDEX	1	16.1971830985915	101	1
3	PXML_Store_Demographics	256000	0	PRIMARY XML INDEX	6	98.4627996046454	9113	64
4	PXML_Store_Demographics	256000	1	PRIMARY XML INDEX	1	15.0976031628367	64	1
5	SXML_Store_Demographics	256001	0	XML INDEX	4	97.7339510748703	9113	41
6	SXML_Store_Demographics	256001	0	XML INDEX	NULL	0	0	1
7	SXML_Store_Demographics	256001	1	XML INDEX	1	23.400049419323	41	1

Figure 4-5. Physical stats after creating Secondary XML index

Although `sys.dm_db_index_physical_stats` is beneficial for finding information needed to maintain all indexes, including XML indexes, there is a system view specifically for XML indexing named `sys.xml_indexes`. This system view shows all the options that have been applied to an XML index. Information returned by the view can be useful in further maintaining an index, by knowing the type and other options set. This view is inherited from `sys.indexes` and returns the same columns and information as `sys.indexes`. Shown in Figure 4-6, the following additional columns also exist:

- using_xml_index_id: The parent index to a Secondary index. As discussed, Secondary indexes require a Primary index to exist before creation. This column will be NULL for Primary XML indexes and used only for Secondary indexes.

- secondary_type: A flag specifying the type upon which a Secondary index is based. Each Secondary index is based on a specific type (V = VALUE, P = PATH, R = PROPERTY). For Primary XML indexes, this column is NULL.

- secondary_type_desc: A description of the Secondary index type. The values for the description map to those described in the `secondary_type` column.

#	name	index_id	type_desc	using_xml_index_id	secondary_type	secondary_type_desc	xml_index_type	xml_index_type_description	path_id
1	PXML_Store_Demographics	256000	XML	NULL	NULL	NULL	0	PRIMARY_XML	NULL
2	SXML_Store_Demographics	256001	XML	256000	P	PATH	1	SECONDARY_XML	NULL

***Figure 4-6.** Results from sys.xml_indexes query*

We need to consider the storage impact of Primary and Secondary XML indexes because the more data that is in the table and the more often we INSERT, UPDATE, and DELETE that data, the more of an impact these indexes will have on those operations. You'll want to weigh the performance improvement of a Secondary XML index against the time it will take to maintain it to decide whether to create the index. Strive to strike a balance between hardware resources, storage, index usefulness, number of indexes created, and number of times an index may actually be needed when building Primary and Secondary XML indexes.

Selective XML Indexes

Introduced in SQL Server 2012, Selective XML indexes address a significant problem with Primary/Secondary XML indexes. XML documents can be extremely large. Applying an index to the entire document has major performance implications both for creating the index and for maintaining it over time. Also, these excessively large indexes can add to the storage woes that are a frequent problem within organizations. Also, when an index becomes excessively large, it may not function as well as it did when it was smaller. Because of all this, the Selective XML index was introduced.

Selective XML indexes allow you to define a subset of the XML document that you want to index. This makes for smaller, more agile indexes that are targeted to specific paths within the XML. When the index gets created, the document is parsed, and the XML is shredded. The shredded values are then stored in standard relational storage within your database. In addition to the Selective XML index, you can add Secondary indexes based on the nodes within the path that defines the Selective XML index.

Selective XML indexes can achieve large performance benefits over a standard XML index. However, if you have ad hoc queries that may go for all sorts of different elements within the XML document, the standard XML index may perform much better. Also, if you have a large number of node paths, you may see better performance from the standard XML index.

To create a Selective XML index, you must meet the following criteria:

- The table must have a clustered primary key.
- The key size is limited to 128 bytes.
- The key columns are limited to 15.

The Selective XML will not be used for query() or modify() method within your XQuery statements. It will support exist(), value(), and nodes(). If you use query() and modify() together, it will assist in a simple node lookup, but that's all.

To see the Selective XML index in action, you'll need to create one. The script in Listing 4-6 creates a path within the Selective XML index. In this case, since we are only accessing annual sales in the XML document, we'll limit our Selective XML index to that XML path.

Listing 4-6. Script for Creating a Selective XML Index

```
CREATE SELECTIVE XML INDEX [SEL_XML_Store_Demographics_AnnualSales]
ON [Sales].[Store] (Demographics)
WITH XMLNAMESPACES
(DEFAULT 'http://schemas.microsoft.com/sqlserver/2004/07/adventure-works/
StoreSurvey')
FOR (AnnualSales = '/StoreSurvey/AnnualSales');
```

CHAPTER 4　XML INDEXES

After creating the Selective XML index, we'll return to our example query from Listing 4-2 again to see the impact on the execution plan. As shown in Figure 4-7, the estimated subtree cost is comparable to having the Secondary XML index in place, but it's slightly more expensive with the Selective XML index. To understand why SQL Server made this choice, run the code in Listing 4-4 to see the storage footprint. As Figure 4-8 shows, the Selective XML index is substantially smaller than the Secondary XML index. Instead of potentially accessing 41 pages and 9,113 records, the Selective XML index is limited to 701 records across 5 pages, which justifies the extra cost for the clustered index scan on the Selective XML index.

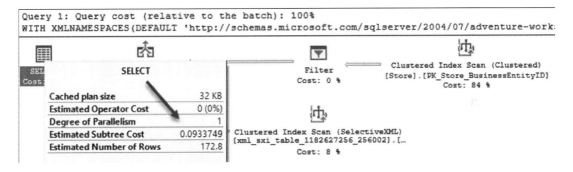

Figure 4-7. XML query cost with Selective XML index

	name	index_id	index_level	index_type_desc	fragment_count	avg_page_space_used_in_percent	record_count	page_count
1	PK_Store_BusinessEntityID	1	0	CLUSTERED INDEX	4	91.902458611317	701	101
2	PK_Store_BusinessEntityID	1	1	CLUSTERED INDEX	1	16.1971830985915	101	1
3	PXML_Store_Demographics	256000	0	PRIMARY XML INDEX	6	98.4627996046454	9113	64
4	PXML_Store_Demographics	256000	1	PRIMARY XML INDEX	1	15.0976031628367	64	1
5	SXML_Store_Demographics	256001	0	XML INDEX	4	97.7339510748703	9113	41
6	SXML_Store_Demographics	256001	0	XML INDEX	NULL	0	0	1
7	SXML_Store_Demographics	256001	1	XML INDEX	1	23.400049419323	41	1
8	SEL_XML_Store_Demographics_AnnualSales	256002	0	XML INDEX	1	90.0469483568075	701	5
9	SEL_XML_Store_Demographics_AnnualSales	256002	1	XML INDEX	1	1.21077341240425	5	1

Figure 4-8. Physical stats after creating Selective XML index

While this provides a much improved opportunity for XML indexing, there is an important restriction that should be considered. If your queries change to the point where the Selective XML index doesn't cover the query, then performance will degrade. While this is an obvious statement, we don't often have to consider this with indexes since traditionally indexes cover all data within a column.

To demonstrate this scenario, let's add another XML element to the query to filter on BusinessType. Shown in Listing 4-7, we'll add the exist() to the WHERE clause and also drop the previously created Primary/Secondary XML indexes to prevent them from interfering with the output. Generally, if you have Selective XML indexes, you would not also have Primary/Secondary XML indexes.

Listing 4-7. Query on [Sales].[Store] for AnnualSales and BusinessType

```
DROP INDEX IF EXISTS [SXML_Store_Demographics] ON [Sales].[Store];
DROP INDEX IF EXISTS [PXML_Store_Demographics] ON [Sales].[Store];
WITH XMLNAMESPACES
(DEFAULT 'http://schemas.microsoft.com/sqlserver/2004/07/adventure-works/StoreSurvey')
SELECT BusinessEntityID, Demographics
FROM [Sales].[Store]
WHERE Demographics.exist('/StoreSurvey/AnnualSales[.=1500000]') = 1
AND Demographics.exist('/StoreSurvey/BusinessType[.="OS"]') = 1
```

After running the code in Listing 4-7, we see that the performance of the query has degraded substantially. The reason for the degradation is the inclusion of the XML Reader with XPath filter, which increases the estimated subtree cost, as shown in Figure 4-9. This isn't as terrible as the first iteration we had with this query, because the Selective XML index is still assisting with reducing the number of records where the entire XML document needs to be scanned with the function. But it is a degradation, and with large tables, this could cause a significant issue.

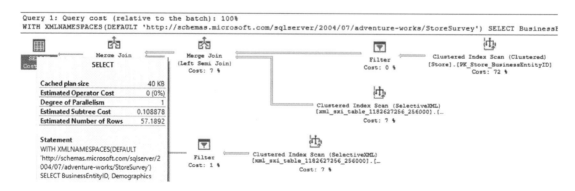

Figure 4-9. *XML query cost with Selective XML index and XML element not included*

CHAPTER 4 XML INDEXES

Fortunately, Selective XML indexes provide flexibility to get around and tune for issues such as this. Specifically, the FOR clause, shown in Listing 4-8, can be extended to include multiple XML nodes and paths. In this case, we are adding BusinessType to the index. As expected, and shown in Figure 4-10, the change in this index improves the performance of the query by dropping the estimated subtree cost to 0.108 by adding a second clustered index scan operation on the Selective XML index.

Listing 4-8. Script for Creating a Selective XML Index

```
DROP INDEX IF EXISTS [SEL_XML_Store_Demographics_AnnualSales] ON [Sales].
[Store];
CREATE SELECTIVE XML INDEX [SEL_XML_Store_Demographics_AnnualSales
BusinessType]
ON [Sales].[Store] (Demographics)
WITH XMLNAMESPACES
(DEFAULT 'http://schemas.microsoft.com/sqlserver/2004/07/adventure-works/
StoreSurvey')
FOR (AnnualSales = '/StoreSurvey/AnnualSales',
BusinessType = '/StoreSurvey/BusinessType');
```

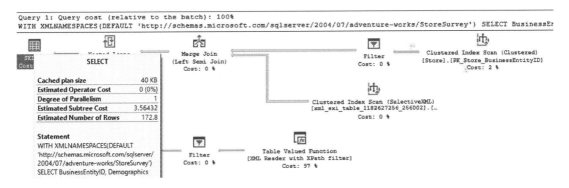

Figure 4-10. *XML query cost with Selective XML index on two elements*

And as we've looked at previously, we'll again review the storage impact of extending the index by running Listing 4-4. Reviewing Figure 4-11, we see that even by increasing the number of elements in the index, we haven't significantly changed the storage footprint of the index. It's still 701 records across 6, instead of 5, pages.

175

	name	index_id	index_level	index_type_desc	fragment_count	avg_page_space_used_in_percent	record_count	page_count
1	PK_Store_BusinessEntityID	1	0	CLUSTERED INDEX	4	91.902458611317	701	101
2	PK_Store_BusinessEntityID	1	1	CLUSTERED INDEX	1	16.1971830985915	101	1
3	SEL_XML_Store_Demographics_AnnualSalesBusinessType	256000	0	XML INDEX	1	95.2433901655547	701	6
4	SEL_XML_Store_Demographics_AnnualSalesBusinessType	256000	1	XML INDEX	1	1.45787002718063	6	1

Figure 4-11. *Physical stats after creating Selective XML index on two elements*

While the Selective XML index is a more complicated aspect of XML indexing, you can see that getting started with it is not that difficult. The Selective XML index also supports more sophisticated XQuery than the examples in this chapter so that you can be extremely precise in exactly which segments of your XML document will be indexed.

Summary

This chapter covered the need to be able to search and index the unstructured and semistructured data that can now be stored within SQL Server. XML indexes provide developers and database administrators with the options to improve the performance of searches through XML documents. This benefits queries both by filtering data in XML documents and by retrieving the data for display. Selective XML indexes offer the opportunity to get a more granular and detailed approach to your XML indexing. Just remember that XML indexes require quite considerable additional disk space, so you should plan your systems accordingly.

CHAPTER 5

Spatial Indexing

The next type of indexing we need to look at is spatial indexing, which relates to the spatial data types. Introduced in SQL Server 2008, spatial data types advance the storage capabilities of SQL Server allowing data that defines shape and location information. Before these enhancements, spatial data was often stored as string or numeric values without meaning within the database and required cumbersome conversions and calculations to resolve the information into something meaningful.

As part of the spatial data support, SQL Server introduced the GEOMETRY and GEOGRAPHY data types. These types support planar and geodetic data, respectively. Planar data is composed of lines, points, and polygons on a 2D plane, while geodetic data is composed of the same but on a geodetic ellipsoid, a fancy term describing a map of Earth. In simple terms, you can look at these two data types like so: GEOMETRY is a flat representation of the shape described, and GEOGRAPHY encompasses a rounded global representation.

Spatial data indexes are unique in how they are created and interpreted. Each index is composed of a set of grids. These grids consist of a set of cells, laid out kind of like a square spreadsheet. The grids can be up to 16 × 16 and as small as 4 × 4. The cells within the grid contain the values that define the objects that define the spatial data being stored. There is a distinct difference between the GEOGRAPHY and GEOMETRY data types in this type of indexing. The GEOMETRY data type requires a bounding box, which is a limit on the size of the area defined by the index. The GEOGRAPHY data type does not have a bounding box since it's basically bound by the size of the planet.

This chapter will explore spatial indexes, their behaviors, and their use within queries to help enhance the performance of your spatial data.

CHAPTER 5 ■ SPATIAL INDEXING

How Spatial Data Is Indexed

The grids that make up a spatial index are actually nested within each other. At the top layer, known as level 1, you can have, for example, a 4 × 4 grid. Each cell within that level 1 grid then contains another grid, consisting of the number of cells defined for that level, in this example 4 × 4. This second grid defines level 2. The cells in level 2 each have a grid that defines level 3, and the cells there contain another grid, level 4. Figure 5-1 shows how a GEOMETRY index consists of these four levels. The index is then made up of these four grids, each one being composed of a series of cells. This layering and grid hierarchy, called *decomposing*, is created when the index is created.

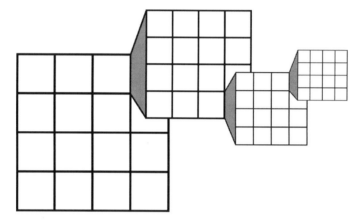

Figure 5-1. *Grid storage representation of the GEOMETRY index storage and cells*

As many as 4 billion cells are possible, as shown in Figure 5-1. This is important when creating the index and determining what density to use at creation. Each layer, or level, can have a specified density. There are three levels of density (low = 4 × 4, medium = 8 × 8, and high = 16 × 16). If the density is omitted at the time an index is created, the default is medium. Manipulating the density is most commonly useful for tuning the actual space of the index. All layers may not be required at a high density. Save space by not using more density than you need.

All this is necessary because the actual storage of the information from within these grids is the same B-tree that is used to store standard indexes. But the definitions within the storage, and obviously the retrieval of those definitions, are radically different within spatial indexes than they are within standard indexes. To get the information into the B-tree, additional processing on top of the grid is necessary.

The next step in the indexing process that SQL Server performs is tessellation. *Tessellation* is the process that places or fits the objects into the grid hierarchy starting at layer 1. This process may require only the first layer of the grid but can require all four depending on the objects involved. Tessellation is essentially taking all the data from the spatial column and placing it onto the grids in cells while retaining each cell that is touched. The index then knows exactly how to go back to find the cells in each grid when a request is evaluated, using the B-tree.

So far, I've gone over how the cells in a grid are filled and how the overall tessellation process is achieved. Having the cells in a grid storage and tessellation process, however, doesn't sit well in theory because there are openings for the cells to be misused or not used efficiently based on the extreme number of touched cells to retain. With the GEOMETRY data type and indexes created on it, the bounding box is required because SQL Server needs a finite space. Creating such a box is done by using the coordinates xmin, xmax and ymin, ymax. The result can be visualized as a square having the x-coordinate and y-coordinate of the lower-left corner and the x-coordinate and y-coordinate of the upper-right corner. What is most critical when determining the bounding box with an index on a GEOMETRY data type is to ensure that all the objects are within the bounding box, without making the bounding box excessively large, with lots and lots of empty cells, a balancing act. An index will be effective only for the objects, or shapes, within the bounding box. Not containing objects within a bounding box could severely impact performance and cause poor performance with spatial queries.

Furthermore, to retain the ability to use an index efficiently in the tessellation process, rules are applied. These rules are as follows:

> ***Covering rule***: The covering rule is the most basic rule applied in tessellation. Not to be confused with the common term *covering index*, this rule states that any cell that is completely covered is not recorded individually for that object. Covered cells are counted for the object. Not storing covered cells saves processing and data storage time and space.
>
> ***Cells-per-object rule***: The cells-per-object rule is a more in-depth rule that applies a limit to the number of cells that can be counted for a specific object. In Figure 5-2, the circle shown covers 2 cells in level 1 and 14 in level 2. The circle is tessellated to the second layer because of a cells-per-object default of 16. If the circle did cover more than 16 cells at level 2, tessellation would not continue

CHAPTER 5 SPATIAL INDEXING

through to level 2. Since the object would cover a lot more than 16 cells at level 3, tessellation stops here. Tuning the cells per object can enhance the accuracy of an index. Tuning this value based on the data stored can be very effective. Given the importance of the cells-per-object rule, the setting is exposed in a dynamic management view, sys.spatial_index_tessellations. You will review this setting later in this chapter.

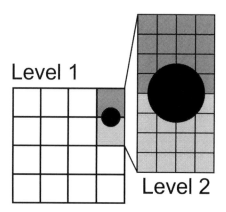

Figure 5-2. *Visual representation of an object and how many cells the object covers within the grid layers*

> **Deepest cell rule**: The last rule of the tessellation process is the deepest cell rule. As discussed, each layer of grids and the cells within them are referenced in each deeper layer. So in Figure 5-2, cells defined in level 2 are the only ones needed to completely refer to any other levels, in this case level 1, effectively. This rule cannot be broken and is built into the optimizer's processing of retrieving the data from the index.

With the GEOGRAPHY type, there is the added challenge of projecting the form in a flattened representation through the tessellation process. This process first divides the GEOGRAPHY grid into two hemispheres. Each hemisphere is projected onto the facets of a quadrilateral pyramid and flattened, and then the two are joined into a non-Euclidean plane. Once this process is complete, the plane is decomposed into the aforementioned grid hierarchy.

Creating Spatial Indexes

The Create Spatial Index statement has most of the same options of a normal clustered or nonclustered index. However, there are specific options that are also required for this index type, as listed in Table 5-1.

Table 5-1. Spatial Index Options

Option Name	Description
USING	The USING clause specifies the spatial data type. This will be GEOMETRY_GRID or GEOGRAPHY_GRID and cannot be NULL.
WITH GEOMETRY_GRID, GEOGRAPHY_GRID	The WITH options include the setting of the tessellation schema for either the GEOMETRY_GRID or the GEOGRAPHY_GRID based on the column data type.
BOUNDING_BOX	The BOUNDING_BOX is used in the GEOMETRY data type to define the bounding box of the cells. This option does not have defaults and must be specified when creating indexes on the GEOMETRY data type. The CREATE SPATIAL INDEX IDX_CITY_GEOM (in Listing 5-1) shows the syntax for this option. Setting the BOUNDING_BOX is done by setting the xmin and ymin and xmax and ymax coordinates, like so: BOUNDING_BOX = (XMIN = xmin, YMIN = ymin, XMAX = xmax, YMAX = ymax).
GRIDS	The GRIDS option is used for altering the density of each grid layer. All layer defaults are medium density but can be altered to low or high to further tune spatial indexes and density settings.

Take the CREATE TABLE statement in Listing 5-1 as an example.

Listing 5-1. CREATE TABLE with a GEOMETRY Data Type

```
USE AdventureWorks2017
GO
```

```
CREATE TABLE CITY_MAPS (
    ID BIGINT PRIMARY KEY
            IDENTITY(1, 1),
    CITYNAME NVARCHAR(150),      CITY_GEOM GEOMETRY
    );
GO
```

This table will consist of the primary key, the city name, and then a GEOMETRY column that holds map data for the city itself. The city's density may affect tuning the cells-per-object rule in tessellation as well as the density of each layer in the grid hierarchy.

To index the CITY_GEOM column, the CREATE statement in Listing 5-2 would be used with a grid layer density of LOW for the first two layers and then MEDIUM and HIGH for the third and fourth layers. This density change allows for tuning the object in the index and the covering cells as the layers go deeper in the grid. The cells-per-object setting is 24 maximum cells an object can cover. The bounding box coordinates are also set.

Listing 5-2. Definition of a Spatial Index on a GEOMETRY Column

```
USE AdventureWorks2017
GO

CREATE SPATIAL INDEX IDX_CITY_GEOM
ON CITY_MAPS (CITY_GEOM)
USING GEOMETRY_GRID
WITH (
BOUNDING_BOX = ( xmin=-50, ymin=-50, xmax=500, ymax=500 ),
GRIDS = (LOW, LOW, MEDIUM, HIGH),
CELLS_PER_OBJECT = 24,
PAD_INDEX  = ON );
```

To utilize and test the index created, you will need to review the estimated and actual execution plans to determine whether the index has been used. In the case of spatial data, reviewing the actual results that a query will yield is also beneficial. SQL Server Management Studio has a built-in spatial data viewer that can be used for reviewing spatial data.

CHAPTER 5 SPATIAL INDEXING

Listing 5-3 creates a table that can benefit from spatial indexing. The table is created to store ZIP codes and other data from the US Census Bureau. This table will be created in the AdventureWorks2014 database.

Listing 5-3. Creating a Table to Hold GEOMETRY-Related Data

```
USE AdventureWorks2017
GO

CREATE TABLE dbo.tl_2017_us_county (
    STATEFP CHAR(2) NULL,
    COUNTYFP CHAR(3) NULL,
    COUNTYNS CHAR(8) NULL,
    GEOID CHAR(5) NULL,
    NAME CHAR(100) NULL,
    NAMELSAD CHAR(100) NULL,
    LSAD CHAR(2) NULL,
    CLASSFP CHAR(2) NULL,
    MTFCC CHAR(5) NULL,
    CSAFP CHAR(3) NULL,
    CBSAFP CHAR(5) NULL,
    METDIVFP CHAR(5) NULL,
    FUNCSTAT CHAR(1) NULL,
    ALAND FLOAT NULL,
    AWATER FLOAT NULL,
    INTPTLAT CHAR(11) NULL,
    INTPTLON CHAR(12) NULL,
    GEOM GEOMETRY NULL
);
```

The GEOM column will store the GEOMETRY data. This column will be used to query the data from SQL Server Management Studio to show the imaging that can be done from other applications.

> **Note** For the examples in this chapter, a shape file and the tool OGR2OGR are required. The shape file will come from TIGER/Line Shapefile, 2017, nation, US, Current County and Equivalent National Shapefile available at www2.census.gov/geo/tiger/TIGER2017/COUNTY/tl_2017_us_county.zip. And OGR2OGR is available in OSGeo4W from http://download.osgeo.org/osgeo4w/osgeo4w-setup-x86_64.exe. When installing the application, only install the GDAL package. After installation, run the PowerShell command [Environment]::SetEnvironmentVariable("GDAL_DATA", "C:\OSGeo4W64\share\gdal", "Machine") to set an environment variable. Finally, from the directory where the geography files were extracted to, run the command C:\OSGeo4W64\bin\ogr2ogr -f "MSSQLSpatial" MSSQL:"server=localhost;database=AdventureWorks2017;trusted_connection=yes;" -nln "tl_2017_us_county" -a_srs "ESPG:4269" -lco "GEOM_TYPE=geography" -lco "GEOM_NAME=geog4269" "tl_2017_us_county.shp" -s_srs EPSG:4269 -t_srs EPSG:26713.

Reviewing the actual data from a query of a GEOMETRY data type column is not useful in the normal grid and tabular resultset from within SSMS. To take advantage of the spatial data features, using the Spatial Results tab in SSMS is much more effective. Given the table from Listing 5-3, a simple SELECT on the column GEOM can be executed, and the results of the SELECT statement will automatically generate the Spatial Results tab. For example, the query in Listing 5-4 will result in an image generated of the state of Washington, coding each county area in a different color.

Listing 5-4. Initial Query for Pulling Back Spatial Data

```
USE AdventureWorks2017
GO

SELECT  *
FROM    dbo.tl_2017_us_county AS tuc
WHERE   tuc.STATEFP = '41';
```

Click the Spatial Results tab in the result window of SSMS to reveal the image generated by the query. You should see something like that in Figure 5-3.

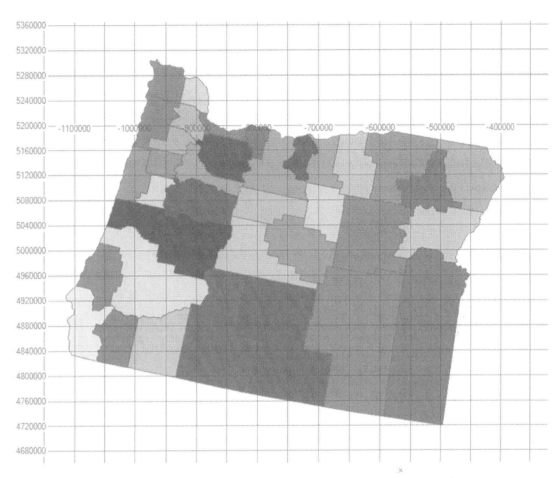

***Figure 5-3.** Output from spatial query against county data*

The query in Listing 5-4 used a standard column, STATEFP, to filter the information so that you are looking only at counties within a particular state. Before using this data, though, it's a good idea to ensure that you are working with only good shapes within the GEOM column. It is possible to have improper data stored, so cleaning your data may be required. To do this, you can use the MakeValid() method to modify any GEOMETRY instances, making them valid. According to the documentation from Microsoft, using the function can cause shapes to "shift slightly," but the extent to which it may affect the shapes under your control is unclear. Executing Listing 5-5 will result in an update to any invalid GEOMETRY instances in the GEOM column.

CHAPTER 5 SPATIAL INDEXING

Listing 5-5. Using MakeValid() to Correct Any Invalid GEOMETRY Instances

```
USE AdventureWorks2017
GO

UPDATE  dbo.tl_2017_us_county
SET     GEOM = GEOM.MakeValid();
```

The MakeValid() method should be used sparingly, and all invalid GEOMETRY instances that are found should be reviewed in a production setting. You should plan on reviewing your shapes after using the MakeValid() function because it could possibly modify those shapes.

You can also use the spatial columns to filter the data being returned based on the behavior of locations and distances. Listing 5-6 shows an example of invoking one of the special methods that have been defined to work with spatial information. The query returns the ten counties closest to the county of Tulsa in Oklahoma (see Figure 5-4).

Listing 5-6. Query for the Top Ten Closest ZIP Codes to a Given Point

```
USE AdventureWorks2017
GO

DECLARE @polygon GEOMETRY;

SELECT  @polygon = tuc.GEOM
FROM    dbo.tl_2017_us_county AS tuc
WHERE   tuc.NAME = 'Tulsa';

SELECT TOP 10
        tuc.GEOM,
        tuc.GEOM.STDistance(@polygon),
        tuc.NAME
FROM    dbo.tl_2017_us_county AS tuc
WHERE   tuc.GEOM.STDistance(@polygon) IS NOT NULL
        AND tuc.GEOM.STDistance(@polygon) < 1
ORDER BY tuc.GEOM.STDistance(@polygon);
```

CHAPTER 5 SPATIAL INDEXING

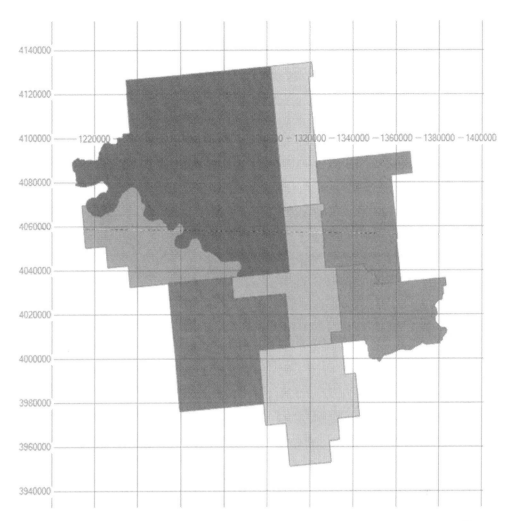

Figure 5-4. *Narrowing the results of the ZIP code data using STDistance()*

The query from Listing 5-6 creates the execution plan shown in Figure 5-5.

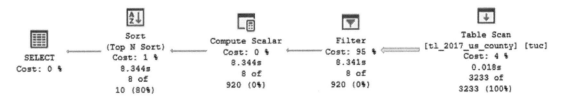

Figure 5-5. *Execution plan generated from STDistance() without indexing*

CHAPTER 5 SPATIAL INDEXING

If you review the Spatial Results tab, the northeast corner of Oklahoma containing the ten counties will look like Figure 5-4. However, the query's execution plan shown in Figure 5-5 is less than ideal, with an index scan on the clustered index created from the primary key and a high-cost filter operation. With the use of the STDistance predicate, the query is a candidate for using an index on the GEOMETRY column, so an index should be added.

Supporting Methods with Indexes

With GEOMETRY and GEOGRAPHY data types, only certain methods are supported with the use of indexes. The STDistance() method will support indexing, which would benefit the query shown in Listing 5-6. Before diving deeply into indexing the query, the methods that do support indexing should be pointed out. These methods have rules in how respective predicates are written. The following is a list of supported methods for the GEOMETRY type:

- GEOMETRY.STContains() = 1
- GEOMETRY.STDistance() < number
- GEOMETRY.STDistance() <= number
- GEOMETRY.STEquals() = 1
- GEOMETRY.STIntersects() = 1
- GEOMETRY.STOverlaps() = 1
- GEOMETRY.STTouches() = 1
- GEOMETRY.STWithin() = 1

And the following are the supported methods for the GEOGRAPHY *type:*

- GEOGRAPHY.STIntersects() = 1
- GEOGRAPHY.STEquals() = 1
- GEOGRAPHY.STDistance() < number
- GEOGRAPHY.STDistance() <= number

For both GEOMETRY and GEOGRAPHY, to return any result that is not null, the first parameter and the second parameter must have the same spatial reference identifier (SRID), which is a spatial reference system based on a specific ellipsoid used to flatten or round the earth.

CHAPTER 5 SPATIAL INDEXING

Recall that the query used in Figure 5-6 to return the counties around Tulsa uses the STDistance() method in the expression STDistance(@polygon) < 1. Based on the methods supported and analyzing the options and CREATE syntax for spatial indexing, you could use the INDEX CREATE statement shown in Listing 5-7 in an attempt to optimize the query.

Listing 5-7. CREATE Statement for a Spatial Index

```
USE AdventureWorks2017
GO

CREATE SPATIAL INDEX IDX_COUNTY_GEOM ON dbo.tl_2017_us_county
(
GEOM
) USING  GEOMETRY_GRID
WITH (
BOUNDING_BOX =(-91.513079, -87.496494, 36.970298, 36.970298),
GRIDS =(LEVEL_1 = LOW,LEVEL_2 = MEDIUM,LEVEL_3 = MEDIUM,LEVEL_4 = HIGH),
CELLS_PER_OBJECT = 16,
PAD_INDEX   = OFF, SORT_IN_TEMPDB = OFF, DROP_EXISTING = OFF,
ALLOW_ROW_LOCKS  = ON, ALLOW_PAGE_LOCKS  = ON) ON [PRIMARY];
GO
```

Executing the query in Listing 5-6 results in the much different execution plan, shown in Figure 5-6. It results in a shorter duration when executing and returning the results, plus spatial results. The largest difference in the execution plan is the use of the index IDX_COUNTY_GEOM.

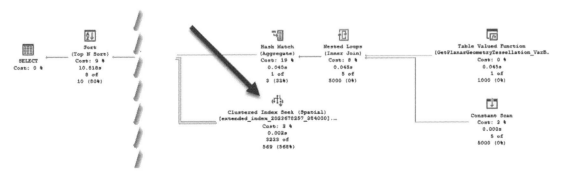

Figure 5-6. *Optimized details of a tuned execution plan using spatial data*

You can see an overall improvement and more optimal execution plan from the creation of the spatial index. The index and optimal execution plan are good, but validating the actual improvement by checking the overall duration in execution time should not be skipped. Capturing the execution time using Extended Events, an overall review of the execution of the statement can be retrieved. In the case of the query that searches for the counties near Tulsa, the results with the index in place return 500 milliseconds. Dropping the index and executing the same query returns 1,500 milliseconds for total execution time. This test is extremely basic, but it's a solid foundation upon which you can begin to form a strategy for indexing existing spatial data to improve overall performance.

Understanding Statistics, Properties, and Information

Indexes in general have many data management views and functions that make the administration of the indexes much easier and more efficient than manual statistics gathering. With spatial indexes, there are additional catalog views that are added to assist in the unique settings and administration of them. In addition to the views, there are also some built-in procedures that you can invoke to get information about spatial indexes.

The Views

There are two catalog views: `sys.spatial_index` and `sys.spatial_index_tessellation`. The `sys.spatial_index` view provides the type and tessellation scheme as well as basic information about each spatial index. The `spatial_index_type` column returned by `sys.spatial_index` returns a 1 for GEOMETRY indexes and a 2 for GEOGRAPHY indexes. Listing 5-8 is an example query against the view, and Figure 5-7 shows the results.

Listing 5-8. Query to Retrieve Metadata About Spatial Indexes

```
USE AdventureWorks2017
GO

SELECT  name,
        type_desc,
        spatial_index_type,
```

```
            spatial_index_type_desc,
            tessellation_scheme
FROM        sys.spatial_indexes;
```

	name	type_desc	spatial_index_type	spatial_index_type_desc	tessellation_scheme
1	IDX_COUNTY_GEOM	SPATIAL	1	GEOMETRY	GEOMETRY_GRID

Figure 5-7. Querying sys.spatial_indexes and results showing IDX_WIZIP_GEOM index

Now query the sys.spatial_index_tessellation view to see the parameters of the index and the tessellation scheme. Listing 5-9 is the query, and Figure 5-8 shows the results.

Listing 5-9. Query to Retrieve Information About Tessellation

```
USE AdventureWorks2017
GO

SELECT  tessellation_scheme,
        bounding_box_xmax,
        bounding_box_xmin,
        bounding_box_ymax,
        bounding_box_ymin,
        level_1_grid_desc,
        level_2_grid_desc,
        level_3_grid_desc,
        level_4_grid_desc,
        cells_per_object
FROM    sys.spatial_index_tessellations;
```

	tessellation_scheme	bounding_box_xmax	bounding_box_xmin	bounding_box_ymax	bounding_box_ymin	level_1_grid_...	...	_4_grid_desc	cells_per_object
1	GEOMETRY_GRID	36.970298	-91.513079	36.970298	-87.496494	LOW			16

Figure 5-8. Querying sys.spatial_index_tessellations and partial results

CHAPTER 5 SPATIAL INDEXING

Both of these catalog views can be joined on the object_id to become extremely useful for tuning and maintenance tasks. At times, it may prove effective to manipulate and re-create indexes as needed when the spatial data dictates.

The Procedures

In addition to the catalog views, four other procedures have been provided internally for further analysis of the spatial indexes. These procedures return a complete listing of properties that are set on the indexes. The four procedures and their parameters are as follows:

```
sp_help_spatial_GEOMETRY_index [ @tabname =] 'tabname'
     [ , [ @indexname = ] 'indexname' ]
     [ , [ @verboseoutput = ] 'verboseoutput'
     [ , [ @query_sample = ] 'query_sample']

sp_help_spatial_GEOMETRY_index_xml [ @tabname =] 'tabname'
     [ , [ @indexname = ] 'indexname' ]
     [ , [ @verboseoutput = ]'{ 0 | 1 }]
     [ , [ @query_sample = ] 'query_sample' ]
     [ ,.[ @xml_output = ] 'xml_output' ]

sp_help_spatial_GEOGRAPHY_index [ @tabname =] 'tabname'
[ , [ @indexname = ] 'indexname' ]
[ , [ @verboseoutput = ] 'verboseoutput' ]
[ , [ @query_sample = ] 'query_sample' ]

sp_help_spatial_GEOGRAPHY_index_xml [@tabname = 'tabname'
[ , [ @indexname = ] 'indexname' ]
[ , [ @verboseoutput = ] 'verboseoutput' ]
[ , [ @query_sample = ] 'query_sample' ]
[ ,.[ @xml_output = ] 'xml_output' ]
```

Listing 5-10 is an example showing how to execute these stored procedures. The example returns information about the GEOMETRY index IDX_COUNTY_GEOM created earlier in Listing 5-7. Figure 5-9 shows the results.

Listing 5-10. Investigating the Geometry Index

```
USE AdventureWorks2017
GO

DECLARE @Sample GEOMETRY
    = 'POLYGON((-90.0 -180.0, -90.0 180.0, 90.0 180.0, 90.0 -180.0,
    -90.0 -180.0))';
EXEC sp_help_spatial_GEOMETRY_index 'dbo.tl_2017_us_county', 'IDX_COUNTY_
GEOM', 0, @Sample;
```

	propname	propvalue
1	Total_Number_Of_ObjectCells_In_Level0_For_QuerySa...	1
2	Total_Number_Of_ObjectCells_In_Level0_In_Index	3233
3	Total_Number_Of_ObjectCells_In_Level1_For_QuerySa...	16
4	Total_Number_Of_Interior_ObjectCells_In_Level1_For_...	12
5	Total_Number_Of_Intersecting_ObjectCells_In_Level1_...	4
6	Total_Number_Of_Border_ObjectCells_In_Level0_For_...	1
7	Total_Number_Of_Border_ObjectCells_In_Level0_In_In...	3233
8	Number_Of_Rows_Selected_By_Primary_Filter	3233
9	Number_Of_Rows_Selected_By_Internal_Filter	0
10	Number_Of_Times_Secondary_Filter_Is_Called	3233
11	Number_Of_Rows_Output	0
12	Percentage_Of_Rows_NotSelected_By_Primary_Filter	0
13	Percentage_Of_Primary_Filter_Rows_Selected_By_Inte...	0
14	Internal_Filter_Efficiency	0.0
15	Primary_Filter_Efficiency	0

Figure 5-9. *sp_help_spatial_GEOMETRY_index example and results (results may vary)*

This information can be useful for adjusting the index to make it function better. The information returned functions in a similar way to the statistics for an index. You can see how many objects are available in each of the levels of the index. You can also see how it returns data that matches the provided query sample. Seeing that a particular number of intersecting objects match the query sample shows you whether a given object will be returned by the index. You can also see the percentage of objects in the index that are not returned from the query sample by comparing the objects in the index to the ones that match. All this helps you understand how well the index is meeting your query requirements.

CHAPTER 5 SPATIAL INDEXING

Tuning Spatial Indexes

As you saw in Listing 5-7, when a spatial index is created, you have some options. Manipulating these options allows you to adjust the behavior of your spatial index. Some experimentation will be necessary to arrive at the right set of options for the optimal behavior of your index. Use a combination of the execution plan and the query performance metrics just as you did earlier in this chapter.

For a GEOMETRY column, you can add a bounding box to the index. This limits the area that the index covers, which can allow you to create an index that can help satisfy certain query criteria better than a general index. For example, if I change the bounding box and re-create the index as in Listing 5-11, I see about a 10 percent reduction in execution time.

Listing 5-11. Adjusting the Bounding Box of the Spatial Index

```
USE AdventureWorks2017
GO

CREATE SPATIAL INDEX IDX_COUNTY_GEOM ON dbo.tl_2017_us_county
(
GEOM
)USING  GEOMETRY_GRID
WITH (
BOUNDING_BOX =(-96.9, -95.3, 36.4, 36.6),
GRIDS =(LEVEL_1 = LOW,LEVEL_2 = MEDIUM,LEVEL_3 = MEDIUM,LEVEL_4 = HIGH),
CELLS_PER_OBJECT = 16,
PAD_INDEX  = OFF, SORT_IN_TEMPDB = OFF, DROP_EXISTING = ON,
ALLOW_ROW_LOCKS  = ON, ALLOW_PAGE_LOCKS  = ON) ON [PRIMARY];
GO
```

By changing the bounding box, some objects are excluded from the index. Depending on your data and the parameters used in the index, performance may not improve with more items filtered out from the index. Due to this complexity with spatial indexes, it is important to test and verify that you achieve the performance improvements you are seeking. Of course, making changes to improve the queries for one set of counties could lead to poor performance for other counties in the United States. As you can see, there is no easy answer here.

Another adjustment you can make is to change the grids of the index. The choice made in the examples so far is a fairly standard choice if you're not sure how your data is distributed and if you're unsure of how many matches you're likely to get from any one query. If your query has a higher percentage of inclusive results, a different distribution on the grids can result in higher speed. It's largely a question of experimentation. But, just as with the bounding box, changing the grid distribution for one dataset could hurt another. You'll have to perform rigorous testing to get this right.

Using the same example, if I were to make the level 1 grid into a HIGH detailed grid, I would lose 10 percent of my performance, making the query run slower. Changing it to MEDIUM neither benefited nor hurt the execution time. In this case, adjusting the grid levels in any combination didn't result in a significant improvement in speed, but having the HIGH level of detail on either level 1 or level 2 of the grid would negatively impact performance. With this experiment complete, I would choose to leave the default grids alone in this instance.

Restrictions on Spatial Indexes

Spatial indexes provide some unique features and restrictions. The following is a comprehensive list of restrictions for spatial indexing:

- Spatial indexes require an existing clustered index.
- A spatial index can be created only on a column of type GEOMETRY or GEOGRAPHY.
- Spatial indexes can be defined only on a table that has a primary key. The maximum number of primary key columns on the table is 15.
- The maximum size of index key records is 895 bytes. Larger sizes raise an error.
- The use of Database Engine Tuning Advisor is not supported.
- You cannot perform an online rebuild of a spatial index.
- Spatial indexes cannot be specified on indexed views.

CHAPTER 5 SPATIAL INDEXING

- You can create only up to 249 spatial indexes on any of the spatial columns in a supported table. Creating more than one spatial index on the same spatial column can be useful, for example, to index different tessellation parameters in a single column.

- You can create only one spatial index at a time.

- An index build of spatial data cannot use available process parallelism.

Summary

Indexing spatial data is a complicated form of data storage and manipulation. This chapter covered the main points of how spatial data is processed and stored to help in managing and reviewing an implementation of the spatial data types in databases.

With spatial indexes, you now have the ability to quickly determine whether points lie within regions or whether regions overlap other regions. Instead of having to fully render each spatial artifact, spatial indexes allow queries to quickly calculate the results of the spatial function. Remember to always examine the execution plan to ensure that the spatial index is actually being used.

CHAPTER 6

Indexing Memory-Optimized Tables

The past few chapters have focused on specialized indexing-related data types in SQL Server. SQL Server also offers specialized tables that reside in memory called memory-optimized, or in-memory, tables. Introduced in SQL Server 2014, these tables reside fully within memory while SQL Server is running relying on disk-based structures only for ensuring the ability to recover from service restarts.

With memory-optimized tables being primarily memory based, this has a significant impact on the traditional structures of a table and its indexes. In this chapter, you'll look at how the changes for memory-optimized tables affect your ability to index these tables and how to create the ideal indexes.

> **Note** Depending on the source and conversation, memory-optimized tables are also referred to as in-memory OLTP and Hekaton. This book will use the term *memory-optimized tables* since it aligns to the terminology used in Microsoft Books Online.

Memory-Optimized Tables Overview

Before digging into the indexing options for memory-optimized tables, let's start with the basics of memory-optimized tables. A memory-optimized table is a new table type introduced in SQL Server 2014. Unlike traditional tables, along with their indexes, memory-optimized tables reside entirely in memory. Memory-optimized tables are supported through disk structures but are not reliant on them for transactional processing. This differs compared to traditional tables, where the table is based on disk storage and typically only a portion of the table and its indexes are in memory.

The value provided by memory-optimized tables is the performance gains that creating tables in this fashion provides for a database. By hosting and managing the entire table in memory, transactions do not need to wait for the disk to bring data to memory for transaction processing to proceed.

The implementation of memory-optimized tables results in a few changes to the way in which tables are architected in SQL Server. First, since the tables are now memory resident, it makes more sense for them to be structured in a manner that is optimal for accessing the data in memory vs. retrieving a subset of the data from disk. For this reason, memory-optimized tables use hash and range indexes vs. B-trees for storing data. Additionally, the tables don't synchronize to disk or move around in memory like a traditional table, removing the need for latching between disk and memory structures.

To create memory-optimized tables in a database, there are a few things that need to be prepared within a database. To begin, a filegroup dedicated to memory-optimized data needs to be added to the database with a file to support the memory-optimized tables. Additionally, the database should have the property MEMORY_OPTIMIZED_ELEVATE_TO_SNAPSHOT enabled in most scenarios. This property hints to all transactions against memory-optimized tables to set the isolation level to SNAPSHOT. In Listing 6-1, the database MemOptIndexing is prepared using these settings.

Listing 6-1. Preparing Database for Memory-Optimized Tables

```
USE master
GO

IF EXISTS(SELECT * FROM sys.databases WHERE name = 'MemOptIndexing')
DROP DATABASE MemOptIndexing
GO

CREATE DATABASE MemOptIndexing
GO

ALTER DATABASE MemOptIndexing
ADD FILEGROUP memoryOptimizedFG CONTAINS MEMORY_OPTIMIZED_DATA
```

CHAPTER 6 INDEXING MEMORY-OPTIMIZED TABLES

```
--This file location may change in your environment
ALTER DATABASE MemOptIndexing
ADD FILE (name='memoryOptimizedData',
filename= 'C:\Program Files\Microsoft SQL Server\MSSQL15.MSSQLSERVER\MSSQL\
DATA\memoryOptimizedData')
    TO FILEGROUP memoryOptimizedFG

ALTER DATABASE MemOptIndexing SET MEMORY_OPTIMIZED_ELEVATE_TO_SNAPSHOT=ON
GO
```

> **Note** The file location for the filestream indicated in Listing 6-1 may need to change to fit your environment.

To see how to create a memory-optimized table, review the code in Listing 6-2. In this code example, you create the table dbo.SalesOrderHeader. There are two items to be aware of in the table schema. First, the option that creates the table as a memory-optimized table is the MEMORY_OPTIMIZED=ON option. The second is the inclusion of a NONCLUSTERED HASH index on the table to index the data within memory. Other than those items, the table is much like any other table created in SQL Server.

Listing 6-2. Create Memory-Optimized Table

```
USE MemOptIndexing
GO
IF OBJECT_ID('dbo.SalesOrderHeader') IS NOT NULL
    DROP TABLE dbo.SalesOrderHeader

CREATE TABLE dbo.SalesOrderHeader(
    SalesOrderID int NOT NULL,
    OrderDate datetime,
    DueDate datetime,
    ShipDate datetime,
    [Status] tinyint,
    CONSTRAINT IX_SalesOrderHeader_Hash PRIMARY KEY
        NONCLUSTERED HASH (SalesOrderID)
        WITH (BUCKET_COUNT = 35000))
    WITH (MEMORY_OPTIMIZED = ON)
```

```
IF  OBJECT_ID('tempdb..#tempHeader') IS NOT NULL
    DROP TABLE #tempHeader

SELECT SalesOrderID
    ,OrderDate
    ,DueDate
    ,ShipDate
    ,[Status]
INTO #tempHeader
FROM AdventureWorks2017.sales.SalesOrderHeader

INSERT INTO dbo.SalesOrderHeader
SELECT SalesOrderID
    ,OrderDate
    ,DueDate
    ,ShipDate
    ,[Status]
FROM #tempHeader

SET STATISTICS IO ON
SET STATISTICS TIME ON
PRINT 'Memory Optimized Table'
SELECT *
FROM dbo.SalesOrderHeader
ORDER BY SalesOrderID

PRINT 'Traditional Table'
SELECT *
FROM AdventureWorks2017.sales.SalesOrderHeader
ORDER BY SalesOrderID

SET STATISTICS IO OFF
SET STATISTICS TIME OFF
```

The additional code in Listing 6-2 inserts data into MemOptIndexing.dbo. SalesOrderHeader and queries that same data. To demonstrate the impact of querying the data in a memory-optimized table, a similar query against AdventureWorks2017. sales.SalesOrderHeader is included. Examining the results, shown in Listing 6-3,

CHAPTER 6　INDEXING MEMORY-OPTIMIZED TABLES

provides a few insights into memory-optimized tables. First, there is no I/O impact from the memory-optimized tables. While the AdventureWorks2017.sales. SalesOrderHeader query requires 689 reads, there are no reads for MemOptIndexing. dbo.SalesOrderHeader. Second, the amount of CPU time for MemOptIndexing.dbo. SalesOrderHeader is much lower, at 16 ms, than the CPU time for the query against AdventureWorks2017.sales.SalesOrderHeader, which is 78 ms.

Listing 6-3. Output from Creating and Querying Memory-Optimized Table

```
(31465 row(s) affected)

(31465 row(s) affected)
Memory Optimized Table

 SQL Server Execution Times:
   CPU time = 0 ms,  elapsed time = 0 ms.
SQL Server parse and compile time:
   CPU time = 0 ms, elapsed time = 0 ms.

(31465 row(s) affected)

 SQL Server Execution Times:
   CPU time = 16 ms,  elapsed time = 310 ms.
Traditional Table

 SQL Server Execution Times:
   CPU time = 0 ms,  elapsed time = 0 ms.

(31465 row(s) affected)
Table 'SalesOrderHeader'. Scan count 1, logical reads 689, physical reads 0, read-ahead reads 0, lob logical reads 0, lob physical reads 0, lob read-ahead reads 0.

 SQL Server Execution Times:
   CPU time = 78 ms,  elapsed time = 785 ms.

 SQL Server Execution Times:
   CPU time = 0 ms,  elapsed time = 0 ms.
```

CHAPTER 6 INDEXING MEMORY-OPTIMIZED TABLES

While there are many more aspects of memory-optimized tables that can be discussed, this overview is intended to provide some of the most basic aspects. The rest of this chapter will examine indexing of memory-optimized tables. While memory-optimized tables are completely in memory, indexes are still required. Being in memory doesn't prevent the need to find specific data or filter resultsets. And as mentioned in Chapter 1, indexes provide the mechanism for providing a path to data.

To support indexing of memory-optimized tables, SQL Server supports two indexing options. These are hash and range indexes. Each memory-optimized table can support up to eight indexes. If a primary key is defined, this will be supported by one of the two index types and be one of the allowed indexes. If there is no primary key defined, the table must be created with at least one index. Additionally, memory-optimized tables do not allow indexing changes after creation, so you will need to define all indexes for a memory-optimized table when it is created.

The remainder of this chapter will focus on the hash and range types of indexes with considerations for building each of them against a memory-optimized table.

> **Note** Index operations for memory-optimized tables are nonlogged activities since they occur only within memory and have no impact on the state of the data stored in the table.

Hash Indexes

The first index type for memory-optimized tables is the hash index. Hash indexes separate the data in the table into a fixed number of buckets. Rows inserted into the table then use a hash function to assign rows to the available buckets. These buckets provide the ability for queries to return specific rows based on the point lookup operations. Hash indexes are designed for types of query workloads where individual rows from the tables need to be retrieved.

When creating hash indexes, the number of buckets to create is a function of the number of rows planned, or expected, for the table. If there will be a large number of rows, a larger bucket count is required. This is an important part of creating and tuning hash indexes on memory-optimized tables. As the number of rows in each bucket increases, the time required to retrieve data increases. The ratio of rows to buckets is something that needs to be carefully considered.

CHAPTER 6 ■ INDEXING MEMORY-OPTIMIZED TABLES

It is generally recommended to over-allocate buckets to hash indexes, with the range of buckets recommended to be between two and five times the number of rows. While this is the recommended practice, it is important to consider how you will be using the tables within your environment and size the buckets accordingly.

To demonstrate the impact of bucket size, Listing 6-4 creates two memory-optimized tables. Both tables have 1,000,000 rows in them, with the first table having 1,000 buckets and the second having 1,000,000 buckets. With this configuration, there will be approximately 1,000 rows per bucket for the first table and 1 row per bucket in the second table.

Listing 6-4. Create Memory-Optimized Tables with Hash Indexes

```
USE MemOptIndexing
GO

IF OBJECT_ID('dbo.SalesOrderHeader_low') IS NOT NULL
    DROP TABLE dbo.SalesOrderHeader_low

CREATE TABLE dbo.SalesOrderHeader_low(
    SalesOrderID int NOT NULL
    ,Column1 uniqueidentifier
    ,CONSTRAINT IX_SalesOrderHeader_Hash_low PRIMARY KEY
        NONCLUSTERED HASH (SalesOrderID)
        WITH (BUCKET_COUNT = 1000))
    WITH (MEMORY_OPTIMIZED = ON);

WITH L1(z) AS (SELECT 0 UNION ALL SELECT 0)
, L2(z) AS (SELECT 0 FROM L1 a CROSS JOIN L1 b)
, L3(z) AS (SELECT 0 FROM L2 a CROSS JOIN L2 b)
, L4(z) AS (SELECT 0 FROM L3 a CROSS JOIN L3 b)
, L5(z) AS (SELECT 0 FROM L4 a CROSS JOIN L4 b)
, L6(z) AS (SELECT TOP 1000000 0 FROM L5 a CROSS JOIN L5 b)
INSERT INTO dbo.SalesOrderHeader_low
SELECT ROW_NUMBER() OVER (ORDER BY z) AS RowID, NEWID()
FROM L6;
GO
```

```
IF OBJECT_ID('dbo.SalesOrderHeader_high') IS NOT NULL
    DROP TABLE dbo.SalesOrderHeader_high

CREATE TABLE dbo.SalesOrderHeader_high(
    SalesOrderID int NOT NULL
    ,Column1 uniqueidentifier
    ,CONSTRAINT IX_SalesOrderHeader_hash_high PRIMARY KEY
        NONCLUSTERED HASH (SalesOrderID)
        WITH (BUCKET_COUNT = 1000000))
    WITH (MEMORY_OPTIMIZED = ON);
WITH L1(z) AS (SELECT 0 UNION ALL SELECT 0)
, L2(z) AS (SELECT 0 FROM L1 a CROSS JOIN L1 b)
, L3(z) AS (SELECT 0 FROM L2 a CROSS JOIN L2 b)
, L4(z) AS (SELECT 0 FROM L3 a CROSS JOIN L3 b)
, L5(z) AS (SELECT 0 FROM L4 a CROSS JOIN L4 b)
, L6(z) AS (SELECT TOP 1000000 0 FROM L5 a CROSS JOIN L5 b)
INSERT INTO dbo.SalesOrderHeader_high
SELECT ROW_NUMBER() OVER (ORDER BY z) AS RowID, NEWID()
FROM L6;
```

> **Warning** The code in Listing 6-4 can take up to 5 minutes to execute.

Prior to executing the next piece of code for this demo, create an Extended Events session based on the Query Detail Tracking template. The session should be created with the default configuration and then launched to the Extended Events live data viewer. Add the columns `session_id`, `statement`, `writes`, `physical_reads`, `logical_reads`, `duration`, and `cpu_time` to the live viewer window. Lastly, filter the `session_id` in the output by the `session_id` values for Listing 6-5, 6-6, 6-8, and 6-9 and the event name `sql_statement_completed`.

When you execute a query against both tables to return the same row, shown in Listing 6-5, you get a slight performance difference between the two. In this sample execution, the execution time for the first query was 359 μs vs. 48 μs, shown in Figure 6-1. While this difference is small in total duration, the difference between them for the same query is significant. In solutions where memory-optimized tables will be used to retrieve results, this kind of performance difference can be important.

CHAPTER 6 INDEXING MEMORY-OPTIMIZED TABLES

Listing 6-5. Query Memory-Optimized Tables with Hash Indexes

```
USE MemOptIndexing
GO

SET STATISTICS TIME ON

PRINT 'Memory Optimized Table with 1000 buckets'
SELECT *
FROM dbo.SalesOrderHeader_low
WHERE SalesOrderID = 42
ORDER BY SalesOrderID

PRINT 'Memory Optimized Table with 1,000,000 buckets'
SELECT *
FROM dbo.SalesOrderHeader_high
WHERE SalesOrderID = 42
ORDER BY SalesOrderID

SET STATISTICS TIME OFF
```

name	timestamp	session_id	statement	writes	physical_reads	logical_reads	duration	cpu_time
sql_statement_completed	2019-07-21 23:11:24.0169838	88	SELECT @@SPID	0	0	0	22	0
sql_statement_completed	2019-07-21 23:11:24.0196896	88	USE MemOptIndexing	0	0	0	379	0
sql_statement_completed	2019-07-21 23:11:24.0227290	88	SET STATISTICS TIME ON	0	0	0	38	0
sql_statement_completed	2019-07-21 23:11:24.0227445	88	PRINT 'Memory Optimized Table with 1000 buckets'	0	0	0	7	0
sql_statement_completed	2019-07-21 23:11:24.0231529	88	SELECT * FROM dbo.SalesOrderHeader_low WHERE	0	0	0	359	0
sql_statement_completed	2019-07-21 23:11:24.0231590	88	PRINT 'Memory Optimized Table with 1,000,000 buckets'	0	0	0	2	0
sql_statement_completed	2019-07-21 23:11:24.0232204	88	SELECT * FROM dbo.SalesOrderHeader_high WHERE	0	0	0	48	0
sql_statement_completed	2019-07-21 23:11:24.0232235	88	SET STATISTICS TIME OFF	0	0	0	0	0

Figure 6-1. *Duration for memory-optimized table queries with hash indexes*

It's important not to interpret the results of the last script to indicate that a 1:1 ratio of buckets to rows is the best practice. If you run another set of queries that retrieves more than a single row, in this case the rows between 42 and 420 being returned as shown in Listing 6-6, the performance profile changes. In this case, the performance advantage shifts to buckets with more rows. The results now are 86,973 μs for the query on the first table vs. 101,127 μs for the second table's query, as shown in Figure 6-2.

Listing 6-6. Query Memory-Optimized Tables with Hash Indexes

```
USE MemOptIndexing
GO

SET STATISTICS TIME ON

PRINT 'Memory Optimized Table with 1000 buckets'
SELECT *
FROM dbo.SalesOrderHeader_low
WHERE SalesOrderID BETWEEN 42 AND 420
ORDER BY SalesOrderID

PRINT 'Memory Optimized Table with 1,000,000 buckets'
SELECT *
FROM dbo.SalesOrderHeader_high
WHERE SalesOrderID BETWEEN 42 AND 420
ORDER BY SalesOrderID

SET STATISTICS TIME OFF
```

name	timestamp	session_id	statement	writes	physical_reads	logical_reads	duration	cpu_time
sql_statement_completed	2019-07-21 23:16:36.6736500	88	SELECT @@SPID	0	0	0	0	0
sql_statement_completed	2019-07-21 23:16:36.8963304	88	USE MemOptIndexing	0	0	0	43	0
sql_statement_completed	2019-07-21 23:16:36.9075833	88	SET STATISTICS TIME ON	0	0	0	2	0
sql_statement_completed	2019-07-21 23:16:36.9075957	88	PRINT 'Memory Optimized Table with 1000 buckets'	0	0	0	6	0
sql_statement_completed	2019-07-21 23:16:36.9946255	88	SELECT * FROM dbo.SalesOrderHeader_low WHERE...	0	0	0	86973	139000
sql_statement_completed	2019-07-21 23:16:36.9946399	88	PRINT 'Memory Optimized Table with 1,000,000 buckets'	0	0	0	4	0
sql_statement_completed	2019-07-21 23:16:37.0957947	88	SELECT * FROM dbo.SalesOrderHeader_high WHERE...	0	0	0	101127	110000
sql_statement_completed	2019-07-21 23:16:37.0958079	88	SET STATISTICS TIME OFF	0	0	0	2	0

Figure 6-2. Duration for memory-optimized table queries with hash indexes

When working with hash indexes, it is important to understand how SQL Server is using the buckets in the hash. One important thing to note is that just because there are enough buckets for each table to have their own bucket, that doesn't mean each row will get its own bucket. To review the statistics for hash indexes created in this chapter, run the query in Listing 6-7 that accesses the DMV sys.dm_db_xtp_hash_index_stats. This DMV provides information on the number of buckets and how those buckets are populated.

CHAPTER 6 INDEXING MEMORY-OPTIMIZED TABLES

Listing 6-7. Query to Review Hash Index Statistics

```
USE MemOptIndexing
GO

SELECT OBJECT_NAME(hs.object_id) AS object_name
,i.name as index_name
,hs.total_bucket_count
,hs.empty_bucket_count
,FLOOR((CAST(empty_bucket_count as float)/total_bucket_count) * 100) AS
empty_bucket_percent
,hs.avg_chain_length
,hs.max_chain_length
FROM sys.dm_db_xtp_hash_index_stats AS hs
INNER JOIN sys.indexes AS i ON hs.object_id=i.object_id AND hs.index_id=i.
index_id
```

Reviewing the results of Listing 6-7, provided in Figure 6-3, you can see there are a few interesting items to notice. To start, the first index with the 1,000 buckets specified (SalesOrderHeader_low) actually has 1,024 buckets for the index. This is because buckets are created in allocations that align to the power of two. This is the same reason there are 1,048,576 buckets for the 1,000,000 bucket index on SalesOrderHeader_high. The next interesting piece is the number of empty buckets in the hash index on SalesOrderHeader_high. With 1,000,000 rows and more than a million buckets, there are still 37 percent of the buckets that are empty. This happens because with the deterministic hashing function, some hashed values are repeated within the range of values before all the buckets are utilized. This is something to consider when building hash indexes, especially when aiming to have a 1:1 ratio of buckets to rows.

	object_name	index_name	total_bucket_count	empty_bucket_count	empty_bucket_percent	avg_chain_length	max_chain_length
1	SalesOrderHeader_low	IX_SalesOrderHeader_Hash_low	1024	0	0	976	1035
2	SalesOrderHeader	IX_SalesOrderHeader_Hash	65536	40674	62	1	7
3	SalesOrderHeader_high	IX_SalesOrderHeader_hash_high	1048576	398369	37	1	8

Figure 6-3. *Output from hash bucket statistics query*

> **Note** The query performance details were captured using an Extended Events session based on the Query Detail Tracking template with a filter for the session that included the demonstration queries. You can find more information on building sessions at www.simple-talk.com/sql/database-administration/getting-started-with-extended-events-in-sql-server-2012/.

Hash indexes with memory-optimized tables are an important indexing choice when there will be many queries that will access individual rows and seek operations that will provide optimal plans. When building the tables and hash indexes, focus on setting the number of buckets to a size that presents a reasonable ratio of rows to buckets with consideration for the number of rows that will be retrieved through queries.

Range Indexes

The second type of index that is supported for memory-optimized tables is the range index. Range indexes are used to support, as the name implies, range scans of data, along with ordered scans. They leverage a variation of a B-tree, which Microsoft is calling a Bw-tree. The key difference between these two structures is the reference between the nodes in the Bw-tree, which refers to memory locations vs. physical page location. When it comes to determining whether to include a range index on a memory-optimized table, the primary consideration will be whether there will be range scans or ORDER BY statements that the table needs to support.

> **Note** You can find more information on Bw-trees at http://research.microsoft.com/pubs/178758/bw-tree-icde2013-final.pdf.

To create a range index on a memory-optimized table, you declare the index within the schema of the table by indicating a NONCLUSTERED index with the key values. As shown in Listing 6-8, the index IX_SalesOrderHeader is a range index on the SalesOrderID column. Unlike hash indexes, there are no other configuration items to consider, and the indexes don't need any bucket consideration when they are created.

Listing 6-8. Create Table with Range Index

```
USE MemOptIndexing
GO

IF OBJECT_ID('dbo.SalesOrderHeader_high_range') IS NOT NULL
    DROP TABLE dbo.SalesOrderHeader_high_range

CREATE TABLE dbo.SalesOrderHeader_high_range(
    SalesOrderID int NOT NULL
    ,Column1 uniqueidentifier
    ,CONSTRAINT IX_SalesOrderHeader_hash_high_range PRIMARY KEY
        NONCLUSTERED HASH (SalesOrderID)
        WITH (BUCKET_COUNT = 1000000)
    ,INDEX IX_SalesOrderHeader NONCLUSTERED (SalesOrderID)
    )
    WITH (MEMORY_OPTIMIZED = ON);

WITH L1(z) AS (SELECT 0 UNION ALL SELECT 0)
, L2(z) AS (SELECT 0 FROM L1 a CROSS JOIN L1 b)
, L3(z) AS (SELECT 0 FROM L2 a CROSS JOIN L2 b)
, L4(z) AS (SELECT 0 FROM L3 a CROSS JOIN L3 b)
, L5(z) AS (SELECT 0 FROM L4 a CROSS JOIN L4 b)
, L6(z) AS (SELECT TOP 1000000 0 FROM L5 a CROSS JOIN L5 b)
INSERT INTO dbo.SalesOrderHeader_high_range
SELECT ROW_NUMBER() OVER (ORDER BY z) AS RowID, NEWID()
FROM L6;
```

To demonstrate the value of the range index on memory-optimized tables, let's use the table created in Listing 6-8 on some queries that will leverage range scans. For this, you will use Listing 6-9, which queries the new table (dbo.SalesOrderHeader_high_range) and the table previously created with just a hash index (dbo.SalesOrderHeader_high). By executing a query against both of those tables for the rows with SalesOrderID between 100 and 10,000, you can see there is a big difference in the execution time. The query with just the hash index on the table runs in 216 ms (see Figure 6-4), while the query against the table with the range index runs in 97 ms. In this case, range indexes provide a substantial performance improvement.

CHAPTER 6　INDEXING MEMORY-OPTIMIZED TABLES

Listing 6-9. Query Memory-Optimized Tables with Range Scan

```
USE MemOptIndexing
GO

SET STATISTICS TIME ON

SELECT *
FROM dbo.SalesOrderHeader_high
WHERE SalesOrderID BETWEEN 100 AND 10000
ORDER BY SalesOrderID

SELECT *
FROM dbo.SalesOrderHeader_high_range
WHERE SalesOrderID BETWEEN 100 AND 10000
ORDER BY SalesOrderID

SET STATISTICS TIME OFF
```

name	timestamp	session_id	statement	writes	physical_reads	logical_reads	duration	cpu_time
sql_statement_completed	2019-07-21 23:55:47.8218210	88	SELECT @@SPID	0	0	0	0	0
sql_statement_completed	2019-07-21 23:55:47.8410257	88	USE MemOptIndexing	0	0	0	51	0
sql_statement_completed	2019-07-21 23:55:47.8446218	88	SET STATISTICS TIME ON	0	0	0	2	0
sql_statement_completed	2019-07-21 23:55:48.0552792	88	SELECT * FROM dbo.SalesOrderHeader_high WHERE				210643	124000
sql_statement_completed	2019-07-21 23:55:48.1523803	88	SELECT * FROM dbo.SalesOrderHeader_high_range W				97080	0
sql_statement_completed	2019-07-21 23:55:48.1523887	88	SET STATISTICS TIME OFF	0	0	0	1	0

Figure 6-4. *Duration for memory-optimized table queries with range scan*

In a similar fashion, ORDER BY statements are also greatly improved when range indexes on memory-optimized tables are available. Using the code in Listing 6-10, you run two queries against the same tables from the previous demonstration. In this case, using the output in Figure 6-5, you see that the range scan took 462 µs compared to the 240,733 µs that the hash index requires. Again, you get a substantial performance improvement through the use of the range index.

Listing 6-10. Query Memory-Optimized Tables with ORDER BY Statement

```
USE MemOptIndexing
GO

SET STATISTICS TIME ON
```

```
SELECT TOP 100 *
FROM dbo.SalesOrderHeader_high
ORDER BY SalesOrderID

SELECT TOP 100 *
FROM dbo.SalesOrderHeader_high_range
ORDER BY SalesOrderID

SET STATISTICS TIME OFF
```

Figure 6-5. Duration for memory-optimized table queries with TOP clause and ORDER BY

Similar to hash indexes, range indexes provide a substantial performance improvement opportunity when creating memory-optimized tables. The need to perform range scans and order results is a common scenario in many applications. These operations are greatly improved by the use of range indexes.

Summary

This chapter looked at the types of indexes available for memory-optimized tables. These options, which include hash and range indexes, are the power behind the ability for memory-optimized tables to provide the incredible performance that they deliver. As demonstrated, each index type aligns to different querying patterns on your tables, and it is important to understand those patterns to build the right indexes for your memory-optimized tables and the workloads that they support.

CHAPTER 7

Full-Text Indexing

SQL Server supports mechanisms that allow you to store large amounts of unstructured text information. Since SQL Server 2008, one of those mechanisms has been the MAX lengthused with the variable-length character data types VARCHAR and NVARCHAR. This means you can store up to 2 GB worth of character information within a single column. While SQL Server can store this information, the 1,700-byte limit for nonclustered indexes and 900-byte limit on clustered indexes make indexing through traditional means a challenge. Fortunately, SQL Server offers another indexing mechanism for searching within these large data types, where full-text indexing comes into play.

Full-Text Indexing

Full-text search indexing is another indexing feature in SQL Server, outside the normal indexing methods and objects. This chapter will briefly describe the full-text search architecture, storage, and indexing for optimal performance.

Full-text search (FTS) allows you to store large amounts of text-based content. This content can include a number of document types including formats such as Word document (.docx) files. This storage is then in BLOB (binary large object) columns instead of plain-text data. The ability to search and store content of an unstructured nature provides a number of opportunities in a database management system.

Document retention is one such opportunity; it allows you to store documents for vast lengths of time at a much lower cost. The search abilities allow for querying this content for all types of needs. Imagine a shipping company that creates thousands of shipping documents from a template created in plain text. Those documents create a massive initiative for retention purposes to ensure shipments can be tracked for later needs. Storage warehouse rooms cost money to maintain. When the task of researching a specific shipment arises, the hours taken for that task are significant.

Now imagine this shipping company is using the FTS feature and an indexing structure. The documents are scanned with systems that read the text into a system that later inserts this data into a SQL Server database. This allows for a full-text search of specific account numbers, shipping invoices, and any distinct text in the documents needed for later review. An index just like a book index can be created, making it even quicker to find specific documents. Going further, FTS lets you search for specific content in the documents themselves. If a request comes in to find all shipping documents that were sent by a specific freight company on a specific trailer, the FTS capabilities allow the information to be retrieved in a fraction of the time as compared to a manual process.

Creating a Full-Text Example

Now that you understand the concept of FTS, let's look at the indexing strategy. Full-text indexes are essentially the backbone of searching and querying the data. This data can be a number of data types including `char`, `varchar`, `nchar`, `nvarchar`, `xml`, and `varbinary`. While it is possible to use `text`, `ntext`, and `image,` `it's best to avoid their use since they are on the deprecation list`. The data types varchar, nvarchar, and varbinary provide equivalent types, respectively. In fact, utilizing `varchar(max)` on most 64-bit systems has outperformed other data types in tests by the DataCAT team, as described in "Best Practices for Integrated Full Text Search (iFTS) in SQL 2008" (`https://techcommunity.microsoft.com/t5/DataCAT/Best-Practices-for-Integrated-Full-Text-Search-iFTS-in-SQL-2008/ba-p/305000`).

For the remainder of this section on full-text search indexing, the contents of the white paper "Optimizing Your Query Plans with the SQL Server 2014 Cardinality Estimator" by Joseph Sack have been inserted into the sample table using the script in Listing 7-1. I'll use the document to demonstrate full-text indexing. You can find the document in Books Online or download it from `http://bit.ly/1II5UfU` and place it in the directory `c:\temp`. Additionally, the full-text catalog feature needs to be installed in order to successfully run all the code in this chapter. Full-text catalog is not a feature that is installed by default, so you may need to address that first.

CHAPTER 7 FULL-TEXT INDEXING

> **Note** For all versions of SQL Server, to build full-text index on Microsoft Office documents, the Filter Pack IFilters must be installed. Download and install Microsoft Office 2010 Filter Packs from https://support.microsoft.com/en-us/help/945934/how-to-register-microsoft-filter-pack-ifilters-with-sql-server. Be sure to follow the additional steps to run sp_fulltext_service and restart the SQL Server instance.

Creating a Full-Text Catalog

Using AdventureWorks2017, a table can be prepared that will be used for full-text searching. Using the varbinary(max) data type allows the import of most document types and images. In Listing 7-1, the CREATE TABLE and INSERT statements prepare the objects needed to create a full-text search index.

Listing 7-1. CREATE TABLE and INSERT Statements Used with Full-Text Search

```
USE AdventureWorks2017
GO

DROP TABLE IF EXISTS dbo.SQLServerDocuments;

CREATE TABLE dbo.SQLServerDocuments (
    SQLServerDocumentsID INT IDENTITY(1, 1),
    DocType VARCHAR(6),
    DOC VARBINARY(MAX),
    CONSTRAINT PK_SQLServerDocuments PRIMARY KEY CLUSTERED
        (SQLServerDocumentsID)
    );
GO
DECLARE @worddoc VARBINARY(MAX);
SELECT  @worddoc = CAST(bulkcolumn AS VARBINARY(MAX))
FROM    OPENROWSET(BULK 'c:\temp\Optimizing Your Query Plans with the SQL Server 2014 Cardinality Estimator.docx', SINGLE_BLOB) AS x;
```

```
INSERT  INTO dbo.SQLServerDocuments
        (DocType, DOC)
VALUES  ('docx', @worddoc);
GO
```

When creating an FTS index, a full-text catalog must first be created. Since SQL Server 2008, the catalog is now contained in the database as a definition. The catalog itself is now a virtual object and greatly enhances the performance by eliminating I/O bottlenecks. A catalog contains all the properties that are searchable.

The catalog is the link to the full-text index. Before we get started, let's review the syntax for CREATE FULLTEXT CATALOG, which is shown in Listing 7-2.

Listing 7-2. The CREATE FULLTEXT CATALOG Syntax

```
CREATE FULLTEXT CATALOG <catalog name>
WITH <catalog specific options>
AS DEFAULT
AUTHORIZATION <the owners name - ownership>
ACCENT_SENSITIVITY = <ON|OFF>;
```

The first option that should be considered in the creation of a catalog is the AS DEFAULT setting. Commonly, full-text indexes are created without thought of the catalog to which they should be applied. If the catalog is omitted in the index creation, the catalog that has been set as the default will be used.

Authorization and accent sensitivity are specific in the CREATE command. When omitting the authorization option, ownership will fall under dbo. This is the same for most objects in SQL Server when ownership is not declared. It is recommended that you assign ownership for managing security and grouping objects under the proper areas. When specifying a user for ownership, you must specify a username matching one of the following:

- The name of the user running the statement
- The name of a user that the user executing the command has impersonate permissions for
- The database owner or system administrator

Accent sensitivity dictates whether the catalog will be accent sensitive or insensitive. For example, with accent insensitive, the words "piñata" and "pinata" will be treated as the same words. Be sure to research whether accent sensitivity should be on or off prior to the creation of the catalog. If this option is changed, the full-text indexes on the catalog must be rebuilt.

For creating a full-text catalog on the white paper, execute the statement in Listing 7-3. For this catalog, we'll use the default options for the syntax, which sets accent sensitivity to the collation of the table.

Listing 7-3. Creating a New Full-Text Catalog

```
CREATE FULLTEXT CATALOG WhitePaperCatalog AS DEFAULT;
```

Creating a Full-Text Index

With the catalog created and the decision made for how you want to handle catalogs, accent sensitivity, and ownership, now you need to make some decisions and apply some restrictions to the creation of the full-text index. The most critical of these decisions is the requirement of a key index.

Syntax

The syntax in Listing 7-4 is used to create the full-text index. Table 7-1 describes the different options available.

Listing 7-4. CREATE FULLTEXT INDEX Syntax

```
CREATE FULLTEXT INDEX ON <table name>
(<column name>)
KEY INDEX <index name [must be specified]>
ON <catalog filegroup>
WITH <index options>
CHANGE_TRACKING = <Manual | Auto | Off>
STOPLIST = <default system or specified StopList name>;
```

In most other `CREATE INDEX` statements, the basic syntax and options are alike with slight modifications. With FTS index creation, you can see there is a completely different set of options and considerations. The initial `CREATE FULLTEXT INDEX` is the same as any `CREATE INDEX`, with the given table required and then column to index. After this, the other options are not typical to normal index creations.

Table 7-1. *Full-Text Index Options*

Option Name	Description
TYPE COLUMN	Specifies the name of the column that holds the document type for documents loaded in BLOB types, such as `.doc`, `.pdf`, and `.xls`. This option is used only for `varbinary`, `varbinary(max)`, and `image` data types. If this option is specified on any other data type, the `CREATE FULLTEXT INDEX` statement will throw an error.
LANGUAGE	Alters the default language that is used for the index with the following variations and options: • The language can be specified as string, integer, or hexadecimal. • If a language is specified, the language is used when a query is run using the index. • When a language is specified as a string value, the `syslanguages` system table must correspond to the language. • If a double-byte value is used, it is converted to hexadecimal at creation time. • Word breakers and stemmers for the specific language must be enabled, or an SQL Server error will be generated. • Non-BLOB and non-XML columns containing multiple languages should follow the 0 x 0 neutral language setting. • For BLOB and XML types, language types in the documents themselves will be used. For example, a Word document with a language type of Russian or LCID 1049 will force the same setting in the index. Use `sys.fulltext_languages` to review all the language types and LCID codings available.

(continued)

Table 7-1. (*continued*)

Option Name	Description
KEY INDEX	Every full-text index requires an adjoining unique, single-key, non-null column to be designated. Specify the column in the same table using this option.
FULLTEXT_CATALOG_NAME	If the full-text index is not to be created using the default catalog, specify the catalog name using this option.
CHANGE_TRACKING	Determines how and when an index is populated. Options are MANUAL, AUTO, and OFF [NO_POPULATION]. The MANUAL setting requires ALTER FULLTEXT INDEX ... START UPDATE POPULATION to be executed before the index is populated. The AUTO setting populates the index at creation time and automatically updates based on changes that are made ongoing. This is the default setting if CHANGE_TRACKING is omitted in the CREATE statement. The OFF [NO_POPULATION] setting is used to completely turn population off for the index, and SQL Server will not retain a list of changes. The index is populated upon creation one time unless the NO_POPULATION is specified.
STOPLIST	Specifies a StopList that will essentially stop certain words from being indexed. OFF, SYSTEM, and a custom StopList are available options. The OFF setting will not use a StopList and will have more overhead on performance of population of the index. The SYSTEM is the default StopList created already. A user-created StopList is a StopList that was created that can be used in association with an index.
SEARCH PROPERTY LIST	Specifies the search property list to associate with the full-text index. Property lists allow greater control of full-text search by allowing differentiation of search between properties of a document, such as title or tags.

Key Indexes

Choosing the key index can be a straightforward choice given the restrictions of the key index being a unique, single-key, and non-nullable column. A primary key will commonly work well for this, like the primary key shown in Listing 7-1 on the dbo.SQLServerDocuments table. However, consideration should be given to the size of the key.

Ideally, a 6-byte key is recommended and documented as optimal to reduce overhead on I/O and CPU resource consumption. Recall that one of the restrictions of the unique key is that it cannot exceed 900 bytes. If this maximum restriction is met, the population will fail. Resolving the problem could force a new index and alteration of the table itself to occur. This could create costly downtime for tables that are in high-use situations.

Population

Change tracking in full-text indexing should be weighed heavily when creating full-text indexes. The default setting of AUTO may have overhead that can affect the performance negatively if the contents of the column being indexed change frequently. For example, a system that is storing shipping invoices that never change and are inserted only once a month would not likely benefit from AUTO being set. A MANUAL population would most likely be better run at a given time by using the SQL Server Agent based on the loading of the contents in the table. Although not common, some systems are static and loaded only one time. This would be an ideal situation for using the OFF setting, with the initial population being performed only at that time.

The last option for population is incremental population. It is an alternative to manual population. Incremental population is the same concept as an incremental update to data. As you run through the data and changes are made, they are tracked. Think of merge replication as a comparison. Merge replication retains changes by the use of triggers and insert/update/delete tracking rows into merge system tables. At a given point in time, a DBA can set a synchronization schedule to process those changes and replicate them to the subscribers. This is the same way incremental population functions. By using a `timestamp` column in the table, the changes are tracked. Only those that are found needing a change are processed. This does mean the requirement for a timestamp column on the table must be met in order to perform incremental populations. For data that has an extreme amount of change, this may not be ideal. However, for data that changes randomly and seldomly, incremental population may be suited for the installation.

StopLists

StopLists are extremely useful in managing what not to populate. This can improve the population performance by bypassing what are known as *noise words*. As an example, consider the sentence "A dog chewed through the fiber going to the SAN causing the disaster and recovery plans to be used for the SQL Server instance." In this sentence,

CHAPTER 7 ■ FULL-TEXT INDEXING

you would most likely want *fiber*, *SAN*, *disaster*, *recovery*, and *SQL* or *Server* indexed. The *A*, *the*, *to*, and *be* words would not be ideal. These are considered noise words and are not part of the population process. As you can imagine, the use of StopList can be extremely helpful in the overall population performance and parsing of the content. Use of the StopList can be specific to languages as well. For example, *la* in French would be specified over *the* in English.

To create a custom StopList, use the `CREATE FULLTEXT STOPLIST` statement as shown in Listing 7-5. The system default StopList can be used to pregenerate all the noise words already identified as such. For the white paper example, the name of the StopList would be `WhitePaperStopList`.

Listing 7-5. Creating a Full-Text StopList

```
CREATE FULLTEXT STOPLIST WhitePaperStopList FROM SYSTEM STOPLIST;
```

To view the StopList, use the system views `sys.fulltext_stoplists` and `sys.fulltext_stopwords`. The `sys.fulltext_stoplists` view will hold metadata related to the stoplists that are created on the SQL Server instance. Determine the `stoplist_id` to join to `sys.fulltext_stopwords` to show a complete listing of the words. Alone, this StopList is no better than the system default StopList. To add words to the StopList, use the `ALTER FULLTEXT STOPLIST` statement in Listing 7-6's example. That example removes *Downtime* as a word to be excluded.

Listing 7-6. Modifying a Full-Text Stoplist

```
ALTER FULLTEXT STOPLIST WhitePaperStopList ADD 'Downtime' LANGUAGE 1033;
```

To review the StopList words, run the query shown in Listing 7-7.

Listing 7-7. Using sys.fulltext_stoplists to Review StopList Words

```
SELECT  lists.stoplist_id,
        lists.name,
        words.stopword
FROM    sys.fulltext_stoplists AS lists
JOIN    sys.fulltext_stopwords AS words
        ON lists.stoplist_id = words.stoplist_id
WHERE   words.language = 'English'
ORDER BY lists.name;
```

You can see the query results in Figure 7-1; the word *Downtime* has been successfully added.

stoplist_id		name	stopword
13	5	WhitePaperStopList	B
14	5	WhitePaperStopList	C
15	5	WhitePaperStopList	D
16	5	WhitePaperStopList	Downtime

Figure 7-1. *Query results of a StopList*

With the catalog, StopList, and key index availability within the primary key SQLServerDocumentsID in the table created in Listing 7-1, you can create a full-text index on the DOC column in the same table from Listing 7-1. To create a full-text index, use the CREATE FULLTEXT INDEX statement (see Listing 7-8).

Listing 7-8. CREATE FULLTEXT INDEX Statement

```
CREATE FULLTEXT INDEX ON dbo.SQLServerDocuments
(
DOC
TYPE COLUMN DocType
)
KEY INDEX PK_SQLServerDocuments
ON WhitePaperCatalog
WITH STOPLIST = WhitePaperStopList;
```

Once the index is created, population will begin since there was no option added for CHANGE_TRACKING. Later in the chapter, I'll show how to monitor the catalog and see the status. It might take a while to load depending on the size of your document. The default AUTO setting takes effect. To query the content of the SQLServerDocuments table and DOC column, you can run a CONTAINS statement to return a specific word. Listing 7-9 shows an example of such a statement.

Listing 7-9. Using CONTAINS to Query for a Specific Word

```
SELECT   ssd.DOC,
         ssd.DocType
FROM     dbo.SQLServerDocuments AS ssd
WHERE    CONTAINS (ssd.DOC, 'statistic');
```

Figure 7-2 shows the execution plan from the query.

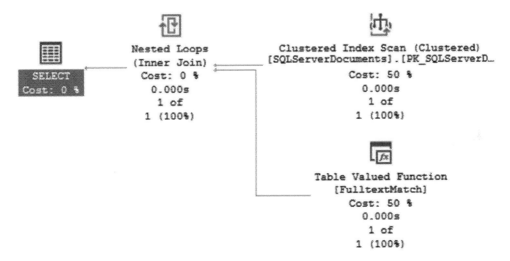

Figure 7-2. *Execution plan of CONTAINS and FTS index usage*

By searching by means of CONTAINS(ssd.DOC,'statistic'), the execution plan in Figure 7-2 shows the operation on FulltextMatch. It also returns the white paper with a document type of .docx as a match for this word search.

Full-Text Search Index Catalog Views and Properties

SQL Server provides a wealth of information about indexes in general. Performance, configurations, usage, and storage are just a few. As with normal index objects, full-text indexes require the same attention and detail to maintenance and options set to ensure they consistently benefit the overall performance rather than hinder it.

Table 7-2 describes the catalog views available to full-text search.

Table 7-2. Full-Text Catalog Views

Catalog View Name	Description
sys.fulltext_catalogs	Lists all full-text catalogs and high-level properties.
sys.fulltext_document_types	Returns a complete list of document types that are available for indexing. Each of these document types will be registered on the instance of SQL Server.
sys.fulltext_index_catalog_usages	
sys.fulltext_index_columns	Lists all columns that are indexed.
sys.fulltext_index_fragments	Lists all details of the full-text index fragments (storage of the inverted index data).
sys.fulltext_indexes	Lists every full-text index and properties set on the indexes.
sys.fulltext_languages	Lists all the available languages on the instance to full-text indexing.
sys.fulltext_semantic_language_statistics_database	Lists semantic language statistics databases installed.
sys.fulltext_semantic_languages	List all of the languages with statistics models registered.
sys.fulltext_stoplists	Lists every StopList created.
sys.fulltext_stopwords	Lists all StopWords in the database.
sys.fulltext_system_stopwords	Lists the preloaded system StopWords.

For informational purposes, while reviewing catalogs, properties, and status results for population, invoke the FULLTEXTCATALOGPROPERTY function, as shown in Listing 7-10.

Listing 7-10. Querying Properties from Full-Text Index

```
FULLTEXTCATALOGPROPERTY ('catalog_name' ,'property')
```

The returned information will provide a wealth of detail on the state of the catalog including population status. The catalog_name parameter will take any catalog created, and then a listing of properties can be utilized to return the specific information required. Table 7-3 lists the properties you can pass.

Table 7-3. *Full-Text Catalog Properties*

Property Name	Description
AccentSensitivity	Catalog's current accent sensitivity setting. This returns 0, which means insensitive, and 1, which means sensitive.
IndexSize	Logical size in megabytes of the catalog.
ItemCount	The total items that have been indexed in the catalog.
LogSize	Backward capability property. This returns 0.
MergeStatus	Returns 0 if no master merge is in progress and 1 if a master merge is in progress.
PopulateCompletionAge	The elapsed time since index population, in seconds, measured since 01/01/1990 00:00:00. This will always return 0 if the population has not run yet.
PopulateStatus	PopulateStatus can return ten different values: *0*: Idle. *1*: Full population in progress. *2*: Paused. *3*: The population has been throttled. *4*: The population is recovering. *5*: The status is shut down. *6*: Incremental population is currently in progress. *7*: The status is currently building an index. *8*: The disk is full. *9*: Change tracking.
UniqueKeyCount	Number of individual full-text index keys in the catalog.
ImportStatus	Returns 0 when the full-text catalog is not being imported and 1 when it is being imported.

For example, to show the population status of the `WhitePaperCatalog` catalog used earlier, you can use the statement in Listing 7-11. The result should be 0 for idle, since the index only has the single document and no other queries are running against the index.

Listing 7-11. *FULLTEXTCATALOGPROPERTY to Return Population Status of a Catalog*

```
SELECT FULLTEXTCATALOGPROPERTY('WhitePaperCatalog','PopulateStatus');
```

Catalogs and the referencing indexes can be reviewed by executing `sys.fulltext_index_catalog_usages`. This catalog view returns all the indexes that have been referenced from it, as shown in Listing 7-12.

Listing 7-12. *Utilizing sys.fulltext_index_catalog_usages*

```
SELECT  OBJECT_NAME(ficu.object_id) [Object Name],
        ficu.index_id,
        ficu.fulltext_catalog_id
FROM    sys.fulltext_index_catalog_usages AS ficu;
```

Figure 7-3 shows the results, which show SQLServerDocuments is using a catalog associated with itself, while JobCandidate, ProductReview, and Document are using a shared full-text catalog. It is important to note that you are able to use a single catalog across multiple tables.

	Object Name	index_id	fulltext_catalog_id
1	JobCandidate	1	5
2	ProductReview	1	5
3	Document	1	5
4	SQLServerDocuments	1	8

Figure 7-3. *Results from sys.fulltext_index_catalog_usages*

For detailed information on all catalogs and settings currently applied to them, query `sys.fulltext_catalogs`. This catalog view is helpful in determining the default catalog and property status indicators, such as `is_importing` that shows whether the catalog is in the process of being imported.

For a detailed review of the full-text indexes in the database, you can use `sys.fulltext_indexes` along with joining catalog views to create a more meaningful resultset. Important information from this catalog view consists of the full-text catalog name and properties; change tracking property, crawl type, and state; and the StopList set to be used.

The query in Listing 7-13 returns an information resultset of all indexes including catalog and StopList information for the index.

Listing 7-13. Using All the Catalog Views for Full-Text Index Information

```
SELECT  idx.is_enabled,
        idx.change_tracking_state,
        idx.crawl_type_desc,
        idx.crawl_end_date [Last Crawl],
        cat.name,
        CASE WHEN cat.is_accent_sensitivity_on = 0 THEN 'Accent
        InSensitive'
            WHEN cat.is_accent_sensitivity_on = 1 THEN 'Accent Sensitive'
        END [Accent Sensitivity],
        lists.name,
        lists.modify_date [Last Modified Date of StopList]
FROM    sys.fulltext_indexes idx
INNER JOIN sys.fulltext_catalogs cat
        ON idx.fulltext_catalog_id = cat.fulltext_catalog_id
INNER JOIN sys.fulltext_stoplists lists
        ON idx.stoplist_id = lists.stoplist_id;
```

Figure 7-4 shows the results of the catalog view query. This can be extremely useful when tuning full-text catalogs. For instance, if the index is out-of-date, you'll be able to identify when it was last updated or crawled. Or if you'd tuned a full-text index to remove noise by adding to the StopList, knowing when that change occurred in relation to the last crawl can help identify why the performance did not improve.

	is_enabled	change_tracking_state	crawl_type_desc	Last Crawl	name	Accent Sensitivity	name	Last Modified Date of StopList
1	1	A	UPDATE_CRAWL	2019-05-01 22:49:37.933	WhitePaperCatalog	Accent Sensitive	WhitePaperStopList	2019-05-01 22:24:43.213

Figure 7-4. *Query results for full-text index information*

CHAPTER 7　FULL-TEXT INDEXING

Summary

This chapter outlined how to create and query from a full-text index. The need to be able to filter and query on large documents and free-form text is just as important as being able to use traditional structured indexes. With full-text indexing, you can examine not only the contents of a column but also the contents of a file within a column, allowing applications to much better identify documents and other artifacts that match contextually with the requests being submitted.

CHAPTER 8

Indexing Myths and Best Practices

In the past few chapters, we've defined indexes and showed how they are structured. In the upcoming chapters, you'll be looking at strategies to build indexes and ensure that they behave as expected. In this chapter, we'll dispel some common myths and show how to build the foundation for creating indexes.

Myths result in an unnecessary burden when attempting to build an index. Knowing the myths associated with indexes can prevent you from using indexing strategies that will be counterproductive. The following are the indexing myths discussed in this chapter:

- Databases don't need indexes.
- Primary keys are always clustered.
- Online index operations don't block.
- Any column can be filtered in multicolumn indexes.
- Clustered indexes store records in physical order.
- Indexes always output in the same order.
- Fill factor is applied to indexes during inserts.
- Deleting from heaps results in unrecoverable space.
- Every table should be a heap or have a clustered index.

When reviewing myths, it's also a good idea to take a look at best practices. Best practices are like myths in many ways in the sense that they are commonly held beliefs. The primary difference is that best practices stand up to scrutiny and are useful recommendations when building indexes. This chapter will examine the following best practices:

- Index to your current workload.
- Use clustered indexes on primary keys by default.
- Properly target database-level fill factors.
- Properly target index-level fill factors.
- Index unique and foreign key columns.
- Balance index count.

Index Myths

One of the problems that people encounter when building databases and indexes is dealing with myths. Indexing myths originate from many different places. Some come from previous versions of SQL Server and its tools or are based on former functionality. Others come from the advice of others, based on conditions in a specific database that don't match those of other databases.

The trouble with indexing myths is that they cloud the water of indexing strategies. In situations where an index can be built to resolve a serious performance issue, a myth can sometimes prevent the approach from being considered. Throughout the next few sections, we'll cover a number of myths regarding indexing, and I'll do my best to dispel them.

Myth 1: Databases Don't Need Indexes

Usually, in an application that is being developed, one or more databases are created to store data for the application. In many development processes, the focus is on adding new features with the expectation that "performance will work itself out." An unfortunate result is that there are many databases that get developed and deployed without indexes being built because of the belief that they aren't needed.

Along with this, there are database developers who believe their databases are somehow unique from other databases. The following are some reasons that are heard from time to time:

- "It's a small database that won't get much data."
- "It's just a proof of concept and won't be around for long."
- "It's not an important application, so performance isn't important."
- "The whole database already fits into memory; indexes will just make it require more memory."
- "I am going to use this database only for inserting data; I will never look at the results."

Each of these reasons is easy to break down. In today's world of big data, even databases that are expected to be small can start growing quickly as they are adopted. Besides that, small in terms of a database is definitely in the eye of the beholder. Any proof of concept or unimportant database and application wouldn't have been created if there wasn't a need or someone wasn't interested in expending resources for the features. Those same people likely expect that the features they asked for will perform as expected. Lastly, fitting a database into memory doesn't mean it will be fast. As was discussed in previous chapters, indexes provide alternative access paths for data, with the aim of decreasing the number of pages required to access the data. Without these alternative routes, data access will likely require reading every page of a table.

These reasons may not be the ones you hear concerning your databases, but they will likely be similar. The general idea surrounding this myth is that indexes don't help the database perform better. One of the strongest ways to break apart this excuse is by demonstrating the benefits of indexing against a given scenario.

To demonstrate, let's look at the code in Listing 8-1. This code sample creates the table MythOne. Next, you will find a query similar to one in almost any application. In the output from the query, in Listing 8-2, the query generated 1,496 reads.

CHAPTER 8 INDEXING MYTHS AND BEST PRACTICES

Listing 8-1. Table with No Index

```
USE AdventureWorks2017;
GO

SELECT * INTO MythOne
FROM Sales.SalesOrderDetail;
GO

SET STATISTICS IO ON
SET NOCOUNT ON
GO

SELECT SalesOrderID, SalesOrderDetailID, CarrierTrackingNumber, OrderQty,
ProductID, SpecialOfferID, UnitPrice, UnitPriceDiscount, LineTotal
FROM MythOne
WHERE CarrierTrackingNumber = '4911-403C-98';
GO

SET STATISTICS IO OFF
GO
```

Listing 8-2. I/O Statistics for Table with No Index

```
Table 'MythOne'. Scan count 1, logical reads 1496, physical reads 0, read-ahead reads 0,
lob logical reads 0, lob physical reads 0, lob read-ahead reads 0.
```

It could be argued that 1,496 isn't a lot of input/output (I/O). This might be true given the size of some databases and the amount of data in today's world. But the I/O of a query shouldn't be compared to the performance of the rest of the world; it needs to be compared to its potential I/O, the needs of the application, and the platform on which it is deployed.

Improving the query from the previous demonstration is as simple as adding an index on the table on the `CarrierTrackingNumber` column. To see the effect of adding an index to `MythOne`, execute the code in Listing 8-3. With the index created, the reads for the query were reduced from 1,496 to 15 reads, shown in Listing 8-4. With just a single index, the I/O for the query was reduced by nearly two orders of magnitude. Suffice it to say, an index in this situation provides a significant amount of value.

Listing 8-3. *Adding an Index to MythOne*

```
CREATE INDEX IX_CarrierTrackingNumber ON MythOne (CarrierTrackingNumber)
GO

SET STATISTICS IO ON
SET NOCOUNT ON
GO

SELECT SalesOrderID, SalesOrderDetailID, CarrierTrackingNumber, OrderQty,
ProductID, SpecialOfferID, UnitPrice, UnitPriceDiscount, LineTotal
FROM MythOne
WHERE CarrierTrackingNumber = '4911-403C-98';
GO

SET STATISTICS IO OFF
GO
```

Listing 8-4. *I/O Statistics for Table with an Index*

```
Table 'MythOne'. Scan count 1, logical reads 15 physical reads 0, read-
ahead reads 0, lob logical reads 0, lob physical reads 0, lob read-ahead
reads 0.
```

I've shown in these examples that indexes do provide a benefit. If you encounter a situation where there is angst for building indexes on a database, try to break down the real reason for the pushback and provide an example similar to the one presented in this section. In Chapter 11, we'll discuss approaches that can be used to determine what indexes to create in a database.

Myth 2: Primary Keys Are Always Clustered

The next myth that is quite prevalent is the idea that primary keys are always clustered. While this is true in many cases, you cannot assume that all primary keys are also clustered indexes. Earlier in this book, we discussed how a table can have only a single clustered index on it. If a primary key is created after the clustered index is built, then the primary key is to be created as a nonclustered index.

CHAPTER 8   INDEXING MYTHS AND BEST PRACTICES

To illustrate the indexing behavior of primary keys, we'll use a script that includes building two tables. We'll build the first table, named dbo.MythTwo1, and then create a primary key on the RowID column. For the second table, named dbo.MythTwo2, after it is created, the script will build a clustered index before creating the primary key. The code for this is in Listing 8-5.

Listing 8-5. Two Ways to Create Primary Keys

```
USE AdventureWorks2017;
GO

CREATE TABLE dbo.MythTwo1
    (
    RowID int NOT NULL
    ,Column1 nvarchar(128)
    ,Column2 nvarchar(128)
    );

ALTER TABLE dbo.MythTwo1
ADD CONSTRAINT PK_MythTwo1 PRIMARY KEY (RowID);
GO

CREATE TABLE dbo.MythTwo2
    (
    RowID int NOT NULL
    ,Column1 nvarchar(128)
    ,Column2 nvarchar(128)
    );
CREATE CLUSTERED INDEX CL_MythTwo2 ON dbo.MythTwo2 (RowID);

ALTER TABLE dbo.MythTwo2
ADD CONSTRAINT PK_MythTwo2 PRIMARY KEY (RowID);
GO

SELECT OBJECT_NAME(object_id) AS table_name
    ,name
    ,index_id
    ,type
```

```
    ,type_desc
    ,is_unique
    ,is_primary_key
FROM sys.indexes
WHERE object_id IN (OBJECT_ID('dbo.MythTwo1'),OBJECT_ID('dbo.MythTwo2'));
```

After running the code segment, the final query will return results like those shown in Figure 8-1. This figure shows that PK_MythTwo1, which is the primary key on the first table, was created as a clustered index. Then on the second table, PK_MythTwo2 was created as a nonclustered index.

	table_name	name	index_id	type	type_desc	is_unique	is_primary_key
1	MythTwo1	PK_MythTwo1	1	1	CLUSTERED	1	1
2	MythTwo2	CL_MythTwo2	1	1	CLUSTERED	0	0
3	MythTwo2	PK_MythTwo2	2	2	NONCLUSTERED	1	1

Figure 8-1. Primary key sys.indexes output

The behavior discussed in this section is important to remember when building primary keys and clustered indexes. If you have a situation where they need to be separated, the primary key will need to be defined after the clustered index or as a NONCLUSTERED index.

Myth 3: Online Index Operations Don't Block

One of the advantages of SQL Server Enterprise Edition is the ability to build indexes online. During an online index build, the table on which the index is being created will still be available for queries and data modifications. This feature is extremely useful when a database needs to be accessed and maintenance windows are short to nonexistent.

A common myth with online index rebuilds is that they don't cause any blocking. Of course, like any of these myths, this one is false. When using an online index operation, there is an intent shared lock held on the table for the main portion of the build. At the finish, either a shared lock, for a nonclustered index, or a schema modification lock, for a clustered index, is held for a short time while the operation moves in the updated index. This differs from an offline index build where the shared or schema modification lock is held for the duration of the index build.

CHAPTER 8 INDEXING MYTHS AND BEST PRACTICES

Of course, you will want to see this in action; to accomplish this, you will create a table and use Extended Events to monitor the locks that are applied to the table while creating indexes with and without the ONLINE options. To start this demo, execute the code in Listing 8-6. This script creates the table dbo.MythThree and populates it with 10 million records. The last item it returns is the object_id for the table, which is needed for the subsequent parts of the demo. For this example, the object_id for dbo.MythThree is 624721278.

> **Note** The demos for this myth all require SQL Server Enterprise or Developer Edition.

Listing 8-6. MythThree Table Create Script

```
USE AdventureWorks2017
GO

CREATE TABLE dbo.MythThree
  (
  RowID int NOT NULL
  ,Column1 uniqueidentifier
  );
WITH L1(z) AS (SELECT 0 UNION ALL SELECT 0)
, L2(z) AS (SELECT 0 FROM L1 a CROSS JOIN L1 b)
, L3(z) AS (SELECT 0 FROM L2 a CROSS JOIN L2 b)
, L4(z) AS (SELECT 0 FROM L3 a CROSS JOIN L3 b)
, L5(z) AS (SELECT 0 FROM L4 a CROSS JOIN L4 b)
, L6(z) AS (SELECT TOP 10000000 0 FROM L5 a CROSS JOIN L5 b)
INSERT INTO dbo.MythThree
SELECT ROW_NUMBER() OVER (ORDER BY z) AS RowID, NEWID()
FROM L6;
GO

SELECT OBJECT_ID('dbo.MythThree')
GO
```

CHAPTER 8 INDEXING MYTHS AND BEST PRACTICES

To monitor those events in this scenario, you'll use Extended Events to capture the lock_acquired and lock_released events fired during index creation. Open sessions in SSMS for the code in Listing 8-7 and Listing 8-8. Before running, update the session_id from Listing 8-8 for the session_id in Listing 8-7; for this scenario, the session_id is 42. Apply the same update with the object_id. After the Extended Events session is running, you can use the live view to monitor the locks as they occur.

Listing 8-7. Extended Events Session for Lock Acquired and Released

```
IF EXISTS(SELECT * FROM sys.server_event_sessions WHERE name =
'MythThreeXevents')
    DROP EVENT SESSION [MythThreeXevents] ON SERVER
GO

CREATE EVENT SESSION [MythThreeXevents] ON SERVER
ADD EVENT sqlserver.lock_acquired(SET collect_database_name=(1)
  ACTION(sqlserver.sql_text)
  WHERE [sqlserver].[session_id]=(42) AND [object_id]=(624721278)),
ADD EVENT sqlserver.lock_released(
  ACTION(sqlserver.sql_text)
  WHERE [sqlserver].[session_id]=(42) AND [object_id]=(624721278))
ADD TARGET package0.ring_buffer
GO

ALTER EVENT SESSION [MythThreeXevents] ON SERVER STATE = START
GO
```

In the example from Listing 8-8, two indexes are created, one built ONLINE and the other with the default option, or offline. To see what locks are acquired and released, observe the locking behavior in the live viewer. By default, only the name and timestamp appear in the live viewer. The live viewer allows for customizing the columns that are displayed. In Figure 8-2, the columns object_id, mode, resource_type, and sql_text have been added to the defaults name and timestamp. To add additional columns, right-click a column header and select "Choose columns."

CHAPTER 8   INDEXING MYTHS AND BEST PRACTICES

Listing 8-8. Online Index Operations on Nonclustered Index Creation

```
USE AdventureWorks2017
GO

CREATE INDEX IX_MythThree_ONLINE ON MythThree (Column1) WITH (ONLINE = ON);
GO

CREATE INDEX IX_MythThree ON MythThree (Column1);
GO
```

When the index is created with the ONLINE option, note that in Figure 8-2 SCH_S (Schema_Shared) and S (Shared) locks are acquired and released within milliseconds of each other. Because these locks are acquired and released throughout the index creation process, other transactions can continue to occur against the table. The SCH_S locks ensure that the schema of the table does not change, while the S locks pages from inserts, updates, and deletes. Because these locks are acquired for very short amounts of time, they allow the table to be available throughout the index creation process.

Note If you do not see any results from the Extended Events session, it's likely due to a mismatch between the object_id for MythThree and the object_id traced through the Extended Events session.

object_id	name	mode	timestamp	sql_text
624721278	lock_acquired	SCH_S	2019-07-28 22:44:20.9149557	CREATE INDEX IX_MythThree_ONLINE ON MythThree (Column1) WITH (ONLINE = ON);
624721278	lock_released	SCH_S	2019-07-28 22:44:20.9151786	CREATE INDEX IX_MythThree_ONLINE ON MythThree (Column1) WITH (ONLINE = ON);
624721278	lock_acquired	IS	2019-07-28 22:44:20.9152222	CREATE INDEX IX_MythThree_ONLINE ON MythThree (Column1) WITH (ONLINE = ON);
624721278	lock_acquired	IS	2019-07-28 22:44:20.9152328	CREATE INDEX IX_MythThree_ONLINE ON MythThree (Column1) WITH (ONLINE = ON);
624721278	lock_acquired	SCH_S	2019-07-28 22:44:20.9152778	CREATE INDEX IX_MythThree_ONLINE ON MythThree (Column1) WITH (ONLINE = ON);
624721278	lock_acquired	S	2019-07-28 22:44:20.9371600	CREATE INDEX IX_MythThree_ONLINE ON MythThree (Column1) WITH (ONLINE = ON);
624721278	lock_acquired	SCH_S	2019-07-28 22:44:22.2173570	CREATE INDEX IX_MythThree_ONLINE ON MythThree (Column1) WITH (ONLINE = ON);
624721278	lock_released	S	2019-07-28 22:44:22.2176549	CREATE INDEX IX_MythThree_ONLINE ON MythThree (Column1) WITH (ONLINE = ON);
624721278	lock_acquired	SCH_S	2019-07-28 22:44:22.2187790	CREATE INDEX IX_MythThree_ONLINE ON MythThree (Column1) WITH (ONLINE = ON);

Figure 8-2. *Index creation with ONLINE option*

With the default index creation, which does not use the ONLINE option, the S locks are held for the entirety of the index build. Shown in Figure 8-3, the S lock is taken before the SCH_S lock and isn't released until after the index is build. The result is that the index is unavailable during the index build.

CHAPTER 8   INDEXING MYTHS AND BEST PRACTICES

object_id	name	mode	timestamp	sql_text
624721278	lock_acquired	SCH_S	2019-07-28 22:45:15.2028196	CREATE INDEX IX_MythThree ON MythThree (Column1);
624721278	lock_released	SCH_S	2019-07-28 22:45:15.2378991	CREATE INDEX IX_MythThree ON MythThree (Column1);
624721278	lock_acquired	S	2019-07-28 22:45:15.2496446	CREATE INDEX IX_MythThree ON MythThree (Column1);
624721278	lock_acquired	S	2019-07-28 22:45:15.2591628	CREATE INDEX IX_MythThree ON MythThree (Column1);
624721278	lock_acquired	SCH_S	2019-07-28 22:45:15.2670049	CREATE INDEX IX_MythThree ON MythThree (Column1);
624721278	lock_released	SCH_S	2019-07-28 22:45:24.4915553	CREATE INDEX IX_MythThree ON MythThree (Column1);
624721278	lock_released	S	2019-07-28 22:45:24.4915625	CREATE INDEX IX_MythThree ON MythThree (Column1);

Figure 8-3. *Index creation without ONLINE option*

Myth 4: Any Column Can Be Filtered in Multicolumn Indexes

The next common myth with indexes is that regardless of the position of the column in an index, the index can use that column in an ordered search to filter data within the index. As with the other myths discussed so far in this chapter, this one is also incorrect. An index does not need to use all the columns in an index. It does, however, need to start with the leftmost column in an index when performing an ordered search and use the columns from left to right, in their order, within the index. This is why the order of the columns in an index is so important.

To demonstrate this myth, you will run through a few examples, shown in Listing 8-9. In the script, a table is created based on `Sales.SalesOrderHeader` with a primary key on `SalesOrderID`. To test the myth of searching all columns through multicolumn indexes, an index with the columns `OrderDate`, `DueDate`, and `ShipDate` is created.

Listing 8-9. Multicolumn Index Myth

```
USE AdventureWorks2017
GO
IF OBJECT_ID('dbo.MythFour') IS NOT NULL
    DROP TABLE dbo.MythFour
GO

SELECT SalesOrderID, OrderDate, DueDate, ShipDate
INTO dbo.MythFour
FROM Sales.SalesOrderHeader;
GO
```

CHAPTER 8   INDEXING MYTHS AND BEST PRACTICES

```
ALTER TABLE dbo.MythFour
ADD CONSTRAINT PK_MythFour PRIMARY KEY CLUSTERED (SalesOrderID);
GO

CREATE NONCLUSTERED INDEX IX_MythFour ON dbo.MythFour (OrderDate, DueDate,
ShipDate);
GO
```

With the test objects in place, the next thing to check is the behavior of the queries against the table that could potentially use the nonclustered index. First, we'll run a query that uses the leftmost column in the index. Listing 8-10 gives the code for this. As shown in Figure 8-4, by filtering on the leftmost column, the query uses a seek operation on IX_MythFour.

Listing 8-10. Query Using Leftmost Column in Index

```
USE AdventureWorks2017
GO

SELECT OrderDate FROM dbo.MythFour
WHERE OrderDate = '2011-07-17 00:00:00.000'
```

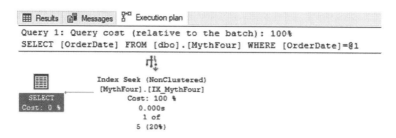

Figure 8-4. *Execution plan for leftmost column in index*

Next, you'll look at what happens when querying from the other side of the index key columns. In Listing 8-11, the query filters the results on the rightmost column of the index. The execution plan for this query, shown in Figure 8-5, uses a scan operation on IX_MythFour. Instead of being able to go directly to the records that match the OrderDate, the query needs to check all records to determine which match the filter. While the index is used, it isn't able to filter the rows based on the sort within the index.

Listing 8-11. Query Using Rightmost Column in Index

```
USE AdventureWorks2017
GO

SELECT ShipDate FROM dbo.MythFour
WHERE ShipDate = '2011-07-17 00:00:00.000'
```

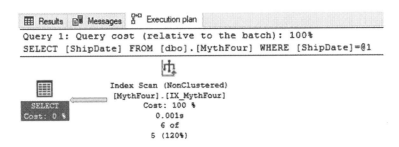

Figure 8-5. Execution plan for rightmost column in index

At this point, we've seen that the leftmost column can be used for filtering and that filtering on the rightmost column can use the index but cannot use it optimally with a seek operation. The last validation is to check the behavior of columns in an index that are not on the left or right side of the index. In Listing 8-12, a query is included that uses the middle column in the index IX_MythFour. As with any execution plan, the execution plan for the middle column query, shown in Figure 8-6, uses the index but also uses a scan operation. The query is able to use the index but not in an optimal fashion.

Listing 8-12. Query Using Middle Column in Index

```
USE AdventureWorks2017
GO

SELECT DueDate FROM dbo.MythFour
WHERE DueDate = '2011-07-17 00:00:00.000'
```

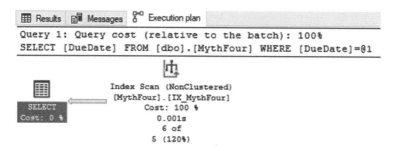

Figure 8-6. *Execution plan for middle column in index*

The myth of how columns in a multicolumn index can be used is one that can sometimes be confusing. As the examples showed, queries can use the index regardless of which columns of the index are being filtered. The key is to effectively use the index. To accomplish this goal, filtering must start on the leftmost column of the index. And when that isn't the typical use case, either reorder the columns of the index or create additional indexes.

Myth 5: Clustered Indexes Store Records in Physical Order

One of the more pervasive myths commonly held is the idea that a clustered index stores the records in a table in their physical order when on disk. This myth seems to be primarily driven by confusion between what is stored on a page and where records are stored on those pages. As was discussed in Chapter 2, there is a difference between data pages and records. As a refresher, you'll see a simple demonstration that dispels this myth.

To begin this example, execute the code in Listing 8-13. The code in the example will create a table named dbo.MythFive. Then, it will add three records to the table. The last part of the script will output, using sys.dm_db_database_page_allocations, the page location for the table. In this example, the page with the records inserted into dbo.MythFive is page 59624, shown in Figure 8-7.

Note The dynamic management function sys.dm_db_database_page_allocations is a replacement for DBCC IND. This function, introduced in SQL Server 2012, provides an improved interface to examining page allocations for objects in a database over its DBCC predecessor.

Listing 8-13. Create and Populate MythFive Table

```
USE AdventureWorks2017
GO

IF OBJECT_ID('dbo.MythFive') IS NOT NULL
    DROP TABLE dbo.MythFive

CREATE TABLE dbo.MythFive
(
RowID int PRIMARY KEY CLUSTERED
,TestValue varchar(20) NOT NULL
);
GO

INSERT INTO dbo.MythFive (RowID, TestValue) VALUES (1, 'FirstRecordAdded');
INSERT INTO dbo.MythFive (RowID, TestValue) VALUES (3, 'SecondRecordAdded');
INSERT INTO dbo.MythFive (RowID, TestValue) VALUES (2, 'ThirdRecordAdded');
GO

SELECT database_id, object_id, index_id, extent_page_id, allocated_page_page_id, page_type_desc
FROM sys.dm_db_database_page_allocations(DB_ID(), OBJECT_ID('dbo.MythFive'), 1, NULL, 'DETAILED')
WHERE page_type_desc IS NOT NULL
GO
```

	database_id	object_id	index_id	extent_page_id	allocated_page_page_id	page_type_desc
1	8	2071678428	1	59616	59620	IAM_PAGE
2	8	2071678428	1	59624	59624	DATA_PAGE

Figure 8-7. *sys.dm_db_database_page_allocations output*

The evidence to dispel this myth can be uncovered with the DBCC PAGE command. To do this, use the PagePID identified in Listing 8-13 with page_type_desc of DATA_PAGE. Since there is only a single data page for this table, that is where the data will be located. (For more information on DBCC commands, see Chapter 2.)

For this example, Listing 8-14 shows the T-SQL required to look at the data in the table. This command outputs a lot of information that includes some header information that isn't useful in this example. The portion that you need is at the end, with the memory dump of the page, as shown in Figure 8-8. In the memory dump, the records are shown in the order in which they are placed on the page. As the dump shows from reading the far-right column, the records are in the order in which they are added to the table, not the order that they will appear in the clustered index.

Listing 8-14. Create and Populate MythFive Table

```
DBCC TRACEON (3604);
GO

DBCC PAGE (AdventureWorks2017, 1, 59624, 2);
GO
```

```
Memory Dump @0x000000C8721F8000

000000C8721F8000:   01010000 00000001 00000000 00000800 00000000    ................
000000C8721F8014:   00000300 44020000 3c1fbe00 e8e80000 01000000    ....D...<.¾.èè......
000000C8721F8028:   6d000000 72460000 02000000 00000000 00000000    m...rF..............
000000C8721F803C:   00000000 01000000 00000000 00000000 00000000    ....................
000000C8721F8050:   00000000 00000000 00000000 00000000 30000800    ................0...
000000C8721F8064:   01000000 02000001 001f0046 69727374 5265636f    ...........FirstReco
000000C8721F8078:   72644164 64656430 00080003 00000002 00000100    rdAdded0............
000000C8721F808C:   20005365 636f6e64 5265636f 72644164 64656430    .SecondRecordAdded0
000000C8721F80A0:   00080002 00000002 00000100 1f005468 69726452    ..............ThirdR
000000C8721F80B4:   65636f72 64416464 65640000 21212121 21212121    ecordAdded..!!!!!!!!
000000C8721F80C8:   21212121 21212121 21212121 21212121 21212121    !!!!!!!!!!!!!!!!!!!!
000000C8721F80DC:   21212121 21212121 21212121 21212121 21212121    !!!!!!!!!!!!!!!!!!!!
```

Figure 8-8. Page contents portion of DBCC PAGE output

Based on this evidence, it is easy to discern that clustered indexes do not store records in the physical order of the index. If this example were expanded, you would be able to see that the pages are in physical order, but the rows on the pages are not.

Myth 6: Indexes Always Output in the Same Order

One of the more common myths that pertain to indexes is that they guarantee the output order of results from queries. This is not correct. As previously described in this book, the purpose of indexes is to provide an efficient access path to the data. That purpose does

CHAPTER 8 INDEXING MYTHS AND BEST PRACTICES

not guarantee the order in which the data will be accessed. The trouble with this myth is that, oftentimes, SQL Server will appear to maintain order when queries are executed under certain conditions, but when those conditions change, the execution plans change, and the results are returned in the order that the data is processed vs. the order that the end user might desire.

To explore this myth, you'll first look at how conditions can change on a query that is using clustered index. In Listing 8-15, there is a single query, repeated twice, for the Sales.SalesOrderHeader and Sales.SalesOrderDetail tables that is performing a simple aggregation. This is something that might appear in many types of use cases for SQL Server.

Listing 8-15. Unordered Results with Clustered Index

```
USE AdventureWorks2017
GO

SELECT soh.SalesOrderID, COUNT(*) AS DetailRows
FROM Sales.SalesOrderHeader soh
    INNER JOIN Sales.SalesOrderDetail sod ON soh.SalesOrderID = sod.
    SalesOrderID
    GROUP BY soh.SalesOrderID;
GO

DBCC FREEPROCCACHE
DBCC SETCPUWEIGHT(1000)
GO

SELECT soh.SalesOrderID, COUNT(*) AS DetailRows
FROM Sales.SalesOrderHeader soh
    INNER JOIN Sales.SalesOrderDetail sod ON soh.SalesOrderID = sod.
    SalesOrderID
    GROUP BY soh.SalesOrderID;
GO

DBCC FREEPROCCACHE
DBCC SETCPUWEIGHT(1)
GO
```

The conditions in which the two queries execute vary a bit. The first query is running under the standard SQL Server cost model and generates an execution that performs a couple index scans and a stream aggregation to return the results, shown in Figure 8-9. The results from the query, provided in Figure 8-10, provide support that SQL Server will return data in the desired output, provided that the SaleOrderID column is the column that the user wants sorted.

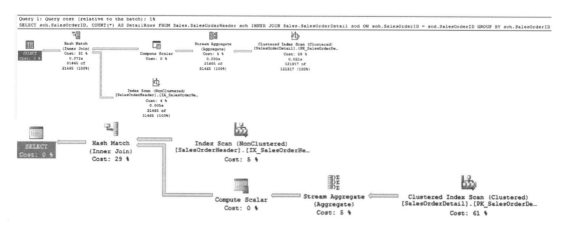

Figure 8-9. Default aggregation execution plan

	SalesOrderID	DetailRows
1	43697	1
2	43698	1
3	43699	1
4	43700	1
5	43701	1
6	43702	1
7	43703	1
8	43704	1
9	43705	1
10	43706	1

Figure 8-10. Results from default aggregation execution plan

But what happens if the conditions on the SQL Server change but the business rules do not? The second query executed in Listing 8-15 is the same query, but with a change in conditions. For this example, the DBCC command SETCPUWEIGHT is leveraged to change the cost of the execution plan. The change in cost results in the use of the parallel execution plan, shown in Figure 8-11. A side effect of the parallel plan is a change in the order in which the results of the query are returned, shown in Figure 8-12. While the results appear to still be ordered and the logic of the query hasn't changed, the first records returned are different. This occurs because one of the parallel threads returned its results faster than some others.

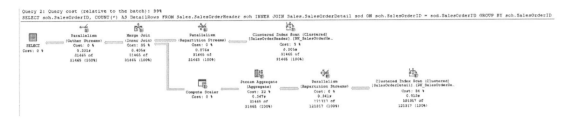

Figure 8-11. Aggregation execution plan with parallelism

	SalesOrderID	DetailRows
1	43659	12
2	43660	2
3	43661	15
4	43666	6
5	43667	4
6	43668	29
7	43669	1
8	43674	1
9	43675	9
10	43676	5

Figure 8-12. Aggregation execution plan with parallelism

Warning Do not use DBCC SETCPUWEIGHT in production code to control parallelism or for any other reason. This DBCC command is strictly available to control environmental variables within SQL Server to test and validate execution plans.

The second condition to consider is when business rules change for a query. For instance, maybe a set of results wasn't originally filtered, but after a change to the application, the query may change to using a different set of indexes. This can also result in a change in the order of the results, such as when a query changes from using a clustered index to a nonclustered index.

CHAPTER 8 INDEXING MYTHS AND BEST PRACTICES

To demonstrate this change in behavior, execute the code in Listing 8-16. This code runs two queries. Both of the queries return `SalesOrderID`, `CustomerID`, and `Status`. For the purposes of the example, the business rule dictates that the results must be sorted by `SalesOrderID`. In this case, the results from the first query are sorted as the business rule states, shown at the top of Figure 8-13. But in the second query, when the logic changes to request fewer rows by adding a filter, the results are no longer ordered, shown at the bottom of Figure 8-13. The cause of the change comes from a change in the indexes that SQL Server is using to execute the query. The change in indexes drives the results to be processed, and ordered, in the manner in which those indexes sort the data.

Listing 8-16. Unordered Results with Nonclustered Index

```
USE AdventureWorks2017
GO

SELECT SalesOrderID, CustomerID, Status
FROM Sales.SalesOrderHeader soh
GO

SELECT SalesOrderID, CustomerID, Status
FROM Sales.SalesOrderHeader soh
WHERE CustomerID IN (11020, 11021, 11022)
GO
```

#	SalesOrderID	CustomerID	Status
1	43659	29825	5
2	43660	29672	5
3	43661	29734	5
4	43662	29994	5
5	43663	29565	5
6	43664	29898	5
7	43665	29580	5
8	43666	30052	5
9	43667	29974	5
10	43668	29614	5

#	SalesOrderID	CustomerID	Status
1	51193	11020	5
2	51610	11021	5
3	51556	11022	5

Figure 8-13. *Query results demonstrating effect of filtering on order*

In these examples, you looked at just a couple of the conditions that can change when it comes to how SQL Server will stream the results from a query. While an index might provide results from the query in the order desired this time, there is no guarantee that this will not change. Don't rely on indexes to enforce ordering. Don't rely on being clever to get the results ordered as desired. Rely on the ORDER BY clause to get the results ordered as required.

Myth 7: Fill Factor Is Applied to Indexes During Inserts

When the fill factor is set on an index, it is applied to the index when the index is built, rebuilt, or reorganized. Unfortunately, with this myth, many people believe that fill factor is applied as records are inserted into a table. In this section, we'll investigate this myth and see that it is not correct.

To begin pulling this myth apart, let's look at what most people believe. In the myth, the thought is that if a fill factor has been specified when rows are added to a table, the fill factor is used during the inserts. To dispel this portion of the myth, execute the code in Listing 8-17. In this script, the table dbo.MythSeven is created with a clustered index with a 50 percent fill factor. That means that 50 percent of every page in the index should be left empty. With the table built, you'll insert records into the table. Finally, you'll check the average amount of space available on each page through the sys.dm_db_index_physical_stats DMV. Looking at the results of the script, included in Figure 8-14, the index is using 95 percent of every page vs. the 50 percent that was specified in the creation of the clustered index.

Listing 8-17. Create and Populate MythSeven Table

```
USE AdventureWorks2017
GO

IF OBJECT_ID('dbo.MythSeven') IS NOT NULL
    DROP TABLE dbo.MythSeven;
GO

CREATE TABLE dbo.MythSeven
  (
  RowID int NOT NULL
  ,Column1 varchar(500)
  );
GO
```

CHAPTER 8   INDEXING MYTHS AND BEST PRACTICES

```
ALTER TABLE dbo.MythSeven ADD CONSTRAINT
    PK_MythSeven PRIMARY KEY CLUSTERED (RowID) WITH(FILLFACTOR = 50);
GO

WITH L1(z) AS (SELECT 0 UNION ALL SELECT 0)
, L2(z) AS (SELECT 0 FROM L1 a CROSS JOIN L1 b)
, L3(z) AS (SELECT 0 FROM L2 a CROSS JOIN L2 b)
, L4(z) AS (SELECT 0 FROM L3 a CROSS JOIN L3 b)
, L5(z) AS (SELECT 0 FROM L4 a CROSS JOIN L4 b)
, L6(z) AS (SELECT TOP 1000 0 FROM L5 a CROSS JOIN L5 b)
INSERT INTO dbo.MythSeven
SELECT ROW_NUMBER() OVER (ORDER BY z) AS RowID, REPLICATE('X', 500)
FROM L6;
GO

SELECT object_id, index_id, avg_page_space_used_in_percent
FROM sys.dm_db_index_physical_stats(DB_ID(),OBJECT_ID('dbo.MythSeven'),
NULL,NULL,'DETAILED')
WHERE index_level = 0;
```

	object_id	index_id	avg_page_space_used_in_percent
1	736721677	1	95.3103286384976

Figure 8-14. *Fill factor myth on inserts*

Sometimes when this myth is dispelled, the belief is reversed, and it is believed that fill factor is broken or doesn't work. This is also incorrect. Fill factor isn't applied to indexes during data modifications. As stated previously, it is applied when the index is rebuilt, reorganized, or created. To demonstrate this, you can rebuild the clustered index on dbo.MythSeven with the script included in Listing 8-18.

Listing 8-18. Rebuild Clustered Index on MythSeven Table

```
USE AdventureWorks2017
GO

ALTER INDEX PK_MythSeven ON dbo.MythSeven REBUILD

SELECT object_id, index_id, avg_page_space_used_in_percent
```

```
FROM sys.dm_db_index_physical_stats(DB_ID(),OBJECT_ID('dbo.MythSeven'),
NULL,NULL,'DETAILED')
WHERE index_level = 0
```

After the clustered index is rebuilt, the index will have the specified fill factor, or close to the value specified, as shown in Figure 8-15. The average space used on the table, after the rebuild, changed from 95 to 51 percent. This change is in alignment with the fill factor that was specified for the index.

object_id	index_id	avg_page_space_used_in_percent
736721677	1	51.0748702742772

Figure 8-15. *Fill factor myth after index rebuild*

When it comes to fill factor, there are a number of myths surrounding the index property. The key to understanding fill factor is to remember when and how it is applied. It isn't a property enforced on an index as it is used. It is, instead, a property used to distribute data within an index when it is created or rebuilt.

Myth 8: Deleting from Heaps Results in Unrecoverable Space

Heaps are an interesting structure in SQL Server. In Chapter 2, you examined how they aren't really an index but just a collection of pages for storing data. One of the index maintenance tasks that will be a part of the next chapter is recovering space from heap tables. As will be more deeply discussed in that chapter, when rows are deleted from a heap, the pages associated with those rows are not removed from the heap. This is generally referred to as *bloat* within the heap.

An interesting side effect of the concept of heap bloat is the myth that bloat never gets reused. The space stays in the heap and is not recoverable until the heap is rebuilt. Fortunately, for heaps and database administrators, this isn't the case. When data is removed from a heap, the space that the data previously held is made available for future inserts into the table.

To demonstrate how this works, you'll build a table using the code in Listing 8-19. The demonstration creates a heap named MythEight and then inserts 400 records, which results in 100 pages of data. This page count can be validated with the page_count column in the first resultset in Figure 8-16. The next part of the script deletes every other

CHAPTER 8 INDEXING MYTHS AND BEST PRACTICES

row that was inserted into the heap. Generally, this should leave each page with half as many rows as it had previously, shown in the second resultset in Figure 8-16. The last part of the script reinserts 200 rows into the MythEight table, returning the row count to 400 records and reusing the previously used pages that had data removed from them. There is a slight growth in the page count from the last resultset in Figure 8-16, but most of the new rows fit into the space already allocated.

Listing 8-19. Reusing Data from the MythEight Heap

```
USE AdventureWorks2017
GO

IF OBJECT_ID('dbo.MythEight') IS NOT NULL
    DROP TABLE dbo.MythEight;

CREATE TABLE dbo.MythEight
(
    RowId INT IDENTITY(1,1)
    ,FillerData VARCHAR(2500)
);

INSERT INTO dbo.MythEight (FillerData)
SELECT TOP 400 REPLICATE('X',2000)
FROM sys.objects;

SELECT OBJECT_NAME(object_id), index_type_desc, page_count, record_count,
forwarded_record_count
FROM sys.dm_db_index_physical_stats (DB_ID(), OBJECT_ID('dbo.MythEight'),
NULL, NULL, 'DETAILED');

DELETE FROM dbo.MythEight
WHERE RowId % 2 = 0;

SELECT OBJECT_NAME(object_id), index_type_desc, page_count, record_count,
forwarded_record_count
FROM sys.dm_db_index_physical_stats (DB_ID(), OBJECT_ID('dbo.MythEight'),
NULL, NULL, 'DETAILED');
```

```sql
INSERT INTO dbo.MythEight (FillerData)
SELECT TOP 200 REPLICATE('X',2000)
FROM sys.objects;

SELECT OBJECT_NAME(object_id), index_type_desc, page_count, record_count,
forwarded_record_count
FROM sys.dm_db_index_physical_stats (DB_ID(), OBJECT_ID('dbo.MythEight'),
NULL, NULL, 'DETAILED');
```

	(No column name)	index_type_desc	page_count	record_count	forwarded_record_count
1	MythEight	HEAP	100	400	0

	(No column name)	index_type_desc	page_count	record_count	forwarded_record_count
1	MythEight	HEAP	100	200	0

	(No column name)	index_type_desc	page_count	record_count	forwarded_record_count
1	MythEight	HEAP	111	400	0

Figure 8-16. Heap reuse query results

As the demonstration for this myth shows, space in a heap that previously held data is released for reuse by the table. For heaps that have a lot of data coming in and out of the table, there isn't a significant need to monitor for page reuse, and the myth can be considered inaccurate. With heaps that have a lot of data removed without the intention to replace the data, you are able to recover the space with ALTER TABLE ... REBUILD. The syntax and impact of this statement are discussed in the next chapter.

Myth 9: Every Table Should Have a Heap/Clustered Index

The last myth to consider is twofold. On the one hand, some people will recommend you should build all your tables with heaps. On the other hand, others will recommend that you create clustered indexes on all your tables. The trouble is that this viewpoint will exclude considering the benefits that each of the structures can offer on a table. The viewpoint makes a religious-styled argument for or against ways to store data in your databases without any consideration for the actual data that is being stored and how it is being used.

Some of the arguments against the use of clustered indexes are as follows:

- Fragmentation negatively impacts performance through additional I/O.

- The modification of a single record can impact multiple records in the clustered index when a page split is triggered.

- Excessive key lookups will negatively impact performance through additional I/O.

Of course, there are some arguments against using heaps:

- Excessive forwarded records negatively impact performance through additional I/O.

- Removing forwarded records requires a rebuild of the entire table.

- Nonclustered indexes are required for efficient filtered data access.

- Heaps don't automatically release pages when data is removed.

The negative impacts associated with either clustered indexes or heaps aren't the only things to consider when deciding between one and the other. Each has circumstances where they will outperform the other.

For instance, clustered indexes perform best in the following circumstances:

- The key on the table is a unique, ever-increasing key value.

- The table has a key column that has a high degree of uniqueness.

- Ranges of data in a table will be accessed via queries.

- Records in the table will be inserted and deleted at a high rate.

On the other hand, heaps are ideal for some of the following situations:

- Data in the table will be used only for a limited amount of time where index creation time exceeds query time on the data.

- Key values will change frequently, which in turn would change the position of the record in an index.

- You are inserting copious numbers of records into a staging table.

- The primary key is a nonascending value, such as a unique identifier.

Although this section doesn't include a demonstration of why this myth is false, it is important to remember that both heaps and clustered indexes are available and should be used appropriately. Knowing which type of index to choose is a matter of testing, not a matter of doctrine.

A good resource to consider for those in the "cluster everything camp" is the Fast Track Data Warehouse Architecture white paper (https://msdn.microsoft.com/en-us/library/hh918452.aspx). The white paper addresses some significant performance improvements that can be found with heaps and also the point in which these improvements dissipate. The white paper helps show how changes in I/O system technologies, with flash and cache-based devices, can change patterns and practices in regard to heaps and clustered indexes. This helps to promote the idea of validating myths and best practices from time to time.

Index Best Practices

Similar to myths are the indexing best practices. A best practice should be considered the default recommendation that can be applied when there isn't enough information available to validate proceeding in another direction. Best practices are not the only option and are just a place to start from when working with any technology.

When using a best practice provided from someone else, such as those appearing in this chapter, it is important to check them out for yourself first. Always take them with a grain of salt. You can trust that best practices will steer you in the correct direction, but you need to verify that it is appropriate to follow the practice.

Given the preceding precautions, there are a number of best practices that can be considered when working with indexes. This section will review these best practices and discuss what they are and what they mean.

Index to Your Current Workload

The most important aspect of indexing your databases is to index to how you are using your databases today, not based on yesterday, not based on the data you expect years in the future, but today.

The indexing that you build for today will likely not be the indexing that will be needed in databases in the future. For this reason, the first best practice is to continuously review, analyze, and implement changes to the indexes in your environment. Realize that regardless of how similar two databases are, if the data in the databases and users are not the same, then the indexing for the two databases will likely need to be different. A detailed conversation on monitoring and analyzing indexes is in Chapters 13 and 14.

With this bit out of the way, let's look at some other best practices for indexing.

Use Clustered Indexes on Primary Keys by Default

The next best practice is to use clustered indexes on primary keys by default. This may seem to run contrary to the nineth myth presented in this chapter. Myth 9 discussed whether to choose clustered indexes or heaps as a matter of doctrine. Whether the database was built with one or the other, the myth would have you believe that if your table design doesn't match the myth, it should be changed regardless of the situation. This best practice recommends using clustered indexes on primary keys as a starting point.

By clustering the primary key of a table by default, there is an increased likelihood that the indexing choice will be appropriate for the table. As stated earlier in this chapter, clustered indexes control how the data in a table is stored. Many primary keys, possibly most, are built on a column that utilizes the identity property that increments as each new record is added to the table. Choosing a clustered index for the primary key will provide the most efficient method to access the data.

Specify Fill Factors

Fill factor controls the amount of free space left on the data pages of an index after an index is built or defragmented. This free space is made available to allow for records on the page to expand with the risk that the change in record size may result in a page split. This is an extremely useful property of indexes to use for index maintenance. Modifying the fill factor can mitigate the risk of fragmentation. A more thorough discussion of fill factor is presented in Chapter 6. For the purposes of best practices, you are concerned with the ability to set the fill factor at the database and index levels.

Database-Level Fill Factor

As already mentioned, one of the properties of SQL Server is the option to set a default fill factor for indexes. This setting is a SQL Server-wide setting and can be altered in the properties of SQL Server on the Database Properties page. By default, this value is set to zero, which equates to 100. Do not modify the default fill factor to anything other than 0, or 100, which has the same impact. Doing so will change the fill factor for every index in the database to the new value; this will add the specified amount of free space to all indexes the next time indexes are created, rebuilt, or reorganized.

On the surface, this may seem like a good idea, but this will blindly increase the size of all indexes by the specified amount. The increased size of the indexes will require more I/O to perform the same work as before the change. For many indexes, making this change would result in a needless waste of resources.

Index-Level Fill Factor

At the index level, you should modify the fill factor for indexes that are frequently becoming heavily fragmented. Decreasing the fill factor will increase the amount of free space in the index and provide additional space to compensate for the changes in record length leading to fragmentation. Managing fill factor at the index level is appropriate since it provides the ability to tune the index precisely to the needs of the database.

Index Foreign Key Columns

When a foreign key is created on a table, the foreign key column in the table should be indexed. This is necessary to assist the foreign key in determining which records in the parent table are constrained to each record in the referenced table. This is important when changes are being made against the referenced table. The changes in the referenced table may need to check all the rows that match the record in the parent table. If an index does not exist, then a scan of the column will occur. On a large parent table, this could result in a significant amount of I/O and potentially some concurrency issues.

An example of this issue would be state and address tables. There would likely be thousands or millions of records in the address table and maybe a hundred records in the state table. The address table would include a column that is referenced by the state table. Consider whether one of the records in the state table needed to be deleted. If there wasn't an index on the foreign key column in the address table, then how would the address table identify the rows that would be affected by deleting the state record? Without an index, SQL Server would have to check every record in the address table. If the column is indexed, SQL Server would be able to perform a range scan across the records that match to the value being deleted from the state table.

By indexing your foreign key columns, performance issues, such as the one described in this section, can be avoided. The best practice with foreign keys is to index their columns. Chapter 11 includes more details on this best practice and a code example.

Balance Index Count

As previously discussed in this book, indexes are extremely useful for improving the performance when accessing information in a record. Unfortunately, indexes are not without costs. The costs to having indexes go beyond just space within your database. When you build an index, you need to consider some of the following:

- How frequently will records be inserted or deleted?
- How frequently will the key columns be updated?
- How often will the index be used?
- What processes does the index support?
- How many other indexes are on the table?

These are just some of the first considerations that need to be accounted for when building indexes. After the index is built, how much time will be spent updating and maintaining the index? Will you modify the index more frequently than the index is used to return results for queries? How many columns are in the table, and are there more indexes than columns?

The trouble with balancing the index count on a table is that there is no precise number that can be recommended. Deciding on the number of indexes that it makes sense to have on a table is a per-table decision. You don't want too few, which may result in excessive scans of the clustered index or heap to return results. Also, the table shouldn't have too many indexes, where more time is being spent keeping the index current than returning results. My rule of thumb on transactional systems is that if a table has more than ten indexes on it, it is increasingly likely that there are too many indexes on the table.

Summary

This chapter looked at some myths surrounding indexes as well as some best practices. For both areas, you investigated what some commonly held beliefs are and were presented some details around each of them.

With the myths, you looked at a number of ideas that are generally believed about indexes that are in fact not true. The myths covered clustered indexes, fill factor, the column makeup of indexes, and more. The key to how to view anything that is believed about indexes that may be a myth is to take it upon yourself to test it.

You also looked at best practices. The best practices provided in the chapter should be the basis on which indexes for your databases can be built. I defined what a best practice is and what it is not. Then I discussed a number of best practices that can be considered when indexing your databases.

CHAPTER 9

Index Maintenance

Like anything in life, indexes require maintenance. Over time, the performance benefits of indexes can wane or, through data modifications, their sizes and the underlying statistics can drift and bloat. To prevent these issues, indexes must be maintained. If you do so, your database will remain a lean, mean query-running machine.

When it comes to maintenance, there are five areas to consider:

- Index fragmentation
- Heap bloat and forwarding
- Columnstore fragmentation
- Statistics
- In-memory statistics

Each plays a key role in maintaining a properly indexed and well-performing database.

This chapter explores all these areas. You'll learn about issues that arise from not maintaining indexes and review strategies for implementing a maintenance process. To illustrate how fragmentation occurs, there will be a number of simple demos. The statistics conversation will expand on the items discussed in Chapter 3 and lay out how to update statistics to keep them accurate.

Index Fragmentation

The first maintenance issue that can lead to a degradation of index performance is index fragmentation. Fragmentation happens when the pages in an index are no longer physically sequential.

While index fragmentation generated a much greater concern in previous versions of SQL Server and with old storage systems, it is still something to be concerned with in SQL Server. The main issue that arises with fragmentation is an increase in the amount of space required to store the index due to pages being split and in many cases left half empty. This excess space impacts the amount of space the database uses on disk, within memory, and through the CPU as it processes the data.

There are a few events in SQL Server that can lead to index fragmentation:

- INSERT operations
- UPDATE operations
- DELETE operations
- DBCC SHRINKDATABASE operations

As you can see, except for selecting data from the database, pretty much everything that you can do to an index can lead to fragmentation. Unless your database is read-only, you must pay attention to fragmentation and address it in an index before it becomes an issue.

Fragmentation Operations

The best way to understand fragmentation is to see it in action. In Chapter 3, you looked at the information returned by the dynamic management object (DMO) sys.dm_index_physical_stats. In this section, you'll review a number of scripts that cause fragmentation and then use the DMO to investigate the amount of fragmentation that has occurred.

As mentioned, fragmentation occurs when physical pages within an index are not sequential. When an insert occurs and the new row is not placed at the ending of the pages for the index, the new row will be placed on a page that already has other rows on it. If there is not enough room on the page for the new row, then the page will split—leading to fragmentation of the index. Fragmentation is the physical result of page splits in the index.

Insert Operations

The first operation that can lead to index fragmentation is an INSERT operation. This isn't usually considered the most likely operation to result in fragmentation, but there are database design patterns that can lead to fragmentation. There are two areas in which INSERT operations can lead to fragmentation: clustered and nonclustered indexes.

The most common pattern for designing clustered indexes is to place the index on a single column with a value that is ever-increasing. This is often done using an int data type and the IDENTITY property. When this pattern is followed, the chances of fragmentation occurring during inserts are relatively rare. Unfortunately, this isn't the only clustered index pattern that exists, and the others lead to fragmentation. For example, using business keys or uniqueidentifier data type values often causes fragmentation.

Clustered indexes that use uniqueidentifier data type values often use the NEWID() function to generate a random, unique value to serve as the clustering key. This value is unique but not ever-increasing. The most recent value generated may or may not be after the previous value. Because of this, when a new row is inserted into the clustered index, it is most likely to be placed between a number of other rows already in the index. And, as mentioned, if there isn't enough room in the index, fragmentation will occur.

To demonstrate fragmentation caused by the use of uniqueidentifier data type values, try the code in Listing 9-1. This code creates a table named dbo.UsingUniqueidentifier. It is populated with rows from sys.columns, and then a clustered index is added. At this point, all the pages in the indexes are physically sequential. Run the code in Listing 9-2 to view the results shown in Figure 9-1; these results show that the average fragmentation for the index is 0.00 percent.

Listing 9-1. Populate Uniqueidentifier Table

```
USE AdventureWorks2017
GO

IF OBJECT_ID('dbo.UsingUniqueidentifier') IS NOT NULL
    DROP TABLE dbo.UsingUniqueidentifier;

CREATE TABLE dbo.UsingUniqueidentifier
(
RowID uniqueidentifier CONSTRAINT DF_GUIDValue DEFAULT NEWID()
,Name sysname
,JunkValue varchar(2000)
);
```

CHAPTER 9 INDEX MAINTENANCE

```
INSERT INTO dbo.UsingUniqueidentifier (Name, JunkValue)
SELECT name, REPLICATE('X', 2000)
FROM sys.columns

CREATE CLUSTERED INDEX CLUS_UsingUniqueidentifier ON dbo.UsingUnique
identifier(RowID);
```

Listing 9-2. View INSERT Index Fragmentation

```
USE AdventureWorks2017
GO

SELECT index_type_desc
    ,index_depth
    ,index_level
    ,page_count
    ,record_count
    ,CAST(avg_fragmentation_in_percent as DECIMAL(6,2)) as avg_frag_in_percent
    ,fragment_count AS frag_count
    ,avg_fragment_size_in_pages AS avg_frag_size_in_pages
    ,CAST(avg_page_space_used_in_percent as DECIMAL(6,2)) as avg_page_space_
    used_in_percent
FROM sys.dm_db_index_physical_stats(DB_ID(),OBJECT_ID('dbo.UsingUnique
identifier'),NULL,NULL,'DETAILED')
```

	index_type_desc	index_depth	index_level	page_count	record_count	avg_frag_in_percent	frag_count	avg_frag_size_in_pages	avg_page_space_used_in_percent
1	CLUSTERED INDEX	3	0	665	1994	0.00	4	166.25	76.03
2	CLUSTERED INDEX	3	1	3	665	0.00	3	1	76.66
3	CLUSTERED INDEX	3	2	1	3	0.00	1	1	1.01

Figure 9-1. *Starting fragmentation results (results may vary)*

With the table built with a clustered index based on uniqueidentifier data types, you are now ready to perform an INSERT into the table to see the effect that the insert has on the index. To demonstrate, insert all the rows in sys.objects into dbo.UsingUniqueidentifier using the code in Listing 9-3. After the insert, you can review the fragmentation of the index in the results, using Listing 9-2 again. Your results should be similar to those shown in Figure 9-2, which shows fragmentation in the clustered index at over 70 percent at index level 0 after adding 689 rows to the table.

Listing 9-3. INSERT into Uniqueidentifier Table

```sql
USE AdventureWorks2017
GO

INSERT INTO dbo.UsingUniqueidentifier (Name, JunkValue)
SELECT name, REPLICATE('X', 2000)
FROM sys.objects
```

As this code sample demonstrated, clustered indexes that are based on values that are not ever-increasing result in fragmentation. The best example of this type of behavior is through the use of uniqueidentifiers. This can also happen when the clustering key is a computed value or based on a business key. When looking at business keys, if a random purchase order is assigned to an order, then that value will likely behave similar to a uniqueidentifier data type value.

	index_type_desc	index_depth	index_level	page_count	record_count	avg_frag_in_percent	frag_count	avg_frag_size_in_pages	avg_page_space_used_in_percent
1	CLUSTERED INDEX	3	0	1191	2683	70.28	846	1.40780141843972	57.35
2	CLUSTERED INDEX	3	1	5	1191	80.00	5	1	82.38
3	CLUSTERED INDEX	3	2	1	5	0.00	1	1	1.70

Figure 9-2. *Post-INSERT fragmentation results (percentage results may vary)*

The other way in which INSERT operations can affect fragmentation is on the nonclustered indexes. While the clustered index values may be ever-increasing values, the values for the columns in the nonclustered index won't necessarily have that same quality. A good example of this is when indexing the name of a product in a nonclustered index. The next record inserted into the table may start with the letter *M* and will need to be placed near the middle of the nonclustered index. If there isn't room at that location, a page split will occur, and fragmentation will result.

To demonstrate this behavior, add a nonclustered index to the table dbo.UsingUniqueidentifier that you used in the previous demonstrations. Listing 9-4 shows the schema for the new index. Before inserting more records to see the effect of inserting into a nonclustered index, run Listing 9-2 again. Your results should be similar to those in Figure 9-3.

Listing 9-4. Create Nonclustered Index

```
USE AdventureWorks2017
GO

CREATE NONCLUSTERED INDEX IX_Name ON dbo.UsingUniqueidentifier(Name)
INCLUDE (JunkValue);
```

	index_type_desc	index_depth	index_level	page_count	record_count	avg_frag_in_percent	frag_count	avg_frag_size_in_pages	avg_page_space_used_in_percent
1	CLUSTERED INDEX	3	0	1191	2683	70.28	846	1.40780141843972	57.35
2	CLUSTERED INDEX	3	1	5	1191	80.00	5	1	82.38
3	CLUSTERED INDEX	3	2	1	5	0.00	1	1	1.70
4	NONCLUSTERED INDEX	3	0	895	2683	0.00	2	447.5	76.22
5	NONCLUSTERED INDEX	3	1	7	895	0.00	2	3.5	96.36
6	NONCLUSTERED INDEX	3	2	1	7	0.00	1	1	4.20

Figure 9-3. Nonclustered index fragmentation results

At this point, you need to insert more records into `dbo.UsingUniqueidentifier`. Use Listing 9-3 again to insert more records into the table and then use Listing 9-4 to view the state of fragmentation in the nonclustered index. With this complete, your nonclustered index has gone from no fragmentation to more than 40 percent fragmentation, as shown in Figure 9-4.

	index_type_desc	index_depth	index_level	page_count	record_count	avg_frag_in_percent	frag_count	avg_frag_size_in_pages	avg_page_space_used_in_percent
1	CLUSTERED INDEX	3	0	1566	3372	85.76	1353	1.15742793791574	54.95
2	CLUSTERED INDEX	3	1	9	1566	88.89	7	1.28571428571429	60.17
3	CLUSTERED INDEX	3	2	1	9	0.00	1	1	3.09
4	NONCLUSTERED INDEX	3	0	1354	3372	43.13	592	2.28716216216216	63.47
5	NONCLUSTERED INDEX	3	1	18	1354	83.33	4	4.5	63.53
6	NONCLUSTERED INDEX	3	2	1	18	0.00	1	1	15.96

Figure 9-4. Nonclustered Post-INSERT fragmentation results

Whenever you perform INSERT operations, there is always a way in which fragmentation can occur. This will happen on both clustered and nonclustered indexes.

Update Operations

Another operation that can lead to fragmentation is an UPDATE operation. There are two main ways in which an UPDATE operation will result in fragmentation. First, the data in the record no longer fits on the page on which it currently resides. Second, the key value for the index changes, and the index location for the new key value is not on the same page or doesn't fit on the page where the record is destined. In both of these cases, the page splits, and fragmentation occurs.

CHAPTER 9 INDEX MAINTENANCE

To demonstrate how these situations lead to fragmentation, you'll first look at how increasing the size of a record in an update can lead to fragmentation. For this, you'll create a new table and insert a number of records into it. Then you'll add a clustered index to the table. The code for this is in Listing 9-5. Using the script from Listing 9-6 again, you can see that there is no fragmentation on the clustered index, as the results in Figure 9-5 show. One thing to pay attention to with these fragmentation results is that the average page space used is almost 90 percent. Because of this, any significant growth in record size will likely fill the available space on the pages.

Listing 9-5. Create Table for UPDATE Operations

```
USE AdventureWorks2017
GO

IF OBJECT_ID('dbo.UpdateOperations') IS NOT NULL
    DROP TABLE dbo.UpdateOperations;

CREATE TABLE dbo.UpdateOperations
(
RowID int IDENTITY(1,1)
,Name sysname
,JunkValue varchar(2000)
);

INSERT INTO dbo.UpdateOperations (Name, JunkValue)
SELECT name, REPLICATE('X', 1000)
FROM sys.columns

CREATE CLUSTERED INDEX CLUS_UsingUniqueidentifier ON dbo.UpdateOperations(RowID);
```

Listing 9-6. View UPDATE Index Fragmentation

```
USE AdventureWorks2017
GO

SELECT index_type_desc
    ,index_depth
    ,index_level
    ,page_count
```

CHAPTER 9 INDEX MAINTENANCE

```
    ,record_count
    ,CAST(avg_fragmentation_in_percent as DECIMAL(6,2)) as avg_
    fragmentation_in_percent
    ,fragment_count
    ,avg_fragment_size_in_pages
    ,CAST(avg_page_space_used_in_percent as DECIMAL(6,2)) as avg_page_
    space_used_in_percent
FROM sys.dm_db_index_physical_stats(DB_ID(),OBJECT_ID('dbo.UpdateOperations'),
NULL,NULL,'DETAILED')
```

	index_type_desc	index_depth	index_level	page_count	record_count	avg_fragmentation_in_percent	fragment_count	avg_fragment_size_in_pages	avg_page_space_used_in_percent
1	CLUSTERED INDEX	2	0	286	1997	0.35	4	71.5	89.77
2	CLUSTERED INDEX	2	1	1	286	0.00	1	1	45.91

Figure 9-5. *Initial UPDATE fragmentation results*

Now increase the size of some of the rows in the index. To accomplish this, execute the code in Listing 9-7. This code will update the JunkValue column for every five rows from a 1,000-character value to a 2,000-character value. Using Listing 9-2 to view current index fragmentation, you can see that, through the results in Figure 9-6, the clustered index is now more than 99 percent fragmented and the average page space used has dropped to about 50 percent. As this code demonstrates, when a row increases in size during an UPDATE operation, there can be significant amount of fragmentation.

Listing 9-7. Create Table for UPDATE Operations

```
USE AdventureWorks2017
GO

UPDATE dbo.UpdateOperations
SET JunkValue = REPLICATE('X', 2000)
WHERE RowID % 5 = 1
```

	index_type_desc	index_depth	index_level	page_count	record_count	avg_fragmentation_in_percent	fragment_count	avg_fragment_size_in_pages	avg_page_space_used_in_percent
1	CLUSTERED INDEX	2	0	571	1997	99.65	571	1	53.61
2	CLUSTERED INDEX	2	1	1	571	0.00	1	1	91.69

Figure 9-6. *UPDATE fragmentation results after record length increase*

CHAPTER 9 INDEX MAINTENANCE

As mentioned, the second way in which an index can incur fragmentation is by changing the key values for the index. When the key values for an index change, the record may need to change its position in the index. For instance, if an index is built on the name of the product, then changing the name from Acme Mop to XYZ Mop will change where the product name will be placed in the sorting for the index. Changing the location of the record in the index may place the record on a different page, and if there isn't sufficient space on the new page, then a page split and fragmentation may occur.

To demonstrate this concept, execute Listing 9-8 and then use Listing 9-6 to obtain the results shown in Figure 9-7. You will see that for the new nonclustered index, there is no fragmentation.

> **Note** If key values for a clustered index change often, that may indicate that the key values selected for the clustered index are inappropriate.

Listing 9-8. Create Nonclustered Index for UPDATE Operations

```
USE AdventureWorks2017
GO

CREATE NONCLUSTERED INDEX IX_Name ON dbo.UpdateOperations(Name) INCLUDE
(JunkValue);
```

	index_type_desc	index_depth	index_level	page_count	record_count	avg_fragmentation_in_percent	fragment_count	avg_fragment_size_in_pages	avg_page_space_used_in_percent
1	CLUSTERED INDEX	2	0	571	1997	99.65	571	1	53.61
2	CLUSTERED INDEX	2	1	1	571	0.00	1	1	91.69
3	NONCLUSTERED INDEX	3	0	351	1997	0.00	3	117	87.01
4	NONCLUSTERED INDEX	3	1	2	351	0.00	1	2	80.81
5	NONCLUSTERED INDEX	3	2	1	2	0.00	1	1	0.57

Figure 9-7. *UPDATE fragmentation results after adding nonclustered index*

At this point, you need to modify some key values. Using Listing 9-9, perform UPDATE activity on the table and update one of every nine rows. To simulate changing the key values, the UPDATE statement reverses the characters in the column. This small amount of activity is enough to cause a significant amount of fragmentation. As the results in Figure 9-8 illustrate, the nonclustered index went from no fragmentation to more than 30 percent fragmentation.

One thing to note is that the fragmentation on the clustered index did not change with these updates. Not all updates will result in fragmentation—only those that move data around because of space being unavailable on the pages where the records are currently stored.

Listing 9-9. UPDATE Operation to Change Index Key Value

```
USE AdventureWorks2017
GO

UPDATE dbo.UpdateOperations
SET Name = REVERSE(Name)
WHERE RowID % 9 = 1
```

	index_type_desc	index_depth	index_level	page_count	record_count	avg_fragmentation_in_percent	fragment_count	avg_fragment_size_in_pages	avg_page_space_used_in_percent
1	CLUSTERED INDEX	2	0	571	1997	99.65	571	1	53.61
2	CLUSTERED INDEX	2	1	1	571	0.00	1	1	91.69
3	NONCLUSTERED INDEX	3	0	438	1997	29.45	135	3.24444444444444	69.72
4	NONCLUSTERED INDEX	3	1	3	438	66.67	2	1.5	66.96
5	NONCLUSTERED INDEX	3	2	1	3	0.00	1	1	1.27

Figure 9-8. *UPDATE fragmentation results after changing index key values*

Delete Operations

The third type of operation that causes fragmentation is DELETE operation. Deletes are a bit different in nature in that they create fragmentation within a database. Instead of relocating pages because of page splits, a delete can lead to pages being removed from an index. Gaps will then appear in the physical sequence of pages for the index. Since the pages are no longer physically sequential, they are considered fragmented—especially since once the pages are deallocated from the index, they can be reallocated to other indexes for a more traditional form of fragmentation.

To demonstrate this type of behavior, create a table, populate it with a number of records, and then add a clustered index. Listing 9-10 shows the script for these tasks. Run the script followed by the script from Listing 9-11 to get the current fragmentation for the clustered index. Your results should match those in Figure 9-9. As you can see from the average fragmentation in percent column (`avg_fragmentation_in_percent`), there is no fragmentation currently in the index.

Listing 9-10. Creating a Table for DELETE Operation

```
USE AdventureWorks2017
GO

IF OBJECT_ID('dbo.DeleteOperations') IS NOT NULL
    DROP TABLE dbo.DeleteOperations;

CREATE TABLE dbo.DeleteOperations
(
RowID int IDENTITY(1,1)
,Name sysname
,JunkValue varchar(2000)
);

INSERT INTO dbo.DeleteOperations (Name, JunkValue)
SELECT name, REPLICATE('X', 1000)
FROM sys.columns

CREATE CLUSTERED INDEX CLUS_UsingUniqueidentifier ON dbo.DeleteOperations(RowID);
```

Listing 9-11. View DELETE Index Fragmentation

```
USE AdventureWorks2017
GO

SELECT index_type_desc
    ,index_depth
    ,index_level
    ,page_count
    ,record_count
    ,CAST(avg_fragmentation_in_percent as DECIMAL(6,2)) as avg_fragmentation_in_percent
    ,fragment_count
    ,avg_fragment_size_in_pages
    ,CAST(avg_page_space_used_in_percent as DECIMAL(6,2)) as avg_page_space_used_in_percent
FROM sys.dm_db_index_physical_stats(DB_ID(),OBJECT_ID('dbo.DeleteOperations'),
NULL,NULL,'DETAILED')
```

	index_type_desc	index_depth	index_level	page_count	record_count	avg_fragmentation_in_percent	fragment_count	avg_fragment_size_in_pages	avg_page_space_used_in_percent
1	CLUSTERED INDEX	2	0	286	2000	0.00	3	95.3333333333333	89.91
2	CLUSTERED INDEX	2	1	1	286	0.00	1	1	45.91

Figure 9-9. Fragmentation results before DELETE operation

Now, to demonstrate fragmentation caused by DELETE operations, you'll delete every other 50 records in the table using the code in Listing 9-12. As before, you'll use Listing 9-11 to view the state of fragmentation in the index. The results, shown in Figure 9-10, indicate that the DELETE operation resulted in about 13 percent fragmentation. With DELETE operations, the rate in which fragmentation usually occurs isn't too fast. Also, since the fragmentation is not the result of page splits, the order of the pages does not become physically out of order. Instead, there are gaps in the contiguous pages. However, pages left empty could be reused in future INSERT and UPDATE transactions which could result in the pages then being physically out of order.

Listing 9-12. Performing DELETE Operation

```
USE AdventureWorks2017
GO

DELETE dbo.DeleteOperations
WHERE RowID % 100 BETWEEN 1 AND 50
```

	index_type_desc	index_depth	index_level	page_count	record_count	avg_fragmentation_in_percent	fragment_count	avg_fragment_size_in_pages	avg_page_space_used_in_percent
1	CLUSTERED INDEX	2	0	161	1000	12.42	22	7.31818181818182	79.97
2	CLUSTERED INDEX	2	1	1	161	0.00	1	1	25.83

Figure 9-10. Fragmentation results after DELETE

As a final note on DELETE operations, the fragmentation may not appear immediately after the DELETE operation. When records are to be deleted, they are first marked for deletion before the record itself is actually deleted. While it is marked for deletion, the record is considered to be a ghost record. During this stage, the record is logically deleted but is physically still present in the index. At a future point, after the transaction has been committed and a CHECKPOINT has completed, the ghost cleanup process will physically remove the row. At this time, the fragmentation will show in the index.

CHAPTER 9 INDEX MAINTENANCE

Shrink Operations

The last type of operation that leads to fragmentation is when databases are shrunk. Databases can be shrunk using either DBCC SHRINKDATABASE or DBCC SHRINKFILE. These operations can be used to shrink the size of a database or its files. When they are used, the pages at the end of a data file are relocated toward the beginning of the data file. For their intended purpose, shrink operations can be effective tools.

Unfortunately, these shrink operations do not take into account the nature of the data pages that are being moved. To the shrink operation, a data page is a data page. The priority of the operation is that pages at the end of the data file find a place at the beginning of the data file. As discussed, when the pages of an index are not physically stored in order, the index is considered fragmented.

To demonstrate the fragmentation damage that a shrink operation can cause, you'll create a database and perform a shrink on it; the code appears in Listing 9-14. In this example, there are two tables: FirstTable and SecondTable. Some records will be inserted into each table. The inserts will alternate back and forth with three inserts into FirstTable and two inserts into SecondTable. Through these inserts, there will be alternating bands of pages allocated to the two tables. Next, SecondTable will be dropped, which will result in unallocated data pages between each of the bands of pages for FirstTable. Using Listing 9-13 again will show that a small amount of fragmentation exists on FirstTable, shown in Figure 9-11.

Listing 9-13. View Index Fragmentation from Shrink

```
Use Fragmentation
GO

SELECT index_type_desc
    ,index_depth
    ,index_level
    ,page_count
    ,record_count
    ,CAST(avg_fragmentation_in_percent as DECIMAL(6,2)) as avg_
    fragmentation_in_percent
    ,fragment_count
```

```
    ,avg_fragment_size_in_pages
    ,CAST(avg_page_space_used_in_percent as DECIMAL(6,2)) as avg_page_
space_used_in_percent
FROM sys.dm_db_index_physical_stats(DB_ID(),OBJECT_ID('dbo.FirstTable'),
NULL,NULL,'DETAILED')
```

Listing 9-14. Shrink Operation Database Preparation

```
USE master
GO
IF EXISTS (SELECT * FROM sys.databases WHERE name = 'Fragmentation')
DROP DATABASE Fragmentation
GO

CREATE DATABASE Fragmentation
GO

Use Fragmentation
GO

IF OBJECT_ID('dbo.FirstTable') IS NOT NULL
    DROP TABLE dbo.FirstTable;

CREATE TABLE dbo.FirstTable
(
RowID int IDENTITY(1,1)
,Name sysname
,JunkValue varchar(2000)
,CONSTRAINT PK_FirstTable PRIMARY KEY CLUSTERED (RowID)
);

INSERT INTO dbo.FirstTable (Name, JunkValue)
SELECT TOP 750 name, REPLICATE('X', 2000)
FROM sys.columns

IF OBJECT_ID('dbo.SecondTable') IS NOT NULL
    DROP TABLE dbo.SecondTable;
```

```sql
CREATE TABLE dbo.SecondTable
(
RowID int IDENTITY(1,1)
,Name sysname
,JunkValue varchar(2000)
,CONSTRAINT PK_SecondTable PRIMARY KEY CLUSTERED (RowID)
);

INSERT INTO dbo.SecondTable (Name, JunkValue)
SELECT TOP 750 name, REPLICATE('X', 2000)
FROM sys.columns
GO

INSERT INTO dbo.FirstTable (Name, JunkValue)
SELECT TOP 750 name, REPLICATE('X', 2000)
FROM sys.columns
GO

INSERT INTO dbo.SecondTable (Name, JunkValue)
SELECT TOP 750 name, REPLICATE('X', 2000)
FROM sys.columns
GO

INSERT INTO dbo.FirstTable (Name, JunkValue)
SELECT TOP 750 name, REPLICATE('X', 2000)
FROM sys.columns
GO

IF OBJECT_ID('dbo.SecondTable') IS NOT NULL
    DROP TABLE dbo.SecondTable;
GO
```

	index_type_desc	index_depth	index_level	page_count	record_count	avg_fragmentation_in_percent	fragment_count	avg_fragment_size_in_pages	avg_page_space_used_in_percent
1	CLUSTERED INDEX	3	0	750	2250	2.27	21	35.7142857142857	75.38
2	CLUSTERED INDEX	3	1	2	750	0.00	2	1	60.21
3	CLUSTERED INDEX	3	2	1	2	0.00	1	1	0.30

Figure 9-11. Fragmentation of FirstTable after inserts

With the database prepared, the next step is to shrink the database, the purpose of which is to recover the space that SecondTable has been allocated and trim down the size of the database to only what is needed. To perform the shrink operation, use the code in Listing 9-15. When the SHRINKDATABASE operation completes, you can see in Figure 9-12 that running the code from Listing 9-13 causes the fragmentation for the index to increase from just over 2 percent fragmentation to more than 35 percent fragmentation. This is a significant change in fragmentation on a database with just a single table. Consider the effect of a shrink operation on a database with dozens, hundreds, or thousands of indexes.

Listing 9-15. Shrink Operation

```
DBCC SHRINKDATABASE (Fragmentation)
```

	index_type_desc	index_depth	index_level	page_count	record_count	avg_fragmentation_in_percent	fragment_count	avg_fragment_size_in_pages	avg_page_space_used_in_percent
1	CLUSTERED INDEX	3	0	750	2250	35.47	269	2.78810408921933	75.38
2	CLUSTERED INDEX	3	1	2	750	0.00	2	1	60.21
3	CLUSTERED INDEX	3	2	1	2	0.00	1	1	0.30

Figure 9-12. *Fragmentation of FirstTable after shrink operation*

This has been a simple example of the damage in terms of fragmentation that a shrink operation can have on an index. As was evident even with this example, the shrink operation led to a significant amount of fragmentation. Most SQL Server database administrators will agree that shrink operations should be an extremely rare operation on any database. Many DBAs are also of the opinion that this operation should never be used on any database for any reason. The guideline that is most often recommended is to be extremely cautious when shrink database operations are performed. Also, don't get caught in a cycle of shrinking a database to recover space and causing fragmentation and then expanding the database through defragmenting the indexes. This is only a waste of time and resources that could be better spent on real performance and maintenance issues.

Fragmentation Variants

Traditionally, when people discuss index fragmentation, the primary focus is on fragmentation within the clustered or nonclustered index. This isn't the only consideration to keep in mind when considering index fragmentation. You also need to consider whether the table or index has bloat, forwarding, or segmentation, each of which is a variation on the idea of index fragmentation. In this section, we'll review two other areas in which fragmentation-type maintenance can be required on tables:

- Heap bloat and forwarding
- Columnstore fragmentation

Heap Bloat and Forwarding

The first area we'll cover is heap bloat and forwarding. As discussed in Chapter 3, heaps are collections of unordered pages in which data for a table is stored. As new rows are added to the table, the heap grows, and new pages are allocated. Insert and update operations can cause changes to heaps that can require maintenance on the table.

To begin, you'll look at bloating within a heap. For heaps, bloating occurs when records are deleted from the heap without being reused for new records. As discussed in Chapter 8, this isn't a matter of records going to new pages but an overall decline in the number of records in the table. The pages will be reused, but when they aren't, the pages remain allocated, and this can have an impact on performance.

To demonstrate this activity, let's review the script in Listing 9-16. In the script, it starts with a heap table that has 400 records inserted into it, and then half the records are deleted, leaving 200 records in the table. As shown in Figure 9-13, the record count for the table reflects these changes, but in both cases the DMV results show that there are 100 pages associated with the table. This is because pages are not removed from a heap unless maintenance activities force this to occur. Through the ALTER TABLE statement on dbo.HeapTable with the REBUILD option, the table is rebuilt, and the excess pages are flushed.

Listing 9-16. Impact of Deletes on Heap Page Allocations

```
USE AdventureWorks2017
GO

IF OBJECT_ID('dbo.HeapTable') IS NOT NULL
    DROP TABLE dbo.HeapTable;

CREATE TABLE dbo.HeapTable
(
    RowId INT IDENTITY(1,1)
    ,FillerData VARCHAR(2500)
);
```

```sql
INSERT INTO dbo.HeapTable (FillerData)
SELECT TOP 400 REPLICATE('X',2000)
FROM sys.objects;

SELECT OBJECT_NAME(object_id), index_type_desc, page_count, record_count,
forwarded_record_count
FROM sys.dm_db_index_physical_stats (DB_ID(),OBJECT_ID('dbo.HeapTable'),
NULL,NULL,'DETAILED');

SET STATISTICS IO ON;
SELECT COUNT(*) FROM dbo.HeapTable;
SET STATISTICS IO OFF;

DELETE FROM dbo.HeapTable
WHERE RowId % 2 = 0;

SELECT OBJECT_NAME(object_id), index_type_desc, page_count, record_count,
forwarded_record_count
FROM sys.dm_db_index_physical_stats (DB_ID(),OBJECT_ID('dbo.HeapTable'),
NULL,NULL,'DETAILED');

SET STATISTICS IO ON;
SELECT COUNT(*) FROM dbo.HeapTable;
SET STATISTICS IO OFF;

ALTER TABLE dbo.HeapTable REBUILD;

SELECT OBJECT_NAME(object_id), index_type_desc, page_count, record_count,
forwarded_record_count
FROM sys.dm_db_index_physical_stats (DB_ID(),OBJECT_ID('dbo.HeapTable'),
NULL,NULL,'DETAILED');

SET STATISTICS IO ON;
SELECT COUNT(*) FROM dbo.HeapTable;
SET STATISTICS IO OFF;
```

	(No column name)	index_type_desc	page_count	record_count	forwarded_record_count
1	HeapTable	HEAP	100	400	0

	(No column name)
1	400

	(No column name)	index_type_desc	page_count	record_count	forwarded_record_count
1	HeapTable	HEAP	100	200	0

	(No column name)
1	200

	(No column name)	index_type_desc	page_count	record_count	forwarded_record_count
1	HeapTable	HEAP	50	200	0

	(No column name)
1	200

Figure 9-13. Results from deleting from a heap

To help emphasize that the pages are still in the table, Figure 9-14 shows the pages that are read when counting all rows in the table, further demonstrating that there are 100 pages being accessed. When considering the impact on performance for heaps after a delete, if there is an excessive number of pages in a heap compared to the amount of data, this will increase the amount of effort required by SQL Server to execute the query. In the case of this demonstration, the COUNT(*) queries are processing twice the amount of data that is required.

```
Table 'HeapTable'. Scan count 1, logical reads 100, physical reads 0, read-ahead reads 0, lob logical reads 0,
Table 'HeapTable'. Scan count 1, logical reads 100, physical reads 0, read-ahead reads 0, lob logical reads 0,
Table 'HeapTable'. Scan count 1, logical reads 50, physical reads 0, read-ahead reads 0, lob logical reads 0,
```

Figure 9-14. I/O impact from deletes on a heap

The other area of consideration for the maintenance of heaps is the volume of forwarded records in the table. Forwarded records, discussed in Chapter 3, are records within a heap that no longer fit in the original location in which they were added to the heap. To accommodate the change in the size of the record, the record is stored on another page, and the previous record location includes a pointer to the new location.

The impact of this change is an increase in the number of pages in the heap, because new pages are added for existing records, and it takes an additional I/O operation to go from the first page to the forwarded page when looking up a record. While this may not

CHAPTER 9 INDEX MAINTENANCE

appear to be a huge issue, in aggregate the accumulated impact of forwarded records increases the amount of I/O for a system and adds to latency in query execution.

To demonstrate the impact of forwarded records on queries, execute the code in Listing 9-17. This script creates a table with a heap, runs a number of queries, updates the records to cause forwarding of heap records to occur, and then completes by reexecuting the previous collection of queries.

Listing 9-17. Forwarded Record Impact on Query Performance

```
SET NOCOUNT ON

IF OBJECT_ID('dbo.ForwardedRecords') IS NOT NULL
    DROP TABLE dbo.ForwardedRecords;

CREATE TABLE dbo.ForwardedRecords
    (
    ID INT IDENTITY(1,1)
    ,VALUE VARCHAR(8000)
    );

CREATE NONCLUSTERED INDEX IX_ForwardedRecords_ID ON dbo.ForwardedRecords(ID);

INSERT INTO dbo.ForwardedRecords (VALUE)
SELECT REPLICATE(type, 500)
FROM sys.objects;

SET STATISTICS IO ON
PRINT '*** No forwarded records'
SELECT * FROM dbo.ForwardedRecords;

SELECT * FROM dbo.ForwardedRecords
WHERE ID = 40;

SELECT * FROM dbo.ForwardedRecords
WHERE ID BETWEEN 40 AND 60;
SET STATISTICS IO OFF
```

CHAPTER 9 INDEX MAINTENANCE

```
UPDATE dbo.ForwardedRecords
SET VALUE =REPLICATE(VALUE, 16)
WHERE ID%3 = 1;

SET STATISTICS IO ON
PRINT '*** With forwarded records'
SELECT * FROM dbo.ForwardedRecords;

SELECT * FROM dbo.ForwardedRecords
WHERE ID = 40;

SELECT * FROM dbo.ForwardedRecords
WHERE ID BETWEEN 40 AND 60;
SET STATISTICS IO OFF
```

There are three queries from Listing 9-17 that are included to demonstrate the impact of forwarded records on heaps:

- SELECT *: To demonstrate the impact of an index scan

- SELECT with equality predicate: To demonstrate the impact on a singleton lookup

- SELECT with inequality predicate: To demonstrate the impact on a range lookup

For the SELECT * query, before the forwarded records are in the heap, the query executes with 99 reads, shown in Figure 9-15. After the forwarded records are introduced, the reads increase to 561. This increase is because of the new pages added to the heap to accommodate the increases in the row sizes. With the second query, the singleton lookup grows from three reads to four reads, which represents the additional read required to go from the original location for the record to the forwarding location. In the last query, the range query with the lookup executes with 23 reads, but after the forwarded records are added to the table, the reads jump to 30 reads.

CHAPTER 9   INDEX MAINTENANCE

```
*** No forwarded records
Table 'ForwardedRecords'. Scan count 1, logical reads 99, physical reads 0,
Table 'ForwardedRecords'. Scan count 1, logical reads 3, physical reads 0,
Table 'ForwardedRecords'. Scan count 1, logical reads 23, physical reads 0,
*** With forwarded records
Table 'ForwardedRecords'. Scan count 1, logical reads 561, physical reads 0
Table 'ForwardedRecords'. Scan count 1, logical reads 4, physical reads 0,
Table 'ForwardedRecords'. Scan count 1, logical reads 30, physical reads 0,
```

Figure 9-15. *I/O statistics for forwarded record queries*

The overall effect of the forwarded records is an increase in reads. While the increase may not be significant from a per-query basis, over time the impact adds up. Scans of heaps with forwarded records access more pages, and lookups require an extra I/O. Reducing the impact of forwarded records in heaps is an important part of maintaining indexes and maintaining performance.

Columnstore Fragmentation

Columnstore indexes are one of SQL Server's newer features. An interesting component of columnstore indexes is the read-only nature of the segments. As discussed in Chapter 2, when new columnstore indexes are added to a delta table, the delta table is eventually compressed into a columnstore format. Also, since the segments are read-only, deletes don't immediately impact the segments, resulting in fragments of the read-only segments that contain data that is no longer part of the table.

To demonstrate both of these concepts, execute the code in Listing 9-18 to prepare a table with a clustered columnstore index. After the table is built, the two sets of rows are inserted. The first set contains 1,000 rows, and the index is reorganized to force the rowgroup to compress to columnstore format. The second set contains 105,000 rows, which is more than the 104,000 threshold that automatically triggers use of the columnstore format. As shown in Figure 9-16, the inserted records are all compressed to columnstore format.

Note   Depending on your environment, the script in Listing 9-18 can take a while to run.

Listing 9-18. Prepare Columnstore Table

```sql
USE ContosoRetailDW
GO

IF OBJECT_ID('dbo.FactOnlineSalesCI') IS NOT NULL
    DROP TABLE dbo.FactOnlineSalesCI

CREATE TABLE dbo.FactOnlineSalesCI(
    [OnlineSalesKey] [int] NOT NULL,
    [DateKey] [datetime] NOT NULL,
    [StoreKey] [int] NOT NULL,
    [ProductKey] [int] NOT NULL,
    [PromotionKey] [int] NOT NULL,
    [CurrencyKey] [int] NOT NULL,
    [CustomerKey] [int] NOT NULL,
    [SalesOrderNumber] [nvarchar](20) NOT NULL,
    [SalesOrderLineNumber] [int] NULL,
    [SalesQuantity] [int] NOT NULL,
    [SalesAmount] [money] NOT NULL,
    [ReturnQuantity] [int] NOT NULL,
    [ReturnAmount] [money] NULL,
    [DiscountQuantity] [int] NULL,
    [DiscountAmount] [money] NULL,
    [TotalCost] [money] NOT NULL,
    [UnitCost] [money] NULL,
    [UnitPrice] [money] NULL,
    [ETLLoadID] [int] NULL,
    [LoadDate] [datetime] NULL,
    [UpdateDate] [datetime] NULL
)
INSERT INTO dbo.FactOnlineSalesCI
SELECT *
FROM dbo.FactOnlineSales
```

CHAPTER 9 INDEX MAINTENANCE

```sql
CREATE CLUSTERED COLUMNSTORE INDEX FactOnlineSalesCI_CCI ON dbo.
FactOnlineSalesCI

DECLARE @we int= 1

WHILE @we <= 5
BEGIN
    INSERT INTO dbo.FactOnlineSalesCI
    SELECT TOP 1000 *
    FROM dbo.FactOnlineSales
    ALTER INDEX ALL ON dbo.FactOnlineSalesCI REORGANIZE
        WITH (COMPRESS_ALL_ROW_GROUPS =ON)
    SET @we += 1
END

WHILE @we <= 10
BEGIN
    INSERT INTO dbo.FactOnlineSalesCI
    SELECT TOP 105000 *
    FROM dbo.FactOnlineSales
    SET @we += 1
END

SELECT*
FROM sys.column_store_row_groups
WHERE object_id=OBJECT_ID('dbo.FactOnlineSalesCI')
ORDER BY row_group_id DESC
```

	object_id	index_id	partition_number	row_group_id	delta_store_hobt_id	state	state_description	total_rows	deleted_rows	size_in_bytes
1	366624349	1	1	33	NULL	3	COMPRESSED	105000	0	1425752
2	366624349	1	1	32	NULL	3	COMPRESSED	105000	0	1425752
3	366624349	1	1	31	NULL	3	COMPRESSED	105000	0	1425752
4	366624349	1	1	30	NULL	3	COMPRESSED	105000	0	1425752
5	366624349	1	1	29	NULL	3	COMPRESSED	105000	0	1425752
6	366624349	1	1	28	NULL	3	COMPRESSED	48696	0	516640
7	366624349	1	1	27	NULL	3	COMPRESSED	1000	0	21144
8	366624349	1	1	26	72057594051100672	4	TOMBSTONE	1000	NULL	188416
9	366624349	1	1	25	NULL	4	TOMBSTONE	47696	0	0
10	366624349	1	1	24	NULL	4	TOMBSTONE	1000	0	0

Figure 9-16. *Columnstore rowgroup resultset*

CHAPTER 9 INDEX MAINTENANCE

The piece that is interesting at this point is that the rowgroups created are much smaller than the max size for a rowgroup, of about 1 million rows. And since they are smaller, there may be an opportunity to optimize the number of pages that they use by increasing the number of records per rowgroup. This can be done by maintaining the columnstore index and rebuilding it. To show the value in rebuilding columnstore indexes, execute the code in Listing 9-19. Through this, you can see that the logical reads before the rebuild are 83,423 over two scan operations and then drop to 833 logical reads after the rebuild, shown in Figure 9-17. This is an almost 100 percent drop in pages accessed. If you consider the effect of this type of maintenance over large fact tables using columnstore indexes, these types of excessive allocation of pages will greatly impact performance. Additionally, comparing Figures 9-16 and 9-18, the table also has far fewer rowgroups, from 34 to 14 after the columnstore index rebuild.

Listing 9-19. Impact of Inserts on Columnstore Table

```
USE ContosoRetailDW
GO

SET STATISTICS IO ON

SELECT DateKey,COUNT(*)
FROM dbo.FactOnlineSalesCI
GROUP BY DateKey

ALTER INDEX ALL ON dbo.FactOnlineSalesCI REBUILD

SELECT DateKey,COUNT(*)
FROM dbo.FactOnlineSalesCI
GROUP BY DateKey

SET STATISTICS IO OFF

SELECT *
FROM sys.column_store_row_groups
WHERE object_id = OBJECT_ID('dbo.FactOnlineSalesCI')
ORDER BY row_group_id DESC
```

CHAPTER 9　INDEX MAINTENANCE

```
Warning: The join order has been enforced because a local join hint is used.

(1096 rows affected)
Table 'FactOnlineSalesCI'. Scan count 2, logical reads 0, physical reads 0, read-ahead reads 0, lob logical reads 449, lob physical reads 0, lob read-ahead reads 0.
Table 'FactOnlineSalesCI'. Segment reads 18, segment skipped 0.
Table 'Worktable'. Scan count 0, logical reads 0, physical reads 0, read-ahead reads 0, lob logical reads 0, lob physical reads 0, lob read-ahead reads 0.
Table 'FactOnlineSalesCI'. Scan count 3, logical reads 0, physical reads 0, read-ahead reads 0, lob logical reads 82974, lob physical reads 375, lob read-ahead reads 143315.
Table 'FactOnlineSalesCI'. Segment reads 21, segment skipped 0.

(1096 rows affected)
Table 'FactOnlineSalesCI'. Scan count 2, logical reads 0, physical reads 0, read-ahead reads 0, lob logical reads 833, lob physical reads 0, lob read-ahead reads 1311.
Table 'FactOnlineSalesCI'. Segment reads 14, segment skipped 0.
Table 'Worktable'. Scan count 0, logical reads 0, physical reads 0, read-ahead reads 0, lob logical reads 0, lob physical reads 0, lob read-ahead reads 0.

(14 rows affected)
```

Figure 9-17. *I/O statistics for columnstore table inserts*

	object_id	index_id	partition_number	row_group_id	delta_store_hobt_id	state	state_description	total_rows	deleted_rows	size_in_bytes
1	366624349	1	1	13	NULL	3	COMPRESSED	710	0	14552
2	366624349	1	1	12	NULL	3	COMPRESSED	573986	0	7236192
3	366624349	1	1	11	NULL	3	COMPRESSED	1048576	0	12770312
4	366624349	1	1	10	NULL	3	COMPRESSED	1048576	0	12597528
5	366624349	1	1	9	NULL	3	COMPRESSED	1048576	0	12710856
6	366624349	1	1	8	NULL	3	COMPRESSED	1048576	0	12640272
7	366624349	1	1	7	NULL	3	COMPRESSED	1048576	0	11976416
8	366624349	1	1	6	NULL	3	COMPRESSED	1048576	0	12349392
9	366624349	1	1	5	NULL	3	COMPRESSED	1048576	0	11560104
10	366624349	1	1	4	NULL	3	COMPRESSED	1048576	0	11566808

Figure 9-18. *Rowgroup statistics after columnstore index rebuild*

The next type of fragmentation that occurs with columnstore indexes is through delete operations. While this is called *fragmentation*, in actuality when deletes occur on columnstore indexes, the rows are not removed from the indexes; they are only marked as deleted. Because of this, pages allocated to a clustered columnstore index that have all their records deleted will still be active within the index.

To show how this impacts, you'll use the script in Listing 9-20 to delete all the 2007 data from the table. Then another statement will rebuild the columnstore index. Between these operations, you'll run an aggregate query to provide an operation to see the impact of deletes on the I/O of queries.

Listing 9-20. Delete Operations on a Clustered Columnstore Index

```
USE ContosoRetailDW
GO

SET STATISTICS IO ON

SELECT DateKey,COUNT(*)
FROM dbo.FactOnlineSalesCI
GROUP BY DateKey
```

CHAPTER 9 ■ INDEX MAINTENANCE

```
DELETE FROM dbo.FactOnlineSalesCI
WHERE DateKey <'2008-01-01'

SELECT DateKey,COUNT(*)
FROM dbo.FactOnlineSalesCI
GROUP BY DateKey

ALTER INDEX ALL ON dbo.FactOnlineSalesCI REBUILD

SELECT DateKey,COUNT(*)
FROM dbo.FactOnlineSalesCI
GROUP BY DateKey

SET STATISTICS IO OFF
```

After running these queries and the index is rebuilt, the results are fairly interesting. If you start with the first query, there are 659 logical reads for the aggregate query, shown in Figure 9-19. Deleting a year's worth of data results in the aggregate query requiring 79,982 logical reads, which is an increase from the original query with 365 fewer rows returned. This is because of the pages required to manage the deleted rows. After rebuilding, the number of I/Os drops significantly to 444 logical reads.

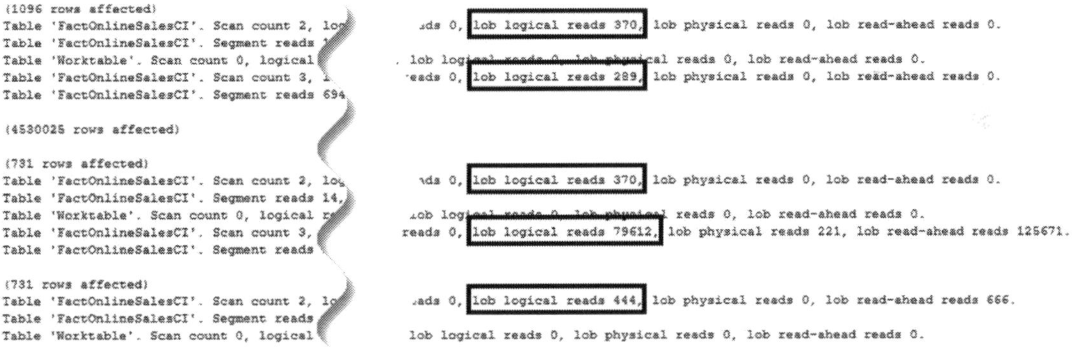

Figure 9-19. Statistics I/O results for delete operation demonstration

Through the addition of new rows and the deletion of existing rows, there are reasons to consider the maintenance requirements of columnstore indexes. The issues that affect these indexes are not the same as those of traditional clustered indexes, but they are significant nonetheless.

Fragmentation Issues

You've seen a number of ways in which indexes can become fragmented, but there hasn't been a discussion about why this is important. There are a couple important reasons why fragmentation within indexes can be a problem:

- Index I/O
- Contiguous reads

As the fragmentation of an index increases, each of these two areas affects the index's ability to perform well. In some worst-case scenarios, the level of fragmentation can be so severe that the query optimizer will stop using the index in query plans.

Index I/O

I/O is an area of SQL Server where it is easy to have performance bottlenecks; likewise, there are a multitude of solutions to help mitigate the bottlenecks. From the perspective of this chapter, you are concerned with the effect of fragmentation on I/O.

Since page splits are often the cause of fragmentation, they provide a good place to start investigating the effect of fragmentation on I/O. To review, when a page split occurs, half the contents on the page are moved off the page and onto another page. Generally speaking, if the original page was 100 percent full, then both pages would be about 50 percent full. In essence, it will take two I/Os to read from storage the same amount of information that required one I/O prior to the page split. This increase in I/Os will drive up reads and writes and thus can have a negative effect on performance.

To validate that effect of fragmentation on I/O, let's walk through another fragmentation example. This time you'll build a table, populate it with some data, and perform an update to generate page splits and fragmentation. The code in Listing 9-22 will perform these operations. The last portion of the script will query `sys.dm_db_partition_stats` to return the number of pages that have been reserved for the index. Execute the fragmentation script from Listing 9-21. You'll see the index at this point is more than 99 percent fragmented, and the results from Listing 9-14 show the index is using 209 pages. See Figure 9-20 for the results.

Listing 9-21. View Index Fragmentation for I/O Example

```
SELECT index_type_desc
    ,index_depth
    ,index_level
    ,page_count
    ,record_count
    ,CAST(avg_fragmentation_in_percent as DECIMAL(6,2)) as avg_
    fragmentation_in_percent
    ,fragment_count
    ,avg_fragment_size_in_pages
    ,CAST(avg_page_space_used_in_percent as DECIMAL(6,2)) as avg_page_
    space_used_in_percent
FROM sys.dm_db_index_physical_stats(DB_ID(),OBJECT_ID('dbo.IndexIO'),NULL,
NULL,'DETAILED')
```

Listing 9-22. Script to Build Index I/O Example

```
USE AdventureWorks2017
GO

IF OBJECT_ID('dbo.IndexIO') IS NOT NULL
    DROP TABLE dbo.IndexIO;

CREATE TABLE dbo.IndexIO
(
RowID int IDENTITY(1,1)
,Name sysname
,JunkValue varchar(2000)
);

INSERT INTO dbo.IndexIO (Name, JunkValue)
SELECT name, REPLICATE('X', 1000)
FROM sys.columns

CREATE CLUSTERED INDEX CLUS_IndexIO ON dbo.IndexIO(RowID);
```

```
UPDATE dbo.IndexIO
SET JunkValue = REPLICATE('X', 2000)
WHERE RowID % 5 = 1

SELECT we.name, ps.in_row_reserved_page_count
FROM sys.indexes we
INNER JOIN sys.dm_db_partition_stats ps ON we.object_id = ps.object_id AND
we.index_id = ps.index_id
WHERE we.name = 'CLUS_IndexIO'
```

	name	in_row_reserved_page_count
1	CLUS_IndexIO	585

Figure 9-20. *Fragmentation of CLUS_IndexIO*

But would removing the fragmentation from the index have a noticeable impact on the number of pages in the index? As the demo will demonstrate, reducing fragmentation does have an impact.

Continuing, the next thing to do is to remove the fragmentation from the index. To accomplish this, execute the ALTER INDEX statement in Listing 9-23 to remove the fragmentation. In the rest of the chapter, we'll discuss the mechanics of removing fragmentation from an index, so for the time being, this statement won't be explained. The effect of this command is that all the fragmentation has been removed from the index. Figure 9-21 shows the results from Listing 9-23. They show that the number of pages that the index is using dropped from 585 to 417. The effect of removing the fragmentation is an impressive reduction of almost 30 percent in pages in the index.

Listing 9-23. Script to Rebuild Index to Remove Fragmentation

```
USE AdventureWorks2017
GO

ALTER INDEX CLUS_IndexIO ON dbo.IndexIO REBUILD

SELECT we.name, ps.in_row_reserved_page_count
FROM sys.indexes we
INNER JOIN sys.dm_db_partition_stats ps ON we.object_id = ps.object_id AND
we.index_id = ps.index_id
WHERE we.name = 'CLUS_IndexIO'
```

	name	in_row_reserved_page_count
1	CLUS_IndexIO	417

Figure 9-21. *Page count resulting from rebuild operations*

This proves that fragmentation can have an effect on the number of pages in an index. The more pages in an index, the more reads are required to get the data you need. Reducing the count of pages can help with allowing SQL Server databases to process more data in the same number of reads or to improve the speed in which they read the same information across fewer pages.

Contiguous Reads

The other negative effect that fragmentation can have on performance relates to contiguous reads. Within SQL Server, contiguous reads affect its ability to utilize read-ahead operations. Read-ahead allows SQL Server to request pages into memory that are expected to be used. Rather than waiting for an I/O request to be generated for the page, SQL Server can read large blocks of pages into memory with the expectation that the data pages will be used by the query in the future.

Going back to indexes, we previously discussed how fragmentation within an index occurs as a result of breaks in the continuity of physical data pages in an index. Every time there is a break in the physical pages, I/O operations must change the place in which data is being read from SQL Server. This is how fragmentation creates a hindrance in contiguous reads.

Defragmentation Options

SQL Server offers a number of ways in which fragmentation can be removed or mitigated within an index. Each of the methods has pros and cons associated with using it. In this section, you'll look at the options and the reasons for using each one.

Index Rebuild

The first method for removing fragmentation from an index is to rebuild the index. Rebuilding an index builds a new contiguous copy of the index. When the new index is complete, the existing index is dropped. Index rebuild operations are accomplished through either a CREATE INDEX or ALTER INDEX statement. Typically, indexes with more than 30 percent fragmentation are considered good candidates for index rebuilds. Note that 30 percent and lower levels of fragmentation in most databases will not show as a large negative impact on performance. The usage of 30 percent is a good starting point, but each database and index usage should be reviewed and adjusted if performance shows more negative effects with less than 30 percent fragmentation of the index.

The chief benefit of performing an index rebuild is that the resulting new index has contiguous pages. When an index is highly fragmented, sometimes the best way to resolve the fragmentation is to simply start over with the index and rebuild. Another benefit of rebuilding an index is that the index options can be modified during the rebuild. Lastly, for most indexes, the index can remain online while it is being rebuilt.

Note Since SQL Server 2012, clustered indexes with `varchar(max)`, `nvarchar(max)`, `varbinary(max)`, and XML data types can be rebuilt online. Clustered indexes still cannot be rebuilt online when they contain the following data types: `image`, `ntext`, or `text`. Also, online rebuilds are limited to SQL Server Enterprise, Developer, and Evaluation Editions. Additionally, online rebuilds require double the space for the index since both the old and new versions of the index need to exist to complete the rebuild, which can be a problem with larger tables.

The first option for rebuilding an index is to use the CREATE INDEX statement, shown in Listing 9-24. This is accomplished through the use of the DROP_EXISTING index option. There are a few reasons to choose the CREATE INDEX option instead of ALTER INDEX:

- The index definition needs to be changed, such as when the columns need to be added or removed or their order needs to change.
- The index needs to be moved from one filegroup to another.
- The index partitioning needs to be modified.

Listing 9-24. Index Rebuild with CREATE INDEX

```
CREATE [ UNIQUE ] [ CLUSTERED | NONCLUSTERED ] INDEX index_name
    ON <object> ( column [ ASC | DESC ] [ ,...n ] )
    [ INCLUDE ( column_name [ ,...n ] ) ]
    [ WHERE <filter_predicate> ]
    [ WITH ( <relational_index_option> [ ,...n ] ) ]
```

```
    [ ON { partition_scheme_name ( column_name )
        | filegroup_name
        | default
        }
    ]
    [ FILESTREAM_ON { filestream_filegroup_name | partition_scheme_name |
    "NULL" } ]
[ ; ]
<relational_index_option> ::=
    DROP_EXISTING = { ON | OFF }
    | ONLINE = { ON | OFF }
    | RESUMABLE = {ON | OF }
    | MAX_DURATION = <time> [MINUTES]
```

The other option is the ALTER INDEX statement, shown in Listing 9-25. This option utilizes the REBUILD option in the syntax. Conceptually, this accomplishes that same thing as the CREATE INDEX statement but with the following benefits:

- More than one index on a table can be rebuilt in a single statement.
- A single partition of an index can be rebuilt.

Listing 9-25. Index Rebuild with ALTER INDEX

```
ALTER INDEX { index_name | ALL }
    ON <object>
    { REBUILD
        [ [PARTITION = ALL]
            [ WITH ( <rebuild_index_option> [ ,...n ] ) ]
            | [ PARTITION = partition_number
                [ WITH ( <single_partition_rebuild_index_option>
                    [ ,...n ] )
                ]
            ]
        ]
    }
```

The primary downside to index rebuilds is the amount of space that is required for the index during the rebuild operation. At a minimum, there should be 120 percent of the size of the current index available within the database for the rebuilt index. The reason for this is that the current index will not be dropped until after the rebuild is completed. For a short time, the index will exist twice in the database.

There are two ways to mitigate some of the space required for an index during a rebuild. First, the SORT_IN_TEMPDB index option can be used to reduce the amount of space needed for intermediate results. You will still need room in the database for two copies of the index, but the 20 percent buffer won't be necessary. The second way to mitigate space is to disable the index prior to the rebuild. Disabling an index drops the index and data pages from an index while retaining the index metadata. This will allow a rebuild of the index in the space that the index previously occupied. Be aware that the disabling option applies only to nonclustered indexes.

A new option with SQL Server 2019 is the ability to resume index builds. When you are building an index online, you can set the RESUMABLE option to ON and the MAX_DURATION to the number of minutes you want the index to run until it should stop. When the index rebuild stops, the old index remains available, and the completed portion of the rebuild is stored until a time when the rebuild is restarted. Additionally, if an index rebuild fails with the RESUMABLE option set to ON, this will allow the index rebuild to be restarted. This can be extremely useful if the transaction log runs out of space or someone kills the index rebuild operation.

Index Reorganization

An alternative to an index rebuild is to reorganize an index. This type of defragmentation happens just as it sounds. Data pages in the index are reordered across the pages already allocated to the index. After the reorganization is complete, the physical order of pages in an index matches the logical order of pages. Indexes should be reorganized when they are not heavily fragmented. In general, indexes fragmented less than 30 percent are reorganization candidates.

To reorganize an index, the ALTER INDEX syntax is used (see Listing 9-26) with the REORGANIZE option. Along with that option, the reorganization allows for a single partition to be reorganized. The REBUILD option does not allow this.

Listing 9-26. Index Reorganization with ALTER INDEX

```
ALTER INDEX { index_name | ALL }
   ON <object>
   | REORGANIZE
       [ PARTITION =partition_number ]
       [ WITH ( LOB_COMPACTION = { ON | OFF } ) ]
```

There are a couple of benefits to using the REORGANIZE option. First, indexes are online or available for use by the optimizer in a new execution plan or in cached execution plans for the duration of the reorganization. Second, the process is designed around minimal resource usage, which significantly lowers the chance that locking and blocking issues will occur during the transaction.

The downside to index reorganizations is that the reorganization uses only the data pages already allocated to the index. With fragmentation, the extents allocated to one index can often be intertwined with the extents allocated to other indexes. Reordering the data pages won't make the data pages any more contiguous than they currently are, but it will make certain that the pages allocated are sorted in the same order as the data itself.

Drop and Create

The third way to defragment an index is to simply drop the index and re-create it. We include this option for completeness, but note that it is not widely practiced or advised. There are a few reasons that illustrate why dropping and creating can be a bad idea.

First, if the index is a clustered index, then all the other indexes will need to be rebuilt when the clustered index is dropped. Clustered indexes and heaps use different structures for identifying rows and storing data. The nonclustered indexes on the table will need information on where the record is and will need to be re-created to obtain this information.

Second, if the index is a primary key or unique, there are likely other dependents on the index. For instance, the index may be referenced in a foreign key. Also, the index could be tied to a business rule, such as uniqueness, that cannot be removed from the table, even in a maintenance window.

The third reason to avoid this method is that it requires knowledge of all properties on an index. With the other strategies, the index retains all the existing index properties. By having to re-create the index, there is a risk that a property or two may not be retained in the DDL for the index and important aspects of an index could be lost.

Lastly, after an index is dropped from that table, it cannot be used. This should be an obvious issue, but it's often overlooked when considering this option. The purpose of an index is usually the performance improvements that it brings; removing it from the table takes those improvements with it.

Defragmentation Strategies

So far we've discussed how fragmentation occurs, why it is an issue, and how it can be removed from indexes. It is important to apply this knowledge to the indexes in your databases. In this section, you will learn two ways in which the defragmentation of indexes can be automated.

Maintenance Plans

The first automation option available is defragmentation through maintenance plans, which offer the opportunity to quickly create and schedule maintenance for your indexes that will either reorganize or rebuild your indexes. For each of the types of index defragmentation, there is a task available in the maintenance plans.

There are a couple of ways in which maintenance plans can be created. For the purposes of brevity, we will assume you are familiar with maintenance plans in SQL Server and thus will focus on the specific tasks related to defragmenting indexes.

Reorganize Index Task

The first task available is the Reorganize Index Task. This task provides a wrapper for the `ALTER INDEX REORGANIZE` syntax from the previous section. Once configured, this task will reorganize all the indexes that match the criteria for the task.

There are a few properties that need to be configured when using the Reorganize Index Task (see Figure 9-22):

- **Connection**: The SQL Server instance the task will connect to when it executes.

- **Database(s)**: The databases the task will connect to for reorganizing. The options for this property are

    - All databases.

    - All system databases.

    - All user databases.

    - These specific databases (a list of available databases is included and one must be selected).

    - Ignore databases where the state is not online.

- **Object**: Determines whether the reorganization will be against tables, views, or tables and views.

- **Selection**: Specifies the tables or indexes affected by this task. This is not available when Tables and Views is selected in the Object box.

- **Compact large objects**: Determines whether the reorganization uses the option ALTER INDEX LOB_COMPACTION = ON.

- **Scan type**: Indicates how you want SQL Server to gather the statistics for the remaining options. The available options are Fast, Sampled, or Detailed.

- **Optimize index only if**: Provides ability to limit reorganization by percent fragmentation, page count, and whether the index was used in the last 7 days.

CHAPTER 9 INDEX MAINTENANCE

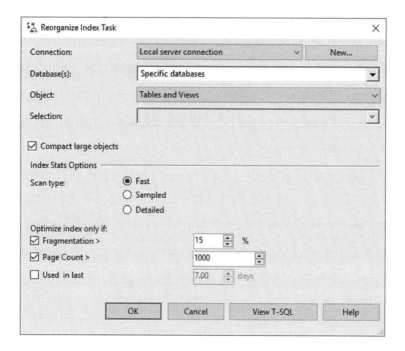

Figure 9-22. *Properties window for Reorganize Index Task*

The index stats options were new for SQL Server 2016 and are a great addition to this feature. In environments that don't have DBAs actively managing the indexes within a server, this is a great option for ensuring indexes are being maintained.

Rebuild Index Task

The other task available is the Rebuild Index Task. This task provides a wrapper for the `ALTER INDEX REBUILD` syntax. Once configured, this task rebuilds all the indexes that match the criteria for the task.

Similar to the Reorganize Index Task, the Rebuild Index Task has a number of properties that need to be configured before using it (see Figure 9-23):

- ***Connection***: The SQL Server instance the task will connect to when it executes.

- ***Database(s)***: The databases the task will connect to for rebuilding. The options for this property are

  - All databases.

  - All system databases.

- All user databases.

- These specific databases (a list of available databases is included and one must be selected).

- Ignore databases where the state is not online.

- **Object**: Determines whether the rebuild will be against tables, views, or tables and views.

- **Selection**: Specifies the tables or indexes affected by this task. This is not available when Tables and Views is selected in the Object box.

- **Default free space per page**: Specifies whether the rebuild should use the current fill factor on the index.

- **Change free space per page to**: Allows the rebuild to specify a new fill factor when the index is rebuilt.

- **Sort results in tempdb**: Determines whether the rebuild uses the option ALTER INDEX SORT_IN_TEMPDB = ON.

- **MAXDOP**: Determines the max degree of parallelism for the rebuild, which determines the max number of CPU threads SQL Server can use to rebuild the index.

- **Keep index online while re-indexing**: Determines whether the rebuild uses the option ALTER INDEX ONLINE = ON. For indexes that cannot be rebuilt online, there is an option to determine whether to skip or rebuild the index offline. Along with that, you can set Low Priority Used to determine if blocking will cancel an index rebuild and whether it cancels itself or blockers and after how much time.

- **Scan type**: Indicates how you want SQL Server to gather the statistics for the remaining options. The available options are Fast, Sampled, or Detailed.

- **Optimize index only if**: Provides ability to limit rebuild by percent fragmentation, page count, and whether the index was used in the last 7 days.

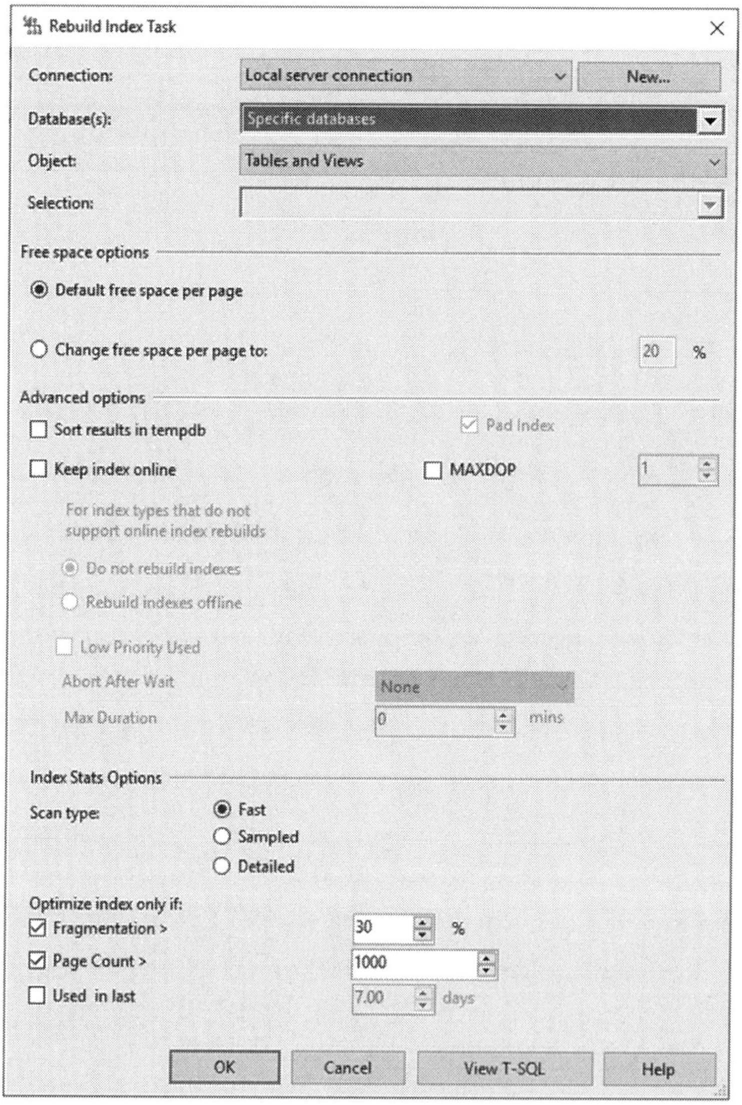

Figure 9-23. Properties window for Rebuild Index Task

And like the reorganization task, the index stats options were added in with SQL Server 2016. And in similar fashion, these changes make the rebuild task a viable option for environments that don't have dedicated database administration resources or when you are looking to keep the index maintenance simple and without custom code to manage the process.

Maintenance Plan Summary

Maintenance plans offer a way to get started with removing fragmentation from your indexes right away. The tasks can be configured and scheduled in a matter of minutes. Since the addition of the SQL Server 2016 enhancements, there are a great choice for managing index maintenance. The only real reason to use other options, such as T-SQL scripts, is when you need additional functionality like custom logging or custom resume logic.

T-SQL Scripts

An alternative approach to defragmenting databases is to use a T-SQL script to defragment the indexes intelligently. In this section, we'll walk through the steps necessary to defragment all the indexes in a single database. The main advantage of this choice is the ability to keep everything in a single process, and there's no chance that both tasks could affect an index. The script will pick the indexes that will best benefit from defragmentation, determine whether to rebuild or reorganize, and ignore those that would receive little or no benefit.

To accomplish the filtering, you'll apply some defragmentation best practices that help determine whether to defragment the index and what method should be applied. The guidelines that you will use are the following:

- Reorganize indexes with less than 30 percent fragmentation.
- Rebuild indexes with 30 percent or more fragmentation.
- Ignore indexes that have less than 1,000 pages.
- If you have Enterprise Edition, use online rebuilds when the data needs to be accessible during maintenance.
- If the clustered index is being rebuilt, rebuild all indexes in the table.

Note Just because an index is fragmented doesn't mean that it should be always be defragmented. When dealing with indexes for small tables, there isn't always a lot of benefit in defragmenting the index. For instance, an index having fewer than eight pages will fit into one extent, and thus there is no benefit in terms of reduced I/O from defragmenting that index. Some Microsoft documentation and SQL Server experts recommend not defragmenting tables with fewer than 1,000 pages. Whether that value is appropriate for your database is dependent on your database, but it is a starting point for building index maintenance strategies.

CHAPTER 9 ■ INDEX MAINTENANCE

There are a few steps that a defragmentation script will perform to intelligently defragment the indexes:

1. Collect fragmentation data.
2. Determine what indexes to defragment.
3. Build the defragmentation statement.

Before starting on the fragmentation steps, you need a template for the index maintenance script. The template, shown in Listing 9-27, declares a number of variables and utilizes a CURSOR to loop through each of the indexes and perform the necessary index maintenance. The variables are set at the DECLARE statement with the thresholds defined at the start of this section. Also in the template is a table variable that is used to store intermediate results on the state of fragmentation in the database.

Listing 9-27. Index Defragmentation Script Template

```
DECLARE @MaxFragmentation TINYINT=30
,@MinimumPages SMALLINT=1000
,@SQL nvarchar(max)
,@ObjectName NVARCHAR(300)
,@IndexName NVARCHAR(300)
,@CurrentFragmentation DECIMAL(9, 6)

DECLARE @FragmentationState TABLE
(
SchemaName SYSNAME
,TableName SYSNAME
,object_id INT
,IndexName SYSNAME
,index_id INT
,page_count BIGINT
,avg_fragmentation_in_percent FLOAT
,avg_page_space_used_in_percent FLOAT
,type_desc VARCHAR(255)
)
```

CHAPTER 9 ■ INDEX MAINTENANCE

```
INSERT INTO @FragmentationState
<Script to Collect Fragmenation Data (Listing 9-28)>

DECLARE INDEX_CURSE CURSOR LOCAL FAST_FORWARD FOR
<Script to Identify Fragmented Indexes (Listing 9-29)>

OPEN INDEX_CURSE

WHILE 1=1
BEGIN
    FETCH NEXT FROM INDEX_CURSE INTO @ObjectName, @IndexName
        ,@CurrentFragmentation

    IF @@FETCH_STATUS <> 0
        BREAK

<Script to Build Index Defragmentation Statements(Listing 9-30)>

    EXEC sp_ExecuteSQL @SQL
END

CLOSE INDEX_CURSE
DEALLOCATE INDEX_CURSE
```

To get started, you need to collect fragmentation data on the indexes and populate them into the `table` variable. In the script in Listing 9-28, the DMF `sys.dm_db_index_physical_stats` is used with the `SAMPLED` option. This option is used to minimize the impact that executing the DMF will have on the database. Included in the results are the schema, table, and index names to identify the index that is being reported on, along with the `object_id` and `index_id`. Statistical columns on the index fragmentation from the DMF are included in the columns `page_count`, `avg_fragmentation_in_percent`, and `avg_page_space_used_in_percent`. The last column in the results is `has_LOB_column`. This column is the result of a correlated subquery that determines whether any of the columns in the index are LOB types, which disallow online index rebuilds.

Listing 9-28. Script to Collect Fragmentation Data

```
SELECT
    s.name as SchemaName
    ,t.name as TableName
    ,t.object_id
    ,we.name as IndexName
    ,we.index_id
    ,x.page_count
    ,x.avg_fragmentation_in_percent
    ,x.avg_page_space_used_in_percent
    ,we.type_desc
FROM sys.dm_db_index_physical_stats(db_id(), NULL, NULL, NULL, 'SAMPLED') x
    INNER JOIN sys.tables t ON x.object_id = t.object_id
    INNER JOIN sys.schemas s ON t.schema_id = s.schema_id
    INNER JOIN sys.indexes we ON x.object_id = we.object_id AND x.index_id = we.index_id
WHERE x.index_id > 0
AND x.avg_fragmentation_in_percent > 0
AND alloc_unit_type_desc = 'IN_ROW_DATA'
```

The results of the query in Listing 9-28 will vary for every reader. In general, the results should be similar to those in Figure 9-24, which include clustered, nonclustered, and XML indexes from the AdventureWorks2017 database.

	SchemaName	TableName	object_id	IndexName	index_id	page_count	avg_fragmentation_in_percent	avg_page_space_used_in_percent	type_desc
1	HumanResources	EmployeePayHistory	2089048	PK_EmployeePayHistory_BusinessEntityID_RateChange...	1	2	50	74.1536940943909	CLUSTERED
2	Sales	SalesOrderHeaderSalesReason	30623152	PK_SalesOrderHeaderSalesReason_SalesOrderID_Sales...	1	86	0	99.2700642451198	CLUSTERED
3	Sales	SalesPerson	62623266	PK_SalesPerson_BusinessEntityID	1	1	0	16.3577958981962	CLUSTERED
4	Sales	SalesPerson	62623266	AK_SalesPerson_rowguid	2	1	0	5.43612552508031	NONCLUSTERED
5	Production	Illustration	66099275	PK_Illustration_IllustrationID	1	1	0	4.78131949592291	CLUSTERED

Figure 9-24. *Query results for table fragmentation data*

The next step in the defragmentation script is to build the list of indexes that need to be defragmented. The list of indexes, created through Listing 9-29, is used to populate the cursor. The cursor then loops through each of the indexes to perform the defragmentation. One point of interest in the script is that for clustered indexes, all the underlying indexes will be rebuilt. This isn't a requirement when defragmenting indexes, but it is something that can be considered. When there are just a few indexes on a table, this may be a worthwhile way to manage them. As the count of indexes increases, this may become less appealing. The results from this query should look similar to those in Figure 9-25.

Listing 9-29. Script to Identify Fragmented Indexes

```
SELECT  QUOTENAME(x.SchemaName)+'.'+QUOTENAME(x.TableName)
    ,CASE WHEN x.type_desc = 'CLUSTERED' THEN 'ALL'
        ELSE QUOTENAME(x.IndexName) END
    ,x.avg_fragmentation_in_percent
FROM    @FragmentationState x
LEFT OUTER JOIN @FragmentationState y ON x.object_id = y.object_id AND y.index_id = 1
WHERE   (
        x.type_desc = 'CLUSTERED'
        AND y.type_desc = 'CLUSTERED'
        )
        OR y.index_id IS NULL
ORDER BY x.object_id
        ,x.index_id
```

	(No column name)	(No column name)	avg_fragmentation_in_percent
1	[HumanResources].[EmployeePayHistory]	ALL	50
2	[HumanResources].[JobCandidate]	ALL	9.09090909090909
3	[dbo].[AllocationCycle]	ALL	30.8965377195654
4	[dbo].[PageCompression]	ALL	2
5	[Sales].[SalesPersonQuotaHistory]	ALL	50
6	[dbo].[LOBAccess]	ALL	25
7	[Person].[Person]	ALL	2.10498960498961

Figure 9-25. *Indexes for rebuild/reorganize operations*

The last part of the template is where the magic happens. In other words, the script in Listing 9-30 is used to construct the ALTER INDEX statement that is used to defragment the index. At this point, the level of fragmentation is checked to determine whether to issue a REBUILD or REORGANIZATION. For indexes that can support ONLINE index rebuilds, a CASE statement adds the appropriate syntax.

Listing 9-30. Script to Build Index Defragmentation Statements

```
SET @SQL = CONCAT('ALTER INDEX ', @IndexName,' ON ',@ObjectName,
  CASE WHEN @CurrentFragmentation <= 30 THEN ' REORGANIZE;'
  ELSE ' REBUILD' END,
  CASE WHEN CONVERT(VARCHAR(100), SERVERPROPERTY('Edition')) LIKE
  'Enterprise%'
  OR CONVERT(VARCHAR(100), SERVERPROPERTY('Edition')) LIKE 'Developer%'
  THEN ' WITH (ONLINE=ON, SORT_IN_TEMPDB=ON) ' END, ';');
```

Note One of the improvements to SQL Server 2017 Enterprise Edition is the ability to perform online index rebuilds when the index contains columns with large object (LOB) data types.

Combining all these pieces into the template from the beginning of this section to create an index defragmentation script provides similar functionality to that of the maintenance plan tasks. With the ability to set the size and fragmentation levels in which the defragmentation occurs, this script removes the fragmentation from indexes that really need the work done on them vs. just defragmenting every index in the database. Using Extended Events on AdventureWorks2017 to trace the output of the script reveals that the ALTER INDEX syntax for the results of the previous queries is similar to that in Listing 9-31.

Listing 9-31. Index Defragmentation Statements

```
ALTER INDEX ALL ON [HumanResources].[EmployeePayHistory] REBUILD WITH
(ONLINE=ON, SORT_IN_TEMPDB=ON) ;
ALTER INDEX ALL ON [HumanResources].[JobCandidate] REORGANIZE; WITH
(ONLINE=ON, SORT_IN_TEMPDB=ON) ;
ALTER INDEX ALL ON [dbo].[AllocationCycle] REBUILD WITH (ONLINE=ON, SORT_
IN_TEMPDB=ON) ;
ALTER INDEX ALL ON [dbo].[PageCompression] REORGANIZE; WITH (ONLINE=ON,
SORT_IN_TEMPDB=ON) ;
ALTER INDEX ALL ON [Sales].[SalesPersonQuotaHistory] REBUILD WITH
(ONLINE=ON, SORT_IN_TEMPDB=ON) ;
```

As the code in this section demonstrated, using a T-SQL script can be much more complicated than just using the maintenance plan tasks. The upside to the complexity is that once the script is complete, it can be wrapped in a stored procedure and used on all your SQL Server instances. This script is meant as a first step in automating defragmentation with T-SQL scripts. It doesn't account for partitioned tables and doesn't check to see whether the index is being used before rebuilding or reorganizing the index. On the upside, rather than driving a truck through your databases and re-indexing everything, a scripted solution can intelligently decide how and when to defragment your indexes.

Note For a complete index defragmentation solution, check out Ola Hallengren's index maintenance scripts at `https://ola.hallengren.com`.

Preventing Fragmentation

Fragmentation within an index is not always a foregone conclusion. There are some methods that can be utilized to mitigate the rate in which fragmentation occurs. When you have indexes that are often affected by fragmentation, it is advisable to investigate why the fragmentation is occurring. There a few strategies that can help mitigate fragmentation; these are fill factor, data typing, and default values.

Fill Factor

Fill factor is an option that can be used when building or rebuilding indexes. This property is used to determine how much space per page should be left available in the index when it is first created or the next time it is rebuilt. For instance, with a fill factor of 75, about 25 percent of every data page is left empty.

If an index encounters a significant or frequent amount of fragmentation, it is worthwhile to adjust the fill factor to mitigate the fragmentation. By doing this, the activities that are causing fragmentation should be less impactful, which should reduce the frequency that the index needs to be defragmented.

By default, SQL Server creates all indexes with a fill factor of 0. This is a recommended value for both the server and database levels. Not all indexes are created equal, and fill factor should be applied as it is needed, not as a blanket insurance policy. Also, a fill factor of 0 is the same as a fill factor of 100.

The one downside of fill factor is that leaving space available in data pages means that the index will require more data pages for all the records in the index. More pages means more I/O and possibly less utilization of the index if there are alternate indexes to select from.

Data Typing

Another way to avoid fragmentation is through appropriate data typing. This strategy applies to data types that can change length depending on the data that they contain. These are data types such as VARCHAR and NVARCHAR, which have lengths that can change over time.

In many cases, variable-length data types are a great fit for columns in a table. Issues arise when the volatility of the data is high and the length of the data is volatile as well. As the data changes length, there can be page splits, which lead to fragmentation. If the length volatility occurs across significant portions of the index, then there may also be significant numbers of page splits and thus fragmentation.

A great example of bad data typing comes from my experience with the first data warehouse that I worked with. The original design for many of the tables included a column with a data type of VARCHAR(10). The column was populated with dates in the format of yyyymmdd, with values similar to 20191011. As part of the import process, the date values were updated into a format of yyyy-mm-dd. When the import was moved to production and millions of rows were being processed at a time, the increase in the length of the column from eight to ten characters led to an astounding level of fragmentation because of page splits. Resolving the problem was as simple as changing the data type of the column from VARCHAR(10) to CHAR(10).

Such simple solutions can apply to many databases. It just requires a bit of investigation into why the fragmentation is occurring.

Default Values

The proper application of default values may not seem to be something that can assist in preventing fragmentation, but there are some scenarios in which it can have a significant effect on fragmentation. The poster child for this type of mitigation is when databases utilize the uniqueidentifier data type.

In most cases, `uniqueidentifier` values are generated using the `NEWID()` function. This function creates a globally unique identifier (GUID) that should be unique across the entire planet. This is useful for generating unique identifiers for rows but is likely scoped larger than that of your database. In many cases, the unique value probably needs to be unique for the server or just the table.

The main problem with the `NEWID()` function is that generating the GUID is not a sequential process. As demonstrated at the beginning of the chapter, using this function to generate values for the clustered index key can lead to severe levels of fragmentation.

An alternative to the `NEWID()` function is the `NEWSEQUENTIALID()` function. This function returns a GUID just like the other function but with a couple variations on how the values are generated. First, each GUID generated by the function on a server is sequential to the last value. The second variation is that the GUID value generated is unique only to the server that is generating it. If another SQL Server instance generates a GUID with this function for the same table, it is possible that duplicate values will be generated and the values will not be sequential since these are scoped to the server level.

With these restrictions in mind, if a table must use the `uniqueidentifier` data type, the `NEWSEQUENTIALID()` function is an excellent alternative to the `NEWID()` function. The values will be sequential, and the amount of fragmentation encountered will be much lower and less frequent.

Index Statistics Maintenance

In Chapter 3, we discussed the statistics collected on indexes. These statistics provide crucial information that the query optimizer uses to compile execution plans for queries. When this information is out-of-date or inaccurate, the database will provide suboptimal or inaccurate query plans.

For the most part, index statistics do not require much maintenance. In this section, we'll look at the processes within SQL Server that can be used to create and update statistics. We'll also look at how you can maintain statistics in situations where the automated processes cannot keep up with the rate of data change within an index.

Automatically Maintaining Statistics

The easiest way to build and maintain statistics in SQL Server is to just let SQL Server do it. There are three database properties that control whether SQL Server will automatically build and maintain statistics:

- AUTO_CREATE_STATISTICS
- AUTO_UPDATE_STATISTICS
- AUTO_UPDATE_STATISTICS_ASYNC

By default, the first two properties are enabled in databases. The last option is disabled by default. In most cases, all three of these properties should be enabled.

Automatic Creation

The first database property is AUTO_CREATE_STATISTICS. This database property directs SQL Server to automatically create single-column statistics that do not have statistics. From the perspective of indexes, this property does not have an impact. When an index is created, a statistics object is created for the index.

Automatic Updating

The next two properties are AUTO_UPDATE_STATISTICS and AUTO_UPDATE_STATISTICS_ASYNC. At a high level, these two properties are quite similar. When an internal threshold is surpassed, SQL Server will initiate an update of the statistics object. The update occurs to keep the values within the statistics object current with the cardinality of values within the table.

The threshold for triggering a statistics update can change from table to table. The threshold is based on a couple of calculations relating to the number of rows that have changed. For an empty table, when more than 500 rows are added to the table, a statistics update will be triggered. If the table has more than 500 rows, then statistics will be updated when 500 rows plus at most 20 percent of the cardinality of rows have been modified. At this point, SQL Server will schedule an update to the statistics. As the number of rows in the table increases, then the 20 percent threshold decreases, which accommodates the need to update statistics more frequently when there are larger numbers of rows within a table. At about 500,000 rows, the percentage drops to about 5 percent and then less than 1 percent for over 1 billion rows. This is the behavior that was previously available through trace flag 2371, which is on by default since SQL Server 2016.

When the statistics update occurs, there are two modes in which it can be accomplished: synchronously and asynchronously. By default, statistics update synchronously. This means that when statistics are deemed out-of-date and require an update, the query optimizer will wait until after the statistics have been updated before it will compile an execution plan for the query. This is extremely useful for tables that have data that is volatile. For instance, the statistics for a table before and after a TRUNCATE TABLE would be quite different. Optionally, statistics can be built asynchronously through enabling the AUTO_UPDATE_STATISTICS_ASYNC property. This changes how the query optimizer reacts when an update statistics event is triggered. Instead of waiting for the statistics update to complete, the query optimizer will compile an execution plan based on the existing statistics and use the updated statistics for future queries after the update completes. For databases with high volumes of queries and data being pushed through, this is often the preferred manner of updating statistics. Instead of occasional pauses in transactional throughput, the queries will flow through unencumbered, and plans will update as improved information is available.

If you are in an environment that disabled AUTO_UPDATE_STATISTICS in previous SQL Server versions, you should consider enabling it now with AUTO_UPDATE_STATISTICS_ASYNC. The most common reason to disable AUTO_UPDATE_STATISTICS in the past was the delay caused by the update of statistics. With the option to enable AUTO_UPDATE_STATISTICS_ASYNC, those performance concerns can likely be mitigated.

Preventing Auto Update

Depending on the indexes on a table, there will be times in which automatically updating the indexes will do more harm than good. For instance, an automatic statistics update on a large table may lead to performance issues while the statistics object is updated. In that situation, the existing statistics object may be good enough until the next maintenance window. There are a number of ways in which AUTO_UPDATE_STATISTICS can be disabled on an individual statistics object rather than across the entire database:

- Executing an sp_autostats system store procedure on the statistics object

- Using the NORECOMPUTE option on the UPDATE STATISTICS or CREATE STATISTICS statement

- Using STATISTICS_NORECOMPUTE on the CREATE INDEX statement

Each of these options can be used to disable or enable the AUTO_UPDATE_STATISTICS option on indexes. Before disabling this feature, always be sure to validate that the statistics update is truly necessary.

In-Memory Statistics

When considering statistics, one area where statistics are created and used a bit differently are with in-memory tables. It's important to understand that statistics cannot be generated automatically on in-memory tables and that they always require a full scan. Add to this, natively compiled stored procedures on in-memory tables retrieve statistics only when the stored procedure is compiled or when SQL Server restarts. This means that when considering the impact of statistics on indexes, in-memory tables require additional care in timing the maintenance for the statistics.

Manually Maintaining Statistics

There will be times when the automated processes for maintaining statistics will not be good enough. This is often tied to situations where the data is changing but not enough has changed to trigger a statistics update. A good example of when this can happen is when update statements change the cardinality of the table without affecting a large number of rows. For instance, if 10 percent of a table was changed from a large number of values to a single value, then the plan for querying the data could end up being suboptimal. In situations like this, you need to be able to get in and manually update statistics. As with index fragmentation, there are two methods for manually maintaining statistics:

- Maintenance plans
- T-SQL scripts

In the next sections, you'll look at each of these methods and walk through how they can be implemented.

Maintenance Plans

Within maintenance plans, there is a task that allows statistics maintenance. This task is the Update Statistics Task, aptly named for exactly what it accomplishes. When using this task, there are a number of properties that can be configured to control its behavior (see Figure 9-26):

- **Connection**: The SQL Server instance the task will connect to when it executes.

- **Database(s)**: The databases the task will connect to for rebuilding. The options for this property are

    - All databases.

    - All system databases.

    - All user databases.

    - These specific databases (a list of available databases is included and one must be selected).

    - Ignore databases where the state is not online.

- **Object**: Determines whether the rebuild will be against tables, views, or tables and views.

- **Selection**: Specifies the tables or indexes affected by this task. This is not available when Tables and Views is selected in the Object box.

- **Update**: For each table, determines whether all existing statistics, column statistics only (using WITH COLUMN clause), or index statistics only (using WITH INDEX clause) are updated.

- **Scan type**: A choice between a full scan of all leaf-level pages of the indexes and "Sample by," which will scan a percentage or number of rows to build the statistics object.

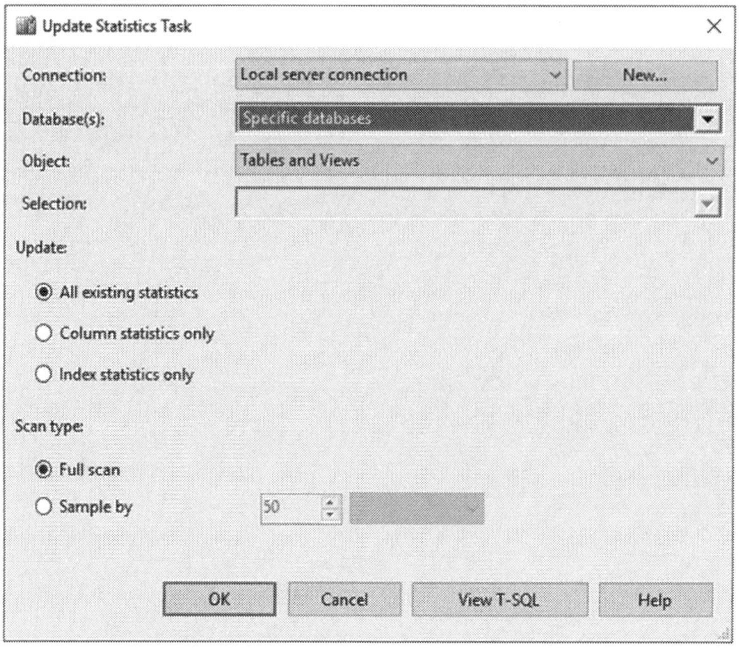

Figure 9-26. Properties window for Update Statistics Task

Unlike the maintenance plans previously discussed, the Update Statistics Task doesn't have deeper controls to help determine whether the statistics should be updated. A useful option would be to limit the statistics updates to a specified date range, which would reduce the number of statistics updated during each execution. For the most part, the lack of that option is not a deal-breaker. Statistics updates aren't like indexes where each update requires enough space to rebuild the entire index. However, it would be good to be able to retain the current sample scan type since that can have an effect on performance and may not result in desired performance with a one-size-fits-all approach.

T-SQL Scripts

Through T-SQL, there are a couple alternative approaches for updating statistics: using stored procedure or using DDL statements. Each of these approaches has pros and cons. In the next sections, you'll look at each one and why it may be a worthwhile approach.

Stored Procedure

Within the master database, there is a system stored procedure named `sp_updatestats` that allows for updating all statistics within a database. Since it is a system stored procedure, it can be called from any database to update the statistics in the database in which it is called from.

When `sp_updatestats` is executed, it runs the UPDATE STATISTICS statement, described in the next section, using the ALL option. The stored procedure accepts a single parameter named `resample`, shown in Listing 9-32. The `resample` parameter accepts only the value `resample`. If this value is supplied, then the stored procedure uses the RESAMPLE option of UPDATE STATISTICS. Otherwise, the stored procedure uses the default sampling algorithm in SQL Server.

Listing 9-32. sp_updatestats Syntax

```
sp_updatestats [ [ @resample = ] 'resample' ]
```

One benefit to using `sp_updatestats` is that it will update the statistics only for items in which there have been modifications to the data. The internal counter that is used to trigger automatic statistics updates is checked to make certain that only statistics that have been changed will be updated. Additionally, the resample option uses the most recently used sample rate for the statistics.

In situations where a statistics update is needed, the `sp_updatestats` is a great tool for updating statistics on just those that have the potential for being out-of-date since the last update. Where the Update Statistics Task is an oversized blanket that smothers the entire database, `sp_updatestats` is a comforter that covers just the right places.

DDL Command

The other option for updating statistics is through the DDL command UPDATE STATISTICS, shown in Listing 9-33. The UPDATE STATISTICS statement allows for finely tuned statistics updates on a per-statistics basis with a number of options for how to collect and build statistics information.

Listing 9-33. UPDATE STATISTICS Syntax

```
UPDATE STATISTICS table_or_indexed_view_name
    [
        {
            { index_or_statistics_name }
          | ( { index_or_statistics_name } [ ,...n ] )
        }
    ]
    [   WITH
        [
        FULLSCAN
            [ [ , ] PERSIST_SAMPLE_PERCENT = { ON | OFF } ]
          | SAMPLE number { PERCENT | ROWS }
            [ [ , ] PERSIST_SAMPLE_PERCENT = { ON | OFF } ]
          | RESAMPLE
            [ ON PARTITIONS ( { <partition_number> | <range> } [, ...n] ) ] ]
            [ [ , ] [ ALL | COLUMNS | INDEX ]
            [ [ , ] NORECOMPUTE ]
            [ [ , ] INCREMENTAL = { ON | OFF } ]
            [ [ , ] MAXDOP = max_degree_of_parallelism ]
    ] ;
```

The first parameter to set when using UPDATE STATISTICS is table_or_indexed_view_name. This parameter references the table in which the statistics will be updated. With the UPDATE STATISTICS command, only one table or view can have its statistics updated at a time.

The next parameter is index_or_statistics_name. This parameter is used to determine whether a single statistic, list of statistics, or all statistics on a table will be updated. To update just a single statistic, include the name of the statistic after the name of the table or view. For a list of statistics, the names of the statistics are included in a comma-separated list within parentheses. If no statistics are named, then all statistics will be considered for updating.

After the parameters are set, it is time to add applicable options to the UPDATE STATISTICS command. This is where the power and flexibility of the syntax really shines.

These parameters allow the statistics to be finely tuned to the data available in them to get the right statistics for the right table and the right index:

- FULLSCAN: When the statistics object is built, all rows and pages in the table or view are scanned. For large tables, this may have an effect on performance while creating the statistics. Basically, this is the same as performing a SAMPLE 100 PERCENT operation.

- SAMPLE: The statistics object is created using either a count or a percentage sample of the rows in the table or view. When the sample rate is not selected, SQL Server will determine an appropriate sample rate based on the number of rows in the table.

- RESAMPLE: Updates the statistics using the sample rate from the last time that the statistics were updated. For instance, if that last update used a FULLSCAN, then a RESAMPLE will result in a FULLSCAN as well.

- PERSIST_SAMPLE_PERCENT: Determines whether the defined sample rate should be persisted into the statistics as their future default value for when default values are not specified.

- ALL | COLUMNS | INDEX: Determines whether column statistics, index statistics, or both should be updated.

- NORECOMPUTE: Disables the option for the query optimizer to request an automatic update to the statistics. This is useful for locking in statistics that shouldn't change or are optimal with the current sample. Take caution when using this on tables that have frequent data modifications and make certain there are other mechanisms in place to update the statistics as needed.

- INCREMENTAL: When enabled, statistics are created as per-partition statistics which allows statistics to be updated per partition using the ON PARTITIONS clause.

- MAXDOP: Determines the max degree of parallelism for the statistics update operation and overrides the max degree of parallelism configuration for the server.

The first three options in this list are mutually exclusive. You are able to select only one of the options. Selecting more than one of those options will generate an error.

Since UPDATE STATISTICS is a DDL command, it can easily be automated in a fashion similar to that used to defragment indexes. For brevity, a sample script is not included, but the template for the index fragmentation maintenance could be used as a starting point. As mentioned in the previous section, sp_updatestats uses UPDATE STATISTICS under the covers. This DDL command is a powerful way to update statistics as needed in your databases without doing more than is really necessary. To continue the analogy from the previous section, using UPDATE STATISTICS replaces the blanket and comforter with a handmade sweater.

Summary

In this chapter, you learned about a number of maintenance considerations that are part of indexing a table. These break down to managing the fragmentation of indexes and managing their statistics. With index fragmentation, you saw ways in which indexes can become fragmented, why it is an issue, and strategies to remove the fragmentation. These maintenance tasks are critical for making certain that SQL Server can use indexes to the best of its ability. Along with the maintenance activity, the statistics on the indexes must also be maintained. Out-of-date or inaccurate statistics can lead to execution plans that do not match the data in the table. Without proper execution plans, performance will suffer regardless of the indexes in place.

CHAPTER 10

Indexing Tools

When it comes to indexing, Microsoft currently has two tools built into SQL Server that can be used to help identify indexes that can improve database performance. These are the missing index dynamic management objects (DMOs) and the Database Engine Tuning Advisor (DTA). Both tools are useful to assist with indexing databases and can provide valuable input when working on tuning a database. Microsoft is developing a new Automatic Index Management tool, which is currently available in Azure SQL Database. This is not included in SQL Server 2019 at the time of this writing.

This chapter delves into both the missing index and Database Engine Tuning Advisor indexing tools. The chapter is divided into two sections that each describe the capabilities of each tool. We then walk through how the tools can be used to provide assistance with indexing. Throughout the chapter, you will also learn about the pros and cons of using each of these tools.

Missing Indexes

The missing index DMOs are a set of management objects that provide indexing feedback from the query optimizer. When the query optimizer compiles an execution plan, it can identify when materializing statistics for a set of columns into a physical index would improve performance. In these situations, the query optimizer will compile the results and store the information in the missing index DMOs.

There are a couple of benefits that the missing index DMOs provide. First, the missing index information is collected from the query optimizer without any action required on your part. Unlike Extended Events and other performance monitoring tools, you don't need to configure and enable it in order for information to be collected. The other thing to consider is that the missing index information is based on actual activity occurring on the SQL Server instance. The index suggestions aren't based on a test load you believe might happen in production but rather on the production load itself.

As the usage patterns of the data in a database change, so too will the missing index recommendations.

Despite the benefits provided by the missing index DMOs, you must take into account a few considerations when using them. The limitations on the missing index DMOs can be summarized into the following categories:

- Size of queue
- Depth of analysis
- Accuracy
- Type of indexes

The size of the queue for missing indexes is one of the limitations that is easy to miss. Regardless of the number of databases on the SQL Server instance, there can be no more than 600 missing index groups. Once 600 missing index groups have been identified, the query optimizer will stop reporting new missing index suggestions. It will not make any determinations to decide whether a new possible missing index is of better quality than items already reported; the information is just not collected.

Note As with other dynamic management objects, the information within the missing index DMOs resets when SQL Server restarts and gets dropped for a database whenever the database is brought offline.

When considering the information in missing indexes, the depth of the analysis is a limitation that needs to be considered whenever you are reviewing the suggestions. The query optimizer considers only the current plan and whether the missing index would benefit the execution plan. Sometimes, adding the missing index to the database will result in a new plan with a new missing index suggestion. These suggestions are only a first pass at improving performance on an execution plan. The other half of this limitation is that the missing index details don't include tests to determine whether the order of the columns in the missing index suggestion is optimal. When looking at missing index suggestions, it will be necessary to test in order to determine the proper column order.

The third limitation of the missing index suggestion is the accuracy of the information returned with the statistics. There are two things that need to be considered with this limitation. First, when the queries use inequality predicates, the cost information is less effective than those returned with equality predicates. Second, it is possible to return the same missing index suggestion with multiple cost estimates. How and where the missing index would be leveraged may change the cost estimate that is calculated. For each cost estimate, a missing index suggestion will be logged.

Lastly, the missing index tool is limited in the types of indexes it can suggest. The main limitation is index types and the inability of missing indexes to suggest clustered, XML, spatial, or columnstore indexes. The suggestions also will not include information on when to make an index filtered. Along these same lines, suggestions may, at times, contain only INCLUDE columns. When this happens, one of the INCLUDE columns will need to be designated as the key column.

Note Missing index information for a table will be dropped whenever there are metadata operations made on the table. For instance, when a column is added to a table, the missing index information will be dropped. A less obvious example is when an index on a table changes. In this case as well, the missing index information will be dropped.

Explaining the DMOs

There are four DMOs that can be used to return information on missing indexes. Each DMO provides a portion of the information needed to build indexes that the query optimizer can use to improve the performance of a query. The DMOs for missing indexes are as follows:

- sys.dm_db_missing_index_details
- sys.dm_db_missing_index_columns
- sys.dm_db_missing_index_group_stats
- sys.dm_db_missing_index_group

In the next four sections, I'll review each of the dynamic management objects and look at how each provides information on how to identify missing indexes.

sys.dm_db_missing_index_details

The DMO sys.dm_db_missing_index_details is a dynamic management view that returns a list of missing index suggestions. Each row in the dynamic management view (DMV) provides a single suggested missing index. The columns in Table 10-1 provide information on the database and the table to create the index on. It also includes the columns that should comprise the key and the included columns for the index.

Table 10-1. Columns in sys.dm_db_missing_index_details

Column Name	Data Type	Description
index_handle	int	Unique identifier for each missing index suggestions. This is the key value for this DMV.
database_id	smallint	Identifies the database where the table with the missing index resides.
object_id	int	Identifies the table where the index is missing.
equality_columns	nvarchar(4000)	Comma-separated list of columns that contribute to equality predicates.
inequality_columns	nvarchar(4000)	Comma-separated list of columns that contribute to inequality predicates.
included_columns	nvarchar(4000)	Comma-separated list of columns needed as covering columns for the query.
statement	nvarchar(4000)	Name of the table where the index is missing.

There are two columns in sys.dm_db_missing_index_details that are used to identify key columns on missing index suggestions. These are equality_columns and inequality_columns. The equality_columns are generated when there is a comparison in the query plan that makes a direct comparison. For instance, when the filter for a query is ColumnA = @Parameter, this is an equality predicate. The inequality_columns details are created when any nonequal filter is used in a query plan. Examples of this are when there are greater than, less than, or NOT IN comparisons being used.

When it comes to the included_columns information, this is generated when there are columns that are not part of the filter but that would be used to allow the index to cover the query request using a single index. Included columns are covered in more depth in Chapter 8. Suffice it to say, the use of included columns will help prevent the query plan from having to use a key lookup in the execution plan if the missing index is created.

sys.dm_db_missing_index_columns

The next DMO is sys.dm_db_missing_index_columns, which is a dynamic management function (DMF). This function returns a list of columns for each missing index listed in sys.dm_db_missing_index_details. To use the DMF, an index_handle is passed into the function as a parameter. Each row in the resultset represents a column in the missing index suggestion from sys.dm_db_missing_index_details and repeats the information in equality_columns, inequality_columns, and included_columns. Table 10-2 lists the output for sys.dm_db_missing_index_columns.

Table 10-2. Columns in sys.dm_db_missing_index_columns

Column Name	Data Type	Description
column_id	int	ID of the column.
column_name	sysname	Name of the table column.
column_usage	varchar(20)	Description of how the column will be used in the index.

The primary information in this DMF is the column_usage column. For every row, this column will return one of the following values: EQUALITY, INEQUALITY, or INCLUDE. These values map to equality_columns, inequality_columns, and included_columns in sys.dm_db_missing_index_details. Depending on the type of usage in the former DMV, the use will be the same for this DMF.

sys.dm_db_missing_index_groups

The DMV sys.dm_db_missing_index_groups is the next missing index DMO. The DMV returns a list of missing index groups paired with missing index suggestions. Table 10-3 lists the columns for sys.dm_db_missing_index_groups. Although this DMV supports the ability for many-to-many relationships within missing index suggestions, they are always made in a one-to-one relationship.

Table 10-3. Columns in sys.dm_db_missing_index_groups

Column Name	Data Type	Description
index_group_handle	int	Identifies a missing index group. This value joins to group_handle in sys.dm_db_missing_index_group_stats.
index_handle	int	Identifies a missing index handle. This value joins to index_handle in sys.dm_db_missing_index_details.

sys.dm_db_missing_index_group_stats

The last missing index DMO is the DMV sys.dm_db_missing_index_group_stats. The information in this DMV contains statistics on how the query optimizer would expect to use the missing index if it were built. From this, using the columns in Table 10-4, you can determine which missing indexes would provide the greatest benefit and the scope to which the index will be used.

Table 10-4. Columns in sys.dm_db_missing_index_group_stats

Column Name	Data Type	Description
group_handle	int	Unique identifier for each missing index group. This is the key value for this DMV. All queries that would benefit from using the missing index group are included in this group.
unique_compiles	bigint	Count of the execution plan compilations and recompilations that would benefit from this missing index group.
user_seeks	bigint	Count of seeks in user queries that would have occurred if the missing index had been built.
user_scans	bigint	Count of scans in user queries that would have occurred if the missing index had been built.
last_user_seek	datetime	Date and time of last user seek from user queries that would have occurred if the missing index had been built.
last_user_scan	datetime	Date and time of last user scans from user queries that would have occurred if the missing index had been built.

(continued)

Table 10-4. (*continued*)

Column Name	Data Type	Description
avg_total_user_cost	float	Average cost of the user queries that could be reduced by the index in the group.
avg_user_impact	float	Average percentage benefit that user queries could experience if this missing index group had been implemented.
system_seeks	bigint	Count of seeks in system queries that would have occurred if the missing index had been built.
system_scans	bigint	Count of scans in system queries that would have occurred if the missing index had been built.
last_system_seek	datetime	Date and time of last system seek from system queries that would have occurred if the missing index had been built.
last_system_scan	datetime	Date and time of last system scans from system queries that would have occurred if the missing index had been built.
avg_total_system_cost	float	Average cost of the system queries that could be reduced by the index in the group.
avg_system_impact	float	Average percentage benefit that system queries could experience if this missing index group had been implemented.

Using the DMOs

Now that the missing index DMOs have been explained, it is time to look at how they can be used together to provide missing index suggestions. You may have noticed that the results of the missing index DMOs have been referred to as suggestions instead of recommendations. This variation in wording is intentional. Typically, when someone receives a recommendation, it is fully thought through and ready to be implemented. This is not so with the missing index DMOs; thus, they are referred to as suggestions.

With the suggestions from the missing index DMOs, you have a starting point to begin looking at and building new indexes. There are two things that are important to consider when looking at missing index suggestions. First, variations of each missing index suggestion may appear multiple times in the results. It is not recommended that each of these variations be implemented. Common patterns within the suggestions should be found. An index that covers a few of the suggestions is usually ideal. Second, when more than one column is suggested, the order of the columns needs to be tested to determine which is optimal.

To help explain how the missing index DMOs work and are related to one another, I'll walk you through an example that includes a few SQL statements. These statements, shown in Listing 10-1, execute a few queries against the SalesOrderHeader table in the AdventureWorks2017 database. For each of the queries, the filtering is on either the DueDate or OrderDate column, or both.

Listing 10-1. SQL Statements to Generate Missing Index Suggestions

```
USE AdventureWorks2017
GO

SELECT DueDate FROM Sales.SalesOrderHeader
WHERE DueDate = '2014-07-01 00:00:00.000'
AND OrderDate = '2014-06-19 00:00:00.000'
GO
SELECT DueDate FROM Sales.SalesOrderHeader
WHERE OrderDate Between '20140601' AND '20140630'
AND DueDate Between '20140701' AND '20140731'
GO
SELECT DueDate, OrderDate FROM Sales.SalesOrderHeader
WHERE DueDate Between '20140701' AND '20140731'
GO
SELECT CustomerID, OrderDate FROM Sales.SalesOrderHeader
WHERE OrderDate Between '20140601' AND '20140630'
AND DueDate Between '20140701' AND '20140731'
GO
```

If you examine the execution plan for any of the example queries, you'll see that they each use a clustered index scan to satisfy the query. Figure 10-1 shows the execution plan for the first query. In this execution plan, there is an indication that there is a missing index that could help improve the performance of the query and an index scan across the table's clustered index.

CHAPTER 10 INDEXING TOOLS

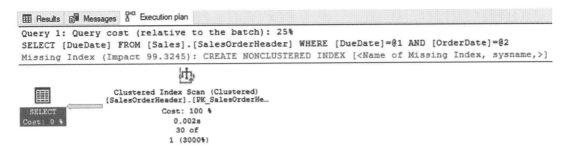

***Figure 10-1.** Execution plan for first query from Listing 10-1*

To see more details on this missing index suggestion, you need to look at the missing index DMOs. A query against the missing index DMOs will look similar to Listing 10-2. The query includes the equality, inequality, and included column information that was described earlier. The query includes two calculations not previously described: the calculations for Impact and Score.

The Impact calculation helps identify missing index suggestions that will have the highest overall impact across multiple query executions. This is calculated by adding the potential seeks and scans on the missing index based on the average impact; the resulting value represents the total improvement across all queries that might have used the index. The higher the value, the more improvement the index could provide.

The Score calculation also helps to identify missing index suggestions that will improve query performance. The difference between Impact and Score is the inclusion of the average total user cost. For the Score calculation, the average total user cost is multiplied by the Impact score and divided by 100. The inclusion of the cost value helps differentiate between expensive and inexpensive queries when deciding whether to consider the missing index. For instance, a missing index suggestion that provides an 80 percent improvement on queries with an average cost value of 1,000 would likely provide a better return that a 90 percent improvement for a query with an average cost value of 1.

***Listing 10-2.** Query for Missing Index DMOs*

```
SELECT
    DB_NAME(database_id) AS database_name
    ,OBJECT_NAME(object_id, database_id) AS table_name
    ,mid.equality_columns
    ,mid.inequality_columns
    ,mid.included_columns
```

```
    ,(migs.user_seeks + migs.user_scans) * migs.avg_user_impact AS Impact
    ,migs.avg_total_user_cost * (migs.avg_user_impact / 100.0) * (migs.
    user_seeks + migs.user_scans) AS Score
    ,migs.user_seeks
    ,migs.user_scans
FROM sys.dm_db_missing_index_details mid
        INNER JOIN sys.dm_db_missing_index_groups mig ON mid.index_handle =
        mig.index_handle
        INNER JOIN sys.dm_db_missing_index_group_stats migs ON mig.index_
        group_handle = migs.group_handle
WHERE DB_NAME(database_id) = 'AdventureWorks2017'
ORDER BY migs.avg_total_user_cost * (migs.avg_user_impact / 100.0) * (migs.
user_seeks + migs.user_scans) DESC
```

Figure 10-2 shows some results from executing this query.

	database_name	table_name	equality_columns	inequality_columns	included_columns	Impact	Score	user_seeks	user_scans
1	AdventureWorks2017	SalesOrderHeader	[OrderDate], [DueDate]	NULL	NULL	99.32	0.568358070973333	1	0
2	AdventureWorks2017	SalesOrderHeader	NULL	[OrderDate], [DueDate]	NULL	94.96	0.561335496986667	1	0
3	AdventureWorks2017	SalesOrderHeader	NULL	[OrderDate], [DueDate]	[CustomerID]	94.21	0.556902034236667	1	0
4	AdventureWorks2017	SalesOrderHeader	NULL	[DueDate]	[OrderDate]	94.79	0.542435174663333	1	0

Figure 10-2. *Results from missing index query*

With the results from the missing index query, shown in Figure 10-2, there are a few items to consider from these suggestions. First, there are quite a few similarities between the suggestions. The predicate columns between each of the suggestions include the OrderDate and DueDate, except for one missing index. Since the column order has not been tested, the optimal column order could go either way. To satisfy the missing index suggestion, one possible index could have the key column DueDate followed by OrderDate. This configuration would create an index that would satisfy all four of the missing index items.

The next item to look at is included_columns. For two of the suggestions, there are included_columns values listed. On the fourth missing index suggestion, it suggests including the column OrderDate. Since it will be one of the key columns of the index, it doesn't need to be included. The other column, from the third missing index suggestion, is the CustomerID column. While only one index needs this column, as an included column, the addition of this column would likely be negligible since it is a narrow column. You would also want to add this column to the index.

After looking at these results, you've seen four missing index suggestions and ended up with a suggestion for one index that can cover all four of the missing index items. If you build the index using a DDL statement similar to that in Listing 10-3, you will end up with an index that solves these missing indexes. If we execute the queries in Listing 10-1 again, we see that all of the queries are using index seeks on the new index, shown in Figure 10-3.

Listing 10-3. Index from Missing Index DMOs

```
CREATE NONCLUSTERED INDEX missing_index_SalesOrderHeader
ON Sales.SalesOrderHeader([DueDate], [OrderDate])
INCLUDE ([CustomerID])
```

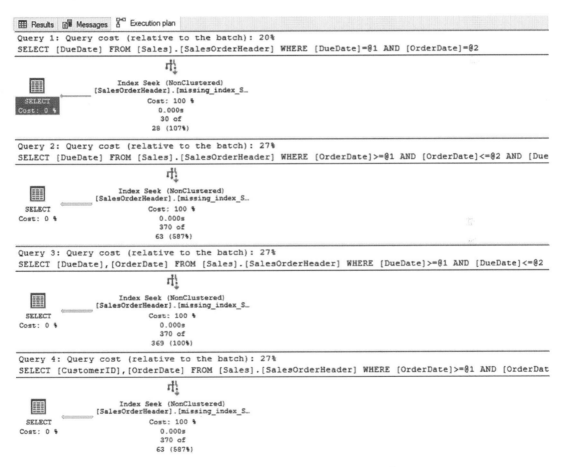

Figure 10-3. *Execution plans for queries after missing index creation*

> **Note** There are many negative opinions regarding the value of the Database Engine Tuning Advisor. In my opinion, this is a tool that fills a role and provided a sufficient workload is used with the tool, it will return worthwhile recommendations. These recommendations provide a better starting point for tuning a database than starting with nothing.

Database Engine Tuning Advisor

The other indexing tool available in SQL Server is the Database Engine Tuning Advisor. This tool allows SQL Server to analyze a workload from a file, a table, the plan cache, or Query Store. The output of the DTA can assist in providing recommendations for indexing and configuring partitions for the workload. The chief benefit of using the tool is that it doesn't require a deep understanding of the underlying databases to make the recommendations.

Whether working with a single query or a full day's workload, DTA provides index recommendations for the following types of objects:

- Rowstore and columnstore tables for both clustered and nonclustered indexes
- Aligned or nonaligned partitions
- Views could support indexing

With the sessions in DTA, you're able to really focus the recommendations on what you expect from your environment. You are able to leverage workload based on your environment, whether transactional or analytical and set the focus on both reads and writes so that you get index recommendations that align to your needs. You even have the ability to modify the environment to look for indexing recommendations for changes in disk space.

Once the analysis is completed, DTA provides a number of reports and outputs. This information allows you to review the recommendations and develop an understanding for how it will impact the database.

Although the DTA has quite a few capabilities, there are also a number of limitations on the tools. The following are some of these limitations:

- Not able to recommend indexes on system tables.
- Cannot add or drop unique indexes or indexes that enforce primary key or unique constraints.
- May provide variations in recommendations on some workloads. The DTA samples data while it executes, which will influence the recommendations.
- Unable to tune trace tables on remote servers.
- Constraints placed on tuning workloads can have a negative impact on suggestions if the tuning session exceeds the constraints.

Note The DTA often suffers a bad rap as an indexing tool. This is mostly because of abuse and misuse by others who have used it. When using the tool, be sure to validate any change that is recommended and test any changes thoroughly before applying them in a production environment.

Explaining the DTA

There are two ways in which users can interact with the DTA. These are the graphical user interface (GUI) and the command-line utility. Both of these methods offer most of the same capabilities. Depending on your comfort level, you can choose either.

The GUI tool, which we will use throughout most of this chapter, provides a wrapper for the DTA. It allows you to select from the available options, and it enables you to view the tuning sessions that were previously executed. If you want to view tuning results, the GUI is well-suited to the task. Tuning sessions can be configured and executed through the GUI.

The command-line utility provides the same capabilities as the GUI when it comes to configuring and executing sessions. The command-line utility can be configured through either switches or an XML configuration file. Both of these options allow database administrators (DBAs) and developers to build processes to automate tuning activities for reviewing and analyzing workloads and to build an index tuning process that allows the DBA to work with results instead of going through the motions of setting up and configuring the tuning sessions. You will learn more about integrating the DTA utility into a performance tuning methodology in Chapter 15.

With both tools, two general areas of configuration need to occur. The first determines how the tuning session will interact and makes suggestions with the physical design structures (PDSs). The second determines which type of partitioning strategy the DTA should employ when trying to tune the database.

There are two parts to the options on how physical design structure suggestions will be generated. The first option you configure is which type of PDS to utilize in the tuning. The physical design structure can be augmented to include considering filtered and columnstore indexes. The options for physical design structure use are as follows:

- Indexes and indexed views.
- Indexes (default option).
- Evaluate utilization of existing PDSs only.
- Indexed views.
- Nonclustered indexes.

The next PDS option is the partitioning to consider in the index tuning. DTA offers to use no partitioning, aligned partitioning, or full partitioning. With full partitioning, recommendations will consider whether a table should include indexes that are partitioned and nonpartitioned.

The last PDS option determines which objects to keep within the database. This option can help ensure that the tuning recommendations do not adversely affect tuning that was previously tested and deployed. The following are the options for PDS items to retain in the database:

- Do not keep any existing PDSs.
- Keep all existing PDSs (default option).
- Keep aligned partitioning.
- Keep indexes only.
- Keep clustered indexes only.

Outside these options, there are some few other options that can be configured. These options configure how long the tuning session will run which can be important if you need to run through a lot of databases, or with a large workload, you want to

CHAPTER 10 INDEXING TOOLS

prevent it from running too long. Additionally, you can define the max disk space for the recommendations and max columns for each index. The last setup option indicates whether index recommendations can or must be able to be deployed online.

> **Note** Before following along in the next section, run the code in Listing 10-1. If the index in Listing 10-3 has been created, drop the index using the DROP INDEX statement provided in Listing 10-4.

Listing 10-4. DDL Statement to Drop Index missing_index_SalesOrderHeader

```
DROP INDEX IF EXISTS Sales.SalesOrderHeader.missing_index_SalesOrderHeader;
```

Using the DTA GUI

As mentioned earlier in the chapter, one of the ways to interact with the DTA is through the GUI. In this section, you'll look at a scenario demonstrating how to use the DTA for index tuning. There are a few methods for launching the tool. The first option is within SQL Server Management Studio (SSMS). Within SSMS, you can choose Tools ➤ Database Engine Tuning Advisor from the menu bar. The other option is to open the Database Engine Tuning Advisor 18 from Microsoft SQL Server Tools 18 on the Start menu.

After launching the DTA, you will be prompted to connect to a SQL Server instance. Once connected, the tool will open a new tuning session for configuration. Figure 10-4 shows a DTA session.

CHAPTER 10   INDEXING TOOLS

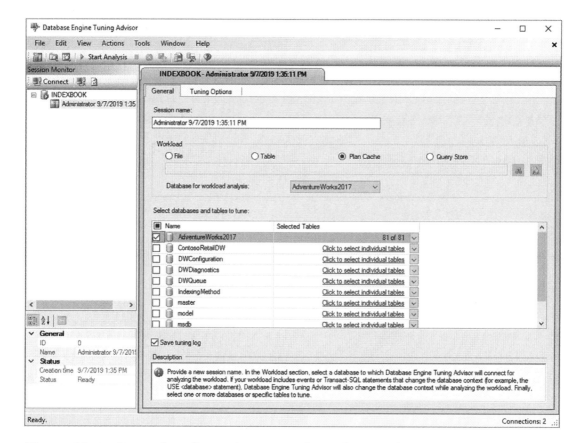

Figure 10-4. *General configuration screen from the Database Engine Tuning Advisor*

In the session launch screen on the General options tab, there are a few things to configure initially. To start, there is the session name. The session name can be any value you desire. The default value includes your username with the date and time. Next, select the type of workload that will be used. There are four options for the workload:

- ***File***: A file containing SQL Trace output, an XML configuration, or SQL scripts.

- ***Table***: SQL Server database table containing SQL Trace output. Before using the table, be sure the trace populating it has been completed.

- ***Plan cache***: The plan cache of the SQL Server that the tuning session is connected to. This capability was introduced in SQL Server 2012 and provides a powerful mechanism to tune execution plans that are being used in your SQL Server environment.

- *Query Store*: The Query Store for the selected database(s) that the tuning session is connected to. This option was introduced in SQL Server 2016 and similar to the plan cache provides an excellent mechanism for tuning a real-world workload with minimal effort.

Each of the workloads can be used to provide recommendations. Through each of these workload sources, there is an opportunity to tune pretty much any type of workload that is needed. For the purposes of this exercise, select the plan cache option.

The next step is to select the database and tables to tune. With large databases, it will be critical to select only the tables that are part of the workload and for which index recommendations are needed. When the DTA executes, it will generate statistics based on information in the table, and the fewer tables that need to be considered, the faster the tuning session can complete. Check the box in the "Select databases and tables to tune" section next to the AdventureWorks2017 database before continuing.

> **Caution** Do not use the DTA in your production SQL Server environment. The tool uses brute-force tactics to identify index recommendations and create hypothetical indexes to support this effort. Running the tool in production can adversely affect the performance of other workloads on the server. Consider running the DTA from a command line and on a remote SQL Server for analyzing production databases. This technique will be demonstrated later in this chapter and discussed further in Chapter 15.

With the General options configured, the next step is to configure the Tuning Options settings. On the screen shown in Figure 10-5, deselect the "Limit tuning time" option. For the other options, leave them as the default selections. These should be as follows:

- *Physical design structures (PDS) to use in database*: Indexes
- *Partitioning strategy to employ*: No partitioning
- *Physical design structures (PDS) to keep in database*: Keep all existing PDS

The next step is to start the Database Engine Tuning Advisor. This can be accomplished through the toolbar or the menu, by selecting Actions ➤ Start Analysis. After starting the DTA, the Progress tab will open, as shown in Figure 10-6.

CHAPTER 10   INDEXING TOOLS

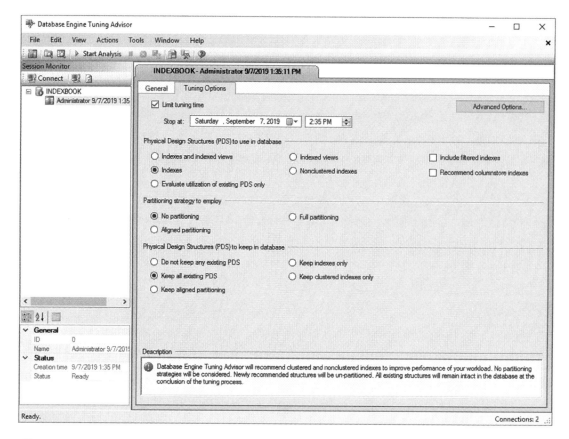

Figure 10-5. *Tuning Options configuration screen from Database Engine Tuning Advisor*

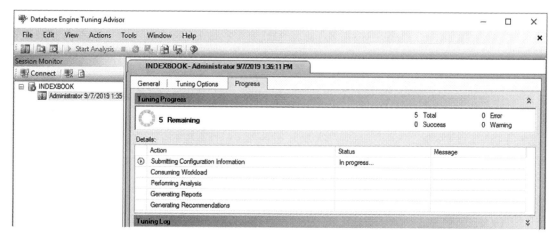

Figure 10-6. *Progress screen from the Database Engine Tuning Advisor*

CHAPTER 10 INDEXING TOOLS

After a few minutes, the tuning session will complete, though this will depend entirely on your computer's workload. With the indexes from Listing 10-1, the results should be similar to those in Figure 10-7. In these results, there are two recommendations. While the names will vary in your environment, the recommendations should be as follows:

- Index on `OrderDate` and then `DueDate` including `CustomerID`
- `Statistics` on `OrderDate` and then `DueDate`

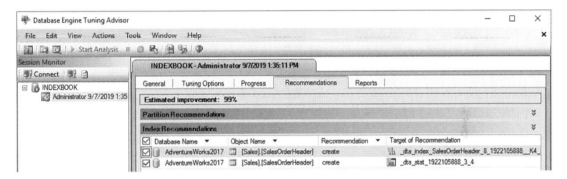

Figure 10-7. *Recommendations from the Database Engine Tuning Advisor*

This index is similar to the suggestion previously found with the missing index DMOs. In situations where there are multiple recommendations provided, you will need to go through the same considerations that were part of reviewing the suggestions from the missing index DMOs, such as "Can the recommendations be consolidated?" Additionally, when statistics are recommended, do they match an index that will be created enough that the index can provide the statistics required for queries? To remove any item from the list of recommendations, simply deselect the check box, and it will not be included in any of the recommendation outputs.

At this point, there are a few options that can be used to apply the indexes:

- ***Apply the indexes***: To apply the indexes, select Actions in the menu bar and select Apply Recommendations. In the Apply Recommendations window that comes up, leave the default, Apply Now, selected and click OK.

- ***Apply the indexes in the future***: To apply the indexes in the future, select Actions in the menu bar and select Apply Recommendations. In the Apply Recommendations window that comes up, select "Schedule for later." Alter the scheduled date as desired and click

CHAPTER 10 INDEXING TOOLS

OK. This will create the SQL Agent job. Ensure the SQL Agent is running and the agent service account has the required permissions to apply the indexes.

- *Save recommendations*: To save recommendations, click the Save Recommendations icon in the menu bar and press the key combination Ctrl+S; or, select Actions ➤ Save Recommendations in the menu bar.

If the recommendations are saved, they will create a script like the one in Listing 10-5. Before applying indexes from the DTA, it is recommended that the names of indexes be changed to match your organization's index naming standards. You will want to also consider whether to apply compression to the index; generally, it is recommended to do so. And when it comes to statistics, it's not as important to add these for a couple reasons. First, SQL Server will create statistics as needed behind the scenes, removing the need for you to build your own statistics. Second, indexes include statistics and usually provide what is required.

Listing 10-5. Database Engine Tuning Advisor Index Recommendations

```
use [AdventureWorks2017]
go

CREATE NONCLUSTERED INDEX [_dta_index_SalesOrderHeader_8_1922105888__K4_K3_11] ON [Sales].[SalesOrderHeader]
(
        [DueDate] ASC,
        [OrderDate] ASC
)
INCLUDE([CustomerID]) WITH (SORT_IN_TEMPDB = OFF, DROP_EXISTING = OFF, ONLINE = OFF) ON [PRIMARY]
go
```

By using the DTA through its GUI, you are able to make quick work of a workload. The recommendations returned provide a level of index tuning above using the missing index DMOs. In essence, they provide a brute-force indexing exercise to improve performance without improving code. Instead of spending many hours on tuning that can be resolved with a few new indexes, you can focus your time on performance tuning issues that are beyond just adding an index.

Note When the DTA is terminated while processing, it will sometimes leave behind hypothetical indexes that were used while it was investigating possible indexes that could improve an environment. A hypothetical index is an index that contains only statistics and no data. These indexes can be identified through the is_hypothetical column in sys.indexes. If they exist in your environment, they should always be dropped.

Using the DTA Utility

The GUI isn't the only way to use the DTA within your SQL Server environment. The other method is through the command line with the DTA utility. What DTA utility lacks in an interactive interface, it makes up for with the flexibility to leverage the DTA utility in scripts and automation.

The syntax for using the DTA utility, shown in Listing 10-6, includes a number of arguments. These arguments, defined in Table 10-5, allow the DTA utility to contain the same features and flexibility of the GUI. Instead of clicking through a number of screens, the configuration information is passed in through the arguments.

Listing 10-6. DTA Utility Syntax

```
dta
[ -? ] |
[
       [ -S server_name[ \instance ] ]
       { { -U login_id [-P password ] } | -E }
       { -D database_name [ ,...n ] }
       [ -d database_name ]
       [ -Tl table_list | -Tf table_list_file ]
       { -if workload_file | -it workload_trace_table_name   | -ip | -ipf }
       { -ssession_name | -IDsession_ID }
       [ -F ]
       [ -of output_script_file_name ]
       [ -or output_xml_report_file_name ]
       [ -ox output_XML_file_name ]
       [ -rl analysis_report_list [ ,...n ] ]
```

```
            [ -ix input_XML_file_name ]
            [ -A time_for_tuning_in_minutes ]
            [ -n number_of_events ]
            [ -m minimum_improvement ]
            [ -fa physical_design_structures_to_add ]
            [ -fi filtered_indexes]
            [ -fc columnstore_indexes]
            [ -fp partitioning_strategy ]
            [ -fk keep_existing_option ]
            [ -fx drop_only_mode ]
            [ -B storage_size ]
            [ -c max_key_columns_in_index ]
            [ -C max_columns_in_index ]
            [ -e | -e tuning_log_name ]
            [ -N online_option]
            [ -q ]
            [ -u ]
            [ -x ]
            [ -a ]
]
```

Table 10-5. DTA Utility Arguments

Argument	Description
-?	Returns help information, including a list of all arguments.
-A	Provides a time limit, in minutes, in which the DTA utility will spend tuning the workload. The default time limit is 8 hours, or 640 minutes. Setting the limit to 0 will result in an unlimited tuning session.
-a	After the workload is tuned, the recommendations are applied without further prompting.
-B	Specifies the maximum size, in megabytes, that recommended indexes can consume. By default, this value is set to either three times the current raw data size or the free space on attached disk drives plus raw data size, whichever is smaller.

(*continued*)

Table 10-5. (*continued*)

Argument	Description
-c	Maximum number of key columns that DTA will recommend in an index. This value defaults to 16. The restriction does not include INCLUDED columns.
-C	Maximum number of columns that DTA will recommend in an index. The value defaults to 16 but can be raised as high as 1024, the maximum columns allowed in an index.
-d	Identifies the database that the DTA session connects to when the session begins. Only a single database can be specified for this argument.
-D	Identifies the databases that the DTA session will tune the workload against. One or more databases can be specified for this argument. To add multiple databases to a session, either include all the database names in a comma-separated list in one argument or add one argument per database.
-e	Identifies the name of the logging table or file where the DTA session will output events that could not be tuned. When specifying a table name, use the three-part naming convention of [database_name].[schema_name].[table_name]. With an output file, the extension for the file should be .xml.
-E	Sets the database connection using a trusted connection. The required argument if -U is not used.
-F	Grants DTA permission to overwrite an output file if it already exists.
-fa	Identifies the types of physical design structures that the DTA session can include in the recommendations. The default value for this argument is IDX. The available values are as follows: • IDX_IV: Indexes and indexed views • IDX: Indexes only • IX: Indexed views only • NCL_IDX: Nonclustered indexes only
-fi	Allows the DTA session to include recommendations for filtered indexes.
-fc	Allows the DTA session to include recommendations for columnstore indexes.

(*continued*)

Table 10-5. (*continued*)

Argument	Description
-fk	Sets the limitations on the existing physical design structures that the DTA session can modify in the recommendations. The available values are as follows: • NONE: No existing structures • ALL: All existing structures • ALIGNED: All partition-aligned structures • CL_IDX: All clustered indexes on tables • IDX: All clustered and nonclustered indexes on tables
-fp	Determines whether partitioning recommendations can be included in the DTA session recommendations. The default value for this argument is NONE. The available values are as follows: • NONE: No partitioning • FULL: Full partitioning • ALIGNED: Aligned partitioning
-fx	Limits the DTA session to only including recommendations to drop existing physical design structures. Lightly used indexes in the session are evaluated, and recommendations for dropping them are provided. This argument cannot be used with the arguments -fa, -fp, and -fk ALL.
-ID	Sets a numerical identifier for the DTA session. Either this argument or -s must be specified.
-ip	Set the source of the workload for the DTA session to the plan cache. The top –n plan cache events for the databases specified with argument –D are analyzed.
-ipf	Sets the source of the workload for the DTA session to the plan cache. The top –n plan cache events for all databases are analyzed.
-if	Sets the source of the workload for the DTA session to a file source. The path and file name are passed in through this argument. The file must be SQL Server Profiler trace file (trc), SQL file (sql), or SQL Server trace file (log).

(*continued*)

Table 10-5. (*continued*)

Argument	Description
-it	Sets the source of the workload for the DTA session to a table. When specifying a table name, use the three-part naming convention of [database_name].dbo.[table_name]. The schema for the table must be dbo.
-ix	Identifies an XML file containing the configuration information for the DTA session. The XML file must conform to the DTASchema.xsd (which is located at http://schemas.microsoft.com/sqlserver/2004/07/dta/dtaschema.xsd).
-m	Sets the minimum percentage of improvement that a recommendation must provide.
-n	Sets the number of events in the workload that the DTA session should tune. When specified for a trace file, the order of the events selected is based on the decreasing order of duration.
-N	Determines whether the physical design structures are created online or offline. The available values are as follows: • OFF: No objects are created online. • ON: All objects are created online. • MIXED: Objects are created where possible.
-of	Configures the DTA session to output the recommendations in a T-SQL format in the path and file specified.
-or	Configures the DTA session to output the recommendations to a report in an XML format. When a file name is not provided, a file name based on the session (-s) name will be used.
-ox	Configures the DTA session to output the recommendations in an XML format in the path and file specified.
-P	Sets the password to be used for the SQL login in the database connection.
-q	Sets the DTA session to execute in quiet mode.

(*continued*)

Table 10-5. (*continued*)

Argument	Description
-rl	Configures the reports that will be generated by the DTA session. One or more reports can be selected in a comma-separated list. The available values are as follows: • ALL: All analysis reports • STMT_COST: Statement cost report • EVT_FREQ: Event frequency report • STMT_DET: Statement detail report • CUR_STMT_IDX: Statement-index relations report (current configuration) • REC_STMT_IDX: Statement-index relations report (recommended configuration) • STMT_COSTRANGE: Statement cost range report • CUR_IDX_USAGE: Index usage report (current configuration) • REC_IDX_USAGE: Index usage report (recommended configuration) • CUR_IDX_DET: Index detail report (current configuration) • REC_IDX_DET: Index detail report (recommended configuration) • VIW_TAB: View-table relations report • WKLD_ANL: Workload analysis report • DB_ACCESS: Database access report • TAB_ACCESS: Table access report • COL_ACCESS: Column access report
-S	Sets the instance of SQL Server to be used for the DTA session.
-s	Sets the name of the DTA session.
-Tf	Identifies the name of a path and file containing a list of tables to be used for tuning. The file should contain one table per line using the three-part naming convention. After each table name, the number of rows can be specified to tune the workload for a scaled version of the table. If -Tf and -Tl is omitted, the DTA session will default to using all tables.
-Tl	Sets a list of tables to be used for tuning. Each table should be listed using the three-part naming convention, with each table name separated by a comma. If -Tf and -Tl are omitted, the DTA session will default to using all tables.
-U	Sets the username to be used for the SQL login in the database connection. The required argument if -E is not used.
-u	Launches the GUI interface for the DTA with all of the configuration values specified the to the DTA utility.
-x	Starts the DTA session and exists upon completion.

Using the DTA utility is fairly easy. You'll look at two scenarios of using the tool that provide different outcomes. In the first scenario, you'll use the DTA utility to recommend indexing changes with allowing only nonclustered indexing changes. For the second scenario, the DTA utility will be configured to recommend any change to the indexing that would improve the performance of the workload. In both scenarios, you'll use the plan cache for SQL Server as the workload source. To populate the plan cache, execute the query in Listing 10-7.

Listing 10-7. Scenario Setup

```
USE AdventureWorks2017
GO

IF OBJECT_ID('dbo.SalesOrderDetail') IS NOT NULL
        DROP TABLE dbo.SalesOrderDetail;
SELECT SalesOrderID, SalesOrderDetailID, CarrierTrackingNumber, OrderQty,
ProductID, SpecialOfferID, UnitPrice, UnitPriceDiscount, LineTotal,
rowguid, ModifiedDate
INTO dbo.SalesOrderDetail
FROM Sales.SalesOrderDetail;

CREATE CLUSTERED INDEX CL_SalesOrderDetail ON dbo.SalesOrderDetail
(SalesOrderDetailID);

CREATE NONCLUSTERED INDEX IX_SalesOrderDetail ON dbo.SalesOrderDetail
(SalesOrderID);
GO

SELECT SalesOrderID, CarrierTrackingNumber
INTO #temp
FROM dbo.SalesOrderDetail
WHERE SalesOrderID = 43660;
DROP TABLE #temp;
GO 1000

SELECT SalesOrderID, OrderQty
INTO #temp
FROM dbo.SalesOrderDetail
```

CHAPTER 10　INDEXING TOOLS

```
WHERE SalesOrderID = 43661;
DROP TABLE #temp;
GO 1000
```

For the first scenario, you'll build a command-line script similar to the one shown in Listing 10-8. For your environment, the server name (-S) will be different. The rest, however, will be the same. The database (-D and -d arguments) will be AdventureWorks2017. The source of the workload will be the plan cache (-ip argument). The name of the session (-s argument) is "First Scenario."

Listing 10-8. First Scenario DTA Utility Syntax

```
"C:\Program Files (x86)\Microsoft SQL Server Management Studio 18\Common7\dta"
-S localhost -E
-D AdventureWorks2017
-d AdventureWorks2017
-ip
-s "First Scenario"
-Tl AdventureWorks2017.dbo.SalesOrderDetail
-of "C:\Temp\First Scenario.sql"
-fa NCL_IDX
-fp NONE
-fk ALL
```

With the DTA utility syntax prepared, the next step is to execute the script through the Command Prompt window. Depending on your SQL Server instance and the amount of information in the plan cache, the execution may take a few minutes. When it completes, the output in the Command Prompt window will look similar to the output shown in Figure 10-8. This output indicates that the file C:\Temp\First Scenario.sql contains the recommendations for tuning the query in Listing 10-7.

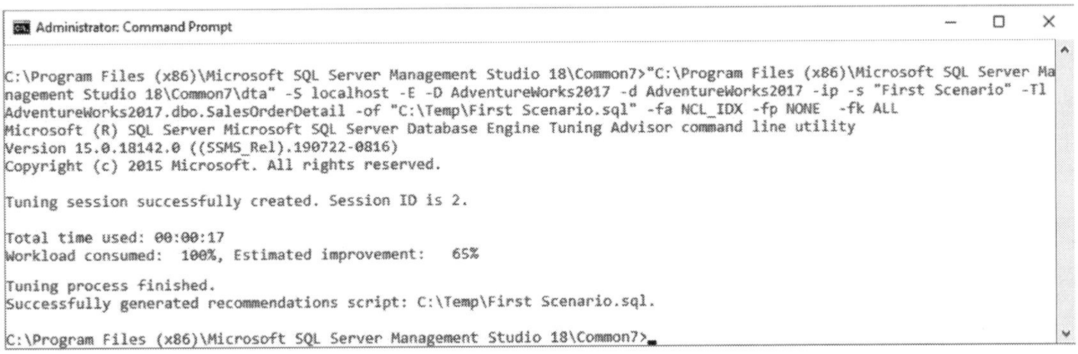

CHAPTER 10 INDEXING TOOLS

```
Administrator: Command Prompt                                          —   □   ×

C:\Program Files (x86)\Microsoft SQL Server Management Studio 18\Common7>"C:\Program Files (x86)\Microsoft SQL Server Ma
nagement Studio 18\Common7\dta" -S localhost -E -D AdventureWorks2017 -d AdventureWorks2017 -ip -s "First Scenario" -Tl
AdventureWorks2017.dbo.SalesOrderDetail -of "C:\Temp\First Scenario.sql" -fa NCL_IDX -fp NONE  -fk ALL
Microsoft (R) SQL Server Microsoft SQL Server Database Engine Tuning Advisor command line utility
Version 15.0.18142.0 ((SSMS_Rel).190722-0816)
Copyright (c) 2015 Microsoft. All rights reserved.

Tuning session successfully created. Session ID is 2.

Total time used: 00:00:17
Workload consumed:  100%, Estimated improvement:   65%

Tuning process finished.
Successfully generated recommendations script: C:\Temp\First Scenario.sql.

C:\Program Files (x86)\Microsoft SQL Server Management Studio 18\Common7>_
```

Figure 10-8. *Command Prompt window for first scenario*

Based on the arguments passed into the DTA utility and the current workload, the recommendation from the first scenario tuning session includes the creation of two nonclustered indexes and statistics on two columns, shown in Listing 10-9. These indexes function as covering indexes for the queries in Listing 10-7; as a result, the key lookup is no longer required as part of the execution plan. The statistics provide information that SQL Server can use to build good plans for queries on the columns used in the query.

> **Note** Listing 10-9 creates the dbo.SalesOrderDetail table.

Listing 10-9. First Scenario DTA Utility Output

```
use [AdventureWorks2017]
go

CREATE NONCLUSTERED INDEX [_dta_index_SalesOrderDetail_8_2119678599__K1_
K2_3] ON [dbo].[SalesOrderDetail]
(
      [SalesOrderID] ASC,
      [SalesOrderDetailID] ASC
)
INCLUDE([CarrierTrackingNumber]) WITH (SORT_IN_TEMPDB = OFF, DROP_EXISTING
= OFF, ONLINE = OFF) ON [PRIMARY]
go
```

CHAPTER 10　INDEXING TOOLS

```sql
CREATE NONCLUSTERED INDEX [_dta_index_SalesOrderDetail_8_2119678599__K1_
K2_4] ON [dbo].[SalesOrderDetail]
(
	[SalesOrderID] ASC,
	[SalesOrderDetailID] ASC
)
INCLUDE([OrderQty]) WITH (SORT_IN_TEMPDB = OFF, DROP_EXISTING = OFF, ONLINE
= OFF) ON [PRIMARY]
go

CREATE STATISTICS [_dta_stat_2119678599_2_1] ON [dbo].[SalesOrderDetail]
([SalesOrderDetailID], [SalesOrderID])
go
```

The downside to the arguments that were selected in the first scenario is that there isn't any information included that helps determine the value in adding this index and the statistics. For the next scenario, you'll learn how to obtain that information along with moving deeper into providing recommendations on the physical structure of your databases.

To begin the next scenario, you'll use the same database and query. The arguments, though, will be modified slightly to accommodate the new goals, as shown in Listing 10-10. First, you'll change the name of the session (-s) to "Second Scenario." Next, change the allowed physical structure changes (argument -fa) from nonclustered indexes only (NCL_IDX) to indexes and indexed views (IDX_IV). The final change, for the reporting output, is to add the report list (argument -rl) to the script with the all analysis reports (ALL) option.

Listing 10-10. Second Scenario DTA Utility Syntax

```
"C:\Program Files (x86)\Microsoft SQL Server Management Studio 18\Common7\dta"
-S localhost
-D AdventureWorks2017
-d AdventureWorks2017
-ip
-s "Second Scenario"
-Tl AdventureWorks2017.dbo.SalesOrderDetail
```

```
-of "C:\Temp\Second Scenario.sql"
-fa IDX_IV
-fp NONE
-fk ALL
-rl ALL
```

Executing the DTA utility using the second scenario produces entirely different results from the first scenario. Instead of recommending nonclustered indexes, the second scenario recommends a change in the clustered key columns. With this solution, the DTA session identified the SalesOrderID column as the column frequently used to access data and recommended that as the clustered index. Listing 10-11 shows these recommendations.

Listing 10-11. Second Scenario DTA Utility Output

```
use [AdventureWorks2017]
go
CREATE NONCLUSTERED INDEX [_dta_index_SalesOrderDetail_8_2119678599__K1_
K2_3] ON [dbo].[SalesOrderDetail]
(
    [SalesOrderID] ASC,
    [SalesOrderDetailID] ASC
)
INCLUDE([CarrierTrackingNumber]) WITH (SORT_IN_TEMPDB = OFF, DROP_EXISTING =
OFF, ONLINE = OFF) ON [PRIMARY]
go

CREATE NONCLUSTERED INDEX [_dta_index_SalesOrderDetail_8_2119678599__K1_
K2_4] ON [dbo].[SalesOrderDetail]
(
    [SalesOrderID] ASC,
    [SalesOrderDetailID] ASC
)
INCLUDE([OrderQty]) WITH (SORT_IN_TEMPDB = OFF, DROP_EXISTING = OFF, ONLINE =
OFF) ON [PRIMARY]
go
```

```
CREATE STATISTICS [_dta_stat_2119678599_2_1] ON [dbo].[SalesOrderDetail]
([SalesOrderDetailID], [SalesOrderID])
go
```

The one other difference with the second scenario is the creation of an XML report file. The session used the ALL option for the -rl argument, which includes all the reports listed for the argument in Table 10-5. These reports provide information regarding the statements that were tuned, the costs associated with the statements, the amount of improvement the recommendations provide, and much more (Figure 10-9). Through these reports, you are provided the information needed to make decisions about which recommendations to apply to your databases.

```
<?xml version="1.0" encoding="UTF-16"?>
- <DTAXML>
  - <DTAOutput>
    - <AnalysisReport>
      + <StatementCostReport>
      + <EventWeightReport>
      + <StatementDetailReport>
      + <StatementIndexReport Current="true">
      + <StatementIndexReport Current="false">
      + <StatementCostRangeReport>
      + <IndexUsageReport Current="true">
      + <IndexUsageReport Current="false">
      - <IndexDetailReport Current="true">
        - <Database>
            <Name>AdventureWorks2017</Name>
          - <Schema>
              <Name>dbo</Name>
            - <Table>
                <Name>MythOne</Name>
              - <Index FilterDefinition="" NumberOfRows="121317" IndexSizeInMB="11.70" FilteredIndex="false" Heap="true" Unique="false" Clustered="false">
                  <Name>MythOne</Name>
                </Index>
              </Table>
            - <Table>
                <Name>AllocationCycle</Name>
              - <Index FilterDefinition="" NumberOfRows="100000" IndexSizeInMB="77.23" FilteredIndex="false" Heap="false" Unique="true" Clustered="true">
                  <Name>PK_AllocationCycle</Name>
                </Index>
              </Table>
            - <Table>
                <Name>ErrorLog</Name>
              - <Index FilterDefinition="" NumberOfRows="0" IndexSizeInMB="0.01" FilteredIndex="false" Heap="false" Unique="true" Clustered="true">
                  <Name>PK_ErrorLog_ErrorLogID</Name>
                </Index>
              </Table>
            - <Table>
                <Name>tl_2017_us_county</Name>
              - <Index FilterDefinition="" NumberOfRows="3233" IndexSizeInMB="136.32" FilteredIndex="false" Heap="true" Unique="false" Clustered="false">
                  <Name>tl_2017_us_county</Name>
                </Index>
              </Table>
```

Figure 10-9. *Sample report output from DTA utility*

One thing to remember with the last two scenarios is that the table being tuned was tuned in a vacuum. There were no constraints or foreign key relationships on the table that need to be considered. In the real world, this won't be the way your database is designed, and foreign key relationships will affect how recommendations are provided. Also, the load for these scenarios contained only two queries. When building your workloads, be sure to use a sample that is representative of your environment.

Through the DTA scenarios provided in this section, you've laid a foundation for using tools in your index tuning activities. Not only can the DTA identify missing indexes, but, given a workload, it can also help identify where clustered indexes and partitioning can assist with performance. The physical changes that DTA can provide could be extremely useful when you quickly need to address performance issues with a database.

Summary

This chapter walked you through using the built-in indexing tools available in SQL Server. Each of these tools can be a great addition to your SQL Server tool belt. They allow you to dig in and start making informed indexing decisions without expending a lot of effort.

When it comes to the missing index DMOs, you are working with index suggestions based on existing activity on the SQL Server instance. These are real-world applications, and they represent areas where you can almost immediately begin to build solutions to improve performance.

The DTA, while not as readily available as the missing index DMOs, allows you to tune indexes from a single query to a full workload with minimal effort. The new option to tune the contents of the plan cache allows you to leverage the work currently being done in an environment to build recommendations without the need to create a workload.

CHAPTER 11

Indexing Strategies

Indexing databases is often thought of as an art where the database is the canvas and the indexes are the paints that come together to form a beautiful tapestry of storage and performance. A little color here, a little color there, and paintings will take shape. In much the same way, a clustered index on a table and then a few nonclustered indexes can result in screaming performance as beautiful as any masterpiece. Going a little too abstract or minimalist with your indexing might make you feel good, but the performance will let you know it isn't too useful.

As colorful as this analogy is, there is more science behind designing and applying indexes than there is artistry. A few columns pulled together because they might work well together is often less beneficial than an index built upon well-established patterns. The indexes that are based on tried-and-true practices are often the best solutions. In this chapter, we'll walk through a number of patterns to help identify potential indexes.

Heaps

There are few valid cases for using heaps in your databases. The general rule of thumb for most DBAs is that all tables in a database should be built with clustered indexes instead of heaps. While this practice rings true in many situations, there are situations when using a heap is acceptable and preferred. This section looks at one of these scenarios and discusses the other situations in generalities. The reason for being generic is that it is difficult to make blanket statements about when to use a heap instead of a clustered index (which will be explained more later in the section).

Temporary Objects

One of the situations in which heaps are useful is with temporary objects, such as temporary tables and table variables. When we use these objects, we often create them without thinking or considering building a clustered index on them. The result is that we use more heaps on tables than we think we do.

Consider for a moment the last time you created a table variable or a temporary table. Did the syntax for the object specifically create a CLUSTERED index or a PRIMARY KEY with the default configuration? If not, then the temporary object was created as a heap. This isn't really a problem. It is common in most workloads—not necessarily a call to arms to change your coding practices. As will be demonstrated in the examples in this section, the performance difference between a temporary object with a heap and a clustered index can be immaterial.

For this example, let's start with a simple use case for a temporary table. The example uses the table `Sales.SalesOrderHeader` from which we'll retrieve a few rows based on a `SalesPersonID` and then insert them into a temporary table. The temporary table will be used to return all rows from `Sales.SalesOrderDetail` that match the results in the temporary table. Two versions of the example will be used to demonstrate how using a heap or a clustered index on the temporary table doesn't change the query execution.

In the first version of the example, shown in Listing 11-1, the temporary table is built using a heap. This is the method that people often use to create temporary objects. As the execution plan in Figure 11-1 shows, when the temporary table is accessed, identified by the arrow, a table scan is used to access the rows in the object. This behavior is expected with a heap. Since the rows aren't ordered, there is no way to access specific rows without checking all the rows first. To find all the rows in `Sales.SalesOrderDetail` that match those in the temporary table, the execution plan uses a nested loop with an index seek.

Listing 11-1. Temporary Object with Heap

```
USE AdventureWorks2017
GO

IF OBJECT_ID('tempdb..##TempWithHeap') IS NOT NULL
    DROP TABLE ##TempWithHeap
```

```
CREATE TABLE ##TempWithHeap
    (
    SalesOrderID INT
    );

INSERT INTO ##TempWithHeap
SELECT SalesOrderID
FROM Sales.SalesOrderHeader
WHERE SalesPersonID = 283;

SELECT sod.* FROM Sales.SalesOrderDetail sod
    INNER JOIN ##TempWithHeap t ON t.SalesOrderID = sod.SalesOrderID;
GO
```

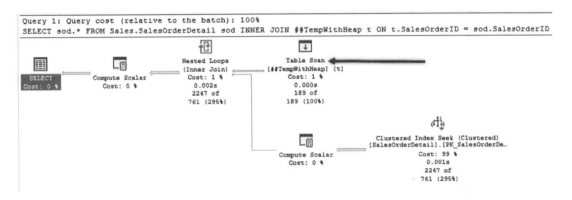

Figure 11-1. Execution plan for heap temporary object

In the second version of the script, shown in Listing 11-2, the temporary table is created instead with a clustered index on the SalesOrderID column. The index is the only difference between the two scripts. This difference results in a slight change in the execution plan. Figure 11-2 shows the clustered index version of the execution plan. The difference between the two plans is that instead of a table scan, there is a clustered index scan against the temporary table. While these are different operations, the work done by both is essentially the same. During query execution, all rows in the temporary object are accessed while joining them to rows in Sales.SalesOrderDetail.

CHAPTER 11 INDEXING STRATEGIES

Listing 11-2. Temporary Object with Clustered Index

```
USE AdventureWorks2017
GO

IF OBJECT_ID('tempdb..##TempWithClusteredIX') IS NOT NULL
    DROP TABLE ##TempWithClusteredIX

CREATE TABLE ##TempWithClusteredIX
    (
    SalesOrderID INT PRIMARY KEY CLUSTERED
    )

INSERT INTO ##TempWithClusteredIX
SELECT SalesOrderID
FROM Sales.SalesOrderHeader
WHERE SalesPersonID = 283

SELECT sod.* FROM Sales.SalesOrderDetail sod
INNER JOIN ##TempWithClusteredIX t ON t.SalesOrderID = sod.SalesOrderID
GO
```

Note Since SQL Server 2014, table variables can have both clustered and nonclustered indexes on them. The requirement is that the indexes are created when the variable is declared. DDL operations are not allowed on table variables after they are defined.

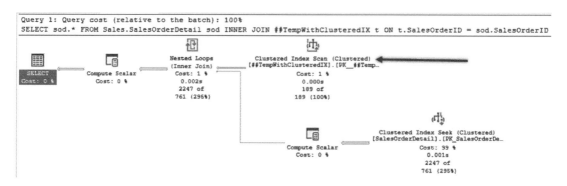

Figure 11-2. *Execution plan for clustered temporary object*

In queries similar to the example in this section, the execution plans for temporary tables with heaps and clustered indexes are nearly the same. As with all rules, there may be exceptions where performance will differ. A good example of when using a heap can affect performance is the T-SQL syntax that leverages a sort in its execution. Listing 11-3 shows a specific example using EXISTS in the WHERE clause. Figure 11-3 shows the execution plan for the query. Before the nested loop joins to resolve the EXISTS predicate, the data must first be sorted. In this case, the use of a heap has hindered the performance of the query because the heap table forces a sort operation. With small datasets, the performance difference may not be noticeable. As the size of the dataset increases, little changes such as the inclusion of a sort operation can compound the performance of your queries.

Listing 11-3. EXISTS Example

```
USE AdventureWorks2017
GO

SELECT sod.* FROM Sales.SalesOrderDetail sod
WHERE EXISTS (SELECT * FROM ##TempWithHeap t WHERE t.SalesOrderID =
sod.SalesOrderID);
GO

SELECT sod.* FROM Sales.SalesOrderDetail sod
WHERE EXISTS (SELECT * FROM ##TempWithClusteredIX t WHERE t.SalesOrderID =
sod.SalesOrderID);
```

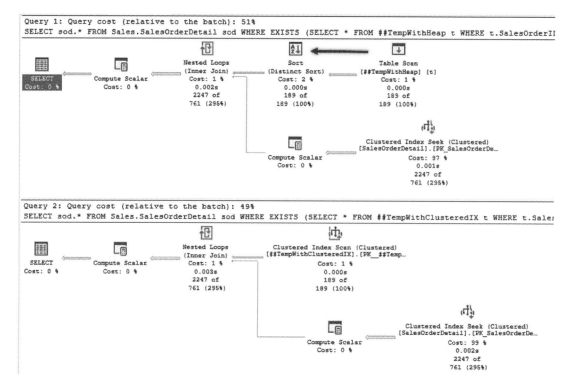

Figure 11-3. EXISTS example execution plan

Other Heap Scenarios

Generally, the other scenarios where using heaps makes sense are few and far between. The reason using temporary objects makes sense is because of the low frequency in which the data will be accessed compared to the amount of time it will take to create a structure, such as a clustered index, to support the performance. This scenario can also carry over the staging tables, since the data is usually inserted and modified a couple times before moving it to its final destination.

In high-insert environments, it might seem to make sense to use heaps to avoid the overhead of maintaining the B-tree. The trouble with this scenario is that the gains on inserts are offset by the need to access the data, which requires other nonclustered indexes, which then have sort orders to maintain.

When confronted with a situation for using heaps on your tables, first look at whether clustered indexes can be proven to be a burden on the storage of the data before using them. And before looking to the heap, also consider whether newer indexing structures such as clustered columnstore indexes or memory-optimized tables provide the performance required.

The main point of this section is that heaps are used more often in the real world than many people realize. While most practices rail against their use, there are some cases and situations where they are a good fit and others where it doesn't matter whether they are there or not. As the discussion moves into clustered indexes, you will see why it is usually a good idea to default to clustered indexes and use heaps in situations where either it won't matter, such as most use cases with temporary objects, or they outperform clustered indexes.

Clustered Indexes

Throughout this book, the value of and preference for using a clustered index as the structure for organizing the data pages of a table has been discussed. Clustered indexes organize the data in their tables based on the key columns for the clustered indexes. All the data pages for the index are stored logically according to the key columns. The benefit of this is optimal access to the data through the key columns.

New tables should almost always be built with clustered indexes. The question, though, when building the tables is what should be selected for the key columns in the clustered index. There are a few characteristics that most often are attributed to well-defined clustered indexes. These characteristics are

- Static
- Narrow
- Unique
- Ever-increasing

There are a number of reasons that each of these attributes helps create a well-defined clustered index.

First, a clustered index should be static. The key columns defined for the clustered index should be expected to be static for the lifetime of the row. By using a static value, the position of the row in the index will not change when the row is updated. When nonstatic key columns are used, the position of the row in the clustered index can change, which may require the row to be inserted on a different page. Also, nonclustered indexes would need to be modified to change the key columns' values stored in those indexes, since clustered index key columns are included in nonclustered indexes. All of this together leads to the potential for fragmentation in the clustered and nonclustered indexes on a table.

The next attribute that a clustered index should have is that it is narrow. Ideally, there should be only a single column for the clustered index key. These columns should be defined with the smallest data type reasonable for that data being stored in the table. Narrow clustered indexes are important because the clustered index key for every row is included in all nonclustered indexes associated with the table. The wider the clustered index key, the wider all nonclustered indexes will be, and the more pages they will require. As discussed in other sections, the more pages in an index, the more resources are required to use the index. This can affect the performance of queries.

Clustered indexes should also be unique. Clustered indexes store a single row in a single location in the index; for duplicate rows within the key columns of a clustered index, the uniquifier provides the uniqueness required for the row. When the uniquifier is added to a row, it is extended by 4 bytes, which changes how narrow the clustered index is and results in the same concerns that are associated with a non-narrow clustered index. You can find more information on the uniquifier in Chapter 2.

Lastly, a well-defined clustered index will be based on an ever-increasing value. Using an ever-increasing clustered key causes new rows to be added to the end of the clustered index. Placing new rows at the end of the B-tree reduces the fragmentation that would likely occur if the rows were inserted in the middle of the clustered index.

One additional consideration when selecting the clustered index key columns is that they represent the columns in the row that will most frequently be used to access the row. Are there specific columns or values that will most often be used to retrieve rows from the table? If so, these columns are good candidates for the clustering index key. In the end, queries against the table will perform best when they can access data through the path of least resistance.

While considering the previous guidelines for selecting clustered index strategies, there are a number of patterns that can be used to identify and model clustered indexes. The clustered index patterns are

- Identity Sequence
- Natural Key
- Foreign Key

- Multiple Column
- Globally Unique Identifier

In the rest of this section, we'll walk you through each of the patterns, describing each and how to identify when to utilize the pattern.

Identity Sequence

The most frequent pattern for building a clustered index is to pair it with a column on a table that has been configured to be ever-increasing using either the IDENTITY property or the SEQUENCE object. In this pattern, the IDENTITY column is often also the PRIMARY KEY on the table. The data type is usually an integer, which includes tinyint, smallint, int, and bigint. The primary benefit of this pattern is that it achieves all the attributes of a well-defined clustered index. It is static, narrow, unique, and ever-increasing. When you consider how the data in the table will be accessed, in most cases the key value will most often be used to access rows in the table.

One distinction of the Identity Sequence pattern is that the column used for the clustered index key has no relationship between the data in the row and the clustered index key. To implement the pattern, a new column is added to the table that contains the IDENTITY property or SEQUENCE default. This column is then set as the clustered index key and often the PRIMARY KEY as well.

Examples of this pattern can be found in nearly all databases. Creating a table with this pattern would look similar to the CREATE TABLE statements in Listing 11-4. Both tables are built to contain fruit: two apple rows, a banana row, and a grape row are inserted. The Color column would not have been a good clustering key since it does not identify the rows in the table. The FruitName column could have identified the rows in the table, except it isn't unique across the table, which would have required the uniquifier and lead to a larger clustering key. Indexing the table to the Identity Sequence pattern, a FruitID column is created.

Listing 11-4. Creating and Populating Table for Identity Sequence Pattern

```
USE AdventureWorks2017
GO

IF OBJECT_ID('IndexStrategiesFruit_Identity') IS NOT NULL
    DROP TABLE IndexStrategiesFruit_Identity
```

CHAPTER 11 INDEXING STRATEGIES

```sql
CREATE TABLE dbo.IndexStrategiesFruit_Identity
(
FruitID int IDENTITY(1,1)
,FruitName varchar(25)
,Color varchar(10)
,CONSTRAINT PK_Fruit_FruitID_Idnt PRIMARY KEY CLUSTERED (FruitID)
);

INSERT INTO dbo.IndexStrategiesFruit_Identity(FruitName, Color)
VALUES('Apple','Red'),('Banana','Yellow'),('Apple','Green'),('Grape','Green');

SELECT FruitID, FruitName, Color
FROM dbo.IndexStrategiesFruit_Identity;

IF OBJECT_ID('IndexStrategiesFruit_Sequence') IS NOT NULL
    DROP TABLE IndexStrategiesFruit_Sequence

IF OBJECT_ID('FruitSequence') IS NOT NULL
    DROP SEQUENCE FruitSequence

CREATE SEQUENCE FruitSequence AS INTEGER
    START WITH 1;

CREATE TABLE dbo.IndexStrategiesFruit_Sequence
(
FruitID int DEFAULT NEXT VALUE FOR FruitSequence
,FruitName varchar(25)
,Color varchar(10)
,CONSTRAINT PK_Fruit_FruitID_Seq PRIMARY KEY CLUSTERED (FruitID)
);

INSERT INTO dbo.IndexStrategiesFruit_Sequence(FruitName, Color)
VALUES('Apple','Red'),('Banana','Yellow'),('Apple','Green'),('Grape','Green');

SELECT FruitID, FruitName, Color
FROM dbo.IndexStrategiesFruit_Sequence;
```

One of the effects of using the Identity Sequence pattern is that the value for the clustering key column has no relationship to the information that it represents. In the query output from Listing 11-1, which is shown in Figure 11-4, the value of 1 is assigned to the first row inserted for both resultsets. Then, a value of 2 is assigned for the next row and so on. As more rows are added, the `FruitID` column increments and doesn't require any single piece of information in the record in order to designate the instance of information.

	FruitID	FruitName	Color
1	1	Apple	Red
2	2	Banana	Yellow
3	3	Apple	Green
4	4	Grape	Green

	FruitID	FruitName	Color
1	1	Apple	Red
2	2	Banana	Yellow
3	3	Apple	Green
4	4	Grape	Green

Figure 11-4. *Results for Identity Sequence pattern*

Note SEQUENCE was a new object in SQL Server 2012. Through sequences, ranges of numeric values can be generated, which are either ascending or descending. A sequence is not associated with any specific table. If you are unfamiliar with using SEQUENCE, it is recommended that you consider using sequences over IDENTITY for performance and control purposes. They are outside the context of this book.

Natural Key

In some cases, using a natural key in the data for the clustering key is as valid as adding an identity column to the table to use for the Identity Sequence pattern. A natural key is a column in the data that can uniquely identify one row from all the other rows. The cases where using a natural key is valid can be identified when there is a natural key in the data that meets the attributes of a well-defined clustering key. When using natural keys for clustering keys, they are not likely to be ever-increasing, but they should still be unique, narrow, and static.

A common example of when a natural key may be used instead of an identity column is when looking at tables that contain one- or two-character abbreviations for the information they represent. These abbreviations may be for the status of an order, the size of a product, or a list of states or provinces. Compared to using an int, which is 4 bytes, in the Identity Column pattern, using a char(1) or char(2) data type with the Natural Key pattern will result in a clustering key that is more narrow than the former. Another example is using dates in the yyyymmdd or timestamp format on date tables.

The Natural Key pattern also has the additional benefit of providing an easier-to-decipher key value. When using the Identity Sequence pattern, there is no inherent meaning when the clustering key has a value of 1 or 7. These values are meaningless—intentionally so. With the Natural Key pattern, the abbreviations of *O* and *C* represent real information (Opened and Closed, respectively).

As a simple example of the Natural Key pattern, let's consider a table that contains states and their abbreviations. We'll also include the name of the country for the states. Listing 11-5 shows the SQL to create and populate the table. The table has a StateAbbreviation column, which is a char(2). Since this is a narrow, unique, and static value for each state, the clustered index is created on the column. Next, a few rows are added to the table for the four states that the fictitious database requires.

Listing 11-5. Creating and Populating Table for Natural Key Pattern

```
USE AdventureWorks2017
GO

CREATE TABLE dbo.IndexStrategiesNatural
(
StateAbbreviation char(2)
,StateName varchar(25)
,Country varchar(25)
,CONSTRAINT PK_State_StateAbbreviation PRIMARY KEY CLUSTERED
(StateAbbreviation)
);
```

```
INSERT INTO dbo.IndexStrategiesNatural(StateAbbreviation, StateName, Country)
VALUES('MN','Minnesota','United States')
,('FL','Florida','United States')
,('WI','Wisconsin','United States')
,('NH','New Hampshire','United States');

SELECT StateAbbreviation, StateName, Country
FROM dbo.IndexStrategiesNatural;
```

In situations where the natural key matches the Natural Key pattern, the technique in Listing 11-5 can be a useful way of selecting the clustering key column. Reviewing the contents of dbo.IndexStrategiesNatural (shown in Figure 11-5), the four rows are in the table, and using StateAbbreviation in another table as a foreign key value can be useful since the value MN has some inherent meaning.

	StateAbbreviation	StateName	Country
1	FL	Florida	United States
2	MN	Minnesota	United States
3	NH	New Hampshire	United States
4	WI	Wisconsin	United States

Figure 11-5. *Results for Natural Key pattern*

This pattern may seem ideal and more worthwhile than the Identity Column pattern—especially since the value of the clustering key helps describe the data. However, there are a few downsides to using this pattern, which relate to the attributes that can make it a well-defined clustering key.

First, let's consider the uniqueness of the clustering key. Provided that the use cases for the database and table never change, there can be trust that the values will remain unique. What happens, though, when the database needs to be used in an international context? If states for other countries such as the Netherlands need to be included, there is a great potential for data issues. In the Netherlands, FL is the abbreviation for Flevopolder, and NH is the abbreviation for Noord-Holland. Sending an order to Florida that should go to Flevopolder can have serious business consequences. To retain the uniqueness, something outside of the two-character abbreviation would need to be added to the natural key and clustering key.

Changing the natural key would then affect the narrowness of the clustering key. There are probably two approaches that could be taken to address this problem. The first option is to add another column to the natural key to identify whether a state abbreviation belongs to one country or another. The second option is to increase the size of the state abbreviation to include a country abbreviation in the same column. With either of the solutions, the size of the clustering key will exceed the 4 bytes used to maintain a narrow clustering key through the use of an int data type and the Identity Column pattern.

Additionally, always consider whether natural keys are truly static. State abbreviations can change. While this doesn't happen too often—the last change in the United States happened in 1987 when state abbreviations were all standardized—it will happen occasionally with nearly all types of natural keys. One example is the country of Yugoslavia with its six republics, which became their own countries. Another is the Soviet Union, which evolved into the Russian Federation, which led to the formation of numerous other countries. As static as values such as state and country abbreviations may seem, on a grander scale there is variance. Also, looking to your applications, status codes that represent the states of a workflow may be accurate today but could have new and different meanings in the future.

Lastly, sometimes apparent natural keys can be made of data that shouldn't be widely distributed. For years, government identifiers, like Social Security Number, were often used for natural keys in databases, often in healthcare and educational systems. While this did an adequate job of identifying an individual, it definitely isn't information that should be easily available to database users. In most modern databases, government identifiers now need to be encrypted, which can cause immense problems when these types of natural keys are used for clustered indexes and potentially as primary keys.

The Natural Key pattern for selecting what an index does is a valid pattern for designing clustered indexes. As the example showed, it can be unique, narrow, and static. Look at the current and future applications of the table before using a natural key for the clustered index.

Foreign Key

One of the most often overlooked patterns for creating clustered indexes is to use a foreign key column in the clustering keys for the table. The Foreign Key pattern is not appropriate for all foreign keys but does have its use in designs where there is a one-to-many relationship between information in a header table and the related detail information. The Foreign Key pattern contains all the attributes that are part of a well-defined clustering key. There are, though, a few caveats with a few of the attributes.

Implementing this pattern is similar to the way you implement the Identity Column pattern. The pattern contains two tables that have columns with the IDENTITY property set on them. Listing 11-6 shows an example. In the example, there are three tables created. The first is the header table, named dbo.IndexStrategiesHeader, with a clustered index built on the HeaderID column. The next table is the first version of the detail table, named dbo.IndexStrategiesDetail_ICP. The table is designed as a child to the header table, the clustered index is built using the Identity Column pattern, and an index on the HeaderID column is used to improve performance. The third table is also a detail table, named dbo.IndexStrategiesDetail_FKP; this table is designed using the Foreign Key pattern. Instead of clustering the table on the column with the IDENTITY property, the clustered index includes two columns. The first column is the column from the parent table, HeaderID, and the second is the primary key for this table, DetailID. To provide sample data, sys.indexes and sys.index_columns are used to populate all the tables.

Listing 11-6. Creating and Populating Tables for Foreign Key Pattern

```
USE AdventureWorks2017
GO

CREATE TABLE dbo.IndexStrategiesHeader
(
HeaderID int IDENTITY(1,1)
,FillerData char(250)
,CONSTRAINT PK_Header_HeaderID PRIMARY KEY CLUSTERED (HeaderID)
);

CREATE TABLE dbo.IndexStrategiesDetail_ICP
(
DetailID int IDENTITY(1,1)
,HeaderID int
,FillerData char(500)
,CONSTRAINT PK_Detail_ICP_DetailID PRIMARY KEY CLUSTERED (DetailID)
,CONSTRAINT FK_Detail_ICP_HeaderID FOREIGN KEY (HeaderID) REFERENCES IndexStrategiesHeader(HeaderID)
);
```

```sql
CREATE INDEX IX_Detail_ICP_HeaderID ON dbo.IndexStrategiesDetail_ICP
(HeaderID)

CREATE TABLE dbo.IndexStrategiesDetail_FKP
(
DetailID int IDENTITY(1,1)
,HeaderID int
,FillerData char(500)
,CONSTRAINT PK_Detail_FKP_DetailID PRIMARY KEY NONCLUSTERED (DetailID)
,CONSTRAINT CLUS_Detail_FKP_HeaderIDDetailID UNIQUE CLUSTERED (HeaderID, DetailID)
,CONSTRAINT FK_Detail_FKP_HeaderID FOREIGN KEY (HeaderID) REFERENCES
IndexStrategiesHeader(HeaderID)
);
GO

INSERT INTO dbo.IndexStrategiesHeader(FillerData)
SELECT CONVERT(varchar,object_id)+name
FROM sys.indexes

INSERT INTO dbo.IndexStrategiesDetail_ICP
SELECT ish.HeaderID, CONVERT(varchar,ic.index_column_id)+'-'+FillerData
FROM dbo.IndexStrategiesHeader ish
        INNER JOIN sys.indexes i ON ish.FillerData = CONVERT(varchar,
        i.object_id)+i.name
        INNER JOIN sys.index_columns ic ON i.object_id = ic.object_id AND
        i.index_id = ic.index_id

INSERT INTO dbo.IndexStrategiesDetail_FKP
SELECT ish.HeaderID, CONVERT(varchar,ic.index_column_id)+'-'+FillerData
FROM dbo.IndexStrategiesHeader ish
        INNER JOIN sys.indexes i ON ish.FillerData = CONVERT(varchar,
        i.object_id)+i.name
        INNER JOIN sys.index_columns ic ON i.object_id = ic.object_id AND
        i.index_id = ic.index_id
```

CHAPTER 11 INDEXING STRATEGIES

At this point, you have three tables designed using the two clustered index patterns, Identity Sequence and Foreign Key. The key to this pattern is to design the table as such that in their common usage patterns the data will be returned as efficiently as possible. There are two use cases that are common in this type of a scenario. The first is returning the header and all the detail rows for one row in the header table. The second is to return multiple rows from the header table and all the related rows from the detail table.

First, let's examine the differences in performance for returning one row from the header table and all the related detail rows. The code in Listing 11-7 executes this use case against both clustered indexing patterns. As expected, the dataset returned by both queries is the same. The difference lies in the statistics and query plan for the two queries. First, let's look at the statistics output when STATISTICS IO is used during the first use case (shown in Figure 11-6). The reads for the Identity Column pattern show that there were four reads as opposed to two reads by the Foreign Key pattern. While these numbers are low, this is a twofold difference that could impact your database significantly if these are highly utilized queries. The big difference in execution, though, can be seen when reviewing the execution plans for the two queries (Figure 11-7). For the first query, to retrieve the results, an index seek, key lookup, and nested loop are required against the detail table. Compare this to the second query, which obtains the same information using a clustered index seek. This example clearly indicates that the Foreign Key pattern performs better than the Identity Column pattern.

Listing 11-7. Single Header Row on Foreign Key Pattern

```
Use AdventureWorks2017
GO

SET STATISTICS IO ON

SELECT  ish.HeaderID, ish.FillerData, isd.DetailID, isd.FillerData
FROM dbo.IndexStrategiesHeader ish
        INNER JOIN dbo.IndexStrategiesDetail_ICP isd ON ish.HeaderID =
        isd.HeaderID
WHERE ish.HeaderID = 10

SELECT  ish.HeaderID, ish.FillerData, isd.DetailID, isd.FillerData
FROM dbo.IndexStrategiesHeader ish
        INNER JOIN dbo.IndexStrategiesDetail_FKP isd ON ish.HeaderID =
        isd.HeaderID
WHERE ish.HeaderID = 10
```

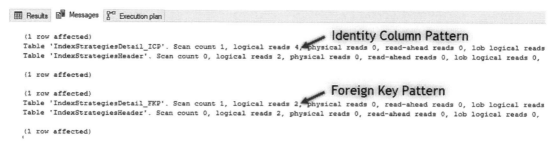

Figure 11-6. Results for single header row on Foreign Key pattern

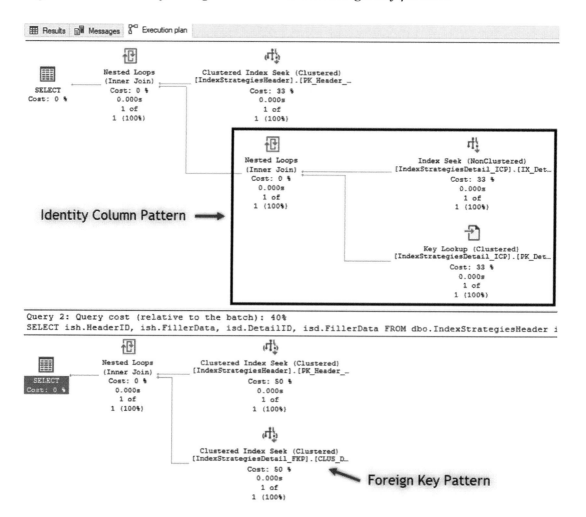

Figure 11-7. Execution plans for single header row on Foreign Key pattern

CHAPTER 11   INDEXING STRATEGIES

With the success of the first use case, let's examine the second use case. In this example, shown in Listing 11-8, the queries will retrieve multiple rows from the header table and will retrieve the data from the detail table that matches the HeaderID from the header rows. Again, the data returned by the queries using both of the clustered index patterns is the same, and there are performance differences between the two executions. The first difference is in the STATISTICS IO output, shown in Figure 11-8. In the first execution, there are 158 reads on the header table and 44 reads on the detail table. Comparing those to the four reads on the header and eight reads on the detail for the Foreign Key pattern, it's clear that the Foreign Key pattern performs better. In fact, the reads are a magnitude lower for the Foreign Key over the Identity Column pattern. The reason for the performance difference can be explained through the execution plan shown in Figure 11-9. In the execution plan, the first query requires a `clustered index scan` on the detail table to return the rows from the detail table. The second query, using the Foreign Key pattern, does not require this and uses a clustered index seek.

Listing 11-8. Multiple Header Row on Foreign Key Pattern

```
Use AdventureWorks2017
GO

SET STATISTICS IO ON

SELECT ish.HeaderID, ish.FillerData, isd.DetailID, isd.FillerData
FROM dbo.IndexStrategiesHeader ish
      INNER JOIN dbo.IndexStrategiesDetail_ICP isd ON ish.HeaderID =
      isd.HeaderID
WHERE ish.HeaderID BETWEEN 10 AND 50;

SELECT ish.HeaderID, ish.FillerData, isd.DetailID, isd.FillerData
FROM dbo.IndexStrategiesHeader ish
      INNER JOIN dbo.IndexStrategiesDetail_FKP isd ON ish.HeaderID =
      isd.HeaderID
WHERE ish.HeaderID BETWEEN 10 AND 50;
```

CHAPTER 11 INDEXING STRATEGIES

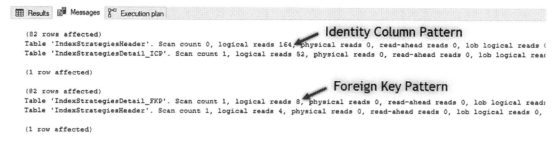

Figure 11-8. Results for multiple header row on Foreign Key pattern

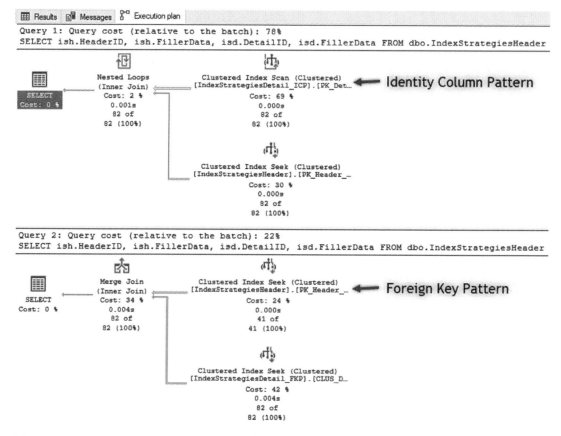

Figure 11-9. Execution plans for multiple header row on Foreign Key pattern

Through the two use cases in this section, we can see how the Foreign Key pattern can outperform the Identity Column pattern. However, there are things that need to be considered in databases before implementing this pattern. The chief question that needs to be answered is whether rows will most often be retrieved going through the primary key of the detail table or its foreign key relationship to the header table. Not all foreign keys are suited for this clustered index pattern; it is valid only when there is a header-to-detail relationship between tables.

As mentioned, there are a few caveats regarding the attributes of a well-defined clustered index when using the Foreign Key pattern. In regard to being narrow, the pattern is not as narrow as the Identity Column pattern. Instead of a single integer-based column, two of them make up the clustering keys. When using the int data type, this will increase the size of the clustering key from 4 bytes to 8 bytes. While not an overly large value, it will impact the size of the nonclustered indexes on the table. In most cases, the clustering keys under the Foreign Key pattern will be static. There is a chance that the header row for some detail rows will need to change from time to time, maybe when two orders are logged and need to be merged for shipping. For this reason, the Foreign Key pattern isn't entirely static. The key can change, but it shouldn't change frequently. If there are frequent changes, you should reconsider using this clustered index pattern. The last attribute that has a caveat is whether the clustering keys are ever-increasing. In general, this should be the case. The typical insert pattern is to create a header and the detail records. In this situation, the header rows are created and inserted sequentially, followed by their detail records. If there is a delay in writing the detail records or more detail records are added to a header row at a later date, the key won't be ever-increasing. As a result, there could be additional fragmentation and maintenance associated with this clustered index pattern.

The Foreign Key pattern is not a clustered index pattern that will be applicable in all databases. When it is, though, it is quite beneficial and can alleviate performance issues that may not be as obvious as other issues. It is important to consider using this pattern when designing clustered indexes and to review the caveats associated with it to determine whether it is the right fit.

Multiple Column

The next pattern that can be used to design clustered indexes is the Multiple Column pattern. In this pattern, two or more tables have a relationship to a third table that allows for many-to-many relationships to exist between the information. For instance, there might be a table that stores employee information and another that contains job roles. To represent the relationship, a third table is used. Through the Multiple Column pattern, instead of using a new column with the IDENTITY property on it, the columns used for the relationship serve as the clustering keys.

CHAPTER 11　INDEXING STRATEGIES

The Multiple Column pattern is similar to the Foreign Key pattern and provides many of the same performance enhancements as the previous pattern. As you will soon see, there is often one column or another in the many-to-many relationship table that is the best candidate for clustering key. Similar to the other patterns, this pattern also adheres to most of the attributes for a well-defined clustered index. The pattern is unique and mostly narrow and static; these properties will be apparent as you walk through an example of the Multiple Column pattern.

To demonstrate the Multiple Column pattern, let's begin by defining a few tables and their relationships. To start, there are tables that will store information about employees and job roles, named dbo.Employee and dbo.JobRole, respectively. Two tables named dbo.EmployeeJobRole_ICP and dbo.EmployeeJobRole_MCP are used to represent the Identity Column and Multiple Column patterns in the example relationships (see Listing 11-9). The example script includes insert statements to provide some sample data to use. Also, nonclustered indexes are created on the tables to provide a real-world scenario.

Listing 11-9. Multiple Column Pattern Script

```
USE AdventureWorks2017
GO

CREATE TABLE dbo.Employee (
EmployeeID int IDENTITY(1,1)
,EmployeeName varchar(100)
,FillerData varchar(1000)
,CONSTRAINT PK_Employee PRIMARY KEY CLUSTERED (EmployeeID));

CREATE INDEX IX_Employee_EmployeeName ON dbo.Employee(EmployeeName);

CREATE TABLE dbo.JobRole (
JobRoleID int IDENTITY(1,1)
,RoleName varchar(25)
,FillerData varchar(200)
,CONSTRAINT PK_JobRole PRIMARY KEY CLUSTERED (JobRoleID));

CREATE INDEX IX_JobRole_RoleName ON dbo.JobRole(RoleName);
```

CHAPTER 11 INDEXING STRATEGIES

```sql
CREATE TABLE dbo.EmployeeJobRole_ICP (
EmployeeJobRoleID int IDENTITY(1,1)
,EmployeeID int
,JobRoleID int
,CONSTRAINT PK_EmployeeJobRole_ICP PRIMARY KEY CLUSTERED
(EmployeeJobRoleID)
,CONSTRAINT UIX_EmployeeJobRole_ICP UNIQUE (EmployeeID, JobRoleID))

CREATE INDEX IX_EmployeeJobRole_ICP_EmployeeID ON dbo.EmployeeJobRole_
ICP(EmployeeID);
CREATE INDEX IX_EmployeeJobRole_ICP_JobRoleID ON dbo.EmployeeJobRole_
ICP(JobRoleID);

CREATE TABLE dbo.EmployeeJobRole_MCP (
EmployeeJobRoleID int IDENTITY(1,1)
,EmployeeID int
,JobRoleID int
,CONSTRAINT PK_EmployeeJobRoleID PRIMARY KEY NONCLUSTERED
(EmployeeJobRoleID)
,CONSTRAINT CUIX_EmployeeJobRole_ICP UNIQUE CLUSTERED (EmployeeID,
JobRoleID));

CREATE INDEX IX_EmployeeJobRole_MCP_JobRoleID ON dbo.EmployeeJobRole_
MCP(JobRoleID);

INSERT INTO dbo.Employee (EmployeeName)
SELECT OBJECT_SCHEMA_NAME(object_id)+'|'+name
FROM sys.tables;

INSERT INTO dbo.JobRole (RoleName)
VALUES ('Cook'),('Butcher'),('Candlestick Maker');

INSERT INTO dbo.EmployeeJobRole_ICP (EmployeeID, JobRoleID)
SELECT EmployeeID, 1 FROM dbo.Employee
UNION ALL SELECT EmployeeID, 2 FROM dbo.Employee WHERE EmployeeID / 4 = 1
UNION ALL SELECT EmployeeID, 3 FROM dbo.Employee WHERE EmployeeID / 8 = 1;
```

```
INSERT INTO dbo.EmployeeJobRole_MCP (EmployeeID, JobRoleID)
SELECT EmployeeID, 1 FROM dbo.Employee
UNION ALL SELECT EmployeeID, 2 FROM dbo.Employee WHERE EmployeeID / 4 = 1
UNION ALL SELECT EmployeeID, 3 FROM dbo.Employee WHERE EmployeeID / 8 = 1;
```

The first test against the example tables will look at querying against all three tables to retrieve information on employee names and job roles. These queries, shown in Listing 11-10, retrieve information based on the RoleName from dbo.JobRole. In the code, the two versions of the EmployeeJobRole table are created with different clustering keys. This results in a drastic difference in the execution plans, shown in Figure 11-10 and Figure 11-11, from the test queries. The first execution plan using the table with the Identity Column pattern applied to it is more complex than the execution plan for the second query and has 61 percent of the cost compared to the other plan. The second plan, which has its clustering keys based on the Multiple Column pattern, has fewer operations and accounts for 39 percent of the execution. The main difference between the two plans is that using the Multiple Column pattern allows the clustered index to cover table access based on a column that is likely to be used to frequently access rows in the table, in this case the JobRoleID column. Using the other pattern does not provide this benefit and represents a data access path that will not likely be used, except maybe when needing to delete the row.

Listing 11-10. Script for Multiple Column Pattern

```
USE AdventureWorks2017
GO

SELECT e.EmployeeName, jr.RoleName
FROM dbo.Employee e
INNER JOIN dbo.EmployeeJobRole_ICP ejr ON e.EmployeeID = ejr.EmployeeID
INNER JOIN dbo.JobRole jr ON ejr.JobRoleID = jr.JobRoleID
WHERE RoleName = 'Candlestick Maker'

SELECT e.EmployeeName, jr.RoleName
FROM dbo.Employee e
INNER JOIN dbo.EmployeeJobRole_MCP ejr ON e.EmployeeID = ejr.EmployeeID
INNER JOIN dbo.JobRole jr ON ejr.JobRoleID = jr.JobRoleID
WHERE RoleName = 'Candlestick Maker'
```

CHAPTER 11 INDEXING STRATEGIES

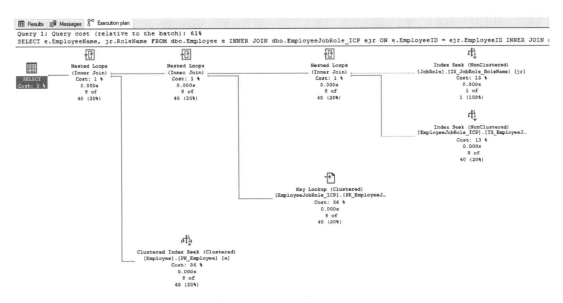

Figure 11-10. *Execution plan for Identity Column pattern*

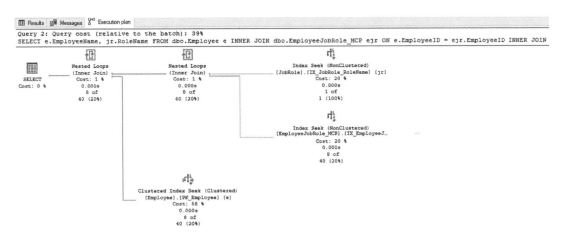

Figure 11-11. *Execution plan for Multiple Column pattern*

While the benefits are significant with the first test results, they are less impressive when looking at some other methods that can be used. For instance, say that instead of using RoleName as the predicate, the EmployeeName was the predicate. The script in Listing 11-11 demonstrates this scenario. Contrary to the last test script, the results this time are no different than the others for either clustered index design (see Figure 11-12 and Figure 11-13). The cause of the identical plans in the figure is based on the decision to optimize the clustering index keys in the Multiple Column pattern to favor the JobRoleID. When the EmployeeID column is used to access the data, the nonclustered

377

index provides most of the heavy lifting, and a good, similar, plan for each query is created. The results of this second test do not discount the use of the Multiple Column pattern, but they do highlight that the column to lead the clustering key should be selected after performing tests with the expected workload.

Listing 11-11. Script for Multiple Column Pattern

```
USE AdventureWorks2017
GO

SELECT e.EmployeeName, jr.RoleName
FROM dbo.Employee e
INNER JOIN dbo.EmployeeJobRole_ICP ejr ON e.EmployeeID = ejr.EmployeeID
INNER JOIN dbo.JobRole jr ON ejr.JobRoleID = jr.JobRoleID
WHERE EmployeeName = 'Purchasing|ShipMethod'

SELECT e.EmployeeName, jr.RoleName
FROM dbo.Employee e
INNER JOIN dbo.EmployeeJobRole_MCP ejr ON e.EmployeeID = ejr.EmployeeID
INNER JOIN dbo.JobRole jr ON ejr.JobRoleID = jr.JobRoleID
WHERE EmployeeName = 'Purchasing|ShipMethod'
```

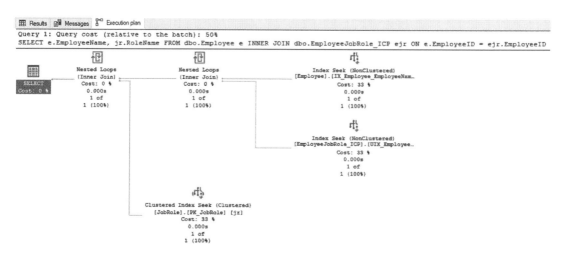

Figure 11-12. *Execution plan for Identity Column pattern*

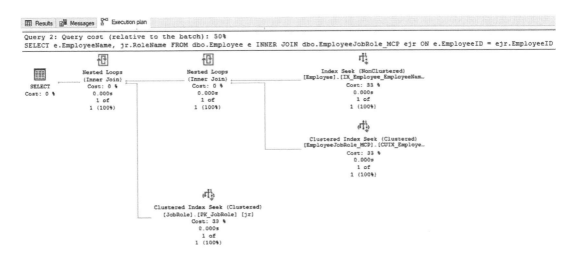

Figure 11-13. Execution plan for Multiple Column pattern

There are various ways in which the Multiple Column pattern can be implemented. The key columns in the clustered index can be reversed, which would change the execution plans generated for the test scripts. While this pattern can be beneficial, be cautious when using it and fully understand the workload expected before using it.

To wrap up the Multiple Column pattern, let's review the attributes of a well-defined clustered index. First, the values are static. If there were to be a change, it would likely be deleting a record and inserting a new record. This is still effectively an update to mitigate this risk attempt to lead the clustered index with the value least likely to change or have variations in population. The second is whether the clustering key is narrow. In this example, the key was mostly narrow. It was comprised of two 4-byte columns. If using larger columns or more than two columns, carefully consider if this is the right approach. The next attribute is whether the values are unique. They are in this scenario and should be in any scenario in the real world. If not, then this pattern is naturally disqualified. Like with the other non-Identity Column patterns, this pattern does not provide an ever-increasing clustering key.

As a final note, fact tables in data warehouses often succumb to the temptation to use the Multiple Column pattern. In these cases, all the dimension keys in the fact table are placed in the clustered index. The aim in doing this is to enforce uniqueness on the fact rows. The effect is the creation of an extremely wide clustering key, which is then added to all the nonclustered indexes on the table. Most likely, each of the dimension columns in the clustered key will have a separate index on the fact table. As a result, these indexes waste a lot of space and, because of their size, perform much worse than if the uniqueness on the fact table were constrained by a nonclustered unique index.

Globally Unique Identifier

The last, and definitely least beneficial, or popular, pattern for selecting a clustered index column is to use a globally unique identifier, also known as a GUID. The GUID pattern involves using a uniquely generated value to provide a unique value for each row in a table. This value is not integer-based and is often chosen because it can be generated at any location (within the topology of an application) and has a guarantee that it will be unique. The problem this pattern solves is the need to be able to generate new unique values while disconnecting from the source that typically controls the list of unique values. Unfortunately, the GUID pattern causes nearly as many issues as it solves.

There are two main methods for generating GUID values. The first is through the NEWID() function. This function generates a 16-byte hexadecimal value that is partially based on the MAC address of the computer creating it at the time. Each value generated is unique and can start with any value from 0 to 9 or a to f. The next value created can be either ahead of or after the previous value in a sort. There is no guarantee that the next value is ever-increasing. The second option for generating a GUID is through NEWSEQUENTIALID(). This function also creates a 16-byte hexadecimal value. Unlike the other function, NEWSEQUENTIALID() creates new values that are greater than the previous value generated since the computer was last started. The last point is important: when the server restarts, it is possible that new values with NEWSEQUENTIALID() will be less than the value created before the restart. The logic for NEWSEQUENTIALID() ensures sequential values only from the time in which the server is started.

As discussed, using the GUID pattern does not provide for an ever-increasing value. With either NEWID() or NEWSEQUENTIALID(), there is no guarantee that the next value will always be greater than the last value. Along with that, it does not provide a narrow index. When storing a GUID as a uniqueidentifier, it requires 16 bytes of storage. This is the size of four ints or two bigints. Comparatively, the GUID is quite large, and that value will be placed in all nonclustered indexes on the table. The space used for the GUID pattern can sometimes be worse than this, though. In some cases, when the GUID pattern is poorly implemented, the GUID value is stored as characters that require 36 bytes to store or 72 bytes if using a Unicode data type.

Even with the failings of the GUID pattern, it does achieve some of the other attributes of a well-defined clustering key. First, the value is unique. With both the NEWID() and NEWSEQUENTIALID() functions, the values generated for the GUID value are unique. The value is also static since the GUID value generated has no business, meaning there is no reason for it to change the value.

CHAPTER 11 INDEXING STRATEGIES

To demonstrate impact of implementing the GUID pattern, let's examine its use on a table with a comparison to a couple other implementations. In this scenario, shown in Listing 11-12, there are three tables. Table dbo.IndexStrategiesGUID_ICP is designed using the Identity Column pattern. Table dbo.IndexStrategiesGUID_UniqueID is built with the GUID pattern using a uniqueidentifier, as best practices dictate. The last script contains table dbo.IndexStrategiesGUID_String, which uses a varchar(36) to store the GUID value. The last method is not the proper way to implement the GUID pattern, and the analysis will help highlight that. With all three tables built, insert statements will populate 250,000 rows to each table. The final statement in the scenario retrieves the number of pages used by each of the tables.

Listing 11-12. Script for GUID Pattern Scenario

```
USE AdventureWorks2017
GO

CREATE TABLE dbo.IndexStrategiesGUID_ICP (
RowID int IDENTITY(1,1)
,FillerData varchar(1000)
,CONSTRAINT PK_IndexStrategiesGUID_ICP PRIMARY KEY CLUSTERED (RowID)
);

CREATE TABLE dbo.IndexStrategiesGUID_UniqueID (
RowID uniqueidentifier DEFAULT(NEWSEQUENTIALID())
,FillerData varchar(1000)
,CONSTRAINT PK_IndexStrategiesGUID_UniqueID PRIMARY KEY CLUSTERED (RowID)
);

CREATE TABLE dbo.IndexStrategiesGUID_String (
RowID varchar(36) DEFAULT(NEWID())
,FillerData varchar(1000)
,CONSTRAINT PK_IndexStrategiesGUID_String PRIMARY KEY CLUSTERED (RowID)
);

INSERT INTO dbo.IndexStrategiesGUID_ICP (FillerData)
SELECT TOP (250000) a1.name+a2.name
FROM sys.all_objects a1 CROSS JOIN sys.all_objects a2
```

```sql
INSERT INTO dbo.IndexStrategiesGUID_UniqueID (FillerData)
SELECT TOP (250000) a1.name+a2.name
FROM sys.all_objects a1 CROSS JOIN sys.all_objects a2

INSERT INTO dbo.IndexStrategiesGUID_String (FillerData)
SELECT TOP (250000) a1.name+a2.name
FROM sys.all_objects a1 CROSS JOIN sys.all_objects a2

SELECT OBJECT_NAME(object_ID) as table_name, in_row_used_page_count, in_
row_reserved_page_count
FROM sys.dm_db_partition_stats
WHERE object_id IN (OBJECT_ID('dbo.IndexStrategiesGUID_ICP')
        ,OBJECT_ID('dbo.IndexStrategiesGUID_UniqueID')
        ,OBJECT_ID('dbo.IndexStrategiesGUID_String'))
ORDER BY 1
```

Figure 11-14 shows some output from this query.

	table_name	in_row_used_page_count	in_row_reserved_page_count
1	IndexStrategiesGUID_ICP	1869	1889
2	IndexStrategiesGUID_String	2959	2977
3	IndexStrategiesGUID_UniqueID	2250	2273

Figure 11-14. *Page counts for GUID pattern*

Unlike the other scenarios, the use of the GUID pattern is much like the Identity Column pattern. There are two primary differences. First, the GUID pattern does not provide a narrow clustering key. For the clustering key with the uniqueidentifier data type, the change in size of the clustering key requires around 400 more pages to store the same information (see Figure 11-14). Even worse, when improperly storing the GUID in the varchar data type, the table requires about 1,100 more pages. Without a doubt, using the GUID pattern amounts to a lot of wasted space in the clustered index, which would also be included in any nonclustered indexes on the table. The second issue with the GUID pattern is tied with the ever-increasing attribute of clustered indexes. As already discussed, GUIDs are not presented in an ordered fashion. The next value can be greater or less than the previous value, and this leads to a random placement of rows within a table, which results in fragmentation. For more information on index fragmentation as a result of GUIDs, read Chapter 6.

In regard to the last two attributes of a well-defined clustering key, the GUID pattern does well with those. The value is static and should not be expected to change over time. The value is also unique. It should, in fact, be unique throughout the entire database. Even though the GUID pattern does achieve the two attributes of a well-defined clustered index, they do not mitigate the aforementioned issues with this pattern. The GUID pattern should be a pattern of last resort when determining how to build the clustered index for a table.

> **Note** Using the new `sp_sequence_get_range` stored procedure in conjunction with SEQUENCEs can be a valid replacement in applications using the `uniqueidentifier` pattern that would like to migrate to using an Identity Column pattern for clustered index design.

Nonclustered Indexes

In the previous two sections, the discussion focused on heaps and clustered indexes, which are used to determine how to store the data. With heaps, the data is stored unsorted. With clustered indexes, data is sorted based on one set of columns. In nearly all databases, there will need to be other ways of accessing the data in the table that don't align with the sort order in which the data is stored. This is where nonclustered indexes come in. Nonclustered indexes provide another method for accessing data in addition to the heap or clustered index to locate data in a table.

In this section, we'll review a number of patterns that are associated with nonclustered indexes. These patterns will help identify when and where to consider building nonclustered indexes. For each pattern, we'll go through the chief components and situations where it may be leveraged. Similar to the clustered index patterns, each nonclustered index pattern will include a scenario or two to demonstrate the benefit of the pattern. The nonclustered index patterns that will be discussed are

- Search Columns
- Index Intersection
- Multiple Column
- Covering Index

- Included Columns
- Filtered Indexes
- Foreign Keys

Before you review the patterns, there are a number of guidelines that will apply to all the nonclustered indexes. These guidelines differ from the attributes of well-defined clustered indexes. With the attributes, one of the key goals was to adhere to them as much as possible. With the nonclustered indexing guidelines, they form a number of considerations that will help strengthen the case for an index but may not disqualify the use of the index. Some of the most common considerations to think of when designing indexes are the following:

- *What is the frequency of change for the nonclustered index key columns?* The more frequent the data changes, the more often the row in the nonclustered may need to change its position in the index.

- *What frequent queries will the index improve?* The greater the overall lift an index provides, the better the database platform will operate as a whole.

- *What business needs does the index support?* Infrequently used indexes that support critical business operations can sometimes be more important than frequently used indexes.

- *What is the cost in time to maintain the index vs. the cost in time to query the data?* There can be a point where the performance gain from an index is outweighed by the time spent creating and defragmenting an index and the space that it requires.

As mentioned in the introduction, indexing can often feel like art. Fortunately, science or statistics can be used to demonstrate the value of indexes. As each of these patterns is reviewed, we'll look at scenarios where they can be applied and use some science, or metrics in this case, to determine whether the index provides value. The two things that will be used to judge indexes will be reads during the execution and complexity of the execution plan.

Search Columns

The most basic and common pattern for designing nonclustered indexes is to build them based on defined or expected search patterns. The Search Columns pattern should be the most widely known pattern but also happens to be easily, and often, overlooked.

If queries will be searching tables with contacts in them by first name, then index the first name column. If the address table will have searches against it by city or state, then index those columns. The primary goal of the Search Columns pattern is to reduce scans against the clustered index and move those operations to a nonclustered index that can provide more direct route to the data through a nonclustered index.

To demonstrate the Search Columns pattern, let's use the first scenario mentioned in this section, a contact table. For simplicity, the examples will use a table named dbo. Contacts that contains data from the AdventureWorks2017 table Person.Person (see Listing 11-13). There should be about 19,972 rows inserted into dbo.Contacts, though this will vary depending on the freshness of your AdventureWorks2017 database.

Listing 11-13. Setup for Search Columns Pattern

```
USE AdventureWorks2017;
GO

CREATE TABLE dbo.Contacts (
    ContactID INT IDENTITY(1, 1),
    FirstName NVARCHAR(50),
    LastName NVARCHAR(50),
    IsActive BIT,
    EmailAddress NVARCHAR(50),
    CertificationDate DATETIME,
    FillerData CHAR(1000),
    CONSTRAINT PK_Contacts PRIMARY KEY CLUSTERED (ContactID));

INSERT INTO dbo.Contacts (
    FirstName,
    LastName,
    IsActive,
    EmailAddress,
    CertificationDate )
```

CHAPTER 11   INDEXING STRATEGIES

```
SELECT pp.FirstName,
       pp.LastName,
       IIF(pp.BusinessEntityID / 10 = 1, 1, 0),
       pea.EmailAddress,
       IIF(pp.BusinessEntityID / 10 = 1, pp.ModifiedDate, NULL)
FROM Person.Person pp
    INNER JOIN Person.EmailAddress pea
        ON pp.BusinessEntityID = pea.BusinessEntityID;
```

With the table dbo.Contacts in place, the first test against the table is to query the table with no nonclustered indexes built on it. In the example, shown in Listing 11-14, the query is searching for rows with the first name of Catherine. Executing the query shows that there are 22 rows in dbo.Contacts that match the criteria (see Figure 11-15). To retrieve the 22 rows, SQL Server ended up reading 2,866 pages, which is all the pages in the table. And as Figure 11-16 indicates, the page reads were the result of an index scan against PK_Contacts on dbo.Contacts. The aim of the query is to retrieve 22 out of the more than 19,000 rows, so checking every page in the table for rows with Catherine for FirstName is not an optimal approach and is one that can be avoided.

Listing 11-14. Search Columns Pattern

```
USE AdventureWorks2017;
GO

SET STATISTICS IO ON;

SELECT ContactID,
       FirstName
FROM dbo.Contacts
WHERE FirstName = 'Catherine';
```

```
(22 rows affected)
Table 'Contacts'. Scan count 1, logical reads 2866, physical reads 0, read-ahead reads 0, lob logical reads 0,

(1 row affected)
```

Figure 11-15. Statistics I/O results for Search Columns pattern

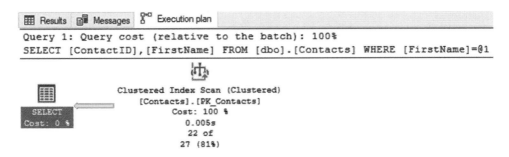

Figure 11-16. Execution plan for Search Columns pattern

Achieving the aim of retrieving all the rows for Catherine optimally is relatively simple by adding a nonclustered index to dbo.Contacts. In the next script (Listing 11-15), a nonclustered index is created on the FirstName column. Besides the filter on FirstName, the query needs to also return ContactID. Since nonclustered indexes include the clustering index key, the value in ContactID is included in the index by default.

Executing the script in Listing 11-15 leads to substantially different results than before the nonclustered index was added to the table. Instead of reading every page in the table, the nonclustered index reduces the number of pages used for the query to two pages (Figure 11-17). The reduction here is significant and highlights the power and value in using nonclustered indexes to provide more direct access to information in your tables on columns other than those in the clustered index keys. There is one other change in the execution: instead of a scan against PK_Index, the execution plan now uses an index seek against IC_Contacts_FirstName, shown in Figure 11-18. The change in the operator is further proof that the nonclustered index helped to improve the performance of the query.

Listing 11-15. Search Columns Pattern

```
USE AdventureWorks2017;
GO

CREATE INDEX IX_Contacts_FirstName ON dbo.Contacts (FirstName);

SET STATISTICS IO ON;

SELECT ContactID,
       FirstName
FROM dbo.Contacts
WHERE FirstName = 'Catherine';
```

CHAPTER 11 INDEXING STRATEGIES

```
(22 rows affected)
Table 'Contacts'. Scan count 1, logical reads 2, physical reads 0, read-ahead reads 0, lob logical reads 0, lob physical reads 0, ]

(1 row affected)
```

Figure 11-17. *Statistics I/O results for Search Columns pattern*

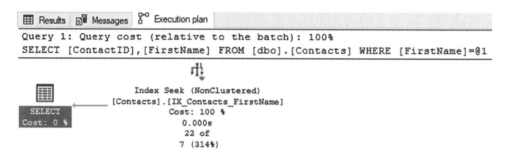

Figure 11-18. *Execution plan for Search Columns pattern*

Using the Search Columns pattern is probably the most important first step in applying nonclustered indexing patterns on your databases. It provides the alternative paths for accessing data that can be the difference between getting your data from a couple pages vs. thousands of pages. The Search Columns example in this section shows building an index on a single column. The next few patterns will expand on this foundation.

Index Intersection

The aim of the Search Columns pattern is to create an index that will minimize the page reads for a query and improve the performance of it. Sometimes, though, the queries go beyond the single column example that was demonstrated. Additional columns may be part of the predicate or returned in the SELECT statement. One of the ways to address this is to create nonclustered indexes that include the additional columns. When there are indexes that can satisfy each of the predicates in the WHERE clause, SQL Server can utilize multiple nonclustered indexes to find the rows between both that match on the clustering key. This operation is called Index Intersection.

To demonstrate the Index Intersection pattern, let's first review what happens when the filtering is expanded to cover multiple columns. The code in Listing 11-16 includes the expanded SELECT statement and WHERE clause, expanding the predicate to include rows where LastName is Cox.

CHAPTER 11 INDEXING STRATEGIES

The change in the query results in a significant change in performance over the previous section's results. With the additional column in the query, there are 68 pages read to satisfy the query vs. the 2 pages when LastName was not included (Figure 11-19). The increase in pages read is because of the change in the execution plan (Figure 11-20). In the execution plan, an additional two operations are added to the execution of the query: a key lookup and a nested loop. These operators are added because the index IX_Contacts_FirstName can't provide all the information needed to satisfy the query. SQL Server determines that it is still cheaper to use IX_Contacts_FirstName and look up the missing information from the clustered index than to scan the clustered index. The problem that you can run into is that for every row that matches on the nonclustered index, a lookup has to be done on the clustered index. While key lookups aren't always a problem, they can drive up the CPU and I/O costs for a query unnecessarily.

Listing 11-16. Index Intersection Pattern

```
USE AdventureWorks2017;
GO

SET STATISTICS IO ON;

SELECT ContactID,
       FirstName,
       LastName
FROM dbo.Contacts
WHERE FirstName = 'Catherine'
    AND LastName = 'Cox';
```

```
(1 row affected)
Table 'Contacts'. Scan count 1, logical reads 68, physical reads 0, read-ahead reads 0, lob logical reads 0, lob physical reads 0,
(1 row affected)
```

Figure 11-19. *Statistics I/O results for Index Intersection pattern*

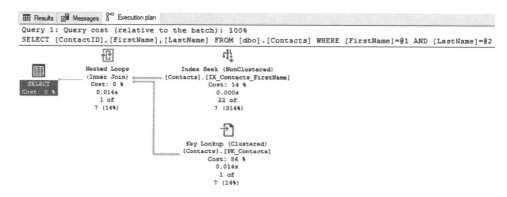

Figure 11-20. *Execution plan for Index Intersection pattern*

Leveraging the Index Intersection pattern is one of a few ways that the performance of the query in Listing 11-16 can be improved. An index intersection occurs when SQL Server can utilize multiple nonclustered indexes on the same table to satisfy the requirements for a query. In the case of the query in Listing 11-16, the most direct path for finding FirstNames was through the index IX_Contacts_FirstName. At that point, though, to filter and return the LastName column, SQL Server used the clustered index and performed a lookup on each row, similar to the image on the left side of Figure 11-21. Alternatively, if there had been an index for the LastName column, SQL Server could have used that index with IX_Contacts_FirstName. In essence, through the Index Intersection pattern, SQL Server is able to perform operations similar to joins between indexes on the same table to find rows that overlap between the two, as shown on the right of Figure 11-21.

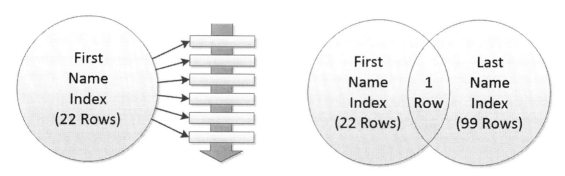

Figure 11-21. *Index seek with key lookup vs. two index seeks using Index Intersection pattern*

To demonstrate the Index Intersection pattern and have SQL Server use index intersection, the next example creates an index on the LastName column (Listing 11-17). With the index IX_Contacts_LastName created, the results change significantly from when the index had not been created. The first significant change is in the number of reads. Instead of the 68 reads that occurred in the previous execution, there are only 5 reads (Figure 11-22). The cause of the reduction in reads is from SQL Server leveraging index intersection in the query plan (Figure 11-23). The indexes IX_Contacts_FirstName and IX_Contacts_LastName were used to satisfy the query without returning to the clustered index to retrieve data for the query. This happened because the two indexes can satisfy the query completely.

Listing 11-17. Index Intersection Pattern

```
USE AdventureWorks2017;
GO

CREATE INDEX IX_Contacts_LastName ON dbo.Contacts (LastName);

SET STATISTICS IO ON;

SELECT ContactID,
       FirstName,
       LastName
FROM dbo.Contacts
WHERE FirstName = 'Catherine'
      AND LastName = 'Cox';
```

```
(1 row affected)
Table 'Contacts'. Scan count 2, logical reads 5, physical reads 0, read-ahead reads 0, lob logical reads 0,

(1 row affected)
```

Figure 11-22. Statistics I/O results for Index Intersection pattern

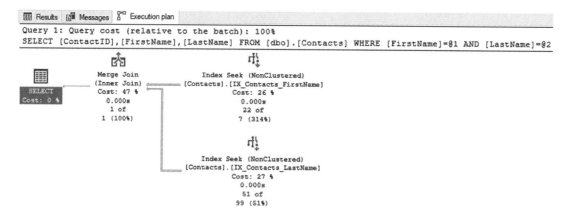

Figure 11-23. *Execution plan for Index Intersection pattern*

Index intersection is a feature of SQL Server that it uses to better satisfy queries when more than one nonclustered index from the same table can provide the results for the queries. When indexing for index intersection, the aim is to have multiple indexes based on the Search Columns pattern that can be used together in numerous combinations to allow for a variety of filters. One key thing to remember with the Index Intersection pattern is that you can't tell SQL Server when to use index intersection; it will opt to use it when it is appropriate for the request, underlying indexes, and data.

Multiple Column

The examples in the previous two sections focused on indexes that included a single key column in the index. Nonclustered indexes, though, can have up to 16 columns. While being narrow was an attribute of a well-defined clustered index, the same does not always apply to nonclustered indexes. Instead, nonclustered indexes should contain as many columns as necessary to be used by the most queries possible. If many queries will use the same columns as predicates, it is often a good idea to include them all in a single index.

A simple method for demonstrating an index using the Multiple Column pattern is to use the same query from the previous section and apply this pattern to it. In that query, two indexes were built, one each on the FirstName and LastName columns. For the Multiple Column pattern, the new index will include both the columns together (Listing 11-18).

CHAPTER 11 INDEXING STRATEGIES

As the statistics indicate (Figure 11-24), by using the Multiple Column pattern, there is a reduction in the number of reads necessary to return the request results. Instead of five reads from the Index Intersection pattern, there are only two reads with the Multiple Column pattern. Additionally, the execution plan (shown in Figure 11-25) has been simplified. There is only an index seek on the index IX_Contacts_FirstNameLastName.

Listing 11-18. Multiple Column Pattern

```
USE AdventureWorks2017;
GO

CREATE INDEX IX_Contacts_FirstNameLastName
  ON dbo.Contacts (FirstName, LastName);

SET STATISTICS IO ON;

SELECT ContactID,
       FirstName,
       LastName
FROM dbo.Contacts
WHERE FirstName = 'Catherine'
      AND LastName = 'Cox';
```

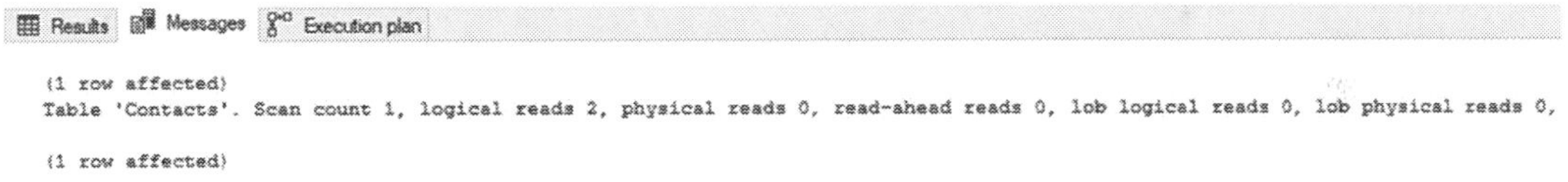

```
(1 row affected)
Table 'Contacts'. Scan count 1, logical reads 2, physical reads 0, read-ahead reads 0, lob logical reads 0, lob physical reads 0,

(1 row affected)
```

Figure 11-24. *Statistics I/O results for Multiple Column pattern*

```
Query 1: Query cost (relative to the batch): 100%
SELECT [ContactID],[FirstName],[LastName] FROM [dbo].[Contacts] WHERE [FirstName]=@1 AND [LastName]=@2
```

```
                    Index Seek (NonClustered)
                    [Contacts].[IX_Contacts_FirstNameLa...
  SELECT                    Cost: 100 %
  Cost: 0 %                   0.000s
                               1 of
                              1 (100%)
```

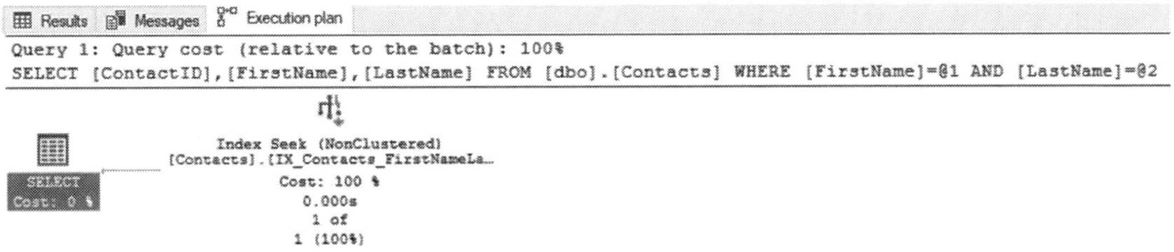

Figure 11-25. *Execution plan for Multiple Column pattern*

CHAPTER 11   INDEXING STRATEGIES

The Multiple Column pattern is as important to implement as the Search Columns pattern when indexing your databases. This pattern can help reduce the number of indexes used by putting the columns together that are most often used in predicates. While this pattern does contradict some of the value of the Index Intersection pattern, the key between them is balance. In some cases, relying on index intersection on single-column indexes will provide the best performance for a table with many variations on the query predicates. In other times, wider indexes with specific orders to the columns will be beneficial. Try both patterns and apply them in the manner that provides the best overall performance. Remember indexes can always be removed if they don't work out.

Covering Index

The next indexing pattern to be aware of is the Covering Index pattern. With the Covering Index pattern, columns outside the predicates are added to an index's key columns to allow those values to be returned as part of the SELECT clauses of queries. This pattern has been a standard indexing practice for a while with SQL Server. Enhancements in how indexes can be created, though, make this pattern less useful than it was in the past. I am discussing it here because it is a common pattern that most already know.

To begin looking at the Covering Index pattern, we'll first need an example to define the problem that the index solves. To show the issue, the next test query will include the IsActive column in the SELECT list (Listing 11-19). With this column added, the I/O statistics increase again from two reads to five reads, shown in Figure 11-26. The change in performance is directly related to the change in the execution plan (see Figure 11-27) that includes a key lookup and a nested loop. As with the previous examples, as items not included in the nonclustered index are added to the query, they need to be retrieved from the clustered index, which contains all the data for the table.

Listing 11-19. Covering Index Pattern

```
USE AdventureWorks2017;
GO

SET STATISTICS IO ON;

SELECT ContactID,
       FirstName,
       LastName,
       IsActive
```

CHAPTER 11 INDEXING STRATEGIES

```
FROM dbo.Contacts
WHERE FirstName = 'Catherine'
      AND LastName = 'Cox';
```

```
(1 row affected)
Table 'Contacts'. Scan count 1, logical reads 5, physical reads 0, read-ahead reads 0, lob logical reads 0,

(1 row affected)
```

Figure 11-26. *Statistics I/O results for Covering Index pattern*

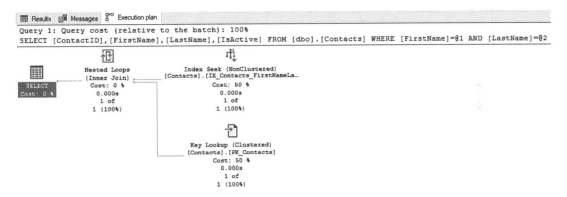

Figure 11-27. *Execution plan for Covering Index pattern*

Ideally, you want an index in place that can accommodate the filters on the index and can also rerun the columns requested in the SELECT list. The Covering Index pattern can fulfill these requirements. Even though IsActive is not one of the predicates for the query, it can be added to the index, and SQL Server can use that key column to return the column values with the query. To demonstrate the Covering Index pattern, let's create an index that has FirstName, LastName, and IsActive as the key columns (see Listing 11-20). With the index IX_Contacts_FirstNameLastName in place, the reads return to two per execution (see Figure 11-28). The execution plan is also now using only an index seek (see Figure 11-29).

CHAPTER 11　INDEXING STRATEGIES

Listing 11-20. Covering Index Pattern

```
USE AdventureWorks2017
GO

CREATE INDEX IX_Contacts_FirstNameLastNameIsActive ON dbo.Contacts(FirstName,
LastName, IsActive);

SET STATISTICS IO ON;

SELECT ContactID,
       FirstName,
       LastName,
       IsActive
FROM dbo.Contacts
WHERE FirstName = 'Catherine'
    AND LastName = 'Cox';
```

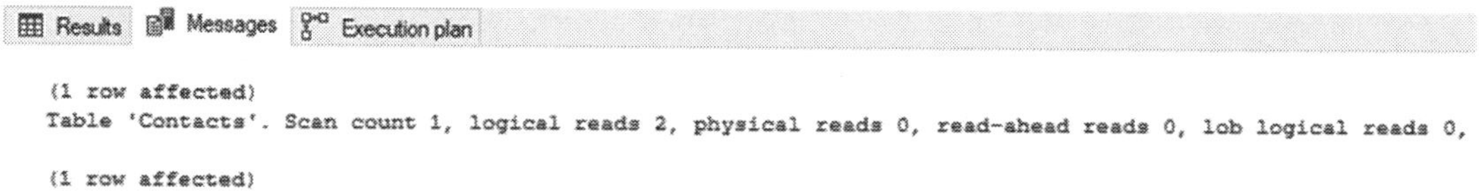

```
(1 row affected)
Table 'Contacts'. Scan count 1, logical reads 2, physical reads 0, read-ahead reads 0, lob logical reads 0,

(1 row affected)
```

Figure 11-28. *Statistics I/O results for Covering Index pattern*

```
Query 1: Query cost (relative to the batch): 100%
SELECT [ContactID],[FirstName],[LastName],[IsActive] FROM [dbo].[Contacts] WHERE [FirstName]=@1 AND [LastName]=@2

                    Index Seek (NonClustered)
                    [Contacts].[IX_Contacts_FirstNameLa...
   SELECT              Cost: 100 %
   Cost: 0 %           0.000s
                       1 of
                       1 (100%)
```

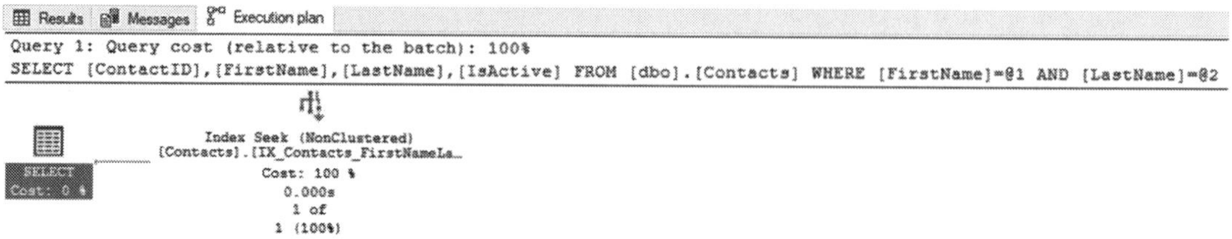

Figure 11-29. *Execution plan for Covering Index pattern*

The Covering Index pattern can be quite useful and has the potential to improve performance in many areas. In the last few years, the use of this pattern has diminished. This change in use is primarily being driven by the availability of the option to include columns in indexes, which was introduced with SQL Server 2005.

Note Some consider covering indexes and indexes with included columns the same thing. While very similar, the key difference between the two is the location of the columns as part of the key or data included in the index.

Included Columns

The Included Columns pattern is a close cousin to the Covering Index pattern. The Included Columns pattern leverages the INCLUDE clause of the CREATE and ALTER INDEX syntax. The clause allows nonkey columns to be added to nonclustered indexes, similar to how nonkey data is stored on clustered indexes. This is the primary difference between the Included Columns and Covering Index patterns, where the additional columns in the Covering Index are key columns on the index. Like clustered indexes, the nonkey columns that are part of the INCLUDE clause are not sorted, although they can be used as predicates in some queries.

The use case for the Included Columns pattern comes from the flexibility that it provides. It is generally the same as the Covering Index pattern, and sometimes the names are used interchangeably. The key difference, which is demonstrated in this section, is that the Covering Index pattern is limited by the sort order of all the columns in the index. The Included Columns pattern can avoid this potential issue by including nonkey data, thereby increasing its flexibility of use.

Before demonstrating the flexibility of the Included Columns pattern, let's first examine another index against the dbo.Contacts table. In Listing 11-21, the query is filtering just on a FirstName value of Catherine and returning the ContactID, FirstName, LastName, and EmailAddress columns. This query request differs from the other examples because it now includes the EmailAddress column. Since this column is not included in any of the other nonclustered indexes, none of them can fully satisfy the query. As a result, the execution plan utilizes IX_Contacts_FirstName to identify the Catherine rows and then looks up the rest of the data from the clustered index, shown in Figure 11-30. With the key lookup, the reads for the query also increase to 68 reads (see Figure 11-31), as they have in previous examples.

CHAPTER 11 INDEXING STRATEGIES

Listing 11-21. Included Columns Pattern

```
USE AdventureWorks2017;
GO

SET STATISTICS IO ON;

SELECT ContactID,
       FirstName,
       LastName,
       EmailAddress
FROM dbo.Contacts
WHERE FirstName = 'Catherine';
```

```
(22 rows affected)
Table 'Contacts'. Scan count 1, logical reads 68, physical reads 0, read-ahead reads 0, lob logical reads 0,
Table 'Worktable'. Scan count 0, logical reads 0, physical reads 0, read-ahead reads 0, lob logical reads 0,

(1 row affected)
```

Figure 11-30. Statistics I/O results for Included Columns pattern

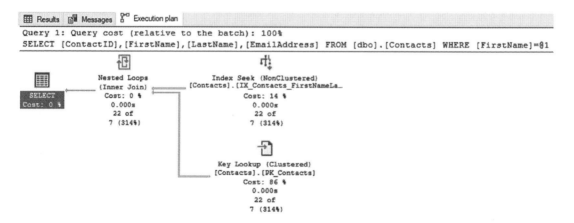

Figure 11-31. Execution plan for Included Columns pattern

To improve the performance of this query, another index based on either the Multiple Column pattern or the Covering Index pattern could be created. The trouble with these options, though, is that the resulting index would have the same limitations as the queries that they could improve. Instead, a new index based on the Included Columns pattern will be created. This new index, shown in Listing 11-22, has FirstName

CHAPTER 11 INDEXING STRATEGIES

as the key column and includes LastName, IsActive, and EmailAddress as the nonkey columns. Even though the IsActive column is not used in the index, it is being included to allow additional flexibility for the index, which a later example in this section will utilize. With the index in place, the performance of the query in Listing 11-22 improves significantly. In this example, the reads drop from the previous 68 per execution to 3 reads (see Figure 11-32). In the execution plan, the key lookup and nested loop are no longer needed; instead, there is just the index seek, which is now using the index IX_Contacts_FirstNameINC (see Figure 11-33).

Listing 11-22. Included Columns Pattern

```
USE AdventureWorks2017
GO

CREATE INDEX IX_Contacts_FirstNameINC ON dbo.Contacts(FirstName)
    INCLUDE (LastName, IsActive, EmailAddress);

SET STATISTICS IO ON;

SELECT ContactID,
       FirstName,
       LastName,
       EmailAddress
FROM dbo.Contacts
WHERE FirstName = 'Catherine';
```

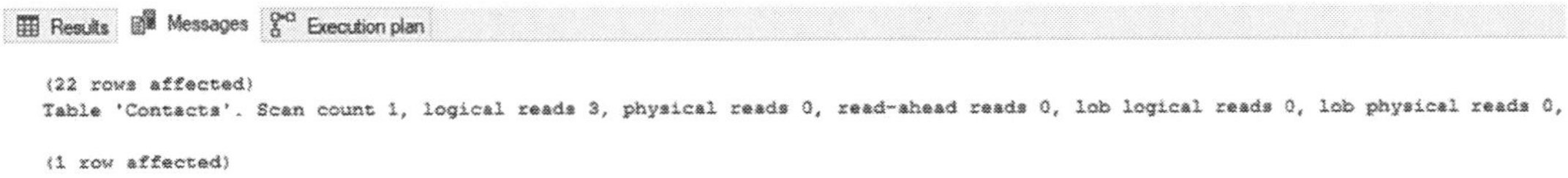

```
(22 rows affected)
Table 'Contacts'. Scan count 1, logical reads 3, physical reads 0, read-ahead reads 0, lob logical reads 0, lob physical reads 0,
(1 row affected)
```

Figure 11-32. Statistics I/O results for Included Columns pattern

```
Query 1: Query cost (relative to the batch): 100%
SELECT [ContactID],[FirstName],[LastName],[EmailAddress] FROM [dbo].[Contacts] WHERE [FirstName]=@1

                        Index Seek (NonClustered)
                        [Contacts].[IX_Contacts_FirstNameIN_
    SELECT              Cost: 100 %
    Cost: 0 %           0.000s
                        22 of
                        7 (314%)
```

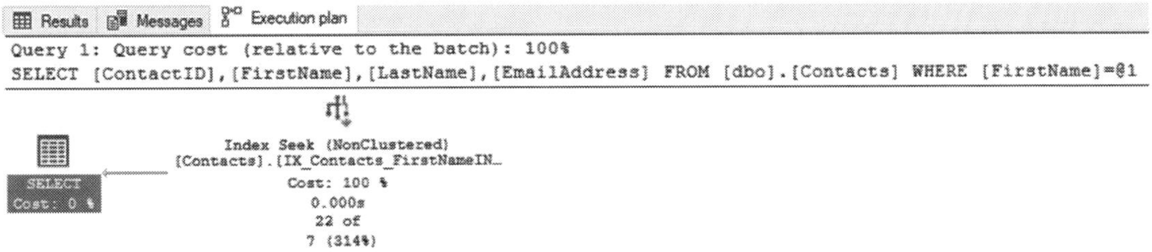

Figure 11-33. Execution plan for Included Columns pattern

While the number of reads is slightly higher with an index created with the Included Columns pattern, there is flexibility with the index that offsets that difference. With each of the examples in this chapter, a new index has been added to the table dbo.Contacts. At this point, there are six indexes on the table, each serving a different purpose and four leading with the same column, FirstName. Each of these indexes takes up space and requires maintenance when the data in dbo.Contacts is modified. In active tables, this amount of indexing could have a negative impact on all activity on the table.

The Included Columns pattern can assist with this issue. In cases where there are multiple indexes with the same leading key column, it is possible to consolidate those indexes into a single index using the Included Columns pattern with some of the key columns added to the index instead as nonkey columns. To demonstrate, first remove all the indexes that start with FirstName, except for the one created using the Included Columns pattern (script provided in Listing 11-23).

Listing 11-23. Dropping Indexes in Included Columns Pattern

```
USE AdventureWorks2017
GO

DROP INDEX IF EXISTS IX_Contacts_FirstNameLastName ON dbo.Contacts
GO

DROP INDEX IF EXISTS IX_Contacts_FirstNameLastNameIsActive ON dbo.Contacts
GO

DROP INDEX IF EXISTS IX_Contacts_FirstName ON dbo.Contacts
GO
```

The dbo.Contact table now has only three indexes on it. There is the clustered index on the ContactID column, a nonclustered index on LastName, and an index on FirstName with the columns LastName, IsActive, and EmailAddress included as data on the index. With these indexes in place, the queries from the previous patterns, shown in Listing 11-24, need to be tested against the table.

There are two points to pay attention to regarding how the queries perform with the Included Columns pattern vs. with the other patterns. First, all the execution plans for the queries, shown in Figure 11-34, are utilizing index seek operations. The seek operation is expected for the query that is just filtering on FirstName, but it can also be used when there is an additional filter on LastName. SQL Server can do this because

CHAPTER 11 INDEXING STRATEGIES

underneath the index seek, it is performing a range scan of the rows that match the first predicate and then removing the LastName results that don't have the value of Cox. The second item to notice is the number of reads for each of the queries, shown in Figure 11-35. The reads increased from two to three. While this constitutes a 50 percent increase in reads, the performance change is not significant enough to justify creating four indexes when one index can adequately provide the needed performance.

Listing 11-24. Other Queries Against Included Columns Pattern

```
USE AdventureWorks2017;
GO

SET STATISTICS IO ON;

SELECT ContactID,
       FirstName
FROM dbo.Contacts
WHERE FirstName = 'Catherine';

SELECT ContactID,
       FirstName,
       LastName
FROM dbo.Contacts
WHERE FirstName = 'Catherine'
    AND LastName = 'Cox';

SELECT ContactID,
       FirstName,
       LastName,
       IsActive
FROM dbo.Contacts
WHERE FirstName = 'Catherine'
    AND LastName = 'Cox';
```

CHAPTER 11 INDEXING STRATEGIES

```
(22 rows affected)
Table 'Contacts'. Scan count 1, logical reads 3, physical reads 0, read-ahead reads 0, lob logical reads 0, lob physical reads 0,

(1 row affected)

(1 row affected)
Table 'Contacts'. Scan count 1, logical reads 3, physical reads 0, read-ahead reads 0, lob logical reads 0, lob physical reads 0,

(1 row affected)

(1 row affected)
Table 'Contacts'. Scan count 1, logical reads 3, physical reads 0, read-ahead reads 0, lob logical reads 0, lob physical reads 0,

(1 row affected)
```

Figure 11-34. *Statistics I/O results for Included Columns pattern*

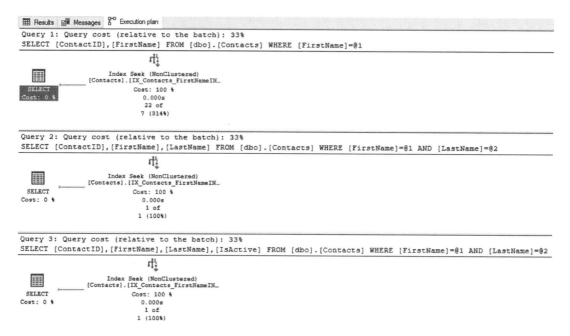

Figure 11-35. *Execution plan for Included Columns pattern*

The Included Columns pattern for building nonclustered indexes is an important pattern to utilize when creating indexes. When used with specific queries that result in lookup operations, it provides improved read and execution performance. It also provides opportunities to consolidate similar queries to reduce the number of indexes on the table while still providing performance improvements over situations where the indexes do not exist.

Filtered Indexes

In some tables in your databases, there are rows with certain values that will rarely, or never, be returned in the resultset as part of the applications using the databases. In these cases, it might be beneficial to remove the rows as an option to be returned by the resultset. In some other situations, it may be useful to identify a subset of data in a table and create indexes. Instead of querying across millions or billions of records in the table, you can utilize indexes that cover the hundreds or thousands of rows that the query needs to return results. Both of these situations identify scenarios where using the Filtered Indexes pattern can help improve performance.

The Filtered Indexes pattern utilizes, as the name suggests, the filtered index feature that was introduced with SQL Server 2005. When using filtered indexes, a WHERE clause is added to a nonclustered index to reduce the rows that are contained within the index. By including only the rows that match the filter of the WHERE clause, the query engine has to consider only those rows in building an execution plan; moreover, the cost of scanning a range of rows is less expensive than if all the rows were included in the index.

To illustrate the value in using filtered indexes, consider a scenario where only a small subset of the table has values in the column that is being filtered. Listing 11-25 considers variations of a query. In the first version, the rows where CertificationDate has a value are returned. The second version returns only rows that have a CertificationDate between January 1, 2005, and February 1, 2005. With both of these queries, there is no index on the table that will provide an optimal plan for execution since all 2,866 pages of the index are accessed during execution (see Figure 11-36). Examining both execution plans (Figure 11-37) shows that a clustered index scan of dbo.Contacts is utilized to find the rows that match the CertificationDate predicate. An index on the CertificationDate column could, as the missing index hint suggests, improve the performance of the query.

Listing 11-25. Filtered Indexes Pattern

```
USE AdventureWorks2017;
GO

SET STATISTICS IO ON;

SELECT ContactID,
       FirstName,
```

        LastName,
        CertificationDate
FROM dbo.Contacts
WHERE CertificationDate IS NOT NULL
ORDER BY CertificationDate;

SELECT ContactID,
       FirstName,
       LastName,
       CertificationDate
FROM dbo.Contacts
WHERE CertificationDate
BETWEEN '20110101' AND '20110201'
ORDER BY CertificationDate;

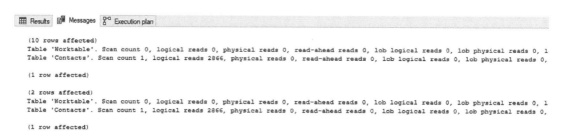

Figure 11-36. *Statistics I/O results for Filtered Indexes pattern*

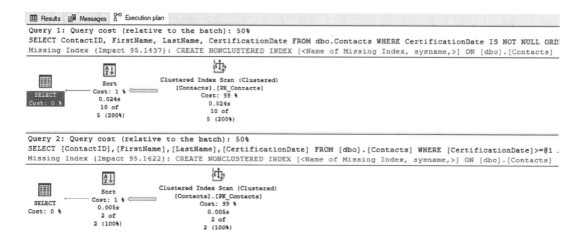

Figure 11-37. *Execution plan for Filtered Indexes pattern*

CHAPTER 11 INDEXING STRATEGIES

Before applying the missing index suggestion, you should consider how the index will be used in this and future queries. In this scenario, assume that there will never be a query that uses CertificationDate when the value is NULL. Does it make sense then to store the empty values for all the NULL rows in the index? Given the stated assumption, it doesn't make sense; doing so would waste space in the database and potentially lead to execution plans that were not optimal if the index on CertificationDate was skipped because the reads for a scan were high enough that other indexes were selected.

In this scenario, it makes sense to filter the rows in the index. To do so, the index is created like any other index, except that a WHERE clause is added to the index (see Listing 11-26). When creating filtered indexes, there are a few things to keep in mind about the WHERE clause. To start with, the WHERE clause must be deterministic. It can't change over time depending on the results of functions within the clause. For instance, the GETDATE() function can't be used since the value returned changes every millisecond. The second restriction is that only simple comparison logic is allowed. This means that the BETWEEN and LIKE comparisons can't be used. For more information on the restrictions and limitations with filtered indexes, refer to Chapter 2.

Executing the CertificationDate queries from Listing 11-26 shows that the filtered index provides a significant impact on the performance for the query. In regard to the reads incurred, there are now only 2 reads as opposed to the 2,866 reads before the index was applied (see Figure 11-38). Also, the execution plans now use index seeks for both queries instead of the clustered index scans, as shown in Figure 11-39. While these results are to be expected, the other consideration with the index is that the new index is comprised of only two pages. As you can see in Figure 11-40, the number of pages required for the entire index is substantially less than the clustered index and the other nonclustered indexes.

Listing 11-26. Filtered Indexes Pattern

```
USE AdventureWorks2017
GO

CREATE INDEX IX_Contacts_CertificationDate ON dbo.
Contacts(CertificationDate)
    INCLUDE (FirstName, LastName)
    WHERE CertificationDate IS NOT NULL;
```

```sql
SET STATISTICS IO ON;

SELECT ContactID,
       FirstName,
       LastName,
       CertificationDate
FROM dbo.Contacts
WHERE CertificationDate IS NOT NULL
ORDER BY CertificationDate;

SELECT ContactID,
       FirstName,
       LastName,
       CertificationDate
FROM dbo.Contacts
WHERE CertificationDate
BETWEEN '20110101' AND '20110201'
ORDER BY CertificationDate;

SET STATISTICS IO OFF;

SELECT OBJECT_NAME(object_id) as table_name
      ,CASE index_id
        WHEN INDEXPROPERTY(object_id , 'IX_Contacts_CertificationDate',
        'IndexID') THEN 'Filtered Index'
       WHEN 1 THEN 'Clustered Index'
       ELSE 'Other Indexes' END As index_type
      ,index_id
      ,in_row_data_page_count
      ,in_row_reserved_page_count
      ,in_row_used_page_count
FROM sys.dm_db_partition_stats
WHERE object_id = OBJECT_ID('dbo.Contacts');
```

CHAPTER 11 INDEXING STRATEGIES

```
(10 rows affected)
Table 'Contacts'. Scan count 1, logical reads 2, physical reads 0, read-ahead reads 0, lob logical reads 0, lob physical reads 0,

(1 row affected)

(2 rows affected)
Table 'Contacts'. Scan count 1, logical reads 2, physical reads 0, read-ahead reads 0, lob logical reads 0, lob physical reads 0,

(1 row affected)

(4 rows affected)

(1 row affected)
```

Figure 11-38. *Statistics I/O results for Filtered Indexes pattern*

```
Query 1: Query cost (relative to the batch): 11%
SELECT ContactID, FirstName, LastName, CertificationDate FROM dbo.Contacts WHERE CertificationDate IS NOT NULL ORDER B
```

Index Scan (NonClustered)
[Contacts].[IX_Contacts_Certificati...
Cost: 100 %
0.000s
10 of
10 (100%)

```
Query 2: Query cost (relative to the batch): 11%
SELECT [ContactID],[FirstName],[LastName],[CertificationDate] FROM [dbo].[Contacts] WHERE [CertificationDate]>=@1 AND
```

Index Seek (NonClustered)
[Contacts].[IX_Contacts_Certificati...
Cost: 100 %
0.000s
2 of
2 (100%)

Figure 11-39. *Execution plan for Filtered Indexes pattern*

	table_name	index_type	index_id	in_row_data_page_count	in_row_reserved_page_count	in_row_used_page_count
1	Contacts	Clustered Index	1	2854	2889	2866
2	Contacts	Other Indexes	5	63	73	65
3	Contacts	Filtered Index	6	1	9	2
4	Contacts	Other Indexes	8	242	267	246

Figure 11-40. *Page count comparison for filtered index*

Including only a subset of the rows in a table within an index has a number of advantages. One advantage is that since the index is smaller, there are fewer pages in the index, which translates directly to lower storage requirements for the database. Along the same lines, if there are fewer pages in the index, there are fewer opportunities for index fragmentation and less effort required to maintain the index. The final advantage of filtered indexes relates to performance and plan quality. Since the values in the filtered index are limited, the statistics for the index are limited as well. Since there are fewer pages to traverse in the filtered index, a scan against a filtered index is almost always less of an issue than a scan on the clustered index or heap.

407

There are a few situations where using the Filtered Indexes pattern can and should be used when creating indexes. The first situation is when you need to place an index on a column that is configured as sparse. In this case, the expected number of rows that will have the value will be small compared to the total number of rows. One of the benefits of using sparse columns is avoiding the storage costs associated with storing NULL values in these columns. Make certain that the indexes on these columns don't store the NULL values by not using filtered indexes. The second situation is when you need to enforce uniqueness on a column that can have multiple NULL values in it. Creating the filtered index as unique where the key columns are not NULL will bypass the restrictions on uniqueness that allow only a single NULL value in the columns. In this case, you can ensure that Social Security Numbers in a table are unique when they are provided.

The last situation that is a good fit for filtered indexes is when queries need to be run that don't fit the normal index profile for a table. In this case, there might be a query for a one-off report that needs to retrieve a few thousand rows from the database. Instead of running the report and dealing with the potential scan of the clustered index or heap, create filtered indexes that mimic the predicates of the query. This will allow the query to be quickly executed, without having to spend the time building indexes that contain values the query would never have considered.

As this section has detailed, the Filtered Indexes pattern is one that can be useful in a variety of situations. Be sure to consider it in your indexing. Often, when the first use for a filtered index is found, there are others that start appearing, and we'll identify situations with selecting and modifying data, as earlier, that can benefit from its use.

Foreign Keys

The last nonclustered index pattern is the Foreign Keys pattern. This is the only pattern that relates directly to objects in the database design. Foreign keys provide a mechanism to constrain values in one table to the values in rows in another table. This relationship provides referential integrity that is critical in most database deployments. However, foreign keys can sometimes be the cause of performance issues in databases without anyone realizing that they are interfering with performance.

Since foreign keys provide a constraint on the values that are possible for a column, there is a check that is done when the values need to be validated. There are two types of validations that can occur with a foreign key. The first happens on the parent table, dbo.ParentTable, and the second happens on the child table, dbo.ChildTable (see Figure 11-41). Validations occur on dbo.ParentTable whenever rows are modified in

CHAPTER 11 INDEXING STRATEGIES

dbo.ChildTable. In these cases, the ParentID value from dbo.ChildTable is validated with a lookup of the value in dbo.ParentTable. Usually, this does not result in a performance issue since ParentID in dbo.ParentTable will likely be the primary key in the table and also the column upon which the table is clustered. The other validations occur on dbo.ChildTable when there are modifications to dbo.ParentTable. For instance, if one of the rows in dbo.ParentTable were to be deleted, then dbo.ChildTable would need to be checked to see whether the ParentID value is being used in that table. This validation is where the Foreign Keys pattern needs to be applied.

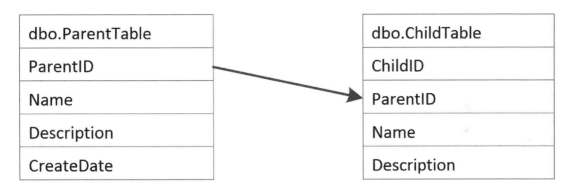

Figure 11-41. Foreign key relationship

To demonstrate the Foreign Keys pattern, you will first need a couple tables for the examples. The code in Listing 11-27 builds two tables, dbo.Customer and dbo.SalesOrderHeader. For these tables, a foreign key relationship exists between them on the CustomerID columns. For every dbo.SalesOrderHeader row, there is a customer associated with the row. Conversely, every row in dbo.Customer can relate to one or more rows in dbo.SalesOrderHeader.

Listing 11-27. Setup for Foreign Keys Pattern

```
USE AdventureWorks2017
GO

CREATE TABLE dbo.Customer(
        CustomerID int
        ,FillterData char(1000)
        ,CONSTRAINT PK_Customer_CustomerID PRIMARY KEY CLUSTERED (CustomerID)
        );
```

```
CREATE TABLE dbo.SalesOrderHeader(
        SalesOrderID int
        ,OrderDate datetime
        ,DueDate datetime
        ,CustomerID int
        ,FillterData char(1000)
        ,CONSTRAINT PK_SalesOrderHeader_SalesOrderID
            PRIMARY KEY CLUSTERED (SalesOrderID)
        ,CONSTRAINT GK_SalesOrderHeader_CustomerID_FROM_Customer
            FOREIGN KEY (CustomerID) REFERENCES dbo.Customer(CustomerID)
        );
INSERT INTO dbo.Customer (CustomerID)
SELECT CustomerID
FROM Sales.Customer;

INSERT INTO dbo.SalesOrderHeader
  (SalesOrderID, OrderDate, DueDate, CustomerID)
SELECT SalesOrderID, OrderDate, DueDate, CustomerID
FROM Sales.SalesOrderHeader;
```

In the example, you want to observe what happens in dbo.SalesOrderHeader when a row in dbo.Customer is modified. To demonstrate activity on dbo.Customer, the script in Listing 11-28 executes a DELETE on the table on the row where CustomerID equals 701. This row should have no rows in dbo.SalesOrderHeader. Even though this is the case, the foreign key does require that a check be made to determine whether there are rows in dbo.SalesOrderHeader for that CustomerID. If so, then SQL Server would error on the delete. Since there are no rows in dbo.SalesOrderHeader, the row in dbo.Customer can be deleted.

The execution identifies a couple potential performance problems with the delete. First, with only one row being deleted, there are a total of 4,516 reads (see Figure 11-42). Of the reads, 3 occur on dbo.Customer, while 4,513 occur on dbo.SalesOrderHeader. The reason for this is the clustered index scan that had to occur on dbo.SalesOrderHeader (shown in Figure 11-43). The scan occurred because the only way to check which rows were using Customer equal to 701 is to scan all the rows in the table. There is no index that can provide a faster path to verifying whether the value was being used.

CHAPTER 11　INDEXING STRATEGIES

Listing 11-28. Foreign Keys Pattern

```
USE AdventureWorks2017
GO

SELECT MAX(c.CustomerID)
    FROM dbo.Customer c
    LEFT OUTER JOIN dbo.SalesOrderHeader soh ON c.CustomerID =
    soh.CustomerID
    WHERE soh.CustomerID IS NULL;

SET STATISTICS IO ON;

DELETE FROM dbo.Customer
WHERE CustomerID = 701;
```

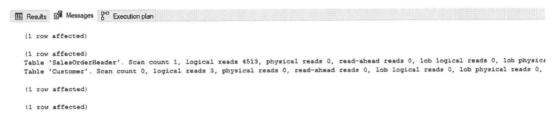

Figure 11-42. Statistics I/O results for Foreign Keys pattern

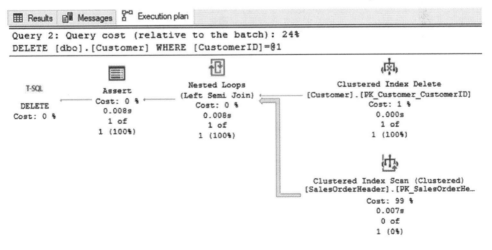

Figure 11-43. Execution plan for Foreign Keys pattern

411

Improving the performance of the DELETE on dbo.Customer can be done simply through the Foreign Keys pattern. An index built on dbo.SalesOrderHeader on the CustomerID column will provide a reference point for validation with the next delete operation (see Listing 11-29). Reviewing the execution with the index in place yields quite different results. Instead of 4,513 reads on dbo.SalesOrderHeader, there are now only two reads against that table (see Figure 11-44). This change is, of course, because of the index that was created on the CustomerID column (see Figure 11-45). Instead of a clustered index scan, the delete operation can utilize an index seek on dbo.SalesOrderHeader.

Listing 11-29. Foreign Keys Pattern

```
USE AdventureWorks2017
GO

CREATE INDEX IX_SalesOrderHeader_CustomerID ON dbo.
SalesOrderHeader(CustomerID);

SELECT MAX(c.CustomerID)
      FROM dbo.Customer c
      LEFT OUTER JOIN dbo.SalesOrderHeader soh ON c.CustomerID =
      soh.CustomerID
      WHERE soh.CustomerID IS NULL;

SET STATISTICS IO ON

DELETE FROM dbo.Customer
WHERE CustomerID = 700
```

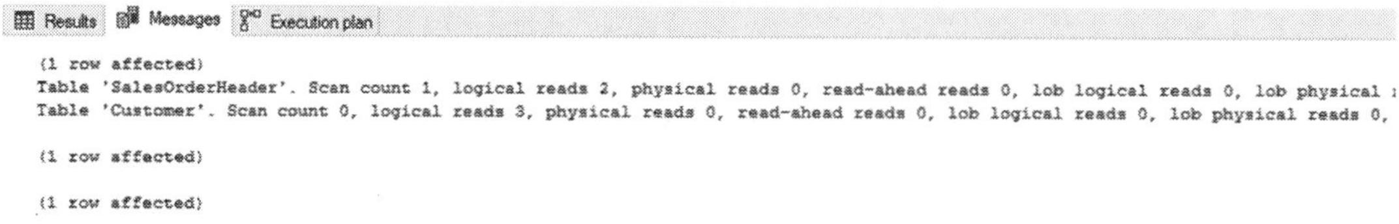

```
(1 row affected)
Table 'SalesOrderHeader'. Scan count 1, logical reads 2, physical reads 0, read-ahead reads 0, lob logical reads 0, lob physical
Table 'Customer'. Scan count 0, logical reads 3, physical reads 0, read-ahead reads 0, lob logical reads 0, lob physical reads 0,

(1 row affected)

(1 row affected)
```

Figure 11-44. Statistics I/O results for Foreign Keys pattern

CHAPTER 11 INDEXING STRATEGIES

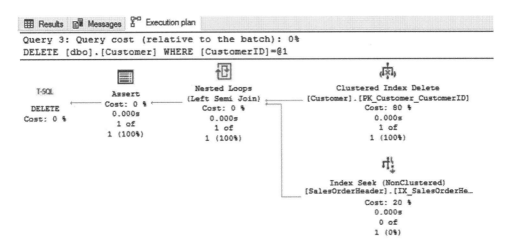

Figure 11-45. *Execution plan for Foreign Keys pattern*

The Foreign Keys pattern is important to keep in mind with building foreign key relationships between tables. The purpose of those relationships is to validate data, and you need to be certain that the indexes to support that activity are in place. Don't use this pattern as an excuse to remove validation from your databases; instead, use it as an opportunity to properly index your databases. If the column needs to be queried to validate and constrain the data, it will likely be accessed by applications when the data needs to be used for other purposes.

Columnstore Index

As the size of databases have grown, there are more and more situations where traditional clustered and nonclustered indexes don't adequately provide the performance needed for calculating results. This is primarily a pain with large data warehouses, and for this problem, the columnstore index was introduced in SQL Server 2012. Previous chapters discussed how the columnstore utilizes column-based storage vs. row-based storage. This section looks at some guidelines with both clustered and nonclustered versions of columnstore indexes and how to recognize when to build a columnstore index. After the guidelines, an example implementing a columnstore index will be provided.

> **Note** The columnstore examples in this section utilize the Microsoft Contoso BI Demo Dataset for Retail Industry. This database has a fact table with more than 8 million records. It is available for download at www.microsoft.com/download/en/details.aspx?displaylang=en&id=18279.

The key to using columnstore indexes is to be able to properly identify the situations where they should be applied. While it could be useful with some OLTP databases to use the columnstore index, this is not the target scenario. While the performance of the columnstore index could be useful in an OLTP database, the restrictions associated with this index type prevent using it in a meaningful way in OLTP databases. The columnstore index is primarily useful for data warehouses, where aggregations across numerous rows are required and few columns will be returned. With the column-wise storage and built-in compression, this index type provides a way to get to the data requested as fast as possible without having to load columns that are not part of the query. Within your data warehouse, columnstore indexes are geared toward fact tables vs. dimension tables. Columnstore indexes really prove their worth when they are used on large tables. The larger the table, the more a columnstore index will be able to improve performance over traditional indexes. Additionally, when considering data warehouse queries, one common quality that they share is aggregations and subsets of the available columns. Through the aggregations, the batch mode processing of columnstore indexes provides greater performance improvements. The fewer columns in the queries means less data is loaded into memory, as only the columns being accessed are used in the context of the query.

When a scenario for using a columnstore index is discovered, there are a couple of things to first consider. Since columnstore indexes can be both clustered and nonclustered, the first decision is which type to use. With clustered columnstore indexes, all the data in the table is stored with the index, meaning that only one copy of the data appears in the database. Since it is all the data, the results in all the columns from the table appear in the columnstore index. In most cases, this will be preferred.

Alternatively, the columnstore index can be nonclustered. This provides the ability to limit the number of columns that are part of the index. In some cases, where the table has many columns, this may be useful. The nonclustered index will rely on a clustered index being part of the table, which means that nonclustered columnstore indexes increase the overall storage footprint of the table.

Nonclustered columnstore indexes have more considerations when creating them, so there are a number of guidelines to remember when building the them. First, the order of the columns in the nonclustered columnstore index does not matter. Each column is stored separate from the other columns, and there are no relationships between them until they are materialized together again during execution. The next thing to remember is that all columns in the table that will be leveraged by the columnstore index must appear in the columnstore index. If a column from a query does not appear in the nonclustered columnstore index, then the index cannot be used.

If you are using SQL Server versions prior to SQL Server 2017, it's important to remember that nonclustered columnstore indexes are read-only, and any table or partition that has a nonclustered columnstore index built upon it will be placed in a read-only state. To modify the table, the nonclustered columnstore index will need to be disabled or dropped and then rebuilt or created after the updates are completed. This limitation does not affect clustered columnstore indexes and was lifted from nonclustered columnstore indexes with SQL Server 2017.

A limitation that affects both types of columnstore indexes is length of time that it takes to create the index. In many cases, it can take four to five times longer to create a columnstore index than it does to build a clustered or nonclustered index. For more information on columnstore indexes, see Chapter 2.

Before demonstrating the value in columnstore indexes, let's look at a demonstration of a query against a data warehouse with traditional indexing. In Listing 11-30, the query is summarizing `SalesQuantity` values by `CalendarQuarter` and `ProductCategoryName`. Executing the query does not take a substantial amount of time; Figure 11-46 shows an elapsed time of 4,293 ms (or 4.2 seconds), with a little less than 20,000 reads on dbo. FactSales. The results are reasonable for the current volume of records, but consider if the table had 10 or 100 times as many rows. At what point would the 4.2 seconds of execution grow outside the acceptable execution time?

Note Because of the size of the execution plans, they are not being included in the columnstore index examples. And since this section is relying on CPU time to demonstrate performance, they are run multiple times to ensure that disk to memory performance is not a factor.

CHAPTER 11　INDEXING STRATEGIES

Listing 11-30. Columnstore Index

```
USE ContosoRetailDW
GO

SET STATISTICS IO ON
SET STATISTICS TIME ON

SELECT dd.CalendarQuarter
      ,dpc.ProductCategoryName
      ,COUNT(*) As TotalRows
      ,SUM(SalesQuantity) AS TotalSales
FROM dbo.FactSales fs
    INNER JOIN dbo.DimDate dd ON fs.DateKey = dd.Datekey
    INNER JOIN dbo.DimProduct dp ON fs.ProductKey = dp.ProductKey
    INNER JOIN dbo.DimProductSubcategory dps ON dp.ProductSubcategoryKey =
    dps.ProductSubcategoryKey
    INNER JOIN dbo.DimProductCategory dpc ON dps.ProductCategoryKey =
    dpc.ProductCategoryKey
GROUP BY dd.CalendarQuarter
        ,dpc.ProductCategoryName;
```

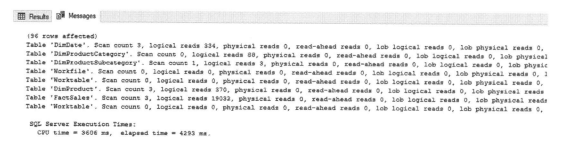

Figure 11-46. *Statistics I/O results for clustered index on fact table*

To test the performance with a nonclustered columnstore index on dbo.FactSales, let's add a new index to the table. As stated in the guidelines in this section, all the columns in dbo.FactSales are added to the columnstore index, shown in Listing 11-31. With the index in place, the performance of the query changes dramatically. From a timing perspective, the query completes in 286 ms, shown in Figure 11-47, which is an improvement of over 15 times the performance without the nonclustered columnstore index. Additionally, the number of I/Os dropped from nearly 20,000 to 2,608.

CHAPTER 11 ■ INDEXING STRATEGIES

Listing 11-31. Adding Nonclustered Columnstore Index

```
USE ContosoRetailDW
GO

CREATE NONCLUSTERED COLUMNSTORE INDEX IX_FactSales_CStore ON dbo.FactSales (
    SalesKey, DateKey, channelKey, StoreKey, ProductKey, PromotionKey,
    CurrencyKey, UnitCost, UnitPrice,
    SalesQuantity, ReturnQuantity, ReturnAmount, DiscountQuantity,
    DiscountAmount, TotalCost, SalesAmount,
    ETLLoadID, LoadDate, UpdateDate);

SET STATISTICS IO ON;
SET STATISTICS TIME ON;

SELECT dd.CalendarQuarter
      ,dpc.ProductCategoryName
      , COUNT(*) As TotalRows
      ,SUM(SalesQuantity) AS TotalSales
FROM dbo.FactSales fs
     INNER JOIN dbo.DimDate dd ON fs.DateKey = dd.Datekey
     INNER JOIN dbo.DimProduct dp ON fs.ProductKey = dp.ProductKey
     INNER JOIN dbo.DimProductSubcategory dps ON dp.ProductSubcategoryKey =
     dps.ProductSubcategoryKey
     INNER JOIN dbo.DimProductCategory dpc ON dps.ProductCategoryKey =
     dpc.ProductCategoryKey
GROUP BY dd.CalendarQuarter
        ,dpc.ProductCategoryName;
```

```
(96 rows affected)
Table 'DimProductSubcategory'. Scan count 1, logical reads 3, physical reads 0, read-ahead reads 0, lob logical reads 0, lob physi
Table 'FactSales'. Scan count 4, logical reads 0, physical reads 0, read-ahead reads 0, lob logical reads 2608, lob physical reads
Table 'FactSales'. Segment reads 5, segment skipped 0.
Table 'DimProduct'. Scan count 3, logical reads 370, physical reads 0, read-ahead reads 0, lob logical reads 0, lob physical reads
Table 'DimProductCategory'. Scan count 0, logical reads 88, physical reads 0, read-ahead reads 0, lob logical reads 0, lob physica
Table 'DimDate'. Scan count 3, logical reads 334, physical reads 0, read-ahead reads 0, lob logical reads 0, lob physical reads 0,
Table 'Worktable'. Scan count 0, logical reads 0, physical reads 0, read-ahead reads 0, lob logical reads 0, lob physical reads 0,
Table 'Worktable'. Scan count 0, logical reads 0, physical reads 0, read-ahead reads 0, lob logical reads 0, lob physical reads 0,

SQL Server Execution Times:
   CPU time = 186 ms,  elapsed time = 286 ms.
```

Figure 11-47. *Statistics I/O results for nonclustered columnstore index*

As mentioned, the clustered columnstore index is preferred; since this is the preference, let's look at the impact of using a clustered columnstore index on dbo.FactSales. Since you are creating a clustered index on the table, we'll use the script in Listing 11-32 to create a new table called dbo.FactSales_CCI, populate it with the same data in dbo.FactSales, and add the clustered columnstore index to it.

When you use the same aggregate query from the previous examples, the performance value of the clustered columnstore is evident. Considering the execution time (shown in Figure 11-48), it drops further to 164 ms, which is more than 26 times faster than the fact table with the clustered index. The I/Os are reduced as well with only 1,309 I/Os for the execution. While the I/O footprint is similar to the nonclustered columnstore, remember that the clustered columnstore is stored only a single time and the values in it can be modified.

Listing 11-32. Create Fact Table with Clustered Columnstore Index

```
USE ContosoRetailDW
GO

IF OBJECT_ID('dbo.FactSales_CCI') IS NOT NULL
    DROP TABLE FactSales_CCI

CREATE TABLE dbo.FactSales_CCI(
    SalesKey int NOT NULL,
    DateKey datetime NOT NULL,
    channelKey int NOT NULL,
    StoreKey int NOT NULL,
    ProductKey int NOT NULL,
    PromotionKey int NOT NULL,
    CurrencyKey int NOT NULL,
    UnitCost money NOT NULL,
    UnitPrice money NOT NULL,
    SalesQuantity int NOT NULL,
    ReturnQuantity int NOT NULL,
    ReturnAmount money NULL,
    DiscountQuantity int NULL,
    DiscountAmount money NULL,
    TotalCost money NOT NULL,
```

```sql
    SalesAmount money NOT NULL,
    ETLLoadID int NULL,
    LoadDate datetime NULL,
    UpdateDate datetime NULL
    )

INSERT INTO dbo.FactSales_CCI
SELECT * FROM dbo.FactSales

CREATE CLUSTERED COLUMNSTORE INDEX FactSales_CStore ON dbo.FactSales_CCI

SET STATISTICS IO ON;
SET STATISTICS TIME ON;

SELECT dd.CalendarQuarter
    ,dpc.ProductCategoryName
    , COUNT(*) As TotalRows
    ,SUM(SalesQuantity) AS TotalSales
FROM dbo.FactSales_CCI fs
    INNER JOIN dbo.DimDate dd ON fs.DateKey = dd.Datekey
    INNER JOIN dbo.DimProduct dp ON fs.ProductKey = dp.ProductKey
    INNER JOIN dbo.DimProductSubcategory dps ON dp.ProductSubcategoryKey =
    dps.ProductSubcategoryKey
    INNER JOIN dbo.DimProductCategory dpc ON dps.ProductCategoryKey =
    dpc.ProductCategoryKey
GROUP BY dd.CalendarQuarter
    ,dpc.ProductCategoryName;
```

```
(96 rows affected)
Table 'DimProductSubcategory'. Scan count 1, logical reads 3, physical reads 0, read-ahead reads 0, lob logical reads 0, lob physic
Table 'FactSales_CCI'. Scan count 2, logical reads 0, physical reads 0, read-ahead reads 0, lob logical reads 1309, lob physical re
Table 'FactSales_CCI'. Segment reads 5, segment skipped 0.
Table 'DimProduct'. Scan count 3, logical reads 370, physical reads 0, read-ahead reads 0, lob logical reads 0, lob physical reads
Table 'DimProductCategory'. Scan count 0, logical reads 88, physical reads 0, read-ahead reads 0, lob logical reads 0, lob physical
Table 'DimDate'. Scan count 3, logical reads 334, physical reads 0, read-ahead reads 0, lob logical reads 0, lob physical reads 0,
Table 'Worktable'. Scan count 0, logical reads 0, physical reads 0, read-ahead reads 0, lob logical reads 0, lob physical reads 0,
Table 'Worktable'. Scan count 0, logical reads 0, physical reads 0, read-ahead reads 0, lob logical reads 0, lob physical reads 0,

SQL Server Execution Times:
   CPU time = 187 ms, elapsed time = 164 ms.
```

Figure 11-48. *Statistics I/O results for clustered columnstore index*

With the recent additions to SQL Server, columnstore indexes are a significant improvement in the way in which data warehouses are indexed. These performance improvements open opportunities to scale the databases even further than is possible with traditional indexes. Scenarios where only millions of rows are able to be summarized in results will now be able to scale to billions of rows. Additionally, since all columns can be included in the columnstore indexes, the effort and requirement for continuous maintenance and tuning of indexes in data warehouses are dramatically reduced.

Note The next section utilizes the WorldWideImporters databases which can be downloaded from https://github.com/Microsoft/sql-server-samples/releases/tag/wide-world-importers-v1.0.

JSON Indexing

SQL Server 2016 introduced the ability to process JSON (JavaScript Object Notation) data within SQL Server. JSON defines methods of structuring data that are easy for both applications and people to read and write. Due to this ease, it's become very popular within application development.

Instead of tags and attributes that are used in XML, JSON leverages brackets, colons, and quotes to define entity-attribute relationships. As an example, Listing 11-33 contains an XML document that defines extra information regarding an employee of WideWorldImporters. That same information represented by JSON is shown in Listing 11-34. Comparing the two, the JSON is quite a bit easier to read and understand than the same data represented as XML.

Listing 11-33. XML Example

```
<CustomFields>
  <OtherLanguages>
    <Language>Polish</Language>
    <Language>Chines</Language>
    <Language>Japanese</Language>
  </OtherLanguages>
```

```
    <HireDate>2008-04-19T00:00:00</HireDate>
    <Title>Team Member</Title>
    <PrimarySalesTerritory>Plains</PrimarySalesTerritory>
    <CommissionRate>0.98</CommissionRate>
</CustomFields>
```

Listing 11-34. JSON Example

```
{
"OtherLanguages": ["Polish","Chinese","Japanese"] ,
"HireDate":"2008-04-19T00:00:00",
"Title":"Team Member",
"PrimarySalesTerritory":"Plains",
"CommissionRate":"0.98"
}
```

While SQL Server can now process JSON data, Microsoft implemented JSON a bit different than how XML and spatial were implemented. Instead of a dedicated data type, JSON data is stored in columns defined with the data types varchar(max) and nvarchar(max). Then the information within the data can be retrieved using the functions JSON_VALUE or JSON_QUERY. The advantage of this implementation is that there are no special indexing types associated with JSON data, which is why there isn't a chapter dedicated to JSON indexing. Instead, JSON data takes advantage of existing indexing capabilities by using computed columns persisted through indexes.

Before we start with how to index JSON data, let's start with an example of how the JSON functions work and their effect on performance. To start, create the table dbo.People from Application.People in WideWorldImporters, provided in Listing 11-35. In that table, we'll include a column for HireDate that retrieves the HireDate from the JSON document in CustomFields.

Listing 11-35. JSON Example Setup

```
USE WideWorldImporters;
GO

DROP TABLE IF EXISTS dbo.People;

CREATE TABLE [dbo].[People]
(
    [PersonID] [INT] NOT NULL,
    [FullName] [NVARCHAR](50) NOT NULL,
    [CustomFields] [NVARCHAR](MAX) NULL,
    [HireDate] AS JSON_VALUE([CustomFields], N'$.HireDate'),
    [Junk] [VARCHAR](4000) NULL,
    CONSTRAINT [PK_People]
        PRIMARY KEY CLUSTERED ([PersonID])
);
GO
INSERT INTO dbo.People
(
    PersonID,
    FullName,
    CustomFields,
    Junk
)
SELECT PersonID,
       FullName,
       CustomFields,
       REPLICATE('x', 4000) AS Junk
FROM Application.People;
GO
```

If we query dbo.People, using the code in Listing 11-36, we'll find that we get the desired results from the JSON data, through the computed column. Unfortunately, to retrieve these results, SQL Server is the clustered index, shown in Figure 11-50. The impact of this scan is that all 1,111 rows in the table are accessed which the statistics output in Figure 11-49 indicates and leads to 762 reads for the query.

Listing 11-36. Query Computed JSON Column

```
USE WideWorldImporters;
GO

SET STATISTICS IO ON;

SELECT PersonID,
       HireDate
FROM dbo.People
WHERE HireDate IS NOT NULL;
```

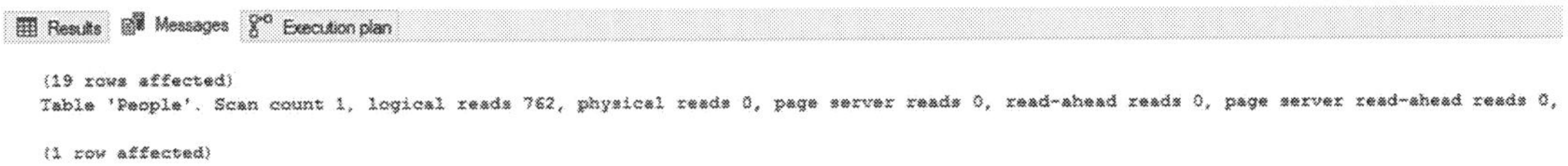

```
(19 rows affected)
Table 'People'. Scan count 1, logical reads 762, physical reads 0, page server reads 0, read-ahead reads 0, page server read-ahead reads 0,

(1 row affected)
```

Figure 11-49. *Statistics I/O results for computed JSON column*

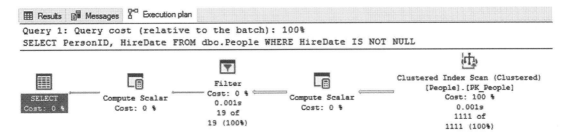

Figure 11-50. *Execution plan for computed JSON column*

To alleviate the performance impact of the computed JSON column, we can add an index to the computed column, as shown in Listing 11-37, and then execute the query against dbo.People again. This time the performance is greatly improved. Instead of 762 reads, Figure 11-51 shows that there are only 3 reads. Additionally, the execution plan in Figure 11-52 indicates that an index seek on the index added was used.

CHAPTER 11 INDEXING STRATEGIES

Listing 11-37. Index and Query JSON Computed Column

```
USE WideWorldImporters;
GO

CREATE INDEX IX_People_HireDate ON dbo.People (HireDate);
GO

SET STATISTICS IO ON;

SELECT PersonID,
       HireDate
FROM dbo.People
WHERE HireDate IS NOT NULL
```

```
(19 rows affected)
Table 'People'. Scan count 1, logical reads 3, physical reads 1, page server reads 0, read-ahead reads 1, page server read-ahead reads 0,

(1 row affected)
```

Figure 11-51. *Statistics I/O results for computed and indexed JSON column*

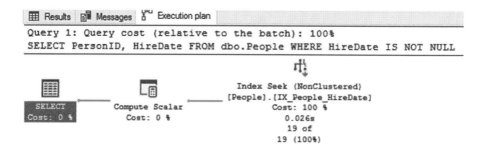

Figure 11-52. *Execution plan for computed and indexed JSON column*

By leveraging computed columns, JSON data can be easily and efficiently accessed within your databases. And rather than needing to learn about new indexing technologies to gain that efficiency, you are able to leverage existing features. This makes it easier to both adopt and support JSON and efficient query access to that data.

Index Storage Strategies

The strategies in the chapter up to this point have primarily focused on improving the performance queries using indexes through the key and nonkey column design of the index. There are other options that can be used in conjunction to column selection that can be considered in the design of indexes. These alternative strategies all relate to the way in which indexes are stored in the database.

There are two options available for addressing how an index stores its data. The basic premise for both of these options is that the smaller the index, the fewer pages that it will contain and the fewer reads and writes that will be required when querying the data. The first option available is row compression, and the second is page compression. Both of these options provide the potential for substantial storage savings and performance improvements.

Note The use of row and page compressions is limited to SQL Server Enterprise Edition.

Row Compression

The first way to reduce the size of an index is by reducing the size of the row on the index. Row compression achieves this by altering the way in which data is stored in a row. Row compression can be used on heaps or clustered and nonclustered indexes. There are a few things that occur on a row when row compression is enabled. These are as follows:

- Modification of the metadata for the row.
- Fixed-length character data is stored in a variable-length format.
- Numeric-based data types are stored in variable-length format.

With the metadata changes, the information stored for each column is generally reduced compared to a nonrow compression record. Excessive bits in the row overhead are removed, and the information is streamlined to reduce waste. There is an exception to this change, though: some of the changes to fixed-length data types may result in a larger row overhead to accommodate for the additional information required for data length and offset values.

CHAPTER 11   INDEXING STRATEGIES

For fixed-length character data, white space is removed from the end of values in the column. This information is not lost, and the behavior of fixed-length data types, such as char and nchar, is unaffected. The difference is only in the manner in which the data is stored. For binary data, trailing zeros on the value are removed, similar to white space. Information on the characters removed from a column is stored in the row overhead.

Numeric data types are probably the most changed data types with row compression. For these data types, the data type is stored in the smallest form possible for the data type. This means a column with the bigint data type, which typically requires 8 bytes, would require only 1 byte if the value stored is between 0 and 255. At the value 256, the column would then store the value in 2 bytes. This progression continues until the need to store the value in 8 bytes is reached. This applies to all the numeric-based data types, including smallint, int, bigint, decimal, numeric, smallmoney, money, float, real, datetime, datetime2, datetimeoffset, and timestamp.

To demonstrate, you first need a table on which to implement compression, which is provided in Listing 11-38. This script creates two tables, dbo.NoCompression and dbo.RowCompression. Let's use these tables to demonstrate the effect of row compression on the size of the table, through the clustered index, and on query performance.

Listing 11-38. Setup for Row Compression

```
USE AdventureWorks2017
GO

IF OBJECT_ID('dbo.NoCompression') IS NOT NULL
    DROP TABLE dbo.NoCompression;

IF OBJECT_ID('dbo.RowCompression') IS NOT NULL
    DROP TABLE dbo.RowCompression;

SELECT SalesOrderID
    ,SalesOrderDetailID
    ,CarrierTrackingNumber
    ,OrderQty
    ,ProductID
    ,SpecialOfferID
    ,UnitPrice
    ,UnitPriceDiscount
    ,LineTotal
```

```
    ,rowguid
    ,ModifiedDate
INTO dbo.NoCompression
FROM Sales.SalesOrderDetail;

SELECT SalesOrderID
    ,SalesOrderDetailID
    ,CarrierTrackingNumber
    ,OrderQty
    ,ProductID
    ,SpecialOfferID
    ,UnitPrice
    ,UnitPriceDiscount
    ,LineTotal
    ,rowguid
    ,ModifiedDate
INTO dbo.RowCompression
FROM Sales.SalesOrderDetail;
```

Implementation of row compression relies on the use of DATA_COMPRESSION index options on the CREATE or ALTER INDEX statement. Compression can be used on either clustered or nonclustered indexes. For row compression, the ROW option is shown in Listing 11-39. In this example, a clustered index is added to both of the example tables. The impact of using row compression on this table is impressive; there is a reduction of more than 35 percent in the number of pages required for the clustered index (see Figure 11-53).

Listing 11-39. Implementing Row Compression

```
USE AdventureWorks2017
GO

CREATE CLUSTERED INDEX CLIX_NoCompression ON dbo.NoCompression
    (SalesOrderID, SalesOrderDetailID);

CREATE CLUSTERED INDEX CLIX_RowCompression ON dbo.RowCompression
    (SalesOrderID, SalesOrderDetailID)
    WITH (DATA_COMPRESSION = ROW);
```

```
SELECT OBJECT_NAME(object_id) AS table_name
    ,in_row_reserved_page_count
FROM sys.dm_db_partition_stats
WHERE object_id IN (OBJECT_ID('dbo.NoCompression'),OBJECT_ID('dbo.
RowCompression'));
```

	table_name	in_row_reserved_page_count
1	NoCompression	1531
2	RowCompression	971

Figure 11-53. *Row compression output*

Storage isn't the only place where there is an improvement; there is also an improvement in query performance. To demonstrate this benefit, execute the code in Listing 11-40. In this script, two queries are executed against the tables from the previous example. While the business rules for the queries are identical, there is more than a 36 percent reduction in page reads for the table with row compression. By just adding compression to the index, the resources required for the query are reduced, and performance is improved without a change to the query design (Figure 11-54).

Listing 11-40. Row Compression Query

```
USE AdventureWorks2017
GO

SET STATISTICS IO, TIME ON

SELECT SalesOrderID, SalesOrderDetailID, CarrierTrackingNumber
FROM dbo.NoCompression
WHERE SalesOrderID BETWEEN 51500 AND 52000;

SELECT SalesOrderID, SalesOrderDetailID, CarrierTrackingNumber
FROM dbo.RowCompression
WHERE SalesOrderID BETWEEN 51500 AND 52000;
```

```
 Results   Messages
SQL Server parse and compile time:
   CPU time = 0 ms, elapsed time = 0 ms.

(4569 rows affected)
Table 'NoCompression'. Scan count 1, logical reads 66, physical reads 0, read-ahead reads 0, lob logical reads 0, lob physical reads 0,

 SQL Server Execution Times:
   CPU time = 0 ms,  elapsed time = 168 ms.
SQL Server parse and compile time:
   CPU time = 0 ms, elapsed time = 0 ms.

(4569 rows affected)
Table 'RowCompression'. Scan count 1, logical reads 42, physical reads 0, read-ahead reads 0, lob logical reads 0, lob physical reads 0,

 SQL Server Execution Times:
   CPU time = 0 ms,  elapsed time = 93 ms.
```

Figure 11-54. Row compression query statistics

There are a number of things that need to be considered when implementing row compression on an index. First, the amount of compression achieved by any use of compression will vary depending on the data types implemented and the data being stored. The improvement will, and should be expected to, vary per table and over time. Compression can't be enabled if the maximum possible size of the row exceeds 8,060 bytes (including the size of the data and the row overhead). Nonclustered indexes will not inherit the compression settings of the clustered index or heap; this must be specified when the index is created. However, clustered indexes will inherit the compression settings of the heap they are being created on if none is specified.

Row compression is a useful mechanism for altering how indexes are stored. It reduces the size of rows, which has the dual benefit of improving query performance and reducing storage requirements for indexes. The main thing to be concerned with when implementing row compression is the additional overhead associated with its use; this overhead materializes as a slight increase in CPU utilization which is usually offset by the reduced effort to process the query, as shown in Figure 11-54. Unless you can prove that row compression is causing issues, it's probably best to always leverage row compression at a minimum on indexes.

Page Compression

The other method to reduce the size of an index is by using variable-length data types and removing repeating values on a page. SQL Server accomplishes this through the page compression option on indexes. Like row compression, this compression type can be applied to heaps or clustered and nonclustered indexes. There are three components of page compression:

- Row compression
- Prefix compression
- Dictionary compression

The row compression component of page compression is identical to the row compression option. Before compressing a page, the row on the page is first compressed.

The next step in page compression is accomplished through prefix compression. Prefix compression scans columns and removes similar values and groups them in the page header. For instance, if a number of columns start with abc, this value is placed in the page header, and the value is replaced in the column with a location identifying what values have been replaced. If another column contains the value abcd, a reference to the abc value in the page header is included, changing the column value to 0d. This is continued for all columns to remove the most prevalent patterns and reduce the information stored per row of the column.

The last step in page compression is the dictionary compression. Through dictionary compression, the values in all columns are checked for repeating values. Continuing the previous example, if there are values in two columns across multiple rows that match the 0d value, then that value is placed in the page header, and a reference to the value is stored in those columns. This is done across the entire page, reducing the repeated prefix-compressed values.

For a demonstration of the benefits of page compression, let's expand on the example from the row compression section. To start the example, execute the script in Listing 11-41. This creates the dbo.PageCompression table similar to the tables from the previous example.

Listing 11-41. Setup for Page Compression

```
USE AdventureWorks2017
GO

IF OBJECT_ID('dbo.PageCompression') IS NOT NULL
    DROP TABLE dbo.PageCompression;

SELECT SalesOrderID
    ,SalesOrderDetailID
    ,CarrierTrackingNumber
```

```
    ,OrderQty
    ,ProductID
    ,SpecialOfferID
    ,UnitPrice
    ,UnitPriceDiscount
    ,LineTotal
    ,rowguid
    ,ModifiedDate
INTO dbo.PageCompression
FROM Sales.SalesOrderDetail;
```

Implementing page compression is nearly the same as row compression. Both utilize the DATA_COMPRESSION option, with the PAGE option for page compression. To see the effect of page compression on the tables, execute the code in Listing 11-42. In this example, the effect of page compression has significantly more impact on the table than was observed with row compression. This time the number of pages used by the table decreases by 55 percent, as shown in Figure 11-55.

Listing 11-42. Implementing Page Compression

```
USE AdventureWorks2017
GO

CREATE CLUSTERED INDEX CLIX_PageCompression ON dbo.PageCompression
    (SalesOrderID, SalesOrderDetailID)
    WITH (DATA_COMPRESSION = PAGE);

SELECT OBJECT_NAME(object_id) AS table_name
    ,in_row_reserved_page_count
FROM sys.dm_db_partition_stats
WHERE object_id IN (OBJECT_ID('dbo.NoCompression'),OBJECT_ID('dbo.
PageCompression'));
```

	table_name	in_row_reserved_page_count
1	NoCompression	1531
2	PageCompression	683

Figure 11-55. Page compression output

The improvements from page compression are not limited to just storing the index. These improvements continue to querying the table. Comparing the previous results against dbo.NoCompression to those against dbo.PageCompression (Listing 11-43) shows that the savings in reads continue with page compression. In this case, the reads decreased to 29 (see Figure 11-56), which is more than a 55 percent decrease in I/O cost.

Listing 11-43. Page Compression Query

```
USE AdventureWorks2017
GO

SET STATISTICS IO, TIME ON

SELECT SalesOrderID, SalesOrderDetailID, CarrierTrackingNumber
FROM dbo.PageCompression
WHERE SalesOrderID BETWEEN 51500 AND 52000;
```

```
(4569 rows affected)
Table 'PageCompression'. Scan count 1, logical reads 29, physical reads 0, read-ahead reads 0, lob logical reads 0, lob physical reads 0,

SQL Server Execution Times:
   CPU time = 0 ms,  elapsed time = 187 ms.
```

Figure 11-56. *Page compression query statistics*

The considerations for page compression are similar in nature to those for row compression with the addition of a few additional items. First, because of the nature in which page compression is implemented, there are times when SQL Server will decide that the rate of compression for a page is not sufficient to justify the cost of compressing the page. In these cases, SQL Server will attempt to compress the page but will record a failure of the page compression and store the page without the benefit of page compression over row compression. It is important to monitor the rate in which page compression attempts do not succeed since they can indicate when there is low value in using page compression on an index. This is discussed further in Chapter 3.

Next, the CPU cost for page compression is much higher than with row compression or without compression. If there are not sufficient CPU resources available, this can lead to other performance issues. Lastly, page compression is not ideal for tables and indexes that expect frequent data modifications. Compressing and uncompressing a page to modify a single row can have a significant impact on CPU.

Both row and page compression can provide substantial cost savings to indexing solutions. Consider both when looking at index designs. Doing so will provide performance improvements in situations where other solutions may not have yielded the desired results.

Note You can find additional considerations related to compression in the Books Online topic "Data Compression" at https://docs.microsoft.com/en-us/sql/relational-databases/data-compression/data-compression.

Indexed Views

In many cases, the way in which data is stored in the database does not fully represent the information that the users need to retrieve from the database. To solve this, you can build queries to pull the data that users need together into resultsets that they can more easily consume. In the process of performing these activities, you can aggregate data to provide the results at the level of detail in which users require.

As an example, users may want to see the total amount sold for a product across all the orders in a database but without including information on the detail items. In most situations, retrieving this information is not an issue. However, in some cases, performing that aggregation on the fly can create bottlenecks in the database. While indexes can assist in streamlining the aggregations, they sometimes do not provide the needed cost improvement to achieve the required performance.

One possible solution for this issue is to create indexes on a view in the database. The view can be created to provide the summary and aggregations that are required, and an index can be used to materialize the information in the view into an aggregated form. When indexing a view, the results of the query are stored in the database in much the same way as any table is stored. By storing this information ahead of time, queries that use the aggregations in the view can obtain improved response time.

Before looking at how to implement a view, let's first walk through the problem outlined earlier with retrieving summary information for products. In this case, suppose that there is a need for summary information for all products at the product subcategory level. The query for this, provided in Listing 11-44, would need to provide a sum aggregation of the `LineTotal OrderQty` values and then an average of the `UnitPrice`. While the number of reads for the query isn't substantially high (see Figure 11-57),

CHAPTER 11 INDEXING STRATEGIES

suppose that in this database it was considered too high for a query to be released into production. Examining the execution plan, provided in Figure 11-58, you see that while not overly complicated, the plan includes a number of steps and would not be considered a trivial plan.

Listing 11-44. Expensive Aggregation Query

```
USE AdventureWorks2017
GO

IF OBJECT_ID('dbo.ProductSubcategorySummary') IS NOT NULL
    DROP VIEW dbo.ProductSubcategorySummary;

SET STATISTICS IO ON;

SELECT psc.Name
    ,SUM(sod.LineTotal) AS SumLineTotal
    ,SUM(sod.OrderQty) AS SumOrderQty
    ,AVG(sod.UnitPrice) AS AvgUnitPrice
FROM Sales.SalesOrderDetail sod
    INNER JOIN Production.Product p ON sod.ProductID = p.ProductID
    INNER JOIN Production.ProductSubcategory psc ON p.ProductSubcategoryID =
    psc.ProductSubcategoryID
GROUP BY psc.Name
ORDER BY psc.Name;
```

```
(35 rows affected)
Table 'Worktable'. Scan count 0, logical reads 0, physical reads 0, read-ahead reads 0, lob logical reads 0, lob physical reads 0, lob read
Table 'Workfile'. Scan count 0, logical reads 0, physical reads 0, read-ahead reads 0, lob logical reads 0, lob physical reads 0, lob read-
Table 'SalesOrderDetail'. Scan count 1, logical reads 1240, physical reads 0, read-ahead reads 0, lob logical reads 0, lob physical reads 0
Table 'Product'. Scan count 1, logical reads 15, physical reads 0, read-ahead reads 0, lob logical reads 0, lob physical reads 0, lob read-
Table 'ProductSubcategory'. Scan count 1, logical reads 2, physical reads 0, read-ahead reads 0, lob logical reads 0, lob physical reads 0,

(1 row affected)
```

Figure 11-57. *Statistics I/O results for expensive aggregation*

CHAPTER 11 INDEXING STRATEGIES

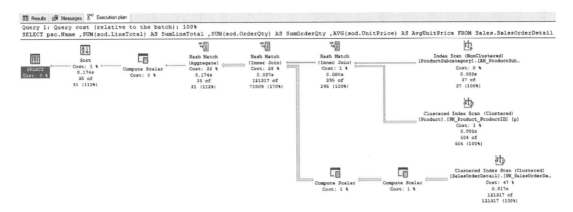

Figure 11-58. *Execution plan for expensive aggregation*

As mentioned, a solution for this performance problem can be found through creating a view for the query in Listing 11-43 and adding an index to the view. There are a number of things to consider when adding indexes to views. Some of the more important considerations are the following:

- All columns in the view must be deterministic.
- The view must be created using the SCHEMA_BINDING view option.
- The clustered index must be created as unique.
- Tables referenced in the view must use two-part naming.
- If aggregating values, the COUNT_BIG() function must be included.
- Some aggregations, such as AVG(), are disallowed in indexed views.

Additional consideration when creating indexed views is included in the Books Online topic "Create Indexed Views" (https://docs.microsoft.com/en-us/sql/relational-databases/views/create-indexed-views?).

The first step in creating an indexed view is to create the underlying view. Given the considerations listed, the query in Listing 11-44 cannot be directly turned into a view. The query must be changed to remove the AVG function and include the COUNT_BIG function. While this change removes one of the required data elements from the output, you will be able to calculate that value after indexing the view. Along with that, the view definition must include the WITH SCHEMABINDING option. The end result is the view definition in Listing 11-45. The last step is to create a unique clustered index on the table using the Name column from the Production.ProductSubcategory table.

435

Listing 11-45. Indexed View

```
USE AdventureWorks2017
GO

CREATE VIEW dbo.ProductSubcategorySummary
WITH SCHEMABINDING
AS
SELECT psc.Name
    ,SUM(sod.LineTotal) AS SumLineTotal
    ,SUM(sod.OrderQty) AS SumOrderQty
    ,SUM(sod.UnitPrice) AS TotalUnitPrice
    ,COUNT_BIG(*) AS Occurrences
FROM Sales.SalesOrderDetail sod
    INNER JOIN Production.Product p ON sod.ProductID = p.ProductID
    INNER JOIN Production.ProductSubcategory psc ON p.ProductSubcategoryID =
    psc.ProductSubcategoryID
GROUP BY psc.Name;
GO

CREATE UNIQUE CLUSTERED INDEX CLIX_ProductSubcategorySummary
    ON dbo.ProductSubcategorySummary(Name)
```

With the indexed view in place, the next step is to test how the view performs compared to the original query. Before executing the code in Listing 11-46, first look at the second query that is using the `TotalUnitPrice` and `Occurrences` columns to generate `AvgUnitPrice`. While you can't include the AVG function in the definitions for indexed views, you can arrive at the same results with minimal effort.

After executing the queries in Listing 11-46, you will notice that the queries performed substantially better than in the example in Listing 11-44. Instead of more than 1,200 reads, there are only 2 reads required (see Figure 11-59), and the execution plan (Figure 11-60) is quite a bit simpler. Instead of numerous operators, the plan was simplified to three operators.

CHAPTER 11 INDEXING STRATEGIES

Listing 11-46. Indexed View

```
USE AdventureWorks2017;
GO

SET STATISTICS IO ON;

SELECT psc.Name,
       SUM(sod.LineTotal) AS SumLineTotal,
       SUM(sod.OrderQty) AS SumOrderQty,
       AVG(sod.UnitPrice) AS AvgUnitPrice
FROM Sales.SalesOrderDetail sod
    INNER JOIN Production.Product p
        ON sod.ProductID = p.ProductID
    INNER JOIN Production.ProductSubcategory psc
        ON p.ProductSubcategoryID = psc.ProductSubcategoryID
GROUP BY psc.Name
ORDER BY psc.Name;

SELECT Name,
       SumLineTotal,
       SumOrderQty,
       TotalUnitPrice / Occurrences AS AvgUnitPrice
FROM dbo.ProductSubcategorySummary
ORDER BY Name;
```

```
(35 rows affected)
Table 'ProductSubcategorySummary'. Scan count 1, logical reads 2, physical reads 0, read-ahead reads 0, lob logical reads 0, lob physical reads 0,

(1 row affected)

(35 rows affected)
Table 'ProductSubcategorySummary'. Scan count 1, logical reads 2, physical reads 0, read-ahead reads 0, lob logical reads 0, lob physical reads 0,

(1 row affected)
```

Figure 11-59. *Statistics I/O results for Indexed View pattern*

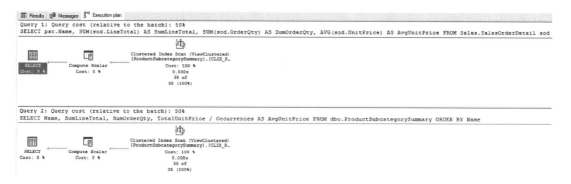

Figure 11-60. *Execution plan for Indexed View pattern*

Another peculiar thing occurred in the execution that you may notice. Both the query against the base tables and the query against the view performed identically after implementing the indexed view. This is one of the added benefits of indexed views. When SQL Server is determining the execution plan for the first query, it is able to deduce that there is an indexed view that can cover the same logic as the query, even though the calculation for the average column is not the same.

Indexed views are an extremely useful tool when multiple tables need to be joined together in a single unit to reduce the I/O required to join the data at runtime. While there are a number of restrictions associated with indexed views, there are numerous benefits, including the ability to use indexed views in situations like the one in Listing 11-46. When you have views and queries with the same shape that are used frequently, consider whether an inclusion of the view can provide the benefit that indexes on the base tables do not provide.

Summary

This chapter focused on how and when to apply indexes to tables in a number of situations. Each example demonstrated how to apply a particular index pattern to the situation to improve the performance with indexing. The chapter covered the limited, yet valid, instances for using heaps. It then went on to identify the various options and manners for building clustered indexes. With nonclustered indexes, the example demonstrated the options for adding to your clustered indexes in order to add performance on columns outside of the clustering key. The chapter also included an example of implementing columnstore indexes and discussed when to apply this type of index. Overall, these patterns provide the groundwork for identifying the types of indexes that are required on tables in databases, and they provide the basis for being able to compare and contrast one index to another.

CHAPTER 12

Query Strategies

In the previous chapter, we looked at strategies to identify potential indexes for your databases. That, though, is often only half the story. Once the indexes have been created, you would expect performance within the database to improve, leading you then to the next bottleneck. Unfortunately, coding practices and selectivity can sometimes negatively influence the application of indexes to queries. And sometimes how the database and tables are being accessed will prevent the use of some of the most beneficial indexes in your databases.

This chapter covers a number of querying strategies where indexes may not be used as you may have expected. These scenarios are

- LIKE comparison
- Concatenation
- Computed columns
- Scalar functions
- Data conversions

In each scenario, we'll look at the circumstances around them and why they don't work as expected. Then we'll see some ways to mitigate the issues and some tips on how to use the right index in the right place. By the end of the chapter, we'll be more prepared to recognize situations that will hamper your ability to index the database for performance, and we'll have the tools to begin mitigating these risks.

LIKE Comparison

When looking at the impact of queries on the use of indexes, the first place to start is with the LIKE comparison. The LIKE comparison allows searches in columns on any single character or pattern. If you need to find all the values in a table that start with the

CHAPTER 12 QUERY STRATEGIES

letters *AAA* or *BBB*, the LIKE comparison provides this functionality. In these searches, the query can read through the index and find the values that match to the characters or pattern, since the index is sorted. Problems can arise when using this comparison in queries to find values that contain or end with a character or pattern.

In this situation, the sort of the index becomes immaterial because statistics are collected only on the left edge of character values. The likelihood that the letter *B* appears in the first value in the index is equal to it appearing in the last value in the index. To determine which records in the table have a *B* in the column, all rows must be checked. There are no statistics available to identify the likelihood or location occurrences. Without reliable statistics to use, SQL Server will not know what index to use to satisfy a query and may end up using a poor execution plan.

To understand the problems that can occur with the LIKE comparison, we'll walk through a few demonstrations that show both scenarios and their related statistics. Let's start with querying the Person.Address table for records where AddressLine1 starts with 710 (see Listing 12-1). A review of the STATISTICS IO output in Figure 12-1 shows the query required three logical reads. Examining the execution plan in Figure 12-2 shows an index seek on the nonclustered index, which results in three logical reads.

Listing 12-1. Query for Addresses Beginning with 710

```
USE AdventureWorks2017
GO

SET STATISTICS IO ON;

SELECT AddressID, AddressLine1, AddressLine2, City, StateProvinceID,
PostalCode
FROM Person.Address
WHERE AddressLine1 LIKE '710%';
```

```
(15 rows affected)
Table 'Address'. Scan count 1, logical reads 3, physical reads 0, read-ahead reads 0, lob logical reads 0,

(1 row affected)
```

Figure 12-1. *STATISTICS IO for addresses beginning with 710*

CHAPTER 12 QUERY STRATEGIES

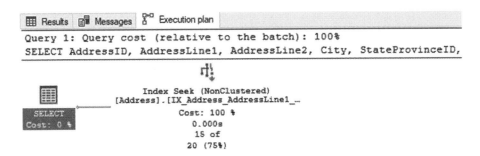

Figure 12-2. *Execution plan for addresses beginning with 710*

In this situation, the LIKE comparison worked well and the execution plan, statistics, and I/O were all appropriate for the request. Unfortunately, as mentioned, this isn't the only manner in which LIKE comparisons can be used. The comparison can be used to find values within a column. Consider a scenario where you need to find all the addresses that match a specific street name of a road, such as Longbrook (see Listing 12-2). With this query, the execution plan uses a scan on the nonclustered index and requires 216 logical reads, as shown in Figure 12-3. Figure 12-4 shows the execution plan.

Listing 12-2. Query for Addresses Containing "Longbrook

```
USE AdventureWorks2017
GO

SET STATISTICS IO ON;

SELECT AddressID, AddressLine1, AddressLine2, City, StateProvinceID,
PostalCode
FROM Person.Address
WHERE AddressLine1 LIKE '%Longbrook%';
```

```
(6 rows affected)
Table 'Address'. Scan count 1, logical reads 216, physical reads 0, read-ahead reads 0, lob logical reads 0,

(1 row affected)
```

Figure 12-3. *STATISTICS IO for addresses containing "Longbrook"*

CHAPTER 12 QUERY STRATEGIES

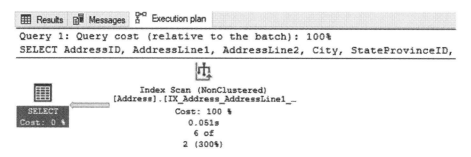

Figure 12-4. Execution plan for addresses containing "Longbrook"

In this scenario, the table and index were both small. The difference between an index seek and an index scan was not too extreme. Consider if this scenario was happening in your production system with one of the larger tables in your databases. Instead of being able to quickly filter out records that match the search values, SQL Server is required to look through all rows. And while that time may be just tens of seconds to complete, it opens the opportunity for blocking and deadlocking issues, which will further slow down queries in your environment.

A popular method of avoiding this situation is to declare that wildcards are never allowed on the left edge of searches. Unfortunately, this is a fairly unrealistic expectation. There are few business managers in the world that would agree to require their users to enter all possible street number combinations in an attempt to find every address that matched the street name search. Just reading it here sounds silly.

A less popular but much more appropriate and useful solution to this scenario is to create a full-text index on the table. A contributing factor to full-text indexes being less popular than nonclustered indexes is because of the difference in building and creating them, which has made them less familiar to most people. With a full-text index, words within one or more columns are cataloged, along with their position in the table. This enables the query to search quickly for the discrete values within a column value without having to check all the records in an index.

To use a full-text index on the Person.Address table, you must first build a full-text catalog, as shown in Listing 12-3. After that, the full-text index is created and includes the column that will be searched in the queries. Lastly, the query needs to be modified to use one of the full-text predicate functions. In this example, you will be using the CONTAINS function.

Listing 12-3. Query for Addresses Using CONTAINS

```
USE AdventureWorks2017
GO

SET STATISTICS IO ON;

CREATE FULLTEXT CATALOG ftQueryStrategies AS DEFAULT;

CREATE FULLTEXT INDEX ON Person.Address(AddressLine1)
KEY INDEX PK_Address_AddressID;
GO

SELECT AddressID, AddressLine1, AddressLine2, City, StateProvinceID,
PostalCode
FROM Person.Address
WHERE CONTAINS (AddressLine1,'Longbrook');
```

With the full-text index in place, the performance of the search for streets named Longbrook is similar to the first search where the query was looking for addresses starting with 710. In the execution plan in Figure 12-6, instead of a scan of the nonclustered index, the query is using a seek operation on the clustered index with a table-valued function lookup against the full-text index. As a result, instead of the 216 logical reads when using the LIKE comparison, using the full-text index requires only 12 logical reads (shown in Figure 12-5). The difference in reads provides a substantial improvement in performance over the first search attempt.

For more information on full-text indexes, read Chapter 6.

```
(6 rows affected)
Table 'Address'. Scan count 0, logical reads 12, physical reads 0, read-ahead reads 0, lob logical reads 0,

(1 row affected)
```

Figure 12-5. *STATISTICS IO for addresses using CONTAINS*

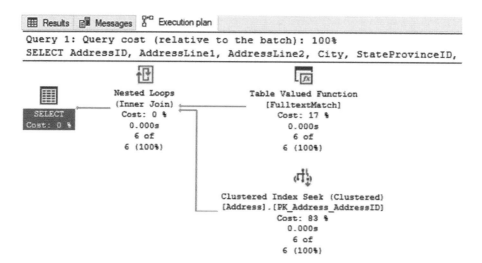

Figure 12-6. *Execution plan for addresses using CONTAINS*

Concatenation

Another scenario that can wreak havoc on indexing strategies is the use of concatenation. *Concatenation* is when two or more values are appended to one another. When this happens in a WHERE clause, it can often lead to poor performance that wasn't expected.

To demonstrate this scenario, consider a query for someone with the name Gustavo Achong. Searching for this value requires using the FirstName and LastName columns, which are concatenated together with a space between the columns. Listing 12-4 shows the query. A script to build an index on these columns is also included in the code listing. The execution plan generated for this query, shown in Figure 12-8, shows that the new index is used but operation is a scan instead of a seek, which would be more desirable. Even though the leading left edge of the index matches the left-side values of the concatenated values, the index is not able to determine where to find the values in the index. This results in the index using 99 logical reads to return the query results, shown in Figure 12-7.

CHAPTER 12   QUERY STRATEGIES

Listing 12-4. Query with Concatenation

```
USE AdventureWorks2017
GO

SET STATISTICS IO ON;

CREATE INDEX IX_PersonContact_FirstNameLastName ON Person.Person
(FirstName, LastName)
GO

SELECT BusinessEntityID, FirstName, LastName
FROM Person.Person
WHERE CONCAT(FirstName,' ',LastName) = 'Gustavo Achong'
```

```
Table 'Worktable'. Scan count 0, logical reads 0, physical reads 0, read-ahead reads 0, lob logical reads
Table 'Person'. Scan count 1, logical reads 106, physical reads 0, read-ahead reads 0, lob logical reads 0

(1 row affected)
Table 'Person'. Scan count 1, logical reads 99, physical reads 0, read-ahead reads 0, lob logical reads 0,

(1 row affected)
```

Figure 12-7. STATISTICS IO for concatenation

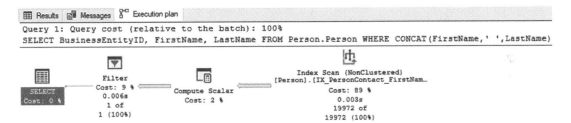

Figure 12-8. Execution plan for concatenation

As mentioned, using a scan on the index is not necessarily a bad thing. However, using a scan when there are a lot of concurrent users or data modifications occurring could lead to a performance issue. When it comes to larger tables with millions or more records, this can possibly lead to a lack of scalability for the database.

You might think that removing the space between the first and last names is a good idea (see Listing 12-5), since then it's using the two columns from the index we created. The major issue with this solution is that it doesn't work. As the execution plan in Figure 12-10 shows, it's nearly identical to the one with the space in the concatenated value with the same 99 reads as well (shown in Figure 12-9).

445

CHAPTER 12   QUERY STRATEGIES

Listing 12-5. Concatenation Without Spaces

```
USE AdventureWorks2017
GO

SET STATISTICS IO ON;

SELECT BusinessEntityID, FirstName, LastName
FROM Person.Person
WHERE CONCAT(FirstName, LastName)= 'GustavoAchong';
```

```
(1 row affected)
Table 'Person'. Scan count 1, logical reads 99, physical reads 0, read-ahead reads 0, lob logical reads 0,

(1 row affected)
```

Figure 12-9. *STATISTICS IO for concatenation without spaces*

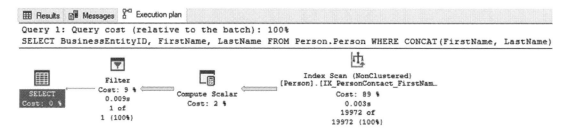

Figure 12-10. *Execution plan for concatenation without spaces*

Probably the best way to fix issues with concatenated values is to remove the need to concatenate. Instead of searching for the value Gustavo Achong, search for the first name Gustavo and the last name Achong (see Listing 12-6). When this change is made, the query is then able to use a seek operation on the nonclustered index and return the results with only two logical reads (see Figure 12-11). These results are a definite improvement over when the values were concatenated together. See Figure 12-12 for the execution plan.

CHAPTER 12　QUERY STRATEGIES

Listing 12-6. Query with Concatenation Removed

```
USE AdventureWorks2017
GO

SET STATISTICS IO ON;

SELECT BusinessEntityID, FirstName, LastName
FROM Person.Person
WHERE FirstName = 'Gustavo'
AND LastName = 'Achong';
```

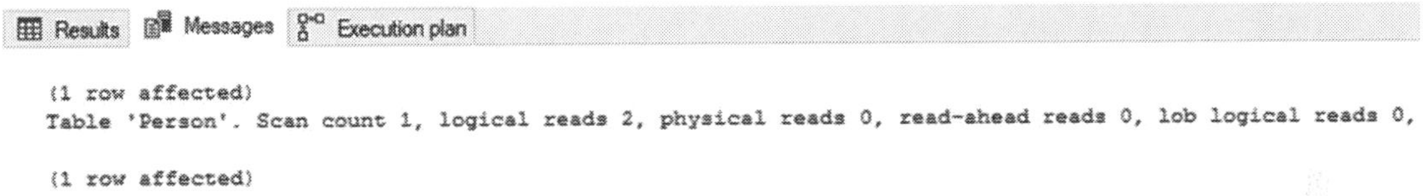

```
(1 row affected)
Table 'Person'. Scan count 1, logical reads 2, physical reads 0, read-ahead reads 0, lob logical reads 0,

(1 row affected)
```

Figure 12-11. *STATISTICS IO for concatenation removed*

```
Query 1: Query cost (relative to the batch): 100%
SELECT [BusinessEntityID],[FirstName],[LastName] FROM [Person].[Person] WHERE [FirstName]=@1 AND [LastName]

                    Index Seek (NonClustered)
                    [Person].[IX_PersonContact_FirstNam...
SELECT              Cost: 100 %
Cost: 0 %           0.000s
                    1 of
                    1 (100%)
```

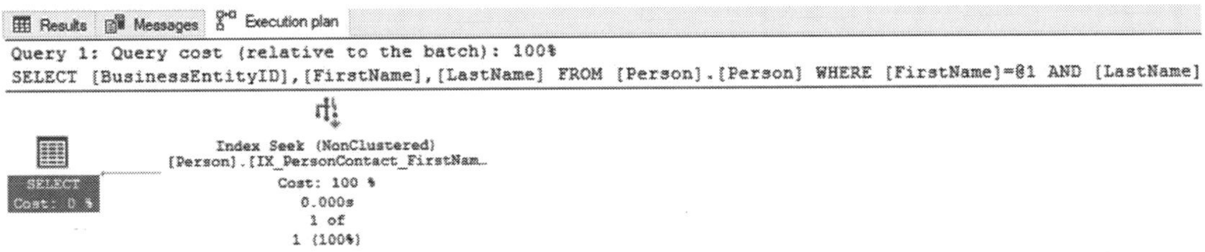

Figure 12-12. *Execution plan with concatenation removed*

At times, you won't have the option to remove concatenation from a query. In these cases, there is another way to resolve index performance issues: the concatenated values can be added to the table as a computed column. This solution, along with some of its issues, is discussed in the next section.

Computed Columns

Sometimes one or more columns in a table are defined as an expression. These types of columns are referred to as *computed columns*. Computed columns can be useful when you need a column to hold the result of a function or calculation that will change over time based on the other columns in the table. Rather than spending the CPU cycles to

CHAPTER 12 QUERY STRATEGIES

make certain that all modifications to a table always include changes to all the related columns, the components can be changed and the results computed when queried.

Note that computed columns cannot leverage the indexes on the source columns for the computed column. To demonstrate, add two computed columns to the Person.Person table using Listing 12-7. The first column will concatenate FirstName and LastName together, as they were concatenated in the previous section. The second column will multiply ContactID by EmailPromotion; this calculation doesn't mean anything, but it will show how this can be used with other calculation types.

Listing 12-7. Add Computed Columns to Person.Person

```
USE AdventureWorks2017
GO

ALTER TABLE Person.Person
ADD FirstLastName AS (FirstName + ' ' + LastName)
,CalculateValue AS (BusinessEntityID * EmailPromotion);
```

With the columns in place, the next step is to execute a couple of queries against the table. Execute two queries against the table using Listing 12-8. The first query is similar to the first and last name query from the previous section (when searching for Gustavo Achong). The second query will return all records with the CalculatedValue of 198.

Listing 12-8. Computed Column Queries

```
USE AdventureWorks2017
GO

SET STATISTICS IO ON

SELECT BusinessEntityID, FirstName, LastName, FirstLastName
FROM Person.Person
WHERE FirstLastName = 'Gustavo Achong';

SELECT BusinessEntityID, CalculateValue
FROM Person.Person
WHERE CalculateValue = 198;
```

CHAPTER 12 QUERY STRATEGIES

After executing both queries, the execution plans in Figure 12-14 show that both used scan operations to return the query results. These results are less than ideal for the same reasons mentioned earlier in this chapter, since they can lead to blocking and utilize more I/O than should be necessary for the query request. By more I/O, the query results for both require read I/Os from scanning the entire table, shown in Figure 12-13.

```
(1 row affected)
Table 'Person'. Scan count 1, logical reads 99, physical reads 0, read-ahead reads 0, lob logical reads 0, l

(1 row affected)

(1 row affected)
Table 'Person'. Scan count 1, logical reads 3858, physical reads 0, read-ahead reads 0, lob logical reads 0,

(1 row affected)
```

Figure 12-13. STATISTICS IO for computed columns

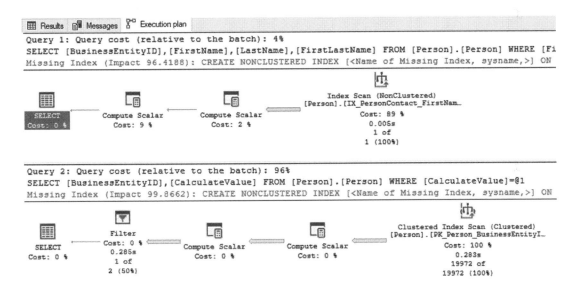

Figure 12-14. Computed column execution plans

An indexing option available for computed columns is to index the computed columns themselves, which even SQL Server suggests as missing indexes in Figure 12-4. As the query for FirstLastName shows, the query can use any of the indexes on the table. The restriction is that they can't use them any better than if the expression for the

CHAPTER 12 QUERY STRATEGIES

computed column was in the query itself. Indexing the computed columns, as shown in Listing 12-9, provides the necessary distribution and record information to allow queries, such as those in Listing 12-8, to use seeks instead of scans. The index materializes the values in the computed column, allowing quick access to the data, which results in a significant reduction in I/O from 99 to 5 reads and 3,878 to 2 reads, shown in Figure 12-15. Figure 12-16 shows the execution plan.

> **Note** When indexing a computed column, the expression for the column must be deterministic. This means that every time the expression executes with the same variables, it will always return the same results. As an example, using GETDATE() in a computed column expression would not be deterministic.

Listing 12-9. Computed Column Indexes

```
USE AdventureWorks2017
GO

CREATE INDEX IX_PersonPerson_FirstLastName ON Person.Person(FirstLastName);
CREATE INDEX IX_PersonPerson_CalculateValue ON Person.Person(CalculateValue);
```

```
(1 row affected)
Table 'Person'. Scan count 1, logical reads 5, physical reads 0, read-ahead reads 0, lob logical reads 0,

(1 row affected)

(1 row affected)
Table 'Person'. Scan count 1, logical reads 2, physical reads 0, read-ahead reads 0, lob logical reads 0,

(1 row affected)
```

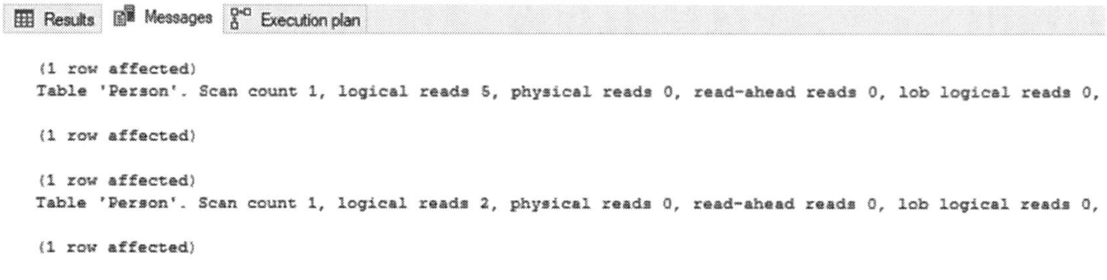

Figure 12-15. *STATISTICS IO for indexed computed column*

CHAPTER 12 QUERY STRATEGIES

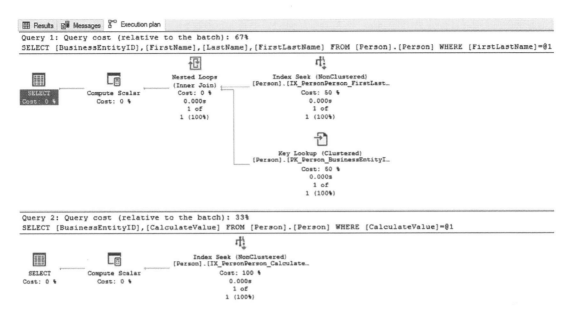

Figure 12-16. *Indexed computed column execution plans*

As this section demonstrates, computed columns can be extremely useful when expressions are needed to define values as part of a table. For instance, if an application can only send in searches where the first and last names were combined, computed columns can provide the data in the format that the application is sending. The columns can use underlying indexes to return results but usually can't fully use the statistics and underlying sort of the data in those indexes because of the expression in the column definition. By leveraging and indexing computed columns, you gain the benefit of having the data in the state the application needs it while maintaining the best performance possible.

Scalar Functions

The previous few sections discussed filtering query results by searching within column values or by combining values across columns. This section looks at the effect of scalar functions used in the WHERE clauses of queries. Scalar functions provide the ability to transform values to other values that can be more useful than the original value when querying the database.

User-defined scalar functions can also be created and used in the WHERE clause. The trouble with both system- and user-defined scalar functions is that if they transform the column where the index exists, then SQL Server is unable to use them efficiently.

Because the values of the calculations are not known until runtime, the query optimizer does not have statistics to determine the frequency of values in the index or information on where the calculated values are located in the index or table.

To demonstrate the effect of scalar functions on queries, consider the two queries in Listing 12-10 that return information from Person.Person. Both queries will return all rows that have the value Gustavo in the FirstName column. The difference between the two queries is that the second query will use the RTRIM function in the WHERE clause on the FirstName column.

Listing 12-10. Queries on FirstName Gustavo

```
USE AdventureWorks2017
GO

SET STATISTICS IO ON

SELECT BusinessEntityID, FirstName, LastName
FROM Person.Person
WHERE FirstName = 'Gustavo';

SELECT BusinessEntityID, FirstName, LastName
FROM Person.Person
WHERE RTRIM(FirstName) = 'Gustavo';
```

As the second execution plan in Figure 12-18 shows, when the scalar function is added to the WHERE clause, the execution plan continues to use the same index as the first plan did, but leverages an index scan instead of an index seek. This change increases the I/Os from 2 to 99 (shown in Figure 12-17), which is similar to other examples. In this example, just excluding the scalar function, as in the first query, can provide the same results as with the function in place. That won't be the case for all queries, but the way to allow indexes to be best used is to move the scalar function from the key columns to the parameters of a query.

CHAPTER 12 QUERY STRATEGIES

```
(2 rows affected)
Table 'Person'. Scan count 1, logical reads 2, physical reads 0, read-ahead reads 0, lob logical reads 0,

(1 row affected)

(2 rows affected)
Table 'Person'. Scan count 1, logical reads 99, physical reads 0, read-ahead reads 0, lob logical reads 0,

(1 row affected)
```

Figure 12-17. *Execution plans for Gustavo queries*

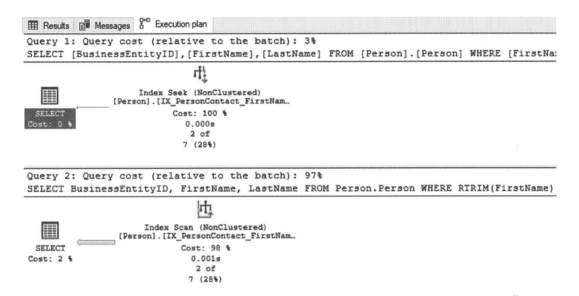

Figure 12-18. *Execution plans for Gustavo queries*

A good example of how scalar functions can be moved off of key columns and into the parameters is when the functions MONTH and YEAR are used. Suppose a query needs to return all the sales orders for the year 2001 and for December. This could be accomplished with the first SELECT query in Listing 12-11. Unfortunately, using the MONTH and YEAR functions changes the value of OrderDate, and the index that was built is used but with a scan instead of a seek (see the first execution plan in Figure 12-20). This issue can be avoided by changing the query in such a way that, instead of using the functions, you filter against a range of values, such as in the second SELECT statement in Listing 12-11. As the second execution shows, the query is able to return the results with a seek instead of a scan, providing a significant reduction in reads, from 73 to 3, as shown in Figure 12-19.

453

CHAPTER 12 QUERY STRATEGIES

Listing 12-11. Queries on FirstName Gustavo

```
USE AdventureWorks2017
GO

CREATE INDEX IX_SalesSalesOrderHeader_OrderDate ON Sales.
SalesOrderHeader(OrderDate);

SET STATISTICS IO ON;

SELECT SalesOrderID, OrderDate
FROM Sales.SalesOrderHeader
WHERE MONTH(OrderDate) = 12
AND YEAR(OrderDate) = 2012;

SELECT SalesOrderID, OrderDate
FROM Sales.SalesOrderHeader
WHERE OrderDate BETWEEN '20121201' AND '20121231';

SET STATISTICS IO OFF;
```

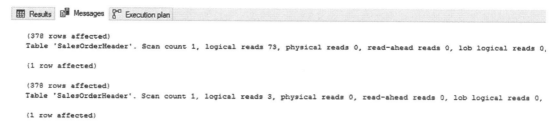

Figure 12-19. *Execution plans for date queries*

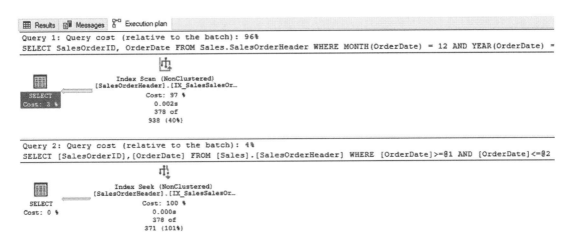

Figure 12-20. Execution plans for date queries

It won't always be possible to remove scalar functions from the WHERE clause of queries. One good example of this is if leading spaces were added to a column that should not be included when comparing the column values to parameters. In such a situation, you will need to think a little more "outside the box." One possible solution is to use a computed column with an index on it, as suggested in the previous section.

The important thing to remember when dealing with scalar functions in the WHERE clause is that if the function changes the value of a column, any index on the column most likely won't be able to be used as efficiently as possible with the query. If the table is small and the queries will be infrequent, this may not be a significant problem. For larger systems, this may be the reason behind unexpected high numbers of scans on indexes and can lead to issues with blocking and deadlocks.

Data Conversion

One last area where queries can negatively affect how indexes are used is when the data types of columns change within a JOIN operation or WHERE clause. When data types don't match in either of those conditions, SQL Server needs to convert the values in the columns to the same data types. If the data conversion is not included in the syntax of the query, SQL Server will attempt the data conversion behind the scenes.

The reason that data conversions can have a negative effect on query performance is along the same lines as the issues related to scalar functions. If a column in an index needs to be changed from varchar to int, the statistics and other information for this index won't be useful in determining the frequency and location of values. For instance, the number 10 and the string "10" would likely be sorted into entirely different positions in the same index. To illustrate the effect that data conversions can have on a query, start by executing the code in Listing 12-12.

Listing 12-12. Data Conversion Setup

```
USE AdventureWorks2017
GO

SELECT BusinessEntityID
    ,CAST(FirstName as varchar(50)) as FirstName
    ,CAST(MiddleName as varchar(50)) as MiddleName
    ,CAST(LastName as varchar(50)) as LastName
INTO PersonPerson
FROM Person.Person;

CREATE CLUSTERED INDEX IX_PersonPerson_ContactID ON PersonPerson
(BusinessEntityID);

CREATE INDEX IX_PersonContact_FirstName ON PersonPerson(FirstName);
```

Listing 12-12 will create a table with `varchar` data in it. It will then add two indexes to the table that will be used in the demonstration queries. The two sample queries, shown in Listing 12-13, will be used to show how data conversions can affect the performance and utilization of an index. For both queries, the `RECOMPILE` option is being utilized to prevent bad parameter sniffing, which occurs when the option is not being used.

> **Note** For more information on parameter sniffing, read Paul White's "Parameter Sniffing, Embedding, and the RECOMPILE Options" article on SQLPerformance.com at http://sqlperformance.com/2013/08/t-sql-queries/parameter-sniffing-embedding-and-the-recompile-options.

The first `SELECT` query uses the `@FirstName` variable with the `nvarchar` data type. This data type does not match the data type for the column in the table `PersonContact`, so the column in the table must be converted from `varchar` to `nvarchar`. The execution plan for the query (Figure 12-21) shows that the query is using an index seek on the nonclustered index to satisfy the query, and the predicate is converting the data in the column to nvarchar, with a key lookup on the clustered index for the columns not in the nonclustered index. Also note that the cost for the first query is 40 percent of the total batch, which is just the two queries.

Listing 12-13. Implicit Conversion Queries

```
USE AdventureWorks2017
GO

SET STATISTICS IO ON
DECLARE @FirstName nvarchar(100)
SET @FirstName = 'Gail';

SELECT FirstName, LastName FROM PersonPerson
WHERE FirstName = @FirstName
OPTION (RECOMPILE);

GO
DECLARE @FirstName varchar(100)
SET @FirstName = 'Gail';

SELECT FirstName, LastName FROM PersonPerson
WHERE FirstName = @FirstName
OPTION (RECOMPILE);
```

Note The additional information shown for the operators in the execution plans is available in the Properties window in SQL Server Management Studio. The Properties windows is full of useful information about the operations from the columns that are used for estimated and actual row counts.

CHAPTER 12   QUERY STRATEGIES

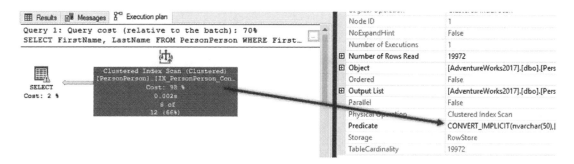

Figure 12-21. *Execution plans with implicit data conversion*

One other item to note in the execution plan in Figure 12-22 is the warning included on the SELECT operation for the first query. With the release of SQL Server 2012, there are now new warning messages included in execution plans that contain implicit conversions. The warning message appears as a yellow triangle with an exclamation point in it. Checking the properties for the operator will include properties of the operator and the warning message. These messages include information detailing what column is being converted and the issue associated with the problem. In this case, the issue is SeekPlan ConvertIssue. In other words, SQL Server doesn't have statistics on the converted data to build an execution plan that knows the frequency of the values in the predicate.

Figure 12-22. *Warning included with implicit conversion*

The second SELECT query in Listing 12-13 uses a variable with a varchar data type. Since this data type already matches the data type of the column in the table, the nonclustered index can be used. As the execution plan in Figure 12-23 shows, with matching data types the query optimizer can build a plan that knows where the rows in the index are and can perform a seek to obtain them.

CHAPTER 12   QUERY STRATEGIES

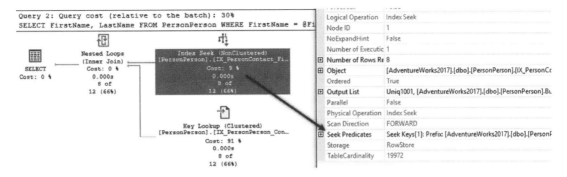

Figure 12-23. Execution plans without data conversion

Even though there are more operations in the second query and the complexity seems higher which might be expected to perform worse, especially with the inclusion of the key lookup, this isn't the case. We can see this if we review the logical reads from STATISTICS IO, shown in Figure 12-24. For the first query, the number of reads was 89 logical reads with an index scan on the clustered index. The second query had only 18 reads while accessing two indexes. The difference in the reads is because scanning the clustered index requires more reads than it takes to find the subset of rows required in the results and looking up missing columns from the clustered index.

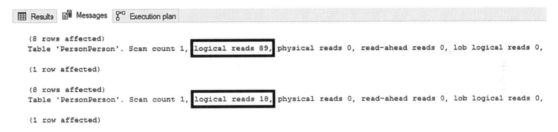

Figure 12-24. STATISTICS IO for implicit conversion queries

In this section, the discussion mostly focused on implicit data conversions. While these can be more silent than explicit data conversions, the same concepts and mitigations apply to these data conversions. Since they are more intentional, they should be less frequent. Even so, when performing data conversions, pay close attention to the data types because how they are changed will impact query performance and index utilization.

Summary

In this chapter, we examined the effect that queries can have on whether indexes can provide the expected performance improvements. There are times when a specific type of index may not be appropriate for a situation, such as searching for values within character values in large tables. In other situations, applying the right type of index or function in the right place can have a significant impact on whether the query can utilize an index.

In many of the examples in this chapter, the offending usage of an index was when it utilized a scan on the index instead of a seek operation. For these scenarios, index seeks were the ideal index operation. This won't always be the case and there are situations where scans against an index are significantly more ideal than seek operations. It's important to remember what type of transactions the environment is geared for and the size of the tables that are being accessed.

The main takeaway from this chapter is that you should take care when writing queries. The choices made when developing database code can completely unravel the work done to properly index a database. Be sure to complement your indexes with code that leverages them to their max.

CHAPTER 13

Monitoring Indexes

Throughout this book, we've discussed what indexes are, what they do, patterns for building them, and many other aspects for determining how a SQL Server database should be indexed. All of that information is necessary for the final piece in indexing your databases, analyzing your databases to determine which indexes are required. For this, this chapter and the two following will pull together the information we need to implement an indexing methodology.

To start, in this chapter, we'll discuss a general practice that can be used for monitoring indexes. It'll include steps that can be taken to observe the behavior of indexes and understand how they impact your environment. This methodology can be applied to a single database, a server, or your entire SQL Server environment. Regardless of the type of operations or business that the database supports, similar monitoring processes can be used.

The main goal behind monitoring indexes is creating the ability to collect information about indexes. This information will come from a variety of sources. The sources for monitoring should be familiar because they are often used with tasks similar to indexing, such as performance tuning. For some sources, the information will be collected over time to provide an idea of general trends. For other sources, a snapshot at a specific point in time is sufficient. It is important to collect information over time to provide a baseline against which to compare performance; this will help us know when changes in index usage and effectiveness have occurred.

As mentioned, there are a number of sources from which information will be collected to monitor your indexes. The sources that will be discussed in this chapter are

- Performance counters
- Dynamic management objects
- Event tracing

For each of these sources, the subsequent sections will describe what is to be collected and will provide guidance on how to collect this information. At the end of the chapter, we will have a framework that is capable of providing the information necessary to start the Analyze phase.

Note All the monitoring information from this chapter will be collected in a database named `IndexingMethod`. The scripts can be run in that database or your own performance monitoring database.

Performance Counters

The first source of monitoring information for indexes is SQL Server performance counters. Performance counters are metrics provided by Microsoft to measure the rate of events or state of resources within applications and hardware on the server. With some of the performance counters, there are general guidelines that can be used to indicate when a problem with indexing may exist. For the others, changes in the rate or level of the performance counter may indicate a need to change the indexing on a server.

The primary issue with using performance counters is that they represent the server-level, or SQL Server instance–level, state of the counters. They do not indicate at a database or table level where possible indexing issues are occurring. This level of detail, though, is acceptable and useful when considering the other tools available for monitoring your indexing and identifying potential indexing needs. One advantage to collecting counter information at this level is that we are forced to consider the whole picture and the effect of all the indexes on performance. In an isolated situation, a couple of poorly performing indexes on a table might be acceptable. However, in conjunction with other tables with poor indexing, the aggregate performance may reach a tipping point where indexes need to be addressed. With the server-level statistics provided by performance counters, we will be able to identify when this point has been reached.

There are a large number of performance counters available for both SQL Server and Windows Server. From the perspective of indexing, though, many of the performance counters can be eliminated. The performance counters that are most useful are those that map to operations related to how indexes operate or are accessed, such as forwarded records and index searches. For a definition of the performance counters that are most useful with indexing, see Table 13-1. The reasons for collecting each of the counters and how they impact indexing decisions will be discussed in the next chapter.

Table 13-1. Index-Related Performance Counters

Option Name	Description
Access Methods\Forwarded Records/sec	Number of records per second fetched through forwarded record pointers.
Access Methods\FreeSpace Page Fetches/sec	Number of pages fetched per second within allocated pages to an object to insert or modify a record.
Access Methods\FreeSpace Scans/sec	Number of scans per second initiated to search for free space within allocated pages to an object to insert or modify a record.
Access Methods\Full Scans/sec	Number of unrestricted full scans per second. These can be either base-table or full-index scans.
Access Methods\Index Searches/sec	Number of index searches per second. These are used to start range scans and single index record fetches and to reposition an index.
Access Methods\Page compression attempts/sec	Number of page compression attempts per second using PAGE compression, this will include failed page compressions.
Access Methods\Pages compressed/sec	Number of pages compressed per second using PAGE compression
Access Methods\Page Splits/sec	Number of page splits per second that occur as the result of overflowing index pages.
Buffer Manager\Page Lookups/sec	Number of requests to find a page in the buffer pool.
Locks(*)\Lock Wait Time (ms)	Total wait time (in milliseconds) for locks in the last second.
Locks(*)\Lock Waits/sec	Number of lock requests per second that required the caller to wait.
Locks(*)\Number of Deadlocks/sec	Number of lock requests per second that resulted in a deadlock.
SQL Statistics\ Batch Requests/sec	Number of Transact-SQL command batches received per second.

There are a number of ways to collect performance counters. For the monitoring in this chapter, we'll use the DMV `sys.dm_os_performance_counters`. This DMV returns a row for all the SQL Server counters for an instance. The values returned are the raw values for the counters, so depending on the type of counter, the value can be a point-in-time state value or an ever-accumulating aggregate.

To begin collecting performance counter information for monitoring, we'll first need to create a table for storing this information. The table definition in Listing 13-1 provides for this need. When collecting the performance counters, we will use a table that stores the counter name with the value and then datestamps each row to identify when the information was collected.

Listing 13-1. Performance Counter Snapshot Table

```
USE IndexingMethod;
GO

CREATE TABLE dbo.IndexingCounters
    (
    counter_id INT IDENTITY(1, 1),
    create_date DATETIME2(0),
    server_name VARCHAR(128) NOT NULL,
    object_name VARCHAR(128) NOT NULL,
    counter_name VARCHAR(128) NOT NULL,
    instance_name VARCHAR(128) NULL,
    Calculated_Counter_value FLOAT NULL,
    CONSTRAINT PK_IndexingCounters
        PRIMARY KEY CLUSTERED (counter_id)
    );
GO

CREATE NONCLUSTERED INDEX IX_IndexingCounters_CounterName
ON dbo.IndexingCounters (counter_name)
INCLUDE (create_date, server_name, object_name, Calculated_Counter_value);
```

For the purposes of collecting information for monitoring indexing, we'll take the information from sys.dm_os_performance_counters and calculate the appropriate values from the DMV. These would be the same values that are available when viewing performance counter information from other tools, such as Performance Monitor. There are a few steps required to populate dbo.IndexingCounters. As mentioned, the DMV contains raw counter values. To calculate these values properly, it is necessary to take a snapshot of the values in the DMV and then wait a number of seconds before calculating the counter value. In Listing 13-2, the counter value is calculated after 10 seconds. Once the time has expired, the counters are calculated and inserted into the dbo.IndexingCounters tables. This script should be scheduled and executed frequently. Ideally, we should collect this information every 1–5 minutes.

Note Performance counter information can be collected more frequently. For instance, Performance Monitor defaults to every 15 seconds. For the purposes of index monitoring, that frequency is not necessary.

Listing 13-2. Performance Counter Snapshot Script

```
DROP TABLE IF EXISTS #Counters;

SELECT pc.object_name,
    pc.counter_name
INTO #Counters
FROM sys.dm_os_performance_counters pc
WHERE pc.cntr_type IN ( 272696576, 1073874176 )
  AND (
      pc.object_name LIKE '%:Access Methods%'
    AND (
         pc.counter_name LIKE 'Forwarded Records/sec%'
      OR pc.counter_name LIKE 'FreeSpace Scans/sec%'
      OR pc.counter_name LIKE 'FreeSpace Page Fetches/sec%'
      OR pc.counter_name LIKE 'Full Scans/sec%'
      OR pc.counter_name LIKE 'Index Searches/sec%'
      OR pc.counter_name LIKE 'Page Splits/sec%'
      OR pc.counter_name LIKE 'Page compression attempts/sec%'
      OR pc.counter_name LIKE 'Pages compressed/sec%'
    )
  )
  OR (
      pc.object_name LIKE '%:Buffer Manager%'
    AND (
         pc.counter_name LIKE 'Page life expectancy%'
      OR pc.counter_name LIKE 'Page lookups/sec%'
    )
  )
```

```sql
    OR (
        pc.object_name LIKE '%:Locks%'
    AND (
           pc.counter_name LIKE 'Lock Wait Time (ms)%'
        OR pc.counter_name LIKE 'Lock Waits/sec%'
        OR pc.counter_name LIKE 'Number of Deadlocks/sec%'
      )
    )
    OR (
        pc.object_name LIKE '%:SQL Statistics%'
    AND pc.counter_name LIKE 'Batch Requests/sec%'
    )
GROUP BY pc.object_name,
    pc.counter_name;

DROP TABLE IF EXISTS #Baseline;

SELECT GETDATE() AS sample_time,
    pc1.object_name,
    pc1.counter_name,
    pc1.instance_name,
    pc1.cntr_value,
    pc1.cntr_type,
    x.cntr_value AS base_cntr_value
INTO #Baseline
FROM sys.dm_os_performance_counters pc1
INNER JOIN #Counters c ON c.object_name = pc1.object_name
                      AND c.counter_name = pc1.counter_name
OUTER APPLY (
    SELECT cntr_value
    FROM sys.dm_os_performance_counters pc2
    WHERE pc2.cntr_type              = 1073939712
      AND UPPER(pc1.counter_name)    = UPPER(pc2.counter_name)
      AND pc1.object_name            = pc2.object_name
      AND pc1.instance_name          = pc2.instance_name
) x;
```

CHAPTER 13 ■ MONITORING INDEXES

```sql
WAITFOR DELAY '00:00:15';

INSERT INTO dbo.IndexingCounters (
    create_date,
    server_name,
    object_name,
    counter_name,
    instance_name,
    Calculated_Counter_value
)
SELECT GETDATE(),
    LEFT(pc1.object_name, CHARINDEX(':', pc1.object_name) - 1),
    SUBSTRING(pc1.object_name, 1 + CHARINDEX(':', pc1.object_name),
    LEN(pc1.object_name)),
    pc1.counter_name,
    pc1.instance_name,
    CASE
        WHEN pc1.cntr_type = 65792 THEN pc1.cntr_value
        WHEN pc1.cntr_type = 272696576 THEN
            COALESCE((1. * pc1.cntr_value - x.cntr_value) /
            NULLIF(DATEDIFF(s, sample_time, GETDATE()), 0), 0)
        WHEN pc1.cntr_type = 537003264 THEN COALESCE((1. * pc1.cntr_value)
        / NULLIF(base.cntr_value, 0), 0)
        WHEN pc1.cntr_type = 1073874176 THEN
            COALESCE(
                (1. * pc1.cntr_value - x.cntr_value) / NULLIF(base.cntr_
                value - x.base_cntr_value, 0)
                / NULLIF(DATEDIFF(s, sample_time, GETDATE()), 0),
                0
            ) END AS real_cntr_value
FROM sys.dm_os_performance_counters pc1
INNER JOIN #Counters c ON c.object_name = pc1.object_name
                    AND c.counter_name = pc1.counter_name
OUTER APPLY (
    SELECT cntr_value,
        base_cntr_value,
```

```
            sample_time
    FROM #Baseline b
    WHERE b.object_name    = pc1.object_name
      AND b.counter_name   = pc1.counter_name
      AND b.instance_name  = pc1.instance_name
) x
OUTER APPLY (
    SELECT cntr_value
    FROM sys.dm_os_performance_counters pc2
    WHERE pc2.cntr_type               = 1073939712
      AND UPPER(pc1.counter_name)     = UPPER(pc2.counter_name)
      AND pc1.object_name             = pc2.object_name
      AND pc1.instance_name           = pc2.instance_name
) base;
```

The first time we collect performance counters for your indexes, we won't be able to compare the counters to other reasonable values for your SQL Server. As time goes on, though, we can retain previous performance counter samples to make comparisons. As part of monitoring, we will be responsible for identifying periods in which values for the performance counters represent the typical activity for your environment. To store these values, insert them into a table similar to the one in Listing 13-3. This table has start and end dates to indicate the range that the baseline represents. Also, there are minimum, maximum, average, and standard deviation columns to store values from the collected counters. The minimum and maximum values will allow for an understanding of how the performance counters vary. The average value provides an idea of what the counter value will be when it is "good." The standard deviation allows us to understand the variability of the counter values. The lower the number, the more frequently the counter values cluster around the average value. Higher values indicate that the counter values vary more frequently and are often nearer to the minimum and maximum values.

Listing 13-3. Performance Counter Baseline Table

```
USE IndexingMethod;
GO

CREATE TABLE dbo.IndexingCountersBaseline
    (
```

```
    counter_baseline_id INT IDENTITY(1, 1),
    start_date DATETIME2(0),
    end_date DATETIME2(0),
    server_name VARCHAR(128) NOT NULL,
    object_name VARCHAR(128) NOT NULL,
    counter_name VARCHAR(128) NOT NULL,
    instance_name VARCHAR(128) NULL,
    minimum_counter_value FLOAT NULL,
    maximum_counter_value FLOAT NULL,
    average_counter_value FLOAT NULL,
    standard_deviation_counter_value FLOAT NULL,
    CONSTRAINT PK_IndexingCountersBaseline
        PRIMARY KEY CLUSTERED (counter_baseline_id)
    );
GO
```

When populating the values into dbo.IndexingCountersBaseline, there are two steps to the population process. First, we need to collect a sample from the performance counters that represents a typical week. If there are no typical weeks, pick this week and collect samples for it. Once we have the typical week, the next step is to aggregate the information into the baseline table. Aggregating the information is a matter of summarizing the information in the table dbo.IndexingCounters for a range of days. In Listing 13-4, the data is from August 1 to August 15, 2019. The next step is to validate the baseline. Just because the average for the past week states that the Forwarded Records/sec value is at 100 doesn't mean that value is good for your baseline. Use your experience with your servers and databases to influence the values in the baseline. Make adjustments to the baseline as needed if there is a recent trend below or above what is normal.

Listing 13-4. Populate Counter Baseline Table

```
USE IndexingMethod;
GO

DECLARE @StartDate DATETIME = '20190911',
    @EndDate    DATETIME = '20190918';
```

```sql
INSERT INTO dbo.IndexingCountersBaseline (
    start_date,
    end_date,
    server_name,
    object_name,
    counter_name,
    instance_name,
    minimum_counter_value,
    maximum_counter_value,
    average_counter_value,
    standard_deviation_counter_value
)
SELECT MIN(create_date),
    MAX(create_date),
    server_name,
    object_name,
    counter_name,
    instance_name,
    MIN(Calculated_Counter_value),
    MAX(Calculated_Counter_value),
    AVG(Calculated_Counter_value),
    STDEV(Calculated_Counter_value)
FROM dbo.IndexingCounters
WHERE create_date BETWEEN @StartDate AND @EndDate
GROUP BY server_name,
    object_name,
    counter_name,
    instance_name;
```

There are other ways to collect and view performance counters for your SQL Server instances. We can use the Windows application Performance Monitor to view performance counters in real time. It can also be used to log performance counters to a binary or text file. The command-line utility Logman can also be used to interact with Performance Monitor to create data collectors and start and stop them as needed. Also, PowerShell is a possibility for assisting in the collection of performance counters.

CHAPTER 13 MONITORING INDEXES

All these alternatives are valid options for collecting performance counters on your databases and indexes. The key is that if we want to monitor your indexes, we must collect the information necessary to know when potential indexing issues may arise. Pick a tool that is most comfortable to use and start collecting these counters today.

Dynamic Management Objects

Some of the best index performance information for monitoring is included in dynamic management objects (DMOs). The DMOs contain information on logical and physical uses for the indexes and overall physical structure. For monitoring, there are four DMOs that provide information on the usage of the indexes: sys.dm_db_index_usage_stats, sys.dm_db_index_operational_stats, sys.dm_db_index_physical_stats, and sys.dm_os_wait_stats. In this section, we'll walk through a process to monitor your indexes using each of these DMOs.

The first three following sections will discuss the sys.dm_db_index_* DMOs. Chapter 3 defined and demonstrated the contents of the DMOs. One thing to remember with these DMOs is that they can be flushed through various operations on the server, such as restarting the service or recreating the index. The fourth DMO, sys.dm_os_wait_stats, relates to index monitoring and provides information that can help during index analysis.

Warning The indexing DMOs don't have information at the row level to precisely indicate when the information collected for the index has been reset. Because of this, there can be situations where the statistics reported can be slightly higher or lower than they actually are. While this shouldn't greatly affect the outcome during analysis, it is something to keep in mind.

Index Usage Stats

The DMO sys.dm_db_index_usage_stats provides information on how indexes are being used and when the index was last used. This information can be useful when we want to track whether indexes are being used and which operations are being executed against the index.

The monitoring process for this DMO, which is similar to the other DMOs, consists of the following steps:

1. Create a table to hold snapshot information.

2. Insert the current state of the DMO into the snapshot table.

3. Compare the most recent snapshot to the previous snapshot and insert the delta between the rows in the output into a history table.

To build the process, we'll first need to create the snapshot and history tables. The schema for these tables will be identical and will contain all the columns from the DMO and a create_date column (see Listing 13-5). For consistency with the source DMO, the columns for the table will match the schema of the DMO.

Listing 13-5. Index Usage Stats Snapshot Tables Stats

```
USE IndexingMethod;
GO

CREATE TABLE dbo.index_usage_stats_snapshot
    (
    snapshot_id INT IDENTITY(1, 1),
    create_date DATETIME2(0),
    database_id SMALLINT NOT NULL,
    object_id INT NOT NULL,
    index_id INT NOT NULL,
    user_seeks BIGINT NOT NULL,
    user_scans BIGINT NOT NULL,
    user_lookups BIGINT NOT NULL,
    user_updates BIGINT NOT NULL,
    last_user_seek DATETIME,
    last_user_scan DATETIME,
    last_user_lookup DATETIME,
    last_user_update DATETIME,
    system_seeks BIGINT NOT NULL,
    system_scans BIGINT NOT NULL,
    system_lookups BIGINT NOT NULL,
```

```sql
    system_updates BIGINT NOT NULL,
    last_system_seek DATETIME,
    last_system_scan DATETIME,
    last_system_lookup DATETIME,
    last_system_update DATETIME,
    CONSTRAINT PK_IndexUsageStatsSnapshot
        PRIMARY KEY CLUSTERED (snapshot_id),
    CONSTRAINT UQ_IndexUsageStatsSnapshot
        UNIQUE (create_date, database_id, object_id, index_id)
    );

CREATE TABLE dbo.index_usage_stats_history
    (
    history_id INT IDENTITY(1, 1),
    create_date DATETIME2(0),
    database_id SMALLINT NOT NULL,
    object_id INT NOT NULL,
    index_id INT NOT NULL,
    user_seeks BIGINT NOT NULL,
    user_scans BIGINT NOT NULL,
    user_lookups BIGINT NOT NULL,
    user_updates BIGINT NOT NULL,
    last_user_seek DATETIME,
    last_user_scan DATETIME,
    last_user_lookup DATETIME,
    last_user_update DATETIME,
    system_seeks BIGINT NOT NULL,
    system_scans BIGINT NOT NULL,
    system_lookups BIGINT NOT NULL,
    system_updates BIGINT NOT NULL,
    last_system_seek DATETIME,
    last_system_scan DATETIME,
    last_system_lookup DATETIME,
    last_system_update DATETIME,
    CONSTRAINT PK_IndexUsageStatsHistory
        PRIMARY KEY CLUSTERED (history_id),
```

CHAPTER 13 ■ MONITORING INDEXES

```
    CONSTRAINT UQ_IndexUsageStatsHistory
        UNIQUE (create_date, database_id, object_id, index_id)
);
```

The next piece in capturing a history of index usage stats is collecting the current values in `sys.dm_db_index_usage_stats`. Similar to the performance monitor script, the collection query, shown in Listing 13-6, needs to be scheduled to run about every 4 hours. The activity in your environment and rate in which indexes are modified should help determine the frequency in which the information is captured. Be certain to schedule a snapshot prior to any index defragmentation processes to capture information that might be lost when indexes are rebuilt.

Listing 13-6. *Index Usage Stats Snapshot Population*

```
USE IndexingMethod;
GO

INSERT INTO dbo.index_usage_stats_snapshot
SELECT GETDATE(),
    database_id,
    object_id,
    index_id,
    user_seeks,
    user_scans,
    user_lookups,
    user_updates,
    last_user_seek,
    last_user_scan,
    last_user_lookup,
    last_user_update,
    system_seeks,
    system_scans,
    system_lookups,
    system_updates,
    last_system_seek,
    last_system_scan,
```

```
        last_system_lookup,
        last_system_update
FROM sys.dm_db_index_usage_stats;
```

After populating the snapshot for the index usage stats, the delta between the most recent and the previous snapshot needs to be inserted into the index_usage_stats_history table. Since there isn't anything in the rows from sys.dm_db_index_usage_stats to identify when the stats for the index have been reset, the process for identifying when a delta between two entries for an index exists is to remove the row if any of the statistics on the index return a negative value. The resulting query, shown in Listing 13-7, implements this logic along with removing any rows where no new activity has happened.

Listing 13-7. Index Usage Stats Snapshot Population

```
USE IndexingMethod;
GO

WITH IndexUsageCTE
  AS (SELECT DENSE_RANK() OVER (ORDER BY create_date DESC) AS HistoryID,
            create_date,
            database_id,
            object_id,
            index_id,
            user_seeks,
            user_scans,
            user_lookups,
            user_updates,
            last_user_seek,
            last_user_scan,
            last_user_lookup,
            last_user_update,
            system_seeks,
            system_scans,
            system_lookups,
            system_updates,
            last_system_seek,
            last_system_scan,
```

```
            last_system_lookup,
            last_system_update
    FROM dbo.index_usage_stats_snapshot)
INSERT INTO dbo.index_usage_stats_history
SELECT i1.create_date,
    i1.database_id,
    i1.object_id,
    i1.index_id,
    i1.user_seeks - COALESCE(i2.user_seeks, 0),
    i1.user_scans - COALESCE(i2.user_scans, 0),
    i1.user_lookups - COALESCE(i2.user_lookups, 0),
    i1.user_updates - COALESCE(i2.user_updates, 0),
    i1.last_user_seek,
    i1.last_user_scan,
    i1.last_user_lookup,
    i1.last_user_update,
    i1.system_seeks - COALESCE(i2.system_seeks, 0),
    i1.system_scans - COALESCE(i2.system_scans, 0),
    i1.system_lookups - COALESCE(i2.system_lookups, 0),
    i1.system_updates - COALESCE(i2.system_updates, 0),
    i1.last_system_seek,
    i1.last_system_scan,
    i1.last_system_lookup,
    i1.last_system_update
FROM IndexUsageCTE i1
LEFT OUTER JOIN IndexUsageCTE i2 ON i1.database_id = i2.database_id
    AND i1.object_id   = i2.object_id
    AND i1.index_id    = i2.index_id
    AND i2.HistoryID   = 2
    --Verify no rows are less than 0
    AND NOT (
            i1.system_seeks - COALESCE(i2.system_seeks, 0) < 0
            AND i1.system_scans - COALESCE(i2.system_scans, 0) < 0
            AND i1.system_lookups - COALESCE(i2.system_lookups, 0) < 0
            AND i1.system_updates - COALESCE(i2.system_updates, 0) < 0
```

```
                AND i1.user_seeks    - COALESCE(i2.user_seeks, 0)   < 0
                AND i1.user_scans    - COALESCE(i2.user_scans, 0)   < 0
                AND i1.user_lookups  - COALESCE(i2.user_lookups, 0) < 0
                AND i1.user_updates  - COALESCE(i2.user_updates, 0) < 0
           )
    WHERE i1.HistoryID                                              = 1
      --Only include rows are greater than 0
      AND (
             i1.system_seeks   - COALESCE(i2.system_seeks, 0)    > 0
          OR i1.system_scans   - COALESCE(i2.system_scans, 0)    > 0
          OR i1.system_lookups - COALESCE(i2.system_lookups, 0)  > 0
          OR i1.system_updates - COALESCE(i2.system_updates, 0)  > 0
          OR i1.user_seeks     - COALESCE(i2.user_seeks, 0)      > 0
          OR i1.user_scans     - COALESCE(i2.user_scans, 0)      > 0
          OR i1.user_lookups   - COALESCE(i2.user_lookups, 0)    > 0
          OR i1.user_updates   - COALESCE(i2.user_updates, 0)    > 0
    );
    GO
```

Index Operational Stats

The DMO sys.dm_db_index_operational_stats provides information on the physical operations that happen on indexes during plan execution. This information can be useful for tracking the physical plan operations that occur when indexes are used and the rates for those operations. One of the other things this DMO monitors is the success rate in which compression operates.

As mentioned in the previous section, the process for monitoring this DMO involves a few simple steps. First, we'll create tables to store snapshot and history information on the DMO output. Then, periodic snapshots of the DMO output are inserted into the snapshot table. After the snapshot is retrieved, the delta between the current and previous snapshot is inserted into the history table.

The process utilizes a snapshot and history table that is nearly identical to the schema of sys.dm_db_index_operational_stats. The chief variance in the schema is the addition of a create_date column, used to identify when the snapshot occurred. The code in Listing 13-8 provides the schema required for the snapshot and history tables.

CHAPTER 13 MONITORING INDEXES

Note The columns version_generated_inrow, version_generated_offrow, ghost_version_inrow, ghost_version_offrow, insert_over_ghost_version_inrow, and insert_over_ghost_version_offrow are new in SQL Server 2019. If using the code in previous versions of SQL Server, the code will need to be adjusted.

Listing 13-8. Index Operational Stats Snapshot Tables Stats

```
USE IndexingMethod;
GO

CREATE TABLE dbo.index_operational_stats_snapshot
    (
    snapshot_id INT IDENTITY(1, 1),
    create_date DATETIME2(0),
    database_id SMALLINT NOT NULL,
    object_id INT NOT NULL,
    index_id INT NOT NULL,
    partition_number INT NOT NULL,
    hobt_id BIGINT NOT NULL,
    leaf_insert_count BIGINT NOT NULL,
    leaf_delete_count BIGINT NOT NULL,
    leaf_update_count BIGINT NOT NULL,
    leaf_ghost_count BIGINT NOT NULL,
    nonleaf_insert_count BIGINT NOT NULL,
    nonleaf_delete_count BIGINT NOT NULL,
    nonleaf_update_count BIGINT NOT NULL,
    leaf_allocation_count BIGINT NOT NULL,
    nonleaf_allocation_count BIGINT NOT NULL,
    leaf_page_merge_count BIGINT NOT NULL,
    nonleaf_page_merge_count BIGINT NOT NULL,
    range_scan_count BIGINT NOT NULL,
    singleton_lookup_count BIGINT NOT NULL,
    forwarded_fetch_count BIGINT NOT NULL,
    lob_fetch_in_pages BIGINT NOT NULL,
    lob_fetch_in_bytes BIGINT NOT NULL,
```

```
    lob_orphan_create_count BIGINT NOT NULL,
    lob_orphan_insert_count BIGINT NOT NULL,
    row_overflow_fetch_in_pages BIGINT NOT NULL,
    row_overflow_fetch_in_bytes BIGINT NOT NULL,
    column_value_push_off_row_count BIGINT NOT NULL,
    column_value_pull_in_row_count BIGINT NOT NULL,
    row_lock_count BIGINT NOT NULL,
    row_lock_wait_count BIGINT NOT NULL,
    row_lock_wait_in_ms BIGINT NOT NULL,
    page_lock_count BIGINT NOT NULL,
    page_lock_wait_count BIGINT NOT NULL,
    page_lock_wait_in_ms BIGINT NOT NULL,
    index_lock_promotion_attempt_count BIGINT NOT NULL,
    index_lock_promotion_count BIGINT NOT NULL,
    page_latch_wait_count BIGINT NOT NULL,
    page_latch_wait_in_ms BIGINT NOT NULL,
    page_io_latch_wait_count BIGINT NOT NULL,
    page_io_latch_wait_in_ms BIGINT NOT NULL,
    tree_page_latch_wait_count BIGINT NOT NULL,
    tree_page_latch_wait_in_ms BIGINT NOT NULL,
    tree_page_io_latch_wait_count BIGINT NOT NULL,
    tree_page_io_latch_wait_in_ms BIGINT NOT NULL,
    page_compression_attempt_count BIGINT NOT NULL,
    page_compression_success_count BIGINT NOT NULL,
    version_generated_inrow BIGINT NOT NULL,
    version_generated_offrow BIGINT NOT NULL,
    ghost_version_inrow BIGINT NOT NULL,
    ghost_version_offrow BIGINT NOT NULL,
    insert_over_ghost_version_inrow BIGINT NOT NULL,
    insert_over_ghost_version_offrow BIGINT NOT NULL,
    CONSTRAINT PK_IndexOperationalStatsSnapshot
        PRIMARY KEY CLUSTERED (snapshot_id),
    CONSTRAINT UQ_IndexOperationalStatsSnapshot
        UNIQUE (create_date, database_id, object_id, index_id, partition_
        number)
);
```

CHAPTER 13 MONITORING INDEXES

```
CREATE TABLE dbo.index_operational_stats_history
    (
    history_id INT IDENTITY(1, 1),
    create_date DATETIME2(0),
    database_id SMALLINT NOT NULL,
    object_id INT NOT NULL,
    index_id INT NOT NULL,
    partition_number INT NOT NULL,
    hobt_id BIGINT NOT NULL,
    leaf_insert_count BIGINT NOT NULL,
    leaf_delete_count BIGINT NOT NULL,
    leaf_update_count BIGINT NOT NULL,
    leaf_ghost_count BIGINT NOT NULL,
    nonleaf_insert_count BIGINT NOT NULL,
    nonleaf_delete_count BIGINT NOT NULL,
    nonleaf_update_count BIGINT NOT NULL,
    leaf_allocation_count BIGINT NOT NULL,
    nonleaf_allocation_count BIGINT NOT NULL,
    leaf_page_merge_count BIGINT NOT NULL,
    nonleaf_page_merge_count BIGINT NOT NULL,
    range_scan_count BIGINT NOT NULL,
    singleton_lookup_count BIGINT NOT NULL,
    forwarded_fetch_count BIGINT NOT NULL,
    lob_fetch_in_pages BIGINT NOT NULL,
    lob_fetch_in_bytes BIGINT NOT NULL,
    lob_orphan_create_count BIGINT NOT NULL,
    lob_orphan_insert_count BIGINT NOT NULL,
    row_overflow_fetch_in_pages BIGINT NOT NULL,
    row_overflow_fetch_in_bytes BIGINT NOT NULL,
    column_value_push_off_row_count BIGINT NOT NULL,
    column_value_pull_in_row_count BIGINT NOT NULL,
    row_lock_count BIGINT NOT NULL,
    row_lock_wait_count BIGINT NOT NULL,
    row_lock_wait_in_ms BIGINT NOT NULL,
    page_lock_count BIGINT NOT NULL,
    page_lock_wait_count BIGINT NOT NULL,
```

```
    page_lock_wait_in_ms BIGINT NOT NULL,
    index_lock_promotion_attempt_count BIGINT NOT NULL,
    index_lock_promotion_count BIGINT NOT NULL,
    page_latch_wait_count BIGINT NOT NULL,
    page_latch_wait_in_ms BIGINT NOT NULL,
    page_io_latch_wait_count BIGINT NOT NULL,
    page_io_latch_wait_in_ms BIGINT NOT NULL,
    tree_page_latch_wait_count BIGINT NOT NULL,
    tree_page_latch_wait_in_ms BIGINT NOT NULL,
    tree_page_io_latch_wait_count BIGINT NOT NULL,
    tree_page_io_latch_wait_in_ms BIGINT NOT NULL,
    page_compression_attempt_count BIGINT NOT NULL,
    page_compression_success_count BIGINT NOT NULL,
    version_generated_inrow BIGINT NOT NULL,
    version_generated_offrow BIGINT NOT NULL,
    ghost_version_inrow BIGINT NOT NULL,
    ghost_version_offrow BIGINT NOT NULL,
    insert_over_ghost_version_inrow BIGINT NOT NULL,
    insert_over_ghost_version_offrow BIGINT NOT NULL,
    CONSTRAINT PK_IndexOperationalStatsHistory
        PRIMARY KEY CLUSTERED (history_id),
    CONSTRAINT UQ_IndexOperationalStatsHistory
        UNIQUE (create_date, database_id, object_id, index_id, partition_
        number)
);
```

With the tables in place, the next step is to capture a current snapshot of the information in sys.dm_db_index_operational_stats. The information can be populated using the script in Listing 13-9. Since the Indexing Method is geared toward capturing information on indexing for all databases on the server, the values for the parameters for sys.dm_db_index_operational_stats are set to NULL. This will return results for all partitions of all indexes on all tables in all databases on the server. Like the index usage stats, this information should be captured about every 4 hours, with one of the scheduled points being before the index maintenance on the server.

Listing 13-9. Index Operational Stats Snapshot Population

```
USE IndexingMethod;
GO

TRUNCATE TABLE dbo.index_operational_stats_snapshot

INSERT INTO dbo.index_operational_stats_snapshot
SELECT GETDATE(),
    database_id,
    object_id,
    index_id,
    partition_number,
    hobt_id,
    leaf_insert_count,
    leaf_delete_count,
    leaf_update_count,
    leaf_ghost_count,
    nonleaf_insert_count,
    nonleaf_delete_count,
    nonleaf_update_count,
    leaf_allocation_count,
    nonleaf_allocation_count,
    leaf_page_merge_count,
    nonleaf_page_merge_count,
    range_scan_count,
    singleton_lookup_count,
    forwarded_fetch_count,
    lob_fetch_in_pages,
    lob_fetch_in_bytes,
    lob_orphan_create_count,
    lob_orphan_insert_count,
    row_overflow_fetch_in_pages,
    row_overflow_fetch_in_bytes,
    column_value_push_off_row_count,
    column_value_pull_in_row_count,
    row_lock_count,
```

```
    row_lock_wait_count,
    row_lock_wait_in_ms,
    page_lock_count,
    page_lock_wait_count,
    page_lock_wait_in_ms,
    index_lock_promotion_attempt_count,
    index_lock_promotion_count,
    page_latch_wait_count,
    page_latch_wait_in_ms,
    page_io_latch_wait_count,
    page_io_latch_wait_in_ms,
    tree_page_latch_wait_count,
    tree_page_latch_wait_in_ms,
    tree_page_io_latch_wait_count,
    tree_page_io_latch_wait_in_ms,
    page_compression_attempt_count,
    page_compression_success_count,
    version_generated_inrow,
    version_generated_offrow,
    ghost_version_inrow,
    ghost_version_offrow,
    insert_over_ghost_version_inrow,
    insert_over_ghost_version_offrow
FROM sys.dm_db_index_operational_stats(NULL, NULL, NULL, NULL)
WHERE database_id > 4;
```

The step after populating the snapshot is populating the history table. As before, the purpose of the history table is to store statistics on the deltas between two snapshots. The deltas provide information on which operations occurred, and they also help to timebox those operations so that, if needed, more focus can be placed on operations during core vs. noncore hours. The business rule identifying when the statistics have been reset is similar to index usage stats: if any of the statistics on the index return a negative value, the row from the previous snapshot will be ignored. Also, any rows that return all zero values will not be included. Listing 13-10 shows the code used to generate the history delta.

Listing 13-10. Index Operational Stats Snapshot Population

```
USE IndexingMethod;
GO

WITH IndexOperationalCTE
  AS (SELECT DENSE_RANK() OVER (ORDER BY create_date DESC) AS HistoryID,
            create_date,
            database_id,
            object_id,
            index_id,
            partition_number,
            hobt_id,
            leaf_insert_count,
            leaf_delete_count,
            leaf_update_count,
            leaf_ghost_count,
            nonleaf_insert_count,
            nonleaf_delete_count,
            nonleaf_update_count,
            leaf_allocation_count,
            nonleaf_allocation_count,
            leaf_page_merge_count,
            nonleaf_page_merge_count,
            range_scan_count,
            singleton_lookup_count,
            forwarded_fetch_count,
            lob_fetch_in_pages,
            lob_fetch_in_bytes,
            lob_orphan_create_count,
            lob_orphan_insert_count,
            row_overflow_fetch_in_pages,
            row_overflow_fetch_in_bytes,
            column_value_push_off_row_count,
            column_value_pull_in_row_count,
            row_lock_count,
            row_lock_wait_count,
```

```
            row_lock_wait_in_ms,
            page_lock_count,
            page_lock_wait_count,
            page_lock_wait_in_ms,
            index_lock_promotion_attempt_count,
            index_lock_promotion_count,
            page_latch_wait_count,
            page_latch_wait_in_ms,
            page_io_latch_wait_count,
            page_io_latch_wait_in_ms,
            tree_page_latch_wait_count,
            tree_page_latch_wait_in_ms,
            tree_page_io_latch_wait_count,
            tree_page_io_latch_wait_in_ms,
            page_compression_attempt_count,
            page_compression_success_count,
            version_generated_inrow,
            version_generated_offrow,
            ghost_version_inrow,
            ghost_version_offrow,
            insert_over_ghost_version_inrow,
            insert_over_ghost_version_offrow
        FROM dbo.index_operational_stats_snapshot)
INSERT INTO dbo.index_operational_stats_history
SELECT i1.create_date,
    i1.database_id,
    i1.object_id,
    i1.index_id,
    i1.partition_number,
        i1.hobt_id,
    i1.leaf_insert_count - COALESCE(i2.leaf_insert_count, 0),
    i1.leaf_delete_count - COALESCE(i2.leaf_delete_count, 0),
    i1.leaf_update_count - COALESCE(i2.leaf_update_count, 0),
    i1.leaf_ghost_count - COALESCE(i2.leaf_ghost_count, 0),
    i1.nonleaf_insert_count - COALESCE(i2.nonleaf_insert_count, 0),
    i1.nonleaf_delete_count - COALESCE(i2.nonleaf_delete_count, 0),
```

```
i1.nonleaf_update_count - COALESCE(i2.nonleaf_update_count, 0),
i1.leaf_allocation_count - COALESCE(i2.leaf_allocation_count, 0),
i1.nonleaf_allocation_count - COALESCE(i2.nonleaf_allocation_count, 0),
i1.leaf_page_merge_count - COALESCE(i2.leaf_page_merge_count, 0),
i1.nonleaf_page_merge_count - COALESCE(i2.nonleaf_page_merge_count, 0),
i1.range_scan_count - COALESCE(i2.range_scan_count, 0),
i1.singleton_lookup_count - COALESCE(i2.singleton_lookup_count, 0),
i1.forwarded_fetch_count - COALESCE(i2.forwarded_fetch_count, 0),
i1.lob_fetch_in_pages - COALESCE(i2.lob_fetch_in_pages, 0),
i1.lob_fetch_in_bytes - COALESCE(i2.lob_fetch_in_bytes, 0),
i1.lob_orphan_create_count - COALESCE(i2.lob_orphan_create_count, 0),
i1.lob_orphan_insert_count - COALESCE(i2.lob_orphan_insert_count, 0),
i1.row_overflow_fetch_in_pages - COALESCE(i2.row_overflow_fetch_in_
pages, 0),
i1.row_overflow_fetch_in_bytes - COALESCE(i2.row_overflow_fetch_in_
bytes, 0),
i1.column_value_push_off_row_count - COALESCE(i2.column_value_push_off_
row_count, 0),
i1.column_value_pull_in_row_count - COALESCE(i2.column_value_pull_in_
row_count, 0),
i1.row_lock_count - COALESCE(i2.row_lock_count, 0),
i1.row_lock_wait_count - COALESCE(i2.row_lock_wait_count, 0),
i1.row_lock_wait_in_ms - COALESCE(i2.row_lock_wait_in_ms, 0),
i1.page_lock_count - COALESCE(i2.page_lock_count, 0),
i1.page_lock_wait_count - COALESCE(i2.page_lock_wait_count, 0),
i1.page_lock_wait_in_ms - COALESCE(i2.page_lock_wait_in_ms, 0),
i1.index_lock_promotion_attempt_count - COALESCE(i2.index_lock_
promotion_attempt_count, 0),
i1.index_lock_promotion_count - COALESCE(i2.index_lock_promotion_
count, 0),
i1.page_latch_wait_count - COALESCE(i2.page_latch_wait_count, 0),
i1.page_latch_wait_in_ms - COALESCE(i2.page_latch_wait_in_ms, 0),
i1.page_io_latch_wait_count - COALESCE(i2.page_io_latch_wait_count, 0),
i1.page_io_latch_wait_in_ms - COALESCE(i2.page_io_latch_wait_in_ms, 0),
i1.tree_page_latch_wait_count - COALESCE(i2.tree_page_latch_wait_
count, 0),
```

```
            i1.tree_page_latch_wait_in_ms - COALESCE(i2.tree_page_latch_wait_
            in_ms, 0),
            i1.tree_page_io_latch_wait_count - COALESCE(i2.tree_page_io_latch_wait_
            count, 0),
            i1.tree_page_io_latch_wait_in_ms - COALESCE(i2.tree_page_io_latch_
            wait_in_ms, 0),
            i1.page_compression_attempt_count - COALESCE(i2.page_compression_
            attempt_count, 0),
            i1.page_compression_success_count - COALESCE(i2.page_compression_
            success_count, 0),
            i1.version_generated_inrow - COALESCE(i2.version_generated_inrow, 0),
            i1.version_generated_offrow - COALESCE(i2.version_generated_offrow, 0),
            i1.ghost_version_inrow - COALESCE(i2.ghost_version_inrow, 0),
            i1.ghost_version_offrow - COALESCE(i2.ghost_version_offrow, 0),
            i1.insert_over_ghost_version_inrow - COALESCE(i2.insert_over_ghost_
            version_inrow, 0),
            i1.insert_over_ghost_version_offrow - COALESCE(i2.insert_over_ghost_
            version_offrow, 0)
FROM IndexOperationalCTE i1
LEFT OUTER JOIN IndexOperationalCTE i2 ON i1.database_id = i2.database_id
AND i1.object_id = i2.object_id
AND i1.index_id = i2.index_id
AND i1.partition_number = i2.partition_number
AND i2.HistoryID = 2
--Verify no rows are less than 0
AND NOT (i1.leaf_insert_count - COALESCE(i2.leaf_insert_count, 0) < 0
        AND i1.leaf_delete_count - COALESCE(i2.leaf_delete_count, 0) < 0
        AND i1.leaf_update_count - COALESCE(i2.leaf_update_count, 0) < 0
        AND i1.leaf_ghost_count - COALESCE(i2.leaf_ghost_count, 0) < 0
        AND i1.nonleaf_insert_count - COALESCE(i2.nonleaf_insert_count, 0) < 0
        AND i1.nonleaf_delete_count - COALESCE(i2.nonleaf_delete_count, 0) < 0
        AND i1.nonleaf_update_count - COALESCE(i2.nonleaf_update_count, 0) < 0
        AND i1.leaf_allocation_count - COALESCE(i2.leaf_allocation_count, 0) < 0
        AND i1.nonleaf_allocation_count - COALESCE(i2.nonleaf_allocation_
        count, 0) < 0
```

```
        AND i1.leaf_page_merge_count - COALESCE(i2.leaf_page_merge_count, 0) < 0
        AND i1.nonleaf_page_merge_count - COALESCE(i2.nonleaf_page_merge_
        count, 0) < 0
        AND i1.range_scan_count - COALESCE(i2.range_scan_count, 0) < 0
        AND i1.singleton_lookup_count - COALESCE(i2.singleton_lookup_
        count, 0) < 0
        AND i1.forwarded_fetch_count - COALESCE(i2.forwarded_fetch_count, 0) < 0
        AND i1.lob_fetch_in_pages - COALESCE(i2.lob_fetch_in_pages, 0) < 0
        AND i1.lob_fetch_in_bytes - COALESCE(i2.lob_fetch_in_bytes, 0) < 0
        AND i1.lob_orphan_create_count - COALESCE(i2.lob_orphan_create_
        count, 0) < 0
        AND i1.lob_orphan_insert_count - COALESCE(i2.lob_orphan_insert_
        count, 0) < 0
        AND i1.row_overflow_fetch_in_pages - COALESCE(i2.row_overflow_fetch_
        in_pages, 0) < 0
        AND i1.row_overflow_fetch_in_bytes - COALESCE(i2.row_overflow_fetch_
        in_bytes, 0) < 0
        AND i1.column_value_push_off_row_count - COALESCE(i2.column_value_
        push_off_row_count, 0) < 0
        AND i1.column_value_pull_in_row_count - COALESCE(i2.column_value_
        pull_in_row_count, 0) < 0
        AND i1.row_lock_count - COALESCE(i2.row_lock_count, 0) < 0
        AND i1.row_lock_wait_count - COALESCE(i2.row_lock_wait_count, 0) < 0
        AND i1.row_lock_wait_in_ms - COALESCE(i2.row_lock_wait_in_ms, 0) < 0
        AND i1.page_lock_count - COALESCE(i2.page_lock_count, 0) < 0
        AND i1.page_lock_wait_count - COALESCE(i2.page_lock_wait_count, 0) < 0
        AND i1.page_lock_wait_in_ms - COALESCE(i2.page_lock_wait_in_ms, 0) < 0
        AND i1.index_lock_promotion_attempt_count - COALESCE(i2.index_lock_
        promotion_attempt_count, 0) < 0
        AND i1.index_lock_promotion_count - COALESCE(i2.index_lock_promotion_
        count, 0) < 0
        AND i1.page_latch_wait_count - COALESCE(i2.page_latch_wait_count, 0) < 0
        AND i1.page_latch_wait_in_ms - COALESCE(i2.page_latch_wait_in_ms, 0) < 0
        AND i1.page_io_latch_wait_count - COALESCE(i2.page_io_latch_wait_
        count, 0) < 0
```

```
        AND i1.page_io_latch_wait_in_ms - COALESCE(i2.page_io_latch_wait_in_
        ms, 0) < 0
        AND i1.tree_page_latch_wait_count - COALESCE(i2.tree_page_latch_wait_
        count, 0) < 0
        AND i1.tree_page_latch_wait_in_ms - COALESCE(i2.tree_page_latch_wait_
        in_ms, 0) < 0
        AND i1.tree_page_io_latch_wait_count - COALESCE(i2.tree_page_io_
        latch_wait_count, 0) < 0
        AND i1.tree_page_io_latch_wait_in_ms - COALESCE(i2.tree_page_io_
        latch_wait_in_ms, 0) < 0
        AND i1.page_compression_attempt_count - COALESCE(i2.page_compression_
        attempt_count, 0) < 0
        AND i1.page_compression_success_count - COALESCE(i2.page_compression_
        success_count, 0) < 0
        AND i1.version_generated_inrow - COALESCE(i2.version_generated_
        inrow, 0) < 0
        AND i1.version_generated_offrow    - COALESCE(i2.version_generated_
        offrow, 0) < 0
        AND i1.ghost_version_inrow - COALESCE(i2.ghost_version_inrow, 0) < 0
        AND i1.ghost_version_offrow - COALESCE(i2.ghost_version_offrow, 0) < 0
        AND i1.insert_over_ghost_version_inrow    - COALESCE(i2.insert_over_
        ghost_version_inrow, 0) < 0
        AND i1.insert_over_ghost_version_offrow - COALESCE(i2.insert_over_
        ghost_version_offrow, 0) < 0
)
WHERE i1.HistoryID = 1
--Only include rows are greater than 0
AND (
    i1.leaf_insert_count - COALESCE(i2.leaf_insert_count, 0) > 0
    OR i1.leaf_delete_count - COALESCE(i2.leaf_delete_count, 0) > 0
    OR i1.leaf_update_count - COALESCE(i2.leaf_update_count, 0) > 0
    OR i1.leaf_ghost_count - COALESCE(i2.leaf_ghost_count, 0) > 0
    OR i1.nonleaf_insert_count - COALESCE(i2.nonleaf_insert_count, 0) > 0
    OR i1.nonleaf_delete_count - COALESCE(i2.nonleaf_delete_count, 0) > 0
    OR i1.nonleaf_update_count - COALESCE(i2.nonleaf_update_count, 0) > 0
```

```
    OR i1.leaf_allocation_count - COALESCE(i2.leaf_allocation_count, 0) > 0
    OR i1.nonleaf_allocation_count - COALESCE(i2.nonleaf_allocation_
count, 0) > 0
    OR i1.leaf_page_merge_count - COALESCE(i2.leaf_page_merge_count, 0) > 0
    OR i1.nonleaf_page_merge_count - COALESCE(i2.nonleaf_page_merge_
count, 0) > 0
    OR i1.range_scan_count - COALESCE(i2.range_scan_count, 0) > 0
    OR i1.singleton_lookup_count - COALESCE(i2.singleton_lookup_count, 0) > 0
    OR i1.forwarded_fetch_count - COALESCE(i2.forwarded_fetch_count, 0) > 0
    OR i1.lob_fetch_in_pages - COALESCE(i2.lob_fetch_in_pages, 0) > 0
    OR i1.lob_fetch_in_bytes - COALESCE(i2.lob_fetch_in_bytes, 0) > 0
    OR i1.lob_orphan_create_count - COALESCE(i2.lob_orphan_create_
count, 0) > 0
    OR i1.lob_orphan_insert_count - COALESCE(i2.lob_orphan_insert_
count, 0) > 0
    OR i1.row_overflow_fetch_in_pages - COALESCE(i2.row_overflow_fetch_in_
pages, 0) > 0
    OR i1.row_overflow_fetch_in_bytes - COALESCE(i2.row_overflow_fetch_in_
bytes, 0) > 0
    OR i1.column_value_push_off_row_count - COALESCE(i2.column_value_push_
off_row_count, 0) > 0
    OR i1.column_value_pull_in_row_count - COALESCE(i2.column_value_pull_
in_row_count, 0) > 0
    OR i1.row_lock_count - COALESCE(i2.row_lock_count, 0) > 0
    OR i1.row_lock_wait_count - COALESCE(i2.row_lock_wait_count, 0) > 0
    OR i1.row_lock_wait_in_ms - COALESCE(i2.row_lock_wait_in_ms, 0) > 0
    OR i1.page_lock_count - COALESCE(i2.page_lock_count, 0) > 0
    OR i1.page_lock_wait_count - COALESCE(i2.page_lock_wait_count, 0) > 0
    OR i1.page_lock_wait_in_ms - COALESCE(i2.page_lock_wait_in_ms, 0) > 0
    OR i1.index_lock_promotion_attempt_count - COALESCE(i2.index_lock_
promotion_attempt_count, 0) > 0
    OR i1.index_lock_promotion_count - COALESCE(i2.index_lock_promotion_
count, 0) > 0
    OR i1.page_latch_wait_count - COALESCE(i2.page_latch_wait_count, 0) > 0
    OR i1.page_latch_wait_in_ms - COALESCE(i2.page_latch_wait_in_ms, 0) > 0
```

```
        OR i1.page_io_latch_wait_count - COALESCE(i2.page_io_latch_wait_
        count, 0) > 0
        OR i1.page_io_latch_wait_in_ms - COALESCE(i2.page_io_latch_wait_in_
        ms, 0) > 0
        OR i1.tree_page_latch_wait_count - COALESCE(i2.tree_page_latch_wait_
        count, 0) > 0
        OR i1.tree_page_latch_wait_in_ms - COALESCE(i2.tree_page_latch_wait_
        in_ms, 0) > 0
        OR i1.tree_page_io_latch_wait_count - COALESCE(i2.tree_page_io_latch_
        wait_count, 0) > 0
        OR i1.tree_page_io_latch_wait_in_ms - COALESCE(i2.tree_page_io_latch_
        wait_in_ms, 0) > 0
        OR i1.page_compression_attempt_count - COALESCE(i2.page_compression_
        attempt_count, 0) > 0
        OR i1.page_compression_success_count - COALESCE(i2.page_compression_
        success_count, 0) > 0
        OR i1.version_generated_inrow - COALESCE(i2.version_generated_
        inrow, 0) > 0
        OR i1.version_generated_offrow - COALESCE(i2.version_generated_
        offrow, 0) > 0
        OR i1.ghost_version_inrow - COALESCE(i2.ghost_version_inrow, 0) > 0
        OR i1.ghost_version_offrow - COALESCE(i2.ghost_version_offrow, 0) > 0
        OR i1.insert_over_ghost_version_inrow - COALESCE(i2.insert_over_ghost_
        version_inrow, 0) > 0
        OR i1.insert_over_ghost_version_offrow - COALESCE(i2.insert_over_ghost_
        version_offrow, 0) > 0
);
```

Index Physical Stats

The last indexing DMO for monitoring indexes is sys.dm_db_index_physical_stats. This DMO provides statistics on the current physical structure of the indexes in the databases. The value of this information is in determining the fragmentation of the index, which is discussed more in Chapter 6. From a monitoring perspective, we are collecting the physical statistics to aid with later analysis. The goal is to identify potential issues that may be affecting the efficiency in how the index is stored, or vice versa, thus impacting query performance because of how the index is stored.

With the physical stats DMO, the statistics are collected a bit differently than with the other DMOs. The main difference between this DMO and the others is the impact that can be placed on the database while collecting the information. While the other two reference in-memory tables, `index_physical_stats` reads the pages in the index to determine the actual fragmentation and physical layout of the indexes. Reference back to Chapter 3 for more about the impact of using `sys.dm_db_index_physical_stats`. To accommodate this difference, the statistics are stored only in a history table; the deltas between the points in which the history is retrieved are not determined. Also, because of the nature of the statistics contained in the DMO, there would be little value in calculating delta values.

The first piece needed to begin collecting statistics on index physical stats is the previously mentioned history table. This table, shown in Listing 13-11, uses the same schema as the DMO, with the addition of the `create_date` column.

> **Tip** When generating the table schema needed for the DMOs, a table-valued function first introduced in SQL Server 2012 was utilized. The function `sys.dm_exec_describe_first_result_set` can be used to identify the column names and data types for a query.

Listing 13-11. Index Physical Stats History Table

```
USE IndexingMethod;
GO

CREATE TABLE dbo.index_physical_stats_history
    (
    history_id INT IDENTITY(1, 1),
    create_date DATETIME2(0),
    database_id SMALLINT,
    object_id INT,
    index_id INT,
    partition_number INT,
    index_type_desc NVARCHAR(60),
    alloc_unit_type_desc NVARCHAR(60),
```

```
index_depth TINYINT,
index_level TINYINT,
avg_fragmentation_in_percent FLOAT,
fragment_count BIGINT,
avg_fragment_size_in_pages FLOAT,
page_count BIGINT,
avg_page_space_used_in_percent FLOAT,
record_count BIGINT,
ghost_record_count BIGINT,
version_ghost_record_count BIGINT,
min_record_size_in_bytes INT,
max_record_size_in_bytes INT,
avg_record_size_in_bytes FLOAT,
forwarded_record_count BIGINT,
compressed_page_count BIGINT,
hobt_id BIGINT NULL,
columnstore_delete_buffer_state TINYINT NULL,
columnstore_delete_buffer_state_desc NVARCHAR(60) NULL,
version_record_count BIGINT NULL,
inrow_version_record_count BIGINT NULL,
inrow_diff_version_record_count BIGINT NULL,
total_inrow_version_payload_size_in_bytes BIGINT NULL,
offrow_regular_version_record_count BIGINT NULL,
offrow_long_term_version_record_count BIGINT NULL,
CONSTRAINT PK_IndexPhysicalStatsHistory
    PRIMARY KEY CLUSTERED (history_id),
CONSTRAINT UQ_IndexPhysicalStatsHistory
    UNIQUE
    (
        create_date,
        database_id,
        object_id,
        index_id,
        partition_number,
        alloc_unit_type_desc,
```

```
            index_depth,
            index_level
        )
);
```

The collection of the history for `index_physical_stats` differs from the previous two DMOs. Since it's just history, there is no need to capture the snapshot information to build the delta between the two snapshots for the history. Instead, the current statistics are inserted directly into the history table, as shown in Listing 13-12. Also, since `index_physical_stats` performs physical operations on the index while collecting the statistics, there are a few things to keep in mind when generating the history information. First, the script will collect information from each database independently from the other databases through a CURSOR-drive loop. This provides a batched separation between the collections of statistics for each database and limits the impact of the DMO. Second, we should be certain that the query is executed during noncore hours. The start of the daily maintenance window would be ideal. It is important that this information is collected prior to defragmentation or re-indexing since these operations will change the information provided by the DMO. Usually, this information is collected as a step in the defragmentation process, which is discussed in Chapter 6. If so, there's no need to collect the information twice. Collect it for defragmentation and store it for later use in monitoring indexes.

Listing 13-12. Index Physical Stats History Population

```
USE IndexingMethod;
GO

DECLARE @DatabaseID INT;

DECLARE DatabaseList CURSOR FAST_FORWARD FOR
SELECT database_id
FROM sys.databases
WHERE state_desc = 'ONLINE'
AND database_id > 4;

OPEN DatabaseList;
FETCH NEXT FROM DatabaseList
INTO @DatabaseID;
```

```
WHILE @@FETCH_STATUS = 0
BEGIN

    INSERT INTO dbo.index_physical_stats_history (
        create_date,
        database_id,
        object_id,
        index_id,
        partition_number,
        index_type_desc,
        alloc_unit_type_desc,
        index_depth,
        index_level,
        avg_fragmentation_in_percent,
        fragment_count,
        avg_fragment_size_in_pages,
        page_count,
        avg_page_space_used_in_percent,
        record_count,
        ghost_record_count,
        version_ghost_record_count,
        min_record_size_in_bytes,
        max_record_size_in_bytes,
        avg_record_size_in_bytes,
        forwarded_record_count,
        compressed_page_count,
        hobt_id,
        columnstore_delete_buffer_state,
        columnstore_delete_buffer_state_desc,
        version_record_count,
        inrow_version_record_count,
        inrow_diff_version_record_count,
        total_inrow_version_payload_size_in_bytes,
        offrow_regular_version_record_count,
        offrow_long_term_version_record_count
    )
```

```
    SELECT GETDATE(),
        database_id,
        object_id,
        index_id,
        partition_number,
        index_type_desc,
        alloc_unit_type_desc,
        index_depth,
        index_level,
        avg_fragmentation_in_percent,
        fragment_count,
        avg_fragment_size_in_pages,
        page_count,
        avg_page_space_used_in_percent,
        record_count,
        ghost_record_count,
        version_ghost_record_count,
        min_record_size_in_bytes,
        max_record_size_in_bytes,
        avg_record_size_in_bytes,
        forwarded_record_count,
        compressed_page_count,
        hobt_id,
        columnstore_delete_buffer_state,
        columnstore_delete_buffer_state_desc,
        version_record_count,
        inrow_version_record_count,
        inrow_diff_version_record_count,
        total_inrow_version_payload_size_in_bytes,
        offrow_regular_version_record_count,
        offrow_long_term_version_record_count
    FROM sys.dm_db_index_physical_stats(@DatabaseID, NULL, NULL, NULL,
    'SAMPLED');
```

```
    FETCH NEXT FROM DatabaseList
    INTO @DatabaseID;
END;

CLOSE DatabaseList;
DEALLOCATE DatabaseList;
```

Wait Statistics

One other DMO that provides information related to indexing is sys.dm_os_wait_stats. This DMO collects information related to resources that SQL Server is waiting on in order to start or continue executing a query or other request. Most performance tuning methodologies include a process for collecting and analyzing wait statistics. From an indexing perspective, there are a number of wait resources that can indicate that there may be indexing issues on the SQL Server instance. By monitoring these statistics, we can be informed when these issues may exist. Table 13-2 provides a short list of wait types that most often indicate that indexing issues may exist.

Similar to performance counters, wait statistics are general indicators of health that reflect information about the SQL Server instance as a whole. They do not point directly to resources; instead, they collect information on when there was a wait for a specific resource on the SQL Server instance.

Note Many performance monitoring tools from third-party vendors collect wait statistics as a part of their monitoring. If there is a tool already installed in your environment, check to see whether wait statistics information can be retrieved from that tool.

Table 13-2. Index-Related Wait Statistics

Option Name	Description
CXPACKET	Synchronizes threads involved in a parallel query. This wait type means a parallel query is attempting to synchronize data within a paralle query between operators and can indicate an unbalanced workload or a worker is blocked by a preceding request.
IO_COMPLETION	Indicates a wait for I/O for operation (typically synchronous) like sorts and various situations where the engine needs to do a synchronous I/O. This wait type represents nondata page I/Os.
LCK_M_*	Occurs when a task is waiting to acquire a lock on an index or table.
PAGEIOLATCH_*	Occurs when a task is waiting on a latch for a buffer that is in an I/O request. Long waits may indicate problems with the disk subsystem.

The process for collecting wait statistics follows the pattern of using snapshot and history tables. To do this, the data will be collected first in a snapshot table with the deltas between snapshots stored in a history table. The snapshot and history tables, shown in Listing 13-13, contain the columns needed to support the snapshot and history patterns.

Listing 13-13. Wait Statistics Snapshot and History Table

```
USE IndexingMethod;
GO

CREATE TABLE dbo.wait_stats_snapshot
    (
    wait_stats_snapshot_id INT IDENTITY(1, 1),
    create_date DATETIME2(0),
    wait_type NVARCHAR(60) NOT NULL,
    waiting_tasks_count BIGINT NOT NULL,
    wait_time_ms BIGINT NOT NULL,
    max_wait_time_ms BIGINT NOT NULL,
    signal_wait_time_ms BIGINT NOT NULL,
    CONSTRAINT PK_wait_stats_snapshot
        PRIMARY KEY CLUSTERED (wait_stats_snapshot_id)
    );
```

CHAPTER 13 ■ MONITORING INDEXES

```
CREATE TABLE dbo.wait_stats_history
    (
    wait_stats_history_id INT IDENTITY(1, 1),
    create_date DATETIME2(0),
    wait_type NVARCHAR(60) NOT NULL,
    waiting_tasks_count BIGINT NOT NULL,
    wait_time_ms BIGINT NOT NULL,
    max_wait_time_ms BIGINT NOT NULL,
    signal_wait_time_ms BIGINT NOT NULL,
    CONSTRAINT PK_wait_stats_history
        PRIMARY KEY CLUSTERED (wait_stats_history_id)
    );
```

To collect the wait statistics information, the output from sys.dm_os_wait_stats is queried. Unlike the other DMOs discussed in this chapter, there is some summarization of the information that needs to occur prior to inserting the data. In a previous version of SQL Server, the wait_stats DMO contains two rows for the wait type MISCELLANEOUS. To accommodate for this variance, the sample script in Listing 13-14 uses aggregations to get around the issue. Another difference between wait_stats_snapshot and the other snapshots is the frequency in which the information should be collected. Wait_stats reports information on when requested resources were not available. Being able to tie this information to specific times of the day can be critical. As such, wait_stats information should be collected about once every hour.

Listing 13-14. Wait Statistics Snapshot Population

```
USE IndexingMethod;
GO

TRUNCATE TABLE dbo.wait_stats_snapshot

INSERT INTO dbo.wait_stats_snapshot (
    create_date,
    wait_type,
    waiting_tasks_count,
    wait_time_ms,
```

```
        max_wait_time_ms,
        signal_wait_time_ms
    )
SELECT GETDATE(),
    wait_type,
    waiting_tasks_count,
    wait_time_ms,
    max_wait_time_ms,
    signal_wait_time_ms
FROM sys.dm_os_wait_stats;
```

With each snapshot collected, the delta between it and the previous snapshot needs to be added in the wait_stats_history table. For determining when the information in sys.dm_os_wait_stats has been reset, the column waiting_tasks_count is utilized. If the value in the column is lower than the previous snapshot, the information in the DMO is reset. Listing 13-15 provides the code for populating the history table.

While there are only a few wait types that point toward indexing issues, the history table will show results for all the wait types that are encountered. The reason is that waits on resources need to be compared to the total number of other waits that occur. For instance, if CXPACKET is the lowest relative wait on the server, there isn't much value in researching the queries and determining the indexing that could reduce the occurrence of this wait type since other issues would likely impact performance more significantly.

Listing 13-15. Wait Statistics History Population

```
USE IndexingMethod;
GO

WITH WaitStatCTE
  AS (SELECT create_date,
        DENSE_RANK() OVER (ORDER BY create_date DESC) AS HistoryID,
        wait_type,
        waiting_tasks_count,
        wait_time_ms,
        max_wait_time_ms,
        signal_wait_time_ms
    FROM dbo.wait_stats_snapshot)
```

```
INSERT INTO dbo.wait_stats_history
SELECT w1.create_date,
    w1.wait_type,
    w1.waiting_tasks_count - COALESCE(w2.waiting_tasks_count, 0),
    w1.wait_time_ms - COALESCE(w2.wait_time_ms, 0),
    w1.max_wait_time_ms - COALESCE(w2.max_wait_time_ms, 0),
    w1.signal_wait_time_ms - COALESCE(w2.signal_wait_time_ms, 0)
FROM WaitStatCTE w1
LEFT OUTER JOIN WaitStatCTE w2 ON w1.wait_type = w2.wait_type
                                AND w1.waiting_tasks_count >= COALESCE(w2.
                                waiting_tasks_count, 0)
                                AND w2.HistoryID = 2
WHERE w1.HistoryID = 1
AND w1.waiting_tasks_count - COALESCE(w2.waiting_tasks_count, 0) > 0;
```

Data Cleanup

While all the information for monitoring is needed for the index analysis, this information is not needed indefinitely. The process for monitoring would not be complete without tasks in place to clean up the information collected after a reasonable amount of time. A generally acceptable schedule for cleaning up information is to purge snapshots after 3 days and history information after 90 days.

The snapshot information is used simply to prepare the history information and is really not needed after the delta is created. Since SQL Agent jobs can error and collection points may be a day apart from the previous, a 3-day window generally provides the leeway needed to support the process and accommodate any issues that may arise.

The data in the history tables is more crucial than the snapshot information and needs to be kept longer. This information feeds the activities during index analysis. The window for retaining this information should match the amount of time that it generally takes to go through the Indexing Method three or more times. This way, the information retained can be used for reference in a few cycles of the process.

When scheduling the cleanup process, it should be at least daily and during noncore processing hours. This will minimize the amount of information deleted in each execution and reduce the possible contention of the delete with other activity on the server. The delete script, shown in Listing 13-16, covers each of the tables discussed throughout this section.

Listing 13-16. Index Monitoring Snapshot and History Cleanup

```
USE IndexingMethod
GO

DECLARE @SnapshotDays INT = 3
    ,@HistoryDays INT = 90

DELETE FROM dbo.index_usage_stats_snapshot
WHERE create_date < DATEADD(d, -@SnapshotDays, GETDATE())

DELETE FROM dbo.index_usage_stats_history
WHERE create_date < DATEADD(d, -@HistoryDays, GETDATE())

DELETE FROM dbo.index_operational_stats_snapshot
WHERE create_date < DATEADD(d, -@SnapshotDays, GETDATE())

DELETE FROM dbo.index_operational_stats_history
WHERE create_date < DATEADD(d, -@HistoryDays, GETDATE())

DELETE FROM dbo.index_physical_stats_history
WHERE create_date < DATEADD(d, -@HistoryDays, GETDATE())

DELETE FROM dbo.wait_stats_snapshot
WHERE create_date < DATEADD(d, -@SnapshotDays, GETDATE())

DELETE FROM dbo.wait_stats_history
WHERE create_date < DATEADD(d, -@HistoryDays, GETDATE())
```

Event Tracing

The last set of information that should be collected for monitoring indexes is event tracing. The trace information collects SQL statements that represent production activity that can be used during index analysis to identify indexes that could be useful based on the query activity in your production environment and on the data that is being stored there. While the statistics collected so far provide information on the effect of activity on indexes and other resource use on the SQL Server instance, event tracing collects the activity that is causing those statistics. With SQL Server, there are two methods that can be used to collect event tracing data:

- SQL Trace
- Extended Events

For the purposes of completeness, both methods will be discussed. In my opinion, only Extended Events should be used to collect event tracing data in SQL Server. This is due to how well Extended Events are incorporated into SQL Server to help prevent it from causing performance issues while monitoring. And the level of detail that it can retrieve goes far beyond the capabilities of SQL Trace.

SQL Trace

SQL Trace, and by extension SQL Profiler, is the original tracing tool for SQL Server. It's one of the most common tools that DBAs have in their back pockets and can easily collect events in SQL Server. With SQL Trace, there are a number of areas to be careful of when collecting information. First, SQL Trace will likely collect a lot of information, and this will need to be accommodated. In other words, the more active the server and the databases, the larger the trace (.trc) files will be. Along these same lines, don't collect the trace information on drives that are already heavily used or dedicated to data or transaction log files. Doing this can, and likely will, impact the performance of I/O on those drives. The end goal for monitoring is to improve the performance of the system; care needs to be taken to minimize the impact of monitoring.

Finally, SQL Trace and SQL Profiler were deprecated in SQL Server 2012. This doesn't mean that these tools no longer function, but they are slated for removal in a future SQL Server release. While SQL Trace is deprecated, it is still the ideal tool in some scenarios for collecting trace information, such as for building workloads for the Database Engine Tuning Advisor.

Note It is always advisable to keep apprised of deprecated features within SQL Server. For more information on deprecated features, see SQL Docs at `https://docs.microsoft.com/en-us/sql/database-engine/deprecated-database-engine-features-in-sql-server-2017?view=sql-server-ver15`.

There are four basic steps to creating a SQL Trace session:

1. Build the trace session.
2. Assign the events and columns to the session.
3. Add filters to the session.
4. Start the SQL Trace session.

The next few pages will cover these steps and describe the components used in creating the SQL Trace session in SQL Server 2019. The script should work in earlier versions of SQL Server.

To begin monitoring with SQL Trace, a trace session must first be created. Sessions are created using the `sp_trace_create` stored procedure. This procedure accepts a number of parameters that configure how the session will collect information. In the example session, shown in Listing 13-17, the SQL Trace session will create files that automatically failover when they reach the 50 MB file size limit. The file size is limited to allow for better file management. In most environments, it's easier to copy many 50 MB files compared to files that are 1 GB or more. Also, the trace files are being created in `c:\temp` with the file name `IndexingMethod`. Be sure to create this folder if it doesn't exist. Note that this name can be changed to anything that suits the needs of the server and databases where the monitoring is being set up.

Listing 13-17. Create SQL Trace Session

```
USE master;
GO

DECLARE @rc INT,
    @TraceID INT,
    --Maximum .trc file size in MB
    @maxfilesize BIGINT = 50,
    --File name and path, minus the extension
    @FileName NVARCHAR(256) = N'c:\temp\IndexingMethod';

EXEC @rc = sp_trace_create @TraceID OUTPUT, 0, @FileName, @maxfilesize, NULL;
```

```
IF (@rc <> 0)
    RAISERROR('Error creating trace file', 16, 1);
SELECT *
FROM sys.traces
WHERE id = @TraceID;
```

After creating the SQL Trace session, the next step is to add events to the session. There are two events that will collect the information that is of most value to index monitoring: RPC:Completed and SQL:BatchCompleted. RPC:Completed returns results whenever a remote procedure call completes; the best example of this is the completion of a stored procedure. The other event, SQL:BatchCompleted, occurs when ad hoc and prepared batches are completed. Between these two events, all the completed SQL statements on the server will be collected.

To add events to the SQL Trace session, we use the sp_trace_set event stored procedure. The stored procedure adds events and the column requested from the event to the trace with each execution of the stored procedure. For two events with 15 columns each, the stored procedure will need to be executed 30 times. For the example session, shown in Listing 13-18, the following columns are being collected for each of the sessions:

- ApplicationName
- ClientProcessID
- CPU
- DatabaseID
- DatabaseName
- Duration
- EndTime
- HostName
- LoginName
- NTUserName
- Reads
- SPID

CHAPTER 13 ■ MONITORING INDEXES

- StartTime
- TextData
- Writes

We can find the codes for the events and columns in system catalog views. Events are listed in view sys.trace_events. The columns available are listed in sys.trace_columns. The columns view also includes an indicator to identify whether the values from the column can be filtered, which is useful in the next step in creating SQL Trace sessions.

Listing 13-18. Add Events and Columns to SQL Trace Session

```
USE master;
GO

DECLARE @on INT = 1,
    @FileName NVARCHAR(256) = N'c:\temp\IndexingMethod',
    @TraceID INT;

SET @TraceID = (
    SELECT id FROM sys.traces WHERE path LIKE @FileName + '%'
);
-- RPC:Completed
EXEC sp_trace_setevent @TraceID, 10, 1, @on;
EXEC sp_trace_setevent @TraceID, 10, 10, @on;
EXEC sp_trace_setevent @TraceID, 10, 11, @on;
EXEC sp_trace_setevent @TraceID, 10, 12, @on;
EXEC sp_trace_setevent @TraceID, 10, 13, @on;
EXEC sp_trace_setevent @TraceID, 10, 14, @on;
EXEC sp_trace_setevent @TraceID, 10, 15, @on;
EXEC sp_trace_setevent @TraceID, 10, 16, @on;
EXEC sp_trace_setevent @TraceID, 10, 17, @on;
EXEC sp_trace_setevent @TraceID, 10, 18, @on;
EXEC sp_trace_setevent @TraceID, 10, 3, @on;
EXEC sp_trace_setevent @TraceID, 10, 35, @on;
EXEC sp_trace_setevent @TraceID, 10, 6, @on;
```

```
EXEC sp_trace_setevent @TraceID, 10, 8, @on;
EXEC sp_trace_setevent @TraceID, 10, 9, @on;

--SQL:BatchCompleted
EXEC sp_trace_setevent @TraceID, 12, 1, @on;
EXEC sp_trace_setevent @TraceID, 12, 10, @on;
EXEC sp_trace_setevent @TraceID, 12, 11, @on;
EXEC sp_trace_setevent @TraceID, 12, 12, @on;
EXEC sp_trace_setevent @TraceID, 12, 13, @on;
EXEC sp_trace_setevent @TraceID, 12, 14, @on;
EXEC sp_trace_setevent @TraceID, 12, 15, @on;
EXEC sp_trace_setevent @TraceID, 12, 16, @on;
EXEC sp_trace_setevent @TraceID, 12, 17, @on;
EXEC sp_trace_setevent @TraceID, 12, 18, @on;
EXEC sp_trace_setevent @TraceID, 12, 3, @on;
EXEC sp_trace_setevent @TraceID, 12, 35, @on;
EXEC sp_trace_setevent @TraceID, 12, 6, @on;
EXEC sp_trace_setevent @TraceID, 12, 8, @on;
EXEC sp_trace_setevent @TraceID, 12, 9, @on;
```

The next step is to filter out unneeded events from the SQL Trace session. There is no need to collect all statements all the time for all databases and all applications with every SQL Trace session. In fact, in Listing 13-19, events from the system databases, those with a database ID less than 5, are removed from the session. The stored procedure for filtering SQL Trace sessions is sp_trace_setfilter. The stored procedure accepts the ID for columns from sys.trace_columns. Columns not included in the events can be filtered, and filters apply to all events.

Listing 13-19. Add Filters to SQL Trace Session

```
USE master;
GO

DECLARE @intfilter INT = 5,
    @FileName NVARCHAR(256) = N'c:\temp\IndexingMethod',
    @TraceID INT;
```

```
SET @TraceID = (
    SELECT id FROM sys.traces WHERE path LIKE @FileName + '%'
);

--Remove system databases from output
EXEC sp_trace_setfilter @TraceID, 3, 0, 4, @intfilter;
```

The last step in setting up the monitoring for SQL Trace is to start the trace. This task is accomplished using the sp_trace_setstatus stored procedure, shown in Listing 13-20. Through this procedure, SQL Trace sessions can be started, paused, and stopped. Once the trace is started, it will start to create .trc files in the file location provided, and the configuration for SQL Trace monitoring will be complete. When the collection period for the SQL Trace session completes, this script will be used with the status code 2 instead of 1 to terminate the session. Listing 13-21 provides this script.

Listing 13-20. Start SQL Trace Session

```
USE master;
GO

DECLARE @FileName NVARCHAR(256) = N'c:\temp\IndexingMethod',
    @TraceID INT;

SET @TraceID = (
    SELECT id FROM sys.traces WHERE path LIKE @FileName + '%'
);

-- Set the trace status to start
EXEC sp_trace_setstatus @TraceID, 1;
```

Note SQL Server experts often find it unfashionable to use the Database Engine Tuning Advisor, preferring instead to manually analyze the database and determine the indexes needed. This bias misses the opportunity to uncover low-hanging fruit or situations where changing the location of the clustered index can improve performance.

Listing 13-21. Stop SQL Trace Session

```
USE master;
GO

DECLARE @FileName NVARCHAR(256) = N'c:\temp\IndexingMethod',
    @TraceID INT;

SET @TraceID = (
    SELECT id FROM sys.traces WHERE path LIKE @FileName + '%'
);

-- Set the trace status to stop
EXEC sp_trace_setstatus @TraceID, 0;
```

The SQL Trace session example in this section is fairly basic. In your environment, we may need to have a more intelligent process that collects information in each trace file for a specified amount of time instead of using a file size to control the file rollover rate. These types of changes to collecting information from SQL Trace for monitoring indexes should have no impact on your ability to use the SQL Trace information for the purposes intended later in this chapter. There is one last item to consider with the SQL Trace information. Trace information does not need to constantly be gathered, like performance counter and DMO information. Instead, the SQL Trace information is often better suited to being collected for a 4–8-hour period that represents a regular day of activity on your database platform. With SQL Trace, we can collect too much information, which can overwhelm the analyze phase and delay indexing recommendations.

Extended Events

Extended Events, introduced in SQL Server 2008, is the preferred tracing tool in SQL Server; it's more functional but oddly less popular than SQL Trace. Given the opportunity to choose, create traces with Extended Events over SQL Trace. There are two ways to create Extended Events sessions. The first is through T-SQL, which will be demonstrated in this chapter. The second uses a GUI in SQL Server Management Studio that includes wizards for building a new session; the GUI was introduced in SQL Server 2012, so it's been around quite some time. The best practices in session creation are the same as SQL Trace for the most part. For instance, be sure to collect session logs on drives other than those in which data and log files are stored.

The trace we'll create in Extended Events will collect the same general information as SQL Trace. The main differences will be how the session is created and some of the names of events and columns. Instead of RPC:Completed and SQL:BatchCompleted, the events to capture in Extended Events are `rpc_completed` and `sql_batch_completed`, respectively. Each of these events captures their own set of columns, or data elements, which are listed in Table 13-3.

Table 13-3. *Extended Events Columns*

Event	Columns
`rpc_completed`	• `connection_reset_option` • `cpu_time` • `data_stream` • `duration` • `logical_reads` • `object_name` • `output_parameters` • `physical_reads` • `result` • `row_count` • `statement` • `writes`
`sql_batch_completed`	• `batch_text` • `cpu_time` • `duration` • `logical_reads` • `physical_reads` • `result` • `row_count` • `writes`

Additionally, we'll include some additional data in the Extended Events session that is available as global fields, or actions, which can be used to extend the default information included in each event. These are similar to the elements included in the SQL Trace session from the previous session. The global fields to be included are

- client_app_name
- client_hostname
- database_id
- database_name
- nt_username
- process_id
- session_id
- sql_text
- username

With the session defined, the next step is to create the sessions. Extended Events leverages the T-SQL data definition language (DDL) instead of stored procedures to create sessions. The code in Listing 13-22 provides the DDL for the session and starts the session. For each event added, the ADD EVENT syntax is used, and the ACTION clause is used to include the global fields. For convenience, the session is designed to store the output in the default log folder for SQL Server in the file EventTracingforIndexTuning.

Listing 13-22. Create and Start Extended Events Session

```
USE master;
GO

IF EXISTS (
    SELECT *
    FROM sys.server_event_sessions
    WHERE name = 'EventTracingforIndexTuning'
)
    DROP EVENT SESSION [EventTracingforIndexTuning] ON SERVER;

CREATE EVENT SESSION [EventTracingforIndexTuning]
ON SERVER
```

```
    ADD EVENT sqlserver.rpc_completed
    (ACTION (
        package0.process_id,
        sqlserver.client_app_name,
        sqlserver.client_hostname,
        sqlserver.database_id,
        sqlserver.database_name,
        sqlserver.nt_username,
        sqlserver.session_id,
        sqlserver.sql_text,
        sqlserver.username
     )
    ),
    ADD EVENT sqlserver.sql_batch_completed
    (ACTION (
        package0.process_id,
        sqlserver.client_app_name,
        sqlserver.client_hostname,
        sqlserver.database_id,
        sqlserver.database_name,
        sqlserver.nt_username,
        sqlserver.session_id,
        sqlserver.sql_text,
        sqlserver.username
     )
    )
    ADD TARGET package0.event_file
    (SET filename = N'EventTracingforIndexTuning')
WITH (
    STARTUP_STATE = ON
);
GO

ALTER EVENT SESSION [EventTracingforIndexTuning] ON SERVER STATE = START;
GO
```

CHAPTER 13 MONITORING INDEXES

Similar to SQL Trace sessions, Extended Events sessions can be started and stopped. There is no need to pause them since the metadata for a session exists independent from whether the session is running. Listing 13-22 includes the syntax for starting the trace. Listing 13-23 shows the code to stop the trace. Additionally, if SQL Server restarts, the Extended Events tracing session will be retained and can be configured to restart, unlike SQL Trace which disappears on restart.

Listing 13-23. Create and Start Extended Events Session

```
USE master;
GO

ALTER EVENT SESSION [EventTracingforIndexTuning] ON SERVER STATE = STOP;
GO
```

This Extended Events session is pretty simple. The nice thing about it is its ability to easily capture workloads from your SQL Server instances. Using the workloads from tracing, we can begin to understand how the SQL Server is being queried and the types of indexes that will help improve the performance of our environment.

Query Store

Introduced in SQL Server 2016, Query Store is a per-database data store that contains execution plan information and related execution statistics. While it doesn't necessarily provide direct index tuning information, advances in this feature may provide automated indexing capabilities in the future. This is based on the existing changes available to SQL Server in Azure SQL Database, which is detailed at https://docs.microsoft.com/en-us/sql/relational-databases/automatic-tuning/automatic-tuning?view=sql-server-ver15#automatic-index-management. As previously noted, this feature is not available in SQL Server 2019 at the time of this writing.

Despite the lack of direct index monitoring benefits, there are a few things that can be useful for indexing within the Query Store. The first is that since it is similar to the plan cache, queries used against the plan cache can be modified to use with the Query Store. In most cases, this will return the same information as the plan cache. An additional benefit to using Query Store is that in situations where execution plans are being replaced by other execution plans for improved performance, this can sometimes be index-related. This could be due to poor statistics available for the indexes or a lack of the best indexes to provide desired performance without replace plans. For either scenario, identifying these performance issues by monitoring Query Store activity can provide insight into indexes needed in an environment.

For the purposes of monitoring indexes, those reasons provide an additional worthwhile reason to leverage Query Store. To enable Query Store on a database, leverage the code in Listing 13-24. While a deep dive into Query Store is itself outside the context of this book, there is a lot of flexibility that can be leveraged around how frequently data is collected, how much data is stored, what the rate of dropping data is, and whether the Query Store is currently writable. It is definitely worthwhile to read further in Query Store for SQL Server 2019 by Apress.

Listing 13-24. Enable Query Store on AdventureWorks2017

```
USE [master]
GO
ALTER DATABASE [AdventureWorks2017] SET QUERY_STORE = ON
GO
ALTER DATABASE [AdventureWorks2017] SET QUERY_STORE
(OPERATION_MODE = READ_WRITE)
GO
```

Summary

In this chapter, we walked through the steps to monitor your indexes. Monitoring indexes is an extension of general platform monitoring but an important part of providing the foundation for determining whether we have the right indexes and for analyzing your indexes. Through the monitoring, I reviewed how to gather dynamic management data and performance counters. In the next chapter, we'll look at how we can apply this information to analyze whether we have the right indexes.

CHAPTER 14

Index Analysis

In the previous chapter, we discussed what information should be collected when monitoring indexes. All of that information is necessary for the next piece of indexing your databases, which is determining which indexes to apply. In this chapter, we will take all the information gathered while monitoring and use it to analyze the state of performance and the value of the existing indexes. The end goal of the index analysis is to build a list of indexes to create, modify, and, potentially, drop from the databases. In many cases, the analysis of the indexes will appear to border on art. There are many decisions in which you will use previous performance to anticipate future indexing needs. In the end, though, with every change proposed, there will be supporting evidence before and after the indexing solutions to statistically support or disprove the value of the index which makes index analysis more science than art.

The general process of index analysis is broken out into a number of components. Each component contains a process in which the analysis will start from high levels to identify the needed focus and hone the analysis into existing issues. The analysis components are as follows:

- Review of server state
- Schema discovery
- Database Engine Tuning Advisor
- Unused indexes
- Index plan usage

Before any exercise in analyzing the indexes of a database can take place, we first need to know the current deployment state. The tactics that can be used for a database in deployment vs. a database already deployed to the production environment will be roughly the same. There is a significant difference between the two, though, when it comes to where and how the statistics are gathered.

CHAPTER 14 INDEX ANALYSIS

For a database that has not been developed, the focus will be on how users are expected to use the database and application after it is deployed. Tests and workloads against the database will focus on validating that the indexing in the database supports those activities. The activity that is chosen for the testing will likely be the result of estimations and projections of what users will do with the application. Determining the activity will be the responsibility of the business analysts who develop the requirements for the application.

Once the database has been deployed, the monitoring shifts from what the activity could be to what the activity is. The rate in which users adopt features and what the distribution of the data is with that activity will be known. At this point, the indexes developed during testing and planning may not be correct for the workload. The first round of using the Indexing Method on the database after deployment may lead to significant indexing changes. The key with indexing databases that have been deployed is that the analysis needs to be against the statistics of the workload in production. Doing so will provide the necessary guidance for implementing indexes that provide the best benefit to the database and pair them with the features that users are using and the frequency in which they use them.

Going through the index analysis with databases in either deployment state will provide a set of indexes that are optimal for what is currently known and understood about the database. When the indexes are applied, your mileage with them can, and will, vary. An index may provide the perfect access path for data for the activity in the database last month. But with the new release, new clients, or changes in user behavior, they may not continue to be optimal. As is often heard with stock purchases, past performance does not dictate future results.

Fortunately, with a well-practiced use of the Indexing Method, we will be able to provide the indexing your environment needs. In this chapter, the focus is on databases that are already deployed to production. As mentioned, these tactics will work with databases and servers in both states, development and production, but for simplicity, a production environment will be the default perspective and approach.

As we move through each of the areas in the index analysis, we will get a list of indexes to either create, modify, delete, or investigate further. For the indexes that require further investigation, we will use subsequent portions of the index analysis process to determine how to progress and handle the index.

Note In this chapter, it will be important to run the monitoring scripts from Chapter 13 between the scripts that create the workload and the queries to review the statistics. Depending on the schedule used for collecting the statistics, it could be hours before the statistics are collected which will prevent the queries for statistics from providing the anticipated results.

Review of Server State

The first step in index analysis is to review the state of the server. Review both the host server environment and the SQL Server instance environment to identify whether there are conditions indicating that there may be indexing issues. By starting at a high level and not looking directly at tables and individual indexes, we can avoid getting blinded by the trees in the forest. Often, when there are hundreds of indexes in dozens of databases, it is easy to get overly focused on an index or table that looks poorly indexed, only to later discover that the table has fewer than a hundred rows in a database with billions of rows in other tables.

When analyzing the server state, we will look at the following three areas:

- Performance counters
- Wait statistics
- Buffer allocation

Each of these areas provides an idea of where to start focusing the index analysis process. They let the database platform determine where the performance issues related to indexing may reside.

Performance Counters

The first set of information collected for index monitoring included the performance counters. Naturally, we want to look at these performance counters first when performing index analysis. Tracking performance counters over a monitoring period and over time will not provide prescriptive guidance on what to do about indexing issues, but it will provide a point for discovering performance issues and thus where to begin.

For each of the counters, we'll discuss some general guidelines. These guidelines are generalities that should be taken with a grain of salt. Use them to initially guide whether the counter is outside what might be normal on other database platforms. If there is a reason that counters on your platform trend higher than typical, that is the purpose of maintaining the baseline tables. Work with the counter values that are valid for your environment as opposed to those that work best for others.

There are two ways in which performance counters should be analyzed. The first is to use Excel and/or Power BI to view graphs and trend lines based on the performance counters. The second is to review the performance counters with a query that takes a snapshot of the information in the performance counter table. The second approach is the approach used in this chapter. The guidelines for the snapshot queries apply to both approaches.

Note For simplicity, the snapshot analysis queries in this section will be scoped to the database level. In most cases, we will need to execute them against every database on the SQL Server instance. Options for accomplishing this are using sp_MSForEachDB and extending the cursors.

Forwarded Records per Second

As discussed in Chapter 2, forwarded records occur when heap records are updated and no longer fit on the page in which they were originally stored. In these situations, a pointer is placed in the original record to the new record location. The performance counter Forwarded Records/sec measures the rate in which forwarded rows are accessed on the server. Generally, the ratio of Forwarded Records/sec should not exceed 10 percent of Batch Requests/sec. This ratio can be a misnomer since Forwarded Records represents the access of data at the row level and Batch Requests represents a higher-scoped operation. The ratio, though, provides an indicator of when the balance of Forwarded Records/sec may be exceeding an advisable level.

The snapshot query for forwarded records, shown in Listing 14-1, provides columns for the Forwarded Records/sec counter and the ratio calculation. In this query, the values are aggregated into minimum, average, and maximum values. The ratio is calculated on each set of collected counters and aggregated after that calculation. The final column, PctViolation, shows the percentage of time in which the Forward Records to Batch Requests ratio exceeds the 10 percent guideline.

Listing 14-1. Forwarded Records Counter Analysis

```
USE IndexingMethod;
GO

WITH CounterSummary
  AS (SELECT create_date,
        server_name,
        MAX(IIF(counter_name = 'Forwarded Records/sec', Calculated_
        Counter_value, NULL)) AS ForwardedRecords,
        MAX(IIF(counter_name = 'Forwarded Records/sec', Calculated_
        Counter_value, NULL))
        / (NULLIF(MAX(IIF(counter_name = 'Batch Requests/sec',
        Calculated_Counter_value, NULL)), 0) * 10) AS ForwardedRecordRatio
    FROM dbo.IndexingCounters
    WHERE counter_name IN ( 'Forwarded Records/sec', 'Batch Requests/sec' )
    GROUP BY create_date,
        server_name)
SELECT server_name,
    MIN(ForwardedRecords) AS MinForwardedRecords,
    AVG(ForwardedRecords) AS AvgForwardedRecords,
    MAX(ForwardedRecords) AS MaxForwardedRecords,
    MIN(ForwardedRecordRatio) AS MinForwardedRecordRatio,
    AVG(ForwardedRecordRatio) AS AvgForwardedRecordRatio,
    MAX(ForwardedRecordRatio) AS MaxForwardedRecordRatio,
    FORMAT(1. * SUM(IIF(ForwardedRecordRatio > 1, 1, NULL)) / COUNT(*),
    '0.00%') AS PctViolation
FROM CounterSummary
GROUP BY server_name;
```

When reviewing the output from the snapshot query, there are a few things to ask about the information returned. First, review the minimum and maximum values for the counter and ratio. Is the minimum value close to or at zero? How high is the maximum? How does it compare to previous values collected during monitoring? Is the average value for the counter and ratio closer to the minimum or maximum value? If the volume and peaks of forwarded records is increasing, then further analysis is warranted.

CHAPTER 14 INDEX ANALYSIS

Next, consider the PctViolation column. Is the percentage greater than 1 percent? If so, further analysis of forwarded records is warranted. If there is a need to dig deeper into Forward Records, the next step is to move the analysis from the server level to the databases.

To provide an example of some forwarded record activity, execute the script in Listing 14-2. This script will create a table with a heap. Then it will insert records into the table and update those records, causing records to be expanded and leading to record forwarding. Finally, a query will access the forwarded records, causing forwarded record access operations.

Listing 14-2. Forwarded Records Example

```
USE AdventureWorks2017
GO

DROP TABLE IF EXISTS dbo.HeapExample;
GO

CREATE TABLE dbo.HeapExample (
    ID INT IDENTITY,
    FillerData VARCHAR(2000)
    );

INSERT INTO dbo.HeapExample (FillerData)
SELECT REPLICATE('X',100)
FROM sys.all_objects

UPDATE dbo.HeapExample
SET FillerData = REPLICATE('X',2000)
WHERE ID % 5 = 1
GO

SELECT *
FROM dbo.HeapExample
WHERE ID % 3 = 1
GO 2
```

CHAPTER 14　INDEX ANALYSIS

Once determining that Forwarded Records/sec analysis needs to go into the database, the process will leverage information available in the DMO. There are two DMOs that will help to determine the scope and extent of forwarded record issues. These are sys.dm_db_index_physical_stats and sys.dm_db_index_operational_stats. For the analysis, the sys.dm_db_index_operational_stats information will come from the monitoring table dbo.index_operational_stats_history. The analysis process, shown in Listing 14-3, involves identifying all the heaps in a database and then checking the physical structure of the heap. This information is then joined to the information collected in dbo.index_operational_stats_history. The physical stature of the index is retrieved from sys.dm_db_index_operational_stats because the DETAILED option for the DMO is required to get the forwarded record information.

Listing 14-3. Forwarded Records Snapshot Query

```
USE AdventureWorks2017
GO
IF OBJECT_ID('tempdb..#HeapList') IS NOT NULL
    DROP TABLE #HeapList

CREATE TABLE #HeapList
    (
     database_id int
    ,object_id int
    ,page_count INT
    ,avg_page_space_used_in_percent DECIMAL(6,3)
    ,record_count INT
    ,forwarded_record_count INT
    )

DECLARE HEAP_CURS CURSOR FORWARD_ONLY FOR
    SELECT object_id
    FROM sys.indexes i
    WHERE index_id = 0

DECLARE @IndexID INT

OPEN HEAP_CURS
FETCH NEXT FROM HEAP_CURS INTO @IndexID
```

```
WHILE @@FETCH_STATUS = 0
BEGIN
    INSERT INTO #HeapList
    SELECT
        DB_ID()
        ,object_id
        ,page_count
        ,CAST(avg_page_space_used_in_percent AS DECIMAL(6,3))
        ,record_count
        ,forwarded_record_count
    FROM
        sys.dm_db_index_physical_stats(DB_ID(), @IndexID, 0,
        NULL,'DETAILED') ;

    FETCH NEXT FROM HEAP_CURS INTO @IndexID
END

CLOSE HEAP_CURS
DEALLOCATE HEAP_CURS

SELECT
    QUOTENAME(DB_NAME(database_id))
    ,QUOTENAME(OBJECT_SCHEMA_NAME(object_id)) + '.'
        + QUOTENAME(OBJECT_NAME(object_id)) AS ObjectName
    ,page_count
    ,avg_page_space_used_in_percent
    ,record_count
    ,forwarded_record_count
    ,x.forwarded_fetch_count
    ,CAST(100.*forwarded_record_count/record_count AS DECIMAL(6,3)) AS
    forwarded_record_pct
    ,CAST(1.*x.forwarded_fetch_count/forwarded_record_count AS
    DECIMAL(12,3)) AS forwarded_row_ratio
FROM #HeapList h
    CROSS APPLY(
        SELECT SUM(forwarded_fetch_count) AS forwarded_fetch_count
        FROM IndexingMethod.dbo.index_operational_stats_history i
```

```
        WHERE h.database_id = i.database_id
        AND h.object_id = i.OBJECT_ID
        AND i.index_id = 0) x
WHERE forwarded_record_count > 0
ORDER BY page_count DESC
```

The results of the snapshot query, shown in Figure 14-1, provide information on all the heaps in a database that have any forwarded records. Through these results, the heaps that have issues with forwarding and forwarded records can be identified. The first columns to pay attention to are page_count and record_count. Heaps with many records with forwarded record issues will be more important than those with few rows. It is worthwhile to focus on those tables that will provide the greatest relief to forwarded records when investigating this counter. The columns forwarded_record_count and forwarded_fetch_count provide a count of the number of records in a table that have been forwarded and the number of times those forwarded records have been accessed, respectively. These columns provide a scope to the size of the problem. The last columns to look at are forwarded_record_pct and forwarded_row_ratio. These columns detail the percentage of columns that are forwarded and how many times each of the forwarded rows has been accessed.

In the example table, the statistics indicate that there is an issue with forwarded records. The table has more than 16 percent of its rows forwarded. Each of these rows has been accessed three times, based on the forwarded_fetch_count. From the code sample, there have been only three queries executed on the table, meaning that every time there has been data access, all of the forwarded rows are being accessed. When analyzing the indexes in this database, mitigating the forwarded records for this table would be worthwhile. Do pay special attention to whether forwarded records are being accessed. Mitigating forwarded records on a table that has very high forwarded records but no forwarded record access would not be worth the effort and would have no impact on the Forwarded Records/sec counter.

(No column name)	ObjectName	page_count	avg_page_space_used_in_percent	record_count	forwarded_record_count	forwarded_fetch_count	forwarded_record_pct	forwarded_row_ratio
[AdventureWorks2017]	[dbo].[HeapExample]	239	76.314	3530	589	1767	16.686	3.000

Figure 14-1. Forwarded record snapshot query results

When heaps that have forwarded record issues have been identified, there are generally two ways in which the forwarded record can be mitigated. The first approach is to change the data types for the columns that are variable to fixed-length data types. For instance, the `varchar` data type would be changed to `char`. This approach is not always ideal since it can result in more space being required by the table, and some queries may not accommodate the extra space at the end of character fields and could return incorrect results. The second option is to add a clustered index to the table, which would remove the heap as the organizational method for storing the data in the table. The downside to this approach is in identifying the appropriate key column to cluster the table on. If there is a primary key on the table, it can usually suffice as the clustering index key. There is a third option. The heap can be rebuilt, which will rewrite the heap back to the database file and remove all the forwarded records (using the script in Listing 14-4). This is generally considered a poor approach to resolving forwarded records in heaps since it doesn't provide a meaningful permanent fix to the issue. Remember, forwarded records aren't necessarily bad. They do, though, provide a potential performance problem when the ratio of operations for forwarded records starts to increase as compared to batch requests.

Listing 14-4. Rebuild Heap Script

```
USE AdventureWorks2017
GO

ALTER TABLE dbo.HeapExample REBUILD
```

FreeSpace Scans and Page Fetches per Second

The performance counter FreeSpace Scans/sec is another performance counter that is related to heaps. This counter represents the activity that happens when records are being inserted into a table with a heap. During inserts into heaps, there can be activity on the GAM, SGAM, and PFS pages. If the rate of inserts is high enough, contention can happen on these pages. Analyzing the values of the FreeSpace Scans/sec and FreeSpace Page Fetches/sec counters provides an opportunity to keep track of this activity, determine when the volume of activity is increasing, and determine when heaps may need to be analyzed further. Used in conjunction, FreeSpace Scans/sec and FreeSpace Page Fetches/sec counters indicate the frequency and volume of scan activity on heaps, respectively.

CHAPTER 14 ■ INDEX ANALYSIS

Listing 14-5 provides the query to analyze the FreeSpace Scans/sec counter. It provides a snapshot of FreeSpace Scans activity on the SQL Server instance. The query provides aggregations of the counter with minimum, average, and maximum values. Similar to the previous counter, this counter also follows recommended guidelines of one FreeSpace Scans/sec for every ten Batch Requests. The PctViolation column measures the percentage of time that the counter exceeds the guideline.

Listing 14-5. FreeSpace Scans Counter Analysis

```
USE IndexingMethod;
GO

WITH CounterSummary
  AS (SELECT create_date,
        server_name,
        MAX(IIF(counter_name = 'FreeSpace Scans/sec', Calculated_Counter_
        value, NULL)) FreeSpaceScans,
        MAX(IIF(counter_name = 'FreeSpace Page Fetches/sec', Calculated_
        Counter_value, NULL)) FreeSpacePageFetches,
        MAX(IIF(counter_name = 'FreeSpace Scans/sec', Calculated_Counter_
        value, NULL))
        / (NULLIF(MAX(IIF(counter_name = 'Batch Requests/sec',
        Calculated_Counter_value, NULL)), 0) * 10) AS ForwardedRecordRatio
      FROM dbo.IndexingCounters
      WHERE counter_name IN ( 'FreeSpace Scans/sec', 'FreeSpace Page
      Fetches/sec', 'Batch Requests/sec' )
      GROUP BY create_date,
        server_name)
SELECT server_name,
    MIN(FreeSpaceScans) AS MinFreeSpaceScans,
    AVG(FreeSpaceScans) AS AvgFreeSpaceScans,
    MAX(FreeSpaceScans) AS MaxFreeSpaceScans,
    MIN(FreeSpacePageFetches) AS MinFreeSpacePageFetches,
    AVG(FreeSpacePageFetches) AS AvgFreeSpacePageFetches,
    MAX(FreeSpacePageFetches) AS MaxFreeSpacePageFetches,
    MIN(ForwardedRecordRatio) AS MinForwardedRecordRatio,
```

```
        AVG(ForwardedRecordRatio) AS AvgForwardedRecordRatio,
        MAX(ForwardedRecordRatio) AS MaxForwardedRecordRatio,
        FORMAT(1. * SUM(IIF(ForwardedRecordRatio > 1, 1, NULL)) / COUNT(*),
        '0.00%') AS PctViolation
FROM CounterSummary
GROUP BY server_name;
```

When the FreeSpace Scans/sec number is high, the analysis will focus on determining which heaps in the databases have the highest rate of inserts. To identify the tables with the highest inserts on heaps, use the information in the monitoring tables from sys.dm_db_index_operational_stats. The column with the information on inserts is leaf_insert_count. The query in Listing 14-6 provides a list of the heaps in the monitoring table dbo.index_operational_stats_history with the most indexes.

Listing 14-6. FreeSpace Scans Snapshot Query

```
USE IndexingMethod
GO

SELECT
    QUOTENAME(DB_NAME(database_id)) AS database_name
    ,QUOTENAME(OBJECT_SCHEMA_NAME(object_id, database_id)) + '.'
        + QUOTENAME(OBJECT_NAME(object_id, database_id)) AS ObjectName
    , SUM(leaf_insert_count) AS leaf_insert_count
    , SUM(leaf_allocation_count) AS leaf_allocation_count
FROM dbo.index_operational_stats_history
WHERE index_id = 0
AND database_id > 4
and QUOTENAME(OBJECT_NAME(object_id, database_id)) IS NOT NULL
GROUP BY object_id, database_id
ORDER BY leaf_insert_count DESC
```

Reviewing the table in the demonstration script in Listing 14-3 with the FreeSpace Scans snapshot query yields the results in Figure 14-2. As this example shows, there were thousands of inserts into the heap. While only a single table is shown in the results, the tables that appear at the height of this list are going to be the ones most often contributing to FreeSpace Scans/sec.

	database_name	ObjectName	leaf_insert_count	leaf_allocation_count
1	[AdventureWorks2017]	[dbo].[HeapExample]	2941	197
2	[AdventureWorks2017]	[sys].[sysfiles1]	0	0

Figure 14-2. *FreeSpace Scans per second snapshot query results*

Once the contributing heaps are identified, the best method for mitigating the heaps is to create a clustered index on the tables with the most inserts. Since the counter is based on scans of free space on the GAM, SGAM, and PFS pages, building clustered indexes on the heap tables will move the allocation of pages to IAM pages, which are dedicated to each clustered index, as compared to heaps where they will compete for page allocations with other heaps.

Full Scans per Second

Through the performance counter Full Scans/sec, the number of full scans on clustered and nonclustered indexes and heaps is measured. Within execution plans, this counter is triggered during index scans and table scans. The higher the rate in which full scans are performed, the more likely that there can be performance issues related to full scans. From a performance perspective, this can impact the Page Life Expectancy value as data is churned in memory, and there may be I/O contention as data needs to be brought into memory.

Using the query in Listing 14-7, the current state of Full Scans/sec can be analyzed for the current monitoring window. As with the previous counters, it is important to consider the relationship between this counter and the Batch Requests/sec counter. When the ratio of Full Scans/sec to Batch Requests/sec exceeds one for every thousand, there may be an issue with Full Scans/sec, which merits further review.

Listing 14-7. Full Scans Counter Analysis

```
USE IndexingMethod;
GO

WITH CounterSummary
  AS (SELECT create_date,
         server_name,
         MAX(IIF(counter_name = 'Full Scans/sec', Calculated_Counter_
         value, NULL)) FullScans,
```

CHAPTER 14   INDEX ANALYSIS

```
            MAX(IIF(counter_name = 'Full Scans/sec', Calculated_Counter_
            value, NULL))
            / (NULLIF(MAX(IIF(counter_name = 'Batch Requests/sec',
            Calculated_Counter_value, NULL)), 0) * 1000) AS FullRatio
    FROM dbo.IndexingCounters
    WHERE counter_name IN ( 'Full Scans/sec', 'Batch Requests/sec' )
    GROUP BY create_date,
            server_name)
SELECT server_name,
    MIN(FullScans) AS MinFullScans,
    AVG(FullScans) AS AvgFullScans,
    MAX(FullScans) AS MaxFullScans,
    MIN(FullRatio) AS MinFullRatio,
    AVG(FullRatio) AS AvgFullRatio,
    MAX(FullRatio) AS MaxFullRatio,
    FORMAT(1. * SUM(IIF(FullRatio > 1, 1, 0)) / COUNT(*), '0.00%') AS
PctViolation
FROM CounterSummary
GROUP BY server_name;
```

Before demonstrating how to examine the underlying causes for high Full Scans/sec counter values, let's set up some example statistics. Listing 14-8 will provide a number of full scans that can be collected through the monitoring process detailed in the previous section. Be certain to execute the scripts that collect the monitoring information after executing the example script.

Listing 14-8. Full Scans Example Query

```
USE AdventureWorks2017
GO

SET NOCOUNT ON

EXEC ('SELECT * INTO #temp FROM Sales.SalesOrderHeader')
GO 1000
```

CHAPTER 14 ■ INDEX ANALYSIS

The primary goal is to identify which indexes the Full Scans/sec counter is being affected by. Once the indexes are identified, they need to be analyzed to determine whether they are the proper indexes for that operation or whether there are other performance tuning tactics required to reduce the use of the index in a full-scan operation. The DMO to use for investigating full scans is sys.dm_db_index_usage_stats from the monitoring tables; from the monitoring, this is stored in the dbo.index_usage_stats_history table.

The indexes can be identified using the query shown in Listing 14-9. The snapshot results exclude any indexes with no rows in them. Those indexes are still being utilized for full scans, but mitigating the scans on those indexes would not greatly impact performance. To sort the results, the number of scans on the indexes is multiplied by the number of rows in the table. Sorting in this manner weighs the output to put focus on those indexes that might not have a high impact on reducing the Full Scans/sec value but will provide the greatest lift to index performance.

Listing 14-9. Full Scans Snapshot Query

```
USE IndexingMethod;
GO

SELECT QUOTENAME(DB_NAME(uh.database_id)) AS database_name,
    QUOTENAME(OBJECT_SCHEMA_NAME(uh.object_id, uh.database_id)) + '.'
    + QUOTENAME(OBJECT_NAME(uh.object_id, uh.database_id)) AS ObjectName,
    uh.index_id,
    SUM(uh.user_scans) AS user_scans,
    SUM(uh.user_seeks) AS user_seeks,
    x.record_count
FROM dbo.index_usage_stats_history uh
CROSS APPLY (
    SELECT DENSE_RANK() OVER (ORDER BY ph.create_date DESC) AS RankID,
        ph.record_count
    FROM dbo.index_physical_stats_history ph
    WHERE ph.database_id = uh.database_id
    AND ph.object_id = uh.object_id
    AND ph.index_id = uh.index_id
) x
```

```
WHERE uh.database_id > 4
AND uh.database_id <> DB_ID()
AND OBJECT_NAME(uh.object_id, uh.database_id) IS NOT NULL
AND x.RankID = 1
GROUP BY uh.database_id,
    uh.object_id,
    uh.index_id,
    x.record_count
ORDER BY SUM(uh.user_scans) * x.record_count DESC;
GO
```

The results of the Full Scans snapshot query will look similar to the output in Figure 14-3. With this output, the next step is to identify which indexes require further analysis. The purpose of the current analysis is to identify problem indexes for later analysis. Once identified, the next step is to determine where they are being utilized and how to mitigate the full scans in those places, which is demonstrated later in this chapter in the Index Plan Usage section.

#	database_name	ObjectName	index_id	user_scans	user_seeks	record_count
1	[AdventureWorks2017]	[Sales].[SalesOrderHeader]	1	1000	0	31465
2	[AdventureWorks2017]	[dbo].[HeapExample]	0	3	0	2941
3	[AdventureWorks2017]	[Production].[Document]	1	0	1	13
4	[AdventureWorks2017]	[Production].[Document]	1	0	1	40
5	[AdventureWorks2017]	[HumanResources].[JobCandidate]	1	0	1	4
6	[AdventureWorks2017]	[HumanResources].[JobCandidate]	1	0	1	13
7	[AdventureWorks2017]	[Production].[ProductReview]	1	0	1	4

Figure 14-3. Full Scans snapshot query results

Index Searches per Second

The alternative to scanning indexes is to perform a seek against the index. The performance counter Index Searches/sec provides reporting on the rate of index seek on the SQL Server instance. This can include operations such as range scans and key lookups. In most environments, it is preferable to see high Index Searches/sec counter values. Along those lines, the higher this performance counter is in relationship to Full Scans/sec, the better.

The analysis of Index Searches/sec will begin with reviewing the performance counter information collected over time (shown in Listing 14-10). As mentioned, the ratio of Index Searches/sec to Full Scans/sec is one of the metrics that can be used to evaluate whether Index Searches/sec is indicating a potential indexing issue. The guideline for evaluating the ratio between the two counters is to look for 1,000 Index Searches/sec for every one Full Scans/sec. The analysis query provides this calculation, along with determining the amount of time in which the counter values exceeded this ratio, through the column PctViolation.

Listing 14-10. Index Searches Counter Analysis

```
USE IndexingMethod;
GO

WITH CounterSummary
  AS (SELECT create_date,
         server_name,
         MAX(IIF(counter_name = 'Index Searches/sec', Calculated_Counter_
         value, NULL)) IndexSearches,
         MAX(IIF(counter_name = 'Index Searches/sec', Calculated_Counter_
         value, NULL))
         / (NULLIF(MAX(IIF(counter_name = 'Full Scans/sec', Calculated_
         Counter_value, NULL)), 0) * 1000) AS SearchToScanRatio
     FROM dbo.IndexingCounters
     WHERE counter_name IN ( 'Index Searches/sec', 'Full Scans/sec' )
     GROUP BY create_date,
         server_name)
SELECT server_name,
    MIN(IndexSearches) AS MinIndexSearches,
    AVG(IndexSearches) AS AvgIndexSearches,
    MAX(IndexSearches) AS MaxIndexSearches,
    MIN(SearchToScanRatio) AS MinSearchToScanRatio,
    AVG(SearchToScanRatio) AS AvgSearchToScanRatio,
    MAX(SearchToScanRatio) AS MaxSearchToScanRatio,
    FORMAT(1. * SUM(IIF(SearchToScanRatio > 1, 1, NULL)) / COUNT(*),
    '0.00%') AS PctViolation
FROM CounterSummary
GROUP BY server_name;
```

If the analysis indicates an issue with index searches, the first step is to verify that the analysis for Full Scans/sec in the previous section was completed. That analysis will provide the most insight into which indexes have many full scans, which would contribute to high ratios for Index Searches/sec.

To help demonstrate how to examine the Index Searches/sec counter values, we'll run the query in Listing 14-11. This query will provide a number of full scans that can be collected through the monitoring process detailed in the previous section. Be certain to execute the scripts that collect the monitoring information after executing the example script.

Listing 14-11. Full Scans Example Query

```
USE AdventureWorks2017
GO

SET NOCOUNT ON

EXEC('SELECT SOH.SalesOrderID, SOD.SalesOrderDetailID
INTO #temp
FROM Sales.SalesOrderHeader SOH
INNER JOIN Sales.SalesOrderDetail SOD ON SOH.SalesOrderID =
SOD.SalesOrderID
WHERE SOH.SalesOrderID = 43659')
GO 1000
```

Once that analysis is complete, we can begin to identify where there are issues with the ratios of scans to seeks at the index level. Using the query in Listing 14-12, indexes with a high ratio of scans to seeks can be identified. Similar to the performance counter guideline of 1,000 seeks to every one scan, the query returns results for those indexes with fewer than 1,000 seeks for every scan. Since full-scan issues should have been identified in the previous section, the analysis also removes any indexes that do not have seeks against them.

Listing 14-12. Index Searches Snapshot Query

```
USE IndexingMethod;
GO

SELECT QUOTENAME(DB_NAME(uh.database_id)) AS database_name,
    QUOTENAME(OBJECT_SCHEMA_NAME(uh.object_id, uh.database_id)) + '.'
    + QUOTENAME(OBJECT_NAME(uh.object_id, uh.database_id)) AS ObjectName,
    uh.index_id,
    SUM(uh.user_scans) AS user_scans,
    SUM(uh.user_seeks) AS user_seeks,
    1. * SUM(uh.user_seeks) / NULLIF(SUM(uh.user_scans), 0) AS
    SeekScanRatio,
    x.record_count
FROM dbo.index_usage_stats_history uh
CROSS APPLY (
    SELECT DENSE_RANK() OVER (ORDER BY ph.create_date DESC) AS RankID,
        ph.record_count
    FROM dbo.index_physical_stats_history ph
    WHERE ph.database_id = uh.database_id
    AND ph.object_id = uh.object_id
    AND ph.index_id = uh.index_id
) x
WHERE uh.database_id > 4
AND uh.database_id <> DB_ID()
AND x.RankID = 1
AND x.record_count > 0
GROUP BY uh.database_id,
    uh.object_id,
    uh.index_id,
    x.record_count
HAVING 1. * SUM(uh.user_seeks) / NULLIF(SUM(uh.user_scans), 0) < 1000
AND SUM(uh.user_seeks) > 0
ORDER BY 1. * SUM(uh.user_seeks) / NULLIF(SUM(uh.user_scans), 0) DESC,
    SUM(uh.user_scans) DESC;
GO
```

Viewing the results of the snapshot query, shown in Figure 14-4, there is just a single index identified where the seek-to-scan ratio is close to 1. This is the case since in the previous section we executed about 1,000 scans against Sales.SalesOrderHeader, but none against Sales.SalesOrderDetail, even though both of these tables and their indexes were accessed in Listing 14-11. The advantage of considering Index Searches in conjunction with Full Scans is they help to offset the severity by identifying the frequency in which more desirable activity is occurring.

database_name	ObjectName	index_id	user_scans	user_seeks	SeekScanRatio	record_count
[AdventureWorks2017]	[Sales].[SalesOrderHeader]	1	1005	1002	0.997014925373134 32	31465

Figure 14-4. *Index search snapshot query sample results*

When delving into further analysis, there are a few things we'll want to pay attention to that might indicate an issue with the indexes identified. First is the current seek vs. scan behavior new to the index; in other words, has the variance been on a common trend that has slowly been getting worse? If the change is sudden, there could be a plan that is no longer using the index as it once did, maybe because of a coding change or bad parameter sniffing. Second is when the change has been gradual; look at increased data volumes and whether a query or feature within the database is being used more than it was previously. This can also hint at changes in how people are using the database and its applications, which is sometimes gradual until it reaches the point where indexing, and the performance the indexes support, suffers.

Page Splits per Second

Similar to how clustered indexes are the other side of heaps, page splits are the other side of forwarded records. An in-depth discussion of page splits is included in Chapter 2. For the purposes of this chapter, though, page splits occur when a clustered or nonclustered index needs to make room in the ordering of the pages of the index to place data into its proper position. Page splits can be resource-intensive because the single page is divided into two or more pages and involves locking and, potentially, blocking. The more frequent the page splits, the more likely that indexes will incur blocking and performance will suffer. Also, the fragmentation caused by page splits reduces the size of reads that can be performed in single operations.

To begin analyzing the performance counters for a page split, the counter Page Splits/sec is utilized. The query in Listing 14-13 provides a method for summarizing page

CHAPTER 14 ■ INDEX ANALYSIS

split activity. The query includes the minimum, maximum, and average levels of the performance counter. Along with that, a ratio of Page Splits/sec to Batch Requests/sec is included. When identifying whether there are issues with page splits on a SQL Server instance, the general rule of thumb is to look for times in which there is more than one page split/sec for every 20 batch requests/sec. Of course, as with the other counter, pay attention to the amount of time, through `PctViolation`, that the counter exceeded the threshold.

Listing 14-13. Page Splits Counter Analysis

```
USE IndexingMethod;
GO
WITH CounterSummary
  AS (SELECT create_date,
          server_name,
          MAX(IIF(counter_name = 'Page Splits/sec', Calculated_Counter_
          value, NULL)) PageSplits,
          MAX(IIF(counter_name = 'Page Splits/sec', Calculated_Counter_
          value, NULL))
          / (NULLIF(MAX(IIF(counter_name = 'Batch Requests/sec',
          Calculated_Counter_value, NULL)), 0) * 20) AS FullRatio
      FROM dbo.IndexingCounters
      WHERE counter_name IN ( 'Page Splits/sec', 'Batch Requests/sec' )
      GROUP BY create_date,
          server_name)
SELECT server_name,
    MIN(PageSplits) AS MinPageSplits,
    AVG(PageSplits) AS AvgPageSplits,
    MAX(PageSplits) AS MaxPageSplits,
    MIN(FullRatio) AS MinFullRatio,
    AVG(FullRatio) AS AvgFullRatio,
    MAX(FullRatio) AS MaxFullRatio,
    FORMAT(1. * SUM(IIF(FullRatio > 1, 1, 0)) / COUNT(*), '0.00%') AS
    PctViolation
FROM CounterSummary
GROUP BY server_name;
```

To determine the indexes that are being affected by page splits, we can consider a few values. A couple of the values come from sys.dm_db_index_operational_stats or dbo.index_operational_stats_history from the index monitoring process. These columns report each page allocation that occurs on an index, whether from inserts at the end of the B-tree or page splits in the middle of it. Since we care only about operations that are part of page splits, the next two columns provide information on whether fragmentation from page splits is occurring. To determine fragmentation, the column avg_fragmentation_in_percent from sys.dm_db_index_physical_stats is included in the monitoring table dbo.index_physical_stats_history. For the average fragmentation, there are two values returned. The first is the last fragmentation value reported for the index; the second is the average of all the fragmentation values collected. See Listing 14-14.

Listing 14-14. Page Splits Snapshot Query

```
USE IndexingMethod;
GO

SELECT QUOTENAME(DB_NAME(database_id)) AS database_name,
    QUOTENAME(OBJECT_SCHEMA_NAME(object_id, database_id)) + '.' +
    QUOTENAME(OBJECT_NAME(object_id, database_id)) AS ObjectName,
    SUM(leaf_allocation_count) AS leaf_insert_count,
    SUM(nonleaf_allocation_count) AS nonleaf_allocation_count,
    MAX(IIF(RankID = 1, x.avg_fragmentation_in_percent, NULL)) AS last_
    fragmenation,
    AVG(x.avg_fragmentation_in_percent) AS average_fragmenation
FROM dbo.index_operational_stats_history oh
CROSS APPLY (
    SELECT DENSE_RANK() OVER (ORDER BY ph.create_date DESC) AS RankID,
        CAST(ph.avg_fragmentation_in_percent AS DECIMAL(6, 3)) AS avg_
        fragmentation_in_percent
    FROM dbo.index_physical_stats_history ph
    WHERE ph.database_id = oh.database_id
    AND ph.object_id = oh.object_id
    AND ph.index_id = oh.index_id
) x
```

```
WHERE database_id > 4
AND database_id <> DB_ID()
AND oh.index_id <> 0
AND (
    leaf_allocation_count > 0
    OR nonleaf_allocation_count > 0
)
GROUP BY object_id,
    database_id
ORDER BY leaf_insert_count DESC;
```

Investigating page splits in this manner provides a way to see the number of allocations and pairs that information with fragmentation. A table with low fragmentation and a high `leaf_insert_count`, such as the table dbo.IndexingCounters shown in Figure 14-5, is not a concern from a page split perspective. On the other hand, dbo.index_operational_stats_history does show a high amount of fragmentation and `leaf_insert_count`. It would be worthwhile to investigate that index further. While the scripting in Listing 14-14 doesn't typically show index results for the IndexingMethod database, the script was modified from what is in the listing to provide some results to examine.

	database_name	ObjectName	leaf_insert_count	nonleaf_allocation_count	last_fragmentation	average_fragmentation
1	[IndexingMethod]	[dbo].[IndexingCounters]	11660	160	99.671	74.399480
2	[IndexingMethod]	[dbo].[index_operational_stats_snapshot]	7300	100	75.000	32.422925
3	[IndexingMethod]	[dbo].[wait_stats_snapshot]	4465	0	7.631	13.039000
4	[IndexingMethod]	[dbo].[index_physical_stats_history]	3640	0	36.842	33.724625
5	[IndexingMethod]	[dbo].[index_operational_stats_history]	1620	80	60.000	21.307964
6	[IndexingMethod]	[dbo].[index_usage_stats_snapshot]	600	40	42.857	16.722300
7	[IndexingMethod]	[dbo].[index_usage_stats_history]	300	40	75.000	20.938920
8	[IndexingMethod]	[dbo].[wait_stats_history]	171	19	36.364	43.689947

Figure 14-5. Page Split snapshot query sample results

With the indexes requiring more analysis identified, the next step is mitigation. There are a number of ways to mitigate page splits on indexes. The first is to review the fragmentation history for the index. If the index needs to be rebuilt on a regular basis, one of the first things that can be done is to decrease the fill factor on the index. Reducing the fill factor will increase the space remaining on pages after rebuilding indexes, which will reduce the likelihood for page splits. The second strategy for reducing fragmentation is to consider the columns in the index. Are the columns highly volatile and do the values change dramatically? For instance, an index on `create_date` would likely not have page split issues. But one on `update_date` would be prone to fragmentation. If the usage rates for the index don't justify the index, it might be worthwhile to remove that index. Or, in multicolumn indexes, move the volatile columns to the right side of the index or add them as included columns. A third approach to mitigating page splits can be to identify where the index is being used. One final approach to mitigating page splits on indexes is to review the data types being used by the index. In some cases, a variable data type might be better suited to being a fixed-length data type.

Page Lookups per Second

The performance counter Page Lookups/sec measures the number of requests made in the SQL Server instance to retrieve individual pages from the buffer pool. When this counter is high, it often means that there is inefficiency in query plans, which can often be addressed through execution plan analysis. Often, high levels of Page Lookups/sec are attributed to plans with large numbers of page lookups and row lookups per execution. Generally speaking, in terms of performance issues, the value of Page Lookups/sec should not exceed a ratio of 100 operations for each Batch Request/sec.

The initial analysis of Page Lookups/sec involves looking at both Page Lookups/sec and Batch Request/sec. To start, use the query shown in Listing 14-15; the analysis will include the minimum, maximum, and average Page Lookups/sec values over the data from the monitoring period. Next, the minimum, maximum, and average values of the ratio are included, with the `PctViolation` column, for the ratio of Page Lookups/sec to Batch Request/sec in each time period. The violation calculation verified whether the ratio of operations exceeds 100 to 1.

Listing 14-15. Page Lookups Counter Analysis

```
USE IndexingMethod;
GO

WITH CounterSummary
  AS (SELECT create_date,
        server_name,
        MAX(IIF(counter_name = 'Page Lookups/sec', Calculated_Counter_
        value, NULL)) PageLookups,
        MAX(IIF(counter_name = 'Page Lookups/sec', Calculated_Counter_
        value, NULL))
```

```
            / (NULLIF(MAX(IIF(counter_name = 'Batch Requests/sec',
                Calculated_Counter_value, NULL)), 0) * 100) AS PageLookupRatio
        FROM dbo.IndexingCounters
        WHERE counter_name IN ( 'Page Lookups/sec', 'Batch Requests/sec' )
        GROUP BY create_date,
            server_name)
SELECT server_name,
    MIN(PageLookups) AS MinPageLookups,
    AVG(PageLookups) AS AvgPageLookups,
    MAX(PageLookups) AS MaxPageLookups,
    MIN(PageLookupRatio) AS MinPageLookupRatio,
    AVG(PageLookupRatio) AS AvgPageLookupRatio,
    MAX(PageLookupRatio) AS MaxPageLookupRatio,
    FORMAT(1. * SUM(IIF(PageLookupRatio > 1, 1, 0)) / COUNT(*), '0.00%') AS
    PctViolation
FROM CounterSummary
GROUP BY server_name;
```

As with the other counters, when the analysis dictates that there are potential problems with the counter, the next step is to dig deeper. There are three approaches that can be taken to address high Page Lookups/sec values. The first is to query sys.dm_exec_query_stats to identify queries that are executed often with high I/O; we can find more information on this DMV at http://msdn.microsoft.com/en-us/library/ms189741.aspx. Those queries need to reviewed, and a determination needs to be made whether the queries are utilizing an excessive amount of I/O. Another approach is to review the database in the SQL Server instance for missing indexes. The third approach, which will be detailed in this section, is to review the occurrences of lookups on clustered indexes and heaps.

To investigate lookups on clustered indexes and heaps, the primary source for this information is the DMO sys.dm_db_index_usage_stats. Thanks to the monitoring implemented in the previous chapter, this information is available in the table dbo.index_usage_stats_history. To perform the analysis, use the query in Listing 14-16; we'll review lookups, seeks, and scans that have occurred from a user perspective. With these values, the query calculates the ratio of user lookups to user seeks and returns all that have a ratio higher than 100 to 1.

Listing 14-16. Page Lookups Snapshot Query

```
USE IndexingMethod;
GO

SELECT QUOTENAME(DB_NAME(uh.database_id)) AS database_name,
    QUOTENAME(OBJECT_SCHEMA_NAME(uh.object_id, uh.database_id)) + '.'
    + QUOTENAME(OBJECT_NAME(uh.object_id, uh.database_id)) AS ObjectName,
    uh.index_id,
    SUM(uh.user_lookups) AS user_lookups,
    SUM(uh.user_seeks) AS user_seeks,
    SUM(uh.user_scans) AS user_scans,
    x.record_count,
    CAST(1. * SUM(uh.user_lookups) / IIF(SUM(uh.user_seeks) = 0, 1,
    SUM(uh.user_seeks)) AS DECIMAL(18, 2)) AS LookupSeekRatio
FROM dbo.index_usage_stats_history uh
CROSS APPLY (
    SELECT DENSE_RANK() OVER (ORDER BY ph.create_date DESC) AS RankID,
        ph.record_count
    FROM dbo.index_physical_stats_history ph
    WHERE ph.database_id = uh.database_id
    AND ph.object_id = uh.object_id
    AND ph.index_id = uh.index_id) x
WHERE uh.database_id > 4
AND x.RankID = 1
AND x.record_count > 0
GROUP BY uh.database_id,
    uh.object_id,
    uh.index_id,
    x.record_count
HAVING CAST(1. * SUM(uh.user_lookups) / IIF(SUM(uh.user_seeks) = 0, 1,
SUM(uh.user_seeks)) AS DECIMAL(18, 2)) > 100
ORDER BY 1. * SUM(uh.user_lookups) / IIF(SUM(uh.user_seeks) = 0, 1,
SUM(uh.user_seeks)) DESC;
GO
```

Once indexes with issues are identified, the next step is to determine how and where the indexes are being used, the process for which is described later in this chapter.

Page Compression

The performance counters Page compression attempts/sec and Pages compressed/sec measure the number of pages compressed and attempted to be compressed. When the rate of Pages Compressed/sec decreases in comparison to the Page Compressions/sec, it indicates failures in SQL Server compression algorithm to save data pages in a compressed state. While there is data that is better off uncompressed, in cases where the CPU cost to decompress exceeds the point where there is value in compressing the data, which often happens on data that appears random like the raw output of an image file. The trouble with compression failures is that SQL Server already spent time, specifically CPU resources, attempting compress the page. Generally, when more than 5 percent of page compression attempts start to fail, it's worthwhile identifying what indexes the failures are occurring on.

To analyze if there is an issue with page compression, we'll first want to look at the counters for page compression. Using the query shown in Listing 14-17, we can review the minimum, maximum, and average Page compression attempts/sec and Pages compressed/sec values from the monitoring period. Additionally, the ratio of Pages compressed/sec to Page compression attempts/sec is included with the minimum, maximum, and average values. The `PctViolation` column lets us know the percentage of time the 5 percent threshold is violated.

Listing 14-17. Page Compression Counter Analysis

```
USE IndexingMethod;
GO

WITH CounterSummary
  AS (SELECT create_date,
         server_name,
         MAX(IIF(counter_name = 'Page compression attempts/sec',
           Calculated_Counter_value, NULL)) PageCompressionAttempts,
         MAX(IIF(counter_name = 'Pages compressed/sec', Calculated_
           Counter_value, NULL)) PagesCompressed,
```

```sql
            MAX(IIF(counter_name = 'Page compression attempts/sec',
            Calculated_Counter_value, NULL))
            / (NULLIF(MAX(IIF(counter_name = 'Pages compressed/sec',
            Calculated_Counter_value, NULL)), 0) * 100.) AS CompressionRate
    FROM dbo.IndexingCounters
    WHERE counter_name IN ( 'Page compression attempts/sec', 'Pages
    compressed/sec')
    GROUP BY create_date,
        server_name)
SELECT server_name,
    MIN(PageCompressionAttempts) AS MinPageCompressionAttempts,
    AVG(PageCompressionAttempts) AS AvgPageCompressionAttempts,
    MAX(PageCompressionAttempts) AS MaxPageCompressionAttempts,
    MIN(PagesCompressed) AS MinPagesCompressed,
    AVG(PagesCompressed) AS AvgPagesCompressed,
    MAX(PagesCompressed) AS MaxPagesCompressed,
    MIN(CompressionRate) AS MinCompressionRate,
    AVG(CompressionRate) AS AvgCompressionRate,
    MAX(CompressionRate) AS MaxCompressionRate,
    FORMAT(1. * SUM(IIF(CompressionRate < 95, 1, 0)) / COUNT(*), '0.00%')
AS PctViolation
FROM CounterSummary
GROUP BY server_name;
```

If there is an indication that page compression failures are high or gaining in frequency, it's worth digging deeper within the databases to determine which tables and indexes are failing to page compress. Using the data that we've been storing for the indexes, we can determine which specific index has page compression failure, or the lowest page compression success rate, using the query in Listing 14-18. The results would look similar to those in Figure 14-6. That index was created with all of the columns from Person.Person, which included some XML and varchar(max) columns. The success rate for page compressions for this index is just over 50 percent which is a rather terrible result.

Listing 14-18. Page Compression Snapshot Query

```
USE IndexingMethod;
GO

SELECT QUOTENAME(DB_NAME(database_id)) AS database_name,
    QUOTENAME(OBJECT_SCHEMA_NAME(object_id, database_id)) + '.' +
    QUOTENAME(OBJECT_NAME(object_id, database_id)) AS ObjectName,
    oh.index_id,
    SUM(oh.page_compression_attempt_count) AS page_compression_attempt_
    count,
    SUM(oh.page_compression_success_count) AS page_compression_success_
    count,
    SUM(1. * oh.page_compression_success_count / NULLIF(oh.page_
    compression_attempt_count, 0)) AS page_compression_success_rate
FROM dbo.index_operational_stats_history oh
WHERE database_id > 4
AND database_id <> DB_ID()
AND oh.page_compression_attempt_count > 0
GROUP BY object_id,
    database_id,
    index_id;
```

database_name	ObjectName	index_id	page_compression_attempt_count	page_compression_success_count	page_compression_success_rate
[AdventureWorks2017]	[Person].[Person]	4	4649	2332	0.50161325016132501

Figure 14-6. Page Split snapshot query sample results

Once indexes with issues are identified, the next step is to determine whether page compression is appropriate for the index. Indexes that contain data types such as XML or varchar(max) are poor candidates for page compression, as we saw in Figure 14-6.

Lock Wait Time

Some performance counters can be used to determine whether there is pressure on the indexes based on their usage. One such counter is Lock Wait Time (ms). This counter measures the amount of time, in milliseconds, that SQL Server spends waiting to implement a lock on a table, index, or page. There aren't any good guidance values for this counter. Generally, the lower this value, the better, but what "low" means is entirely dependent on the database platform and the applications that are accessing it.

Since there are no guidelines for the level at which the values from Lock Wait Time(ms) are good or bad, the best method for evaluating the counter is to compare it to the baseline values. In this case, collecting a baseline becomes incredibly important in terms of being able to monitor when index performance related to Lock Wait Time has occurred. Using the query in Listing 14-19, the Lock Wait Time (ms) value is compared to the available baseline values. For both the baseline and the values from the monitoring period, an aggregate of the counter values is provided for the minimum, maximum, average, and standard deviation. These aggregations assist in providing a profile of the state of the counter and whether it has increased or decreased compared to the baseline.

Listing 14-19. Lock Wait Time Counter Analysis

```
USE IndexingMethod;
GO

WITH CounterSummary
  AS (SELECT create_date,
            server_name,
            instance_name,
            MAX(IIF(counter_name = 'Lock Wait Time (ms)', Calculated_Counter_
            value, NULL)) / 1000 LockWaitTime
      FROM dbo.IndexingCounters
      WHERE counter_name = 'Lock Wait Time (ms)'
      GROUP BY create_date,
            server_name,
            instance_name)
SELECT CONVERT(VARCHAR(50), MAX(create_date), 101) AS CounterDate,
    server_name,
    instance_name,
    MIN(LockWaitTime) AS MinLockWaitTime,
    AVG(LockWaitTime) AS AvgLockWaitTime,
    MAX(LockWaitTime) AS MaxLockWaitTime,
    STDEV(LockWaitTime) AS StdDevLockWaitTime
```

```
FROM CounterSummary
GROUP BY server_name,
    instance_name
UNION ALL
SELECT 'Baseline: ' + CONVERT(VARCHAR(50), start_date, 101) + ' --> ' +
CONVERT(VARCHAR(50), end_date, 101),
    server_name,
    instance_name,
    minimum_counter_value / 1000,
    maximum_counter_value / 1000,
    average_counter_value / 1000,
    standard_deviation_counter_value / 1000
FROM dbo.IndexingCountersBaseline
WHERE counter_name = 'Lock Wait Time (ms)'
ORDER BY instance_name,
    CounterDate DESC;
```

As an example, in Figure 14-7, the average and maximum Lock Wait Times have decreased from the baseline values which is what would be desired. In the case where there was an increase in the average lock wait over the baseline, there could be a cause for concern, especially if that increase is in tens of milliseconds. Also, if there were an increase in the range to the maximum value, it would be something else to investigate. The more the duration of time spent waiting to acquire locks increases, the more it is likely going to impact users.

	CounterDate	server_name	instance_name	MinLockWaitTime	AvgLockWaitTime	MaxLockWaitTime	StdDevLockWaitTime
1	Baseline: 08/14/2019 -> 08/15/2019	SQLServer	_Total	0	0.0016	3.07692307692308E-05	0.000221880078490092
2	08/16/2019	SQLServer	_Total	0	6.55737704918033E-06	0.0016	0.0001024295039463617
3	Baseline: 08/14/2019 -> 08/15/2019	SQLServer	AllocUnit	0	0	0	0
4	08/16/2019	SQLServer	AllocUnit	0	0	0	0
5	Baseline: 08/14/2019 -> 08/15/2019	SQLServer	Application	0	0	0	0
14	08/16/2019	SQLServer	HoBT	0	0	0	0
15	Baseline: 08/14/2019 -> 08/15/2019	SQLServer	Key	0	0	0	0
16	08/16/2019	SQLServer	Key	0	0	0	0
17	Baseline: 08/14/2019 -> 08/15/2019	SQLServer	Metadata	0	0.0016	3.07692307692308E-05	0.000221880078490092
18	08/16/2019	SQLServer	Metadata	0	6.55737704918033E-06	0.0016	0.0001024295039463617

Figure 14-7. *Lock Wait Time counter analysis sample results*

When investigating Lock Wait Time, it is important to identify which indexes are generating the most Lock Wait Time by using the query in Listing 14-20. This information is found in the DMO sys.dm_db_index_operational_stats or the monitoring table dbo.index_operational_stats_history. The columns reviewed for Lock Wait Time are row_lock_wait_count, row_lock_wait_count, row_lock_wait_count, and page_lock_wait_in_ms. These columns report the number of waits per index and the time for those waits. As the columns indicate, there are locks at both the row and page levels; most often the variations between the lock types correlate with seek and scan operations on the index.

Listing 14-20. Lock Wait Time Snapshot Query

```
USE IndexingMethod;
GO

SELECT QUOTENAME(DB_NAME(database_id)) AS database_name,
    QUOTENAME(OBJECT_SCHEMA_NAME(object_id, database_id)) + '.' +
    QUOTENAME(OBJECT_NAME(object_id, database_id)) AS ObjectName,
    index_id,
    SUM(row_lock_wait_count) AS row_lock_wait_count,
    SUM(row_lock_wait_in_ms) / 1000. AS row_lock_wait_in_sec,
    ISNULL(SUM(row_lock_wait_in_ms) / NULLIF(SUM(row_lock_wait_count), 0) /
    1000., 0) AS avg_row_lock_wait_in_sec,
    SUM(page_lock_wait_count) AS page_lock_wait_count,
    SUM(page_lock_wait_in_ms) / 1000. AS page_lock_wait_in_sec,
    ISNULL(SUM(page_lock_wait_in_ms) / NULLIF(SUM(page_lock_wait_count), 0)
    / 1000., 0) AS avg_page_lock_wait_in_sec
FROM dbo.index_operational_stats_history oh
WHERE database_id > 4
AND database_id <> DB_ID()
AND (
    row_lock_wait_in_ms > 0
    OR page_lock_wait_in_ms > 0
)
GROUP BY database_id,
    object_id,
    index_id;
```

Looking at the results of the snapshot query, shown in Figure 14-8, there are a couple things to point out. First, in this example, all the locks are occurring across the pages of the table, not at the row level. This can result in larger-scale blocking since more than the rows being accessed will be locked. Also, the average page lock is about 7 seconds. For most environments, this is an excessive amount of time for locking. Based on this information, we should definitely further investigate the clustered index (index_id=1) on the table Sales.SalesOrderDetail.

database_name	ObjectName	index_id	row_lock_wait_count	row_lock_wait_in_sec	avg_row_lock_wait_in_sec	page_lock_wait_count	page_lock_wait_in_sec	avg_page_lock_wait_in_sec
[AdventureWorks2017]	[Sales].[SalesOrderHeader]	1	1	52.719000	52.719000	0	0.000000	0.000000

***Figure 14-8.** Lock Wait Time index analysis sample results*

When we need to dig deeper into an index and its usage, the next step is to determine which execution plans are utilizing the index. Then optimize either the queries or the index to reduce locking. In some cases, if the index is not critical to the table, it might be better to remove the index and allow other indexes to satisfy the queries.

Lock Waits per Second

The next counter, Lock Waits/sec, has a similar approach for analysis to that of Lock Wait Time (ms). With Lock Waits/sec, the counter measures the number of lock requests that could not be satisfied immediately. For these requests, SQL Server waited until the row or page was available for the lock before granting the lock. As with the other counter, this counter does not have any specific guidelines on what "good" values are. For these, we should turn to the baseline and compare and contrast against it to determine when the counter is outside normal operations.

The analysis of Lock Waits/sec includes the same minimum, maximum, average, and standard deviation aggregations as used for Lock Wait Time(ms). These values are aggregated for both the per-counter table dbo.IndexingCounters and the baseline table dbo.IndexingCountersBaseline, shown in Listing 14-21. Figure 14-9 displays the results from the query.

Listing 14-21. Lock Waits Counter Analysis

```
USE IndexingMethod;
GO

WITH CounterSummary
  AS (SELECT create_date,
           server_name,
           instance_name,
           MAX(IIF(counter_name = 'Lock Waits/sec', Calculated_Counter_
           value, NULL)) LockWaits
      FROM dbo.IndexingCounters
      WHERE counter_name = 'Lock Waits/sec'
      GROUP BY create_date,
           server_name,
           instance_name)
SELECT CONVERT(VARCHAR(50), MAX(create_date), 101) AS CounterDate,
    server_name,
    instance_name,
    MIN(LockWaits) AS MinLockWait,
    AVG(LockWaits) AS AvgLockWait,
    MAX(LockWaits) AS MaxLockWait,
    STDEV(LockWaits) AS StdDevLockWait
FROM CounterSummary
GROUP BY server_name,
    instance_name
UNION ALL
SELECT 'Baseline: ' + CONVERT(VARCHAR(50), start_date, 101) + ' --> ' +
CONVERT(VARCHAR(50), end_date, 101),
    server_name,
    instance_name,
    minimum_counter_value / 1000,
    maximum_counter_value / 1000,
    average_counter_value / 1000,
    standard_deviation_counter_value / 1000
```

CHAPTER 14　INDEX ANALYSIS

```
FROM dbo.IndexingCountersBaseline
WHERE counter_name = 'Lock Waits/sec'
ORDER BY instance_name,
    CounterDate DESC;
```

There will be times, such as those included in Figure 14-9, when Lock Wait/sec is not an issue, but there were issues with Lock Wait Time(ms). Those cases point to long duration blocking situations. On the other hand, Lock Wait/sec is important to monitor since it will indicate when there is widespread blocking. The blocking may not be long in duration, but it is widespread; a single long block can cause significant performance issues.

	CounterDate	server_name	instance_name	MinLockWait	AvgLockWait	MaxLockWait	StdDevLockWait
1	Baseline: 08/14/2019 -> 08/15/2019	SQLServer	_Total	0	8E-05	1.53846153846154E-06	1.10940039245046E-05
2	08/16/2019	SQLServer	_Total	0	0.0003715170278637	0.08	0.0049705399048934
3	Baseline: 08/14/2019 -> 08/15/2019	SQLServer	AllocUnit	0	0	0	0
4	08/16/2019	SQLServer	AllocUnit	0	0	0	0
5	Baseline: 08/14/2019 -> 08/15/2019	SQLServer	Application	0	0	0	0
14	08/16/2019	SQLServer	HoBt	0	0	0	0
15	Baseline: 08/14/2019 -> 08/15/2019	SQLServer	Key	0	0	0	0
16	08/16/2019	SQLServer	Key	0	0	0	0
17	Baseline: 08/14/2019 -> 08/15/2019	SQLServer	Metadata	0	8E-05	1.53846153846154E-06	1.10940039245046E-05
18	08/16/2019	SQLServer	Metadata	0	0.000247678018575851	0.08	0.00445131907259726

Figure 14-9. Lock Waits counter analysis sample results

In a situation with widespread blocking, as indicated by high values for Lock Wait/sec, the analysis will require investigating the statistics of indexes using the DMO sys.dm_db_index_operational_stats. With the monitoring process, this information will be available in the table dbo.index_operational_stats_history. Using the query in Listing 14-22, the count and percentage of locks that wait can be determined. As with Lock Wait Time(ms), this counter analysis also looks at statistics at the row and page levels.

549

Listing 14-22. Lock Waits Snapshot Query

```
USE IndexingMethod;
GO

SELECT QUOTENAME(DB_NAME(database_id)) AS database_name,
    QUOTENAME(OBJECT_SCHEMA_NAME(object_id, database_id)) + '.' +
    QUOTENAME(OBJECT_NAME(object_id, database_id)) AS ObjectName,
    index_id,
    SUM(row_lock_count) AS row_lock_count,
    SUM(row_lock_wait_count) AS row_lock_wait_count,
    ISNULL(SUM(row_lock_wait_count) / NULLIF(SUM(row_lock_count), 0), 0) AS
    pct_row_lock_wait,
    SUM(page_lock_count) AS page_lock_count,
    SUM(page_lock_wait_count) AS page_lock_wait_count,
    ISNULL(SUM(page_lock_wait_count) / NULLIF(SUM(page_lock_count), 0), 0)
    AS pct_page_lock_wait
FROM dbo.index_operational_stats_history oh
WHERE database_id > 4
AND (
    row_lock_wait_in_ms > 0
    OR page_lock_wait_in_ms > 0
)
GROUP BY database_id,
    object_id,
    index_id;
```

Indexes that have a high percentage of lock waits to locks are prime for index tuning. Often, when there are excessive lock waits on a database, the end users will see slowness in the applications and, in some of the worse cases, time-outs in the applications. The aim of analyzing this counter is to identify indexes that can be optimized and then to investigate where the indexes are being used. Once this is done, address the causes for the locks and tune the indexes and queries to reduce the locking on the index.

Number of Deadlocks per Second

In extreme cases, poor indexing and excessive lock blocking can lead to deadlocks. Deadlocks occur in situations where locks have been placed by two or more transactions in which the locking order of one of the transactions is prevented from acquiring and/or releasing its locks because of the locks of the other transactions. There are a number of ways to address deadlocking, one of which is to improve indexing.

To determine whether deadlocks are occurring on the SQL Server instance, review the performance counters collected during the monitoring process. The query in Listing 14-23 provides an overview of the deadlock rate during the monitoring window. The query returns aggregate values for the minimum, average, maximum, and standard deviation for the deadlocks on the server.

Listing 14-23. Number of Deadlocks Counter Analysis

```
USE IndexingMethod;
GO

WITH CounterSummary
  AS (SELECT create_date,
         server_name,
         Calculated_Counter_value AS NumberDeadlocks
     FROM dbo.IndexingCounters
     WHERE counter_name = 'Number of Deadlocks/sec')
SELECT server_name,
    MIN(NumberDeadlocks) AS MinNumberDeadlocks,
    AVG(NumberDeadlocks) AS AvgNumberDeadlocks,
    MAX(NumberDeadlocks) AS MaxNumberDeadlocks,
    STDEV(NumberDeadlocks) AS StdDevNumberDeadlocks
FROM CounterSummary
GROUP BY server_name;
```

In general, a well-tuned database platform should not have any deadlocks occurring. When they occur, each should be investigated to determine the root cause for the deadlock. Before a deadlock can be examined, though, the deadlock first needs to be retrieved. There are a number of ways in which deadlock information can be collected from SQL Server. These include trace flags, SQL Profiler, and event notifications.

CHAPTER 14 INDEX ANALYSIS

Another method is through Extended Events, using the built-in `system_health` session. The query in Listing 14-24 returns a list of all the deadlocks that are currently in the `ring_buffer` for that session.

Listing 14-24. System-Health Deadlock Query

```
USE IndexingMethod;
GO

WITH deadlock
  AS (SELECT CAST(target_data AS XML) AS target_data
      FROM sys.dm_xe_session_targets st
      INNER JOIN sys.dm_xe_sessions s ON s.address = st.event_session_address
      WHERE name = 'system_health'
      AND target_name = 'ring_buffer')
SELECT c.value('(@timestamp)[1]', 'datetime') AS event_timestamp,
    c.query('data/value/deadlock')
FROM deadlock d
CROSS APPLY target_data.nodes('//RingBufferTarget/event') AS t(c)
WHERE c.exist('.[@name = "xml_deadlock_report"]') = 1;
```

When deadlocks have been identified, they are returned in an XML document. For most, reading the XML documents is not a natural way to examine a deadlock. Instead, it is often preferable to review the deadlock graph that is associated with the deadlock, such as the one shown in Figure 14-10. To obtain a deadlock graph for any of the deadlocks returned by Listing 14-22, open the deadlock XML document in SQL Server Management Studio and then save the file with an `.xdl` extension. When the file is reopened, it will open with the deadlock graph instead of as an XML document.

Figure 14-10. *Deadlock graph in SQL Server Management Studio*

Once deadlocks are identified, it is important to determine why they occur to prevent them from reoccurring. A common issue that causes deadlocks is the order of operations between numerous transactions. This cause is often difficult to resolve since it may require rewriting parts of applications. To address deadlocks, one of the easiest approaches is to decrease the amount of time in which the transaction occurs. Indexing the tables that are accessed is a typical approach that can resolve deadlocks in many cases by shrinking the window in which deadlocks can be created.

Wait Statistics

The analysis process for wait statistics is similar to that of performance counters. For both sets of data, the information points to areas where resources are potentially being taxed, identifying the resources and indicating next steps. A lot of the same processes for performance counters apply to wait statistics. One main difference between the two sets of information is that wait statistics are looked at as a whole, and their value is determined as a relationship of themselves to other wait statistics on the SQL Server instance.

Because of this difference, when reviewing wait statistics, there is only a single query required for analysis of the wait stats. Before using the wait statistics analysis query, provided in Listing 14-25, there are a few aspects to wait statistics analysis that should be explained. First, as the list of ignore wait stats shows, there are some wait states that accumulate regardless of the activity on the server. For these, there isn't any value in investigating behavior related to them, either because they are just the ticking of CPU time on the server or they are related to internal operations that can't be affected. Second, the value in wait statistics is in looking at them in relationship to the time that has transpired on the server. While one wait state being higher than another is important, without knowing the amount of time that has transpired, there is no scale by which to measure the pressure the wait state is having on the server. To accommodate for this, the waits from the first set of results in the monitoring table are ignored, and the date between them and the last collection point is used to calculate the time that has transpired. The length of time that a wait state occurred compared to the total time provides the values needed to determine the pressure of the wait state on the SQL Server instance.

CHAPTER 14 INDEX ANALYSIS

Note The pct columns in the results for Listing 14-25 will be null if there is only a single sample in the table dbo.wait_stats_history.

Listing 14-25. Wait Statistics Analysis Query

```
USE IndexingMethod;
GO

WITH WaitStats
  AS (SELECT DENSE_RANK() OVER (ORDER BY w.create_date ASC) AS RankID,
         create_date,
         wait_type,
         waiting_tasks_count,
         wait_time_ms,
         max_wait_time_ms,
         signal_wait_time_ms,
         MIN(create_date) OVER () AS min_create_date,
         MAX(create_date) OVER () AS max_create_date
      FROM dbo.wait_stats_history w
      WHERE wait_type NOT IN ( 'BROKER_EVENTHANDLER', 'BROKER_RECEIVE_
      WAITFOR', 'BROKER_TASK_STOP', 'BROKER_TO_FLUSH', 'BROKER_TRANSMITTER',
      'CHECKPOINT_QUEUE', 'CHKPT', 'CLR_AUTO_EVENT', 'CLR_MANUAL_EVENT',
      'CLR_SEMAPHORE', 'CXCONSUMER', 'DBMIRROR_DBM_EVENT', 'DBMIRROR_
      EVENTS_QUEUE', 'DBMIRROR_WORKER_QUEUE', 'DBMIRRORING_CMD', 'DIRTY_
      PAGE_POLL', 'DISPATCHER_QUEUE_SEMAPHORE', 'EXECSYNC', 'FSAGENT',
      'FT_IFTS_SCHEDULER_IDLE_WAIT', 'FT_IFTSHC_MUTEX', 'HADR_CLUSAPI_
      CALL', 'HADR_FILESTREAM_IOMGR_IOCOMPLETIO,', 'HADR_LOGCAPTURE_WAIT',
      'HADR_NOTIFICATION_DEQUEUE', 'HADR_TIMER_TASK', 'HADR_WORK_QUEUE',
      'KSOURCE_WAKEUP', 'LAZYWRITER_SLEEP', 'LOGMGR_QUEUE', 'MEMORY_
      ALLOCATION_EXT', 'ONDEMAND_TASK_QUEUE', 'PARALLEL_REDO_DRAIN_
      WORKER', 'PARALLEL_REDO_LOG_CACHE', 'PARALLEL_REDO_TRAN_LIST',
      'PARALLEL_REDO_WORKER_SYNC', 'PARALLEL_REDO_WORKER_WAIT_WORK',
      'PREEMPTIVE_HADR_LEASE_MECHANISM', 'PREEMPTIVE_SP_SERVER_DIAGNOSTICS',
      'PREEMPTIVE_OS_LIBRARYOPS', 'PREEMPTIVE_OS_COMOPS', 'PREEMPTIVE_OS_
      CRYPTOPS', 'PREEMPTIVE_OS_PIPEOPS', 'PREEMPTIVE_OS_AUTHENTICATIONOPS',
```

```sql
        'PREEMPTIVE_OS_GENERICOPS', 'PREEMPTIVE_OS_VERIFYTRUST', 'PREEMPTIVE_
        OS_FILEOPS', 'PREEMPTIVE_OS_DEVICEOPS', 'PREEMPTIVE_OS_QUERYREGISTRY',
        'PREEMPTIVE_OS_WRITEFILE', 'PREEMPTIVE_XE_CALLBACKEXECUTE',
        'PREEMPTIVE_XE_DISPATCHER', 'PREEMPTIVE_XE_GETTARGETSTATE',
        'PREEMPTIVE_XE_SESSIONCOMMIT', 'PREEMPTIVE_XE_TARGETINIT',
        'PREEMPTIVE_XE_TARGETFINALIZE', 'PWAIT_ALL_COMPONENTS_INITIALIZED',
        'PWAIT_DIRECTLOGCONSUMER_GETNEXT', 'PWAIT_EXTENSIBILITY_CLEANUP_TASK',
        'QDS_PERSIST_TASK_MAIN_LOOP_SLEEP', 'QDS_ASYNC_QUEUE', 'QDS_CLEANUP_
        STALE_QUERIES_TASK_MAIN_LOOP_SLEEP', 'REQUEST_FOR_DEADLOCK_SEARCH',
        'RESOURCE_QUEUE', 'SERVER_IDLE_CHECK', 'SLEEP_BPOOL_FLUSH', 'SLEEP_
        DBSTARTUP', 'SLEEP_DCOMSTARTUP', 'SLEEP_MASTERDBREADY', 'SLEEP_
        MASTERMDREADY', 'SLEEP_MASTERUPGRADED', 'SLEEP_MSDBSTARTUP', 'SLEEP_
        SYSTEMTASK', 'SLEEP_TASK', 'SLEEP_TEMPDBSTARTUP', 'SNI_HTTP_ACCEPT',
        'SOS_WORK_DISPATCHER', 'SP_SERVER_DIAGNOSTICS_SLEEP', 'SQLTRACE_
        BUFFER_FLUSH', 'SQLTRACE_INCREMENTAL_FLUSH_SLEEP', 'SQLTRACE_WAIT_
        ENTRIES', 'STARTUP_DEPENDENCY_MANAGER', 'WAIT_FOR_RESULTS', 'WAITFOR',
        'WAITFOR_TASKSHUTDOW', 'WAIT_XTP_HOST_WAIT', 'WAIT_XTP_OFFLINE_CKPT_
        NEW_LOG', 'WAIT_XTP_CKPT_CLOSE', 'WAIT_XTP_RECOVERY', 'XE_BUFFERMGR_
        ALLPROCESSED_EVENT', 'XE_DISPATCHER_JOI,', 'XE_DISPATCHER_WAIT', 'XE_
        LIVE_TARGET_TVF', 'XE_TIMER_EVENT'))
SELECT wait_type,
    DATEDIFF(ms, min_create_date, max_create_date) AS total_time_ms,
    SUM(waiting_tasks_count) AS waiting_tasks_count,
    SUM(wait_time_ms) AS wait_time_ms,
    CAST(1. * SUM(wait_time_ms) / NULLIF(SUM(waiting_tasks_count),0) AS
    DECIMAL(18, 3)) AS avg_wait_time_ms,
    CAST(100. * SUM(wait_time_ms) / NULLIF(DATEDIFF(ms, min_create_date,
    max_create_date),0) AS DECIMAL(18, 3)) AS pct_time_in_wait,
    SUM(signal_wait_time_ms) AS signal_wait_time_ms,
    CAST(100. * SUM(signal_wait_time_ms) / NULLIF(SUM(wait_time_ms), 0) AS
    DECIMAL(18, 3)) AS pct_time_runnable
FROM WaitStats
GROUP BY wait_type,
    min_create_date,
    max_create_date
ORDER BY SUM(wait_time_ms) DESC;
```

CHAPTER 14 INDEX ANALYSIS

The query includes a number of calculations to help identify when there are issues with specific wait types. To best understand the information provided, see the definitions provided in Table 14-1. These calculations and their definitions will help focus the performance issues related to wait statistics.

When reviewing the results of the wait statistics query, shown in Figure 14-11, there are two thresholds to watch. First, if any of the waits exceed 5 percent of the total wait time, there is likely a bottleneck related to that wait type, and further investigation into the wait should happen. Similarly, if any of the waits exceed 1 percent of the time, they should be considered for further analysis but not before reviewing the items with higher waits. One thing to pay close attention to when reviewing wait statistics is that if the time spent on the wait is mostly because of signal wait time, then the resource contention can be better resolved by first focusing on CPU pressure on the server.

Table 14-1. Wait Statistics Query Column Definitions

Option Name	Description
wait_type	Wait statistics that incurred the wait.
total_time_ms	Total amount of time measured by the query in milliseconds.
waiting_tasks_count	Count of the number of waits for this wait type.
wait_time_ms	Time in milliseconds accumulated for this wait type. This includes the time spent on signal_wait_time_ms.
avg_wait_time_ms	Average time per wait type in milliseconds.
pct_time_in_wait	Percent of total time spent for this wait type.
signal_wait_time_ms	Time in milliseconds accumulated after the wait type was available and no longer waiting before it was running. This is the time spent in the RUNNABLE state.
pct_time_runnable	Percentage of time spent for this wait type in the RUNNABLE state.

CHAPTER 14 INDEX ANALYSIS

	wait_type	total_time_ms	waiting_tasks_count	wait_time_ms	avg_wait_time_ms	pct_time_in_wait	signal_wait_time_ms	pct_time_runnable
1	HADR_FILESTREAM_IOMGR_IOCOMPLETION	611513000	560610	281775535	502.623	46.078	45293	0.016
2	PAGEIOLATCH_SH	611513000	174404	1474528	8.455	0.241	26994	1.831
3	PAGEIOLATCH_EX	611513000	61824	160722	2.600	0.026	1005	0.625
4	RESOURCE_SEMAPHORE	611513000	2	122020	61010.000	0.020	0	0.000
5	SOS_SCHEDULER_YIELD	611513000	794601	120025	0.151	0.020	117740	98.096
6	SLEEP_BUFFERPOOL_HELPLW	611513000	3704	58742	15.859	0.010	1116	1.900
7	WRITELOG	611513000	60691	52737	0.869	0.009	7270	13.785
8	LCK_M_IX	611513000	1	48706	48706.000	0.008	81	0.166
9	BACKUPTHREAD	611513000	27	46966	1739.481	0.008	6	0.013
10	BACKUPIO	611513000	2567	45905	17.883	0.008	1543	3.361

***Figure 14-11.** Wait statistics analysis output*

Once wait states with issues have been identified, the next step is to review the wait and the recommended courses of actions for the wait. Since this chapter focuses on more index-centric wait types, we'll focus on those definitions. To learn more about the other wait types, review the Books Online topic for `sys.dm_os_wait_stats` (Transact-SQL).

CXPACKET

The CXPACKET wait type occurs when there are waits due to parallel query execution, otherwise known as *parallelism*. There are two main scenarios when parallel queries can experience CXPACKET waits. The first is when an operator in a parallel query is waiting due from being able to execute due to other threads already running on the scheduler. The second is when a thread from an operator in a parallel thread takes longer to execute than the rest of the threads and the rest of the threads have to wait for the slower thread to complete. The first cause is the more common cause for parallel waits, but it is outside the scope of this book and generally tied to configuration settings and query tuning. The second cause, though, can be addressed through indexing. And often, by addressing the second reason for CXPACKET waits, the first cause of parallel waits can be mitigated.

> **Note** There is a second parallelism wait named CXCONSUMER that identifies waits associated with parallel operators waiting for threads to send rows to the operator. This is generally not an actionable wait and is outside the context of this book.

Two approaches that are common for addressing CXPACKET waits are to adjust the max degree of parallelism and cost threshold for parallelism server properties. As with the first cause of parallelism waits, addressing parallelism with these server properties is outside the context of the book. There are valid approaches for utilizing these two properties, but the focus here is on indexing rather than constraining the

557

degree and cost of parallelism. For a simple explanation, the max degree of parallelism limits the total number of cores that any single query can use during parallel processing. Alternatively, the cost threshold for parallelism increases the threshold in which SQL Server determines that a query can use parallelism, without limiting the scope of the parallelism.

What is within the context here is mitigating CXPACKET waits through indexing, which can be paired with query tuning. To address the indexing for queries running in parallel, we need to first identify the queries that are using parallelism. There are a number of ways that we can identify queries and indexes participating in parallel operations.

The first method is to examine execution plans that have used parallelism in previous executions. For this approach, the plan cache is able to be queried to identify the execution plans that were created that contain parallel operators. This provides an ideal list of queries that tune to reduce the I/O consumed or remove the need for a parallel query. The need for the parallel query can sometimes be attributed to improper indexing on the underlying tables. For instance, a parallel operation on a table that leverages a scan may be alleviated with an index that supports the predicates or sorts within the query. The query in Listing 14-26 provides a list of execution plans in the plan cache that utilize parallelism.

Listing 14-26. Execution Plans in the Plan Cache That Utilize Parallelism

```
SET TRANSACTION ISOLATION LEVEL READ UNCOMMITTED;

WITH XMLNAMESPACES (
    DEFAULT 'http://schemas.microsoft.com/sqlserver/2004/07/showplan'
)
SELECT COALESCE(
        DB_NAME([p].[dbid]),
        [p].[query_plan].[value]('(//RelOp/OutputList/ColumnReference/
        @Database)[1]', 'nvarchar(128)')
    ) AS [database_name],
    IIF([p].[objectid] <> 0,
      CONCAT(
        QUOTENAME(DB_NAME([p].[dbid])),
        '.',
```

```
            QUOTENAME(OBJECT_SCHEMA_NAME([p].[objectid], [p].[dbid])),
            '.',
            QUOTENAME(OBJECT_NAME([p].[objectid], [p].[dbid]))
        ),
        NULL) AS [object_name],
    [cp].[objtype],
    [p].[query_plan],
    [cp].[usecounts] AS [use_counts],
    [cp].[plan_handle],
    CAST('<?query --' + CHAR(13) + [q].[text] + CHAR(13) + '--?>' AS XML)
    AS [sql_text]
FROM [sys].[dm_exec_cached_plans] AS [cp]
CROSS APPLY [sys].[dm_exec_query_plan]([cp].[plan_handle]) AS [p]
CROSS APPLY [sys].[dm_exec_sql_text]([cp].[plan_handle]) AS [q]
WHERE [cp].[cacheobjtype] = 'Compiled Plan'
AND [p].[query_plan].[exist]('//RelOp[@Parallel = "1"]') = 1
ORDER BY COALESCE(
            DB_NAME([p].[dbid]),
            [p].[query_plan].[value]('(//RelOp/OutputList/
            ColumnReference/@Database)[1]', 'nvarchar(128)')
        ),
    [cp].[usecounts] DESC;
```

Warning This chapter features a number of queries that are executed against the plan cache and Query Store. These are accessed through DMOs that provide access to the execution plans in SQL Server, which allows for investigations into current and recent execution activity on the server. While this information is extremely useful, take care when executing this code on production systems. An overly expensive query against these can impact the performance of your SQL Server. Be sure to monitor these types of queries and test them in nonproduction environments before using in a production environment.

The next method is similar to using the plan cache, but instead to query the Query Store. Provided this is running on the database, there is a column in sys.query_store_plan that identifies parallel plans. Using this with a few other DMOs gets you a list of T-SQL statements that have parallel operators. A query that returns parallel queries from the Query Store is provided in Listing 14-27, which includes a count of the number of executions for the T-SQL statement. One advantage to using the Query Store is that it limits the results down to a single database.

Listing 14-27. Execution Plans in the Query Store That Utilize Parallelism

```
SET TRANSACTION ISOLATION LEVEL READ UNCOMMITTED;
SELECT IIF([qsq].[object_id] <> 0,
            CONCAT(
                QUOTENAME(DB_NAME()),
                '.',
                QUOTENAME(OBJECT_SCHEMA_NAME([qsq].[object_id])),
                '.',
                QUOTENAME(OBJECT_NAME([qsq].[object_id]))
            ),
            NULL) AS [object_name],
    CAST([qsp].[query_plan] AS XML) AS [query_plan],
    [deqs].[execution_count],
    CAST('<?query --' + CHAR(13) + [qsqt].[query_sql_text] + CHAR(13) +
    '--?>' AS XML) AS [sql_text],
    [qsp].[engine_version],
    [qsp].[compatibility_level],
    [qsq].[query_parameterization_type_desc],
    [qsp].[is_forced_plan],
    [deqs].[total_worker_time]
FROM [sys].[query_store_plan] AS [qsp]
INNER JOIN [sys].[query_store_query] AS [qsq] ON [qsp].[query_id] = [qsq].[query_id]
INNER JOIN [sys].[query_store_query_text] AS [qsqt] ON [qsq].[query_text_id] = [qsqt].[query_text_id]
INNER JOIN sys.[dm_exec_query_stats] AS deqs ON [last_compile_batch_sql_handle] = [deqs].[sql_handle]
```

```
WHERE [qsp].[is_parallel_plan] = 1
ORDER BY [deqs].[execution_count] DESC,
    [deqs].[total_worker_time] DESC;
```

Another method for parallelism waits is to investigate plans that are currently executing. This information is available in the DMO sys.dm_os_tasks which returns waits which are currently using multiple workers; a sample query to retrieve this information is provided in Listing 14-28. This query provides a list of currently executing parallel plans.

Listing 14-28. Parallel Queries Currently Executing

```
WITH executing
  AS (SELECT er.session_id,
        er.request_id,
        MAX(ISNULL(exec_context_id, 0)) AS number_of_workers,
        er.sql_handle,
        er.statement_start_offset,
        er.statement_end_offset,
        er.plan_handle
    FROM sys.dm_exec_requests er
    INNER JOIN sys.dm_os_tasks t ON er.session_id = t.session_id
    INNER JOIN sys.dm_exec_sessions es ON er.session_id = es.session_id
    WHERE es.is_user_process = 0x1
    GROUP BY er.session_id,
        er.request_id,
        er.sql_handle,
        er.statement_start_offset,
        er.statement_end_offset,
        er.plan_handle)
SELECT QUOTENAME(DB_NAME(st.dbid)) AS database_name,
    QUOTENAME(OBJECT_SCHEMA_NAME(st.objectid, st.dbid)) + '.' +
    QUOTENAME(OBJECT_NAME(st.objectid, st.dbid)) AS object_name,
    e.session_id,
    e.request_id,
    e.number_of_workers,
```

```
    SUBSTRING(
        st.text,
        e.statement_start_offset / 2,
        (CASE
                WHEN e.statement_end_offset = -1 THEN
                LEN(CONVERT(NVARCHAR(MAX), st.text)) * 2
                ELSE e.statement_end_offset END - e.statement_start_offset
        ) / 2
    ) AS query_text,
    qp.query_plan
FROM executing e
CROSS APPLY sys.dm_exec_sql_text(e.plan_handle) st
CROSS APPLY sys.dm_exec_query_plan(e.plan_handle) qp
WHERE number_of_workers > 0;
```

The second way is to start an Extended Events session, capture transaction information, and then group that information on the available call stack. The session, defined in Listing 14-29, retrieves all the parallel waits as they occur and groups them by their T-SQL stack. Before running the script, ensure that the value for the CXPACKET wait type matches the value in the query; for SQL Server 2019, the value is 265. The T-SQL stack contains all the SQL statements that contribute to a final execution point. For example, drilling through an execution stack can provide information on a stored procedure that is executing a function that executes a single T-SQL statement. This provides information that can be used to track where the parallel wait is occurring. These statements are grouped using the histogram target, which allows us to minimize the size of the collection and focus on the items causing the most CXPACKET waits on the system.

Listing 14-29. Extended Events Session for CXPACKET

```
USE master;
GO

SELECT name,
    map_key,
    map_value
```

```
FROM sys.dm_xe_map_values
WHERE name = 'wait_types'
AND map_value = 'CXPACKET';
GO

IF EXISTS (
    SELECT *
    FROM sys.server_event_sessions
    WHERE name = 'ex_cxpacket'
)
    DROP EVENT SESSION ex_cxpacket ON SERVER;
GO

CREATE EVENT SESSION [ex_cxpacket]
ON SERVER
    ADD EVENT sqlos.wait_info
    (ACTION (
        sqlserver.plan_handle,
        sqlserver.tsql_stack)
     WHERE ([wait_type] = (265)
         AND [sqlserver].[is_system] = (0)))
    ADD TARGET package0.histogram
    (SET filtering_event_name = N'sqlos.wait_info', slots = (2048), source =
    N'sqlserver.tsql_stack', source_type = (1))
WITH (STARTUP_STATE = ON);
GO

ALTER EVENT SESSION ex_cxpacket ON SERVER STATE = START;
GO
```

Once the Extended Events session has collected data for a while, the sessions with the most waits can be looked at more closely. Listing 14-30 provides a list of all the CXPACKET waits that have been collected and the statements and query plans associated with them. Once we know these, investigate the indexes being used to determine which are resulting in low selectivity or unexpected scans.

CHAPTER 14 ■ INDEX ANALYSIS

Listing 14-30. Query to View CXPACKET Extended Events Session

```
WITH XData
  AS (SELECT CAST(target_data AS XML) AS TargetData
      FROM sys.dm_xe_session_targets st
      INNER JOIN sys.dm_xe_sessions s ON s.address = st.event_session_address
      WHERE name = 'ex_cxpacket'
      AND target_name = 'histogram'),
ParsedEvent
  AS (SELECT c.value('(@count)[1]', 'bigint') AS event_count,
        c.value('xs:hexBinary(substring((value/frames/frame/@handle)
        [1],3))', 'varbinary(255)') AS sql_handle,
        c.value('(value/frames/frame/@offsetStart)[1]', 'int') AS
        statement_start_offset,
        c.value('(value/frames/frame/@offsetEnd)[1]', 'int') AS
        statement_end_offset
      FROM XData d
      CROSS APPLY TargetData.nodes('//Slot') t(c) )
SELECT QUOTENAME(DB_NAME(st.dbid)) AS database_name,
    QUOTENAME(OBJECT_SCHEMA_NAME(st.objectid, st.dbid)) + '.' +
    QUOTENAME(OBJECT_NAME(st.objectid, st.dbid)) AS object_name,
    e.event_count,
    SUBSTRING(
        st.text,
        e.statement_start_offset / 2,
        (IIF(e.statement_end_offset = -1, LEN(CONVERT(NVARCHAR(MAX),
        st.text)) * 2, e.statement_end_offset)
          - e.statement_start_offset
        ) / 2
    ) AS query_text,
    qp.query_plan
FROM ParsedEvent e
CROSS APPLY sys.dm_exec_sql_text(e.sql_handle) st
```

```
CROSS APPLY (
    SELECT plan_handle
    FROM sys.dm_exec_query_stats qs
    WHERE e.sql_handle = qs.sql_handle
    GROUP BY plan_handle
) x
CROSS APPLY sys.dm_exec_query_plan(x.plan_handle) qp
ORDER BY e.event_count DESC;
```

IO_COMPLETION

The IO_COMPLETION wait type happens when SQL Server is waiting for I/O operations to complete for non–data page I/Os, such as index pages. Even though this wait is related to nondata operations, there are still some indexing-related actions that can be taken when this wait is high for the SQL Server instance.

First, review the state of Full Scans/sec on the server. If there is an issue with that performance counter, the operations under that counter could bleed through to nondata pages that are being used to manage the indexes. In cases where the two of these are high, place additional emphasis on analyzing Full Scans/sec issues.

The second action that we can take is to review the missing index information within the SQL Server instance. That information is discussed in Chapter 7. Adding missing indexes can shift the pressure of the data being consumed to new structures where the query may no longer need to wait for the nondata I/Os to complete since the query now leverages a different index.

Next, consider the volume of page splits occurring on the index; page splits affect nondata pages when they reallocate the pages to new pages. Heavy page split activity will result in high non–data page I/Os which can be the source of or related to these waits.

Finally, if the cause of the IO_COMPLETION issues is not apparent, investigate them with an Extended Events session. This type of analysis is outside the scope of this book since these causes would likely be non-index-related. The method used for investigating CXPACKET could apply and would be a place to start the investigation.

LCK_M_*

The LCK_M_* collection of wait types refers to waits that are occurring on the SQL Server instance. These are not just the use of locks but also the times when locks have waits associated with them. Each wait type in LCK_M_* references a distinct type of lock, such as exclusive or shared locks. To decipher the different wait types, use Table 14-2. When the LCK_M_* wait types increase, they will always be in conjunction with increases in Lock Wait Time(ms) and Lock Waits/sec, allowing these counters to help investigate this wait type.

When investigating increases in either the performance counters or the different lock types, see Table 14-2. Use the combination of the wait types and the performance counters to hone in on specific issues. For instance, when the performance counters are pointing to Lock Wait Time(ms) issues, look for long-running waits on LCK_M_*. Use the wizard in SQL Server Management Studio to create the Count Query Lock session and determine which lock and which queries, through the query_hash, are causing the issue. Similarly, if the issue is with Lock Waits/sec, look for those with the most numerous locks.

Table 14-2. LCK_M_* Wait Types

Wait Type	Lock Type
LCK_M_BU	Bulk Update.
LCK_M_IS	Intent Shared.
LCK_M_IU	Intent Update.
LCK_M_IX	Intent Exclusive.
LCK_M_RIn_NL	Insert Range lock between the current and previous key with NULL lock on the current key value.
LCK_M_RIn_S	Insert Range lock between the current and previous key with Shared lock on the current key value.
LCK_M_RIn_U	Insert Range lock between the current and previous key with Update lock on the current key value.
LCK_M_RIn_X	Insert Range lock between the current and previous key with Exclusive lock on the current key value.

(continued)

Table 14-2. (*continued*)

Wait Type	Lock Type
LCK_M_RS_S	Shared Range lock between the current and previous key with Shared lock on the current key value.
LCK_M_RS_U	Shared Range lock between the current and previous key with Update lock on the current key value.
LCK_M_RX_S	Exclusive Range lock between the current and previous key with Shared lock on the current key value.
LCK_M_RX_U	Exclusive Range lock between the current and previous key with Update lock on the current key value.
LCK_M_RX_X	Exclusive Range lock between the current and previous key with Exclusive lock on the current key value.
LCK_M_S	Shared.
LCK_M_SCH_M	Schema Modify.
LCK_M_SCH_S	Schema Share.
LCK_M_SIU	Shared with Intent Update.
LCK_M_SIX	Shared with Intent Exclusive.
LCK_M_U	Update.
LCK_M_UIX	Update with Intent Exclusive.
LCK_M_X	Exclusive.

All of the locks in Table 14-2 can appear with the suffixes _ABORT_BLOCKERS and _LOW_PRIORITY which are related to the low priority options added to online index and partition switching operations. This capability has been available since SQL Server 2014. If you see locks with these suffixes, review the index maintenance operations that are occurring. When the waits are excessive, the schedule of the maintenance will likely need to be adjusted.

PAGEIOLATCH_*

The final index-related wait is PAGEIOLATCH_* wait types. This wait refers to the waits that occur when SQL Server is retrieving data pages from indexes and placing them into memory. The time in which the query is ready to retrieve the data pages and when they are available in memory is tracked by SQL Server with these counters. As with LCK_M_* waits, there are a number of different PAGEIOLATCH_*, which are defined in Table 14-3.

First, monitor the indexes that are currently in the buffer cache to identify which indexes are available. Also, review the Page Life Expectancy/sec (PLE) counter, which is not currently collected in the monitoring section. Reviewing the allocation of pages to indexes in the buffer before and after changes in the PLE can help identify which indexes are pushing information out of memory. Then investigate query plans and tune the queries or indexes to reduce the amount of data needed to satisfy the queries.

Table 14-3. PAGEIOLATCH_* Wait Types

Wait Type	Lock Type
PAGEIOLATCH_DT	IO Latch in Destroy mode.
PAGEIOLATCH_EX	IO Latch in Exclusive mode.
PAGEIOLATCH_KP	IO Latch in Keep mode.
PAGEIOLATCH_SH	IO Latch in Shared mode.
PAGEIOLATCH_UP	IO Latch in Update mode.

The second tactic to addressing PAGEIOLATCH_* is to put more emphasis on the Full Scans/sec analysis. Often, indexes that lead to increases in this wait type are related to full scans that are in use by the database. By placing more emphasis on reducing the need for full scans in execution plans, less data will need to be pulled into memory, leading to a decrease in this wait type.

In some cases, the issues related to PAGEIOLATCH_* are unrelated to indexing. The issue can simply be a matter of slow disk performance. To verify whether this is the case, monitor the performance of the server counters for Physical disk: disk seconds/read and Physical disk: disk seconds/write and the virtual file stats for SQL Server. If these statistics are continually high, expand the investigation outside of indexing to hardware and the I/O storage level. Besides improving disk performance, this wait statistic can be reduced by increasing the available memory, which can decrease the likelihood that the data page will be pushed out of memory.

Buffer Allocation

The final area to look at when determining the server state with indexing is to look at the data pages that are in the buffer cache. This isn't a typical area that people usually look at when considering indexing, but it provides a wealth of information regarding what SQL Server is putting into memory. The basic question that this can answer for the SQL Server instance is, does the data in the buffer represent the data most important to the applications using the SQL Server?

The first part of answering this question is to review which databases have how many pages in memory. This might not seem that important, but the amount of memory being used by the different databases can sometimes be surprising. Before indexes were added to the backup tables in the MSDB database, it wouldn't be uncommon for those tables to push all the data in the backup tables into memory. If the data in the tables wasn't trimmed often, this could be a lot of information not critical to the business applications consuming an unnecessary amount of data.

For the second part of the question, we will need to engage the owners and subject-matter experts for the applications using the SQL Server instance. If the answers from these folks don't match the information that is in the buffer, this provides a list of databases for which we can focus the index tuning effort.

Along those same lines, many applications have logging databases where error and processing events are stored for troubleshooting at a later date. When issues arise, instead of going to log files, the developers can simply query the database and extract the events they need to perform their troubleshooting. But what if these tables aren't properly indexed or the queries aren't SARGable? Log tables with millions or billions of rows may be pushed into memory, pushing the data from the line-of-business applications out of memory and potentially causing worse issues. If the data in the buffer isn't being checked, there is no way to know what is in memory and if it is the right stuff.

Checking the data in memory is a relatively simple task that utilizes the DMO `sys.dm_os_buffer_descriptors`. This DMO lists each data page that is in memory and describes the information on the page. By counting each page for each database, the total number of pages and the size of memory allocated to the database can be determined. Using the query in Listing 14-31, we can see in Figure 14-12 that the `ContsoRetailDW` database occupies the most memory on the server with the `IndexingMethod` database currently using 8.84 MB of space.

Listing 14-31. Buffer Allocation for Each Database

```
SELECT LEFT(CASE database_id
                WHEN 32767 THEN 'ResourceDb'
                ELSE DB_NAME(database_id) END, 20) AS Database_Name,
    COUNT(*) AS Buffered_Page_Count,
    CAST(COUNT(*) * 8 / 1024.0 AS NUMERIC(10, 2)) AS Buffer_Pool_MB
FROM sys.dm_os_buffer_descriptors
GROUP BY DB_NAME(database_id),
    database_id
ORDER BY Buffered_Page_Count DESC;
```

	Database_Name	Buffered_Page_Count	Buffer_Pool_MB
1	ContosoRetailDW	8115	63.40
2	AdventureWorks2017	2006	15.67
3	IndexingMethod	1132	8.84
4	tempdb	784	6.13
5	master	226	1.77
6	ResourceDb	136	1.06
7	msdb	94	0.73

Figure 14-12. *Results for buffer allocation for each database query*

Once the databases in memory have been identified, it is also useful to determine what objects in the database are in memory. For the similar reason as looking to see what databases are in memory, identifying the objects in memory helps with identifying the tables and indexes to focus on when indexing. Retrieving the memory use per table and index also utilizes `sys.dm_os_buffer_descriptors` but includes mapping the rows to `allocation_unit_id` values in the catalog views `sys.allocation_units` and `sys.partitions`.

Through the query in Listing 14-32, the memory used by each of the user tables and indexes is returned. In the results in Figure 14-13, the tables FactSales and FactOnlineSales are taking up a substantial amount of memory. If this was unexpected and it wasn't obvious these were fact tables, we would definitely want to understand more about why they were taking up so much memory. This can lead us to other questions, such as: What is this data? Why is it so large? Is the space used by the table impacting the ability of other databases to use memory optimally with their indexes? In these cases, we need to investigate the indexes on these tables because the tables that are most in memory ought to have the best-honed indexing profiles.

Listing 14-32. Buffer Allocation by Table/Index

```
WITH BufferAllocation
  AS (SELECT object_id,
             index_id,
             allocation_unit_id
        FROM sys.allocation_units AS au
        INNER JOIN sys.partitions AS p ON au.container_id = p.hobt_id
                                       AND (au.type = 1 OR au.type = 3)
      UNION ALL
      SELECT object_id,
             index_id,
             allocation_unit_id
        FROM sys.allocation_units AS au
        INNER JOIN sys.partitions AS p ON au.container_id = p.hobt_id
                                       AND au.type = 2)
SELECT t.name,
    we.name,
    we.type_desc,
    COUNT(*) AS Buffered_Page_Count,
    CAST(COUNT(*) * 8 / 1024.0 AS NUMERIC(10, 2)) AS Buffer_MB
FROM sys.tables t
INNER JOIN BufferAllocation ba ON t.object_id = ba.object_id
LEFT JOIN sys.indexes we ON ba.object_id = we.object_id
                        AND ba.index_id = we.index_id
INNER JOIN sys.dm_os_buffer_descriptors bd ON ba.allocation_unit_id = bd.allocation_unit_id
WHERE bd.database_id = DB_ID()
GROUP BY t.name,
    we.index_id,
    we.name,
    we.type_desc
ORDER BY Buffered_Page_Count DESC;
```

	name	name	type_desc	Buffered_Page_Count	Buffer_MB
1	FactSales	PK_FactSales_SalesKey	CLUSTERED	18918	147.80
2	FactOnlineSales	PK_FactOnlineSales_SalesKey	CLUSTERED	17208	134.44
3	FactITSLA	PK_FactITSLA_ITSLAKey	CLUSTERED	9	0.07
4	FactStrategyPlan	PK_FactStrategyPlan_StrategyPlanKey	CLUSTERED	7	0.05
5	DimMachine	PK_DimMachine_MachineKey	CLUSTERED	5	0.04
6	FactITMachine	PK_FactITMachine	CLUSTERED	3	0.02
7	FactInventory	PK_FactInventory_InventoryKey	CLUSTERED	2	0.02
8	DimAccount	PK_DimAccount_AccountKey	CLUSTERED	2	0.02
9	DimGeography	PK_DimGeography_GeographyKey	CLUSTERED	1	0.01
10	DimSalesTerritory	PK_DimSalesTerritory_SalesTerritoryKey	CLUSTERED	1	0.01
11	FactSalesQuota	PK_FactSalesQuota_SalesQuotaKey	CLUSTERED	1	0.01

Figure 14-13. Results for buffer allocation for each table/index query

Schema Discovery

After investigating the state of the server and its indexing needs, the next step in the index analysis process is to investigate the schema of the databases to determine whether there are schema-related indexing issues that can be addressed. For these issues, we are primarily going to focus on a few key details that can be discovered through catalog views.

Identify Heaps

As discussed previously, it is often more ideal to utilize clustered indexes on tables as opposed to storing tables as heaps. When heaps are preferred, it should be when the use of a clustered index has been shown to negatively impact performance as opposed to a heap. When investigating heaps, it is best to consider the number of rows and the utilization of the heap. When a heap has a low number of rows or is not being used, taking the effort to cluster its table may be rather pointless.

To identify heaps, use the catalog views sys.indexes and sys.partitions. The performance information is available in the table dbo.index_usage_stats_history. It can be used in conjunction to form the query in Listing 14-33, which provides the output in Figure 14-14.

The results show that dbo.DatabaseLog has a number of rows. The next step is to review the schema of the table. If there is a primary key already on the table, it's a good candidate for the clustering index key. If not, check for another key column, such as a business key. If there is no key column, it may be worthwhile to add a surrogate key to the table.

Listing 14-33. Query to Identify Heaps

```
SELECT QUOTENAME(DB_NAME()) AS database_name,
    QUOTENAME(OBJECT_SCHEMA_NAME(we.object_id)) + '.' + QUOTENAME(OBJECT_
NAME(we.object_id)) AS object_name,
    we.index_id,
    p.rows,
    SUM(h.user_seeks) AS user_seeks,
    SUM(h.user_scans) AS user_scans,
    SUM(h.user_lookups) AS user_lookups,
    SUM(h.user_updates) AS user_updates
FROM sys.indexes we
INNER JOIN sys.partitions p ON we.index_id = p.index_id
                            AND we.object_id = p.object_id
LEFT OUTER JOIN IndexingMethod.dbo.index_usage_stats_history h ON p.object_
id = h.object_id
                                            AND p.index_id = h.index_id
WHERE type_desc = 'HEAP'
GROUP BY we.index_id,
    p.rows,
    we.object_id
ORDER BY p.rows DESC;
```

	database_name	object_name	index_id	rows	user_seeks	user_scans	user_lookups	user_updates
1	[AdventureWorks2017]	[dbo].[HeapExample]	0	2941	0	5	0	2
2	[AdventureWorks2017]	[dbo].[DatabaseLog]	0	1596	NULL	NULL	NULL	NULL
3	[AdventureWorks2017]	[Production].[ProductProductPhoto]	0	504	NULL	NULL	NULL	NULL

Figure 14-14. *Output for query identifying heaps*

CHAPTER 14 INDEX ANALYSIS

Duplicate Indexes

The next schema issue to review is duplicate indexes. Except for rare occasions, there is no need to have duplicate indexes in your databases. They waste space and cost resources to maintain without providing any benefit. To determine that an index is a duplicate of another, review the key columns and included columns of the index. If these values match, the index is considered a duplicate.

To uncover duplicate indexes, the `sys.indexes` view is used in conjunction with the `sys.index_columns` catalog view. Comparing these views to each other using the code in Listing 14-34 will provide a list of the indexes that are duplicates. The results from the query, displayed in Figure 14-15, show that in the AdventureWorks2017 database the indexes AK_Document_rowguid and UQ__Document__F73921F7C5112C2E are duplicates.

When duplicates are found, one of the two indexes should be removed from the database. While one of the indexes will have index activity, removing either will shift the activity from one to the other. Before removing either index, review the noncolumn properties of the index to make sure important aspects of the index are not lost. For instance, if one of the indexes is designated as unique, be sure that the index retained still has that property.

Listing 14-34. Query to Identify Duplicate Indexes

```
USE AdventureWorks2017;
GO

WITH IndexSchema
  AS (SELECT we.object_id,
        we.index_id,
        we.name,
        ISNULL(we.filter_definition, '') AS filter_definition,
        we.is_unique,
        (
            SELECT QUOTENAME(CAST(ic.column_id AS VARCHAR(10)) + CASE
                            WHEN ic.is_descending_key = 1 THEN '-'
                                                          ELSE '+' END,
                    '('
            )
```

```sql
        FROM sys.index_columns ic
        INNER JOIN sys.columns c ON ic.object_id = c.object_id
                                AND ic.column_id = c.column_id
        WHERE we.object_id = ic.object_id
        AND we.index_id = ic.index_id
        AND is_included_column = 0
        ORDER BY key_ordinal ASC
        FOR XML PATH('')
    ) + COALESCE((
            SELECT QUOTENAME(CAST(ic.column_id AS VARCHAR(10)) + CASE
                            WHEN ic.is_descending_key = 1 THEN '-'
                            ELSE '+' END,
                    '('
                    )
            FROM sys.index_columns ic
            INNER JOIN sys.columns c ON ic.object_id = c.object_id
                                    AND ic.column_id = c.column_id
            LEFT OUTER JOIN sys.index_columns ic_key ON c.object_id =
            ic_key.object_id
                                                    AND c.column_id =
                                                    ic_key.column_id
                                                    AND we.index_id =
                                                    ic_key.index_id
                                                    AND ic_key.is_
                                                    included_column = 0
            WHERE we.object_id = ic.object_id
            AND ic.index_id = 1
            AND ic.is_included_column = 0
            AND ic_key.index_id IS NULL
            ORDER BY ic.key_ordinal ASC
            FOR XML PATH('')
        ),
            ''
    ) + CASE
            WHEN we.is_unique = 1 THEN 'U'
            ELSE '' END AS index_columns_keys_ids,
```

```
            CASE
                WHEN we.index_id IN ( 0, 1 ) THEN 'ALL-COLUMNS'
                ELSE COALESCE((
                    SELECT QUOTENAME(ic.column_id, '(')
                    FROM sys.index_columns ic
                    INNER JOIN sys.columns c ON ic.object_id =
                    c.object_id
                                            AND ic.column_id =
                                            c.column_id
                    LEFT OUTER JOIN sys.index_columns ic_key ON
                    c.object_id = ic_key.object_id
                                            AND c.column_id = ic_key.
                                            column_id
                                            AND ic_key.index_id = 1
                    WHERE we.object_id = ic.object_id
                    AND we.index_id = ic.index_id
                    AND ic.is_included_column = 1
                    AND ic_key.index_id IS NULL
                    ORDER BY ic.key_ordinal ASC
                    FOR XML PATH('')
                ),
                    SPACE(0)
                ) END AS included_columns_ids
    FROM sys.tables t
    INNER JOIN sys.indexes we ON t.object_id = we.object_id
    INNER JOIN sys.data_spaces ds ON we.data_space_id = ds.data_space_id
    INNER JOIN sys.dm_db_partition_stats ps ON we.object_id = ps.object_id
                                            AND we.index_id = ps.index_id)
SELECT QUOTENAME(DB_NAME()) AS database_name,
    QUOTENAME(OBJECT_SCHEMA_NAME(is1.object_id)) + '.' + QUOTENAME(OBJECT_
    NAME(is1.object_id)) AS object_name,
    is1.name AS index_name,
    is2.name AS duplicate_index_name
FROM IndexSchema is1
```

```
INNER JOIN IndexSchema is2 ON is1.object_id = is2.object_id
                          AND is1.index_id <> is2.index_id
                          AND is1.index_columns_keys_ids = is2.index_
                          columns_keys_ids
                          AND is1.included_columns_ids = is2.included_
                          columns_ids
                          AND is1.filter_definition = is2.filter_
                          definition
                          AND is1.is_unique = is2.is_unique;
```

	database_name	object_name	index_name	duplicate_index_name
1	[AdventureWorks2017]	[Production].[Document]	UQ__Document__F73921F7C5112C2E	AK_Document_rowguid
2	[AdventureWorks2017]	[Production].[Document]	AK_Document_rowguid	UQ__Document__F73921F7C5112C2E

Figure 14-15. *Output for query identifying duplicate indexes*

Note The original inspiration for the overlapping index query is from the blog post at http://sqlblog.com/blogs/paul_nielsen/archive/2008/06/25/find-duplicate-indexes.aspx by Paul Nielsen.

Overlapping Indexes

After identifying duplicate indexes, the next step is to look for overlapping indexes. An index is considered to be overlapping another index when its key columns make up all or part of another index's key columns. Included columns are not considered when looking at overlapping columns; the focus for this evaluation is only on the key columns.

To identify overlapping indexes, the same catalog views, sys.indexes and sys.index_columns, are used. For each index, its key columns will be compared using the LIKE operator and a wildcard to the key columns of the other indexes on the table. When there is a match, it will be flagged as an overlapping index. The query for this check is provided in Listing 14-35, with the results from executing against the AdventureWorks2017 database shown in Figure 14-16.

Decisions on handling overlapping indexes are not as cut and dry as the duplicate indexes. To help illustrate overlapping indexes, the index IX_SameAsPK was creating on the column DocumentNode. This is the same column that is used as the clustering key for the table Production.Document. What this example shows, though, is that a nonclustered index can be considered an overlapping index of a clustered index. In some cases, it might be advisable to remove the overlapping nonclustered index. In all reality, the clustered index has the same key, and the pages are sorted in the same manner. We can find the same values in both. The gray area comes in when considering the size of the rows in the clustered index. If the rows are wide enough, if just querying for the clustering key, it will at times be more beneficial to use the nonclustered index. In this manner, we will need to spend more time analyzing indexes. This same gray area will apply to comparisons between two nonclustered indexes as well.

When reviewing overlapping indexes, there are a few other things to note. Be sure to retain the index properties, such as whether the index is unique. Also, watch the included columns. The included columns are not considered in the overlapping comparison. There may be unique sets of included columns between the two indexes. Watch for this and merge the included columns as appropriate.

Listing 14-35. Query to Identify Overlapping Indexes

```
WITH IndexSchema
  AS (SELECT we.object_id,
        we.index_id,
        we.name,
        (
          SELECT CASE key_ordinal
                   WHEN 0 THEN NULL
                   ELSE QUOTENAME(column_id, '(') END
          FROM sys.index_columns ic
          WHERE ic.object_id = we.object_id
          AND ic.index_id = we.index_id
          ORDER BY key_ordinal,
              column_id
          FOR XML PATH('')
        ) AS index_columns_keys
```

CHAPTER 14 INDEX ANALYSIS

```
        FROM sys.tables t
        INNER JOIN sys.indexes we ON t.object_id = we.object_id
        WHERE we.type_desc IN ( 'CLUSTERED', 'NONCLUSTERED', 'HEAP' ))
SELECT QUOTENAME(DB_NAME()) AS database_name,
    QUOTENAME(OBJECT_SCHEMA_NAME(is1.object_id)) + '.' + QUOTENAME(OBJECT_
    NAME(is1.object_id)) AS object_name,
    STUFF((
            SELECT ', ' + c.name
            FROM sys.index_columns ic
            INNER JOIN sys.columns c ON ic.object_id = c.object_id
                                    AND ic.column_id = c.column_id
            WHERE ic.object_id = is1.object_id
            AND ic.index_id = is1.index_id
            ORDER BY ic.key_ordinal,
                ic.column_id
            FOR XML PATH('')
         ),
        1,
        2,
        ''
    ) AS index_columns,
    STUFF((
            SELECT ', ' + c.name
            FROM sys.index_columns ic
            INNER JOIN sys.columns c ON ic.object_id = c.object_id
                                    AND ic.column_id = c.column_id
            WHERE ic.object_id = is1.object_id
            AND ic.index_id = is1.index_id
            AND ic.is_included_column = 1
            ORDER BY ic.column_id
            FOR XML PATH('')
         ),
        1,
        2,
        ''
    ) AS included_columns,
```

```
    is1.name AS index_name,
    SUM(CASE
            WHEN is1.index_id = h.index_id THEN
                ISNULL(h.user_seeks, 0) + ISNULL(h.user_scans, 0) +
                ISNULL(h.user_lookups, 0)
                + ISNULL(h.user_updates, 0) END
    ) index_activity,
    is2.name AS duplicate_index_name,
    SUM(CASE
            WHEN is2.index_id = h.index_id THEN
                ISNULL(h.user_seeks, 0) + ISNULL(h.user_scans, 0) +
                ISNULL(h.user_lookups, 0)
                + ISNULL(h.user_updates, 0) END
    ) duplicate_index_activity
FROM IndexSchema is1
INNER JOIN IndexSchema is2 ON is1.object_id = is2.object_id
                          AND is1.index_id > is2.index_id
                          AND (
                              is1.index_columns_keys LIKE is2.index_
                              columns_keys + '%'
                              AND is2.index_columns_keys LIKE is2.index_
                              columns_keys + '%'
                          )
LEFT OUTER JOIN IndexingMethod.dbo.index_usage_stats_history h ON is1.
object_id = h.object_id
GROUP BY is1.object_id,
    is1.name,
    is2.name,
    is1.index_id;
```

database_name	object_name	index_columns	included_columns	index_name	index_activity	duplicate_index_name	duplicate_index_activity
[AdventureWorks2017]	[Production].[Document]	rowguid	NULL	AK_Document_rowguid	NULL	UQ__Document__F73921F7C5112C2E	209
[AdventureWorks2017]	[Production].[Document]	DocumentNode	NULL	IX_SameAsPK	NULL	PK_Document_DocumentNode	28493

Figure 14-16. Output for query identifying overlapping indexes

Unindexed Foreign Keys

Foreign keys are useful for enforcing constraints within a database. When there are parent and child relationships between tables, foreign keys provide the mechanism to verify that child tables aren't referencing parent values that don't exist. Likewise, the foreign key makes certain that a parent value can't be removed while child values are still in use. To support these validations, the columns for the parent and child values between the tables need to be indexed. If one or the other is not indexed, SQL Server can't optimize the operation with a seek and is forced to use a scan to verify that the values are not in the related table.

Verifying that foreign keys are indexed involves a process similar to the duplicate and overlapping indexes process. Along with the sys.indexes and sys.index_columns catalog views, the sys.foreign_key_columns view is used to provide an index template that the foreign key would rely upon. This is pulled together in the query in Listing 14-36 with results from the AdventureWorks2017 database shown in Figure 14-17.

The common practice is that every foreign key should be indexed, always. This, though, is not actually the case for every foreign key. There are a couple things to consider before adding the index. First, how many rows are in the child table? If the row count is low, adding the index may not provide a performance gain. If the uniqueness of the column is fairly low, statistics may justify a scan of every row regardless of the index. In these cases, it could be argued that if the size of the table is small, the cost of the index is also small, and there is nothing to lose from adding the index. The other consideration is whether data will be deleted from the table and when activities that require validation of the foreign key will occur. With large tables with many columns and foreign keys, performance may suffer from having yet another index to maintain on the table. The index would probably be of value, but is it of enough value to justify creating it?

While those are good considerations when indexing foreign keys, the majority of the time, we will want to index your foreign keys. Similar to the recommendation for clustering tables, index your foreign keys unless we have performance documentation showing that indexing the foreign keys negatively impacts performance.

CHAPTER 14 ■ INDEX ANALYSIS

Listing 14-36. Query to Identify Unindexed Foreign Keys

```
WITH cIndexes
  AS (SELECT we.object_id,
        we.name,
        (
            SELECT QUOTENAME(ic.column_id, '(')
            FROM sys.index_columns ic
            WHERE we.object_id = ic.object_id
            AND we.index_id = ic.index_id
            AND is_included_column = 0
            ORDER BY key_ordinal ASC
            FOR XML PATH('')
        ) AS indexed_compare
      FROM sys.indexes we),
cForeignKeys
  AS (SELECT fk.name AS foreign_key_name,
        'PARENT' AS foreign_key_type,
        fkc.parent_object_id AS object_id,
        STUFF((
                SELECT ', ' + QUOTENAME(c.name)
                FROM sys.foreign_key_columns ifkc
                INNER JOIN sys.columns c ON ifkc.parent_object_id =
                c.object_id
                                            AND ifkc.parent_column_id =
                                                c.column_id
                WHERE fk.object_id = ifkc.constraint_object_id
                ORDER BY ifkc.constraint_column_id
                FOR XML PATH('')
            ),
            1,
            2,
            ''
        ) AS fk_columns,
```

```sql
            (
                SELECT QUOTENAME(ifkc.parent_column_id, '(')
                FROM sys.foreign_key_columns ifkc
                WHERE fk.object_id = ifkc.constraint_object_id
                ORDER BY ifkc.constraint_column_id
                FOR XML PATH('')
            ) AS fk_columns_compare
        FROM sys.foreign_keys fk
        INNER JOIN sys.foreign_key_columns fkc ON fk.object_id = fkc.constraint_object_id
        WHERE fkc.constraint_column_id = 1),
cRowCount
    AS (SELECT object_id,
            SUM(row_count) AS row_count
        FROM sys.dm_db_partition_stats ps
        WHERE index_id IN ( 1, 0 )
        GROUP BY object_id)
SELECT QUOTENAME(DB_NAME()),
    QUOTENAME(OBJECT_SCHEMA_NAME(fk.object_id)) + '.' + QUOTENAME(OBJECT_NAME(fk.object_id)) AS ObjectName,
    fk.foreign_key_name,
    fk_columns,
    row_count
FROM cForeignKeys fk
INNER JOIN cRowCount rc ON fk.object_id = rc.object_id
LEFT OUTER JOIN cIndexes we ON fk.object_id = we.object_id
                            AND we.indexed_compare LIKE fk.fk_columns_compare + '%'
WHERE we.name IS NULL
ORDER BY row_count DESC,
    OBJECT_NAME(fk.object_id),
    fk.fk_columns;
```

	(No column name)	ObjectName	foreign_key_name	fk_columns	row_count
1	[AdventureWorks2017]	[Sales].[SalesOrderDetail]	FK_SalesOrderDetail_SpecialOfferProduct_SpecialOfferIDP...	[SpecialOfferID], [ProductID]	121317
2	[AdventureWorks2017]	[Production].[WorkOrderRouting]	FK_WorkOrderRouting_Location_LocationID	[LocationID]	67131
3	[AdventureWorks2017]	[Sales].[SalesOrderHeader]	FK_SalesOrderHeader_Address_BillToAddressID	[BillToAddressID]	31465
4	[AdventureWorks2017]	[Sales].[SalesOrderHeader]	FK_SalesOrderHeader_CreditCard_CreditCardID	[CreditCardID]	31465
5	[AdventureWorks2017]	[Sales].[SalesOrderHeader]	FK_SalesOrderHeader_CurrencyRate_CurrencyRateID	[CurrencyRateID]	31465
6	[AdventureWorks2017]	[Sales].[SalesOrderHeader]	FK_SalesOrderHeader_ShipMethod_ShipMethodID	[ShipMethodID]	31465
7	[AdventureWorks2017]	[Sales].[SalesOrderHeader]	FK_SalesOrderHeader_Address_ShipToAddressID	[ShipToAddressID]	31465
8	[AdventureWorks2017]	[Sales].[SalesOrderHeader]	FK_SalesOrderHeader_SalesTerritory_TerritoryID	[TerritoryID]	31465
9	[AdventureWorks2017]	[Sales].[SalesOrderHeaderSalesReason]	FK_SalesOrderHeaderSalesReason_SalesReason_SalesR...	[SalesReasonID]	27647
10	[AdventureWorks2017]	[Person].[PersonPhone]	FK_PersonPhone_PhoneNumberType_PhoneNumberTypeID	[PhoneNumberTypeID]	19972

Figure 14-17. Output for query identifying missing foreign key indexes

Uncompressed Indexes

As discussed earlier in this chapter and in other parts of the book, it is usually beneficial to utilize some level of compression on all indexes. With row compression, the indexes generally store fixed-length data as variable length, while page compression examines data and reduces duplication to compress further. In many cases, databases can be compressed to 25–75 percent of their current size through compression. That size reduction increases the amount of data SQL Server can process through the CPU. Often times, the additional CPU cost to compress data is more than offset by the decrease in CPU effort to process the uncompressed data volume.

When examining databases for uncompressed indexes, the query in Listing 14-37 provides a list per database with the filegroup, partition boundary, row count, and size for each index. This information is especially useful because it can help identify the largest indexes where compression could provide the greatest gain. Review the list and determine which indexes to start compressing, keeping in mind whether there are data types, such as varchar(max), that will compress and may lead to compression failures, as discussed earlier in this chapter.

Listing 14-37. Query to Identify Uncompressed Indexes

```
WITH partitioning
  AS (SELECT dds.data_space_id,
        dds.partition_scheme_id,
        ds.name,
        dds.destination_id AS partition_number,
        CASE
```

```
            WHEN prv.value IS NOT NULL THEN
                CONCAT(
                    IIF(pf.boundary_value_on_right = 1, 'Less than ',
                    'Greater than or equal to '),
                    CAST(prv.value AS VARCHAR(MAX))
                )
            WHEN pf.boundary_value_on_right = 1 THEN 'Greater than MAX
            boundary'
            ELSE 'Less than MIN boundary' END AS Boundary
    FROM sys.destination_data_spaces AS dds
    INNER JOIN sys.partition_schemes AS ps ON ps.data_space_id = dds.
    partition_scheme_id
    INNER JOIN sys.partition_functions AS pf ON pf.function_id =
    ps.function_id
    INNER JOIN sys.data_spaces AS ds ON dds.data_space_id = ds.data_
    space_id
    LEFT OUTER JOIN sys.partition_range_values AS prv ON pf.function_id =
    prv.function_id
                                             AND prv.boundary_id =
                                             dds.destination_id)
SELECT S.name AS schema_name,
    T.name AS table_name,
    I.name AS index_name,
    I.index_id,
    P.partition_number,
    P.data_compression_desc,
    I.type_desc,
    IIF(DS.type_desc = 'PARTITION_SCHEME', PS.name, DS.name) AS file_group,
    PS.Boundary AS partition_boundary,
    DS.type_desc AS data_space_type,
    P.rows,
    CAST(dps.reserved_page_count * CAST(8 AS FLOAT) / 1024. AS DECIMAL(20,
    3)) AS mb_size
FROM sys.tables AS T
INNER JOIN sys.schemas AS S ON S.schema_id = T.schema_id
```

```
INNER JOIN sys.indexes AS I ON T.object_id = I.object_id
INNER JOIN sys.partitions AS P ON I.object_id = P.object_id
                              AND I.index_id = P.index_id
INNER JOIN sys.dm_db_partition_stats AS dps ON P.object_id = dps.object_id
                                           AND P.index_id = dps.index_id
                                           AND P.partition_number = dps.partition_number
LEFT OUTER JOIN partitioning AS PS ON I.data_space_id = PS.partition_scheme_id
                                   AND P.partition_number = PS.partition_number
INNER JOIN sys.data_spaces AS DS ON DS.data_space_id = I.data_space_id
WHERE P.data_compression_desc = 'NONE';
GO
```

> **Note** It bears repeating that the DTA is a good tool for determining useful indexes to add to a database. While there may be more pride in designing indexes for a database by hand without the need of a tool, it isn't practical to ignore useful recommendations. Use the DTA as a starting point to discover indexing suggestions that would have taken hours to determine without the tool in place.

Database Engine Tuning Advisor

The Database Engine Tuning Advisor (DTA) was discussed in Chapter 7. In that chapter, we discussed the two modes for using the DTA: the GUI interface and the command-line utility. While tuning queries is often a process of reviewing statistics and evaluating execution plans, the DTA provides means to accelerate this analysis by using the trace files from the monitoring process in the previous chapter to identify potentially useful indexing recommendations. This process is able to accomplish the tuning with minimal impact on the production environment since all the recommendations are derived from analysis on a nonproduction environment.

The basic process for using the DTA index analysis can be broken out into five different steps, shown in Figure 14-18:

1. Collect a workload.
2. Gather the metadata.
3. Perform the tuning.
4. Consider recommendations and review.
5. Deploy changes.

Through this process, we can get a jump start on indexing and begin working with recommendations that relate to existing performance issues.

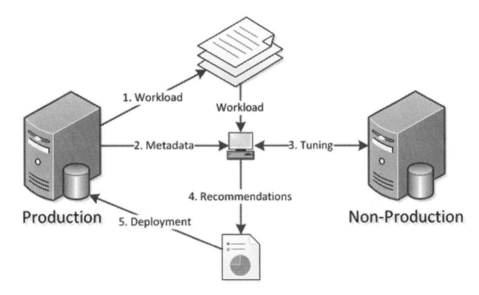

Figure 14-18. *Steps for using the DTA index analysis*

The first step in the process is to collect a workload. If we followed the process in the index monitoring process from the previous chapter, we should have already collected this information. There are two standard scenarios that workloads should represent. To begin, collect a workload that represents a typical day, because even a normal day can have underlying performance issues that tuning can help alleviate. Second, gather a workload during times where performance problems are known to exist. This will be useful for providing recommendations that we may be able to achieve through manual tuning.

After the workload is collected, the next step is to gather the necessary metadata to start the tuning sessions. There are two components to gathering metadata. The first is to create an XML input file for the dta session. The XML input file contains the production and nonproduction server names and information on where the workload is and what type of tuning options to utilize (Listing 14-38 shows a sample). For more information on tuning options, see Chapter 7. The second part of this step is the effect on tuning from the first piece. When the tuning occurs, SQL Server will gather the schema and statistics for the database from the production database(s) and move that information to the nonproduction server. While the database won't have the production data, it will have the information necessary to make indexing recommendations.

Listing 14-38. Sample XML Input File for DTA

```
<?xml version="1.0" encoding="utf-16" ?>
<DTAXML xmlns:xsi="http://www.w3.org/2001/XMLSchema-instance"
xmlns="http://schemas.microsoft.com/sqlserver/2004/07/dta">
  <DTAInput>
    <Server>
      <Name>STR8-SQL-PRD</Name>
      <Database>
        <Name>AdventureWorks2017</Name>
      </Database>
    </Server>
    <Workload>
      <File>c:\temp\IndexingMethod.trc</File>
    </Workload>
    <TuningOptions>
      <TestServer>STR8-SQL-TEST </TestServer>
      <FeatureSet>IDX</FeatureSet>
      <Partitioning>NONE</Partitioning>
      <KeepExisting>NONE</KeepExisting>
    </TuningOptions>
  </DTAInput>
</DTAXML>
```

> **Note** We can find more information on the XML input file configuration in Books Online at `https://docs.microsoft.com/en-us/sql/tools/dta/xml-input-file-reference-database-engine-tuning-advisor?view=sql-server-ver15`.

The next step is the actual execution of the DTA tuning session. To run the session, execute the `dta` command using the `-ix` command-line option, shown in Listing 14-39. Since all the configuration information for the session is located in the XML file, there is no need to add any additional parameters.

Listing 14-39. DTA Command with XML Input File

```
dta -ix "c:\temp\SessionConfig.xml"
```

After the tuning session completes, we will receive a list of index recommendations. This isn't the last step in this portion of the process. Before any recommendations from the DTA can be implemented, they must be reviewed. While using this tool will accelerate the index analysis process, all the recommendations need to be reviewed and vetted to verify that they make sense and don't overload a table with more indexes than SQL Server can support for the workload.

The last step is to deploy the indexing recommendations. This step is technically outside the scope of this phase of the Indexing Method. At this time, though, we should be familiar with the indexing changes that will be implemented. Add these changes to the existing list of indexing changes from other analysis and prepare them for implementation, which is discussed in the next chapter.

Unused Indexes

One of the necessary and potentially dangerous steps during index analysis is the determination of indexes to remove. Some indexes will be removed because of consolidation or because they are duplicates. Often these have less risk than when other indexes are dropped. The indexes in this other category are those that are unused.

The easiest manner for identifying indexes that are not used is to check the list of indexes in each database against the `dbo.index_usage_stats_history` table in the `IndexingMethod` database. If there are any unused indexes in the database, the query in Listing 14-40 will identify them. One word of caution with unused indexes: In this analysis, heaps and clustered indexes are ignored, along with any unique indexes and primary keys. Indexes with these properties are often related to other business rules, and their removal should be based on other factors. Figure 14-19 shows an example of unused indexes in the AdventureWorks2017 database.

Listing 14-40. Query for Unused Indexes

```sql
SELECT OBJECT_NAME(we.object_id) AS table_name,
    COALESCE(we.name, SPACE(0)) AS index_name,
    ps.partition_number,
    ps.row_count,
    CAST((ps.reserved_page_count * 8) / 1024. AS DECIMAL(12, 2)) AS size_in_mb,
    COALESCE(ius.user_seeks, 0) AS user_seeks,
    COALESCE(ius.user_scans, 0) AS user_scans,
    COALESCE(ius.user_lookups, 0) AS user_lookups,
    we.type_desc
FROM sys.all_objects t
INNER JOIN sys.indexes we ON t.object_id = we.object_id
INNER JOIN sys.dm_db_partition_stats ps ON we.object_id = ps.object_id
                                        AND we.index_id = ps.index_id
LEFT OUTER JOIN sys.dm_db_index_usage_stats ius ON ius.database_id = DB_ID()
                                                AND we.object_id = ius.object_id
                                                AND we.index_id = ius.index_id
WHERE we.type_desc NOT IN ( 'HEAP', 'CLUSTERED' )
AND we.is_unique = 0
AND we.is_primary_key = 0
AND we.is_unique_constraint = 0
AND COALESCE(ius.user_seeks, 0) <= 0
AND COALESCE(ius.user_scans, 0) <= 0
AND COALESCE(ius.user_lookups, 0) <= 0
ORDER BY OBJECT_NAME(we.object_id),
    we.name;
```

CHAPTER 14   INDEX ANALYSIS

	table_name	index_name	partition_number	row_count	size_in_mb	user_seeks	user_scans	user_lookups	type_desc
1	Address	IX_Address_StateProvinceID	1	19614	0.38	0	0	0	NONCLUSTERED
2	BillOfMaterials	IX_BillOfMaterials_UnitMeasureCode	1	2679	0.26	0	0	0	NONCLUSTERED
3	BusinessEntityAddress	IX_BusinessEntityAddress_AddressID	1	19614	0.45	0	0	0	NONCLUSTERED
4	BusinessEntityAddress	IX_BusinessEntityAddress_AddressTypeID	1	19614	0.45	0	0	0	NONCLUSTERED
5	BusinessEntityContact	IX_BusinessEntityContact_ContactTypeID	1	909	0.20	0	0	0	NONCLUSTERED
6	BusinessEntityContact	IX_BusinessEntityContact_PersonID	1	909	0.20	0	0	0	NONCLUSTERED
7	CountryRegionCurrency	IX_CountryRegionCurrency_CurrencyCode	1	109	0.07	0	0	0	NONCLUSTERED
8	Customer	IX_Customer_TerritoryID	1	19820	0.38	0	0	0	NONCLUSTERED
9	Document	IX_Document_FileName_Revision	1	13	0.07	0	0	0	NONCLUSTERED
10	Document	IX_SameAsPK	1	13	0.07	0	0	0	NONCLUSTERED

Figure 14-19. *Output for query identifying missing foreign key indexes*

While this section didn't discuss it, there are two additional scenarios for identifying unused indexes. These are lightly used indexes or no longer used indexes. A similar process can be used for these situations: instead of looking for indexes that have never been used, filter for low usage rates or no use in a period of weeks or months. But don't just remove these indexes automatically. If the index is lightly used, verify how the index is being used before dropping it. It may be used once a day, but it might be tied to critical processes. Also, with no longer used indexes, verify that the index isn't part of a seasonal process. Removing indexes tied to seasonal activity can create more of a burden than just maintaining them in off-peak times.

Index Plan Usage

In previous sections of this chapter, we discussed the concept of checking the plan cache to analyze and investigate index usages. While statistics can show that there was a seek or a scan against an index, it doesn't provide us with enough detail to know what columns to add or what caused the index to use a scan over a seek. To gather this information, we need to turn to the execution plan. And the place where we can get some of the best execution plans for your databases and SQL Server instance is the plan cache. In this section, for index analysis, we'll be looking at two queries that can be used to retrieve execution plans from the plan cache.

The first query is one that will be used when we need to retrieve all the plans for a specific index. Suppose we need to determine what processes, or T-SQL statements, are using one of the indexes on a table that is used once or twice a day. For this, we can turn to the plan cache with the query in Listing 14-41 and check whether the plan for that query is still in the cache. To use the query, replace the index name in the variable `@IndexName` and execute it to return a list of plans that use the index. Be cautious if we have a database where there are many indexes with the same name, since index names

CHAPTER 14 ■ INDEX ANALYSIS

need to be unique only on a per-table basis. If all of the indexes are named IX_1 and IX_2, we will need to verify the table name in the search to be sure we have the correct index.

Listing 14-41. Query Plan Cache for Index Usage

```
SET TRANSACTION ISOLATION LEVEL READ UNCOMMITTED;
GO

DECLARE @IndexName sysname = 'PK_SalesOrderHeader_SalesOrderID';
SET @IndexName = QUOTENAME(@IndexName, '[');

WITH XMLNAMESPACES (
    DEFAULT 'http://schemas.microsoft.com/sqlserver/2004/07/showplan'
)
, IndexSearch
  AS (SELECT qp.query_plan,
             cp.usecounts,
             ix.query('.') AS StmtSimple
      FROM sys.dm_exec_cached_plans cp
      OUTER APPLY sys.dm_exec_query_plan(cp.plan_handle) qp
      CROSS APPLY qp.query_plan.nodes('//StmtSimple') AS p(ix)
      WHERE query_plan.exist('//Object[@Index = sql:variable
      ("@IndexName")]') = 1)
SELECT StmtSimple.value('StmtSimple[1]/@StatementText', 'VARCHAR(4000)') AS sql_text,
    obj.value('@Database', 'sysname') AS database_name,
    obj.value('@Schema', 'sysname') AS schema_name,
    obj.value('@Table', 'sysname') AS table_name,
    obj.value('@Index', 'sysname') AS index_name,
    ixs.query_plan
FROM IndexSearch ixs
CROSS APPLY StmtSimple.nodes('//Object') AS o(obj)
WHERE obj.exist('//Object[@Index = sql:variable("@IndexName")]') = 1;
```

CHAPTER 14 ■ INDEX ANALYSIS

At other times, searching for just the name of an index will be too broad of a search of the plan cache. In these cases, we can use the query in Listing 14-42. This query adds in the name of a physical operator to the plan cache search. For instance, suppose we are investigating Full Scans/sec and we know what index is causing the spike in the performance counter. Searching for just the index may return dozens of execution plans. Alternatively, we could add a search for a particular operator, such as an index scan, using the @op variable in the query provided.

Listing 14-42. Query Plan Cache for Index Usage and Physical Operation

```
DECLARE @IndexName sysname = 'IX_SalesOrderHeader_SalesPersonID';
DECLARE @op sysname = 'Index Scan';

;WITH XMLNAMESPACES (
      DEFAULT N'http://schemas.microsoft.com/sqlserver/2004/07/showplan'
 )
SELECT cp.plan_handle,
    DB_NAME(dbid) + '.' + OBJECT_SCHEMA_NAME(objectid, dbid) + '.' +
    OBJECT_NAME(objectid, dbid) AS database_object,
    qp.query_plan,
    c1.value('@PhysicalOp', 'nvarchar(50)'),
    c2.value('@Index', 'nvarchar(max)')
FROM sys.dm_exec_cached_plans cp
CROSS APPLY sys.dm_exec_query_plan(cp.plan_handle) qp
CROSS APPLY query_plan.nodes('//RelOp') r(c1)
OUTER APPLY c1.nodes('IndexScan/Object') AS o(c2)
WHERE c2.value('@Index', 'nvarchar(max)') = QUOTENAME(@IndexName, '[')
AND c1.exist('@PhysicalOp[. = sql:variable("@op")]') = 1;
```

Both of these queries provide mechanisms for getting in and investigating indexes in their environment and seeing exactly how SQL Server is using them. This information can be easily leveraged to identify when problems are occurring and why and then provide a path to resolving indexing issues without a lot of the guesswork that many use today.

Summary

As this chapter showed, we can use the information collected from monitoring indexes to analyze indexes to examine and identify indexes. The results from this analysis help to determine what types of indexes to modify and where. Indexing tools such as the Database Engine Tuning Advisor and missing index DMOs can be leveraged to discover "the low-hanging fruit," giving us a head start on analysis that we may not have discovered otherwise. By following the processes laid out in this index analysis, we can build a stable, repeatable indexing process that can help improve the performance of your database platform and achieve stable performance over time.

CHAPTER 15

Indexing Methodology

Throughout this book, we've discussed what indexes are, what they do, patterns for building them, and many other aspects for determining how a SQL Server database should be indexed. All that information is necessary for the last piece in indexing your databases, which is a methodology for managing indexes. To do this, you need a process for applying that knowledge to determine the indexes that are best for your environment and provide the greatest gain to performance.

In this last chapter, we'll discuss a general practice that can be used to build an indexing methodology. You'll look at the steps necessary to manage indexes. This methodology can be applied to a single database, a server, or your entire SQL Server environment. Regardless of the type of operations or business the database supports, you can use the same methodology for building indexes.

The Indexing Method

Before you can begin creating and dropping indexes, you first need a process to analyze current and potential indexes. This process needs to provide a way to observe your databases and determine the indexes that are appropriate for your databases. As mentioned in previous chapters, indexing should be more of a science than an art. The information needed to properly index a database is available; through some research, you can identify potential indexes. Similar to how scientists use the Scientific Method to prove theories, database administrators and developers can use the Indexing Method to prove what indexes a database requires.

The Indexing Method used in this book is comprised of three phases: Monitor, Analyze, and Implement (see Figure 15-1). Within each component are a number of steps that, when completed, help to provide the appropriate indexing for the database. At the completion of the Implement phase, the Indexing Method restarts the first phase, making indexing a continuous and iterative process.

When starting with the Monitor phase, the primary activity is to observe the indexes. The observations entail reviewing both the performance and the behavior of the indexes (i.e., the indexing concepts described in Chapter 13). SQL Server will use the indexes that it finds most beneficial from those available. By observing this behavior, you can identify the indexes that are most often used and how they are used.

After the observations, the Analyze phase of the Indexing Method begins. In the Analyze phase, detailed in Chapter 14, the statistics collected in the previous phase are used to determine what indexes are best suited for the database. The goal is to identify what indexes need to be created, dropped, and modified. Along with this, the impacts of any indexing changes are also identified.

The last phase of the Indexing Method is the Implementation phase. In this phase, the indexes from the last phase are applied, or deployed, to the databases. For every database and environment, the deployment process may be different. For instance, the process for deploying indexes on third-party databases differs from applications owned by your company. Within this phase, though, there are core concepts that apply to all environments; outside of physically building the indexes, you will need to communicate the change plan and possible effects of the change. Then, you need to track the changes over time. There is more to implementing indexes than just executing a CREATE INDEX statement.

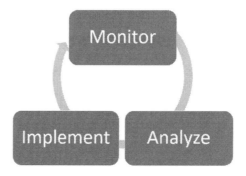

Figure 15-1. *Indexing Method cycle*

After the last phase completes, the Indexing Method begins again with the first phase. In this way, indexing is a continuous and iterative process. The indexes that provide the best performance today may not be the best indexes for tomorrow. Two events primarily contribute to the need for changing indexes over time. The first is data usage, where the functions and features of applications can change over time, so the purpose of the application can also change. Second, the data population and distribution can, and usually will, change over time. With these changes, indexes may shift out of usage, and other data access paths may be required. Data changes aren't the only things that can cause index use to change; the optimization in a future SQL Server version or service pack may change how the optimizer uses indexes.

Now that the basics of the Indexing Method are covered, the remainder of this chapter will focus on the Implement portion. The concepts for the Monitor and Analyze phases are covered in Chapters 13 and 14, respectively. It's important too that as you learn more about indexes, you will discover new patterns that can be used to identify indexes. As you learn more about indexing and your databases, you will find other ways to look at performance and usage statistics that provide more, or better informed, guidance. Use this book and the information you learn to continue to expand your indexing methodology.

Implement

The final phase of the Indexing Method is the Implement phase. This phase does as the name implies: it implements the indexing changes that were determined as necessary through the Analyze phase. There isn't much to this phase from a process perspective, but there are some important steps that need to be done during the Implement phase that will help build out a successful process. The aim of the entire process is to improve the performance of the database environment. With this aim, there are three key points to remember during implementation:

- Communication
- Source code control (e.g., via deployment scripts)
- Execution

While the last step is the only one where the database is modified, the other two help ensure that the changes will be noticed and that you can continue to use the Indexing Method in the future.

CHAPTER 15 INDEXING METHODOLOGY

Communication

The first hurdle in modifying the indexes on any database is the need to communicate with management and users of the database your intent to change the database. Modifications to the database can often raise red flags, especially when they are being prescribed by nonowners of the application the database supports. Preparing for and implementing open lines of communication between the owners of applications and the database administration team will help not only in the indexing process but in other areas of mutual interest. Without this communication, teams can be blindsided by the indexing changes, which may impact something that the analysis did not uncover or a feature that is planned but not yet released.

When it comes to communication, there are basically two items that need to be prepared for the owners of the databases: an impact analysis of the indexing changes and a status report of the changes after implementation.

Impact Analysis

When preparing for changes to indexing on a database, it is important to highlight the intended changes to the application performance. Historically, this has often been a guessing game. There was not a lot of easily accessed information that would indicate where an index is being used, how it is being used, and the frequency of use.

With the processes laid out in the Monitor phase, you gain the ability to confidently know the use of an index. You can determine when it was last used and what operations were included. There is information that can also be used to identify the trend in which an index will no longer be used or is being used more frequently.

Through the Analyze phase, steps were laid out that allow the identification of execution plans that are utilizing different indexes. Use these steps to identify where an index change will have an impact and then perform sample executions of the T-SQL statements before and after the indexing changes are made.

In the end, the impact analysis will function in two important roles within the Implement phase. First, it will communicate to managers and peers the intent of the indexing changes, informing them of the changes to validate what is being done and allowing them the chance for feedback. Second, the impact analysis provides an insurance policy in case an index change has an unexpected negative impact. This isn't to say that there won't be negative repercussions to poor indexing recommendations, but with others involved and the impact documented, it is more likely that a negative impact can be mitigated quicker and possibly identified before actual implementation.

Note In one environment that I worked in, some lightly used indexes were removed from the database. They were generally used once per day. That one time was for a business-critical import process that basically couldn't perform without those indexes. Had an impact analysis been done prior to removing those indexes, a lot of tough questions could have been avoided.

Status Report

On the opposite end of the Implement phase is the status report. As the name implies, the status report is a document that provides feedback to managers and peers about the actual impact of indexes. This document does not need to be very deep, but it does need to cover some key points. The status report should cover the following information:

- All index changes made
- Status on deployment of changes
- Brief performance review
- Information on any regressions noted
- What was learned in the deployment process
- Summary of issues encountered

Don't get too mired in the details while writing the status report. If all goes well, there will be additional Monitor and Analyze phases in the near future. In the end, the status report needs to communicate two things. First, it provides an honest assessment of the successes and failures in the indexing deployment. Second, and most importantly, it lists what benefits are now being realized by the indexing changes. This is most important because it is the ROI that managers need to see to be able to justify the time and effort spent on indexing.

> **Note** One of the most successful things I did as a consultant was constantly updating customers about the impact of indexing changes I'd make. A graph with before and after performance often looked like a "self-pat on the back" with some of the teams I was assisting, but the management that brought me in found it incredibly useful in identifying the ROI of bringing in consultants but also communicating further up the line the effort being placed in resolving business concerns with performance.

Deployment Scripts

The primary deliverable from the Analyze phase is a list of index changes that are planned for the databases in your environment. During the Implement phase, those indexes need to be reviewed and prepared for deployment. As part of preparing the indexes for deployment, three steps need to occur:

1. Prepare the deployment and rollback of the schema.
2. Save index changes to source code control.
3. Share results of peer review with impact analysis.

Prepare Deployment and Rollback of Schema

Usually, at the completion of the Analyze phase, you have a list of the index changes that are being proposed. This list typically is not in a state that can be used for deployment at the end of the phase. Between that point and the execution of the changes, the indexing changes need to be put into a state that can be used for their deployment.

When building the deployment scripts, be sure to observe the idea of "doing no harm" to the database. In other words, you need to build scripts that are intelligent enough that they can be executed multiple times with the identical results. Also, this means that scripts should be available to reverse any indexing changes being made. Never assume that the previous indexing state of a table is being stored in source code control. Check to be certain that the existing state is known and develop scripts to revert to that state if needed.

The deployment scripts also need to be aware of the edition of SQL Server that is being used. For instance, if you are using Enterprise Edition, leverage online index rebuilds for indexes that are being rebuilt with new characteristics. If appropriate for the index, Enterprise Edition also allows for compression on the index, which can save space and improve performance in many cases.

Save Index Changes to Source Code Repository

As mentioned, the current state of the indexes on tables should be in a source code repository. If they are not, then with this iteration through the Implement phase, it's time to do so. Source code repositories offer a place to store the code, or schema, for a database to allow your organization to determine what the index, table, or store procedure schema was at a specific date and time. Source code is often well managed from an application perspective. Developers are usually quick to choose a tool and leverage it for their applications.

Source code repositories allow you to recover to a point in time for the database schema. If there are any development teams within your organization, they likely already have a desired repository in place. This may be an internal repository like Perforce or an externally available solution like GitHub.

Peer Review with Impact Analysis

The last thing to do before the Execution step is to seek a peer review of the indexing changes. There is nothing worse than working in a vacuum and not understanding the whole impact of the changes that are being proposed against the applications that use the databases. It is easy to get a tunnel vision by focusing on the indexing goal and miss the business goals of the current deployment or overlook something that wasn't apparent in the index analysis.

The best way to avoid these pitfalls is to find a peer to review the indexing changes. Bring to the peer the index deployment scripts and the impact analysis and go over the changes. Your peer doesn't necessarily need to know everything about the environment, just a basic understanding of indexing. The aim of the peer review is to explain each change. In this dialogue, your peer serves as a sounding board as you explain the indexing need. This serves a dual role. First, your peer will be able to provide feedback on the indexing change. Second, by discussing the changes, you may hear yourself describe an indexing change that doesn't sound correct when it is explained.

In some environments, you may not have a peer that you can turn to review the indexes. In these cases, consider going to your manager for the peer review. If that is not possible, talk to your manager about leveraging peers in your technical network.

Leverage the forums and social networks to find either a peer or group of peers that will be willing to review your changes with you. Using social networks, such as Twitter, to connect with a technical peer and review some indexing changes is much better than not having a peer review at all.

With the peer review complete, the indexes are ready for the next step in the Implement phase: the step where the indexes are actually applied to the databases.

Note Within the SQL Server community, Twitter is one of the more active social networking tools. Use hashtags `#sql` and `#sqlserver` to find general information on SQL Server. When looking for answers to questions specifically about SQL Server, you can utilize the hashtag `#sqlhelp`. Twitter also allows you to add people to your conversation by including their Twitter handle in the tweet. For instance, the author of this book is available through the twitter handle `@stratesql`.

Execution

The last piece of the Implement phase is the execution of the T-SQL scripts that will apply the indexing changes to the database. These scripts should already be prepared through the Deploy Scripts step, and the scope of the changes should be well known from the Communication step. Thus, the Execution step should be relatively painless as the preparation work is already completed.

From an execution standpoint, the manner of execution is completely dependent on your organization's change control process. In some environments, there are automated processes where scripts can be loaded to a deployment mechanism and executed on a schedule. In others, the DBAs simply open SQL Server Management Studio and execute each script until all the changes are completed. Whatever the mechanism, the key is that at this stage the indexes get deployed.

As the deployment progresses, be sure to catalog the changes made and any issues that arise during execution. Pay attention to unintended blocking on the databases. If indexes are being deployed in an offline state, be sure to select an execution window that is during the database maintenance window. Remember even online index operations can cause short-lived blocking.

CHAPTER 15 INDEXING METHODOLOGY

Repeat

At the beginning of this chapter, the discussion started by looking at the three phases of the Indexing Method. The diagram for the process (Figure 15-1) shows the three phases in an endless loop, with each phase leading to the next. This choice in layout was intentional. Indexing is not a fixed-point activity. Once the first round of the Indexing Method is completed, it is important to start the next round of indexing.

It can be tempting, when databases are properly tuned, to let the practice of indexing slip and to focus on other priorities. Unfortunately, new features are often added to applications as frequently as new data is added to the database. Both of these events will change the way in which indexes are used by the database and the effectiveness of the current state of "good" indexes.

To maintain the desired performance of the database platform, indexes must be continuously reviewed. This isn't to say that a full-time resource always needs to be assigned to monitoring, analyzing, and implementing indexes. There does, though, need to be an acceptance that at some interval an evaluation of the state of indexing will be completed.

Summary

As this chapter showed, the Indexing Method is quite similar to the Scientific Method. Within your database platform, statistics can be collected on indexes in order to identify where indexing issues may exist. These statistics can then be further utilized to determine the types of indexes to modify and where. Indexing tools such as the Database Engine Tuning Advisor and missing index DMOs can be leveraged to discover "the low-hanging fruit," giving you a head start on analysis that you may not have discovered otherwise. By following the phases laid out in the Indexing Method, you can build a stable, repeatable indexing process that can help improve the performance of your database platform and achieve stable performance over time.

Index

A

Aggregation execution plan, 247
Automatically maintaining statistics
    creation, 310
    prevention, 311–312
    updation, 310–311

B

Balance index count, 258
Best practices, Indexing
    balance index count, 258
    change management, 255
    fill factor
        database level, 256
        index level, 257
    indexing foreign key
        columns, 257, 258
    using clustered indexes on primary
        keys, 256
Binary large object (BLOB), 213
Buffer allocation, 572–575
Bulk Changed Map (BCM) page, 37

C

CarrierTrackingNumber column, 232
Clustered indexes, 4, 87, 88
    ever-increasing, 360
    foreign key
        IDENTITY property, 367–369
        multiple header row, 371–373
        single header row, 369, 370
    GUID pattern, 380–383
    identity column, 361–363
    multiple column, 373–379
    narrow, 360
    static, 359
    surrogate key, 363–366
    unique, 360
    use, 254
Columnstore index, 5, 6, 89, 413–420
Columnstore operational stats
    header columns, 161
    statistics columns, 161–162
Columnstore physical stats
    header columns, 159
    statistics columns, 159–160
Computed columns
    execution plans, 449
    indexed computed column, 450, 451
    Person.Person, 448
    queries, 448
    STATISTICS IO, 449
Concatenation
    execution plan for, 445
        concatenation removed, 447
        without spaces, 446

INDEX

Concatenation (*cont.*)
    query, 445, 447, 448
    STATISTICS IO, 445
        concatenation removed, 447
        without spaces, 446
CXPACKET, 557–565

D

Database administrators (DBAs), 331
Database Engine Tuning Advisor (DTA)
    command-line utility
        description, 331
        first scenario, 346–348
        scenario setup, 345
        second scenario, 348–351
        utility arguments, 340–344
        utility syntax, 339, 340
    DDL Statement, 333
    deployment, 589
    GUI tool
        configuration screen, 334
        default selections, 335
        description, 331
        indexes options, 337
        progress screen, 336
        recommendations, 337
        tuning options configuration screen, 336
        workload options, 334, 335
    limitations, 331
    metadata, 588
    PDSs, 332
    recommendations, 588
    tuning, effect on, 588
    workload collection, 587
    XML input file, 588
Database level fill factor, 256

Data conversion
    execution plans, 458, 459
    queries, 457
    setup, 456
    STATISTICS IO for, 459
Data definition language (DDL)
    alter index, 18–21
    command, 315–318
    create index
        index options, 15, 19–21
        syntax, 14, 16
        types, 14
        UNIQUE keyword, 15
    drop index, 22–24
Data storage
    extents
        mixed, 31
        uniform, 32
    pages (*see* Pages)
DBCC PAGE
    allocations, 71
    parameters, 68
    print option
        hex data, 76–77
        hex rows, 74–77
        page header, 72–74
        row data, 77–80
    syntax, 68
dbo.DatabaseLog, 572
dbo.IndexingCounters, 465, 469
Defragmentation, 291
    drop and re-create, 295
    index rebuild, 291–294
    index reorganization, 294, 295
    maintenance plans
        rebuild index task, 298–300
        reorganize index task, 296–298
    T-SQL scripts, 301–307

Differential Change Map (DCM) page, 37
Duplicate indexes, 574–577
Dynamic management function (DMF), 323
Dynamic management objects (DMOs), 91
    data cleanup, 501, 502
    definition, 471
    index operational stats
        snapshot population, 482–491
        snapshot tables stats, 478–481
    index physical stats
        history population, 497–500
        history table, 494–496
    index usage stats
        monitoring steps, 472
        snapshot population, 474, 475
        snapshot tables stats, 472–474
    missing index
        benefits, 319
        feedback, 319
        included_columns, 328
        limitations, 320
        query performance, 326–328
        SQL statements, 326
        sys.dm_db_missing_index_
            columns, 323
        sys.dm_db_missing_index_details,
            322, 323
        sys.dm_db_missing_index_
            groups, 323
        sys.dm_db_missing_index_group_
            stats, 324, 325
    wait statistics
        history population, 500, 501
        index-related, 498
        snapshot and history table, 498, 499
        snapshot population, 499
Dynamic management view
        (DMV), 322, 323

E

Event tracing
    extended events, 509–513
    SQL trace, 503–509
Extended events, 509–513
Extended Events session
    columns, 510
    creating and starting, 511
    global fields, 511
    stop, 513, 514
Extensible Markup Language (XML), 163
    benefits, 164
    cautions, 164
    creation
        Primary index, 167
        Secondary index, 169
        _xml_index_id, 171
    selective, 171–176
    types, 165

F

Fill factor
    database level, 256
    description, 256
    index level, 257
Filtered index, 12
Foreign key, 257, 366–373
Forwarded record pointer, 81
Fragmentation
    columnstore
        delete operations, 286, 287
        impact of inserts, 285
        I/O statistics, 286
        rowgroup resultset, 284
        rowgroup statistics, 286
        statistics I/O results, 287
        table preparation, 282–284

INDEX

Fragmentation (*cont.*)
  default values, 308
  defragmentation
    drop and re-create, 295
    index rebuild, 291–294
    index reorganization, 294, 295
    strategies, 296–307
  events, 262
  heap bloat and forwarding
    delete impact, 277–279
    forward record impact, 280, 281
    I/O impact, 279
    I/O statistics, 281, 282
  issues
    contiguous reads, 291
    index I/O, 288–291
  NEWID() function, 263, 309
  NEWSEQUENTIALID() function, 309
  operations
    delete, 270–272
    insert, 262–266
    shrink, 273
    update, 266–270
  prevention
    data typing, 308
    fill factor, 307
Full-text search (FTS), 6, 9
  creation
    catalog, 215, 216
    CREATE TABLE and INSERT
      statements, 215, 216
    key indexes, 219
    population, 220
    StopLists, 220–223
    syntax, 217–219
  description, 213
  index catalog views and
    properties, 223–227

G

Global Allocation Map (GAM) page, 36
Globally unique identifier
  (GUID), 380–383
Graphical user interface (GUI) tool
  configuration screen, 334
  default selections, 335
  description, 331
  indexes options, 337
  progress screen, 336
  workload options, 334, 335

H

Hash index, 8
Heaps
  scenarios, 358, 359
  temporary objects, 354–358
Heap tables, 3

I

Impact analysis, 598, 599
Implement phase, indexing method
  communication
    impact analysis, 598
    status report, 599, 600
  deployment scripts
    impact analysis review, 601
    preparation and rollback, 600
    source code repository, 601
  execution, 602
Index Allocation Map (IAM) pages, 38
Index analysis
  components, 515
  deployed, 516
  DTA, 589–592
  index plan usage, 591–593

INDEX

schema discovery
    duplicate indexes, 574–577
    heaps identification, 572–574
    overlapping indexes, 577–581
    unindexed foreign keys, 581–586
server state review
    buffer allocation, 572–575
    performance counters, 518–554
    wait statistics, 553–569
unused indexes, 589–591

Indexing
benefits, 231
clustered, 87, 88
columnstore, 89
compression
    page-level, 13
    row-level, 13
DDL (*see* Data definition language (DDL))
heap, 87
metadata, 23–26
nonclustered, 88
overview, 1, 2
types
    clustered index, 4
    columnstore index, 5, 6
    full-text search, 9
    hash index, 8
    heap tables, 3
    nonclustered index, 5
    range index, 8
    spatial index, 7
    XML index, 6, 7
variations
    filtered index, 12
    included columns, 11
    partitioned index, 12, 13

    primary key, 10
    unique index, 10

Indexing databases
clustered indexes (*see* Clustered indexes)
columnstore index
    data warehouse, 414
    guidelines, 415
    performance improvements, 420
    statistics IO results, 416–419
heaps
    scenarios, 358
    temporary objects, 354–358
non-clustered indexes (*see* Non-clustered indexes)
page compression
    benefits, 430
    components, 430
    implementation, 431
    output, 431
    query, 432
    setup, 430
row compression
    benefits, 429
    fixed-length character data, 426
    implementation, 427
    metadata changes, 425
    numeric data types, 426
    output, 428
    query, 428, 429
    setup, 426, 427
views
    benefits, 438
    considerations, 435
    creation, 435, 436
    queries, 436–438
    summary information, 433

INDEX

Indexing method
  cycle, 596
  implement phase
    communication, 598–600
    deployment scripts, 600–602
    execution, 602
  phases, 595, 596
  repeat process, 603
Indexing myths
  best practices (*see* Best practices, Indexing)
  clustered indexes, physically ordered records, 242–244
  column filteration in multicolumn indexes
    index with columns, 239–241
  deleting heaps
    query results, 253
    reusing data, 252
  description, 229
  fill factor
    average space, 251
    on inserts, 250
    rebuilding clustered index, 250
    table creation, clustered index, 249
  index requirement
    adding index, 233
    orders of magnitude, 232
    table without index, 232
  online index operations
    creating table, 236
    index created with ONLINE option, 238
    index created without ONLINE option, 239
    monitoring events, 237
    on nonclustered index creation, 238
  ordering of index output
    default aggregation execution plan, 246
    filtering on order, 248
    parallelism, aggregation execution plan, 247
    unordered results, 245, 248
  primary keys, clustered, 233–235
  table, heap/clustered index, 253–257
Indexing tools
  DMF, 323
  DMOs (*see* Dynamic management objects (DMOs))
  DMV, 322, 323
  DTA (*see* DTA)
  PDSs, 332
Index level fill factor, 257
Index-level statistics
  cardinality, 92
  catalog views, 100, 101
  DBCC SHOW_STATISTICS
    density vector, 95, 96
    histogram, 96–100
    stats header, 93–95
    syntax, 93
  DDL statements, 109
  query optimization, 109
  STATS_DATE function, 101
  sys.dm_db_stats_properties, 102–106
Index maintenance, *see* Fragmentation; Statistics maintenance
Index monitoring
  DMOs
    data cleanup, 501, 502
    definition, 471
    index operational stats, 477–491
    index physical stats, 491–497

610

index usage stats, 471–477
wait statistics, 497–501
event tracing
    Extended Events
        session, 509–513
    SQL Trace session, 503–509
performance counters
    baseline table, 468
    definition, 462
    index-related, 463
    populate counter baseline
        table, 469, 470
    snapshot script, 465–468
    snapshot table, 464, 465
Index operational statistics
    compression, 147–149
    DML activity, 125–129
    header columns, 124
    latch contention, 139
        page I/O latch, 140–142
        page latch, 142–144
    LOB access, 149–152
    locking contention, 132
        lock escalation, 137, 138
        page lock, 135–137
        row lock, 133–135
    page allocation cycle, 144–147
    parameters, 123
    SELECT activity
        forwarded fetch, 131, 132
        range scan, 128, 129
        singleton lookup, 129
    syntax, 123
Index physical statistics
    fragmentation statistics, 157, 158
    header columns, 154
    parameters, 154

row statistics, 155, 156
Index usage statistics
    dynamic management
        view, 110
    header columns, 110–112
    system columns, 119–122
    user columns
        user_lookups, 116–118
        user_scans, 114–116
        user_seeks, 112, 113
        user_updates, 118, 119
Integrated Full Text Search
    (iFTS), 214
International Standard Book Number
    (ISBN), 5
IO_COMPLETION, 565

J, K

JavaScript Object Notation (JSON), 7

L

Large object (LOB) page, 39
LCK_M_*, 566–568
LIKE comparison
    execution plan for
        710, 441
        Longbrook, 442
    query for
        710, 440, 441
        CONTAINS function, 443
        Longbrook, 441
    STATISTICS IO for
        710, 440
        CONTAINS function, 443
        Longbrook, 441

INDEX

M

MakeValid() method, 186
Manually maintaining statistics
    maintenance plans, 313, 314
    methods, 312
    T-SQL scripts
        DDL command, 315–318
        stored procedure, 315
Memory-optimized tables, 197
    aspects, 202
    creation, 199
    hash index, 202
        buckets, 203
        execution time, 204
        extended events session, 204
        statistics query, 206
    implementation, 198
    insert data, 201
    overview, 198
    range index, 208
        NONCLUSTERED index, 208
        ORDER BY statements, 210
        substantial performance, 209
metadata
    sys.column_store_dictionaries, 25
    sys.column_store_segments, 25
    sys.fulltext_catalogs, 26
    sys.fulltext_index_columns, 26
    sys.fulltext_indexes, 26
    sys.hash_indexes, 26
    sys.index_columns, 24
    sys.indexes, 23
    sys.selective_xml_index_paths, 24
    sys.spatial_indexes, 25
    sys.xml_indexes, 24
Minimally Logged (ML), 37
MythEight Heap, 252
MythFive Table, creation, 243, 244

N

Natural key, 363–366
Noise words, 220
Non-clustered indexes, 5, 88
    considerations, 384
    covering index, 394–397
    filtered index, 403–409
    foreign keys, 408–413
    included columns, 397–402
    intersection pattern, 388–392
    multiple column, 392–394
    search columns, 385–388

O

Overlapping indexes, 577–581

P

Page Free Space (PFS), 35
PAGEIOLATCH_*, 568–570
Page Life Expectancy/sec (PLE)
    counter, 568
Pages
    BCM page, 37
    boot page, 34
    data file page, 33, 34
    data pages, 38
    DBCC EXTENTINFO
        allocations, 61, 62
        output columns, 60
        parameters, 60
        syntax, 59
    DBCC IND
        allocations, 64–68
        benefits, 64
        output columns, 63
        page type mappings, 64

parameters, 62
syntax, 62
DBCC PAGE (*see* DBCC PAGE)
DCM page, 37
file header page, 34
GAM page, 36
IAM pages, 38
index pages, 39
LOB page, 40
offset array, 31
organizational structures
    B-tree, 43–45
    columnstore, 45–48
    heap, 41–43
row placement, 31
SGAM page, 36
SQL Server
    forwarded records, 81–83
    page splits, 83–87
sys.dm_db_database_page_allocations
    additional columns, 49, 55
    DBCC IND output, 67
    parameters, 48, 55
    syntax, 48, 51, 54
Partitioned index, 12
Performance counters, 517
Performance counters, index analysis
    deadlocks, 553–555
    Forward Records/sec, 520
        counter analysis, 519
        rebuild heap script, 524
        snapshot query, 521–523
    FreeSpace Scans/sec
        counter analysis, 525, 526
        snapshot query, 526
    Full Scans/sec
        counter analysis, 527, 528
        snapshot query, 529, 530

Index Searches/sec
    counter analysis, 531
    snapshot query, 534, 535
Lock Waits/sec
    counter analysis, 548, 549
    snapshot query, 550
Lock Wait Time
    counter analysis, 545, 546
    index analysis sample
        results, 547
    snapshot query, 546
Page Lookups/sec
    counter analysis, 538, 539, 541, 542
    snapshot query, 540, 543
Page Splits/sec
    counter analysis, 535
    snapshot query, 537, 538, 543, 544
Performance counters, index monitoring
    baseline table, 468
    definition, 462
    index-related, 463
    populate counter baseline
        table, 469, 470
    snapshot script, 465–468
    snapshot table, 464, 465
Physical design structures (PDSs), 332
Primary key, creation, 234, 235

Q

Query Detail Tracking template, 204
Querying strategies
    computed columns, 447–451
    concatenation, 444–448
    data conversions, 459–461
    LIKE comparison, 439–443
    scalar functions, 452–456
Query Store, 514

R

Range index, 8
Rebuild Index Task, 298–300
Reorganize Index Task, 296–298

S

Scalar functions, queries strategies, 452
Schema modification lock, 235
Shared Global Allocation Map (SGAM) page, 36
Spatial data indexes
    adjusting bounding box, 194
    cells-per-object rule, 179, 180
    covering rule, 179
    creation
        GEOMETRY column, 182
        GEOMETRY data type, 181
        index options, 181
        initial query & output, 184, 185
        MakeValid() method, 186
        STDistance(), 187
        supporting methods, 188–190
        table to hold GEOMETRY-related data, 183, 184
        ZIP code data, 186, 187
    deepest cell rule, 180
    description, 177
    GEOMETRY index storage and cells, 178
    procedures, 192, 193
    unique features and restrictions, 195
    views, 190–192
Spatial index, 7
SQL Trace session
    adding events and columns, 506, 507
    adding filters, 507
    columns to be collected, 505
    creation, 504
    start, 508
    stop, 509
Statistics maintenance
    automatic, 310
        creation, 310
        in-memory tables, 312
        prevention, 311, 312
        updation, 310, 311
    manual
        maintenance plans, 313, 314
        methods, 312
        T-SQL scripts, 314–318
Status report, 599
STDistance(), 187
Stored procedure, 315
sys.dm_db_incremental_stats_properties, 109
sys.dm_db_index_operational_stats, 481
sys.dm_db_stats_histogram, 107, 108

T

Tessellation, 179
T-SQL data definition language (DDL), 511
T-SQL scripts
    fragmentation
        building index defragmentation statements, 306
        collecting fragmenation data, 304
        guidelines, 301
        identifying fragmented indexes, 305
        index defragmantion script template, 302, 303
        index defragmentation statements, 306
        properties window, 304

manually maintaining statistics
    DDL command, 315–318
    stored procedure, 315

U, V

User-defined type (UDT), 15
Unindexed foreign keys, 581–586
Unused indexes, 589–591

W

Wait statistics analysis, index monitoring
    history population, 500, 501
    index related, 498
    snapshot and history
        table, 498, 499
    snapshot population, 499
Wait statistics, index analysis
    analysis output, 557
    analysis query, 554, 555
    CXPACKET, 557–565
    definitions, 556
    IO_COMPLETION, 565
    LCK_M_*, 566–568
    PAGEIOLATCH_*, 568–570

X, Y, Z

XML Index, 6, 7

Printed by Amazon Italia Logistica S.r.l.
Torrazza Piemonte (TO), Italy